C000112834

The Lake District

The Ultimate Guide

Gordon Readyhough

with illustrations by

Donald Dakeyne

HAYLOFT

First published 2004

Hayloft Publishing Ltd, Kirkby Stephen,
Cumbria, CA17 4DJ

tel: (017683) 42300
fax. (017683) 41568
e-mail: books@hayloft.org.uk
web: www.hayloft.org.uk

ISBN 1 904524 11 7

A catalogue record for this book is available
from the British Library

Produced in Great Britain
Printed and bound in Hungary

Jacket photography Peter Koronka

To Callum and Emma who, I hope, will come to appreciate and love the Lake District as much as I have done.

ILLUSTRATIONS

CONTENTS

SKETCH MAP OF THE AREA

(Not to Scale)

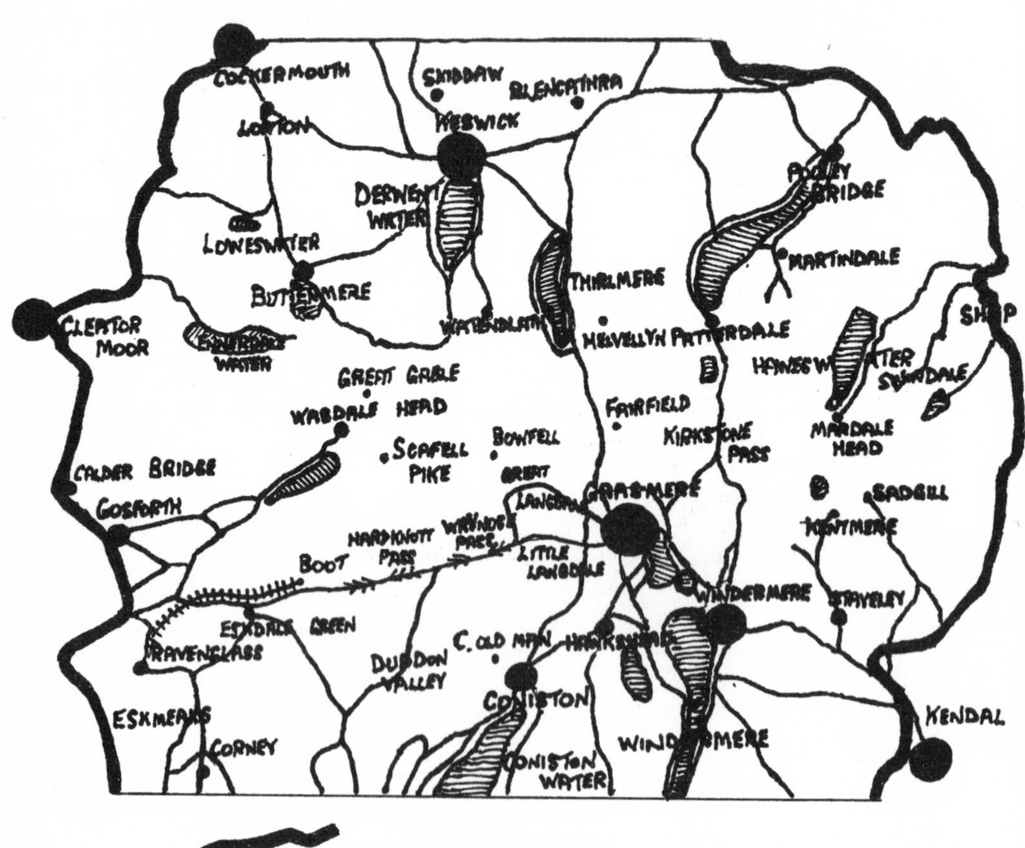

LAKE DISTRICT NATIONAL PARK BOUNDARY

ACKNOWLEDGEMENTS

First and foremost to the Ordnance Survey for many pleasant hours spent consulting and reading the four 1:25000 Outdoor Leisure Maps of the English Lakes. To the English Place Name Society for its admirable works on Cumberland and Westmorland and to the Lake District Search and Mountain Rescue Association for permission to extract information from its mountain accidents year books. Also, to Andrew Humphries, head of department, Agriculture and Land Use, Newton Rigg, for certain particulars on sheep distribution in the Lake District National Park. To the secretary Brathay Hall for an excellent history of that establishment, the headmaster's secretary, St Anne's School, for much information on the history of Elleray and the school and the marketing manager, Calvert Trust, Keswick, for considerable detail on the Trust.

I am also indebted to the late Alfred Wainwright, and the many authors and associations who, over the years, have provided me with information. To Donald Dakeyne for his many excellent illustrations and a depth of gratitude to Nancy Murphy my computer guru who came to my rescue and spent considerable time word processing and printing when my original computer and its printer eventually gave up after many years of service and later for her efforts in adapting my text in a more convenient form. Also, I am extremely grateful to Rob Spedding for his painstaking proof reading and attention to detail.

Finally, many thanks to my wife Annice for her patience and understanding whilst I spent countless hours researching, checking and subsequently computing material.

Gordon Readyhough, 2003

Introduction

This work provides more than a guide book to a specific area of the Lake District, the whole of which attracts somewhere in the region of eighteen million people a year, and of which the Lake District National Park occupies 2292 sq. kms. (885 square miles). General guide books are prolific and range from Celia Fiennes who wrote of the area during her 'great journey' of 1698 to Thomas Gray's *A Tour in the Lake District* published in the 1760s. This was followed by Father Thomas West's *Guide to the Lakes* (1778), *A Tour in the Lakes* (1797) by William Gell, edited by William Rollinson, and subsequent works by Wordsworth, Martineau, Collingwood and Palmer, to more recent works by Norman Nicholson, Penguin, Ward Lock, Geographia, Ordnance Survey, Hunter Davies, Melvyn Bragg, Frank Welsh, the inimitable Alfred Wainwright, and many others.

Items listed here are those in the Lake District National Park based on the 1:25,000 (2.5ins to the mile) single sheet OS Outdoor Leisure Map NE area - Ullswater and Haweswater (1989), SE area - Windermere and Kendal (1993), SW area - Wastwater and Coniston (1988) and NE area - Ennerdale and Derwent (1987/8). Apart from the odd 'pile of stones', cairn, the unnamed bield or sheepfold, items have been six-figure grid referenced. Over and above this, considerable geographical, historical, topographical and other information which I feel will be of interest to readers has been included. The four maps do not cover all the National Park but the area covered is generally considered to be the major part of one of the most beautiful (and many would say the most beautiful) areas in the country. For the fellwalker and climber heights are given in both metres and feet of practically all peaks, hills, crags, tarns, etc. noted on the OS map and others which are not specificed. Most works on the Lake District concentrate on the high peaks but in this case a considerable number of lesser known heights are given. Altogether over 1300 heights are listed under heights in the Reference Section.

In most cases the source and course of a watercourse has been easily identified but in some instances it has been extremely difficult to ascertain the same. Where the latter has occurred, after much deliberation and perusal of other maps, I have given my considered opinion as to its source and possible course. Likewise, the position of individual crags and even some hills is not easily identified and consequently an approximate grid reference has been given and for some places the grid reference spotlights the name on the map. A capital letter C preceding a height represents the nearest contour line. For the origin of place names I am particularly indebted to the English Place Name Society's *The Place Names of Cumberland* and *The Place Names of Westmorland* and Eilert Ekwall's *The Place Names of Lancashire*. Also, the excellent *Lake District Place-Names* by Robert Gambles and *The Place Names of Cumbria* by Joan Lee. For those interested in place name nomenclature and etymology I recommend further study of the above works. Unfortunately, the former area of Lancashire west of Windermere has not been covered by the English Place Name Society (EPNS). It has, however, been included by Ekwall in his *The Place Names of Lancashire* but not to the same degree that the EPNS has covered Westmorland and Cumberland. Consequently, the origin of many minor names in this area has been assumed from their proximity or similarity to Westmorland or Cumberland nomenclature, from other sources, or in a relatively few cases simply my own interpretation after careful consideration of all factors. With regard to place names generally, most were allotted many centuries ago and over the ensuing years have seen changes in their structure as they have passed through various times and inhabitants. Consequently, even linguistic experts cannot now be certain as to the derivation of many original meanings or even agree among themselves as to that meaning. Therefore, sometimes educated guesses or assumptions have had to be made and in many cases two or even more possible derivations have been given.

Throughout the work the choice of facts and general information has been subjective and I only hope that readers will appreciate what has been included and not bemoan what may have been excluded. Furthermore, although every effort has been made to check and double check the information given it is inevitable that with just under 8000 major references in the gazetteer and over 12000 altogether a few errors and mistakes will have crept in. Should this be the case, I can only apologise and ask the reader to bear with me. The work has taken many years to compile and, although every effort has been made to keep it up to date, this obviously has not been possible in certain cases and where information is likely to have changed or the reader believes that it may have changed I suggest that he or she check its up-to-dateness with the appropriate Tourist Information Office or the current leaflet concerning it.

Gordon Readyhough,
Arnside, 2003

High fells, a stone wall and a birch tree, the Lake District epitomised. Illustration by the author.

A-Z OF THE LAKE DISTRICT

A

A5074 A591 (Windermere) to A590 (Gilpin Bridge) via Winster and the Lyth valleys.

A5075 Waterhead (A591) to the Ambleside-Coniston road (A593)

A5084 Torver-Blawith-A5092 at Lowick Green.

A5086 Egremont-Cleator Moor-Cockermouth. A short section borders the NP between 103266 and 109279.

A5091 A66-Troutbeck-Matterdale End-A592. Highest point 342m (1122ft) at 389246

A591 Sizergh roundabout-A595 (Bothel) via Kendal by-pass, Staveley by-pass, Windermere, Ambleside, Grasmere, and Keswick. Highest point Dunmail Raise summit 238m (781ft) at 327117. The old Kendal-Keswick road diverted from the route of the present A591 in four areas. It originally ran from Ings and N of Orrest Head to Troutbeck Bridge via Mislet, Mislet Moors, and Near Orrest. The present route was adopted in the 19th century. From Rydal the old road cut up over White Moss (from near the present-day car parks) and dropped down to Grasmere past Dove Cottage which at one time was an inn, The Dove and Olive Bough. The present deviation at the foot of the hill and alongside Grasmere (the lake) was constructed in 1825/6. The former road alongside the E of Thirlmere is now under the reservoir and the present section was built to replace it in the 1880s. In the 1960s a wide section of northbound carriageway from Shoulthwaite to Dalebottom was constructed while part of the old road was retained as the southbound carriageway and in 1971 the road was straightened and widened to three lanes on the south side of Dunmail Raise and a dual carriageway constructed over the summit of the pass.

A592 Newby Bridge to Penrith via Windermere, Kirkstone Pass, Patterdale, Glenridding and Watermillock. The road over the pass was declared a main road in 1880 but only received its first coat of tarmac in 1930. Highest point, summit of Kirkstone Pass, 455m (1493ft) at 401082.

A593 Ambleside, Skelwith Bridge, Coniston, Torver and Broughton-in-Furness.

A594 see **A66.**

A595 Dalton-Askham-Kirkby-Broughton in Furness-Silecroft-Bootle-Ravenglass-Cleator Moor-Cockermouth-Bothel, Thursby-Carlisle.

A6 for approximately a third of its 26 miles between Kendal and Penrith the A6 skirts the National Park boundary. It crosses Shap summit at 426m (1398ft).

A66(T) Penrith-Workington. Formerly the A594 but given trunk road status and became the A66(T) in 1968. Major reconstruction work took place in the 1970s. Highest point 288m (945ft) NE of junction with A5091 at 395275.

Aaron Crags Seathwaite Fell [231105] ...it has been suggested that the name is derived from the British 'Aran', a high place, or the Welsh 'Aran', a peaked hill, but like Aaron's Bield near Shap and Aaron's Town, Brampton, it could be a personal name along with nearby Aaron Slack.

Aaron Slack stony gully between Great Gable and Green Gable and leading down to Styhead Tarn from Windy Gap [217103] ...see **Aaron Crags**.

Aaron's Bield Mardale Banks, east Haweswater [485129] ...see **Aaron Crags**. Bield is a shelter.

Abbey Bridge bridge across the River Lowther near Shap Abbey [547153].

Abbey Flatts alongside the Calder Bridge to Ennerdale Bridge road and slightly north of the remains of Calder Abbey [051072] ...the Abbey's piece of level ground.

Abbey Gate alongside Little Sandy Beck and the minor road from Low Lorton over Sandybeck Bridge to Abbeygate Bridge [128278] ...unknown origin (EPNS).

Abbeygate Bridge carries minor road over Little Sandy Beck [128278].

Abbott House Rosgill. Alongside the road from Rosgill Head to Rosgill [540170] ...local family of Abbott.

Abbot's Bay on Brandlehow Point west shore Derwentwater [253195].

Abbot's Bay Derwentwater [254194].

Above Beck Fells North Levers Water Beck as opposed to Below Beck Fells to the south of the beck [294999].

Achille Ratti Climbing Club see **Dunmail Raise**.

Acre Gate formerly a gate across the Birker Moor Road. Now replaced by a cattle grid [192945].

Acre Tarn see **Acretarn Plantation**.

Acretarn Plantation between Mickle Moss and the River Kent. Although not named on the map a small tarn hereabouts is known as Acre Tarn [450015].

Adam-A-Cove south of Adam A Crag and Swinsty Gill [245042]. *Hardknott: A National Forest Park Guide* (1949) mentions that Adam-A-Cove "is said to be haunted by the ghosts of three kings who now lie buried with their Golden crowns in the cairns at Iron Gate near Cockley Beck." ...surname + small hollow.

Adam-A-Crag west of Long Top, Crinkle Crags [241050] ...surname + crag.

Adam Seat subsidiary summit of Harter Fell, Mardale. Between Gatescarth Pass and Little Harter Fell. 666m (2185ft) [471091] ...Adam's hillside.

Addacomb Beck rises Addacomb Hole at 193198 and drops steeply down to meet Sail Beck at 197195.

Addacomb Hole hanging valley below Wandope. From it flows Addacomb Beck [191199].

Adder only poisonous snake in Britain. Widespread in the Lake District although very infrequently seen and few people are bitten by this elusive reptile.

Aik Beck rises 469207, joined by Elder Beck at 469235 and flows into Ullswater at 467238 ...oak stream.

Aika Hill north of Haweswater Dam and Burn Banks [501168] ...oak hill.

Aika Sike rises SSE Drybarrows below Aika Hill at 499168 and joins Haweswater Beck at 516162 ...'oak tree/s by the stream.'

Aikbank Farm Irton [095003] ...oak bank farm

Aikbank Mill by the confluence of Mosser Beck and Cat Gill [117260].

Aiken SSW Lord's Seat. W Ullister Hill [201261] ...oaks.

Aiken Beck rises between Lord's Seat and Ullister Hill at 207262. Joined by Drycloff Gill at 199255 and Willycrag Gill at 194258 before dropping over Spout Force then under Scawgill Bridge and shortly afterwards meets Blaze Beck and Sware Gill and later Whit Beck which flows under High Whitbeck and Whitbeck Bridges before entering the River Cocker at 153248.

Aiken Crag overlooks Wall End and lower Deepdale [391140] ...oak trees crag.

Aiken Plantation Thornthwaite Forest [193258].

Aikin Keskadale [215195] ...the first participle refers to oak.

Aikin Knott rocky outcrop below Ard Crags summit. Above Aikin, Keskadale [215199].

Ain House ESE Irton Pike. Off the Santon Bridge to Eskdale Green road [125014] ...possibly from 'ein' meaning bracken.

Ainhouse Plantation Alongside Ain House [127016]

Air accidents many are recorded under the specific mountain, fellside or area in which they occurred but nearly 600 incidents in an extended Lakeland are recorded in *Air crashes in the Lake District 1936-76* by Michael J Hurst (1997).

Aira Beck rises Stybarrow Dodd at 347189. Joined by Browndale Beck, Lurge Gill, Coegill Beck, Little Aira Beck, Blake Sike, Pounder Sike, and Riddings Beck. Flows down Deepdale and on its lower reaches passes over the well-known High Force and Aira Force waterfalls. Enters Ullswater near Aira Point at 400197. The valley through which it flows is the subject of Wordsworth's poem *Airey Force Valley* ...stream with a gravel bank.

Aira Force waterfall with continuous 21m, approximately (70ft), drop on Aira Beck. Near junction of A5091 and A592. The fall, valley and beck provide the setting for two of Wordsworth's poems *The Somnambulist* and *Airey Force Valley*. There is a National Trust car park and cafe below the falls and numerous paths throughout the area. The stone bridges above and below the fall commemorate Sir Cecil Spring-Rice, former diplomat, and his son, Stephen Edward Spring-Rice [399206].

Aira Point Ullswater. Delta formed by Aira Beck [403197].

Airy Crag alongside Gowbarrow Fell [406218].

Airy's Bridge bridge across Styhead Gill.

Alcock Tarn in a fold on the west slope of Heron Pike. Until the 19th century named Butter Crag Tarn after the crags slightly north and sometimes Grey Crag Tarn after the crags WSW of it. Dammed at its southern end by a Mr Alcock of the Hollens, Grasmere. He subsequently stocked it with trout and the tarn thereafter became known as Alcock Tarn. Fishing is free. There is a pleasant but steepish walk to it from Greenhead Gill or a more gradual one from White Moss Common. 365m (1198ft) [349079].

Aldby Farm off the A66. First mention of Aldby is 'Aldebi' nearly 800 years ago. [462278] ...old village or hamlet + farm.

Alice Howe just before the A591 drops down to Windermere village it rises and falls over two distinct humps, the southern slope of Banner Rigg and Alice Howe. Property alongside the A591 is also called Alice Howe. A Victorian reservoir here served as a service reservoir for Windermere and Bowness. [418986].

Alisongrass Crag slightly W of the confluence of Langstrath Beck and Greenup Gill. Alisongrass Hoghouse below [266129] ...the crag above the land owned by Alison. Across Stonethwaite Beck there is a Willygrass Gill.

Alisongrass Hoghouse below Alisongrass Crag, Stonethwaite. [268131] ...the lamb shed on the land belonging to Alison.

Allan Bank large mansion in parkland overlooking Grasmere from the west. Built in 1805 by John Crump, a Liverpool merchant. In its infancy Wordsworth described it as 'a temple of abomination' and Dorothy Wordsworth wrote "...but that Mr Crump's ruinous mansion... stares me in the face whenever I look up..." Be this as it may, by 1808 the Wordsworth family needed more room than was available at Town End and they moved into Allan Bank. Many of the trees below the house were planted by Wordsworth. Here he wrote most of *The Excursion* (not published until 1814). However, Allan Bank turned out to be exceptionally cold and smoke poured from the chimney into the house. Consequently the family moved into the Rectory facing St Oswald's Church. Another notable occupant of

Allan Bank was Canon Rawnsley, a staunch safeguarder of natural beauty, one of the founders of the National Trust, and its first secretary from its inception in 1895 until his death. He died in 1920 and the house came to the National Trust after his wife, Eleanor, renounced her life interest in 1951. It is not open to the public [333077].

Allen Crag NNE Beda Head. [430174].

Allen Crags on the Glaramara to Esk Hause ridge and with excellent views from the summit over the Hause to the Scafell range and particularly Great End and Great Gable. Slightly higher than Glaramara at 785m (2575ft) [236085] ...'Aleyn's/Alein's' crags.

Allen Crags Tarns several small tarns to the NW of Allen Crags summit [236088].

Allen Gill rises between Glaramara and Allen Crags near Lincombe Tarns at 240095 and joins Grains Gill at 235100.

Allen Knott site of an ancient hill fort on the east slope of the Troutbeck valley [415011]. Probably similar to Allen Crags in that it derived from the common personal name 'Alein'. The settlement here and those at Kentmere and High Borrans suggest a sizeable Celtic population in the area.

Allencrags Gill two headstreams rise, one below Esk Hause at 236082 and the other on the NW slope of Esk Pike at 238077. The combined stream joins with Angletarn Gill at 247087 to become Langstrath Beck.

Allerdale Ramble an 88.5 kms (55 mile) walk which commences at Seathwaite, Borrowdale, then proceeds via Seatoller and west of Rosthwaite where it is joined for a time by the Cumbria Way. West of Grange it bifurcates, a path for the more energetic heads along the slopes of Maiden Moor and Cat Bells to Keswick whilst another follows the west shore of Derwentwater. Both meet at Keswick. The Cumbria Way and the Allerdale Way part company at Keswick, the former heading over the northern fells to Carlisle while the latter continues alongside Bassenthwaite Lake (with a detour, if required, over Skiddaw) and on to Cockermouth. From there to Grune Point north of Silloth. See leaflet and also *The Cumbria Way and Allerdale Ramble* by Jim Watson (1997).

Ambleside town alongside the A591, Windermere-Grasmere road, and 1.2kms (0.75 mile) north of Windermere (the lake). A principal tourist centre with a hub of roads radiating to Great and Little Langdale, Hawkshead and Coniston, Grasmere and Keswick, Kirkstone Pass and Ullswater, Windermere and Bowness, while for the walker there is the expanse of Loughrigg to the W, Wansfell to the E and the Fairfield range to the N. The strategic position of Ambleside was much appreciated by the Romans who built a fort (Galava) here between their Hardknott Fort and the route over High Street to Brougham. Excavations can be seen in Borran's Field alongside the River Rothay. Other principal attractions or buildings are the Bridge House over Stock Ghyll; three parks, Borrans, Rothay and Stock Ghyll; Zeffirelli's cafe, cinema and shopping arcade, Hayes Garden World; The Armitt Library and Museum which houses a substantial assembly of books, articles and drawings on local topography, natural history and archaeology, opened in new premises in 1997; and more recently the Homes of Football, an exhibition of 60,000 photographs covering 500 grounds and some 3,000 teams, opened in the town. There are many hotels and guest houses, the two oldest hotels being the Salutation Inn and the Queen's Hotel. For accommodation listings and other information consult *Cumbria: The Lake District* published by the Cumbria Tourist Board, or the local Tourist Information Office. Ambleside is similar to Grasmere in that it holds a rush-bearing festival each year. In the former case this is held in July [376044], see also **Stock Ghyll** ...shieling (pastures) by the river sandbank. Suggested reading *At Lakeland's Heart* by John Carnie (2002).

Ambleside Golf Course founded 1902. Above Deer Hows and at the end of track from Miller Bridge up to and past Browhead Farm. Once described as "a splendid 9-hole course, well drained and surrounded by the most magnificent scenery, within easy reach of the town." Be that as it may, the course closed in the mid-1950s due to lack of support and the club house is now a private residence [362044].

Ambleside Sports centuries old and has been held at its present venue, Rydal Park, for more than 50 years.

Ambleside Youth Hostel alongside the A591 at Waterhead. Earlier in the Queen's Hotel building [377030].

Amethyst Green off the A595 on minor road to Hall Carleton [082982].

Ancient Hill Forts see **Forts, Iron Age**.

Ancrow Brow steep upper slope of hill which rises above Stockdale, Longsleddale [498055] ...either 'Arni's hovel/pen' or 'eagle's eyrie' hilltop.

Angle Tarn large tarn in a corrie under the north spur of Bowfell and below Ore Gap. The source of Angletarn Gill which combines with Allencrags Gill to form Langstrath Beck. Contains small brown trout. Fishing free. 570m (1870ft) [244076] ...see below.

Angle Tarn one of Lakeland's largest tarns. Lies on a shallow ridge NE Hartsop and between Angletarn Pikes and Brock Crags. A pretty tarn with many inlets. Contains two islands. From a certain position on the east shore one can obtain a repetitious echo. Fishing is for eels, perch, pike and trout. 480m (1575ft) above sea level [417144] ...It is a tarn of many angles but the origin is likely to be from 'angel' meaning 'fish hook'.

Angle Wood appropriately named as it lies in the angle between the B5286 and the B5286- High Wray road [364014].

Anglers' Crag a rocky headland at the foot of Crag Fell. Below it passes the path along the south shore of Ennerdale Water. At its base a large block of stone has acquired the name of Robin Hood's Chair [099151].

Anglers Inn/Hotel see **Ennerdale.**

Angletarn Beck flows from Angle Tarn at 416144 and cascades down fellside to be joined by Dubhow Beck and Eden Beck before joining Goldrill Beck at 404144.

Angletarn Gill rises Angle Tarn at 245078 and joins Allencrags Gill at 247087 to become Langstrath Beck.

Angletarn Pikes twin peaks NW Angle Tarn. N summit 567m (1860ft) [413148], S summit 565m (1854ft) [414147].

Annas, River see **River Annas**.

Annas Sike rises near Jeanie Brewster's Well at 480205 and joins Brown Beck at 480201 ...Agnes' stream.

Anna's Wood E Coniston Water [302919].

Anne Riggs Torver Low Common [283927].

Applethwaite one of the five settlements, Millbeck, Applethwaite, Ormathwaite, Brundholme and Thrushwood which comprise the parish of Underskiddaw. Applethwaite lies at the foot of Skiddaw. A woollen mill here provided employment until the 1880s. Today the mill building is a private house. In 1802 Sir George Beaumont gave a small cottage and estate on the site of the present Ghyll alongside Applethwaite Gill to William Wordsworth. The latter never actually lived there although the property remained with his family for some years after his death. He did, however, write a sonnet titled *At Applethwaite, Near Keswick* which refers to Sir George's gift. The present Ghyll was built several years after his death [264257].

Applethwaite Common the township and chapelry of Applethwaite comprised the whole of Windermere (the lake) and much of the parish lying N of Bowness and E of Troutbeck. Applethwaite Common is shown on today's maps as that area of land lying principally between the Dubbs/Garburn Road and Kentmere Park and N of High Borrans. However, before the enclosure of the Common in the first half of the 19th century it occupied a considerable portion of Applethwaite and swept down as far as Windermere. Highest point is Sour Howes [425027] ...apple tree clearing. There is another prominent Applethwaite near Keswick.

Applethwaite Gill two tributaries rise one on each side of Howgill Tongue at 271272 and 273270 (How Gill) respectively. Applethwaite Gill then flows through Applethwaite, is met by Burr Gill at 260250 and flows under the A591 and across the Derwent valley to join Wath Beck and eventually the River Derwent.

Applethwaite Quarry large disused quarry alongside Garburn Road [424034].

Appletree Worth in afforested area between minor road from Broughton Mills and the River Lickle [245925] ...apple tree enclosure.

Appletree Worth Beck rises W High Pike Haw at 258948 and joins the River Lickle at 234918.

Aquarium of the Lakes Lakeside, Newby Bridge.

Ard Crags highest point on the Newlands Hause-Knott Rigg-Ard Crags ridge 581m (1906ft) [207198] ...possibly high rocks.

Ard Gill rises Ard Crags at 207197. Joins Ill Gill at 208193 and the latter enters Keskadale Beck at 214192.

Argent Close W High Cunsey and below Bishop Woods [378942] 'argent' is an archaic and poetic word for silver.

Arlecdon Reservoir see **Cogra Moss**.

Armaside off the B5292 [150276] ...either hermit's head/headland or Hermundr's (personal name) head/headland.

Armaside Farm off the minor road from the B5292 to the Hundith Hill Road [151275].

Armaside How alongside the B5292. 91m (298ft) [148275].

Armathwaite Hall Hotel foot of Bassenthwaite Lake. A house is said to have occupied the site since the 11th century. Between the mid-16th and mid-18th centuries it was the seat of the Highmore family. Subsequently owned by the Spedding family and then the Fletcher-Vanes in 1796 who extended the hall and later sold it to the Boustead family c1850. Remodelled by Thomas Hartley, a mine owner, towards the end of the 19th century. Sold in 1930 and turned into a hotel finally becoming under later owners a well known luxury hotel [206235].

Armboth the hamlet of Armboth is no longer with us having been submerged under the waters of Thirlmere. Armboth today, on the W side of the reservoir, principally comprises two car parks, public toilets, a monkey puzzle tree, and a launching site for rowing boats and dinghies. The latter are allowed on application to the United Utilities. In yester years the former Armboth House was reputed to be haunted by the ghost of a murdered bride and was the scene of much ghostly revelry. A path to Watendlath via High Tove commences at Armboth and Middlesteads Gill and Fisher Gill enter Thirlmere here. The previous lake waisted nearby and a bridge consisting of stone piers supporting a wooden structure crossed it [306171] ...maybe 'Armi's booth' or 'hermit's booth'.

Armboth Fell fell area above Armboth, Thirlmere, and lying principally between Fisher Gill and Launchy Gill. The footpath from Armboth to Watendlath via High Tove ascends initially by Fisher Gill and then across the fell but the actual summit is S of the path at 479m (1571ft) [297160].

Arminghow Gill rises below Great Arming How at 186993 and meets the combined Highford, Little and Smallstone Becks at 176992. Subsequently the watercourse takes the name of Birker Beck.

Armitt Library and Museum Centre Ambleside. Known familiarly as just The Armitt. Began with the formation of the Ambleside Book Club in 1828. On the formation of the Ambleside Ruskin Library in 1882 the latter took over the book club. Thirty years later under the will of Miss Mary Louise Armitt (1851-1911), the youngest of three sisters who retired to Rydal and was an exceptional local historian, the Armitt Trust was founded as a subscription library and took over the Ruskin Library. Its aim "to create a collection of scientific, literary or antiquarian value for the student and book-lover." Over the succeeding years the collection has grown through donations and bequests and in August 1977, the museum moved into new purpose-built premises in the grounds of Charlotte Mason College, Ambleside, followed in September by the library. The whole was officially opened by HRH Princess Alexandra on 15 July 1998.

Armitt, Annie Maria (1850-1933) born Salford and retired to Rydal. Wrote short stories and poetry. She married her cousin, Stanford Harris FRCS, and much of the material by her which is kept in the Armitt Library at Ambleside is under the name of A M Harris.

Armitt, Miss Mary Louise see **Armitt Library & Museum Centre**.

Armitt, Miss Sophia (1847-1908) born in Salford and retired to Rydal. Artist, botanist and amateur scientist. The Armitt Library possesses much material on or by her.

Armont House Eskdale [183007] ...Armithow in 1578 which name is presumably hermit hill.

Arndale Beck rises east of Howe Farm, Winster, and the A5074 at 426934 and joins the River Winster west of Cowmire Hall.

Arnison Crag spur on the east slope of the St Sunday Crag ridge. Overlooks Deepdale and the A592, 433m (1421ft) [394150] ...possibly means 'eagle (erne)' crag or maybe 'Arnison's' (personal name) Crag.

Arnison Gill rises south of Arnison Crag at 394148 and flows down to 399145.

Arnsbarrow Hill Bethecar Moor 322m (1056ft) 312911 ...Arni/Arnison's burial place or stronghold.

Arnsbarrow Moss SE Arnsbarrow Hill [313909].

Arnsbarrow Tarn small circular tarn north of Arnsbarrow Hill. SE Top O'Selside, 295m (968ft) [310917].

Arnside Heights name given to the large tract of fell between Knipe Fold and Barngates which, with adjoining Black Fell and Park Fell, comprises an area of fell land from Tarn Hows, in the S, to Skelwith in the N, to the A593 W and The Drunken Duck Inn to Skelwith Fold road to the E, 297m (974ft) at 337013 ...Arnside, similar to that of the village in the former Westmorland, simply means Arni's or Arnulf's land.

Arnside Intake steep and partially tree-clad hill E A593, Coniston-Skelwith Bridge road. Below it runs a section of the old road from High Cross to Knipe Fold. The Heights tower above Arnside Tarn [334010].

Arnside Plantation Arnside Heights [338015].

Arnside Tarn see **High Arnside Tarn**.

Art in the Lake District over several centuries the Lake District has occupied the minds and actions of countless artists from the 'lowly' amateur to the major professional artists of the day. From the 18/19th century many notable artists including William Bellers (1750-73), Joseph Farrington (1747-1821), Sir George Beaumont (1753-1827), J M W Turner

(1775-1851), Francis Towne (1740?-1816), John Constable (1776-1837), Peter De Wint (1784-1849) and John Ruskin (1819-1900) featured the Lake District in their works. For those interested in tracing the history of art in the Lake District, whether its landscape or its buildings, *The Discovery of the Lake District: A Northern Arcadia and its Uses*, published by the Victoria and Albert Museum in 1984 as a catalogue to a major exhibition, provides an excellent introduction.

Artists in the Lake District see **Painting the Lake District**.

Arthur Wood Claife Heights N [382995].

Arthur, King see **Round Table**.

Arthur's Pike conical knoll surmounted by a large cairn and a wind shelter and situated roughly NE Bonscale Pike and N Loadpot Hill. Not spot-heighted on OS map but generally given as 532m (1745ft) [461207]. There is a Stone Arthur above Grasmere and an Arthur Seat at Bewcastle but who is the Arthur commemorated here? ...possibly derived from the Celtic 'ar torr' meaning 'on the pike'.

Artle Crag NNE of Artlecrag Pike [480102] ...possibly surname + crag.

Artlecrag Pike near the summit of the fell known as Branstree and shown on the OS map as the highest point thereabouts. Surmounted by a large circular cairn 713m (2339ft) [478100].

Ash between Dacrebank Farm and Brockhole Hag [449271].

Ash Bank ENE Turner Hall Farm. S Walna Scar Road [239966].

Ash Crag overlooks the head of Ennerdale [193119].

Ash Crags E slope Steel Fell overlooking Dunmail Raise [323114].

Ash Crags overlook Mere Beck [291097].

Ash Crags Tarn small tarn near Ash Crags [293096].

Ash Gill short stream which rises at 149084 and joins Nether Beck at 151086.

Ash Gill Beck rises as Red Gill Beck and Lee Haw Gutter at 260963 and 263960 respectively. Subsequently joined by Seal Gill, Red Gill and Bull Haw Moss Beck before becoming Tranearth Beck which joins Torver Beck at 283957.

Ash Gill Quarry Honister. In operation for a period from about 1820 [213140].

Ash Hill Rosgill. Alongside the road from Rosgill Head to Rosgill [539169].

Ash Knott Mosedale [505103].

Ash Spring below Cunswick Scar [488941] ...ash 'copse or plantation'.

Ashcrag Holme below Ash Crag, Ennerdale, and alongside the River Liza [192122].

Ashes farm E of the Staveley to Crook road. Eighteenth century but probably a house hereabouts much earlier. An old residence of a branch of the well-known Philipson family but in more recent times owned by a Mather, a partner in the Bolton engineering firm of Mather and Platt [470970] ...ash trees.

Ashes Beck Dale Park Beck rises at the head of the Dale Park valley at 357948. Flows down by Thwaite Head where it becomes Ashes Beck. This joins Grizedale Beck near Rusland and subsequently takes the name Rusland Pool. Later joins the River Leven near Haverthwaite.

Ashes Coppice alongside Ashes Lane [473967].

Ashes Lane from the A591 to the B5284 via Rather Heath, Ashes Coppice and Ashes. Caravan and camping sites adjoining [476965].

Ashley Green off the A593, Ambleside-Skelwith Bridge road [357037] ...ash tree green.

Ashleymore Plantation Lowther Park. Adjoining Buckholme Wood to its S [527250].

Ashness Bridge ancient packhorse bridge which carries the road to Watendlath over

Ashness Gill. A beauty spot, viewpoint and much photographed and painted structure [270197] ...the bridge by the headland where the ash trees grow.

Ashness Farm off the Watendlath road. With Ashness Wood it was acquired by the NT in 1949 [272193].

Ashness Fell between Thwaitehouse Beck and Ashness Gill [276184].

Ashness Gill two streams rise on the slope of High Seat at 283184 and 287185 respectively and combine at 282188 to become Ashness Gill. This drops over spectacular falls in a narrow ravine before journeying under the ancient Ashness Bridge. From here it subsequently becomes Barrow Beck which drops over the Barrow Falls at the rear of Barrow House YHA before entering Derwent Water at 267202.

Ashness How Nether Wasdale. N Woodhow Tarn [138045].

Ashness Wood alongside the road to Watendlath [270188].

Askew Rigg Farm east of road from A66-Mungrisdale [371280] ...probably 'hare wood' farm.

Askham the village of Askham, 7.2kms (4.5 miles) S of Penrith, and 4.8kms (3 miles) from Pooley Bridge runs E-W on either side of a long main street and is crossed centrally by the Penrith-Bampton road. It is a picturesque and pretty village on the W bank of the R Lowther consisting mainly of two rows of 17th and 18th century farm houses and houses facing each other across a succession of village greens. It was purchased by the Lowther family in the early 18th century. Principal buildings are - Askham Hall, originally a 14th century pele tower converted and extended into an Elizabethan manor house in 1574 by Thomas Sandford whose family lived at the hall for over 300 years. Converted into a rectory in 1828 the Hall has been the home of the Earls of Lonsdale since the 1930s and is not open to the public; St Peter's Church, the records of earlier buildings go back to the 13th century, was re-built in 1832/3; one of Askham's cottages has the grandiose title of the 'Lowther Outdoor Activity Centre and Lakeland Country Base Museum'. Facing the village across the River Lowther is the facade of the former Lowther Castle, St Michael's

Church and Lowther Park. Nearby there is much antiquity notably on Moor Divock, two 'settlements' on Skirsgill Hill, a medieval moated 'camp' or 'homestead' moat in Setterah Park and the site of early fortifications in Lowther Park and Yanwath Wood [513237] ...place of the ash trees.

Askham Beck rises 507235 and flows through Askham to join the R Lowther at 518239.

Askham Bridge carries the Askham-Lowther Park-A6 road over the R Lowther [519239].

Askham Fell WSW to SW Askham. With Moor Divock it provides considerable archaeological and antiquarian interest. Routes from Helton to Pooley Bridge and Askham to Howtown traverse it and the Roman Road along the High Street ridge lies to the W [492225]. The Cop Stone [496216] and standing stones [494220], barrows [493222/489224/488225], a Pile of Stones [481220], and Cairn [482219] on Threepow Raise are all scheduled as Ancient Monuments.

Askham Hall see **Askham.**

Askill off the Loweswater to Mockerkin road [121227] ...ash tree hill.

Askill Knott N Loweswater (lake) and E Askill, 284m (932ft) [123227].

Assheton-Stones, Christopher former Cumbria artist and one of Britain's leading pastel painters. Died 1999.

Atkinson Coppice Little Langdale [309027].

Atkinson Ground large property and grounds alongside the connecting road from the B5235 to that along the E side of Coniston Water [321977] ...see **Grounds.**

Atkinson Pike Foule Crag, Blencathra. 845m (2772ft) [324283].

Atkinson's Grain rises SE of the summit of Wether Hill at 460163. Joins Howe Grain at 471175 and shortly afterwards receives Sealhole Grain and becomes Cawdale Beck. In its lower reaches takes the name Howes Beck before flowing into Haweswater Beck at 518180. This subsequently joins the River Lowther ...personal name + 'fork of a river or meeting of streams'.

Ausin Fell Coppice E Low Dale Park Plantation. WNW Graythwaite Hall [363916] ...personal name 'Austin'?

Ausin Fell Wood alongside Home Farm, Graythwaite [364914].

Auestwait Hall see **Dalegarth Hall.**

Auterstone below Auterstone Crag from which it takes its name [457212].

Auterstone Crag line of crags NNW Arthur's Pike and overlooking Ullswater [460212] ...possibly from a supposed resemblance to an altar.

Auterstone Wood adjoining Auterstone and below Auterstone Crag [458214].

B

B5284 from the A5074 S Bowness via Crook to the Plumgarths roundabout.

B5285 A5074-Ferry-Far Sawrey-Near Sawrey-Hawkshead-Hawkshead Hill-Coniston.

B5286 Clappersgate (A593)-Hawkshead (B5285).

B5287 Town End (A591) through Grasmere to Swan Inn (A591).

B5288 A66-Motherby-Greystoke-Penrith.

B5289 A66 (Portinscale)-Keswick-Borrowdale-Buttermere-Low Lorton-B5292.

B5292 A66-Braithwaite-Whinlatter Pass-Lorton-Cockermouth.

B5320 Pooley Bridge (A592)-Eamont Bridge (A6).

B5322 through St John's in the Vale. Links A66-A591. Highest point C170m (C558ft) near junction with A591 at 318190.

B5343 Skelwith Bridge (A593) to the head of Great Langdale.

B5360 A592 to A5074.

Back Greenriggs southern end of Lowther Park. Nearby is Greenriggs Head Plantation and West Greenriggs Plantation [546205].

Back Guards Plantation Coniston. E B5285 [307983] ...the enclosed plantation at the rear.

Back Hawthorn Riggs between the Hawkshead-Newby Bridge road and its connecting road from Far Sawrey. Behind Fore (front) Hawthorn Riggs [373929].

Back Intake Grizedale Forest Park [344972].

Back Lane leaves the B5284 alongside Crook church, passes Milldam and Brow Head and eventually joins the Underbarrow-Crosthwaite road [447947].

Backside off New Road, A5091-Dockray [386228]. Name is at least 350 years old.

Backstone Barrow Applethwaite Common [424029] ...similar to High and Low Bakestones in that it refers to the 'hill where baking stones could be found'.

Baddeley Clock situated alongside the main road between Windermere and Bowness. Erected in 1907 by public subscription in memory of the late John B Baddeley author of a classic guide *The English Lake District* in the late 19th century.

Badger Rock Kentmere. Also known as Brock Stone. Large boulder in field to left of track from Kentmere village to Garburn Pass [453044].

Bailiff Wood E side Coniston Water. Two car parks at the foot of the wood [305934].

Bakerstead Outdoor Pursuits Centre, Miterdale [159023].

Bakestone Barrow Wood National Trust woodland alongside the A593 to Hodge Close road [313015] ...another area where 'baking stones' could be obtained (see also **High Bakestones**).

Bakestones Moss section of ridge route from Dove Crag to Little Hart Crag passes over Bakestones Moss. Lies to the NE of High Bakestones and to the N of Low Bakestones [382102] ...the moss where bakestones were found. A bakestone is a flat stone on which cakes and bread were baked in the oven.

Bald Howe adjacent minor road from A592 to minor road A66-Matterdale End [407237] ...possibly, like several Boat How(e)s means 'booth hill' or could simply mean 'bald hill'.

Baldhowend S of Matterdale End. East of A5091 [396227].

Ball Hall substantial property off a minor road from Broughton Mills [227920].

Balla Wray property, High Wray. Built in 1871 as a holiday home for the Richardson family of Newcastle. Members of that family lived at Balla Wray until the death of James A Richardson in 1959 when the house was sold. Today it is a nursing home. Nearby on the shore of Windermere there was a permanent shingle beach from which fishermen used to haul in their nets with, hopefully, a good catch of char or trout. However, many years ago the shingle disappeared due to erosion [379999] ...Wray a secluded nook or corner. Balla - possibly Belle (see **Belle Grange**).

Bampton village approximately 7.2kms (4.5 miles) WNW Shap and 3.2kms (2 miles) from the foot of Haweswater. Roads from Askham, Haweswater, and Shap converge here. Separated from the community of Bampton Grange by the River Lowther. Through the village flows Howes Beck and the confluence of Haweswater Beck and the River Lowther is nearby. A Free Library was established at Bampton in 1710. Both the Mardale Hunt and the old Shepherds' Meet which were held at the Dun Bull, Mardale Green, until 1935 are now held at the St Patrick's Well Inn. The centuries-old Bampton Hall has been converted into several residences and the old Bampton corn mill is now a private residence. Near the former mill and covered by a stone is St Patrick's Well commonly called Mab Well after a local inhabitant [515181] ...farmstead made of beams or a farm by a tree, see also **Bampton Grange.**

Bampton Bridge Bampton. Carries the Bampton-Haweswater road over Howes Beck [515182].

Bampton Common WSW Bampton. Like Deepdale Common, Glenridding Common, Mardale Common, Martindale Common, Patterdale Common, and Swindale Common, the one near Bampton reminds us of the time when such 'commons' were indeed common grazing lands [473162]. Two cairns on the Common are scheduled as Ancient Monuments as are standing stones and a settlement on Four Stones Hill nearby.

Bampton Grange the community of Bampton Grange is separated from Bampton by Haweswater Beck and the River Lowther. It possesses the church of St Patrick which was erected in 1726 on an earlier church site (first mentioned in 1170). Major restoration work was completed in 1885. The Wesleyan Chapel was built in 1877. Bampton Grange once possessed a grammar school of some renown. This was founded in 1623 and, like Measand, it was often said about Bampton that "they sowed in Latin and reaped in Greek". The school, standing to the W of the church, is now the Church Hall [522180]. There is a fine riverside walk to Rosgill.

Bampton Hall see **Bampton**.

Band, The see **The Band**.

Band End W Haweswater. Above Flakenhow Crags [469123].

Band Knotts rocky scar E Kentmere Reservoir [456083] ...rocky ridge.

Baneriggs see **White Moss Common & Baneriggs**.

Banishead sometimes called Baniside. On moorland S Walna Scar Road. Possesses ancient cairns, homestead and an enclosure [285965] ...Banni's shieling/mountain pasture.

Bank alongside Dockray-Dowthwaitehead road [386219].

Bank Crags W Thirlmere. N middle reaches of Cragsteads Gill [313146].

Bank End off the B5284 [488953].

Bank End alongside the A593 [265928] ...Cat Bank ends nearby.

Bank Fold sheepfold, Borrowdale [531053].

Bank Ground Farm, the 'Holly Howe' of Arthur Ransome's *Swallows and Amazons*. Today a farm and bed and breakfast establishment [316970].

Bank Head off Underbarrow Road [496927].

Bank House on slope below Whiteside End, Kentmere and W Kentmere Tarn [452026].

Bank House just off the Cleator Moor to Ennerdale Bridge road by the bank of the River Ehen [058158].

Bank House Farm Matterdale End. Horse and sheep farm, earlier a dairy farm. Built in the 1850s [393233].

Bank House Farm Gosforth [077045].

Bankend Wood Eskdale Green [142995].

Banking Hows above Black Sike and Low Hall [219951].

Banks Torver High Common 303m (994ft) [269940].

Banks Quarry Lingmoor Fell [316044] ...surname + Quarry.

Banks Wood alongside the A593 [245912].

Banna Fell fell area to the to the N of Ennerdale Water and the Floutern Pass. Two summits one at 411m (1348ft) [108175] and the other 456m (1496ft) at [116174] ...possibly the fell with a peak.

Bannel Head off the A591 just N of the Plumgarths roundabout. Victorian mansion now divided into flats. A coach house forms part of the property [494951] ...origin obscure but possibly a link with the Cornish banal/bannel which refers to broom.

Banner Rigg ridge of land rising to C270m (C886ft) above The Common [427995] ...Banner is possibly similar to that of John Bell's Banner above the Kirkstone Pass in that it refers to a standard, a banner or a flag used at one time as a boundary mark.

Bannerdale one of the four valleys incorporated in the district called Martindale. Separated from Rampsgill in its upper reaches by The Nab. The two dales join lower down to become Howe Grain which in its turn is joined by Boredale near Sandwick. There is the site of an ancient settlement, scheduled as an Ancient Monument, alongside Heck Beck at the head of the valley [423154]. Formerly the highest habitation was Dale Head Farm [434165], rebuilt in the 17th century, and in which Wordsworth in his *Guide to the Lakes* describes "... a room built by Mr Hasell (of Dalemain) for the accommodation of his friends at the annual chase of red deer in his forests at the head of these dales." The road up the dale ends at Dale Head but paths continue to Boredale Hause and Angle Tarn [428158] ...'holly valley' - from early to more recent times the tender sprouts and sprigs of the evergreen holly have been used as nutritious winter fodder for sheep.

Bannerdale small valley leading down to the R Glenderamackin from the impressive Bannerdale Crags [342295].

Bannerdale Beck rises Bannerdale Crags at 333299 and flows down Bannerdale to join the R Glenderamackin at 351295.

Bannerdale Beck rises below Satura Crag at the head of Bannerdale [425138] and on its way down the dale is joined by Heck Beck and Yewgrove Gill. Unites with Rampsgill Beck at 436177 to become Howe Grain Beck. This is subsequently joined by Boredale Beck to become Sandwick Beck which enters Ullswater slightly N of the hamlet of Sandwick at 423200.

Bannerdale Crags NE of Blencathra. The crags overlook the R Glenderamackin and Bannerdale Beck to the E and the R Glenderamackin and Blackhazel Beck to the SW and W respectively. Former mine workings and caves just below the summit, 683m (2241ft) [335290].

Bannerigg Farm southern slope of Banner Rigg and alongside the A591 [425988] ...see **Banner Rigg.**

Bannerside SSE slope St Sunday Crag [372131].

Bannisdale lonely valley N of Kendal and between Longsleddale and Borrowdale. Of the six dales which leave the A6 in a westerly direction between Kendal and Shap Bannisdale is the only one hidden from the gaze of travellers along that highway. At one time the purveyors of water had an idea to flood this 'hidden' valley and trial borings were made. However, there was such considerable resistance to the scheme that as yet Bannisdale remains untouched except for a rain gauge to measure precipitation. Two 'settlements' at 532020 and 520029 and an 'enclosure' at 547006 signify early occupation of the dale presumably by stock rearers. Bannisdale figures in Mrs Humphrey Ward's *Robert Elsmere* under the name of Marrisdale. She describes some of the old beliefs and customs which survived for many years in this remote region. Bannisdale has also given its name to the Bannisdale Slates, a series of the Silurian Period [520033] ...ON nickname 'Banandr', the one who curses, swears, hinders.

Bannisdale Beck rises 503057 on Bannisdale Fell. Flows down Bannisdale where it is joined by Dryhowe Gill and Priest Gill before flowing under the A6 at Bannisdale Low Bridge. Shortly afterwards it meets Ashstead Beck suitably enlarged by Wolfhowe Gill, Kidshowe Beck, and other streams at 553005. Here it takes its grandiose title, River Mint, and subsequently joins the River Kent at 517943.

Bannisdale Fell head of Bannisdale beyond Bannisdale Head. Spot-heighted on Long Crag at 493m (1617ft) [516052].

Bannisdale Head farm, Bannisdale [515043].

Bannisdale High Bridge carries the old road from Kendal to Shap over Bannisdale Beck [541011].

Bannisdale Low Bridge carries the A6 over Bannisdale Beck. Constructed in the early 1820s [542011].

Bannock Stone Bridge Coniston. Carries Lake Road over Church Beck [305973] ...flat stones in the shape of bannocks (flat round loaves). A C Gibson in his *The Old Man: or Ravings and Ramblings Round Conistone* (1849) recalls "a primitive-looking bridge, formed of two huge flags laid upon piers of ancient and substantial mason-work, and named with manifest propriety 'Bannock-stone bridge'".

Barbary Rigg section of the Old Coach Road, St John's in the Vale-Dockray [358227] ...barberry bush + ridge.

Barbaryrigg Fold sheepfold [360227].

Barbaryrigg Moss N Old Coach Road, St John's in the Vale-Dockray [359229].

Barf pyramid-shaped hill on the shoulder of Lord's Seat with cliffs and scree on its E and SE slopes 468m (1535ft) [215268]. See also **Bishop of Barf**. Originally Barrugh Fells and the name simply means 'hill'.

Barf, Bishop of see **Bishop of Barf.**

Bark Butts Blengdale Forest [091065].

Bark House Wood W shore Windermere [377923].

Barkbeth Gill rises at the head of Barkbethdale at 255297. Joins with Southerndale Beck at 342311 and later by a combination of Mill Beck/Cockup Gill before becoming Chapel Beck which enters Bassenthwaite Lake.

Barkbethdale valley which commences below Gibraltar Crag on the Skiddaw ridge and down which flows Barkbeth Gill [254298] ...Barkbeth was Barkboth in the mid-17th century.

Barkbooth E Great Hartbarrow and River Winster [413906] ...probably a place in which bark was stored or used in the tanning process.

Barker Brow on N section of Kirkstone Pass below Smithy Brow [403101] ...the names

Smithy and Barker suggest a smithy/forge and a tannery. However, it is more than likely that these are surnames rather than actual occupations. For the origin of the name Barker see **Barker Hill** below.

Barker Hill W bank River Lowther across from Hegdale [533170] ...named from an earlier member of the family of George or Joseph Barker. 'Barkere' is a Middle English word for a tanner.

Barker Knott Farm alongside the A5074 near its junction with the B5360 [405945] ...Barker's hill farm. Fell to immediate N rises to 158m (518ft).

Barley Bridge Staveley. Carries the road from Staveley to Park House/Staveley Head, and that to Bowston and Garnett Bridge over the River Kent. Two old mills once sited alongside. A house was recently built on one site [470987] ...the bridge by the barley clearing.

Barnes Gill rises below Bull Crag, W face of Maiden Moor, at 236185 and, according to the OS map, ends abruptly at 232184 before it reaches Newlands Beck.

Barnet Wood N Askham alongside the Askham-Yanwath road [514250].

Barngates Tarn otherwise known as Drunken Duck Tarn. Across the road from The Drunken Duck Inn C130m (C426ft) [351011]. Originally constructed some 60 years ago as a water supply for the inn. Fishing, by permission from the inn, is for trout. Likewise, a smaller water, Water Barnetts, behind the hostelry also contains trout.

Barnscar substantial bronze age settlement with attendant ancient cairns on Birkby Fell 2.4kms (1.5 miles) WSW Devoke Water [133959] ...the borran (burial place) on the ridge.

Barras Meadow SW How End [114925] ...the EPNS suggests that the Cumberland 'Barras' usually refers to a gate or other obstacle across a road. Barras on Stainmore, however, is said t mean the house on the hill.

Barrow heather clad hill S Braithwaite and W of the Braithwaite to Buttermere road 455m (1493ft) [227218].

Barrow Bay Derwent Water [269203].

Barrow Beck rises N Naddles Crags at 389298. Joined by Naddles Beck at 378297 and meets the Glenderamackin at 366291 ...In the 16th century was 'Berryerbeke' which came from Berrier meaning hill shieling.

Barrow Beck see **Ashness Gill**; **Barrow Falls.**

Barrow Crag alongside the A595 [091972] ...Barrow (beorg) - hill.

Barrow Door gap between Stile End and Barrow [222217].

Barrow Falls cascades on Barrow Beck at the rear of Barrow House, the Derwentwater YH. Not entirely natural as the falls were enlarged by Joseph Pocklington shortly after he built Barrow Cascade House (the present YHA establishment) in the late 18th century. This enlargement doubled the fall's height and at the same time the stream was diverted [269200].

Barrow Gill rises Barrow Door at 223218 and joins Coledale Beck at Braithwaite.

Barrow House Youth Hostel alongside Derwent Water. Entrance is off the Borrowdale Road 3.2 kms (2 miles) S of Keswick. Earlier named Barrow Cascade House and built by Joseph Pocklington who, in the late 19th century, was often referred to as 'King Pocky' [268200], see also **Barrow Falls.**

Barrow Mine former old lead mine situated alongside the Braithwaite to Buttermere road and near Uzzicar farm at the foot of Barrow. Ore was first mined in the 17th century and the mine closed in 1889 [234217].

Barrow Plantation E Lindeth Lane, S Undermillbeck Common [419948] ...plantation by the hill/mound. Land to immediate NE rises to 169m (554ft).

Barrow Plantation alongside the A595 [093973].

Barrow Plantation Tarn see **Stonehills Tarn**.

Barrowfield farm at the foot of Underbarrow (Scout Scar) [483908] ...open country at the foot of the barrow (hill). In this case Helsington Barrows.

Barrowfield Lot SSE Garthrow, Underbarrow [479907] ...area of land owned by, or adjoining, Barrowfield.

Barrowfield Wood E Garth Row Lane and alongside section of Underbarrow Road [485920].

Bartigills Crags Lover's Walk Plantation. NW Dalemain [472276].

Barton hamlet off the B5320 2.4kms (1.5 miles) NW of Pooley Bridge and 4.8kms (3 miles) WSW Eamont Bridge. At one time the parish of Barton ranked third in extent among the parishes of Westmorland stretching from Eamont Bridge to the top of Kirkstone Pass. The church of St Michael's with its central tower is architecturally unique and dates from the 12-13th centuries with considerable alterations and extensions over the succeeding centuries and with a major reconstruction in the middle of the 19th century. Here are buried William Wordsworth's grandfather, Richard, and his wife, and there are inscriptions and tablets to William's Aunt, Ann Myers, and Captain John Wordsworth's wives, Anne and Elisabeth. Barton Church Farm, previously a Hall, dates from the 16th century and nearby Glebe Farm was built as a parsonage by Dr Lancelot Dawes, Vicar of Barton and Lord of the Manor, in 1637. He never lived at the parsonage but at the nearby Barton Hall. This fact is emphasised by the inscription over the door "Non Miki Sed Svccessoribvs" - "Not for me, but for those who came after me." The parsonage was superseded in the middle of the 19th century by the present vicarage and subsequently became a farmhouse. A Barton Free Grammar School was founded in 1648 [486264] ...barley farm or grange.

Barton Church Farm see **Barton**.

Barton Fell extensive area of fell to the E of the lower reach of Ullswater. Traversed by a section of the Roman road on its way to Tirril. It was the setting of part of Wordsworth's *Resolution and Independence*, published in 1807 but written in 1802 as *The Leechgatherer.* In Verse 3 he writes: "I was a traveller then upon the moor; I saw the hare that raced about with joy;" Adjoins Moor Divock, an antiquarian and archaeologically enriched area [470212].

Barton Hall the present hall was built in 1710 and improved and enlarged later [478251].

Barton Hall Farm adjoining Barton Hall off the B5320 [479252].

Barton House alongside the B5320 between Pooley Bridge and Barton [483252].

Barton Park E Ullswater. Wooded area which in 1650 was described as "a parcel of arable and pasture ground full of eller ('elder') and hazell". Elder Beck flows nearby [468223].

Base Brown large fell which is actually the end of a ridge running NE from Green Gable. The valley of Gillercomb lies to its W, Sourmilk Gill to its N and the River Derwent to its E. The well-trodden path alongside Sourmilk Gill and on to Green Gable passes along its W slope 646m (2119ft) [225115] ...an inversion compound and probably refers either to surnames, Brown/Basbrun or Bruni's cowshed. See also **Baysbrown**.

Basecamp building at High Wray off the Colthouse-High Wray road. Built by the National Trust as a base for organised groups who wish to participate in outdoor pursuits or voluntary conservation work [372995]. Other Basecamps in Cumbria are at Bowderstone and Wasdale.

Basin Barrow N Wallowbarrow Crag [221974].

Baskell alongside the A593 [238905] ...Eckwall notes that the second element is 'hut' but the first is doubtful.

Baskil sometimes Baskell. Farm off the Birker Moor Road. Acquired by the NT in 1963 [193938] ...see above.

Bason Crag adjoining Whelter Crags and above Whelter Bottom and the W shore of Haweswater [462143] ...possibly the crag at the head of the basin or hollow (Whelter Bottom).

Bass How W shore Windermere [388973] ...see **Bass Rock**.

Bass Rock small rocky islet off the W shore Windermere near Belle Grange [388988] ...bass, a fish of the perch family/any of various sea perches.

Bassenthwaite Common large area of 'common' land to the E of the A591 [248298].

Bassenthwaite Lake NW of Derwentwater and the most northerly of the lakes. The only 'lake' as opposed to meres and waters. Wordsworth notes that in his day it was called Broad-Water and Clarke in his *Survey of the Lakes* (1789) makes reference to "Broad Water, commonly called Bassenthwaite Water." The lake is 6.4 kms (4 miles) in length, 1.2 kms (0.75 mile) wide and is one of the shallowest lakes with a depth of 19m (62ft) at its deepest point. It is situated at a height above sea level of 68.8m (226ft). Principally fed by the River Derwent while other suppliers include Newlands Beck, Beckstones Gill, Beck Wythop, Dubwath Beck, Chapel Beck, Pooley Beck and Skill Beck. Bassenthwaite Sailing Club operates from Dubwath near its foot. No power boats are allowed and permits for other craft must be obtained. Fishing is for perch, pike, the occasional vendace, trout and some salmon. Lists of permit outlets for sailing/boating and fishing are given in the LDNP leaflet *Bassenthwaite Lake: A Lake Users Guide* or are obtainable from tourist information offices. The lake has two no-boating zones, at its head and foot. These are wildlife sanctuaries. At one time Bassenthwaite and Derwent Water were joined together and today they are the only two waters in the country where the extremely rare fish, the vendace, live.

In June, 2001, news was released that since April of that year a pair of ospreys had arrived alongside the lake at a special nest platform built by the Forestry Commission. These were the first ospreys to successfully nest in England for over 150 years and, in June, a chick was hatched out. A special observation area was set up in Dodd Wood and this was much frequented by bird watchers and visitors. Live pictures from the nesting platform are beamed on to screens at the Whinlatter Visitor Centre across the lake. The ospreys returned in April 2002 and in 2003 [220285] ...Bastun's clearing by the lake (earlier water). See also **Ospreys**.

Bassenthwaite Village 1.6kms (1 mile) from the lake and at the foot of Skiddaw on the old coaching route from Keswick to Carlisle. A pleasant stream, Hall Beck, flows nearby. Two inns, The Sun, an 18th century coaching inn, and The Castle, originally a licensed farmhouse, serve both locals and visitors. There are two C of E churches, the ancient St. Bega near the lake (see **St. Bega**) and St. John's, built in 1865, and a Methodist Chapel also built in 1865. Three notable buildings hereabouts are Bassenfell Manor [218327], built in 1842, and now a Christian holiday centre, Armathwaite Hall (see **Armathwaite Hall**) and Mirehouse (see **Mirehouse**) [230322].

Baswicks alongside Cunsey-Graythwaite road. Collingwood notes that Baswicks was famous for "an awful 'boggle' that met Graythwaite folk coming home from the ferry of a Saturday night." With the not far distant Bogle Crag and Woods, Beech Hill across the water with its 'awesome wraith', the Cat Crag 'boggart', the Crier of Claife and Devil's

Gallup the area has certainly had its share of hauntings. Perhaps it still does? [376919] ...not known. Perhaps 'bass' and 'wick' meaning the cow shed on the dairy farm?

Bateman Fold W Back Lane, ENE Knipe Tarn. Comprises three residential properties, Fold House, Fold Barn and Fold Cottage, eight stables, a workshop and ten acres of land [432945] ...local family surname.

Bateman Fold Allotment S of and adjoining Knipe Tarn [426942].

Bateman, Robert see **Reston Hall**.

Bats there are 986 species of bats worldwide. Of these fourteen are to be found in the UK and seven in Cumbria. Of the latter the smallest is the pipistrelle and the largest, but rarest, the noctule. The others are the brown long-eared, brandts, whiskered, daubentons and natterers.

Bawd Hall Keskadale [219196].

Baxter Rash Lowther Park [528209] ...local family of Baxter with most likely 'a narrow piece of land left uncultivated.'

Baysbrown variously Baisbrowne, Basebrowne, Basebrun (13th century) and Bays Brown. Farm and camping site Great Langdale. At one time a dairy farm and large estate owned by Conishead Priory [314050] ...Bruni's cowshed.

Baysbrown Pool rises Lingmoor Fell at 304048 and joins Great Langdale Beck at 317053.

Baysbrown Wood on the slope of Lingmoor Fell above Baysbrown [316046].

Baysoar Slack Kirk Fell [196109].

Baystones Wansfell ridge [403053] ...the 'Cragge of Baystones' in the 16th century. Possibly, like High and Low Bakestones, Backstone Barrow and Bakestone Barrow Wood, a place where stones used for baking could be found.

Beacon Crag E Satterthwaite [342923].

Beacon Fell marked on the OS map as Beacon. Highest point of the Blawith Fells 255m (837ft) [278907].

Beacon Plantation Muncaster. Plantation leads up to Newtown Knott on which there is a beacon [094951].

Beacon Tarn Blawith Fells. Large tarn comparable in size to Sunbiggin Tarn, Orton, lying in a broad hollow between Beacon Fell (Beacon) and Wool Knott at an altitude of 163m (535ft). Contains trout, perch and pike [274901].

Beastman's Crag E Swindale. SSE Outlaw Crag. N Fewling Stones [514121].

Beauthorn early 19th century property now divided into two separate homes at Watermillock. Alongside the A592 [446220] ...lovely thorn.

Beck Bank Farm Wythop Mill [178298].

Beck Grains several small streams combine here to become Latterbarrow Beck [078112] ...'grein', a fork of a river or watercourse.

Beck Head col and pass between Great Gable and Kirk Fell and on the Moses Trod track between Honister and Wasdale Head C620 (C2034ft) [206107] ...so called because two becks have their sources just below the col. One, Gable Beck, flows S to Lingmell Beck while the other flows N to the River Liza.

Beck House alongside the B5289 at Brackenthwaite. Liza Beck nearby [157220].

Beck House Farm Embleton [165292].

Beck Leven two major tributaries, one rises W Carron Crag at 322944 and the other at Crag Head at 320958. Enters Coniston Water at Beck Leven Foot at 309952.

Beck Leven Foot small promontory E side Coniston Water [309952]. Here the stream known as Beck Leven enters Coniston Water. There is a car park and picnic site on the E side of the road and nearby are the slag remains of an old bloomery.

Beck Pane Wood W B5286 and WSW Brathay Hall [361028].

Beck Side Crook. The beck which flows alongside the property is dammed to its S to form Rowanthwaite Pond [458956].

Beck Side Intake Grizedale Forest Park [347939] ...the beck alongside flows down to meet Dale Park Beck.

Beck Wythop see **Wythop Beck**.

Beck Wythop property alongside the A66 and at the foot of Beck Wythop [214285].

Beckbottom near Dockray. E bank Aira Beck [383216].

Beckcote Farm off the Calder Bridge to Ennerdale Bridge road and slightly N of the remains of Calder Abbey [053079] ...cottage by the stream + farm. Black Beck flows slightly W and an unnamed watercourse slightly E.

Beckfoot alongside and near the foot of Heltondale Beck which provides its name [510202].

Beckfoot Eskdale. Foot of Whillan Beck which joins the River Esk nearby. Penultimate halt on the Ravenglass and Eskdale railway [169005].

Beckfoot Ennerdale [103162].

Beckfoot Bridge carries the Helton to Bampton road over Heltondale Beck [509204].

Beckfoot Bridge sometimes referred to as Trough House Bridge. Carries the road up Eskdale over Whillan Beck near the latter's confluence with the Esk [169005].

Beckhead Moss source of Crabtree Beck [134229].

Beckhead Tarn Beck Head, the col and pass between Great Gable and Kirk Fell, actually possesses two tarns of which one may or may not hold water depending on prevailing weather conditions. The other possesses water all year, C620 (C2034ft) [205107]. Note: Dalehead Tarn at the foot of Dale Head is sometimes referred to as Beckhead Tarn.

Beckhouse Embleton. Alongside Tom Rudd Beck [163292].

Beckmire Rigg NW Pull Wyke. ESE Skelwith Fold [356026] ...bog alongside the stream by the ridge.

Beckses east of B5288, A66-Motherby [417277] ...'ye Beckeces' in the mid-17th century.

Beckside off the Crook-Underbarrow road and alongside Chapel Beck. This is the lower of the two Becksides shown on the map in the Crook area. Across the beck from the property lies the Beckside Golf Course, earlier a 7-hole course but today a 9-hole undulating scenic course [463938].

Beckside Sandwick [423197].

Beckstones farm alongside the Patterdale-Hartsop track E of Goldrill Beck. Nearby Deepdale Beck joins Goldrill Beck [404150].

Beckstones off the A5084 between Torver and Sunny Bank [286931].

Beckstones alongside Logan Beck Bridge and the road from Duddon Bridge to Ulpha W of the Duddon [183903].

Beckstones Powter How, Thornthwaite. Alongside the gill of the same name [220263].

Beckstones Gill rises Barf at 211266. Joined by two tributaries and drops down to enter Bassenthwaite Lake at 225266.

Beckstones Plantation above Beckstones and Beckstones Gill and below Seat How [215259].

Beckthorns foot of Beckthorns Gill. Off the B5322 [320210].

Beckthorns Gill rises SW slope Clough Head at 328217 and joins St John's Beck at 317209.

Beda Fell ridge running NNE from Angletarn Pikes to the Howtown-Sandwick road. Separates Boredale from Bannerdale and a path from Boredale Hause to Bannerdale crosses it diagonally. Highest point is Beda Head [423164] ...There is apparently no definite interpretation of Beda. Possibly a personal name ie Bede.

Beda Head summit of Beda Fell 509m (1670ft) [428170]. Slightly E of the summit a Lockheed Hudson crashed in 1942 killing its crew of four.

Bedafell Knott Beda Fell [420160].

Bee Holme National Trust property W shore Windermere. Camping site nearby. In his *The National Trust Properties in the Lake District* (1930) Bruce Logan Thompson notes that "Normally Bee Holme is an island and forms part of the county of Westmorland; in dry weather when the lake is low it is connected with the mainland and becomes part of Lancashire." [371020].

Beech Grove W shore Thirlmere between foot of the reservoir and Armboth [308184].

Beech Hill Mosser [110246].

Beech Hill Hotel alongside the A592. Overlooks Windermere with terraced gardens down to the water. Parking and picnic site nearby [390922]. In his *The Lake Counties* (1902) W G Collingwood notes that "at Beech hill was a wraith... terrible of renown." ...Over 200 years ago the hill was known as Bitch Hill, 'the hill haunted by bitches,' (see also **Beech Hill Wood**, Longsleddale) which is obviously derived from the hauntings thereabouts. However, in the late 18th century beech trees were extensively planted around this area and the present title most appropriately also represents the plantings.

Beech Hill Wood Longsleddale [499025] ...According to the *Place Names of Westmorland* (EPNS) 'beech' here stands for 'bitches' (not the beech tree) and therefore the name means 'the wood on the hillside haunted by bitches.'

Beetham Cottage alongside the A592 E Brothers Water. Shown on the map as a climbing hut [406130].

Bell see **The Bell**.

Bell Beck rises SSE Parkamoor at 312922, joins Farra Grain Gill which ultimately joins Grizedale Beck.

Bell Beck rises E Arnsbarrow Tarn at 312917. Joined by Yew Beck at 331892 and the combined watercourse meets Grizedale Beck at 327889.

Bell Cottage Coniston. S of The Bell [288975].

Bell Crag the Screes, Wasdale [153041].

Bell Crags E face Fleetwith Pike [218139].

Bell Crags between Launchy Gill and Mosshause Gill. Rises to 558m (1831ft) [298143].

Bell Grove off the A592 between Watermillock and Pooley Bridge [455236].

Bell Hill Underbarrow, C130m (C426ft) [470940] ...similar to its taller and more famous brothers, Ill Bell and Mardale Ill Bell, in that it means the bell-shaped or rounded hill.

Bell Hill Farm alongside minor road to Saltcoats from the A595 [082980].

Bell Knott crag slightly N of High Hartsop Dodd summit [394110].

Bell Knott crags W Ullswater S Swineside Knott E Brown Hills [380192].

Bell Rib Yewbarrow. Rises to pinnacle on SSW ridge [171076].

Bell Rib Illgill Head [162049].

Bell Stand crags E Brotherilkeld, Eskdale [216015].

Bell, Herbert (1856-1946) son of Thomas Bell, chemist, Lake Road, Ambleside. Well-known local photographer. The Armitt Library, Ambleside, has a very large collection of his photographs. He was honorary librarian of the Armitt Trust from its inception in 1912 until his death.

Belle Grange remote property on W shore Windermere. Dates from the late 17th century and formerly owned by the Curwen family of Belle Isle. At one time a ferry crossed from Low Millerground to Belle Grange and an old packhorse track passes near the house and traverses Claife Heights on its way to Hawkshead [387989] ...either the grange at the foot of the hill (ME Belle) or the beautiful (French 'belle') grange. However, as it was once owned by the Curwen family, as was Belle Isle, it more than likely commemorates Isobel Curwen.

Belle Grange Bay inlet W Windermere and adjoining Belle Grange [388990].

Belle Grange Beck rises on Claife Heights at 373982 and joins Windermere at 387992.

Belle Isle Windermere's largest island. Formerly The Holme, Long Holme and The Island. The famous roundhouse on it, sometimes referred to as the 'tea caddy', was built in 1774 at a cost of £5000 by architect John Plaw. Purchased by Isabella Curwen in 1781 and the island was re-christened Belle Isle in her honour. The house was owned by the Curwen family until 1991 when it was sold to the Leftons. In December 1994, a fire ripped through the building causing considerable interior and structural damage and, after more than three years reconstruction, the grade one listed building was completed in 1998 [393965]. Two of West's 'stations' are on Belle Isle, one on the S side and one on the N side (see also **West's Stations**).

Belles Knott Easedale. An impressive peak from the valley floor (Wainwright called it 'the Matterhorn' of Easedale). Provides an easy scramble up rocks to a grassy ridge which drops down gently to Coledale Tarn [297086].

Bellman Ground alongside the B5360 [400942] ...local Bel(l)man family. See also **Grounds**.

Bellman Houses E Bellman Ground. Approached by track from the A5074 [406942] ...surname Bel(l)man.

Bellman Landing E shore Windermere near Storrs Hall [393938] ...local family of Bel(l)man. See also **Bellman Ground** and **Houses**.

Bellman's Hole W bank Coniston Water [295932].

Bellmount property off the B5360 [400943].

Belmount house off the B5286 between Outgate and Hawkshead Hall. This Georgian property was part of Beatrix Potter's (Mrs Heelis') bequest to the National Trust [352993].

Below Beck Fells S Levers Water Beck as opposed to Above Beck Fells to the N of the Beck [279978].

Belsfield Hotel Bowness-on-Windermere. A prominently sited building erected in the 1840s for the Baroness de Sternberg and owned by the Barrow industrialist, H W Schneider, from 1869-1887 after which it became a hotel. Considerably extended over the years. Requisitioned during the war for RAF Officers [402967].

Belt Ash Coppice Claife Heights [385967].

Belt Knott Langstrath [268125].

Belt Knott above the track from Rosthwaite to Watendlath [262155].

Ben Beck two principal streams, one rising below Great How at 324026 and the other on Oxen Fell at 328018 combine at 328024 to become Ben Beck. This is joined by Washfall Beck at 331029 and joins the River Brathay at 321030.

Ben Gill rises between Crag Fell and Grike 093142 and flows down a deep ravine to 088150.

Ben Place Grasmere. Alongside a side road off the A591. Large house today divided into three apartments [341082].

Bendhue Hill overlooking Crosthwaite village. Rises to 79m (259ft) [439918].

Bengarth alongside the Nether Wasdale to Gosforth road [111046] ...possibly Ben's enclosure.

Benn Mann summit of The Benn. Between Shoulthwaite Gill and the foot of Thirlmere 446m (1463ft) [302193].

Bennesty Knott WSW Clough Head. E St John's in the Vale [326223] ...Benedict's steep path to the knott.

Bennethead farm, Bennethead, alongside minor road from Bennethead to Cove [441238].

Bennethead hamlet, Watermillock. Alongside minor road from the A592 to Sparket and Cove [441238] ...holly headland.

Bennethead Banks fell rising to 295m (968ft) behind Bennethead [444243].

Benny Crag Millbeck [256263].

Benson Lane off minor road from the A595 S to Corney [120942].

Bent Haw E minor road from Broughton Mills [232922] ...bent grass hill.

Benty Howe W Haweswater NNE Whelter Knotts [473140] ...bent grass hill.

Bernard Pike overlooking Ullswater. In the National Trust's Gowbarrow Park [406206].

Berry How Nether Wasdale [119045].

Bessy Gill runs partly along the E boundary of the National Park. Rises as Greenriggs Sike at 540205. Becomes Bessy Gill at 543220 and joins the R Leith at 552217 ...Who was Bessy?

Bessyboot a summit on Rosthwaite Fell. Near Tarn at Leaves C540m (C1772ft) [258125] ...unexplained. Possibly Bessy's sheepfold or booth/shelter. This could fit in with a suggestion for the unusual named Tarn at Leaves nearby ie the tarn by the laithes/barns.

Bessygill Wood Lowther Park [547218].

Bethecar Moor large fell area E Coniston Water. Its highest point is Top o Selside at 335m (1099ft) [309919].

Betsy Crag on Low (Tilberthwaite) Fell N of Tilberthwaite and S of Little Langdale Tarn. There are several disused quarries hereabouts and in one of them the noted Lake District author Harry Griffin discovered a cave once used by the notorious Lanty Slee as an illicit still. For those who would look for the cave I must point out that it is now walled up [307021].

Betsy Crag Quarries several quarries in the vicinity of Betsy Crag.

Betty Fold property alongside the Knipe Fold-High Cross road. Erected on one of the many 'grounds' in the area, in this case Dodgson Ground [340993].

Between Guards Gosforth [093051] ...Between the 'enclosures' of Guards End and Guards Head.

Beulah Pooley Bridge. Off the B5320 [476248].

Bewbarrow Crag overlooks Swindale Beck. N Swindale Foot Crag [520142].

Beyond Fields near Balla Wray [377999] ...a similar meaning to Outgate in that it is the end of the valley fields and the start of the enclosed fell land.

Beyondfields Fell Claife Heights. Fell beyond Beyond Fields [379994].

Bield Crag Little Langdale. Crag above The Bield and High Bield [312039] ...shelter crag.

Bield, The see **The Bield**.

Bields Crag overlooks Woundale [407077] ...the crag which offers shelter.

Big Hill W Bell Cottage, Coniston [285974].

Big Parrocks NW Pull Wyke [359025] ...large paddocks.

Big Stanger Gill rises High Knott, Rosthwaite Fell at 259129 and joins Stonethwaite

Beck at 267134 ...'stang/stanger' - a pole, usually marking a boundary.

Big Wood NNE Soulby Fell Farm. Practically adjoining Occupation Wood [458257].

Bigert Mire properties alongside the ancient track and bridleway between Ulpha and Waberthwaite [179927] ...In the mid-17th century it was 'Biggatmire'. By 1722 'Bigertmyre' and 50 years later Beggar Mire. Possibility of a reference to barley from the ON Bygg.

Bigert Mire Pasture NW Bigert Mire. Crossed by ancient track from Waberthwaite to Ulpha [172933].

Binka Stone W Thirlmere. SSW Dobgill Bridge. A large glaciated outcrop seen prominently from the minor road around the W shore of Thirlmere. Overlooks the head of Thirlmere and across to Longsleddale Pike and the Helvellyn ridge [316138] ...'bink' - a stone table top/narrow ledge of rock/narrow shelf.

Binks Moss W junction with A5091 and New Road to Dockray [388241].

Birch Crag Beckstones Plantation [215262].

Birch Crags W Thirlmere. Overlooks the road between the foot of the reservoir and Armboth [305183].

Birch How E Langstrath [256090].

Bird How Eskdale. Cottage on the approach road to Taw House. Purchased by the NT in 1959 and today used as a holiday cottage [205011].

Bird Dyke Lamplugh [090214] ...birch tree by the dyke.

Birds in the Lake District Cumbria and the Lake District are excellent places to see birds. In his classic work *Vertebrate Fauna of Lakeland* (1892) the Rev H A Macpherson lists and details over 260 species seen in the then Cumberland/Westmorland and Lancashire N of the Sands. 100 years later in *Birds and Wildlife in Cumbria*, (Jan-Dec 1992 edition) 239 species were recorded and, in the January-December 2001 edition of the latter 216 species plus two awaiting confirmation were recorded. Wordsworth was a keen naturalist and in his *Wordsworth Birds* (1986) Stanley Finch notes over 60 species of birds in the poetry of Wordsworth. According to the many place names referring to birds our predecessors obviously had an ornithological eye but not necessarily from a naturalist or conservationist point of view. The RSPB has five nature reserves in Cumbria - Campfield Marsh on the Solway Estuary; Geltsdale, E of Carlisle; Haweswater, W of Shap; Hodbarrow, Millon and St. Bees Head. See also the entries under individual birds in the Reference Section: **Flora & Fauna**.

Birk Bank off the Aikbank Mill-Brandlingill-Randle Cross road [125263].

Birk Crag NNW Gowbarrow Bay, Ullswater. Overlooking minor road from A592 [430217].

Birk Crag W Thirlmere. S Dob Gill. End of spur on Wythburn Fells [315135].

Birk Crag Nether Wasdale Common. WSW Raven Crag and above Swinsty Beck [126080].

Birk Dub on the River Esk near its confluence with Scale Gill [215021] ...birch tree(s) by the pool.

Birk Fell N shoulder of Place Fell and a subsidiary summit of it, C510 (C1673) [401182] ...Birch hill.

Birk Fell NE shoulder of Wetherlam. Shown on most maps and guide books as just Birk Fell but the OS map shows Birk Fell as a large fell area and Birk Fell Man as its summit 526m (1726ft) [296019].

Birk Fell Hawse the hause (pass) below Birk Fell through which the path from Greenburn to Wetherlam traverses before starting the steep rocky ascent to the summit of Wetherlam [293016].

Birk Fell Man see **Birk Fell**.

Birk Field farm off the minor road from Staveley under Craggy Plantation and on to Hall Lane [485990] ...birch field.

Birk Hagg adjoining High Park, Rydal, and alongside Rydal Beck [366069] ...birch clearing.

Birk Haw Torver Low Common [269923].

Birk Haw E Climb Stile [262901].

Birk Haw Tarn below Birk Haw, Torver Low Common. Shown but not named on the OS map, C160m (C525ft) [270924].

Birk How overlooking Matterdale End [398233].

Birk Howe Little Langdale. See **High Birk Howe**.

Birk Knott Lingmoor Fell. ESE Blea Tarn [298042].

Birk Knott E side Coniston Water above the minor road [296903].

Birk Moss property E Back Lane, Crook, WSW High House [440938] ...birch tree(s) in the bog/swamp.

Birk Moss Ennerdale Bridge [071155].

Birk Rigg above Calfhowe Crag and Scales, Kentmere [455053] ...birch tree ridge.

Birk Rigg Over Staveley [470026].

Birk Rigg Potter Fell [513987].

Birk Rigg W side of the Newlands valley. Opposite Birkrigg [224199].

Birk Rigg Park S Elter Water and River Brathay [338035] ...the several 'parks' hereabouts suggest that they were outlying farms created centuries ago by Furness Abbey. 'Park' in this case is of French origin and means an enclosed piece of ground for pasture or arable farming.

Birk Riggs alongside Tranearth Beck [280954].

Birk Side SW/SSW Nethermost Pike. Pony track from Wythburn to Helvellyn ascends via Birk Side [337135].

Birkby earlier Bretteby/Bretby. Area and properties across the River Esk from Muncaster. Includes Barnscar and Birkby Fell [122963] ...farmstead/hamlet/village of the Britons.

Birkby Fell large fell area to the S and SW Devoke Water and to the E of Birkby with White Pike as its centre. I have separated it from the Whitfell group by giving the latter as lying S of a Stainton Beck/Holehouse Gill line and N of the Corney Fell road. What exactly comprises Birkby Fell is, like several other fell areas, open to conjecture but as I stated in the introduction although most peaks or summits fit into a precise geographical pattern there are obviously exceptions to this rule. In the case of Birkby Fell and other similar fells, map makers and certain readers may disagree with my interpretation of what heights comprise the particular fell ranges, but in the interest of practicability I have grouped together those I consider to be part of or allied to that particular range. Highest point of Birkby Fell is Yoadcastle at 494m (1621ft) [157952].

Birkby Fell Range see Reference Section: **Heights**.

Birker Beck Arminghow Gill and the combined Highford, Little and Smallstone Becks become one at 176992 to become Birker Beck. This flows over Stanley Force into the deep wooded ravine of Stanley Gill where it becomes Stanleygill Beck. Meets the River Esk at 173002.

Birker Fell rocky serrated ridge rising above Birker Moor and principally comprising Great Worm Crag, White How, Green Crag, Crook Crag, Great Whinscales, Kepple Crag and several lower summits. Highest point is Green Crag 489m (1604ft) [200983].

Birker Fell Range see Reference Section: **Heights**

Birker Force Eskdale. Waterfall on Low Birker Pool as the latter flows down to meet the River Esk [188999].

Birker Holes Wasdale Fell [197094].

Birker Moor Extensive moorland area stretching from the S slope of Harter Fell, between the valleys of the Esk and Duddon, and to the heights of Rough Crag and Seat How, W of the Birker Moor fell road. Sometimes referred to as Birker Fell but this actually comprises the high ridge E of the Birker Moor road. See also **Birker Fell**.

Birker Moor Road fell road between Ulpha and Eskdale. Rises to C260m (C853ft) [176972]. From here there is a marvellous view looking E over the Moor and Birker Fell to the high mountains.

Birkerthwaite property E of the Birker Moor fell road [179981].

Birket Houses Winster valley. Built early 20th century by Major Birket replacing a centuries-old property. A Grade-II listed building [412930] ...Birket(t), a common Westmorland surname derived from birch hill/headland.

Birket Houses Wood adjoining Birket Houses [410930].

Birkett, Lord a major stalwart in the 1962 battle with Manchester Corporation Waterworks over Ullswater. Consequently, after his death in 1962, a nameless fell, SW of Dowthwaitehead, was named Birkett Fell in his honour and, at the same time, a plaque was affixed to Kailpot Crag overlooking Ullswater.

Birkett Beck rises Threlkeld Common at 333236 and joins lodge alongside the R Glenderamackin at 325249 ...birch covered headland by the stream.

Birkett Cottage off the minor road Low Lorton to Low Swinside [162248].

Birkett Fell on earlier maps shown as Nameless Fell. ENE Hart Side summit. Dedicated to Lord Birkett (d.1962), a major stalwart in the 1962 battle with M/C Corporation Waterworks over Ullswater. The fell is possibly the only Lakeland high fell or mountain to possess its own engraved stone name plate C720m (C2362ft) [365198].

Birkett Field down track from minor road, Guardhouse-Scales [348255].

Birkett Houses Allotment off Ghyll Head Road. Note that the name appears with two t's on the OS map as opposed to the one of Birket Houses [402925] ...an allotment of land made two centuries ago to James Birkett of Birket House(s). At one time a public carriage road linked the 'allotments' with Birket Houses. Today, part track but mainly footpath connects Birket Houses and Winster House with Ghyll Head Road. Part of the allotment is designated as a SSSI for its series of mires and flushes and in 1999 much planting of English native wood took place here.

Birkett Leap alongside the track from Rosthwaite to Watendlath [264156].

Birkett Mire alongside B5322 [319244].

Birkett Wood Farm Ormathwaite [270252].

Birkfell Earth steep craggy area W-N of the summit of Birk Fell, Place Fell [402184].

Birkhead Troutbeck [408029] ...originally Birch Hill. However, this became the personal name Birkett (Birkhead) and that of a well-known Troutbeck family. From the names of the 48 tenements recorded for the manor in 1675 no less than 20 were Birketts.

Birkhouse Moor spur of the Helvellyn range descending from the Hole-in-the-Wall NNE to Glenridding Beck 718m (2356ft) [364160].

Birkie Knott W of Howegrain Beck and the road from Howtown through Martindale to Dale Head, Bannerdale [437188].

Birkmoss Plantation 0.8kms (0.5 mile) ESE Birk Moss [443931].

Birkness Comb see **Burtness Comb**.

Birkrigg property alongiside the Newlands Pass road [227199].

Birkrigg Brow slope between Sleet Hause and Rigg Beck [225204].

Birkriggs Wood Potter Fell [507989].

Birks SE Greenup Edge and between it and Broadstone Head [291102].

Birks summit of NE spur of St Sunday Crag (The Cape). Normally climbed as part of the route from Patterdale via St Sunday Crag and Cofa Pike to Fairfield. Many crags on its N and E faces, 622m (2041ft) [380144].

Birks old farm alongside the Duddon valley and approached across the picturesque Birks Bridge [230991].

Birks Ulpha. Adjoining Birks Wood and alongside the bridleway to Kiln Bank [200929].

Birks Bridge carries minor road over River Winster [413919].

Birks Bridge picturesque and much photographed arched packhorse bridge across the River Duddon where the latter narrows and becomes a deep pool. Car parking nearby. Several tracks and paths through the Dunnerdale Forest and alongside it commence or end at the bridge [234993].

Birks Brow above Birks Bridge [411919].

Birks Coppice Eskdale. Slope Muncaster Fell [129986].

Birks Crag NNW Birks. Overlooks Grisedale [377150].

Birks Crag W Haweswater between Whelter Crags/Hanging Stones and Castle Crag. Overlooks Whelter Beck and Whelter Bottom [467128].

Birks Gill rises E Low White Stones at 289100 and joins Mere Beck at 294103. This eventually becomes the Wyth Burn which enters Thirlmere at 322131.

Birks Head E B5360, NW Rosthwaite Farm [399936].

Birks Plantation Eskdale. SW Birks Coppice [126982].

Birks Road connects the A592 with Birks Bridge [393913].

Birks Wood Ulpha [201931].

Birks Wood Nether Wasdale [120040].

Birkside Gill rises Birk Side at 341132 and joins Raise Beck at 325124.

Birrel Sike originally called Holegatebeck. Rises springs at 079074 and 080073 between Swainson Knott and Ponsonby Fell. Joins Stargreen Beck at 061065.

Birthwaite Road Windermere. Connects the A592 with the A5074 [407985] ...road by or through the birch clearing.

Bishop of Barf on the steep slope of Barf stands a white-washed rock called The Bishop of Barf or just The Bishop which is prominently seen from the A66 travelling N or from the minor road through Thornthwaite. Legend suggests that in 1783 the Bishop of Derry while travelling to Whitehaven en route to Ireland broke his journey at the Swan Hotel, Thornthwaite. After partaking of several drinks he made a bet with his clerk that he could ride his trusty pony to the top of Barf and on to Lord's Seat. Unfortunately the pair only reached the rock where the pony stumbled on the steep slope and fell killing both itself and the Bishop. He is said to be buried at the foot of the scree slope by a smaller rock known as The Clerk. The Bishop rock is painted regularly by the Keswick Mountain Rescue Team on behalf of the landlord of the Swan Hotel [217265].

Bishop Plantation alongside the Ings-Troutbeck road [425004] ...possibly 'Bishop' in this case is a surname.

Bishop Woods W High Cunsey [377943] ...once the property of Bishop Watson of Llandaff.

Biskey Howe Bowness. A short walk from Bowness centre up Crag Brow and then off right up Helm Road leads to Biskey Howe Road and Biskey Howe. A craggy summit set in a public park area. Good view point and a view indicator on the summit was erected to commemorate the Silver Jubilee of Queen Elizabeth II in 1977, 143m (469ft) [407970] ...Known as Biscot-how in the late 18th century. Possibly the name refers to the OE 'biscop' bishop or a later personal name or 'cot' could be the OE 'cottage/hut'.

Black Allens outcrop of rocks W of the foot of Seathwaite Tarn and alongside Tarn Beck [247985] ...'Allan' refers to a water meadow and is also frequently used to refer to a narrow strip of land by a stream. In this case the stream is Tarn Beck.

Black Apple Tree area alongside the Silurian Way, Grizedale Forest Park [342932] ...In its leaflet guide to the Silurian Way the Forest Enterprise suggests that "crab apple trees were often planted near the pitsteads of charcoal burners and maybe the tree (now disappeared) that gave this area its name was blackened by the smoke from a charcoal oven." Over the centuries the crab apple has been popular amongst country folk, a fact emphasised by the many Lake District place names beginning with apple (most of them referring to the crab apple) and other names having 'crab' as the first participle. Much revered and anciently a mythological symbol, the crab apple has been used medicinally and for jellies and preserves.

Black Apron Eskdale Fell [193041].

Black Beck farthest headstream rises Sleddale Forest at 483018 and flows down to meet the River Sprint near Wadshowe Bridge, Longsleddale, at 497032.

Black Beck rises 442020 and joins Park Beck at 451020.

Black Beck rises Grizedale Forest Park at 323963 and joins Coniston Water at 312968.

Black Beck rises N Grigghall Lane at 461913 and joins Underbarrow Pool near Denehead Bridge at 468907.

Black Beck two principal feeders, Thurs Gill and Penrose Beck, rise in Grizedale Forest at 333976 and 333974 respectively while Black Beck itself rises in a swampy area on Arnside Heights below Black Crag at 339013. Thurs Gill joins Black Beck at 346991 and Penrose Beck at 351987. Black Beck then flows E of Hawkshead, under the Hawkshead-Near Sawrey road, alongside Priest Pot which has been isolated from Esthwaite Water by deposits from the beck, and joins Esthwaite Water at 358975.

Black Beck rises slope of Brunt Knott at 487006 and joins Dockernook Gill at 494009. This flows down past Docker Nook to meet the River Sprint in Longsleddale.

Black Beck rises below Red Pike (Wasdale) ridge at 167104 and joins Mosedale Beck at 179102.

Black Beck rises Blackbeck Knotts at 158088 and joins Nether Beck at 155083.

Black Beck rises near Tosh Tarn at 127050 and joins the River Irt at 124039.

Black Beck rises near Field End at 092022. Joined by Hallsenna Beck at 077005. The combined watercourse joins the River Irt at 079997.

Black Beck rises 267911 and flows into Coniston Water at 291918.

Black Beck rises below Wonder Hill, Birker Moor, at 173985. Subsequently joins with Hare Gill to become Red Gill. This is joined by Whis Gill and subsequently enters the River Esk at 146987.

Black Beck rises N Devoke Water at 157982. Joins Linbeck Gill (outflow of Devoke Water) at 148978.

Black Beck rises W Devoke Water at 150967 and combines with Stainton and Samgarth Becks at 121946 to become Mill Gill.

Black Beck rises Thwaites Fell at 160907 and, after a lengthy and winding journey, joins the Duddon Channel at 204842.

Black Beck flows out of Blackbeck Tarn and joins Warnscale Beck at 199138.

Black Beck rises 143173 and joins Scale Beck, Crummock, at 152174.

Black Beck rises 107220 and joins Meregill Beck at 098222.

Black Beck rises below Grey Crags, Skiddaw Little Man, at 264274. For continuation see Tongues Beck.

Black Beck Cottage E side Coniston Water near Black Beck. Date stone 1846 but extended and modernised in the 1980s [316967].

Black Beck Wood alongside the B5360 which connects the A592 with the A5074. The adjoining Black Beck formed part of the old boundary between Westmorland and Lancashire [395935].

Black Bells crags overlooking the head of Swindale [496114].

Black Borrans slightly W of the track alongside Trout Beck to Threshwaite Mouth [422090] ...black 'heap of stones'/'burial place'.

Black Brow wall of crags running NW-NNE of Little Hart Crag [387102].

Black Brows rocky outcrop rising to 268m (879ft), Dale Park [363926].

Black Brows Close below Black Brows [366924].

Black Buttress on craggy spur from Fairfield to Greenhow End [365120].

Black Cat sightings over recent years there have been many sightings of large black cats (thought to be panthers) in the Lake District and particularly Southern Lakeland where, up to July 2002, there had been reports in the *Westmorland Gazette* of sightings from over 20 different areas. Since then there have been many more sightings. A black cat specialist and recorder said that he believed that there could be four black cats, probably panthers, roaming the Lake District.

Black Comb head of Mosedale and source of Mosedale Beck [165113].

Black Crag alongside Kidsty Howes and between the latter and Randale Beck [464126].

Black Crag Bannisdale. Above Blackcrag Plantation [512036].

Black Crag between Wyth Burn and Blackcrag Gill [311117].

Black Crag Black Fell. See **Black Fell**.

Black Crag E face Birks overlooking Glenamara Park [385148].

Black Crag E Swindale. ENE Beastman's Crag. NW Glede Howe [520122].

Black Crag ENE Sheffield Pike. Overlooks Glencoyne and Glencoyne Wood [373183].

Black Crag Hugill Fell. W Scroggs Bridge [463994].

Black Crag impressive crag alongside route over Hartsop above How [378116].

Black Crag Longsleddale. Above Underhill Wood [488041].

Black Crag lower slope E Rydal Fell between Calf Cove and Nettle Cove [361108].

Black Crag Place Fell. SE Low Moss. Overlooks Boredale [417175].

Black Crag W Stonesty Pike [240039].

Black Crag W Swindale. Alongside Black Crag Gill [508131].

Black Crag Wrynose Fell [274037].

Black Crag western outlier of Scafell overlooking Brown Tongue and Hollow Stones [201070].

Black Crag alongside Red Pike ridge. Cairn on ridge above at 801m (2628ft) [166101].

Black Crag W slope Brim Fell [267987].

Black Crag alongside Great Crag, Birker Moor [188979].

Black Crag between Pillar and Little Scoat Fell [164117].

Black Crag huge cliff above Troutdale. Not named on the OS map [263172].

Black Crag line of crags E slope Maiden Moor overlooking Manesty [245186].

Black Crag overlooks Highnook Beck and High Nook Tarn [122196].

Black Crag NE Jenkin Hill [277278].

Black Crag Whinlatter 527m (1729ft) [199241].

Black Crag Gill rises SE slope of Powley's Hill at 506134 and joins Swindale Beck at 512130.

Black Crags adjoining Castle Crag on Wythburn Fells [303117].

Black Crags line of crags between Little Gill and Stake Gill on the Rossett Pike to Mansey Pike ridge. Spot height at rear 588m (1929ft) [256081].

Black Dyke Moss boggy area W Hawkshead Hall Park [329979].

Black Dyke Moss Tarn small tarn, Black Dyke Moss [330980].

Black Fell large fell area to the W of the Outgate-Skelwith Bridge road and E of the A593, Skelwith Bridge-Coniston road. Includes Great Cobble and Black Crag. The highest point is at 323m (1060ft) which is separated from the trig. point on Black Crag at 322m (1056ft) by a wall and high wooden stile. The triangulation column bears the metal symbol of the National Trust. Slightly SE of Black Crag and slightly lower in height is a subsidiary summit bearing a large cairn [340016].

Black Fell Torver High Common [261956].

Black Gill tributaries rise at Miterdale Head Moss at 166016 and White Moss at 170023. Joins the River Mite at 163025.

Black Gill rises at 209254 and joins Comb Gill at 212252. This subsequently joins Comb Beck.

Black Gills three small gills combine at 279108 to form a stream which is joined by others and becomes Greenup Gill.

Black Hall Duddon valley. At one time a YHA Hostel [239012].

Black John Hole gully NNW face Harter Fell. Stream emerges to feed into Small Water Beck [457096].

Black Knott Ullscarf [296121].

Black Knott Watendlath Fell [278147].

Black Mire see **Loughrigg Fell**.

Black Moss Beck rises E Stephenson Haw at 227935. Joined by a lengthy tributary which rises W Stephenson Haw at 225934. The beck joins the River Lickle at 230913.

Black Pots near the source of the River Calder [099135] ...black pits.

Black Quarter see **Easdale**.

Black Sail Hut Black Sail Youth Hostel. Formerly a shepherds' bothy which was altered to a YH in 1933 and is claimed to be the most isolated hostel in the Lake District if not the country. The hut still has its traditional gas lighting but, in 1998, a wind turbine backed up by solar panels was harnessed to provide enough power to run a phone, fax, deep freeze, fridge, microwave and low-energy lighting. Nearby, on the S side of the River Liza stood, until the early 1990s, a wooden hut called Hazel Lodge which acted as a refuge for walkers particularly during the times of the year when Black Sail YH was closed to individual members. Unfortunately, vandalism reached such proportions that the wooden structure had to be removed and a small plaque on its site simply reads "Black Sail Shelter removed due to vandalism" [195124].

Black Sail Shelter see **Black Sail Hut.**

Black Sail Pass pass between Mosedale and Ennerdale. Down its W side flows Gatherstone Beck and on its E slope Sail Beck C550m (C1804ft) [192114] ...Takes its name from Sail Beck which much earlier was Black Sail, the 'dark stream'.

Black Sail YH see **Black Sail Hut**.

Black Sails summit SW Wetherlam C740m (C2428ft) [283007] ...the fell above the 'dark streams' or the 'muddy place'.

Black Scar Seathwaite Fells [251976].

Black Sike rises from spring at 220946 and joins the River Duddon at 209944.

Black Sike several streams combine at Seathwaite and its valley to become Black Sike which joins the River Derwent at 245135.

Black Spouts on Fairfield which lies between Great Carrs and Grey Friar [264008] ...black 'springs'.

Black Star E face Fleetwith Pike [214142].

Black Stone Mire Claife Heights [379971].

Black Stones Dunnerdale Fells. WSW Great Stickle [204913].

Black Tippet behind Black Buttress, Fairfield Crags. 'Tippet' is a long band of cloth. In this case, however, a long narrow band of scree [365118].

Black Wall wall of crags on Stonethwaite Fell overlooking Langstrath [258107].

Black Wars crags slope Pike o'Blisco [267043] ...possibly the dark wall of crags.

Black Waugh crags on the N slope of Seathwaite Fell [233107].

Black Waugh Watendlath Fell [276150].

Black Waugh Watendlath [273163].

Blackbeck Bridge carries the A595 over Black Beck [078010].

Blackbeck Knotts SW Low Tarn and above Black Beck [157088].

Blackbeck Tarn one of three principal tarns on or alongside the Hay Stacks ridge. The source of Black Beck C490m (C1608ft) [202128].

Blackcrag Gill rises 310115 and flows down between Black Crag and Rake Crags to join the Wyth Burn at 313118.

Blackcrag Plantation Bannisdale. SSW Bannisdale Head [513038].

Blackdike Beck rises at 405228. Joined by Todgill Sike, Cooper Beck, Lowthwaite Beck, Mellfell Beck and and ultimately becomes Thackthwaite Beck at confluence with Routing Gill Beck at 412253.

Blackhazel Beck rises Mungrisdale Common just below col between Blencathra and Bannerdale Crags at 327292 and joins the R Caldew at 312312.

Blackmoor Pols between Base Brown and Green Gable [223111] ...pol/poll - pool/stream.

Blackmoss S of the A591 and the Kendal-Windermere railway line [432981].

Blackmoss Pot pool in Langstrath Beck. Its surrounding area is often used as a picnic site and locals, and others, use the pool for bathing [267113].

Blackshaw Sike rises at 391128 and joins Deepdale Beck at 390131.

Blacksmiths Arms see **Broughton Mills**.

Blackstone Point promontory W shore Bassenthwaite Lake [223274].

Blackwell Windermere. Historic house, a classic example of architect Baillie Scott's early designs. The mansion was built between 1897 and 1900 as a holiday home for the Mayor of Manchester, wealthy industrialist and brewer, Sir Edward Holt. From 1941 until 1974 it was a girls' school and its last tenant, the Nature Conservancy Council, moved out in 1997 after nearly 20 years occupancy. Subsequently purchased by the Lakeland Arts Trust and in 1999 the Grade I listed building received £2.25 million from the Heritage Lottery Fund and many donations. Restoration work began in 2000 to turn it into a prestigious arts and crafts house. This opened in July 2001, and was officially opened by the Prince of Wales in September of that year. The house received the prestigious English Civic Trust Award in 2003 [400945].

Bladder Keld spring on slope of Ling Fell [178272].

Blaes Crag lower S slope Glenridding Dodd overlooking Greenside Road and Glenridding [380172] ...bare spot on a hillside + crag.

Blaika Sike rises 485189 and joins Heltondale Beck at 490199 ...stream by the bleak hill.

Blake Bank overlooks Miterdale [154013] ...Bleakbank in the 16th century.

Blake Beck rises from spring at 381278 and joins the R Glenderamackin at 364278.

Blake Brow alongside and to N of Hartsop above How ridge [377118].

Blake Fell generally referred to as just Blake. Situated above Lamplugh Fell and Cogra Moss. Highest of the Loweswater Fells S at 573m (1880ft) [110197].

Blake Fell/Loweswater Range an extensive area of fells bounded on the W by the Croasdale-Fangs Brow road, on the N by Loweswater, on the E by Crummock Water and on the S by the Floutern Pass track. See **Loweswater Fells/Blake Fell** range of fells in Reference Section: **Heights**.

Blake Hill Skiddaw Forest [268298].

Blake Hills Farm W A66-Mungrisdale road [366281].

Blake Holme Windermere's southernmost island. Not listed on the 1:25000 Outdoor Leisure 7: South Eastern area map. However, well worth recording as, according to Arthur Ransome, it was "the island most used as Wild Cat Island" in his *Swallows and Amazons*. Its secret harbour in the book was borrowed from one on Peel Island, Coniston Water. A well-wooded island adjacent to Hill of Oaks Caravan Park.

Blake How NNE Levers Water [283999].

Blake Rigg W Low Tilberthwaite and N Tilberthwaite Gill 423m (1388ft) [301012] ...bleak or black ridge.

Blake Rigg Wrynose Fell [286040] ...bare or black ridge.

Blake Rigg Plantation below Blake Rigg [303013].

Blake Sike rises W Round How at 385205 and joins Aira Beck at 382212 ...black stream.

Blake Sike rises WNW Low How at 373216 and joins Groove Beck at 377224.

Blakebank property off Broom Lane, Underbarrow [456915] ...bleak/black bank.

Blakebank Moss S Blakebank and the Underbarrow-Crosthwaite road [458907].

Blakebeck farm W A66-Mungrisdale road [367277].

Blakefell Screes Blake Fell [109195].

Blakeley fell area whose summit is Blakeley Raise. See also **Blakeley Raise**.

Blakeley Moss NW Blakeley Raise [063139].

Blakeley Raise rounded grassy fell S Ennerdale Bridge and N of the River Calder 389m (1276ft) [070135] ...bleak pasture land with cairn/pile of stones. See also **Blakeley Raise Stone Circle** below.

Blakeley Raise Stone Circle also referred to as Kinniside Stone Circle. Possibly early bronze age but reconstructed in 1925 after several stones had been removed for building purposes. Before vandalism comprised thirteen stones but after reconstruction eleven stones [060140].

Blakerigg Crag N Greenburn Bottom [316110].

Blawith Fells an undulating area of bracken and heather interspersed with hillocks, hills and rocky outcrops lying between the Woodland valley, Blawith and the A5084. Today it is National Park access land. The highest point is Beacon Fell (marked on the OS map as

Beacon) 255m (837ft) with nearby Blawith Knott at 246m (807ft). Nestled between Beacon Fell and Wool Knott is the large and picturesque Beacon Tarn. That early man appreciated the area is shown by the many ancient cairns and other prehistoric sites, including a Giant's Grave, on it and surrounding commons and fells [278906] ...the area was once covered by trees and this is emphasised by the name Blawith which means dark wood.

Blawith Wood Bottom Blawith Fells [282909] ...a reminder of the time when Blawith really was the 'dark wood'.

Blaze Beck Hobcarton Gill and Whinlatter Gill combine at 185247 to become Blaze Beck which eventually becomes Whit Beck when it joins Aiken Beck alongside Scawgill Bridge at 177257 ...the EPNS suggests that it may be derived from one Edward del Blees recorded in the 13th century.

Blaze Bridge carries the minor road from the B5292 to Lorton and Hopebeck over Blaze Beck [182251].

Blaze Hill W Lanshaw Hill, E Bracken Howe [535140] ...similar to Blease of Blease Fell, Blencathra, and Blaika, Bampton, in that it means bare spot on a hill.

Blea Bank opposite side of the minor road from Aikbank Mill [117260].

Blea Beck rises Eskdale at 196017 and joins the River Esk at 194009.

Blea Beck rises as Frith Beck at 179915. Takes the name Blea Beck near Blea Beck Bridge at 188919 and joins the River Duddon at 195920.

Blea Cove below Nab Crag, Birkhouse Moor [368168].

Blea Crag below Brown Crag and overlooking Langstrath [268106].

Blea Crag crag towering above Easedale, Easedale Tarn and paths leading to head of Easedale and Blea Rigg [301080]. The path along Blea Rigg at the rear of the crag cuts across the 530m (1739ft) contour line.

Blea Crag the path from Maiden Moor and over Narrow Moor to High Spy passes between the summit of Blea Crag and the precipitous cliff to its W 630m (2067ft) [237171].

Blea Crag above Scale Force, Scale Beck, Crummock [154169].

Blea Crags on Gategill Fell, Blencathra, below Knott Halloo [321265].

Blea Crags Robinson-High Snab Bank ridge. Overlooking Scope Beck [213179].

Blea Moss swampy area to the S of Blea Tarn through which Bleamoss Beck flows on its way from Blea Tarn to the River Brathay [295035].

Blea Moss between Stone Howe and Rowantree Crag [527127].

Blea Rigg lengthy ridge at the rear of Eagle and Blea Crags. The path up to it from Easedale Tarn joins others on top heading for Great Langdale, Silver How and Sergeant Man. Nearby, alongside the path to the SE and below Great Castle How, are two attractive tarns called appropriately Great Castle How Tarns. It was in the area of Blea Rigg that George and Sarah Green of Blindtarn (Gill) Cottage near the foot of Blindtarn Gill (Dorothy Wordsworth's 'Blentern Gill'), Easedale, lost their way and their lives in a snow storm while returning home from a sale at Langdale Head in March 1808. They had earlier left their daughter of eleven years of age with the care of five other children. The bodies of the parents were discovered several days later. Their grave is near that of William Wordsworth in St Oswald's churchyard, Grasmere. The children were placed with local families 541m (1774ft) [301078].

Blea Rock huge boulder by the side of the path along Langstrath. Sometimes referred to as Gash Rock as one large section of it has broken away leaving a substantial cleft [269114].

Blea Tarn Langdale. One of three prominent Blea Tarns in the Lake District, the others being at Eskdale, Watendlath and a Blea Water at the head of Mardale. A nearly rounded tarn lying in a hollow just below the Little Langdale to Great Langdale road. Tree-lined on its W shore the tarn and surrounding area is much photographed and painted particularly the view of the Langdale Pikes, Wordsworth's 'those lusty twins', from its shore. Along with nearby Blea Tarn House it was given to the NT by Col. H A A Oliver in 1971. Altitude C190m (C623ft) [293044]. Fishing by permit is for brown trout, perch and pike ...dark tarn.

Blea Tarn Eskdale. Large tarn roughly 1.2 kms (0.75 mile) W of Boot, C220m (C722ft) [166010]. Fishing for brown trout and perch is free. Just S of the tarn are the abandoned workings of the Blea Tarn Iron Mine. This closed in the 1880s and, like its near neighbour, the Nab End Mine, was served by the original Ravenglass and Eskdale Railway.

Blea Tarn Watendlath Fell. Large tarn in bowl below Low Saddle and Standing Crag. Alongside the route between Watendlath and Wythburn. Contains trout C480m (C1575ft) [291141].

Blea Water impressive tarn situated in corrie at the head of Mardale and below the crags of Mardale Ill Bell, High Street and Long Stile. An underground pipeline connects the tarn with the Harper Hills Reservoir and subsequently Swindale Water Treatment Works. Blea Tarn Beck flows out from its ENE end to join Small Water Beck to become Mardale Beck which ultimately flows into Haweswater Reservoir. With a maximum depth of 68m (223ft) it is by far the deepest of the Lakeland tarns (next being Grisedale with a mere 35m {115ft} and of the lakes it is only exceeded by Wastwater which is 76m [249ft] deep). Fish content is brown trout. Its altitude is 483m (1585ft) [449108] ...'dark, dark blue' tarn.

Blea Water Beck flows out of the ENE end of Blea Water at 452108 and joins Small Water Beck at 463106. The two combined then become Mardale Beck which flows into Haweswater at 468109.

Blea Water Crag line of crags above and to the S of Blea Water. It is said that in 1787 while following the hunt a man called Dixon fell 305m (1000ft) from the crag, bounced three times, but miraculously suffered only severe bruising. On the other hand some sources emphasise that after the fall Dixon managed to signal to the hunt the whereabouts of the fox before he collapsed and died. Consequent on this fall, however, the crag was often referred to by locals as Dixon's Three Jumps [447103]. Another Dixon, also a huntsman, fell from Striding Edge and is commemorated by a plaque at the spot where he fell.

Bleabank Side on 1947 2.5ins OS Map shown as Bleakbank Side. NNW slope Sheffield Pike. An arm of the Sticks Pass route to Glencoyne passes diagonally across it [367185].

Bleabeck Eskdale. Property alongside Blea Beck and Bleabeck Bridge [194010].

Bleabeck Bridge carries the road up Eskdale over Blea Beck [194010].

Bleabeck Bridge Ulpha. Carries track over Blea Beck [189919].

Bleaberry Crag alongside the path between the Hole-in-the-Wall and Striding Edge. Overlooks Grisedale [358152] ...bilberry crag.

Bleaberry Fell W of footpath and bridleway between Hazelseat and Thwaite Head [363922].

Bleaberry Fell last high summit on the Ullscarf-Coldbarrow Fell-High Tove-High Seat ridge before it drops down to Castlerigg and the A591. Heather clad and an excellent view-point 590m (1936ft) [286196] ...bilberry fell.

Bleaberry Gill rises between Buck Crags and Sleddale Fell at 504071 and joins Crookdale Beck at 517071 ...bilberry gill.

Bleaberry Gill stream which rises on Seathwaite Fells at 258981 and enters Seathwaite

Tarn at 251984.

Bleaberry Gill NE Caw Fell at 126112, met by Long Grain at 102113 and subsequently combines with other streams to become Worm Gill.

Bleaberry Haws between Seal Gill and Bull Haw Moss Beck, Torver High Common. Possesses ancient cairns, a long dyke and an enclosure [265946] ...bilberry hill.

Bleaberry Hill overlooks Dale Park Beck valley [352935].

Bleaberry How N end of Eskdale Fell crags overlooking Oliver Gill [195051].

Bleaberry Knott Birk Fell, Place Fell [404182].

Bleaberry Knott Hartsop above How ridge below Gale Crag [392126].

Bleaberry Knott Wrynose Fell [284042] ...peak on which the bilberrry grows.

Bleaberry Tarn situated in a corrie encircled on three sides by the ridge of Red Pike and High Stile and by Chapel Crags. Believed to occupy the crater of a long-since extinct volcano. The tarn is the source of Sourmilk Gill which drops down over impressive cataracts before reaching the outflow of Buttermere C500m (C1640ft) [166154].

Bleach Green Cottages Ennerdale. Alongside the River Ehen. With nearby The Mill and Croftfoot the name recalls the time when Ennerdale Bridge possessed a thriving spinning, weaving and bleaching industry [085153].

Bleacove Beck rises Blea Cove, NNE face Birkhouse Moor, at 367168 and joins Glenridding Beck at 371172.

Bleacrag Moss Grange Fell. Why not Blackcrag Moss as it is situated at the foot of Black Crag! [264171].

Bleak Dodd WSW Reamer Bank, NW Slate Hill. Path from Wet Sleddale to Keld crosses hereabouts [549129].

Bleak Haw above Ulpha [196935].

Bleak Hill Ralfland Forest. S Great Ladstones, N Gambling Crag 438m (1437ft) [533121].

Bleak How craggy hill at the end of the High Raise-Sergeant's Crag-Eagle Crag ridge. Overlooks the confluence of Greenup Gill and Langstrath Beck [274125].

Bleak Knotts Blawith Fells [277902].

Bleak Rigg Bleak Rigg drops down ESE of the summit of Whiteless Pike and between an unnamed stream and Third Gill to Sail Beck [187186].

Bleamoss Beck commences at the outlet of Blea Tarn, Langdale, at 293043 and before entering flows over Blea Moss where it is swelled by several smaller streams before entering the River Brathay at 302032.

Blease Farm foot of Blease Fell, westerly slope of Blencathra. Pony trekking and carriage driving centre [315259].

Blease Fell western extremity of Blencathra. Rises to Knowe Crags 804m (2638ft) [312270] ...bare spot on a hillside.

Blease Gill rises high on Gategill Fell, Blencathra, at 317271 and flows down between Knowe Crags and Gategill Fell to become Kilnhow Beck which joins the R Glenderamackin at 324251.

Bleatarn Gill its source is Blea Tarn from where it flows by a circuitous route alongside Watendlath Fell to join Watendlath Tarn as its main feeder at 275160.

Bleatarn Hill above Blea Tarn, Eskdale C280m (C919ft) [168013].

Bleatarn House former traditional farmhouse alongside the Little Langdale to Great Langdale Head road. It was given to the NT in 1971 by Col. H A A Oliver and subsequently ceased to be a farm. The place where Wordsworth's Solitary lived in the 'one bare dwelling in the valley' in Book II of *The Excursion.* Today it is a well known guest house [295048].

Bleathwaite Coppice alongside the A593, Torver to Coniston road [290957].

Bleathwaite Crag W Mardale Ill Bell S High Street summit. Overlooks Hall Cove. The River Kent rises E of the High Street ridge between Bleathwaite Crag and Thornthwaite Crag [442101] ...dark clearing crag.

Bleathwaite Pasture adjoining Bleathwaite Coppice [289956].

Bleawick see **Blowick**.

Blelham Beck flows out of Blelham Tarn at 368006 and joins Windermere at 370019.

Blelham Tarn Large tarn, more like a small lake, situated on National Trust land just under 0.8kms (0.5 mile) SW Low Wray. The lowland bog NW side of the tarn was leased by the National Trust to the Nature Conservancy Council as a National Nature Reserve and a SSSI. Fishing for trout and coarse fish is by permit from Hawkshead Angling Club. It stands at a height of 42m (138ft) [367005] ...similar to 'Blea' of Blea Water meaning dark/dark blue accompanied by 'lumm(e)' pool.

Blencathra mountain ridge rising above Threlkeld and the A66, Penrith-Keswick road. More popularly known as Saddleback because of the Saddle between Hall's Fell Top (the highest point on the ridge 868m [2848ft]) and Foule Crag. Separated from the slopes of Skiddaw by Glenderaterra Beck. To the S the major ridge shows three distinct ridges leading from it, Gategill Fell, Hall's Fell and Doddick Fell, while its W flank is Blease Fell and its E flank Scales Fell. Robert Southey (1774-1843) writing in 1829 about Blencathra provides us with a different interpretation to today of major heights on the summit ridge when he says "From Linthwaite Pike, which is the highest point of Blencathra, keeping along the brow, you pass in succession the points called Lilefell, Priestman and Knott Crag."

On its summit ridge between the Saddle and Foule Crag a large white cross on the ground is a memorial. But to whom? Wainwright writing in 1962 says that an earlier smaller cross ('locally ascribed as a memorial to a walker who lost his life on a rough slope adjacent') was extended many years ago by Harold Robinson of Threlkeld, a fell walker and lover of Blencathra. However, John Drews in his *Lakeland High Tarns* (1995) agrees that the cross is a memorial but in this case erected by a fell-runner to a former friend of his, a gamekeeper of Skiddaw House, who was killed in the Second World War. Obviously, a case of 'one pays one's money and makes one's choice'. A smaller white cross nearby is the work of a later unknown builder ...'Blencathra' is said to mean 'peak of demons' but linguistically it means summit shaped like a chair [323277]. The earliest known form of its name, the Rackes of Blenkarthure, 1589, has given rise to a doubtful claim to a connection with Arthurian legend.

Blencathra Centre 5kms (3 miles) NE Keswick on the slope of Blease Fell. A Field Studies Council (FSC) Centre operated in partnership with the Lake District National Park Authority. Accommodation is in either twin, family, or single rooms. Originally a sanatorium it was one of the first built in England (1904) [303255].

Blencathra Range see Reference Section: **Heights**.

Bleng, River see **River Bleng**.

Bleng Bridge bridge across the River Bleng [086055].

Bleng Bridge carries the Gosforth to Santon Bridge road over the River Bleng [084029].

Bleng Fell slope of Ponsonby Fell. Rises to 253m (830ft) at 079060.

Bleng Tongue tongue of land overlooking the River Bleng [092072].

Blengdale property alongside Bleng Bridge [085056].

Blengdale Forest E Ponsonby Fell and bisected by the River Bleng [097067].

Blennerhazel Gosforth [068039].

Blind Cove E Heron Pike [358083] ...the secluded/hidden cove.

Blind Cove W slope Birks [374143].

Blind Lane Wood alongside Blind Lane, Dale Park [347916] ...Blind Lane leads from the Force Mills to Dale Park road and ends abruptly at the edge of the forest before Dale Park Beck. Hence it has a 'blind' ending.

Blind Tarn Eskdale. Small and practically overgrown tarn between Blea and Siney Tarns, C220m (C722ft) [161010] ...either 'overgrown' tarn signifying one covered over/blind or a tarn with no apparent outlet or inlet.

Blind Tarn also referred to as T'Over Tarn. Small tarn on shelf below steep E face Brown Pike. Contains trout and char, C560m (C1837ft) [262967] ...a 'blind' tarn is one with no apparent inlet or outlet.

Blind Tarn Screes above Blind Tarn, E Dow Crag ridge [263970].

Blindtarn (Gill) Cottage see **Blea Rigg**.

Blindtarn Gill see **Blindtarn Moss**.

Blindtarn Moss several streams, including one down Swinescar Hause, flow from the heights above into Blindtarn Moss [316078]. At some stage the tarn hereabouts became overgrown and as the name suggests a mossy/boggy area which covered the tarn and made it 'blind'. From this area Blindtarn Gill (Dorothy Wordsworth's Blentern Gill) flows down to join Easedale Beck at 325083. Near the foot of the Gill is Blindtarn (Gill) Cottage. (See George and Sarah Green tragedy under **Blea Rigg**).

Bloomeries open hearths where iron ore was smelted using charcoal. On page 83 of *The Lake District* by Millward and Robinson (1970) a map, 'Features of the Iron Industry of High Furness', shows the sites of 27 bloomeries between Windermere and the W shore of Coniston Water. In his *The Ancient Ironworks of Coniston Lake* (1902) archaeologist W G Collingwood notes that "in High Furness there are about 30 known sites where iron was smelted in the ancient way with charcoal producing a Bloom, the lump of metal made by blowing in the furnace, hence the name." So far, over a period of some 45 years, noted amateur archaeologist Michael Davies-Shiel has found the sites of 150 forges, 20 blast furnaces and 70 iron smelting workings in Cumbria (see also **The Forge**).

Bloomsmithies bloomeries with water-powered trip hammers.

Blowick formerly Bleawick. Originally a farm at the foot of Place Fell alongside Ullswater, now called Blowick House. Owned by the National Trust it is obviously today much better maintained than when Wordsworth noted it as "... a decaying and uncomfortable building in a place where sublimity and beauty seemed to contend with each other." [395174] ...dark creek.

Blowick Bay E shore upper reach Ullswater [393174].

Blue Gill farthest headstream of Hagg Gill. Rises Froswick at 434085. Flows down deep chasm and ultimately become Hagg Gill which joins Trout Beck at 421054. Two cairns between it and Trout Beck at 425077 are scheduled as ancient monuments.

Blue Gill rises Red Scar at the head of Boredale at 415157 and joins Freeze Beck at 413160.

Blue Screes slate fragments forming an extensive scree area to the W of Foule Crag, Blencathra [324284].

Boardale see **Boredale**.

Boardale Hause see **Boredale Hause**.

Boat Crag Whiteside End [164218] ...probably the crag by or above the booth/shelter.

Boat House Wood W shore Windermere. E Graythwaite Hall and rear of boat house [376913].

Boat How highest point on Eskdale Moor. Several ancient cairns and stone circles hereabouts 337m (1106ft) [177034] ...see **Boat How** below

Boat How S slope Lank Rigg [087104] ...see **Boat Howe** below.

Boat How isolated rocky outcrop on the slope of Kirk Fell overlooking the River Liza and the head of Ennerdale [199114] ...see **Boat Howe** below.

Boat How The Side, Ennerdale 363 (1191ft) [111136] ...booth/shelter.

Boat How Crags NE slope Kirk Fell [200110].

Boathow Crags Ennerdale. Above Boat How [109134].

Boat Howe crag on Brant Street [480111]. There are also Boat Hows on Kinniside Common; The Side, Ennerdale; Eskdale Moor and N of Kirk Fell ...Boat How, Eskdale, is apparently 'booth hill'. The origin of this particular Boat Howe is not given in *The Place Names of Westmorland* but it may mean 'booth hill' or possibly be the same derivation as Baldhow 'bare hill'.

Boating and Sailing:-

Bassenthwaite Lake - No powered craft. Permits required for other craft.

Brothers Water - no boating permitted

Buttermere - no powered craft. A limit of ten craft for canoeing, windsurfers, dinghies and rowing boats. Rowing boats can be hired.

Coniston Water - non-powered craft can be launched from alongside the Monk Coniston car park at the head of the lake and also from the Brown Howe car park at the SW end. Boats of any size can be launched (for a charge) from the Coniston Boating Centre, Lake Road. Boats can also be hired from here and cruises booked.

Crummock Water - As Buttermere.

Derwent Water - Canoes, dinghies, windsurfers and rowing boats. No power craft over 6hp. Rowing boats and small motor boats can be hired.

Easedale Tarn - no boating permitted

Elter Water - no boating allowed.

Ennerdale Water - no boating permitted.

Esthwaite Water - privately owned, only rowing boats are allowed and a permit is required.

Grasmere - rowing boats can be hired in the season from the Boatyard, Pavement End, Grasmere.

Haweswater - no boating permitted.

Hayeswater - no boating permitted.

Little Langdale Tarn - No boating permitted

Loughrigg Tarn - No boating permitted

Loweswater - No private boats. Rowing boats can be hired

Rydal Water - No boating permitted

Tarn Hows - No boating permitted

Thirlmere - launching of light non-powered craft by permit.

Ullswater - Sailing centres catering for yachtsmen, canoeists, kayakers and wind surfers. Ullswater Yacht Club operates from Thwaite Hill off the Pooley Bridge to Howtown road. There are public launching sites at Glenridding, light craft can be launched at Glencoyne Bay and all craft (maximum 20ft) at Howton. The lake, however, has a 10 mph speed limit.

Wastwater - Rowing boats and canoes with a maximum of 15 at any one time. No power boats

Watendlath Tarn - No private craft. Boats can be hired

Windermere - this is the principal boating and sailing lake and one of the busiest stretches of inland water in the country. All motorised craft must be registered. The two main launching sites are Bowness (off Ferry Road) and Waterhead (limit to length and hp) while the National Trust allows launching of non-powered craft from areas of its W shore and from Fell Foot Park, near Newby Bridge, on the payment of fees. There is also a Yacht Club, Motor Boat Club, boat hiring points and many cruises. At the present time a 10 mph speed limit is scheduled to come into operation in 2005.

Yew Tree Tarn - No boats permitted

For more information consult leaflet *Boating and Fishing on National Trust Waters in the Lake District* and that issued by the Sports Council *Boat Access and Slipways in the Northern Region.* Information can also be obtained from the National Park Visitor Centre, Brockhole, Windermere, National Park Information Offices and other Tourist Information Offices. The Lake District National Park Authority also issues a leaflet *Enjoying Water Safely.*

Bob Graham Round in June 1932, Bob Graham completed 42 Lakeland peaks, over 72 miles and a total ascent of more than 27,000ft in 24 hours. To date, well over 1000 runners have completed the course within the 24 hours. Starts and finishes at the Moot Hall, Keswick.

Bobbin Mills see **Stott Park Mill, Thurs Gill Mill**.

Bodle Ground off the A595 alongside minor road to Saltcoats [083985].

Bog House E A66. Alongside Newlands Beck [239245].

Bog Lane minor road between Brathay and Skelwith Fold [357034] ...for much of its route it lies across low lying and boggy marsh land alongside the River Brathay.

Boggles/Bogles spirits more sinister and more to be feared than 'dobbies'. Derived from 'boggart' meaning 'ghost'. Boggles could take human or any other form.

Bogle Crag and Wood Grizedale Forest Park. Three woodland walks start and finish at the Bogle Crag car park and picnic site [337934] ...bogle, a mischievous spirit. In this case the 'bogle' or 'boggart' which gave the crag its name is said to be that of an old woman burnt as a witch.

Bolton Hall Gosforth. 'Boutanam' in the 12th century. The 'Hall' prefix was added at a later date [087026] ...see **Bolton Head**.

Bolton Head Gosforth. Bolton Head Park to its N [088039] ...the word Bolton frequently figures in the counties of Cumbria, Lancashire and Yorkshire and is derived from 'bool' - dwelling and 'tun' - farmstead, village or town.

Bolton Head Park Gosforth [086042] ...'Booltun' - enclosure with buildings/special building.

Bolton Holme WSW slope Swainson Knott [070080] ...'enclosed buildings on an island'. Buildings and reservoir on isolated site here.

Bolton's Tarn a practically completely overgrown tarn between Crook and Crosthwaite and accessible by footpath from either C190m (C623ft) [448935] ...named after a former owner.

Bolton Wood N Nether Wasdale to Gosforth road [105048].

Bomby area S Bampton Grange across the River Lowther [522176] ...No linguistic connection with India. Actually means farmstead of the peasant landowner.

Bomby Farm Bomby [523177].

Bomery Gill rises slope of Burn Edge at 068128 and joins the River Calder at 074126.

Bonfire Hall farm, Underbarrow [475935] ...Originally Boynfierhowe (Bonfire Hill) which in later years became Bonfire Hall.

Bonington, Chris (Christian) (knighted 1996) mountaineer, writer and photographer. Residence: Hesket Newmarket.

Bonning Gate alongside Crook Road (B5284) [480952] ...possibly a surname + gate. One hundred and sixty years ago it was Bunnion Yeat and could therefore refer to person called Bunyan. It may also mean the place/area inhabited by a bondsman, an unfree man.

Bonscale farm, E Ullswater, NNW Bonscale Pike [450206] ...possibly shieling of the peasant freeholder.

Bonscale Pike and Tower two subsidiary summits of Swarth Fell both on crags overlooking Ullswater and both surmounted by cairns. The higher, Bonscale Pike, sometimes referred to as Toughmoss Pike, is 524m (1719ft) [453201] while Bonscale Tower, which possesses a more professionally built cairn, is slightly lower to the NE.

Bonscale Tower see **Bonscale Pike and Tower**.

Boo Tarn small and fast diminishing tarn alongside the Walna Scar Road 280m (919ft) [282968] ...either derived from a personal name or means the tarn by the hut.

Boon Crag Farm Coniston. Under the Marshall family it was the home farm for the Monk Coniston Estate. Monk Coniston Hall is situated just across the B5285. Purchased by the National Trust through an anonymous donor in 1945. Shortly after its acquisition the Trust established a tree nursery there. This is the centre of the Trust's woodland enterprise [306984].

Boonbeck High Lorton [164254].

Boot small village alongside Whillan Beck, Eskdale [176011]. The Ravenglass and Eskdale Railway terminates at Dalegarth nearby. Possesses a church (St. Catherine's), a Post Office, two inns (Burnmoor and Woolpack), a hotel, guest houses, several farms, a restored water-powered corn mill (Eskdale Mill), Fold End Gallery and a packhorse bridge situated on the old corpse route from Wasdale to Boot. There are several notable waterfalls nearby particularly Dalegarth Falls (also known as Stanley Gill Falls) in its wooded ravine

and Gill Force. Boot and its immediate environs once possessed a number of iron mines including Blea Tarn (167007), Christcliff area (185011), Gill Force (180999), Gate Crag (180999), and the largest of them all, Nab Gill (175012). The latter was the last to close. It ended its days in 1917 after several previous closings and reopenings. The others were abandoned in the mid 1880s.

Boot Bank Boot, Eskdale [175015].

Booth Holme Duddon valley [196917].

Booth How N Walna Scar Road. W Bursting Stone Quarry road [281971].

Border End cliffs at the SW end of Hardknott Fell above the pass and the Roman Fort. Rises to 522m (1713ft) at 228019.

Borderside Cartmel Fell. Off the Winster-Bowland Bridge road. William Pearson, naturalist and poet and friend of Wordsworth was born in Crosthwaite but eventually returned to live at Borderside in the 1820s and built the present property in 1848 [416902] ...the old border between Lancashire and Westmorland passed close by.

Boredale one of the four dales incorporated into the district called Martindale. Drops down from Boredale Hause and between Place Fell and Beda Fell to join Howe Grain (formed by the meeting of Bannerdale and Rampsgill) near Sandwick. A road from Sandwick up the dale ends at the highest habitation, Boredale Head Farm [419170], but continues as a track up to and over Boredale Hause. The Hayeswater Aqueduct follows the valley [422179] ...Valley with a dwelling or storehouse. The alternative name Boardale is of much later origin.

Boredale Beck furthest headstream is Freeze Beck which rises below Angletarn Pikes at 413150. On its way down Boredale it is joined by Blue Gill, Redgate Gill, and Hollinhow Gill. Joins Howegrain Beck at 426194 to become Sandwick Beck which enters Ullswater slightly N of the hamlet of Sandwick at 423200.

Boredale Hause many sources quote 'Boardale Hause'. The col between Patterdale and Boredale and between Place Fell and Angletarn Pikes. A meeting place of several tracks and paths. Near the summit the 2.5ins OS map shows 'Chapel in the Hause' and Bartholomew's notes 'shelter'. This, centuries ago, was a chapel for the people of Patterdale and Martindale and some sources even suggest that it was constructed by St Patrick. It was, however, a ruin even in Wordsworth's time and today what looks like a sheepfold that has been derelict for centuries is all that is left to remind us of the religious fervour of our ancestors. Unseen, yet ever present, beneath the surface of the Hause and passed over by countless feet lies the Hayeswater Aqueduct on its way down Boredale 384m (1260ft) [408157] ...see **Boredale**.

Boredale Head Farm see **Boredale**.

Borran's Field Waterhead. National Trust land at the head of Windermere and on the alluvial plain between Waterhead and the Brathay outflow. On it the Romans built their Galava Fort [373033] ...there are several Borrans/Borrens referring to burial mound(s) or ancient heaps of stones.

Borrans Lane from the Ings-Troutbeck road to High Borrans [431004].

Borrans Plantation High Borrans [432012].

Borrans Reservoir High Borrans. Presently owned by United Utilities. Dubbs Beck is a principal supplier C200m (C656ft) [429010].

Borrow Beck furthest headstream rises between Red Crag and Bleaberry Gill at 509068. Flows down Borrowdale where it is joined by West Nab Gill, Willy Gill, Crookdale Beck and Eelman Sike, before joining the R Lune below Low Borrow Bridge at 610015.

Borrowdale not quite as attractive and popular as its namesake S of Derwentwater but nevertheless, a scenic, relatively tourist and traffic-free valley and longer than its namesake. From its eastern end at Low Borrow Bridge to the end of Borrowdale is nearly 11.2kms (7 miles) of which 4kms (2.5 miles), W of the A6, and forming part of Fawcett Forest, lies within the LDNP. The Roman fort alongside Low Borrow Bridge was on the line of a S-N route to Brougham while another road headed up Borrowdale for a short distance before it crossed Whinfell and went on its way to the fort at Watercrook, Kendal [609013-515063] ...fort in a valley or valley with a fort by a stream.

Borrowdale valley of great beauty and variety lying above Dewent Water and down which the River Derwent flows and through which runs the B5289 en route from Keswick to Lorton via the Honister Pass. Towering fells particularly to its E and the picturesque hamlets of Grange-in-Borrowdale, Rosthwaite, Seatoller and the farmstead of Seathwaite alongside the valley with Rosthwaite nearby in a side valley. Castle Crag to the dale's W is an excellent viewpoint up and down and across the valley and is believed to have been an ancient fort and possibly the origin of the name Borrowdale (valley of the fort). At 290m (951ft) the crag is the lowest fell in Wainwright's seven volume *Pictorial Guide to the Lakeland Fells* and he claims that the square mile which encompasses it and where the valley narrows is "the loveliest square mile in Lakeland - the Jaws of Borrowdale."

Borrowdale Church roughly halfway between Rosthwaite and Stonethwaite. Dedicated to St Andrew. A chapel-of-ease was consecrated in 1687. Rebuilt in 1762. Restored in 1825 and 1873. Its site marks the old boundary between the lands held by Furness Abbey and those held by Fountains Abbey. The pulpit from the former Mardale Church was brought here in 1937 [258140].

Borrowdale Fells large horseshoe of high fells at the head of Borrowdale and incorporating Glaramara, Allen Crags, across the head of the Ruddy Gill/Grains Gill valley, by Sprinkling Tarn and over Seathwaite Fells and Base Brown. Marked on the OS map at 253121.

Borrowdale Gates Country House Hotel Grange-in-Borrowdale [251177].

Borrowdale Ground Corney [113910].

Borrowdale Head Farm Borrowdale. Now operated as an outlier of Forest Hall. [544041].

Borrowdale Hole Borrowdale Moss [507064].

Borrowdale Hotel Country House Hotel Grange-in-Borrowdale. Alongside the B5289 [261182].

Borrowdale Lead Mine see Seathwaite.

Borrowdale Moss W of the End of Borrowdale [510062].

Borrowdale Road part of the B5289 leading from Keswick into Borrowdale [270221].

Borrowdale Wood E A595 [103923].

Borrowdale Yews see **Seathwaite**.

Borrowdale YH see **Longthwaite YH**.

Borwick Fold old farmhouse, listed as of 17th century origin, between Ings and the B5284 (Crook). Has its own privately stocked trout tarn [443969] which in the 1930s was made by damming a swampy area. Borwick Fold lies on an ancient packhorse route and is reputed to have been an inn serving the needs of the packhorsemen and other travellers [441970] ...family name + small enclosure.

Borwick Fold Tarn see **Borwick Fold**.

Borwick Lodge formerly Borwick Ground. NW Hawkshead. Large Georgian property. Opposite the lodge the scenic old road from Knipe Fold to High Cross on the Skelwith

Bridge to Coniston road (A593) passes Iron Keld Plantation, the head of Tarn Hows and slightly W of High Arnside Tarn [342996].

Bottom Heads SSE Birk Fell summit, Place Fell [404180].

Bouch House Embleton [147295] ...associated with the family of Bowche.

Boulder Valley valley running S from Levers Water and across which flows Low Water Beck from its source, Low Tarn, high on the E side of Coniston Old Man. The valley is littered with boulders which have fallen from the extensive craggy area above and several are high and huge enough to provide practice for rock climbers. The largest called the Pudding Stone is a 7.5m (25ft) high monolith possessing several climbing routes of varying degrees of difficulty [280987] ...boulders of a rounded or suggested rounded shape are often referred to as pudding stones because their shape suggests a giant pudding.

Boundary Bank between Kendal Fell and the Kendal by-pass [499930].

Bow Mabble Breast wooded escarpment overlooking the bridleway between Thornfields and the A5074 [429938] ...Bow Mabble's slope. Who was Bow Mabble? Suggests a person called Mabel bowed down with a bent back.

Bowder Crag above the Bowder Stone, Borrowdale [256165].

Bowder Stone extremely large boulder weighing nearly 2000 tons perched precariously on one edge and lying in the Jaws of Borrowdale. Whether the result of glacial deposition or a fall from the crags above is debatable but the general concensus plumps for the first mentioned. The Lakeland eccentric Joseph Pocklington realised its value as a tourist attraction and erected a ladder against it, hewed a hole underneath whereby visitors could shake hands with companions or an old woman who lived in a cottage alongside. Today it is owned by the NT and is still a tourist attraction and a ladder is still in position for those who have a head for heights and wish to stand on its summit 11m (36ft) above ground level [254164] ...bowder is dialect for boulder.

Bowderbeck Buttermere [179167] ...boulder stream.

Bowderdale farm, Wasdale. Farmed by Joss Naylor, MBE, noted fell runner and record breaker and a legend in his own lifetime. He has also won the Biggest Liar in the World Competition held annually at Santon Bridge with a story concerning Sheeparoos - Herdwicks crossed with kangaroos to make woolly jumpers. Jos also holds the record time for climbing all 214 summits listed in Wainwright's 7 guides to the Lakeland fells - 6 days, 23 hours, 11 minutes from the first to last summit [165071] ...valley with a booth in it.

Bowdergate Gill rises at 269161 and enters Watendlath Tarn at 275161.

Bowderthwaite Bridge carries path from The Rigg to Kidsty Howes and that along the W bank of Haweswater over Riggindale Beck [467118] ...clearing with a booth or shelter by the bridge.

Bowerbank Pooley Bridge. Off the B5320 [474248] ...cottage or storehouse + bank/slope.

Bowerhouse Bridge carries the Santon Bridge to Eskdale Green road over the River Mite [132003].

Bowerhouse Inn Eskdale Green [131002] see also **Eskdale Green**.

Bowers Wood between Yewbarrow Wood and Grubbings Wood, Longsleddale [507023].

Bowfell Bow Fell on OS map. Large arch-shaped mountain overlooking the head of Mickleden and Eskdale. Wainwright noted Bowfell as number two of his six finest mountains ranking behind Scafell Pike but above Pillar, Great Gable, Blencathra and Crinkle Crags. Climbers are catered for by the impressive Bowfell Buttress, Flat Crags and Bowfell Links while walkers reach its summit by several routes, the most popular being along The

Band 902m (2959ft) [245064] ...the obvious and most accepted explanation is 'the bow-shaped mountain', a title it obviously merits. However, W H Cooper in his *The Tarns of Lakeland* suggests that the name is derived from 'bogr fjell', the mountain of the shoulder referring to its prominent supporting ridge, The Band, while both Robert Gambles and Joan Lee in their respective works indicate a personal name Bowes from its 13th century form Bowesfel.

Bowfell and adjoining fells see Reference Section: **Heights**.

Bowfell Buttress E face Bowfell. Popular with climbers [245067].

Bowfell Links precipitous face S Bowfell summit. Leave it to the rock climbers [246063].

Bowfield Wet Sleddale [546120] ...curving hillside.

Bowkerstead Farm between Satterthwaite and Force Mills. Often referred to as High Bowkerstead to differentiate it from Low Bowkerstead across the valley [359917]. It was from the bend of the road near the track to the farm that Franz von Werra made his escape in October 1940 (see **Grizedale Hall**) ...Bowker's place/site.

Bowman, Joe famous huntsman who was born at Matterdale in 1850 and died at Glenridding in 1940. Became huntsman of the Ullswater Pack in 1879 and held the post until 1911. Returned to the position three years later but eventually retired in 1924. 'Auld Hunty' is immortalised in at least two traditional songs.

Bowmanstead Coniston [300968] Area to the S of Coniston village ...the place where, in earlier times, the bowmen lived and produced their bows and arrows to defend nearby Coniston Hall and to help with the hunts.

Bowness shore of Ennerdale Water. Nearby is the Bowness Knott car park and picnic site [108155] ...curved or bow-shaped headland.

Bowness see **Bowness-on-Windermere**.

Bowness Bay E Windermere [400969] ...bay by the curved or bow-shaped headland.

Bowness Bay E shore Bassenthwaite Lake [223294] ...see **Bowness Bay** above. The headland lies to its S.

Bowness Bay Boating Co. major passenger carrying company operating on Windermere. Purchased the Windermere Iron Steamboat Co (established 1848) in 1993.

Bowness Farm E Bassenthwaite Lake. Nearby are Bowness Bay and Bowness Wood [224291].

Bowness Knott rocky hill above Ennerdale Water and Bowness Knott car park 333m (1093ft) [112155].

Bowness-on-Windermere situated alongside and overlooking Bowness Bay, Windermere. Major 'port' on Windermere it is also a popular holiday resort, fishing and boating centre, and consequently becomes very crowded in high season. Originally a Viking settlement it was called Bulebas in the late 12th and early 13th centuries but by the late 13th century it had become Bulnes, a name more in keeping with its present title. The arrival of the railway to Birthwaite (Windermere) in the middle of the 19th century brought an influx of tourists to the area and many notables, particularly industrialists, either built mansions here or moved into existing ones. Prominent amongst these was H W Schneider who moved to Belsfield and was responsible for much building in the village.

As previously mentioned the arrival of the railway brought many tourists to the area and to cater for these two rival boat operators initially vied with each other for custom. The first steam powered boat *Lady of the Lake* slightly preceded the railway in 1845. It was followed by *Lord of the Isles*, *Firefly*, *Dragonfly* and others. Today, motor vessel services are operated frequently in the season by *MV Swan* (built 1938), *MV Teal* (launched 1936) and *MV Tern* (1891) and infrequently in the winter months. Several launches also ply between Bowness, Lakeside and Waterhead or complete the 21-mile trip round the lake. Boats can also be privately chartered and smaller craft hired. A ferry has operated for over 500 years between Ferry Nab and the opposite shore of Windermere. St Martin's Church dates from the 15th century having replaced a previous edifice. Tourists are well catered for by the many hotels, guest houses and public houses.

Other attractions include The Windermere Steamboat Museum; a permanent World of Beatrix Potter Exhibition; the Old Laundry Theatre; the Royal Cinema; the Amazonian World of Reptiles and The Glebe, an undulating grassy area rising to 56m (185ft) with its Victorian bandstand, putting, miniature golf and tennis courts. A place to just relax and watch the perambulations of visitors or the many craft sailing along the lake and also to appreciate from its vantage points the views across the bay to Belle Isle, Claife Heights and up the lake [403969] ...bull's headland.

Bowness Plantation ESE summit of Bowness Knott, Ennerdale [117153].

Bowness Wood on a headland S of Bowness Bay, Bassenthwaite Lake [222290].

Bowscale N Bowscale Beck. ESE Plough Fell [169909] ...curved or bow-shaped hut.

Bowscale Beck farthest tributary rises between White How and Cloven Stone at 166906 and the Beck meets the lengthy Logan Beck at 176909.

Bowscale Fell Blencathra 702m (2303ft) [333305].

Boxtree Crook. Property off the B5284 [448954] ...Box, of the genus Buxus, are evergreen shrubs or small trees grown mainly as a border, hedge or for topiary work. The common box has, over the centuries, been used for engravings, musical instruments or other articles which can be highly polished.

Bracelet Hall Bracelet Moor [241912] ...possibly the hall on the broad level moor.

Bracelet Moor between a minor road and the A593 [245919] ...broad level moor.

Bracken today, apart from its beauty in autumn when it changes from green to a lovely russet reddish brown, bracken is not particularly liked. Fellwalkers often have trouble walking through it, its speed of encroachment is fantastic and more recently research has shown that its spores are carcinogenic (produce cancer). It is also a harbinger of tics, another nuisance for walkers. However, with over 20 places in the Lake District having bracken as part of their title it is not surprising to learn that in yesteryear bracken was a valuable quantity both in industry and farming. It was used considerably for the manufacture of potash soap used in the local cottage woollen industry. Enormous quantities of bracken were 'sledded' from fellsides or 'brackenriggs' to be burnt in a potash kiln to produce the soap. For the farmer, bracken made excellent bedding for his stock and if it is allowed to rot down for a considerable time it provides a good mulch or compost.

Bracken Gill rises W slope Lingmell at 195084 and joins Lingmell Beck at 193088.

Bracken Hause col between Helm Crag and Gibson Knott and on path between Far Easedale and Easedale [325095].

Bracken How S of Dockray C370m (C1214ft) [393211].

Bracken Howe between Thiefstead and Blaze Hill. Overlooks Tailbert Gill [533140].

Bracken Platt Watendlath [271161].

Bracken Riggs between Brackenrigg and Dodd Crag and above Snipeshow Tarn [296209].

Bracken Wreay off the Ennerdale Bridge to Cleator Moor road [059153].

Brackenbarrow Farm Torver [291944].

Brackenburn Manesty. Famous author Hugh Walpole (later knighted) purchased Brackenburn (built 1909) in 1923 and here he wrote most of his works. He died at Brackenburn in 1941 [249912].

Brackenclose Fell and Rock Climbing Club hut at the head of Wastwater [185073].

Brackenrigg Bowness-on-Windermere. SW Brant Fell [406959].

Brackenrigg E A5074. N Hubbersty Head [424926].

Brackenrigg alongside the A591 at the foot of Bracken Riggs [298210].

Brackenrigg Hotel Watermillock. Formerly known as the Fox and Hounds. At the junction of the A592 and the minor road to Bennethead [449232].

Brackenthwaite Nether Staveley. Fell area to the W of Crook Road [460966] ...One of many 'clearings amongst the bracken' in Cumbria.

Brackenthwaite alongside the Duddon Bridge to Ulpha road W of the Duddon [180923].

Brackenthwaite area to the NE of Loweswater [155221].

Brackenthwaite Fell craggy and scree area to the N of Grasmoor summit [173208].

Brackenthwaite Hows earlier Lanthwaite Hill and one of Thomas West's 'Stations', see **West, Thomas**. Only a small hill 208m (682ft) but an excellent viewpoint of the fells on either side and particularly looking down to Crummock Water and beyond [154214].

Brackenwife Knotts N Stone Arthur [347094] ...wives figure prominently in place names hereabouts. There is Willie Wife Moor below Dollywaggon Pike and Fisher's Wife's Rake, E St John's in the Vale while two former fields in the Grasmere area are called Bessy Backside and Harry Wives respectively ...Bracken, as well as referring to the plant, is an old Westmorland surname.

Bradley Field farm off Brigsteer Road [500919] see also **Underbarrow & Bradleyfield**.

Bradleyfield E slope Underbarrow Scar (Scout Scar) [494916]. See also **Underbarrow & Bradleyfield** and **Kendal Racecourse**.

Bradleyfield House off Underbarrow Road [495925]. See also **Underbarrow & Bradleyfield.**

Braesteads farm in Grisedale [377156].

Bragg, Melvyn (made a Life Peer in 1998. Now Baron Bragg of Wigton). Born at Wigton, Cumbria, in 1939 and now lives at High Ireby. Editor and presenter of the *South Bank Show*, arts programme on TV since 1978. Also a biographer but principally a novelist with most of his works being set in his native Cumbria. These include his first novel, *For Want of a Nail* (1965) followed by others including *The Hired Man*, *A Time to Dance*, *Without a City Wall*, *The Maid of Buttermere*, *The Cumbrian Trilogy, Credo*, *The Soldier's Return* and *A Son of War* (2001). His most recent work is *Adventures in English* (2003).

Braidy Beck rises Bursting Stone Quarry at 280961. Fed by several tributaries before joining Scrow Beck at 290973.

Braithwaite village on the B5292 (A66-Lorton-Cockermouth road) and at the foot of the Whinlatter and Newlands Passes. Many years ago the village possessed a woollen mill, a flour mill and was the original site for the Cumberland Pencil Co. A considerable number of miners and quarry workers once lived here. Coledale Beck flows through the village. The church is just over 100 years old and was originally a Chapel of Ease to the parish church of St. Mary, Thornthwaite. It is dedicated to St. Herbert who lived on the island which bears his name in Derwent Water. Braithwaite boasts two hostelries, the Coledale Inn and the Royal Oak. The former takes its name from the valley down which flows Coledale Beck. It was once used as a woollen mill and later, in 1868, the Cumberland Pencil Co. was founded here in part of the buildings before the firm moved to Keswick after a fire 30 years later. The Royal Oak is a traditional Lakeland inn. Its name commemorates Charles II who hid in an oak tree at Boscobel after the Battle of Worcester in 1651 [230236] ...broad clearing.

Braithwaite How Braithwaite 172m (564ft) [230240].

Braithwaite Lodge Braithwaite [233232].

Braithwaite Moss NNE Braithwaite [234247].

Braithwaite Plantation Grizedale [343947].

Bram Crag E of and overlooking B5322 [321216]. Contains a deep gully of great interest to climbers ...presumably a personal name as it was Brian Cragge in the early 17th century.

Bram Crag farm off B5322 [319214].

Bramcrag Quarry disused. E B5322. St John's in the Vale. Home of the smallest of our three native newt species, the palmate [320220].

Bramley off the Mockerkin to Mosser road [108237].

Bramley Seat rocky outcrop above Bramley [109238].

Brandelhow Bay Derwent Water [252196].

Brandelhow Park W shore Derwent Water. The first acquisition by the NT in the Lake District and opened in October 1902. Funds to purchase it and prevent housing development were raised by a public appeal. Queen Victoria's daughter, Princess Louise, presided at the opening ceremony and four oak trees were planted to mark the occasion [252204].

Brandelhow Point promontory. W shore Derwent Water [253195].

Brandlingill alongside the minor road from Aikbank Mill to Randle Cross [122265].

Brandreth summit on the ridge betwen Grey Knotts and Green Gable usually climbed on the Honister Hause-Grey Knotts-Green Gable-Great Gable route 715m (2346ft) [215119] ...from the ON 'brand-reio' meaning grate/tripod/trivet and suggesting that there was once a beacon here lit in a three-legged recepticle. This is implied by a reference in 1805 to the 'three-footed Brandreth'. Another but possibly more subtle explanation is that the tripod/trivot refers to the fact that the mountain is the culmination of three ridges and occupies a triangular pattern.

Brandreth Three Tarns sometimes referred to as just Three Tarns. Actually four tarns are shown on the OS map lying S of the summit of Brandreth on Gillercombe Head C660m (C2165ft) [215115].

Brandy Crag Dunnerdale Forest. N Grassguards [225989] ...the EPNS notes that it is said that "the name preserves the meaning of a cache for smuggled goods which were brought down from Ravenglass along an old packhorse road."

Branken Wall Muncaster [098970].

Branstree SE of the head of Haweswater and NNE of the summit of Gatescarth Pass. The name is a contraction of Brant Street which is given on the OS map to the steep fellside overlooking Haweswater. The actual summit of Branstree is flat-topped and grassy and is not named on the OS map although Branstree is given to the slope overlooking the Gatescarth Pass. Neither is the sunken trig. point shown. This is sited just N of the junction of the wall up Selside Brow and the wire fence from Gatescarth Pass. A trig. point of this style is most unusual as practically all are set on either concrete or stone pillars. Similar ones not far distant are on Great Yarlside and Seat Robert. Wainwright and others claim the summit as 711m (2333ft). However, the OS suggests that the nearby large-cairned Artlecrag Pike is the highest point at 713m (2339ft) [478100] ...'steep path', possibly referring to the steep track of the Gatescarth Pass up from Mardale Head to its summit.

Brant Brows slope Loughrigg Fell above Pelter Bridge [363058] ...steep slopes.

Brant Fell N B5284. E A5074. Trig. point at 191m (627ft). Writing in his *The Outlying Fells of Lakeland* (1973) Alfred Wainwright notes that on the top of the fell "occur the railings, foundations and a well of a former summerhouse, which was destroyed in a fire" [410962] ...steep hill.

Brant Rake Eskdale [148987].

Brant Street steep fellside below Branstree/Artlecrag Pike. E head of Haweswater [476108].

Brantfell Farm N Brant Fell [410964].

Brantrake Crags between Black Beck and the River Esk. Rises to 259m (850ft) [149982].

Brantrake Moss N Water Crag. Black Beck flows through it [154980].

Brantstocks Ulpha. [199927] ...suggests a steep slope once covered by tree stumps.

Brantwood E side Coniston Water. Former home of John Ruskin (1819-1900), poet, writer, art critic, artist and pro-reformer of the social injustice campaign. Brantwood began as a cottage in the 18th century and when Ruskin bought it from W J Linton and his novelist wife, Eliza Lynn, in 1871 for £1500 it was in a dilapidated state. Over the next 29 years Ruskin repaired and extended the cottage until it became the property we see today. He died at Brantwood in January 1900. The house is open to the public. The gardens comprise eight separate entities ranging from the most recently completed Zig-Zaggy Garden to the Moorland Garden [313958] ...steep wood.

Brathay area adjoining Clappersgate across the River Brathay. Principally comprises Old Brathay (Brathay Farm), Brathay Hall, Brathay Church and a former Sunday School. [367030] ...broad river, that being the River Brathay.

Brathay Bridge bridge which carries the B5286, Clappersgate-Hawkshead road, over the River Brathay. The bridge was probably replaced centuries ago by a packhorse bridge. It collapsed in 1681 and was rebuilt as a much broader structure. In the 20th century levelled out and modified [367034].

Brathay Church Holy Trinity Church, Brathay, stands on a hillock overlooking the River Brathay and facing Loughrigg Fell across the valley. Of Italianate style it was built by Giles Redmayne of Brathay Hall in 1836 [362033].

Brathay Farm alongside the B5286, Clappersgate-Hawkshead road, immediately after the bridge over the Brathay. Variously called Old Brathay/Low Brathay. A large house with farm buildings. In the 17th century the oldest part was an alehouse but in the following century Low Brathay was developed as a country seat and from 1799-1815 was the home of Charles Lloyd, poet and novelist (1775-1839). In 1950 the building was acquired as additional premises for the Brathay Hall Trust and in 1996 after refurbishment, opened as a 30-bed training centre for young people [367034]. See also **Brathay Hall**.

Brathay Garths enclosed woodland ('garth' means enclosure). Part of the Brathay Hall estate [366027].

Brathay Hall S Clappersgate, off the B5286. Today it is the headquarters of the Brathay Hall Trust which organises Leadership and Development Training/Youth and Environment Training/Brathay Explorations Group. The site was originally a small farm before the erection of the hall by George Law towards the end of the 18th century. Over the succeeding years Brathay Hall has been owned, or leased, by several notable families including the Hardens, the Redmaynes, the Bells of Yorkshire and the Irvings of Liverpool. The Brathay Hall Trust was founded by Francis Scott, managing director of the Provincial Insurance Co, the hall's then owner, in 1946, and the Brathay Hall Exploration Group began in 1949. A

Field Studies Centre was formally opened in 1967 [367031]. See also **Brathay Farm**.

Brathay Quarries Great Brathay [358015].

Brathay, River see **River Brathay**.

Brathay Rocks Windermere, near the inflow of the River Brathay [372028].

Brat's Hill see **Brat's Moss**.

Brat's Moss boggy area N Boot, Eskdale. Brat's Hill [173025] slightly to its SW. Several stone circles and cairns in its vicinity [176026].

Braw Crags Deepdale Common [379132].

Breast Route see **Great Gable**.

Breasty Haw area near Satterthwaite. Crossed by the Bogle Crag Blue Walk [345928] ...possibly side of the hill or copse on the side of the hill.

Breasty Haw property at Satterthwaite [339927].

Brewer Wood opposite Force Beck from Force Forge [337905].

Breweries Cumbria possesses several breweries. These comprise *Jennings* - the largest in Cumbria. Established in 1828 at Lorton and which moved to its present site at Cockermouth in 1874; *Barngates Brewery* - established at the Drunken Duck, Barngates, in 1997; *Bitter End Brewery* - brewed since 1995 at the pub of that name at Cockermouth; *Cartmel Brewery* - began brewing beside the Cavendish Arms, Cartmel, in 1994, moved to larger premises at Kendal the following year but ceased brewing there in April, 1998; *Coniston Brewing Co* - established behind the Black Bull, Coniston, in 1995 and won Champion Beer of Britain with its Bluebird Bitter at the 1998 Great Britain Beer Festival; *Dent Brewery* - brewed at Dent since 1990; *Derwent Brewery* - opened at Cockermouth in 1997, now at Silloth; *Foxfield Brewery* - brewed at the Prince of Wales, Foxfield, since 1997; *Great Gable Brewing Co Ltd*, Wasdale Head Inn, Wasdale - brewing began in the first half of 2002; *Hawkshead Brewery* - full brewing began in summer 2002 at an 18th century barn at Town End, Colthouse, Hawkshead, which was previously the Town End Dairy; *Hesket Newmarket Brewery* - brewed since 1988; *Lakeland Brewing Co* - opened in 1990 behind the Masons Arms, Strawberry Bank. Moved to new premises at Kendal in 1997; *Strawberry Bank Brewery* - originally Lakeland Brewing Co but name changed in 1997. Brewed behind the Strawberry Bank Inn; *Loweswater Brewery* - Kirkstile Inn, Loweswater, was established in the summer of 2003; *Tirril Brewer* - Queen's Head Inn, Tirril - commenced in 1999 but production was subsequently moved to Brougham Hall; *Yates Brewery* - started in 1986 and brewed at Westnewton.

Briar Rigg Keswick [268241].

Briar Shot E Hawkshead-Newby Bridge road [374925] ...'shot' is a dialect word for an ill-grown ewe.

Bridge End former farm across bridge over Greenburn Beck. Bequeathed to the National Trust and now run as a holiday cottage [301029].

Bridge End approximately 0.54kms (0.3 mile) SE Sandwick [427193].

Bridge End property alongside footbridge over R Sprint, Longsleddale [510010].

Bridge End off the A593. A bridge across Steers Pool (Lord's Gill) nearby [246903].

Bridge End Waberthwaite. Alongside the bridge which carries the A595 over Mill Gill/Broadoak Beck [114946].

Bridge End Farm N Thirlmere between minor road around the W side of the reservoir and St John's Beck. Nearby the river can be crossed in normal conditions by large stepping stones [314194].

Bridge End Farm Santon Bridge [112016].

Bridge House W bank St John's Beck [310226].

Bridge House Ambleside. See *Stock Ghyll.*

Bridge Lane connects Troutbeck Bridge to Town End, Troutbeck [407015]

Bridge Petton Gosforth [070030] ...probably an inversion compound but the bridge part is unexplained.

Bridgend cottages on A592 1.6kms (1 mile) S Patterdale. Here, at Deepdale Bridge, the A592 crosses Deepdale Beck and from a small car parking area a path leads over a curious double bridge over the beck, across fields and Goldrill Beck, to meet the Patterdale-Hartsop track and one to Boredale Hause. Across the A592, initially a cart track and then a path traverses to the head of Deepdale. Occasionally referred to as Deepdale Bridge [399145].

Bridgend Threlkeld [327252].

Bridges promontory between the River Derwent and Bridges Hole, Bassenthwaite Lake. Two bridges over the Derwent nearby [233271].

Bridges Hole bay alongside Bridges, Bassenthwaite Lake [231271].

Brier's Intake Coppice Claife Heights [382993].

Briery alongside the River Greta [286242].

Briery Close alongside Holbeck Lane. Complex of buildings around a mansion which was the home of John Kay-Shuttleworth, industrialist and educationalist, and where, in 1850, Charlotte Bronte met and befriended her future biographer, novelist Mrs Gaskell. In 1956 the complex became the home of the Briery Close Arabian Stud but this moved to Calgarth Hall in 1991. In its grounds is the large Briery Mount [391019].

Brigham/Low Brigham Keswick [277238] and [273236] respectively ...Brigholm in the 13th century. Therefore holmr (islet or isolated piece of land) by the bridge.

Brighouse farm off the fell road between Ulpha and Eskdale. Acquired by the NT in 1950 [197947].

Brighouse Muncaster [089953].

Bright Beck flows down from the E slope of the plateau-like ridge between Thunacar Knott and High White Stones at 281086 to join Stickle Tarn at 289078 ...bright water stream.

Brigsteer Road Brigsteer to Kendal.

Brigstone Moss on the watershed between Silver How and Lang How [322069] ...On early OS maps boundary stones are shown on the Moss.

Brigstone Tarn not named on the OS map. Near Brigstone Moss and E of Youdell Tarn C370 (C1214ft) [319068].

Brim Fell next summit to Coniston Old Man northwards on the ridge to Swirl How. A slightly curved broad summit with its highest point at 796m (2611ft) just 7m (23ft) below that of the Old Man [271986] ...fell on the brim.

Brim Fell End end of Brim Fell ridge overlooking Levers Water [279989].

Brim Fell Haws Brim Fell [275985].

Brim Fell Rake E slope Brim Fell [272988].

Brimful Beck rises Low Tarn at 161092 and joins Over Beck at 167082.

Brimmer Head Farm Easedale, Grasmere [324085].

Brimming Knott Watendlath Fell [283152].

Brin Crag W Brandreth. Below is Tongue Beck and above this Tongue [209119] ...Centuries ago Tongue was called le Brinttenng.

Brinhowe Crag Easedale. Little Brinhowe Gill flows below [317087]. 'Brimmer' in 1847. Nearby is Brimmer Head Farm ...brow/edge of a hill.

Brink Rigg W Thirlmere. Between Brown Rigg and Hause Gill [313150].

Britannia Inn Elterwater. A farm before 1858 in which year it was owned by a beer retailer. By 1885 it had been named The Britannia. Two schools of thought as to the origin of the name. One - after one of the seven HMS Britannias, possibly that commissioned in 1762 and broken up in 1825. Two - simply as a patriotic gesture by locals [328048].

Broad Crag originally shown on maps as one of the Scafell Pikes along with Scafell Pike and Ill Crag. Lies but a stone's throw from the latter and there are indeed many stones and boulders on its summit. Alfred Wainwright speaks of it as "the roughest summit in Lakeland." In its *The Lakeland Fells*, the Fell and Rock Climbing Club position it as 6th in the hierarchy of the Lakeland mountains. Although its summit is only a very short distance from the well-used path between Esk Hause and Scafell Pike few people make a detour. Consequently, they miss an impressive view NW over the Corridor Route and Piers Gill to Lingmell and N to Great Gable. In 1946 a De Havilland Dominie crashed on the Crag killing its five occupants. At 930m (3051ft) [219076] Broad Crag lies NE of Scafell Pike but there is, or are, Broad Crags equidistant to the SW of the Pike and a Broadcrag Tarn lies on the summit shelf.

Broad Crag S Blea Rigg and overlooking Scale Gill [300074].

Broad Crag to the W of the path from Scandale Pass col up to Red Screes [389093].

Broad Crag Yewbarrow. Adjacent Bell Rib [173079].

Broad Crag Buckbarrow [138060].

Broad Crag The Screes, Wasdale [150039].

Broad Crag Birker Moor. E Great Crag. SW Green Crag 372m (1220ft) [195978].

Broad End end of the ridge which drops down from Caudale Moor over Pike How and alongside Woundale to the A592, Windermere-Kirkstone Pass road [405075].

Broad End Skiddaw N ridge 831m (2726ft) [261298].

Broad End between Skiddaw Little Man and Carl Side [261280].

Broad Gill rises Skiddaw Forest at 281292 and joins the River Caldew at 286296].

Broad Haws E Long House. N Walna Scar Road [243969] ...broad hills.

Broad Haystack Rosthwaite Fell. NNE Bessyboot [260133].

Broad Hollins E Coniston Water [301917].

Broad How see **Rooking**.

Broad Howe overlooks Trout Beck from the W [420088].

Broadmire Intake Claife Heights [378969].

Broad Oak Underbarrow. Off the Underbarrow to Brigsteer road. Built 1565 the same year as nearby Fallen Yew but completed before the latter [469918].

Broad Oak alongside the A595 3.2kms (2 miles) NE then N Waberthwaite [114947]. A large quarry here closed to all intents and purposes in 1946 and is now an SSSI.

Broad Oaks off Bridge Lane, Troutbeck Bridge. A country house hotel [406011].

Broad Piece Grizedale [332944].

Broad Slack rock and scree slope at the head of Greenburn and between Swirl How and Great Carrs [272007] ...broad hollow.

Broad Stand a wall of huge precipitous rocks providing a route up Scafell from Mickledoor for experienced rock climbers but certainly not casual walkers. Samuel Taylor Coleridge is credited with the first descent of Broad Stand and the first recorded rock climb in August 1802. He subsequently wrote "My limbs were all in a tremble." In fact, he was lucky to have escaped with his life from such a perilous descent [210068].

Broad Stone W of Kirkstone Pass Inn across the A592 [399081].

Broad Stone alongside the River Irt [132037].

Broad Tongue NE Burnmoor Tarn between Hardrigg Gill and Oliver Gill [195051].

Broadcrag Tarn surely should be Broadcrags Tarn as it lies on Broad Crags and not Broad Crag. Generally accepted as the highest tarn in the Lake District although Foxes Tarn on Scafell runs it a very close second and, according to the OS "it is not possible to give an accurate height for either." Alt. 820-830m (2690-2723ft) [213069].

Broadfold Nether Staveley. Off the A591 Kendal to Windermere road [476970].

Broadgate Farm alongside the Ings-Troutbeck [435995] ...Broad street/way. Nearby names The Causeway (raised way) and Crosses has led authorities to believe that part of the present Ings-Troutbeck road and that continuing down to Troutbeck Bridge would have been more or less on the line of an old medieval and possibly Roman road.

Broadmoor Ennerdale. Parkland between Ennerdale Bridge and Ennerdale Water [082158].

Broadmoor Hill rear of Dodd Wood. Rises to 286m (938ft) at 143246.

Broadness Farm E Bassenthwaite Lake. The Allerdale Ramble passes alongside [222297].

Broadoak Beck continuation of Mill Gill. Enters the River Esk at 099953. See also **Samgarth** and **Stainton Becks**.

Broadslack SW Caw [228940] ...wide hollow.

Broadslack Beck rises on the SE slope of Caw at 233942. Joins Long Mire Beck at 231933.

Broadslack Crag S Caw (231943].

Broadslack Gill rises below Castle Crag, Borrowdale, at 247157. Two principal tributaries join at 248159 and 248160 respectively. The gill joins the River Derwent at 251166.

Broadstone Head crags at the head of Far Easedale [296099].

Brock Barrow E Kiln Bank Farm. N Tommy Gill 343m (1125ft) [220943].

Brock Bield N King's How, Grange Fell [259171] ...badger's shelter.

Brock Crag Beda Fell. High Brock Crag and Low Brock Crags are also alongside the ridge [425170] ...badger crag.

Brock Crag craggy end of S shoulder of Scafell overlooking Scale Gill, the River Esk and Eskdale 342m (1122ft) [215029].

Brock Crag end of one arm of Sandy Wyke, Windermere [369023].

Brock Crag Longsleddale. SSE Great Howe. Manchester Corporation Waterworks survey post above [491061]. See also **Pillars**.

Brock Crag W Dale Park Beck valley [346923].

Brock Crag W High Street Roman Road and E Cote Farm, Fusedale [451189].

Brock Crag Dodd Wood [242271].

Brock Crags overlooking Hartsop from the ENE. Satura Crag is to the E and Angle Tarn to the N. The Hayeswater Aqueduct passes across its slopes. Four small tarns are shown in the vicinity of its summit cairn 561m (1841ft) [417137] ...badger crags.

Brock How overlooking Tarn Head Beck [264994] ...badger hill.

Brock How Seathwaite Fells [247975].

Brock Stone see **Badger Rock**.

Brocken Spectre a phenomenon occasionally seen in the Lake District by walkers on the summits of mountains or high fells. In conditions where the sun is behind the walker and the valley is mist-filled he or she sometimes sees their huge shadow on the mist below with sometimes halos, rainbows or coloured circles around the figure. So called because it was first observed on the Brocken Mountain, Germany.

Brockhole Hag Hutton John [443271] ...badger set wood.

Brockhole National Park Visitor Centre alongside the A591 between Windermere and Ambleside. Mansion built in 1899 by Manchester businessman, William Gaddum, and gardens laid out by noted landscape gardener, Thomas Mawson. Subsequently the property became a convalescent home before purchase by the Lake District National Park authority in 1966 for £65,000. It opened in June 1969. The spacious gardens are open all year. Admission is free to the centre and gardens but there is a charge for car parking [390010].

Brockle Beck rises NNE of the summit of Bleaberry Fell at 287199 and flows down by Castlerigg then under the B5289 and through The Ings to join Derwent Water at 268220 ...badger sett by the stream.

Brocklebank Ground Torver. Guest house off the A593 [277939] ...badger set bank.

Brockshaw Beck two tributaries rise Whinscales at 197034 and 198033 respectively. Combine at 191028 and the Beck joins Whillan Beck at 184022 ...badger copse/wood stream.

Brockstones Kentmere [467053] ...badger stones.

Broken Rib The Screes, Wasdale [153043].

Brook Farm Thackthwaite, Lorton Vale [149237].

Brook House Boot, Eskdale. Hotel and restaurant [176009].

Brookside Elterwater. Alongside the B5343 [335046] ...as its name implies alongside a brook. This drops down by Low Wood to join Elter Water.

Broom Bank between Stanegarth and Winder Hill [499175].

Broom Fell Lord's Seat Group 511m (1676ft) [194272].

Broom Hill E Ullswater. Between the lake and Barton Park [464227].

Broom Hill side of the Winster valley [415942].

Broom Lane connects the Crook-Underbarrow road with the Underbarrow-Crosthwaite road [457922].

Broom Riggs E Esthwaite Water [365971].

Broom, The see **The Broom**.

Broomhill Plantation one of three plantations in Grisedale [368150].

Brotherilkeld the last farm in Eskdale. Owned by the NT since 1961 when, along with Black Hall Farm, Dunnerdale, it was purchased to prevent the afforestation of the upper Eskdale and Hardknott Pass areas. Earlier Butherulkil or Butterilkelt and at one time a grange farm of Furness Abbey who acquired an already old farmstead in the 13th century. Rebuilt in the 17th century [213014] ...Ulfketil's/Ulkell's booths/bothies/huts.

Brothers Parting Stone see **Grisedale Tarn**.

Brothers Water much earlier Broader Water or Broad Water. At the foot of Kirkstone Pass. Now owned by the National Trust. The present name is said to have been derived from two brothers being drowned in it while skating in December 1785. Smallest of the lakes but at 158m (520ft) above sea level it is the third highest of them. Maximum depth 21m (70ft). So far, along with Ullswater, Haweswater and Red Tarn, confirmed as one of the only waters in England in which the rare schelly lives [403127].

Brotherswater Inn opened in the early 19th century. Then called The Cross Keys. Later, as it is sited at Kirkstone Foot (the foot of Kirkstone Pass), it was renamed the Kirkstone Foot Inn and is still known by many locals as 'The Foot'. Subsequently given its present title, the Brotherswater Inn. When the nearby Hartsop Mine was closed about 1860 stones from the buildings were used to build an extension to the inn [404119].

Broughton Mills hamlet consisting of scattered farms and cottages approx. 3.2 kms (2 miles) by road from Broughton-in-Furness. The River Lickle flows nearby on its way to join the Duddon. The old Blacksmiths Arms dates from the mid 18th century and is one of the relatively few hostelries in the country, and one of two in Cumbria rated by CAMRA as Heritage Pubs because of their unspoilt interior character. Up to 1988 the inn was combined with a farm and shop. Once the hamlet possessed a woollen mill (later to become a bobbin mill) and a corn mill. Walk Mill (a fulling mill) appears on the OS map at 224905. There are remains of former lime kilns in the vicinity and disused quarries on the surrounding fells. The church of Holy Innocents, consecrated in 1888, is situated alongside the start of the fell road to Seathwaite [223906] ...takes its name from the former mills thereabouts.

Broughton Moor moorland area W Torver and NE Broughton Mills. Part is occupied by the large Broughton Moor Quarry [254940].

Broughton Moor Quarry large quarry near Torver. One of the few still operating in the Lake District National Park. Its coarse textured green slate is used particularly for roofing and much is exported [254945].

Brow former farm, Little Langdale. Off the old road from Little Langdale to Elterwater [314037].

Brow, The see **The Brow**.

Brow Coppice alongside minor road from the Outgate-Skelwith Fold road to the A593, Skelwith Bridge-Coniston road [342029].

Brow Gill rises 502061 and flows down alongside Ancrow Brow to meet Stockdale Beck at 492056.

Brow Head old farm alongside Back Lane, Crook. From 1892 until 1905 it was owned by the Home Colonisation Society who provided home and training for epileptic boys and youths. Later the colony moved to Starnthwaite [441945]. See also Starnthwaite Ghyll.

Brow Head Farm properties at the end of a surfaced lane which, after buildings, becomes a track past the former Ambleside Golf Club. It then continues as a path to Loughrigg Fell [367045].

Brow Lane Staveley. From main road through the village to the Kentmere road [467984].

Brow Side hillside above Browside Farm, Duddon valley [238987].

Brow Side Fell SE Grey Friar [262001].

Brow Wood adjoining Highgate Farm. Slightly S of A66(T) [447274].

Browfoot farm alongside Browfoot Lane, Kentmere [455008].

Browfoot Lane Scroggs Bridge, Staveley, to track from The Heights to Kentmere [458005].

Brown Band band of crags NNE Boot, Eskdale [172020].

Brown Band between Tongue Gill and Gowder Crag [140103].

Brown Beck rises 465197. Joined by Wartches Beck, Annas Sike, and meets Heltondale Beck at 486198.

Brown Beck rises High Rigg at 305215 and flows down to Naddle Beck at 300214.

Brown Cove above Keppel Cove and possibly the most enclosed combe in the Lake District. At one time, before a dam was built lower down, the small tarn it contains, fed by a head stream from Helvellyn Lower Man, was dammed and used as a reservoir by the Greenside Mining Co. The tarn, now two linked shallow pools, has no appreciable depth and lies at an altitude of 625m (2051ft) [343160].

Brown Cove Tarn see **Brown Cove**.

Brown Crag between Low White Stones and Thick Side [271103].

Brown Crag E Raise and on lower slope of White Side, Helvellyn range 610m (2001ft) [328177].

Brown Crags Longsleddale. N Goat Scar summit, S Raven Crag [473076].

Brown Dodd Glenridding Common. E of the top of zig zag on pony track from foot of Keppel Cove up to White Side. Excellent views of Brown Cove and crags E Helvellyn Lower Man, Swirral Edge and Catstye Cam [351171].

Brown Dodd a summit on the E ridge of Grange Fell and on the W flank of the Watendlath valley. N Ether Knott [266177].

Brown Edge Blengdale Forest [103072].

Brown Haw between Fox Haw and Park Head Road [222937].

Brown Hill S Keld, WSW Thornship 262m (860ft) [553140]. Path from Wet Sleddale to Keld passes slightly to the W of it.

Brown Hills overlooking Glencoyne, Glencoyne Beck, and Ullswater on section of high-level walkers' route to Hart Side from Dockray C590 (C1936) [372193].

Brown Horse Inn Winster. See **Winster**.

Brown How overlooks Thirlspot and A591. Below Brown Crag [321176].

Brown How spur between Tongue Gills and Greendale Gill [143067].

Brown How between Bowness Knott and Great Borne C320m (C1050ft) [116158].

Brown How Lorton Fells 517m (1696ft) [191251].

Brown How see **Lingmoor Fell**.

Brown How Whinlatter 517m (1696ft) [191251].

Brown Howe Mardale Banks, E Haweswater. E Brownhowe Crag [485124].

Brown Howe on the ridge and alongside the path between Kentmere Pike and The Knowe C700m (C2297ft) [463083] ...either named after a member of the family of one Richard Broune or simply means the brown hill.

Brown Howe overlooks Browney Gill from the E. Path from Oxendale to Red Tarn/Pike o'Blisco/Crinkle Crags passes over it [267047].

Brown Howe W Little Saddle Crag across Brownhowe Gutter. Cairn at C560m (C1837) [519085].

Brown Howe off the A5084, Torver to Blawith road [290908].

Brown Knotts to the E of and above Derwentwater YHA, Borrowdale [273199].

Brown Pike on Dow Crag ridge above Walna Scar Road 682m (2237ft) [261966].

Brown Rigg alongside the head of Aik Beck [470211].

Brown Rigg W Thirlmere 463m (1519ft) [305146].

Brown Rigg alongside the Birker Moor Road [180962].

Brown Tongue at one time comprised a grass ridge vestiges of which still remain. Today steep and eroded and principally brown in colour betwen Lingmell Gill and a major tributary. Ascended by a popular route to Scafell Pike via Hollow Stones and one to Scafell via Lord's Rake [198074].

Browncove Crags WNW/NW Helvellyn Lower Man. An odd name for these particular crags considering that Brown Cove is on the other side of the Helvellyn ridge [331159].

Browndale Beck rises E slope Watson's Dodd at 339195 and joins Aira Beck at 353200.

Brownend Plantation paths from Glenridding which meet that from Patterdale en route to Hole-in-the-Wall and over Striding Edge pass through this plantation SW Lanty's Tarn [381160].

Browney Gill sometimes referred to as Brown or Brownie Gill. Flows out of Red Tarn at 268038. Just before it combines with Buscoe Sike and Crinkle Gill at 264052 to form

Oxendale Beck it is joined by Isaac Gill at 265051 ...'Brown' - surname? Brown Howe overlooks.

Brownhow Hill W of minor road from A66-Matterdale End 305m (100lft) [408266].

Brownhowe Bottom connects Gatescarth Pass with Mosedale [479086].

Brownhowe Crag Mardale Banks, E Haweswater. W Brown Howe [483124].

Brownhowe Gutter rises SW Little Saddle Crag at 524081 and joins Sleddale Beck at 518091.

Brownrigg Farm off minor road from A66-Matterdale End [408245].

Brownrigg Moss W Calf Crag, E Greenup Edge [297104].

Brownrigg Well also known as Whelpside Gill Spring. Approximately 457m (500yds) W Helvellyn summit. Situated at 853m (2799ft) it is the source of Whelpside Gill and is Wordsworth's "the fountain of the mists" claimed by him to be the "...highest fountain known on British Land" [338150] (England).

Brown's Coaches Brown's actually began around 1853 when two Ambleside hotels, the Queens and the Salutation, joined forces to provide horse-drawn carriages for their customers. Between 1902-1993 under the Faulkner family the firm expanded from carriages to up-to-date luxury coaches. For a short period the firm was in the hands of the Mountain Goat Co before the old-established coach proprietors Shaw Hadwin took over. However, still trades under the name of Brown's. In November 1995, after over 142 years in Ambleside the firm moved to new premises in Windermere.

Brownspring Coppice slightly E Fairbank Farm. Alongside part of the Kendal-Windermere railway line [458980] ...family name Broun/Brown.

Brownthwaite Crag on ridge between the head of Fusedale and Ramps Gill, NNW Gowk Hill, 444m (1457ft) [443173].

Browside farm below Brow Side, Troutal, Duddon valley. Along with other Duddon valley farms, Beckstones, Brighouse, Hazel Head, Pike Side and Thrang, Browside was given to the NT in 1950 by the Rev. H H Symonds, a prominent official in the Friends of the Lake District and one-time chairman of the Lake District Farm Estates (formed in 1937 to safeguard landscape and the livelihoods of farmers through careful ownership of especially sensitive farms). Ceased in 1977 when the last holdings were transferred to the NT [236987].

Brumston Bridge bridge over Wythop Beck [185293].

Brund Fell highest point of Grange Fell 415m (1362ft) [264162].

Brund Gill rises at 337171 and flows down to be joined by Sticks Gill at 328180 and from confluence becomes Fisherplace Gill (Fisher Gill).

Brundholme W Wescoe. Alongside Glenderaterra Beck [298250].

Brundholme Wood [288248].

Brundriggs S A591, Kendal-Windermere road [453985] ...more than likely the burnt ridge cleared by burning.

Brunt Crag SSE Dockray. Overlooks A5091 [396209].

Brunt Crag W slope Cat Bells [241192].

Brunt Crags slope Robinson above Little Dale [207168].

Brunt Fells fell area W Long Mire Beck [229933].

Brunt How property alongside Brunt How [350037].

Brunt How wooded hillside N A593 between Clappersgate and Skelwith Bridge [355037] ...originally the hill cleared by burning.

Brunt Knott NE Scales Tarn, Blencathra [331283] ...burnt hillock.

Brunt Knott Sleddale Forest. A path from Staveley to Longsleddale passes to its S Trig.

point at 427m (1401ft) [484006] ...burnt hillock.

Brunt Knott Farm Over Staveley. Below Brunt Knott [478002].

Brunt Stones W of the summit of Loadpot Hill [454180].

Brunt Tongue tongue of land between Mosedale Beck and Little Mosedale Beck [502092] ...burnt tongue of land.

Bruts Moss Matterdale Common [355216].

Bryan Beck property alongside the beck which flows down to meet the River Winster [407902]. See also **Bryan House Farm**.

Bryan House Farm Winster valley. Known as Brime House in the late 17th century and from this property former Westmorland clockmaker, Jonas Baber, carried on his horological trade from 1682-1720. Subsequently he was succeeded by his son and grandson. The latter died in 1802. More detailed information on the Babers appears in Brian Loomes' *Westmorland Clock and Clockmakers* (1974) [416928] ...surname? Across the Winster there is a Bryan Beck on Cartmel Fell at 407902.

Bryan Houses Plantation alongside the A5074 and separated by it and minor road from Bryan House Farm [425931].

Bryant's Gill rises 440054. Joined by Skeel Gill at 449065 and enters the R Kent at 450068. Excavations on its N bank of archaeological sites ...surname + stream.

Bryer's Fold Far Sawrey [382952].

Buck Barrow SSW Whitfell 549m (1801ft) [152910] ...hill frequented by bucks.

Buck Castle W Clough Head. E St John's in the Vale [327225].

Buck Crag adjoining Satura Crag and, similar to the latter, looks down the length of remote Bannerdale. The path from Patterdale to High Street via Angle Tarn and Satura Crag passes just below it to the W [422140].

Buck Crag on Rossett Pike to Mansey Pike ridge 606m (1988ft) [253078].

Buck Crag slightly E of the path from the head of the Garburn Pass to Yoke [440049].

Buck Crag near Birks, Duddon valley [228993].

Buck Crags Shap Fells. SE Harrop Pike. Spot height at rear 579m (1900ft) [506072] ...crags frequented by bucks.

Buck Hole alongside headwater of the River Calder [087133].

Buck Pike central summit on the Brown Pike-Dow Crag ridge 744m (2441ft) [262973] ...rocky outcrop frequented by deer.

Buck Pike Rossett Pike ridge 606m (1988ft) [253078]

Buck Stone large boulder W bank River Lowther [539160] ...stone frequented by bucks or the stone by which deer passed.

Buck Stone boulder WSW summit of Seatallan [131068].

Buck Stones alongside summit of Hartsop above How [386120].

Buckbarrow craggy face of the southern ridge of Seatallan. Provides several rock climbs. 420m (1378ft) [136061] ...hill frequented by bucks or goats.

Buckbarrow former small farm alongside the Gosforth to Wastwater high road and at the foot of Buckbarrow. Along with nearby Gill, Broadgap and Harrowhead farms acquired by the NT in 1977. Excepting Harrowhead Farm the other three are now farmed as one unit [137054].

Buckbarrow Beck rises slope Buck Barrow at 149915 and joins Kinmont Beck at 133901.

Buckbarrow Bridge carries the Corney Fell Road over Buckbarrow Beck [134904].

Buckbarrow Crag substantial crags on lower slope of Tarn Crag, E head of

Longsleddale. Faces Goat Scar across the valley. Many rock climbs covering varying degrees of difficulty [483074] ...crag on the hill frequented by bucks.

Buckbarrow Crag Buck Barrow [153912].

Buckbarrow Moss slope Seatallan. Source of Tongues Gills [140070].

Buckbarrow Well actually a spring alongside the track up Longsleddale and below Buckbarrow Crag [478076].

Buckholme Lodge edge of Buckholme Wood Lowther Park [527257].

Buckholme Slip adjoining Ashleymore Plantation, Lowther Park [529248].

Buckholme Wood Lowther Park [526253] ...water meadow frequented by bucks.

Buckstone Hows overlooks Gatesgarthdale and Honister Pass [219148] ...rocks on the hill frequented by bucks.

Buckstones E Rydal Beck [368083] ...rocks frequented by bucks.

Buckstones Jump waterfall on Rydal Beck at 377077. Nearby are the Buckstones.

Bulatt Bridge footbridge near the N end of Burnmoor Tarn. Crosses over the confluence of Whillan Beck and the Tarn [187046].

Bull Close alongside minor road from the Outgate-Skelwith Fold road to the A593 [347025].

Bull Close Coppice above Bull Close [346023].

Bull Coppice adjoining Stephead Close [232957].

Bull Crag E of Langstrath [271109].

Bull Crag NNW High Hartsop Dodd summit. Overlooks Thin Side and Dovedale [392111].

Bull Crag W Thirlmere. Between the road and Thackwell Crags. One of many fine crags which overlook Thirlmere [310156].

Bull Crag Eskdale. W Boot [169011].

Bull Crag Yewbarrow [172081].

Bull Crag Buckbarrow [138059].

Bull Crag E Craghouse Bridge and the River Irt [108026].

Bull Crag crag overlooking Stonethwaite Beck [267131].

Bull Crag below the summit of Maiden Moor [237183] ...a tall story, (or is it?), recounted by a farmer in 1779 suggests that the name of the crag was derived from the echo thereabouts which was so great that a bull if kept there for a length of time would go mad from hearing the repeated echos of its own roarings.

Bull Crags alongside Red Pike (Wasdale) ridge [174100].

Bull Gill Quarry Honister [216139].

Bull Haw Moss Torver High Common [271947].

Bull Haw Moss Beck rises Bleaberry Haws at 266944 and joins Ash Gill Beck where the latter becomes Tranearth Beck at 276950.

Bull How Eskdale [206020].

Bulman Strands property in the Gilpin valley alongside the river [434931] ...bull pool shores/bull keeper's shores.

Bungalow, The see **The Bungalow**.

Burn Banks above Burnbanks [502164].

Burn Edge between Sillathwaite Wood and the River Calder 311m (1020ft) [066125].

Burn Moor SW Whitfell 543m (1781ft) [151924] ...see **Burn Moor** above.

Burnbank Fell E Owsen Fell. Summit is atopped by a rusty adorned iron straining post 475m (1558ft) [110209].

Burnbanks below the Haweswater Reservoir dam and 2.4kms (1.5 miles) SSW Bampton. There has been an area called Burnbanks for centuries but the houses here [507160] were constructed by Manchester Corporation Waterworks to accommodate workers building the dam and their families. At one time there were over 60 properties and the community boasted a shop, club and mission hall. Only a third of the properties now remain some occupied but many derelict. At the time of writing the LDNP Authority had approved plans to rebuild 12 bungalows providing they were subsequently occupied by local people. At grid reference 505160 are five long oblong tumuli known as Giant's Graves and like those similarly named at Mallerstang, Ravenstonedale, and Waitby and the Giant's Grave at Penrith, legend has it that they contain the bodies of giants.

Burn Moor wild and desolate moorland between Boot and Wasdale. Before the church at Wasdale Head was licensed for burials in 1901 corpses had to be taken over to Boot, Eskdale, along what has become known as the old corpse route. Legend has it that the moor is haunted by a horse which, carrying a coffin, was lost in mist and never found [187042] ...the moor of borrans or ancient remains. There are certainly prehistoric cairn burial mounds and stone circles scattered on or alongside the moor particularly on Boat How, Brat's Moss and alongside Whillan Beck.

Burnmoor Inn Boot, Eskdale. The late Sidney Cross, his wife, and Albert Hargreaves and his wife teamed up in 1945 to buy a run-down inn, The Freemasons Arms at Boot, from its old lady owner. After lengthy negotiations the deal was finally clinched with a Brennand's pork pie. Considerably renovated they renamed it The Burnmoor Inn.

Burnmoor Lodge alongside Burnmoor Tarn. Sometimes referred to as Keeper's Lodge as it was built as a fishing and hunting lodge. Privately owned but covenanted to the NT in 1959. Looks very much neglected and abandoned. On its gable end there is a plaque inscribed with a religious text [183040].

Burnmoor Stake Burn Moor [150926].

Burnmoor Tarn Burn Moor. The largest of the lakeland tarns after Devoke Water and Seathwaite Tarn. Owned by the NT. It is interesting that both its major inflow and outlet enter and leave the tarn within approximately 150m (164yards) of each other. The old corpse road from Wasdale Head to Boot passes alongside its E shore. Fishing for brown trout, pike, perch and eels is free, C250m (C820ft) [184044].

Burns Farm alongside minor road, Threlkeld Bridge-Naddle Bridge-A66 [308242].

Burns Wood S bank of R Greta opposite Wescoe Wood [307245] ...burnt hill.

Burnt Crag between Troughton Gill and Doe House Gill [262013].

Burnt Crag overlooking Seathwaite Tarn and the source of Tarn Beck [247989].

Burnt Horse end of the ridge running NNE from Lonscale Fell [290282].

Burnt House off the Nether Wasdale to Santon Bridge road [119031].

Burnt Intake near High Cross and slightly N of the B5285 [328986].

Burnt Scarth gully on the N face of Fleetwith Pike [210143].

Burnt Wood Plantations alongside Graythwaite-Thwaite Head road [358908].

Burnthwaite farm, the last building in Wasdale. At one time consisted of two farms, High and Low Burnthwaite. The track from Wasdale Head to Sty Head skirts the farm buildings [193091] ...early settlers at the head of Wasdale presumably provided the name when they cleared the area to build and farm. The name means clearing among the stones.

Burr Gill rises 276265 and flows down to meet Applethwaite Gill at 260250.

Burrow Bridge A 592. Here a bridge carries the main road over a beck which rises on Cartmel Fell [387910].

Bursting Gills rises Hardknott Fell at 231026 and joins the River Esk at 225030.

Bursting Knott S slope Great Gable below Lower Kern Knotts [213095].

Bursting Stone large stone ESE of the summit of Coniston Old Man and above Bursting Stone Quarry [280975].

Bursting Stone Quarry large quarry between the Walna Scar Road and Coniston Old Man. One of the few Lakeland quarries still being worked. A small quarry is believed to have been worked in the 19th century. This subsequently closed but in 1959 Mandall's Slate Co. applied for it to be reopened. The present owners, Burlington Slate Co., took over Mandall's and the Lakeland Slate Co. in the 1970s [279973] ...takes its name from the nearby Bursting Stone.

Burthwaite Wythop Dale [185289] ...booth/shelter in or by a clearing or possibly birch tree clearing.

Burthwaite Bridge carries the B5289 along Borrowdale over Combe Gill [255140] ...bridge by the booth/shelter in or adjacent to a clearing or bridge by the birch tree clearing.

Burthwaite Heights ESE Ling Fell. S Low Burthwaite Wood 318m (1043ft) [189283].

Burtness Comb below High Stile. Down it flows Comb Beck. Climbers refer to it as Birkness. The Fell and Rock HQ on the opposite side of the lake is called Birkness and an earlier Bartholomew's map refers to the stream passing through it as Birkness Gill. However the OS and other authorities refer to it as Burtness. Bill Birkett in his *Complete Lakeland Fells* (1994) states categorically that the OS incorrectly calls it Burtness and that it should be Birkness. The gill is one of the few places in Britain where the mineral wulfenite is found [176146].

Burtness Wood W shore Buttermere. Part acquired by the NT in 1937 and the remainder given by Prof. G M Trevelyan in 1940 [177158] ...birch tree headland.

Burtree Bank Lowther Park [534212] ...elder tree bank (slope).

Burtree Bank Pond Burtree Bank, Lowther Park [536211].

Burtree Scar rocky escarpment, Lowther Park. Overlooks the R Lowther [526225] ...elder tree scar.

Buscoe area alongside Buscoe Sike and on the W slope of The Band [255059]. See **Buscoe Sike**.

Buscoe Sike rises by the Three Tarns in the gap between Bowfell and Crinkle Crags at 249060 and flows down through Hell Gill and over Whorneyside Force to join Crinkle Gill and nearby Browney Gill at 264052 and become Oxendale Beck ...possibly from 'bogr scarth', the gap (Three Tarns gap) by the shoulder (The Band) or 'the stream by the Bowes haugr (Bowes Hill)' ie Bowfell.

Busk House former farm, Little Langdale. Foot of Busk Pike. Bequeathed to the National Trust in 1944 [305034] ...see **Busk Pike** below.

Busk Pike Lingmoor Fell [307040] ...bush pike.

Butharlyp Howe Grasmere. Also Butterlip How. This small wooded knoll between Easedale Road and the confluence of Easedale Beck and the River Rothay was a favourite walk of the Wordsworth family and friends. In fact, when the land came up for sale in 1810 the Wordsworths considered purchasing it but could not afford the price. Today it is protected by the National Trust. The Victorian house of the same name at its foot is one of Grasmere's two Youth Hostels 106m (348ft) [336079]. See **Butter Crag** and **Dunmail Raise**.

Butter Crag W Heron Pike and slightly N of Alcock Tarn. The Senior Guides Race at the Grasmere Sports starts from the showground arena and the contestants climb steeply to 294m (966ft) up on the crag before hurtling down back to the showground C400 (C1312)

[350083] ...the adjective 'butter', also in Butharlyp Howe, may be derived from the British chieftain Boethar who fought a savage battle on Dunmail Raise against Norman troops (see **Dunmail Raise**). On the other hand it could be derived from 'butere' (butter) and mean 'the butter pastures' ie the rich pastures for the feeding of cattle. Possibly similar to Buttermere which means 'the lake by the rich grazing lands'. An early 19th century etching by Lake District artist William Green (1760-1823) shows Butharlyp Howe as an idyllic setting with cattle grazing contentedly while a later writer specifically mentions the 'rolling grasslands' around Butter Crag ...possibly similar to Buttermere.

Buttermere small village sited principally on the alluvial plain between Crummock Water and Buttermere (lake) and surrounded by high mountains. Approached by road from the NW via the Newlands Pass, from the E over Honister Pass and from Cockermouth in the W via Lorton. Takes its name from the nearby lake. Comprises four farms, Wilkinsyke, Syke, Croft and Cragg, with Cragg and Wilkinsyke owned by the NT, cottages and other properties, two hostelries, the Fish Hotel and the Bridge Hotel. The former is 18th century and famous as having been the home of Mary Robinson, the 'Beauty of Buttermere', who was tricked into marrying John Hatfield, notorious forger and bigamist, in 1802. He was subsequently executed in September 1803, at Carlisle for forgery. The story of Mary Robinson and John Hatfield is immortalised in Melvyn Bragg's novel *The Maid of Buttermere* first published in 1987. The Bridge Hotel was originally a corn mill (alongside the bridge over Mill Beck which today carries the B5289). The hostelry was licensed in the early 18th century and since then has been called The Bridge, The Queen's, the Victoria and in more recent times has reverted back to The Bridge.

The village school closed in 1950. The present church, dedicated to St. James, dates from 1840 was restored in 1930 but the original chapel was consecrated in 1507. Inside the church is a memorial plaque to Alfred Wainwright. The Buttermere YH, the King George VI Memorial Hostel, was formerly the Buttermere Hotel. In 2002 Buttermere was voted the second most beautiful place in Britain after Salisbury Cathedral. Near the village are two of lakeland's principal waterfalls, Sour Milk Gill and Scale Force, the latter being the highest depth waterfall in the Lake District (see also **Scale Force**) [175170] ...generally accepted as being the mere by the good grazing land, possibly the huts by the lake or even named after a Norse chieftain 'Buthar'.

Buttermere lake in the Buttermere valley with impressive high fells rising on three sides. 2kms long by 0.6 kms wide (1.25 miles x 0.37 mile wide). Owned by the NT since 1930. No power boats allowed and a permit must be obtained for canoeing, windsurfing, dinghy sailing and rowing boats (a limit of 10 craft in each case). Fishing, also by permit, is for trout, char, pike and perch. Depth is 29m (95ft) and the lake is situated at a height of 100m (328ft) [180160].

Buttermere Dubs stream which joins Buttermere (lake) to Crummock Water [169165].

Buttermere Fell fell area to the S of Buttermere [186144].

Buttermere Gully Grasmoor [166203].

Buttermere Moss extremely marshy area between High Snockrigg and Robinson [195168].

Buttermere Valley where Lorton Vale ends the Buttermere valley begins. The valley actually possesses three lakes, Loweswater, Crummock Water and Buttermere and its valley head is Gatesgarthdale which rises to Honister Hause.

Butterwick hamlet W of the road from Helton to Bampton. Gill Beck flows by it and the River Lowther is nearby [507196] ...As Keswick is the 'cheese farm', Butterwick is the 'butter farm'.

BUTTERMERE

Butterwick Crag 18th century cottage with 8 acres of walled ground near Butterwick Crag, Butterwick.

Butterwick Crag Butterwick [505195].

Buzzard bird of prey numerous in Cumbria and often seen circling effortlessly high in the sky while its sharp eyes scan for its prey, small mammals and carrion, on the ground.

Buzzard Crag ESE foot of Seathwaite Tarn [253983].

Buzzard Knott Bassenthwaite Common [250297].

Byerstead off minor road off the Hundith Hill Road [148289] ...piece of land on which a byre/shed stands.

Cabin, The see **The Cabin.**

Caddy Well above Great Bank, Miterdale. A spring from which Merebeck Gill originates [144023] ...possibly centuries ago associated with a local Cady family.

Caerthanoc/Caer-Thannock see **Maiden Castle**.

Caffel Side E flank of the extensive Grange Fell. Below Ether Knott [270173].

Caine, Sir (Thomas Henry) Hall (1853-1931) novelist. His *Shadow of a Crime* (1885) is set in the Dale Head and Thirlspot area.

Caiston Beck sometimes called **Keystone Beck.** Principal headstream rises at 391091 and flows down Caiston Glen to meet Kirkstone Beck at 399109 ...see **Caiston Glen.**

Caiston Glen after the path from Ambleside via the Scandale Pass reaches the col it drops down Caiston Glen to either Hartsop Hall or the Brotherswater Inn [396103] ...the derivation of Caiston is not given in the *Place Names of Westmorland* but may I suggest that it comes from either 'ceaster' meaning ancient fortification (there is a settlement at the foot of the valley) or 'caiton' meaning wood. Similar to many small valleys in the Lake District it would have been well-wooded at one time. The Glen, like Glencoyne and Glenridding, is from the Welsh 'glyn' and not the Scottish derivation.

Caldbeck & Uldale Commons mineral-rich areas in the north of the Lake District beyond Skiddaw and Blencathra. Over-exploitation of minerals such as lead, tungsten, copper, zinc and barytes by collectors resulted in a permit system being put into operation from 1 April 2000. For information on permits, etc. contact the National Park Authority, Blencathra Office, Threlkeld, Keswick, Cumbria, CA12 4TT.

Calder, River see **River Calder.**

Calder Abbey remains of this ancient abbey are situated ENE Calder Bridge and alongside the River Calder. The religious home was founded in the 12th century but was ravaged shortly afterwards by the Scots. Rebuilt, it was, along with other Cumbrian abbeys and priories, dissolved by Henry VIII in the 1530s. Only the 12th century west door, parts of the 13th century nave and parts of the 14th century chapter house remain. The ruin is privately owned [051064].

Calder Bridge ancient bridge which carries the A595 over the River Calder. In her *Complete Guide to the Lakes* (1855) Harriet Martineau writes, "step into the inn garden at the bridge, and see how beautifully the brown waters swirl away under the red bridge and its ivied banks, while the waving ferns incessantly checker the sunshine..." [042060].

Calder Hall Nuclear Power Station see **Sellafield.**

Calderbridge OS map Calder Bridge. Village on the A595 and on the westerly boundary of the LDNP. Takes its name from the bridge which crosses the River Calder here. The village boasts two inns, the Golden Fleece and the Stanley Arms. The parish church, St. Bridget's, dates from the 1840s while not far distant the much older Ponsonby Church stands in the grounds of Pelham Hall (formerly Ponsonby Hall). Even older are parts of the remains of Calder Abbey which are situated alongside the River Calder just outside the actual village [042060].

Caldew, River see **River Caldew.**

Calf Cove slope E Rydal Fell. NE Greatriggs Man [359107] ...'cove where calves were pastured.'

Calf Cove small valley WSW Fairfield [264002].

Calf Cove above Esk Hause. Path to Great End and Scafell Pike passes through it to col above [229080].

Calf Crag W Tarn Head Beck valley [263997].

Calf Crag head of the long ridge (Lancrigg) which stretches from Helm Crag over Gibson Knott, Moment Crag to Calf Crag 530m (1739ft) [302104].

Calf Crag S Beckstones Gill and Beckstones [219261].

Calf Crag Holme Fell [315003]

Calf Hole E Nethermost Pike. S Nethermost Cove [348142].

Calf Screes screes dropping down W of the Hindscarth ridge [215169].

Calfclose Bay Derwent Water [269213] ...So named in the first half of the 17th century but Thomas Gray in 1769 refers to it as Carf-Close-Reeds. Some early guide books refer to it as Scarfclose Bay. Scarf is a Cumbrian dialect word meaning cormorant in which case it could be the bay frequented by cormorants. This is highly probable as to its N is Strandshag Bay (the shore frequented by shag/cormorants) while in the lake nearby is Scarf Rocks.

Calfclose Wood WSW Woodend [218271].

Calfcove Gill rises Calf Clove above Esk Hause at 228080 and joins the upper Esk at its confluence with Little Narrowcove at 228066.

Calfgate Gill rises between Brock Crags and Satura Crag at 432135 and joins Hayeswater Gill alongside the Filter House at 422130.

Calfhow Pike WNW Great Dodd. NW Little Dodd. A rocky outcrop in a wilderness of grass C660m (C2165) [331211] ...calf 'hill' pike.

Calfhowe Crag Kentmere. W of River Kent and off track from Kentmere village to Kentmere Reservoir [459051] ...crag below the hill where calves where pastured or possibly called 'calf' because of its relatively small size in relation to nearby Rainsborrow Crag.

Calflay Wood E of Staveley-Kentmere road [460032] ...calf hill wood.

Calgarth Hall built in the 16th century by the notable and powerful Philips family of Windermere and their home until the 18th century. Later it became a farmer's residence and recently, in 1991, the Briery Close Arabian Stud moved there from Briery Close. The legend of the Calgarth skulls has often been quoted in local histories, etc. and I will not bore readers by reproducing it here [398996] ...Hall by the calf enclosure.

Calgarth Park Troutbeck Bridge. Georgian mansion built in 1789 by Richard Watson (1737-1816), Bishop of Llandaff and host to many prominent persons of his day. Before the First World War the grounds were the setting for many Volunteer Camps and during the war the building was a hospital for wounded soldiers. Continued as a hospital for many years but today consists of flats for retired professional people. It was from in front of the mansion that Leeming and Hinkler took off and successfully landed on Helvellyn in December, 1926. Their Avro 585 Gosport had been forced to land at Calgarth Park owing to a clogged air filter [397002].

Calley Bridge carries the minor road from Sparket Mill to Hutton John and the A66 over Dacre Beck [439265].

Calvert, Raisley (1773-1795) friend and benefactor of William Wordsworth. Died of pulmonory tuberculosis but for six months prior to his death Wordsworth nursed him. In his will he left Wordsworth a legacy of £900 which allowed the latter to concentrate full-time on his poetry. See also **Calvert Trust**.

Calvert's Bridge across the River Greta near Windebrowe [274239] ...associated with the Calvert family. See also **Calvert Trust** and **Windebrowe**.

Calvert Trust the Calvert Trust, named after Raisley Calvert, a great friend and benefactor of William Wordsworth, is a charity which provides outdoor activity courses and holidays for people with disabilities and their families and friends. Today the Trust operates three centres. That at Keswick has two sites, one at Windebrowe (Old Windebrowe) which over 200 years ago was given rent-free to William and Dorothy Wordsworth by Raisley Calvert. In 1974 the then owner of Windebrowe, John Fryer-Spedding, formed a Trust with the object of enabling people with physical, sensory or learning difficulties, to benefit from outdoor activities in the countryside. He also handed over to the Trust Windebrowe to be used as accommodation. The property is adjacent to the Calvert Trust Riding Centre. Another farmstead at Little Crosthwaite was also given to the Trust by the Fryer-Spedding family and the Little Crosthwaite Adventure Centre was formally opened in 1978. Another adventure centre at Kielder was opened in 1984 and accommodation at the third centre, Exmoor, was open for business in 1996. A detailed brochure pack and other information on the Calvert Trust Keswick can be obtained from the Marketing Manager, Calvert Trust Keswick, Little Crosthwaite, Keswick, Cumbria, CA12 4QD (017687 72254).

Cam Crag crag at the end of the ridge which drops down SE from Rosthwaite Cam [261112].

Cam Spout secluded waterfall in deep fissure on How Beck below the N face of Spout Cam Crag. The path from Eskdale to Mickledore passes on the N side of the stream [217060] ...the waterfall below the crest of the hill.

Cam Spout Crag W River Esk with Cam Spout (waterfall) to its N [215056].

Campbell, Donald (1921-1967) land and and water-speed record holder. In 1955 on Ullswater he established a water-speed record of 325.53 kmph (202.33 mph). Later he established records on Coniston Water but, in January 1967, he was killed on that lake while attempting to beat the 480 kmph (300 mph) barrier. On its second run *Bluebird* was travelling at over 480 kmph (300 mph) when it somersaulted 18m (60ft) into the air before practically disintegrating on crashing back down onto the lake's surface. *Bluebird* was recovered in March 2001, and Donald Campbell's body later. Subsequently, his body was laid to rest in Coniston churchyard and his gravestone is inscribed :-

DONALD MALCOLM CAMPBELL C.B.E.
QUEEN'S COMMENDATION FOR BRAVE CONDUCT
March 1921-January 1967
Laid To Rest September 2001
Whose achievements in World Speed Records
Depict His Courage in Life And Death

Campbell, Sir Malcolm (1885-1948) father of Donald Campbell. On 19 August 1939, he established a world water-speed record of 228.11 kmph (141.74 mph) on Coniston Water. This record stood until 1950.

Camping Barns apart from Youth Hostels the YHA also offers simple self-catering accommodation in converted farm buildings sometimes called 'stone tents'. These are owned and operated by farmers. At the time of writing there were 14 camping barns in the Lake District. For detailed information consult *Camping Barns in England* issued by the YHA.

Can Wood alongside the Hawkshead-Newby Bridge road [368935].

Cannon Crag projection E shore Windermere [396950].

Cannon Dub River Derwent. Across the B5289 from the Lodore Hotel [262189]. See **Gowder Crag**.

Canoe Centre foot of Derwent Water [259234].

Canoeing several rivers, lakes and even some streams offer good stretches for canoeists to test their skills. However, initially check whether this sport is allowed on individual waters. Ullswater Canoeing and Kayaking Club at Glenridding provides instruction and equipment for groups or individuals as does the Canoe Centre at the foot of Derwent Water. The possibilities for canoeing on four rivers - the Eamont, Greta, Lowther, and Trout Beck - are outlined in *A Canoeist's Guide: Rivers of Cumbria* by Mike Hayward (1988). For an introduction to moving water there is the River Derwent in Borrowdale. Other waters where canoeing takes place but not for novices include the Brathay at Skelwith Force, the Langdale Beck at Elterwater, the Caldew beneath Carrock Fell, Langstrath Beck from Black Moss Pot, the River Calder from Cold Fell to Calder Bridge, Mosedale Beck from Wolf Crag to Scales, the River Rothay and the River Greta from its confluence with the Glenderamackin to Keswick. At the time of writing this section the notable canoeist Stuart Miller of Braithwaite was compiling the definitive guidebook to canoeing the rivers, etc. of Cumbria and the NW of England. Also consult **Boating & Sailing** in general text.

Cape, The see **St Sunday Crag**.

Capel Crags Place Fell. Between Patterdale Common and the summit of the fell [404167] ...from 'kapall' meaning nag.

Capell Crag Thornythwaite Fell. Overlooks Seathwaite [242121] ...horse crag.

Capell Gill rises Thornythwaite Fell at 244118 and joins Black Sike at 237122.

Caple Crag isolated crag SW slope Lank Rigg [071102] ...horse/nag crag.

Caplecrag Beck rises as two major tributaries at 078107 and 079106 respectively and joins the River Calder at 064102.

Capple Barrow Undermillbeck Common and overlooking Windermere Golf Course C190m (C623ft) [422958] ...horse/nag's hill.

Capple Beck rises 093048 and joins the River Bleng at 084030 ...horse stream.

Capple Howe Applethwaite Common 445m (1460ft) [432029] ...nag's hill.

Capple Rigg S B5284. W Capplerigg Lane 144m (472ft) [474989] ...horse ridge.

Capplebarrow on a grassy ridge between Longsleddale and Bannisdale 512m (1680ft) [509035] ...horse hill.

Capplebarrow Crag Capplebarrow, overlooking Longsleddale [508034].

Capplefall overlooking Bannisdale [527030] ...'horse clearing'.

Capplerigg farm alongside Capplerigg Lane off the B5284 [474945].

Capplerigg Lane off the B5284, Plumgarths to Crook road [476946].

Captain Whelter Beck rises Captain Whelter Bog at 490109, joins Hopgill Beck at 483111. This flows down to join Haweswater at 479118.

Captain Whelter Bog marshy area between Selside Pike and unnamed peak SSW. Captain Whelter Beck rises here [490109] ...whelter is a 'hollow or combe' and Captain

Whelter implies a surname.

Car parking major car parks in the Lake District are operated principally by the LDNP the NT or local councils. Practically all are pay and display although those owned by the NT are free to members. See current leaflet issued by the NT and titled *Car Parks in the Lake District.* Incidentally, the first car park charges by the LDNP were introduced at Waterhead - 1s (5p) per day. In December 2002, the charge was £2.20 for 12 hours.

Caral Beck rises alongside the old coach road from St John's in the Vale-Dockray at 365226 and joins Mosedale Beck at 356239.

Carble Hows SSW Great Carrs, ESE Grey Friar [267002].

Carhullan W Moorahill Farm and N Cawdale Beck [490182] ...W G Collingwood in his *The Lake Counties* (1902) says "Bampton Cundale or Carhullen is in the valley of the Cowdale or Cundale Beck." According to the *Place Names of Westmorland* the first element could be 'fort on the ledge' or 'rocky ledge' and may refer to Towtop Kirk which lies less that 0.4kms (0.25 mile) SE. The second element is not known.

Carl Crag above Garnett Bridge [520992] ...'karl' refers to a 'lower class freemen' and, similar to 'lad' or 'bull', is used figuratively for a rock or crag. It may also refer to a person. See **Carl Side** below.

Carl Side summit in the Skiddaw group. Usually climbed as part of an alternative section of the Allerdale Ramble to the summit of Skiddaw and a direct route from Millbeck to Skiddaw 746m (2447ft) [255281] ...Karl's slope.

Carleton area N Ravenglass and across the River Irt from Drigg. Specifically represented on the OS map by the names of Carleton Green, Hall and Head and Hall Carleton [078984] ...generally accepted as meaning the farm of the freeman or peasant.

Carleton Green alongside the A595 [082986].

Carleton Hall alongside the A595 [083988].

Carleton Head off the A595 on minor road to Hall Carleton [081983].

Carlew Crag projection W shore Windermere between High Cunsey and Low Cunsey [384939] ...curlew crag.

Carlhowe Beck rises Threlkeld Common at 348247 although a much longer tributary rises at 344235. Joins the River Glenderamackin at 335256.

Carling Knott between Sharp Knott and Loweswater. A subsidiary height at 519m (1703ft) with its summit at 544m (1785ft) [121206] ...the rocky hill on or by which the old hag/old woman lives.

Carling Stone overlooks Greendale Tarn [141075] ...possibly old woman's stone.

Carr Howes between the Elterwater-Little Langdale road and Elterwater [331039] ...either brushwood hill or marsh hill.

Carron area below Carron Crag, Grizedale Forest Park [323944].

Carron Crag E of Grizedale and the highest point in Grizedale Forest Park. Trig. point and excellent viewpoint 314m (1030ft) [325943].

Carron Plantation alongside Carron Crag, Grizedale Forest Park [326941].

Carrs head of Far Easedale [306102] ...Valleys and valley heads are notoriously wet and boggy areas and more than likely this name is derived from the ON 'Ki(j)arr' meaning a swamp or marsh.

Carr's Farm alongside Middleton Place on the minor road from the A595 to Monk Moors and the coast [098921].

Carlside Tarn small tarn on the col betwen Skiddaw South Top and Carl Side. Non-existent in dry weather C720m (C2362ft) [256282].

Carsleddam on the ridge descending from Carl Side to Millbeck [259270].

Carter Ground farm off a minor road from Broughton Mills [229924]. See **Stephenson Ground**.

Cartmel Fell undulating and well-wooded fell area between Windermere and the Winster valley to the E and the A592 in the S to Black Beck and Storrs in the N. Picturesque cottages and farms nestle between many plantations. Its highest point is Gummers How 321m (1054ft) [390885] with its excellent viewpoint of and over Windermere. Cartmel Church, dedicated to St Anthony, was built in 1504 by local farmers who, up until then, had to walk seven miles to Cartmel Priory. It became the 'Browhead Chapel' of Mrs Humphrey Ward's *Helbeck of Bannisdale*.

Cartmell Fold Crosthwaite [446915] ...home of the Cartmell family who took their name from Cartmel across the River Winster. Cartmel means the sandbank by the rocky ground.

Caspel Gate slight depression on Riggindale Scar between Rough Crag and Long Stile. A grassy slope leads up to it from Blea Water and there is a small tarn in the depression just below the path up the ridge to High Street. In times of drought this tarn may dry up. Presumably, the name is, like Capel, from kapall meaning nag and it is possibly one way by which horses were taken to the High Street 'meet' [450112].

Caspel Gate Tarn see **Caspel Gate**.

Casshow Wood Lorton Vale. Rises to 101m (331ft) [152270].

Cast Rigg alongside the River Derwent. Rises to 80m (262ft) [250250] ...possibly derived from caester meaning an ancient fort or earthwork. There is no trace today of any fortification or earthworks.

Castle Crag Kentmere. N Crabtree Brow, Garburn Pass 490m (1608ft) [446052] ...its prominent position suggests a castle.

Castle Crag W Haweswater Reservoir and at the end of a ridge leading down to that reservoir along the top of Whelter Crags, over Hanging Stones, and Birks Crag. On its summit are the remains of an ancient hill fort occupying a striking position overlooking Mardale and the foot of Haweswater [469128].

Castle Crag Wythburn Fells. SW Nab Crags and adjoining Black Crags [306119].

Castle Crag above the Jaws of Borrowdale. Believed to be the site of an ancient fort and possibly the origin of the name Borrowdale (valley of the fort). Extensively quarried and by now may have been completely eaten away except that before 1800 Lord William Gordon of Waterend bought the crag to save it from further destruction. Subsequently given to the NT as a memorial to Sir William Hawes and his son and on its summit cairn is a tablet, a memorial to the men of Borrowdale who died in the First World War. Castle Crag is the lowest fell in Wainwright's seven volumed *Pictorial Guide to the Lakeland Fells* and he claims the square mile which encompasses it as "The loveliest square mile in Lakeland - the Jaws of Borrowdale." In a cave in one of the quarries the eccentric Millican Dalton lived for many years, see **Dalton, Millican**, 290m (951ft) [249159].

Castle Crag Hill Fort also called **Shoulthwaite Castle**. Ancient hill fort W Thirlmere behind Raven Crag and overlooking Shoulthwaite Gill. Believed to date from the 7th century AD and to have been used by locals as a refuge in time of invasion. A Scheduled Ancient Monument [300188].

Castle Head summit in Castlehead Wood and excellent viewpoint over Derwent Water to the fells, W, N and S 162m (531ft) [270227]. See also **Castlerigg**.

Castle How Dunnerdale. A rocky eminence which resembles a fortification [237005].

Castle How rocky outcrop N Bleabeck Bridge 144m (472ft) [189921].

Castle Howe at the eastern foot of the Wrynose Pass near Fell Foot. Rocky hillock which certainly suggests its name [297033].

Castle Lane lane leading from the A591 to Goosewell Farm and Castlerigg Stone Circle [289232].

Castle Nook Newlands valley [230169] ...the nook below a crag which even if it did not once possess a castle on its summit certainly has a castle-like appearance.

Castle Rock formerly **Green Crag**. Also known as **Castle Rock of Triermain**, a name perpetuated by Sir Walter Scott as the fictitious castle of his romantic poem *Bridal of Triermain* (1813). At the foot of Watson's Dodd overlooking S end of St John's in the Vale. Popular with climbers both beginners and more experienced. A 13th century document mentions Castelyadolfbek at the foot of Castle Rock which suggests that at one time the rock housed the castle of one Ludolf or Liudolf. 339m (1112ft) [322197].

Castle Side slope of the Castle, Helton Fell [474201].

Castle Wood SSE Near Sawrey [373949].

Castle Wood Hill S of Near Sawrey [371952].

Castle, The (Helton Fell) see **The Castle**.

Castlehead Wood NT woodland surrounding Castle Head to the E of the B5289 [271228].

Castlehow at the E foot of Wrynose Pass near Fell Foot Farm. A rocky hillock which certainly suggests its name [297033].

Castlehow Beck rises Birker Fell below Demming Crag at 223002 and joins the River Duddon at 239002 near Stepping Stones.

Castlehows Point Watermillock. Opposite, on the E shore of Ullswater across the narrows, is Thwaitehill Neb. Pencilmill Beck joins Ullswater here [451226] ...probably from the family of a Thomas Castelhow. A brass plaque in the present Watermillock Church commemorates a John and Margaret Castlehow who lived 'man and wife for LX years (60)' and were 'buryed both on new yerisday'.

Castlenook Mine Newlands valley. Former small lead mine worked from 1860 to 1864 and for a brief period 1917/18 [227170].

Castlerigg area [281225] on a ridge approached by road off the A591. Principally comprises two farms, Castlerigg Hall (282226] and Castlerigg [283224]. Nearby is the Castlerigg Stone Circle ...castle or fort on a ridge. There is no trace of any fortification. However, nearby is the viewpoint of Castle Head which name suggests that it may have been the site of a castle or simply that the hill stands proud like a castle towering above the lake and Keswick. Further S Castlerigg Fell rises above Castle Crag Hill Fort (Shoulthwaite Castle) which is believed to date from the 7th century.

Castlerigg Farm see **Castlerigg**.

Castlerigg Fell a subsidiary fell of Bleaberry Fell and shown on the OS map at 286202 with its highest point at 460m (1509ft) above Dodd Crag at 291206 ...see **Castlerigg**.

Castlerigg Hall Farm see **Castlerigg**.

Castlerigg Stone Circle 2.4kms (1.5 miles) E of Keswick. Originally titled 'Druid's Circle' although it pre-dates the Druids. Also referred to as 'The Carles' which means ring or circle. Believed to date from 3400 to 4000 years ago. A spectacular sited circle of approximately 30m (100 ft) in diameter and consisting of 38 remaining stones with another 10 forming a rectangle on the S side. Owned by the NT but cared for by English Heritage. 210m (689ft) above sea level and towards the end of a lengthy ridge running from Castlerigg

Fell to the River Greta [292236] ...see **Castlerigg**.

Castlesteads near Lowther Castle, Lowther Park. Remains of a fortified site [519241]. There is another Castlesteads 0.8kms (0.5 mile) N in Yanwath Wood.

Castocks Wood E shore Bassenthwaite Lake [227285].

Cat Bank Coniston [302972].

Cat Bank alongside the A593 above Town End [258923] ...slope frequented by wild cats.

Cat Bells conical hill on the Hause End-High Spy ridge. A popular hill walk 451m (1480ft) [244199] ...possibly a corruption of Cat Bields (shelter of the wild cat) or the bell-shaped hill.

Cat Bields subsidiary cairned summit on slope of Seatallan [130070] ...'wild cats' shelters'.

Cat Cove between Whinscales and Cat Crag. A path from Eskdale via Eel Tarn above Stony Tarn and over Slight Side to Scafell passes through the Cove. A feeder of Cowcove Beck rises here [203031].

Cat Crag adjoining Bateman Fold Plantation. WSW Knipe Tarn. [424940] ...crag frequented by wild cats.

Cat Crag immediately SW Angle Tarn, Hartsop [416142].

Cat Crag Sleet Fell, Place Fell. Overlooks Boredale [424188].

Cat Crag Catcove Beck flows to its W and S and Cowcove Beck to its E 369m (1211ft) [209031].

Cat Crag above Ennerdale YH. The address of the youth hostel is Cat Crag, Ennerdale [140144].

Cat Gill rises near Ashness Farm at 272192. Joined by Rampshaw Beck before entering Derwentwater at 267195.

Cat Gill farthest headstream rises on the slope of Fellbarrow at 130244 and the Gill meets Mosser Beck at 117260.

Cat Gill stream between Walla Crag and Falcon Crag. Two major tributaries rise at 280208 and 278206 respectively and the gill drops steeply alongside Great Wood to join Derwent Water at 269209.

Cat Gills the longest of the gills rises at the head of Green Comb at 294118 and joins the Wyth Burn at 298112.

Cat How Nether Wasdale [116049] ...'wild cat hill'.

Catcove Beck rises below Great How, Eskdale Fell, at 200040. Feeder from Cat Cove joins at 205032 and the beck joins Cowcove Beck at 210028. The watercourse then becomes Scale Gill which joins the River Esk at 215022.

Catgill Bridge carries the fell road over Cat Gill [117255].

Cathow slightly W of the Meadley Reservoir, Kinniside [047144].

Cathow Bridge carries the high road from Gosforth to Wastwater over Kid Beck [117048].

Cat's Crag Duddon valley. Overlooks the Duddon Bridge to Ulpha road [202909].

Catstye Cam normally referred to as Catstycam but in the past was Catchedican, Cathedicam, or as Camden referred to it, Casticand. At the end of the Swirral Edge ridge and a very impressive peak particularly when viewed from the E or the N 890m (2920ft) [348158] ...the wild cats steep path to the ridge.

Cauda Brow section of the minor road between Croasdale and Lamplugh [091179] ...cold brow.

Caudale from Caudale Bridge on the A592 up to Caudale Head below Caudale Moor.

Caudale Beck flows down it [410110] ...Most likely means 'cold valley' rather than 'calf valley'.

Caudale Beck rises Caudale Head at 414103 and flows down past the disused Caudale Quarry and under the A592 to join Kirkstone Beck at 399117.

Caudale Beck Farm foot of Kirkstone Pass between Kirkstone Beck and Caudale Beck. Purchased by the National Trust in 1965 [401116].

Caudale Bridge at the foot of Kirkstone Pass. Carries the A592 over Caudale Beck [402115].

Caudale Head steep craggy head of Caudale below Caudale Moor [412103].

Caudale Head/Moor Tarn largest of three tarns on Caudale Moor, 745m (2444ft) [415101].

Caudale Moor sometimes called John Bell's Banner although this is only a section of it. A barren region to the E of Kirkstone Pass consisting of several ridges and an extensive plateau of grass culminating in the cairned summit of Stony Cove Pike. On the summit plateau are three small tarns the largest of which is called Caudale Head/Moor Tarn. A subsidiary summit to the SW of Stony Cove Pike is Pike How. Approximately 640m (700yds) W of this summit is the Atkinson Memorial to the memory of Mark Atkinson who was owner of the Kirkstone Pass Inn for 16 years up to his death in 1930 and his son William who died in 1987. To the E of the summit across Threshwaite Mouth is Thornthwaite Crag with its tall well-built cairn. Stony Cove Pike is 763m (2503ft) at [418100].

Caudale Quarry former quarry approached by steep track up a spur of Caudale Moor [409108].

Causeway Farm see **The Causeway Farm**.

Causeway Foot alongside the A591 [293218] ...foot of the raised way, the latter being the rise over Nest Brow.

Causey Pike summit on the Rowling End to Sail ridge. Its knobbly pike summit is a distinctive landmark 637m (2090ft) [219209] ...sharp pointed peak above the causeway/embankment.

Caw pyramidical-shaped hill on undulating ridge E of the Duddon valley. Trig. point at 529m (1735ft) [230944] ...the name could refer to the hill on which calves were pastured or a small hill next to or near to a larger one.

Caw Fell S Iron Crag, W Haycock. A large mountain mass with several subsidiary summits. Its size is emphasised by the fact that the OS places its title nearly 1.6kms (1 mile) from the principal summit. SW of this summit can still be seen the the remains of an Avro Oxford which crashed in 1941 killing its crew of two, C690 (C2264ft) [132110] ...'hill on which calves are reared'.

Caw Gill rises Stockdale Moor at 106085 and joins Worm Gill at 092092.

Caw Moss ENE Caw [249949].

Caw Moss Tarn sickle-shaped water on Caw Moss, C390m (C1280ft) [252949].

Cawdale sometimes Cowdale or Cundale. Valley W Bampton, E Loadpot Hill. Cawdale Beck flows down it [484178] ...'cold valley'.

Cawdale Beck Howe Grain, Atkinson's Grain and Sealhole Grain become Cawdale Beck at 472175. The latter subsequently becomes Howes Beck below The Howes at approximately 505177. This joins Haweswater Beck at 518180. The latter joins the River Lowther shortly afterwards. A stone bridge over the beck at 496178 is scheduled as an Ancient Monument.

Cawdale Edge escarpment overlooking Cawdale [479179].

Cawell Beck rises Threlkeld Common at 356248 and joins the River Glenderamackin at 340260.

Cawfell Beck rises below Caw Fell at 121100 and joins Worm Gill at 093094.

Cawk Cove below Cofa Pike at the head of Deepdale ...two variants for the origin of the name (1) from 'caw' - calf or calves - and meaning the cove where calves are pastured (2) 'cawk' - corruption of 'gawk', the cuckoo. Therefore the cove where the cuckoo is often heard or seen [363121].

Celleron hamlet on the National Park boundary off the B5320 to Askham road. High Street Roman road is shown on the 2.5ins OS map as passing through Celleron but some authorities suggest that from Heughscar Hill this is a possible rather than a definite route [497252] ...'thicket near a store house'.

Central Gully see **Great End**.

Central Pillar see **Dow Crag**.

Chambers Crag slightly E of the summit of Scafell Pike [217072].

Channel Mire Ralfland Forest [544131].

Chapel Beck of its two principal headstreams one rises from several springs alongside the Crook-Borwick Fold road near Fell Plain at 454961 and flows down to meet another which rises N Hollin Hall and E Crook road at 465965. The combined watercourse passes through Underbarrow where it is joined by Underbarrow Beck at 465917 to become Underbarrow Pool. This is joined by Black Beck at 468907 and Tanyard Beck at 469905 before becoming Helsington Pool and joining the River Gilpin [467879] which in turn joins the River Kent.

Chapel Beck begins life as two major tributaries on the slope of Grisedale Pike namely Sanderson Gill and Grisedale Gill. Subsequently the two watercourses meet on Revelin Moss and become Comb Beck and later Chapel Beck by Chapelbeck Bridge. Shortly after this the stream passes alongside St. Mary's Church (chapel) en route to join Newlands Beck at 232260.

Chapel Bridge Underbarrow. Near All Saints Church. Much earlier believed to have been called Underbarrow Bridge. Carries the Crook-Underbarrow road over Chapel Beck [462927].

Chapel Bridge carries the road to Newlands Church/Chapel over Newlands Beck [231194].

Chapel Crags alongside the ridge between Red Pike and High Stile and overlooking Bleaberrry Tarn [164151].

Chapel Hill Muncaster Fell. On its summit is Muncaster Tarn (Chapel Hill Tarn) and on its lower slope a tall 3-tier monument erected in the 19th century to commemorate the spot where Henry VI was found by shepherds after a battle in 1464. He was taken to Muncaster Castle and given shelter. To show his gratitude the King gave the family a glass drinking bowl 'the Luck of Muncaster' declaring that as long as it remained intact, Penningtons would live and thrive at Muncaster. A replica is on display at the castle. However, it is also said that the King took refuge under a huge oak tree in the grounds of not far distant Irton Hall!! [108977].

Chapel Hill Tarn see **Muncaster Tarn**.

Chapel House Underbarrow. Near Underbarrow Chapel, now a church dedicated to All Saints. The house once belonged to the chapel [463929].

Chapel Stile village in Great Langdale. Grew substantially in the hey day of local quarrying particularly to house the workers at the huge Thrang Quarry behind the village, the nearby Elterwater Quarry and the not far distant Tilberthwaite and Hodge Close Quarries and the many Lingmoor Fell quarries. Less than 0.8kms (0.5 mile) away the former gun-powder works (1824-1931) also provided work for Elterwater and Chapel Stile villagers. Today there are several farms in the vicinity but the main industry is tourism providing bed and breakfast, hotel facilities or catering for the large timeshare complex which took over the old gunpowder works site. Until the first half of the 19th century the Langdale dead were carried over the fells to be buried at Grasmere. However, in 1857 the present church was constructed to supersede an old chapel. Half the cost of its construction was contributed

by the squire of Elterwater Hall and the other half by the squire of High Close. In this day and age the Langdale Cooperative village store, established in 1884, is unique not only for its remarkable stock but for the fact that it has continued to pay dividends to its customers [321055] ...chapel on the 'steep hill'.

Chapel Wood Chapel Hill, Muncaster Fell [110972].

Chapel Wood alongside Wythop Mill old chapel remains [197292].

Chapelbeck Bridge Thornthwaite. Carries road over Chapel Beck [225253].

Char a deep water troutlike fish found in Windermere (the most southerly lake in which Arctic char still survive), Coniston Water, Crummock Water, Buttermere and Ennerdale Water.

Char Dub pool on the River Liza just before the latter enters Ennerdale Water [127143] ...pool frequented by char.

Charlesground off the minor road from the A595 S to Corney [120922].

Charlesground Gill rises Corney Fell at 140924 and joins the River Annas at 129928.

Charlotte Mason College of Education a large white fronted mansion situated on a knoll E of the A591 and just N of the centre of Ambleside town. Built in the early 19th century with modern day extensions. Charlotte Mason was born in 1842 and subsequently became teacher, lecturer and a leading educationalist. She moved to Ambleside in 1891 and opened her 'House of Education' at Ambleside in Springfield House, now the principal's residence, in 1892. Two years later she moved to Greenbank (Scale How) the College's present site. She remained principal until her death in 1923. Much later affiliated from Manchester University to Lancaster University was granted and in 1992 it became part of the university. Recently it has passed to St Martin's College, Lancaster [375049].

Cherry Holm one of Ullswater's four islands [393171] ...Named after an ancient cherry tree which grew there.

Cherry Tree Inn Wythburn. See **Wythburn**.

Chestnut Hill section of the A591, Keswick [280236].

Chicken Rock rock in Windermere [396956].

Chimney Crag N Town Head, Troutbeck.W A591 [414044] ...'crag by the rocky crevice'.

China Plantation Grizedale Forest Park [334965]. Similar to Guinea Hill and New South Wales Plantation in that it was probably named by the Brocklebank family of Grisedale Hall who owned much land hereabouts. The family controlled the Cunard Shipping Line and named areas such as China Plantation, Guinea Hill and New South Wales Plantation after certain distant destinations of their ships.

Christcliffe property, Eskdale [185012] ...'broken' cliff.

Christen Sike Bampton. Rises near (Christ's) Cross Gate at 508184 and according to the 1:25000 map ends at the Bampton-Helton road at 512185 ...Christian's 'small stream'.

Christ's Cross Gate see **Cross Gate**.

Christy Bridge Martindale. Nearby is the old Martindale Church. The bridge carries the minor road, Sandwick to Dalehead, Boredale, over Howe Grain Beck [434183] ...'bridge by the church'.

Church Bank side of the hill above Crosthwaite Church. Rises to 61m (200ft) [444911]

Church Bay Bassenthwaite Lake. St Bega's Chapel/Church nearby [224288].

Church Bridge carries the A592 over Trout Beck near Troutbeck Church [412027].

Church Bridge Loweswater. Carries the track which serves Kirkhead and Kirkgate Farm over Park Beck [141209].

Church House Boot, Eskdale [176004].

Church of the Wayside Grasmere. Alongside the A591.

Churchstile Wood Nether Wasdale [128043].

Churn, The see **Watendlath Beck**.

Churn Hole SSW The Pike. S Pike Side [183929] ...churn is a figurative name similar to cauldron, cup, pulpit holes and usually referring to a deep hollow on a hillside.

Churn How E Lingcove Beck [239053] ...possibly a figurative name.

Cinder Hill hill above Cinderhill Beck and an ancient bloomery. E River Duddon. [202923] ...hill above the slag/cinders (waste from the bloomery).

Cinderdale Beck a bifurcation of Greendale Beck at 143056. Joins the River Irt at 127038 ...former bloomeries or furnaces near the beck have left traces of slag/cinders from which the name has derived.

Cinderdale Beck rises below Lad Hows at 175197 and joins Crummock Water at 162192 ...see above.

Cinderdale Bridge carries the road from Strands to Santon Bridge/Wastwater over Cinderdale Beck [128039].

Cinderdale Common foot of Cinderdale Beck [164194].

Cinderhill Beck rises Dunnerdale Fells at 206925 and flows down past Cinder Hill and an ancient bloomery to join the River Duddon at 200918.

Cistercian Way a 53kms (33 mile) walk along ancient paths and byways from Grange-over-Sands via Ulverston and the low Furness Fells to Roa Island. See leaflet produced by South Lakeland Distict Council *The Cistercian Way* or *The Cistercian Way: the official guide* by Ian Brodie.

Claife Heights comprises the well-wooded slopes and undulating plateau between Far Sawrey and Balla Wray on the W shore of Windermere. Colthouse Heights provides part of its W face. In medieval times the area was a huge deer park. Enclosed at the end of the 18th century and the present extensive afforestation owes much to J C Curwen of Belle Isle who in 1798 planted thirty thousand larches and a considerable number of oaks on the Heights. Today Claife Heights is bisected by numerous paths and a considerable portion including most of its tree-clad E side and approximately 6.4kms (4 miles) of shoreline was acquired by the National Trust in 1962. Latterbarrow, also owned by the NT, is the highest summit in the N reaches and rises to 244m (800ft) but the highest point is High Blind How with its trig. point at 270m (886ft). A major route across Claife Heights known as the White Post route starts at Ash Landing near the ferry and journeys across the top of the Heights to the summit of Latterbarrow. It is marked by 12 white posts and was opened by the Duke of Edinburgh in 1966 [377975] ...'cliff-like/steep hill'. See also **Crier of Claife**.

Clappersgate hamlet 1.6kms (1 mile) SW Ambleside with its cottages and houses alongside the A593 and the River Brathay. In the 16th to the early 19th century Clappersgate was a port from which slate was taken down the Brathay to Windermere and on down the lake. Principal properties are White Craggs, built in 1904 by Leeds surgeon Charles Henry Hough. Its 14 acres of gardens were, until 1979, open to the public. Today the property comprises a house and three apartments. The boat house and harbour to the Croft, the large mansion which dominates the Clappersgate scene, was part of the previously mentioned port. The present Croft, erected about 1830, replaced a previous building, an old farmhouse, and was built for a wealthy Liverpool merchant. The property changed hands several times before the First World War and during that conflict soldiers recovered there. During the Second World War schoolchildren were billeted in the house. Later it became a hotel.

Today it is divided into apartments. The 17th century Rock Cottage has associations with the young Hartley and Derwent Coleridge while Willy Hill was once the home of artist Julius Caesar Ibbotson [367035] ...'rough bridge, possibly of planks and slate, laid on stone' with a 'gata' (road) or 'geat' (opening/gate). Probably the forerunner of one that existed earlier nearby.

Cleabarrow large house sited off the B5284 opposite Windermere Golf Course. Dales Way passes alongside [422963] ...possibly 'the hill on which the burdock grew'.

Cleabarrow Tarn Cleabarrow. Off the B5284. Coarse fishing principally for tench, carp, eels and some trout. Under the control of the WADAA. C170m (C558ft) [424962].

Cleator Moor the town is situated just outside the National Park boundary at the junction of the A5086, the B5295 and the road to Ennerdale Bridge. It is 6.4kms (4 miles) from Whitehaven and 4.8kms (3 miles) from Ennerdale Bridge. The River Ehen flows to its E and S. 1.6kms (1 mile) S on the A5086 is the village of Cleator. Once a thriving mining area but this industry has now disappeared and new industries have sprung up in its place. A small grotto, a replica of the one at Lourdes, built in 1926 and re-dedicated in 1980, stands close to the Roman Catholic Church and is visited by many pilgrims and visitors. In the market square stands a memorial to miners of yesteryear. This was produced by local artist Conrad Atkinson [026146] ...shieling (pasture) by the cliffs or rocks on the moor.

Cleaty Gill rises S of the fell road from Mosser to Low Lorton at 129254 and joins Sandy Beck at 127265 ...rocky ravine.

Cleft Ghyll Longsleddale. Hereabouts the River Sprint cascades over a high rock step between Wren Gill and the upper valley above Sadgill [478077].

Clemety Sike rises at 247029 and joins Moasdale (Mosedale) Beck at 246018 just before the latter enters the River Duddon.

Clerk, The small pinnacle of rock known as The Clerk stands unobtrusively amongst bracken at the foot of scree descending Barf [219264], see also **Bishop of Barf**.

Clewes Gill rises between Great Borne and Starling Dodd at 132162 and joins Smithy Beck at 131149.

Climb Stile SE Haws. W Birk Haw [258901].

Climb Stile Beck rises alongside Climb Stile at 259901 and joins Strands Beck at 243898.

Climbers route to Pillar & Pillar Rock see **High Level Route to Pillar & Pillar Rock**.

Climbing see **Rock Climbing**.

Clint's Wood slightly W Harrot [155275].

Close off the minor road which runs from the A592 up Grisedale [389158].

Close see **The Close**.

Clough Fold sheepfold [332235].

Clough Head northernmost major peak of the Helvellyn range. Excellent viewpoint of the ridges and gullies of Blencathra and extensive views in other directions. A popular spot for paragliding 726m (2382ft) [334225]. In January 1992, two men received multiple injuries and broken legs when a Cessna 172 made a glancing blow to the summit in low cloud.

Cloven Stone a cleft boundary stone at C550m (1804ft) on Long Brow [303288]. ...'cloven' means cleft or split.

Cloven Stone boundary stone near Mellfell Beck. NE Matterdale End [401241].

Cloven Stone SE Plough Fell [168905].

Cloven Stone Looking Stead [187117].

Coal Beck rises 324074 and joins Easedale Beck at 330081 ...the beck alongside the coal/charcoal workings.

Coast to Coast Walk by A Wainwright. See **Wainwright's Coast to Coast Walk**. There are also other guides similar to this walk including *Walney Island to Holy Island; Alternative Coast to Coast* and another alternative *On Foot from Coast to Coast* this being Ravenglass to Scarborough.

Coatlap Point W shore Windermere [390960] ...resembles a coat lap.

Coats Hill W Coniston Water. Above Stable Harvey [284919].

Cock Cove E Dollywaggon Pike. SE The Tongue. NNW Falcon Crag [350131] ...cove of 'the woodcock'.

Cock Hag Crook [447937] ...'clearing frequented by woodcock'.

Cock Moss SE Holmes Wood. SW Underbarrow Moss [462901] ...local family of Cock(e).

Cock Point E shore Coniston Water [308947].

Cocker, River see **River Cocker**.

Cockermouth although situated just outside the NP Cockermouth is a gateway to the Lake District. Roman occupation from Papcastle was followed by a Norman castle below which grew a medieval town that has since grown into the bustling township of today. The first written record of Cockermouth was in the middle of the 12th century when it was Cokyrmoth. Nearly a century later, in 1221, it received its market charter.

The meeting of two fast-flowing rivers, the Cocker and the Derwent, and two substantial streams, Bitter and Tom Rudd Beck both of which join the Cocker provided water power to drive waterwheels for many early mills and by the beginning of the 19th century there were some 40 mills and factories in and around Cockermouth. There was also a thriving hat industry, a tanning industry alongside the woollen industry as well as quarries, mines and of course, agriculture. Apart from agriculture the other industries have to all intents and purposes disappeared with the mills and factories either demolished or adapted for habitations or light industry. Agriculture is still a prime industry with tourism continually expanding. Cumbria's largest independent brewers, Jennings, founded in 1828 moved from Lorton to Cockermouth in 1874 and became a limited company in 1887.

William Wordsworth was born at Cockermouth in 1770 and the house where he lived until 1779 and where his sister Dorothy and brothers Richard, John and Christopher were born is today owned by the NT and open to the public. Just S of Cockermouth on the A66 near the roundabout with the A5086 is the Lakeland Sheep and Wool Centre and the Cumwest Visitor Centre [119306] ...self explanatory.

Cockermouth Mountain Rescue Team celebrated its 50th anniversary late 2002. Covers Ennerdale, Loweswater and the Buttermere valley.

Cockhag Plantation S Cock Hag [449930] ...see **Cock Hag**.

Cocklakes Hill approximately 0.8 kms (0.5 mile) S of A66, C270m (C886ft) 408273 ...place frequented by the Blackcock (Black Grouse).

Cocklaw Fell N Skeggles Water. Crossed by bridleway from Green Quarter, Kentmere, to Longsleddale, 365m (1198ft) [481039] ...place where the woodcock played.

Cockle Hill W of the unfenced road from Heltondale to Rough Hill [494197] ...presumably hill of the cock or woodcock.

Cocklethwaite between Slate Hill and Reamer Bank. Footpath from Wet Sleddale to Steps Hall crosses it [554127].

Cockley Beck farm and the last habitation at the head of the Duddon valley. Situated at the meeting of the Wrynose Pass road and that over the Hardknott Pass [247016] ...stream by the pasture frequented by the Blackcock.

Cockley Beck Bridge single span bridge which carries the Hardknott Pass road over the River Duddon from Cockley Beck [247017].

Cockley Beck Fell E Cockley Beck [257018].

Cockley Beck Gill rises 254011 and joins the River Duddon at 245015.

Cockley Beck Great Intake Cockley Beck [252016].

Cockley How eminence below Blea Crag-Nitting Haws escarpment [243173] ...hill frequented by grouse.

Cockley How W of path leading up to summit of Hartsop above How. Overlooks Deepdale [393132].

Cockley Moor NW Dockray 455m (1493ft) [381225].

Cockley Moss NW Hesk Fell [166955] ...moss frequented by grouse/woodcock.

Cockly Crag near Easedale Tarn and overlooking Sourmilk Gill [312090] ...the crag overlooking the place frequented by woodcock.

Cockly Pike E face Ill Crag, Scafell Pike range. Above Calfcove Gill [229071].

Cockpit Hill S B5284 at Crook [455950] ...site of a former cockfighting pit.

Cockpit, The see **Moor Divock**.

Cockrigg Crags W Thirlmere. Overlooks Armboth, Middlesteads Gill, and Fisher Gill [301169].

Cocks Close near Garnett Bridge, Longsleddale [521996] ...from the family of one James Cocke.

Cockshott Point promontory, Bowness-on-Windermere. Handed over to the National Trust after being purchased by public subscription in 1937. At one time the site of an old aircraft factory and, after the First World War, a base for pleasure and commercial flights (see **Windermere, Lake**). Today, a pleasant place to linger and admire the view across to Belle Isle, Claife Heights and down the lake [396964] ...similar to other Cockshotts/shutts in the country in that it means where woodcock 'shot' and were netted.

Cockshot Wood S bank of the River Kent [486978] ...see **Cockshott Point**.

Cockshott Wood E shore Derwent Water [266226].

Codale see **Codale Tarn**.

Codale Head above Codale and Codale Tarn. NE Sergeant Man C710m (C2329ft) [289092].

Codale Head Tarns three tarns in the vicinity of Codale Head [288091].

Codale Tarn sited W of Easedale Tarn, N of the shapely Belles Knott and S of Lang Crag this attractive tarn lies in the little valley of Codale from which it takes its name, 466m (1529ft) [297088]. Fishing, for those who are willing to undertake the trek to it, is for brown trout and perch. Ghost and ghost stories abound in Lakeland and Codale Tarn is no exception. Its shores are said to be haunted by a wailing spectre ...as the dale faces N the most likely interpretation of the name would seem to be the 'tarn in the cold valley'.

Coegill Beck rises Birkett Fell at 363198 and meets Aira Beck at 371207.

Cofa Pike shown on 1947 OS 2.5 ins map as Cawkhaw Pike. N Fairfield and at the head of Deepdale. Lies on the well-trodden route from Fairfield via Deepdale Hause to St Sunday Crag. Cofa has three possible derivations any of which could be applicable: 1) a variant of Caw meaning the hill where calves are pastured. Below it is Cawk Cove. 2) Cofa meaning Cove hill, the hill above the Cove (Cawk Cove). 3) Cawk, a corruption of gawk - the cuckoo - and therefore the hill above the cove where the cuckoo is seen or heard. C820m (C2690ft) [359121].

Coffin Track see **Whitemoss Common & Baneriggs**.

Cogra Moss Arlecdon Reservoir, pronounced locally as Arlton. Artificial tarn created in the 19th century by the damming of Rakegill Beck to provide a water supply for Arlecdon to its W. Now no longer used to supply drinking water it is in an attractive setting and, stocked with rainbow and brown trout by Cockermouth Angling Society, it is very popular with fishermen, C230m (C755ft) [095195].

Cold Cove cove down which Coldcove Gill flows from Gavel Moss [383139].

Cold Fell W River Calder [058092] ...obviously not generally a warm area.

Cold Gill N slope Whiteside. Source of Coldgill Beck [167229].

Cold Harbour Underbarrow [479931] ...'place offering shelter from the cold'.

Cold Keld between Oakbank and the River Cocker [148222] ...cold spring.

Cold Pike faces Pike o'Blisco across the col which houses Red Tarn. It is actually part of the SE ridge of Crinkle Crags which drops down over Wrynose Breast to Wrynose Pass. Possesses three cairned summits. Two spot-heighted at 701m (2300ft) [263036] and 683m (2241ft) [259036] and the third at C650m (C2132ft) [256037] ...cold peak.

Cold Pike Tarns tarns near the far W summit of Cold Pike.

Cold Well Great Coppice. Short stream which issues from it flows into the River Irt [121037].

Cold Well WSW summit of Seatallan. Source of Gill Beck [133067].

Cold Well Intake N Outgate. W B5286 [355007].

Coldbarrow Fell Ullscarf ridge. NNW summit of Ullscarf. Two principal summits, High Saddle 675m (2215ft) [289129] and Low Saddle 656m (2152ft) [288133].

Coldcove Gill rises Gavel Moss at 376137 and flows down Cold Cove to meet Deepdale Beck at 392136.

Coldfell Road name given to the moorland road between Calder Bridge and Ennerdale Bridge which traverses the W slope of Cold Fell, passes alongside the Kinniside Stone Circle and drops down Scarny Brow to eventually meet the Cleator Moor to Ennerdale Bridge road.

Coldgill Beck rises Cold Gill on the N slope of Whiteside between Wythe Gill and Hope Gill at 170225. Met by Wythe Gill at 156233 and joins Hope Beck just before the latter enters the River Cocker.

Coldkeld Knotts between Great End and Tongue [227079] ...cold 'spring' 'rocky hill'.

Coledale valley down which flows Coledale Beck. At its head are Coledale Hause, Eel Crag and Crag Hill and near its head Force Crag Mine. Braithwaite is situated at its foot [216226] ...possibly Kolli's valley, hazel valley or charcoal burner's valley.

Coledale Beck rises below Eel Crag at 196207. Fed by several tributaries including named Pudding and Birthwaite Becks and flows down the Coledale valley and through Braithwaite to join Newlands Beck at 237234.

Coledale Hause another 'Piccadilly' of the Lake District. Routes from Lanthwaite Green up Gasgale Gill, Whiteless Pike and Wandope, Hopegill Head and Sand Hill, from the Coledale valley and to and from Grasmoor all converge at the head of this hause/pass/col C600m (C1968ft) [189212] ...the col/pass above Coledale.

Colin How S Farra Grain Gill, Grizedale Forest Park [319922].

Collier Hagg N Ullswater and Yew Crag. In National Trust Gowbarrow Park [414211] ...possibly 'the wood of the charcoal burner'. A collier in this case being a person engaged in the charcoal making process.

Collierhagg Beck rises Gowbarrow Park at 410215 and enters Ullswater at 419205.

Collingwood, W G see **Lanehead**.

Colt Howe Quarry Lingmoor Fell [308047].

Colthouse hamlet to the E of Hawkshead and alongside the road from the B5285 to High Wray. Became an important Quaker centre after George Fox's visit to Hawkshead in 1653. Five years later the Colthouse Quaker burial ground (known as Sepulchre Corner) came into existence and the present meeting house dates from 1688. Wordsworth is believed to have lodged with Ann Tyson in one of two houses collectively known as Green End. Today these are owned by the National Trust. On the hill to the N of the hamlet there is mention of a Gallabarrow which by its very name implies the site of a gallows. In the summer of 2002 a micro brewery, the Hawkshead Brewery, began full production at a barn in Colthouse [359983] ...Ekwall simply says that the meaning is 'self explaining' therefore 'the place in which colts were housed/stabled'?

Colthouse Heights part of the W face of Claife Heights. SE Colthouse. Highest point 218m (715ft) [368973].

Colthouse Plantation N Colthouse and E Colthouse-High Wray road [362985].

Colwith Brow on the A593, Skelwith Bridge-Coniston road [331026] ...'colwith' wood on the peak/ridge.

Colwith Force waterfall on the River Brathay between Little Langdale Tarn and Elter Water. Approximately 0.8kms (0.5 mile) from Colwith through woodland. Twin divided falls drop some 17m (56ft) into a pool. In 1910 a then considerable sum of 4d (1.5p) was made to see the falls. Today, viewing is free from National Trust land [328032].

Colwith (High & Low) see **High/Low Colwith**.

Comb Beck rises Mousthwaite Combe at 347278 and joins the River Glenderamackin at 354268.

Comb Beck rises Burtness (Birkness) Comb below High Stile at 174146 and joins Buttermere at 185153.

Comb Beck rises Blakeley at 072134. Joins Stinking Gill which shortly afterwards enters the River Calder at 075129.

Comb Beck Whinlatter, see **Grisedale Gill**.

Comb Bridge carries the B5292 over Comb Beck [209244].

Comb Crags W High Crag, Helvellyn range. Between Middle Tongue and Birk Side [335136].

Comb Crags above Burtness (Birkness) Comb and alongside the High Stile to High Crag ridge [175144].

Comb Crags N Brown Dodd. E Troutdale [266179].

Comb Gill farthest headstream rises Grange Fell at 263164 and the gill joins the River Derwent at Cannon Dub at 263189.

Comb Gill on Bartholomew map called North Birkside Gill. Rises SSW Nethermost Pike at 341132. Prior to flooding of the valley at the end of the last century Comb Gill joined the Wyth Burn. Today it is culverted under the road and enters Thirlmere at 323137.

Comb Gill farthest headstream of Croasdale Beck. Rises Fothergill Head at 113189. See also Croasdale Beck.

Comb Gill rises slightly E of Ullister Hill at 210259. Joined by Black Gill at 212252 and enters Comb Beck at 216249.

Comb Plantation Whinlatter [209247].

Combe Door NE Glaramara. Cleft opening to The Combe [252109].

Combe Door Tarns several tarns/pools alongside Combe Door [253108].

Combe Gill rises Combe Door at 252111 and flows down through The Combe where it is joined by Rottenstone Gill and eventually reaches the River Derwent at 254140. At one time there was a grain mill alongside the gill but this ceased working well over 100 years ago. Later the building was taken over as a saw mill for Honister Quarry.

Combe Head head of The Combe NNE Glaramara [250109].

Combe Head Tarns several tarns below Combe Head [250108].

Common Farm dates from the 17th century. Shown on OS Outdoor Leisure map as The Common Farm but generally known as just Common Farm and so signposted off the A591. Originally two farms, High and Low. The latter was incorporated in outbuildings [422996] ...farm by the common.

Common Fell on Watermillock Common overlooking Dockray C540m (C1772ft) [383204] ...shown as such over 400 years ago.

Common Wood SE Orrest Head [417992] ...According to the EPNS in their *The Place Names of Westmorland* the Common nearby refers to 'common land' but the Common of Common Wood takes its name from the local family of Commune/Common.

Common, The see **The Common**.

Coniston village at the head of Coniston Water with good access to high and low fells. Copper mining and quarrying were thriving industries until early last century and there are still signs of former bloomeries alongside Coniston Water shore. The mining of copper hereabouts dates back to Jacobean times and in its hey day some 600 persons were engaged in the task of wresting the metal from the fells. By 1855 500 tons of copper were transported from Coniston every month for smelting The Copper Mines Valley site is now listed as an ancient monument. To carry copper ore and slate to the outside world a railway opened in 1859 from the main Furness lines (opened 1857) through Torver to Coniston. This also carried tourists. However, years after the demise of its main customer, the copper mines, the railway closed to passenger traffic in 1958 and to freight in 1962. The village centre grew mainly over the 40 years after 1880.

Today tourism is the principle industry and a 'must' for many is to climb the Old Man (see **Coniston Old Man**). The oldest building is the 16th century Coniston Hall and a popular attraction is Brantwood, former home of John Ruskin. A Ruskin Museum was housed in the Coniston Institute from 1901 until 1996. A new purpose-built museum to replace this was opened to the public on 1 May 1999, and officially opened by the Secretary of State for Culture, Media & Sport, Chris Smith in May 2000. This, apart from much detail on Ruskin, also tells the story of Coniston. Ruskin is buried in the churchyard and his tomb is a pilgrimage for many visitors. At the time of writing rivalling Ruskin's grave as a tourists' attraction is a rusty engine part of the remains of a Halifax bomber LL505 which crashed on Great Carrs above Coniston in October 1944, killing its 8 occupants. Its site, however, is only temporary for the engine is ultimately scheduled to be transferred to the new Ruskin museum. The present church, consecrated in 1586, was rebuilt in 1819, later enlarged, and was much restored in 1891.

The village also has strong connections with the late Donald Campbell who used it as his headquarters for his record breaking successes and who died on Coniston Water in 1967. He is buried in the churchyard. Famous author Arthur Ransome lived at The Heald on the E side of Coniston Water from 1940-45, [302976] ...the King's settlement.

There are many works on Coniston itself, its famous personalities and its copper mines including *Book of Coniston* by W G Collingwood (1900), *Coniston Copper* by E G Holland (1987) and *The Story of Coniston* by Alaistair Cameron and Elizabeth Brown (2002).

Coniston Bank see **Thurston**.

Coniston Coppermines Youth Hostel see **Coppermines Youth Hostel**.

Coniston Fells see **Coniston Range**.

Coniston Foxhounds founded about 1825.

Coniston Hall built by William Fleming in the 16th century. A classic example of Lakeland architecture with its four large rounded chimneys. After the Flemings left for Rydal in the 17th century the hall became a dower house and later a farm. In 1819 it was said to be in a ruinous condition and in 1971 when the hall, and 540 acres of land, were acquired at auction by the National Trust it required considerable restoration to make it habitable. Today part of it is a farmhouse and the grounds provide a camping and caravan site with tents and touring vans screened by trees in the neighbouring Park Coppice [304963].

Coniston Hall Park adjoining Coniston Hall [302961].

Coniston Moor N of Coniston [305999].

Coniston Mountain Rescue Team established in 1947. Today its premises are at Railway Terrace, Coniston. In November 1999, a new extension costing £70,000 was opened.

Coniston Old Man shown on the OS Map as The Old Man of Coniston but generally referred to as Coniston Old Man. Popular mountain W of Coniston. Its flanks are scarred by quarry debris but there is a good view from the summit and a fine ridge walk to Swirl How and Great and Little Carrs. It is the Kanchenjunga of Arthur Ransome's *Swallow and Amazons*. Before this part of Lancashire was incorporated into the present Cumbria in 1974 the Old Man was the highest point in Lancashire 803m (2634ft) [272978]

Six months after he had walked out of the Royal Manchester Childrens' Hospital where he worked the body of child specialist Dr Richard Stevens was found in a disused slate mine on the Old Man on 6 January 2004. ...Historian W G Collingwood in his *The Lake Counties*

(1902) provides the best explanation for the name when he says that the "'Old Man' in spite of several guesses as to its meaning is probably nothing more or less than an old cairn on the highest of the Coniston Fells. The present cairn was made by the Ordnance Surveyors, but before that there were three ancient stone heaps 'the old man, his wife and his son'." A 'man' on a summit refers to a pile of stones/a cairn.

Coniston Range (including Wetherlam) see Reference Section: **Heights**.

Coniston Water originally Thorston/Thurston Water which was derived from the surname Thurston/Thorston. Length 8.7kms (5.5 miles) making it the longest lake after Windermere and Ullswater. Its greatest width is 0.8kms (0.5 mile) and with a maximum depth of 56.1m (184ft) it is the fifth deepest lake after Wastwater, Windermere, Ullswater and Haweswater, the latter being slightly less than 1m (3.3ft) deeper. Height above sea level is 43.5m (143ft). The Water contains two islands, Fir and Peel (part of the latter adopted as the Wildcat Island of Arthur Ransome's *Swallows and Amazons*). Main feeders are Yewdale Beck, Church Beck and Torver Beck. Its outlet is at Nibthwaite where it becomes the River Crake which joins the River Leven at Greenodd. On the E side of the lake is Brantwood, former home of John Ruskin and practically opposite on the W shore is the 16th century Coniston Hall.

Over the years Coniston Water has been the scene of several World Water Speed records. In 1939 Malcolm Campbell (later Sir Malcolm who died in 1949 aged 63) established a new world record of 141.74 mph. Later his son Donald returned to Coniston breaking the record several times and raising it to 276.35 mph. In January 1967, in an attempt to raise the record to 300 mph he was killed on the lake. *Bluebird* was recovered in March 2001 and in May of that year Donald Campbell's body was recovered. In August 1997, the body of Mrs Carol Park was discovered in Coniston Water. She had disappeared in 1976. Twenty-eight years later, in January 2004, her husband, Gordon Park, was charged with her murder.

Between March and the end of October the National Trust's Victorian steam yacht *Gondola*, first launched in 1859, provides a scheduled service up and down the lake. Boats can also be hired and trips booked at the Coniston Boating Centre, Coniston Pier. Powered craft must be launched from Coniston Boating Centre. In 1978 the Secretary of State accepted the LD Planning Board's proposal to introduce a 10 mph speed limit on the lake. Small, non-powered craft may be launched from public access land (this is shown in the LDNP's leaflet *A Visitor's Guide to Coniston Water*). Also of interest is the LDNP Authority's *Boating on Coniston Water*. For general information on the use of the lake and the lake shore there is the *Lake User's Guide, Coniston Water*, also issued by the LDNP Authority. There is some free fishing for trout, char, pike and perch [308955] ...see Coniston.

Coniston Youth Hostels Coppermines House, Copper Mines Valley. Once the home of the manager of the Coniston Coppermines [289986]: Holly Howe, Far End [302980].

Cookson Place across the River Irt from Holmrook village [085997].

Coombs, The see **The Coombs**.

Cooper Beck rises 392226 and meets Matterdale Beck at 400234.

Cooper, William Heaton famous Lakeland water-colour artist. Died July 1995, aged 91. The Heaton Cooper Studio is at Grasmere.

Coopers Green Wet Sleddale [556121] ...local family of Cooper or Cowper.

Cop Knott above White Crags, Langstrath [262119] ...rocky hill top.

Cop (Top) Stone see **Moor Divock**.

Cop Stone see **Launchy Gill**.

Copeland Forest one of the Lake District's former medieval forests protected at that time for the pursuit of game including deer, wolves and wild boar. Very extensive, covering the wild area between the Rivers Ehen and Esk. Now exists in name only and shown on the OS map at 155075, see also **Forests, Medieval**. Copeland Borough Council with its HQ in Whitehaven covers the area of Copeland Forest and extends down to Millom.

Copeland Wood E of Garthrow, Underbarrow, and adjoining Barrowfield Lot [481912] ...land acquired by purchase or a surname derived from this.

Copperheap Bay Derwent Water [254217] ...in the 16th century copper and lead ore was shipped from here to Keswick for refining.

Copperheap Hill above Copperhead Bay, Derwent Water [253216].

Coppermines Valley once the scene of much mining activity but today an area of spoil heaps, ruined buildings (some have been restored including the former home of the copper-mines manager which is now a youth hostel, Coppermines Valley Heritage Centre and a row of former miners' cottages), old mine workings, shafts and tunnels (very dangerous and should not be entered). Alfred Wainwright in his *Wainwright in the Valleys of Lakeland* (1992) page 96, and in his *The Southern Fells*, Coniston Old Man 12, provides much information on the valley including a detailed sketch of the area [289986].

Coppermines Youth Hostel Coniston. At one time the home of the manager of the copper mines. Of the first three hostels established in Cumbria in 1931, Coppermines, Kirkby Stephen and Patterdale, Coppermines is the only one which still exists in the original building [289986].

Copthwaite How ESE Cockley Beck [255013].

Copyhill off A66-Mungrisdale road [367299] ...a copped or truncated hill.

Cora Crag W of the head of Brothers Water overlooking Low Wood [396125].

Corbett a Scottish mountain between 762m (2500ft) and 914m (2999ft). The name is often applied to Lakeland mountains in the same height range.

Cork Lad Of Kentmere see **Hird House**.

Cornclose Lane track running S from Green Quarter, Kentmere [462036] ...lane close by the corn field.

Corney small predominately farming community between Waberthwaite and Bootle. Two other major present-day industries one of which is closely allied to the farming community is that of agricultural engineering while another is that of traditional cured and smoked foods. Corney's church, dedicated to St. John the Baptist, was erected in 1882 but a church had existed on the site since the 12th century. The hostelry, the Brown Cow Inn, was built around 1800. Corney's most famous son, Edward Troughton (1753-1835) was brought up at Welcome Nook. He became famous for his work on scientific instruments particularly sextons and naval theodolites. He was awarded the prestigious Copley Medal by the Royal Society. Corney Fell rises to the E of the village and, along with adjoining fells, possesses several ancient cairns [115914] ...possibly heron island.

Corney Fell large fell area to the S of Waberthwaite Fell and E of Corney [135918].

Corney Fell Road road from Corney over Corney Fell and Thwaites Fell which connects with the A595, Duddon Bridge and Ulpha. Rises to 400m (1312ft) near Stoneside Hill at 150896.

Corney Hall Corney [111907].

Cornhow off the B5289 to Scale Hill and Loweswater road [151223] ...probably corn on the projecting piece of land. Here there is a projection into a bend of the River Cocker.

Corpse roads/tracks along these the dead were transported from their place of death to consecrated burial grounds elsewhere. In some cases this process involved long distances over fell and moor. Major routes were:- Wasdale-Burnmoor-Boot; Mardale-Shap; Buttermere-Brigham; Hawkshead-Dalton; Coniston-Ulverston and Ambleside/Rydal-Grasmere.

Corridor Route track from Sty Head along the slopes of Great End and Broad Crag to Scafell Pike. Earlier known as the Guides Route [219086].

Corpse Road see **Old Corpse Road**.

Cote Farm Fusedale [447188] ...'cottage' farm.

Cote Hill Ludderburn. Overlooks the foot of Ghyll Head Road [401916] ...hill with a cottage/hut on it.

Cote How Rydal. Across the R Rothay from Rydal village. Dates from the 15th century and has a spinning gallery [363060] ...cottage on the side of a hill.

Cotehow Martindale. Off road from The Hause up to Dale Head, Bannerdale. In Wordsworth's day was a public house called the Star Inn [435189] ...cottage hill.

Cotra below Steel Fell and Cotra Breast W of the A591 [327108] ...The EPNS in its *Place Names of Westmorland* suggests that it is more than likely 'cold, exposed tree'. Gertrude Simpson in *Grasmere Field-Names* (1928) states that Cowtray or Cotra is a hog-house and intake and that the monks of Furness had a right of way granted in 1280 from Borrowdale to Furness by Castlerigg and Wythburn to the Cotra.

Cotra Breast crags and scree above Cotra. Adjoining Ash Crags and Blakerigg Crags and to the W of the A591 [324108].

Countess Beck Greendale Beck bifurcates at 143056 near Greendale Farm and one arm, Countess Beck, peels off to join Wasterwater at 152054.

Cove ESE Little Mell Fell. Adjacent minor road to Bennethead [431236].

Cove Beck rises head of Gill Cove at 273990 and joins Levers Water at 277993.

Cove Hut old quarry building above The Cove [272969].

Cow Bridge old stone bridge near Hartsop. Carries track over Goldrill Beck. Pre-bypass this track was the road from Patterdale to Hartsop and Kirkstone Pass. There is a car park adjoining the bridge and just over it a metal seat commemorates the Diamond Jubilee of Queen Victoria (1897) [403133]. While resting on the bridge in April 1802, Wordsworth wrote his 10 line poem the first four lines of which are:

The Cock is crowing,
The stream is flowing,
The small birds twitter,
The lake doth glitter.

Cow Brow E side of Coniston Water. Above Bailiff and Dodgson Woods [306931] ...brow of the hill on which the cows grazed.

Cow Close Gill rises above Heald Brow, E side of Coniston Water, at 312940 and drops down by The Heald to meet Coniston Water at 307946.

Cowcove Beck farthest headstream rises W High Scarth Crag at 213043, joined by Damas Dub at 212033, Catcove Beck at 210028 and becomes Scale Gill which enters the River Esk at 215022.

Cowperthwaite Intake E The Drunken Duck Inn [357013] ...possibly the clearing where the cows grazed or the cow path through the clearing + intake land.

Cowrake Head High Rigg, W St John's in the Vale [313207] ...head of the cows' way.

Cowsty Knotts S Pengenet, W Raven Crag, Kentmere [451049] ...more than likely the cow's steep path to the rocky hill top.

Crab Haws wooded area along the E side of Coniston Water [297907]. See also **Grass Paddocks**.

Crabtree Beck rises Beckhead Moss at 136231 and joins Loweswater at 129216.

Crabtree Brow see **Garburn/Garburn Pass**.

Crabtree Cottages alongside Far Sawrey-High Cunsey road [380947].

Crabtree Dale Wood Miterdale [135007].

Crabtreebeck alongside the Loweswater to Mockerkin road. Crabtree Beck flows alongside [130216].

Crackhill Nook alongside Whitbysteads. SSW Askham. NNW Helton [507226] ...presumably the nook alongside the crow hill.

Cracoe Close Pooley Bridge. Alongside the B5320 [478248] ...enclosure by the crow hill.

Crag Troutbeck [408029].

Crag Band S Tarn Beck. W Seathwaite Tarn [243984].

Crag Close alongside the Grizedale-Satterthwaite road near Bogle Crag [338936].

Crag Coppice adjoining Brantwood [314960].

Crag Coppice Eskdale. Adjoining Penny Hill Farm 137m (449ft) [192005].

Crag End off the minor road from Low Lorton to Brandlingill [141265].

Crag Farm off minor road A595 (Holmrook) to Santon Bridge [109998].

Crag Farm House below Crag Fell, Ennerdale, and slightly W of the foot of Ennerdale Water [086150].

Crag Fell impressive line of crags towering over the S shore of Ennerdale Water. Its actual summit is undulating and grassy but N of this the cliffs of Revelin Crag drop for several hundred feet. Below these are the Pinnacles, impressive vertical rock formations rising some 18-20m (60-80ft) above the angled slope. At the foot of the fell is a rocky knoll, Anglers' Crag. ESE of the summit is the site of the former Old Crag Fell Mine [105139] worked in part of the second half of the 19th century. Crag Fell has two spot heights, one at 523m (1716ft) [097144] and the other at 522m (1713ft) [098143].

Crag Head E side Coniston Water. E Brantwood [319958].

Crag Head property W Loughrigg Tarn [342042].

Crag Hill exceedingly craggy mountain second in height to Grasmoor in the large fell area between the Whinlatter and Newland passes. Trig. point at [193204] 839m (2753ft). W G Collingwood refers to it as Eel Crags Rocks and Wainwright as Eel Crag while many climbers still refer to it as Eel Crags. The OS and others, however, differentiate between Crag Hill and Eel Crag by naming Eel Crag nearby as the rocky buttress between Coledale Hause and Sail.

Crag Hills Crook [460942].

Crag Holme island off the W shore Windermere [378917].

Crag House alongside minor road which connects minor road, A66-Matterdale End, to A592 [433232].

Crag House off the B5284 (Cleabarrow) to Borwick Fold road [435966].

Crag House Irton. WNW Santon Bridge. In the 16th century was Santon Craghouse [107025].

Crag Houses Buttermere [173172].

Crag Intake Plantation between Gillbank and Latterbarrow and to the E of the Colthouse-High Wray road [364988].

Crag Lane Winster. Track from minor road alongside Bryan House Farm-A5074 [419929].

Crag o'Stile S slope Coniston Old Man [274972].

Crag Quarter one of the four Quarters of Kentmere the other three being Green, Hallow Bank and Wra(e)y and takes its name from the impressive Rainsborrow Crag nearby ...see **Hallow Bank Quarter**.

Crag Top above Cawdale Edge, Cawdale, and Cawdale Beck [478100].

Crag Wood 0.3kms (0.16 mile) E Middle Fairbank Tarn [454974].

Crag Wood N Colthouse. Principally National Trust [359989].

Crag Wood W of the road from Far Sawrey-Graythwaite [377932].

Crag Wood S of and adjoining Great Intake [252905].

Crag Wood E shore Buttermere. S Hassness [186157].

Cragg Farm Strickland Ketel [486974].

Cragg Farm Eskdale. Off minor road, A595 to Eskdale Green. Foot of craggy area which includes Raven Crag and Latter Barrow [129973].

Cragged Head Lorton Vale 128m (420ft) [160242].

Craggy Plantation below Spy Crag, Over Staveley [476985].

Craghouse Bridge carries the road to Crag House over the River Irt [105025].

Craghouse Wood N Crag House [108028].

Cragside Wood Lowther Park. E Whale and below a crag [527215]. A 'settlement' in the wood is scheduled as an Ancient Monument [525216].

Cragsteads Gill W Thirlmere. Rises Brown Rigg at 308147 and flows S Bank Crags to join Thirlmere at 316144.

Cragwood House early 20th century mansion behind Ecclerigg Crag, E shore Windermere [390006].

Crier of Claife legend says that centuries ago on a stormy night a call from the W shore of Windermere for the ferry resulted in a boatman crossing over the water. Some time later he returned alone struck dumb and terror-stricken. A few days later he died. For some considerable time after strange and horrible sounds were heard from the region of the Nab on stormy nights. Eventually, a local monk exorcised the fiend to a quarry on the Heald marked on the OS map 'Crier of Claife'. However, in more recent times people have spoken of weird sounds on the Heights particularly on stormy nights and sightings of a hooded figure [386982].

Cringlemire property off Holbeck Lane [394020] ...'circular marsh/bog'.

Cringley Hill alongside the fell road from Mosser to Low Lorton [123257] ...circular hill.

Crinkle Crags serrated and mainly rocky ridge overlooking the head of Oxendale. Possesses five pinnacles of which the highest is Long Top, the second 'crinkle' from the S 859m (2818ft) [249049]. The most northerly crinkle is called Gunston Knott. It is generally accepted that Crinkle Crags is, or are, comprised of five crinkles but some people suggests that Shelter Crags should be part of Crinkle Crags and therefore, depending on whether the crags are listed as one peak or two separate peaks, there could be six or even seven 'crinkles'. In 1998 Crinkle Crags was designated an SSSI by English Nature because of its special rock formations ...crinkled, wrinkled crags. Its, or their appearance, certainly suggests this explanation. However, the Norse called it 'Kringla' meaning a circle and which they saw as encircling the valley below.

Crinkle Gill rises below Mickle Door, Crinkle Crags, at 252047 and joins Buscoe Sike at 264052.

Criscliffe Knotts between Piers Gill and Greta Gill and slightly W of the Corridor Route [216084] ...'shattered/broken cliff on the rocky peak'.

Croasdale earlier Crossdale. Valley down which Croasdale Beck flows. Also community alongside the beck [094175] ...valley with a cross.

Croasdale Beck farthest headstream, Comb Gill, rises Fothergill Head at 113189 and joins forces with Ill Gill, Grain Gill and High Bridge Gill to become Croasdale Beck which enters the River Ehen at Ennerdale Bridge.

Croasdale Bridge bridge which carries the Croasdale to Lamplugh road over Croasdale Beck [092174].

Croasdale Farm Croasdale [094176].

Croft see **Clappersgate**.

Croft Coppice Muncaster Castle grounds [104961].

Croft End alongside the A592 [247911].

Croft Head W River Kent. N Hugill Fell [454014].

Croft Head Farm alongside the minor road from Bennethead to Sparket Mill [438253].

Croft Head Farm Applethwaite [264256].

Croft House E Rosgill, near Rosgill Head [543168].

Croftbrow below Meadley Reservoir, Kinniside, dam [048144].

Croftfoot Ennerdale [096168].

Crofts Head off the Colthouse-High Wray road [358986].

Crook peaceful village astride the B5284. The present St Catherine's Church was consecrated in 1887 but replaced a chapel which stood from 1516 to 1887. Only the tower (built about 1620) of the latter remains on a knoll behind the present church. Major structural repair work on the tower was carried out in 1993. One solitary gravestone to a Thomas Hutchinson of Crook who died in 1868 stands in the walled enclosure surrounding the old tower. Another prominent landmark above Yew Tree Farm to the N of the B5284 is the Monument, an ancient look-out point in the time of the Scottish raiders and more recently a look-out post for the Home Guard during the Second World War. Hollin Hall has a 15th century pele tower attached to it and Crook Hall, now a farm, stands on the site of Thwatterden Hall, the seat of the Philipson family in the 17th century.

The village boasts two hotels, the Sun Inn, believed to date back to the 17th century and licensed since the 18th and further along the road towards Bowness the Wild Boar Hotel, built as a farmhouse in the early 1700s, which became an inn towards the end of the 1800s. The Memorial Hall, built in 1873, has become an attractive private residence. Alongside Dobby Lane is the site of a former 16th century fulling mill which later grew in size and in the 19th century traded in worsted cloth. The streams around Crook once provided water supplies for many early fulling mills and later during the 19th century four bobbin mills, a woollen mill and three basket making workshops [464952] ...crook/bend or just 'hill'.

Crook Torver [285947].

Crook Beck combination of two streams one of which rises near Hole Rake at 292993 and the other at 297992. Joins Yewdale Beck in Tilberthwaite Gill at 300007.

Crook Brow Crook [458951].

Crook Crag Birker Fell. Several rocky outcrops rising to 469m (1539ft) [200989].

Crook Crags in afforested area W Duddon valley [233999].

Crook End Crook. Slightly W of the Crook-Fell Plain-Borwick Fold road [455959].

Crook Foot off Back Lane, Crook [432035].

Crook Hall Crook. Farm. The present building dates from the 18th century. Earlier called Thwatterden Hall, the original of which was built by the Philipson family, noted local landowners. Possesses a herd of water buffalo [452945].

Crook Reservoir NW Boxtree. Private fish pond with subsidiary smaller tarn to its SW,

C200m (C656ft) [445957].

Crook Road 1) Minor road Staveley to B5284 [466961]. 2) section of B5284, Plumgarths to Crook road [481951].

Crook roundabout see **Plumgarths Roundabout**.

Crook Wood Duddon valley [206951].

Crookabeck alongside the Patterdale-Hartsop track E Goldrill Beck. At Crookabeck Angora goats are farmed for their Mohair fleeces. Nearby the beck winds like the handle of a shepherd's crook [402166].

Crook-A-Dyke off the Pooley Bridge to Howtown road [460219] ...'crooked ditch'.

Crookdale little known dale to the W of the A6 near to Shap summit and situated between Wasdale and Borrowdale. Begins at the confluence of Borrow Beck and Crookdale Beck and continues up between High House Bank, Robin Hood, and Lord's Seat, to the S and Whatshaw Common, Little Yarlside, and Great Yarlside to the N to slightly E of Harrop Pike. A desolate and lonely valley which Wainwright spoke of in his *The Outlying Fells of Lakeland* as "...a valley without a habitation and the loneliest within the National Park." However, since that pronouncement in 1973 the then uninhabited Hause Foot farmhouse in its lower reach has been occupied but the middle and upper sections of the dale are still desolate, lonely, and extremely boggy. Over and onward from High Borrow Bridge the predecessor of the present A6 still continues as a road to Hause Foot and then proceeds as an extremely wide footpath up the hillside and over the hause (pass) to cross the A6 slightly N of its summit. The Crookdale Hause route was in use until replaced by the present section of the Shap route in the 1820s [533065] ...'crooked valley' or 'valley with many bends'.

Crookdale Beck farthest headstream rises slightly E Harrop Pike at 504078. Joined by Bleaberry Gill and flows down Crookdale to meet Borrow Beck near High Borrow Bridge at 552040.

Crookdale Bridge carries the old Kendal-Shap road over Crookdale Beck [550056].

Crookdale Fold ruined sheepfold alongside Crookdale Beck near its confluence with Bleaberry Gill [516071].

Crookelty Bridge carries the A 591 over Mill Beck [253258].

Crookwath off Dockray-Dowthwaitehead road [381215] ...'ford by a bend in a stream' (Aira Beck).

Crookwath Bridge carries the Askham-Bampton Grange road over the R Lowther. Earlier there was a ford here [517222] ...'ford at the bend' by the bridge.

Cropple How Eskdale. Alongside minor road, A595 to Eskdale Green [129977].

Cropple How Plantation Eskdale. E Cropple How. S High Coppice [139976].

Crosby Bridge carries the road up the Duddon valley over Crosby Gill [201937].

Crosby Gill rises as Woodend Pool W Woodend at 166962 and subsequently, after being joined by many small streams becomes Crosby Gill at 184956. This enters the River Duddon at 201937.

Crosbythwaite off the Birker Moor Road. Alongside Crosby Gill [190950].

Cross, Sidney former noted climber, founder of the Langdale Mountain Rescue Team in the 1950s (this amalgamated with the Ambleside Rescue Team in 1969) and hotelier. The hostelries of which he was a proprietor were the Burnmoor Inn, Eskdale, and the Old Dungeon Ghyll Hotel, Langdale.

Cross alongside minor road from the A595 to Hall Waberthwaite [105947].

Cross Dormont farm E Ullswater off the Pooley Bridge to Howtown road. Lies under the wooded Barton Park. Earlier names include Trostermod and Tre(i)stermo(u)nt

[462225]. Nearby there are traces of a motte-and-bailey which is scheduled as an Ancient Monument ...Romantics suggest that the name of Tristermount is that of the former abode of Sir Tristram of the Knights of the Round Table fame. Be this as it may, the EPNS suggests that 'Cross' is actually 'Tros' which means either a place with much undergrowth or place which holds the remains of tree felling or clearing of woodland + a personal name + river confluence. Several streams do meet in the immediate vicinity.

Cross Gate earlier Christ's Cross Gate [508183] ...surname Christian + croft + road or way.

Cross Gates cross roads at Lorton [156257].

Cross, The see **The Cross**.

Crosses Farm alongside the old road between the Ings-Troutbeck road and Troutbeck Bridge [412001] ...The present farmhouse was built at the end of the 19th century but a 'Crosshouse' is recorded nearly 350 years earlier and the site name more than likely refers to a much earlier wayside cross. Also, the name, coupled with nearby Causeway ('raised way') and Broadgate ('broad way') has led authorities to believe that the present road could have been more or less on the site of an old Roman road from Watercrook, Kendal, to Galava, Ambleside.

Crosshill S of the fell road from Mosser to Low Lorton [130254].

Crossing Plantation one of three plantations in close proximity to each other in Grisedale. A mixed conifer and deciduous wood and the highest now existing in Grisedale [368146].

Crossings Bridge Crosthwaite. The bridge which carries a road over a stream is alongside the junction of two minor roads and the B5289 [259241].

Crosthwaite village comprised principally of farms and old cottages 6.4kms (4 miles) SE of Bowness and 0.8kms (0.5 mile) off the A 5074 (Gilpin Bridge-Bowness road). Notable buildings are the church, dedicated to St Mary and re-built in two stages 1878-9 with the

Crosthwaite, near Underbarrow

tower erected some years later. Earlier chapels had occupied the site since ancient times. In fact, the very name Crosthwaite meaning 'cross in a clearing' suggests that at one time a preaching cross stood hereabouts. Crosthwaite also possesses a large memorial hall; the Punch Bowl Inn; the Damson Dene Hotel; a preserved mill alongside the Gilpin; a village shop and a Post Office [438915]. The first edition of the 1 inch OS map shows Crosthwaite as Church Town with a small portion named Crosthwaite Green. Town Yeat, Underbarrow, but near the border with Crosthwaite means the way/gate to the town (Church Town).

Crosthwaite NW Keswick. The latter actually once formed part of the parish of the diminutive Crosthwaite [262241] ...clearing with a cross.

Crosthwaite Church Great Crosthwaite. Dedicated to St Kentigren who is sometimes referred to as St Mungo. The old parish church of Keswick. Legend says that the church was founded in the 6th century by St Kentigren. Rebuilt in the C12th and again in the C16th and restored in the C19th. Contains a C14th font and C15th effigies. Robert Southey (1774-1843), former Poet Laureate, is buried here as is Canon Rawnsley (1851-1920) vicar of the church for 34 years and a founder of the NT [257243].

Crosthwaite Mill alongside Mill Lane which connects the Underbarrow to Crosthwaite road with the A5074. A former corn mill now a private residence [441908].

Crow Holme Island, Windermere [391958] ...island frequented by crows.

Crow Park Keswick [263230].

Crowberry Haws E slope Coniston Old Man [284981] ...the crowberry is an evergreen shrub locally common in the N and W of England. Possesses small pale pinkish flowers. Its fruit is a berry, green at first, turning pink, purple and finally black.

Crowberry Hill W River Duddon [208959].

Crowhow End Birker Fell [221008].

Crowmire off Bridge Lane, Troutbeck Bridge-Town End, Troutbeck, road [402007] ...mire/bog frequented by crows.

Crown Hotel Bowness-on-Windermere. An advertisement in Jenkinson's *Practical Guide to the English Lakes* 1873-6 refers to it as "Cloudsdale's Crown Hotel (patronised by Royalty and American Presidents)."

Crozier, John (1822-1903) Squire Crozier as he was known was Master of the Blencathra Foxhounds for over 60 years having taken over that position at the age of 18 from his father. Lived for most of his life at The Riddings, Threlkeld, and died there. He is buried in Threlkeld churchyard.

Crummock Water in the 16th century - Cromack. An attractive lake with high fells to its E and W. It is the largest of the three lakes in the Buttermere valley being 4.0 kms (2.5 miles) in length and 1.2 kms (0.75 mile) wide. Serves as a reservoir. Purchased by the NT in 1935 and adjoining Holme Wood was acquired two years later. Situated at an altitude of C100m (C328ft) and has a depth of 44m (144ft). It is nearly twice the size of its nearest neighbour Buttermere to which it was once joined. The lush alluvial plain (from which Buttermere takes its name) between the two lakes has been formed from debris washed down by Sail/Mill Beck. In its S reaches it possesses six small islands, Woodhouse Islands (3), Holme Island (2) and Scale Island. It is linked to Buttermere by Buttermere Dubs and is principally served by Sail/Mill Beck, Rannerdale Beck, Cinderdale Beck, Liza Beck, Park Beck (which joins it from Loweswater), Scale Beck and Far Ruddy Beck. The B5289 passes along its E shore and to its W a path, boggy at times, leads to Lakeland's waterfall with the highest drop, Scale Force. From the lake the River Cocker flows along Lorton Vale to Cockermouth where it meets the Derwent. Boating by permit is similar to Buttermere (see **Buttermere**) and fishing, also by permit, is for char, perch, pike and brown trout with some salmon and sea trout taken at times. In the spring of 1988 the body of Sheena Owlett was found three weeks after her murder at the bottom of Crummock Water. Her husband, Kevin, confessed to strangling her and dumping her body in the lake [160180] ...originally applied to the head of the River Cocker which flows through it and is its outflow. It means the crooked one.

Cubben off the Eskdale Green to Santon Bridge road [130011].

Cuckoo Brow Wood Claife Heights [377962].

Cuddy Beck two tributariess rise at 280229 and 280230 respectively.

Cuddy Crag near Dockray [384217]

Cumberland & Westmorland Wrestling ancient Lakeland sport possibly introduced by the Vikings. However, George Ion in his treatise *Cumberland and Westmorland Wrestling* (1955) notes that the earliest record he could find of the game was in 1656. The competitor's traditional costume is white vest, often embroidered, and hose with gaily embroidered trunks. A 'throw' is effected by a number of skilful moves. Terms used include chip, cross buttock, dog fall. The sport is controlled by the Cumberland and Westmorland Wrestling Association which was founded in 1906.

Cumberland Way an 80-mile walk from Ravenglass to Appleby via Strands, Buttermere, Keswick, Dockray, and Eamont Bridge.

Cumblands off minor road to Saltcoats from the A595 [084978] ...Cumerlands in the late 16th century. Possibly, similar to Cumberland, from the Welsh 'Cymry/Cymru', land of the Celtic Cumbrians or Britons.

Cumbria land of the Cymry or Cymri (the Celts). Until 1974 the area covered by this work comprised part of Cumberland and Westmorland. In that year the two counties and a section of Lancashire were joined to form the present-day Cumbria.

Cumbria Coastal Way a long-distance route from Milnthorpe via coast and country to Carlisle. Ian and Krysia Brodie's book *The Cumbria Coastal Way* covers the whole route. A leaflet detailing the 45-mile section from Milnthorpe to Barrow-in-Furness, promoted by South Lakeland District Council, is obtainable from Tourist Information Offices and a leaflet describing the rest of the way is available from Cumbria County Council.

Cumbria's Top 20 Tourism Attractions in 2000, according to figures supplied by the Cumbria Tourist Board they were, in descending order: Windermere Lake Cruises; Colony Country Store; South Lakes Wild Animal Park; Ullswater Steamers; Aquarium of the Lakes; Adrian Sankey Glass; Carlisle Cathedral; Lakeside & Haverthwaite Railway; Lakes Glass Centre; Sellafield Visitor Centre; Cumberland Pencil Museum; Hill Top, Sawrey; Cartmel Priory; Carlisle Castle; Muncaster Castle; Priests Mill; Sizergh Castle; Birdoswald Fort; Beatrix Potter Gallery; Lakeland Motor Museum.

Cumbria Way 113kms (70-mile) walk from Ulverston through Coniston, Dungeon Ghyll, Borrowdale, Keswick, Caldbeck, to Carlisle. Consult *Cumbria Way* by John Trevelyn (1987) and *Cumbria Way and Allerdale Ramble* by Jim Watson (1997).

Cumbria Wildlife Trust celebrated its 40th anniversary in May 2002, and at that time had acquired its 40th nature reserve and held 8000 acres of reserves throughout Cumbria.

Cummacatta Wood Borrowdale [254172] ...obscure origin.

Cunsey see **Cunsey Beck, Cunsey Bridge, High Cunsey, Low Cunsey Farm**.

Cunsey Beck the outflow of Esthwaite Water at 366952 flows through Out Dubs Tarn and on through drumlin country. After passing under Esthwaite Bridge it flows alongside the Forge (a former bloomsmithy), under Cunsey Bridge where there was once a blast furnace which later became a bobbin mill. The beck enters Windermere at 385936. Garnett's

Travelling Maps of the Lake District (c1865) shows Cunsey Beck as Eel House Pool (see Eel House) ...Ekwall suggests that Cunsey means 'water meadow' while Robert Gambles in his *Lake District Place Names* gives 'The King's river or King's island'. Credence is given to this with the origin of nearby Coniston whereby Con/Cun means King and the whole word refers to the King's farmstead. There is also the possibility that Cunsey Beck means the stream by which there were rabbits.

Cunsey Beck Forge see **Cunsey Bridge**.

Cunsey Bridge carries the Far Sawrey-Graythwaite road over Cunsey Beck. To the N is High Cunsey and to the S Low Cunsey Farm. Near the bridge a furnace was built in the early 18th century. This subsequently became a bobbin mill and at the end of the 19th century a battery recharging works for the various electric launches then operating on Windermere [381936].

Cunsey Wood alongside the lower reaches of Cunsey Beck [377934].

Cunswick Fell the fell behind Cunswick Scar. Highest point at the N end of the ridge overlooking Plumgarths 207m (679ft) [492943] ...see **Cunswick Hall**.

Cunswick Hall a private road off the B5284 and past Halhead Hall leads to Cunswick Hall. Once attached to a pele tower the hall today is a farm. From early times until 1715 the home of the Le(a)ybourne family. In that year it was forfeited to the Crown. Later acquired by Thomas Crowle of Kendal and subsequently acquired by the Lowther family. Little remains of the ancient hall but an old gateway bears on its courtyard side a Royal coat of arms which has given rise to the legend that King Henry VIII stayed there while wooing Katherine Parr who subsequently became his sixth and final wife. There is no proof, however, that Henry visited or stayed at Cunswick Hall or that he actually 'courted' Katherine. His wishes had to be obeyed. In any case she is believed to have been staying at Sizergh Castle after the death of her second husband. A notorious Leybourne is said to haunt the scar above the hall [486934] ...Cunswick is the King's farm and so called long before Henry VIII.

Cunswick Scar N of what is commonly called Scout Scar and separated from it by the declivity of Underbarrow Road. The roughly 2kms (1.25 miles) ridge ends at its highest point on Cunswick Fell overlooking Plumgarths. Good views of the Lakeland fells and eastwards but particularly to the W and looking up the Kentmere valley 207m (679ft) [492943]. See also **Underbarrow Scar**.

Cunswick Tarn below Cunswick Scar. In the past used as a fishpond by the occupants of the nearby hall and probably as a water supply. Served by spring(s) from the escarpment but does not appear to have an outlet. Lies at an altitude of 145m (476ft) [490938].

Curlew Crag rocky islet in Windermere [399969] ...rock frequented by curlews.

Cust's Gully see **Great End**.

D

Dacre ancient village 6.4kms (4 miles) SW Penrith and 2.4kms (1.5 miles) from the foot of Ullswater. The Venerable Bede refers to 'Dacore' as the site of a monastery in 698 AD. This is thought to have stood on the site of the present St Andrew's Church, the tower of which, originally Norman, was rebuilt in the 19th century. There are other examples of the Norman influence and the chancel is of the 13th century. The origin of four 1.5m (5ft) high carved stone bears sited at the corners of the graveyard is a mystery. It is believed, however, that they might originally have stood on top of the nearby castle. Dacre Castle, a moated 14th century pele tower, restored in the 17th century, was anciently the home of the Dacre family later that of the Hasells of Dalemain. One room is called the Kings Chamber from legend that it was the meeting place in 926 AD of the three Kings of England, Scotland and Cumberland. There is no doubt that such a meeting took place nearby, possibly in the then monastery, but certainly not in that room as the castle was not built until 400 years later. Earthworks at the castle are scheduled as an Ancient Monument. The castle is now a private residence and Dacre Castle Farm [459225]. For more information see *Dacre Castle* by E H A Stretton ...takes its name from Dacre Beck, the trickling stream.

Dacre Bank between Dacrebank Farm and the A66(T) [452274].

Dacre Beck stream served by two principal headstreams, Matterdale Beck and Skitwath Beck, which rise at totally different compass points. The source of the former is in Matterdale at 386224. It then flows through Matterdale End to meet Cooper Beck at 400234 after which, according to Bartholomew's 1 inch (1:63360) it is Dacre Beck. Subsequently joined by Blackdike Beck, Mellfell Beck, Routing Gill Beck, where, according to the 2.5 ins

OS map, it adopts the name of Thackthwaite Beck for a section. Joined by Thackthwaite Gill and, at Hutton, Skitwath Beck. Subsequently joined by Greaves Beck and Southwaite Beck it then goes, in the words of Dorothy Wordsworth, from "a little stony-bedded stream" to one "that spreads out to a considerable breadth at the village of Dacre." Finally joins the River Eamont at 478267. Skitwath Beck rises at 416296 and is joined by Swinescales Beck and Wham Sike before its confluence with Dacre Beck at Hutton ...trickling stream.

Dacre Bridge crosses Dacre Beck between Dalemain and West Park [477268].

Dacre Castle see **Dacre**.

Dacre Castle Farm see **Dacre**.

Dacre Church (St Andrew's) see **Dacre**.

Dacre Lodge farm, Dacre [457261].

Dacrebank farm off minor road from Dacre to the A66 (T) [455271].

Daffodils those immortalised by Wordsworth in his famous poem *The Daffodils* were seen by him and Dorothy by the water's edge near Gowbarrow Park, Ullswater, while they were walking home from Eusemere on 15 April 1802. See also **Gowbarrow Park**.

Dale Bottom off the A591. Caravan and camping site here [296218].

Dale End alongside Red Bank Road, Grasmere. In Wordsworth's day and earlier known as Tail End. At one time the home of Mr Benson from whom the Wordsworths rented Dove Cottage [336062] ...'end of a narrow strip of land'.

Dale End farm, Little Langdale. Alongside the old road from Little Langdale to Elterwater. Bequeathed to the National Trust in 1944 [316037].

Dale End Longsleddale. Not at the head of the dale but near the beginning. All depends on whether one is coming or going [518001].

Dale Hause neck of land between Brown Beck and Heltondale Beck [478199].

Dale Head Bannerdale. See **Bannerdale**.

Dale Head alongside the A591 approximately 800m (0.5 mile) N Thirlspot. One of four settlements that constitute the village of Thirlmere. Sir Hall Caine wrote about Dale Head and its environs in his *Shadow of a Crime* (1885) [317185].

Dale Head property near the head of Dunnerdale [241007].

Dale Head mountain N of Honister Hause and at the head of the dale down which flows Newlands Beck. Connected to Hindscarth by the ridge of Hindscarth Edge. On its N slope is Great Gable. Not that of climbing and memorial fame but a much lesser craggy height 753m (2471ft) high [223153].

Dale Head Close E Dale Head, Dunnerdale [245006].

Dale Head Gill rises below Rowan Tree How at 250005 and joins the River Duddon at 240005.

Dale Head Hall an Elizabethan manor house overlooking Thirlmere. Former seat of the Leathes family who gave one of the names, Leatheswater, to the former lake thereabouts. Now a hotel. Approached down a lane from the A591 [314175].

Dale Head Tarn below Dale Head. One of three principal tarns in the immediate area, the others being Launchy and High Scawdel. Sometimes called Beckhead Tarn as Newlands Beck rises nearby. A short stream flows out of the tarn to meet the infant Newlands Beck C500m (C1640ft) [230152].

Dale How hill on Rannerdale Knotts above Rannerdale [167186].

Dale Lodge Grasmere village. Former mansion. Opened as a residential hotel in 1913 it later became a residential home for the elderly and today is a hotel with Tweedies Bar at its rear.

Dale Park large area covering the Dale Park Beck Valley and land to the W and E of it. Highest point is Black Brows 268m (879ft) [363926]. In 1516 Dale Park was enclosed and made into a hunting chase for red deer by the Abbot of Furness. This occupied land with a 8kms (5 miles) circumference. Today, nearly five centuries later, native red deer still roam the area among woodland but they are now protected [360930] ...in many cases 'park' refers to the relatively small enclosed piece of ground for pasture or arable farming but in the case of the large 'parks' these were extensive areas in which deer were confined ie Dale Park, Lowther Park, Martindale Deer Park and Troutbeck Park.

Dale Park Beck rises at the head of Dale Park valley at 358948. Flows down the valley, alongside Thwaite Head and becomes Ashes Beck. This joins Grizedale Beck near Rusland and subsequently takes the name Rusland Pool which joins the River Leven near Haverthwaite.

Dale Park Scar Plantation Dale Park. W Middle Dale Park [348922].

Dalefoot farm, Heltondale [493201].

Dalegarth property E side Buttermere (lake) off the B5289 [187160].

Dalegarth Force see **Stanley Force**.

Dalegarth Hall farm. Called Auestwait Hall in the early 13th century but from the early 16th century known by its present title. A seat of the Stanley family who occupied it until 1690 when they moved to Ponsonby. Much of the hall was demolished in the 18th century but some oak beams and an early plaster ceiling remain. The hall was later restored. Nearby is the delightful Dalegarth Force (Stanley Force) [170001].

Dalegarth Station Boot, Eskdale. Terminus of the Ravenglass and Eskdale Railway ('T'laal Ratty') [173007].

Dalehead Heltondale [485196].

Dalehead Close Rydal. Alongside upper Rydal Beck [361099].

Dalehead Crags N face Dale Head [224156].

Dalemain historic house and gardens 3.2kms (2 miles) from Pooley Bridge and alongside the A592. The earliest known owner was John de Morville whose brother Hugh was granted the barony of Westmorland by Henry II and who was one of the four knights who assassinated Thomas á Becket in 1172. It has been the home of the Hasell family for more than 300 years. The Georgian facade, added by Edward Hasell in the middle of the 18th century, hides much that is Elizabethan and a Norman pele tower. The house and grounds are open to the public daily except Fridays and Saturdays from mid-April to mid-October. Dalemain provided the exterior shots of Gateshead Hall in London Weekend TV's production of *Jane Eyre* shown on 9 March 1997, and the medieval courtyard and 16th century barn were used as exterior and interior shots of the Lowood Institution in the film. A silver fir tree in the grounds is 25m (85ft) high and claimed to be the largest in the United Kingdom [478269] ...probably 'Mani's valley'.

Dales Way a 73-miles, or is it 81 miles, long-distance walk from Ilkley to Bowness or vice versa. The reason for the doubt is that at the Ilkley start the signpost claims 73 miles to Bowness whereas at Bowness a plaque gives the distance to Ilkley as 81 miles. Actually, the most accurate mileage is given as between 81 and 84 miles. The route enters the LDNP between Staveley and Cowan Bridge alongside the River Kent and then journeys just S of Staveley, by Field Close, Fell Plain, Outrun Nook, Cleabarrow and Matson Ground to Brantfell (Bowness) [486979-407967].

Dales Wood E side Coniston Water [302925].

Dalt Wood N Castle Crag, Borrowdale [248166].

Dalton, Millican he was born in Nenthead in 1867 and his family later moved to London and lived in a house on the edge of Epping Forest. After leaving school Millican Dalton worked for a time as an insurance officer before building a hut in the forest where he made and sold camping tents and equipment. At the age of 30 he left London and established himself in the Lake District amongst his beloved mountains. Here he had a brief sojourn as secretary of the Holiday Fellowship in the Newlands valley. Initially he lived in a tent at High Lodore but later moved to more commodious and comfortable quarters in a quarry on Castle Crag, Borrowdale, where he enjoyed a large living area with a smaller adjacent cave as his sleeping quarters. The large cave is now known as Millican Dalton's Cave. An eccentric, he established himself as the self-styled 'Professor of Adventure, Camping Holidays, Mountain Rapid Shooting, Rafting; and Hair-Breadth Escapes' and over the years he imparted enthusiasm, knowledge, a love of the mountains and a spirit of adventure to many he escorted on expeditions and tours. He died in Buckinghamshire in 1947, at the age of 80. Words carved on his cave wall, whether done by Dalton or a Scottish friend, provide an epitaph to this unique character and advice to others. They simply read "Don't!! Waste Words, Jump to Conclusions."

Damas Dubs twin headstreams rise at 218039 and 220039 respectively and flow either through or alongside 'dubs', pools, to join Cowcove Beck at 212033. This becomes Scale Gill at its confluence with Catcove Beck and enters the Esk at 215022.

Damson Dene Hotel Crosthwaite. The building dates back to the 1880s when it was a cottage called New House. Later it became a farm. Subsequently the farmhouse and yard, small barn and shippen, were given the title Damson Dene because of the adjoining orchard of damson and apple trees. In the 1930s the enlarged property became a CTC hostel and later a Youth Hostel. In 1960 it became a hotel and after extensions received a restaurant licence allowing alcohol to be served with meals. Purchased by Methodist Holiday Hotels in 1993 and opened by them in July of that year after considerable refurbishment. From then until July 2000, it was a temperance hotel (apart from the restaurant licence) but since that date and after successive owners it has been granted a full liquor licence [426913].

Damsons Crosthwaite, and the Lyth valley leading up to it, are well-known for their orchards of damson trees which in spring are covered in white blossom and later with damsons, unique to the area and possessing a characteristic flavour. To promote interest in the growing of damsons and safeguard the interest of fruit growers in the district the Kendal and District Damson Growers' Association was formed in the spring of 1939. This was short-lived however owing to the Second World War but more recently, in 1996, another association, the Westmorland Damson Association was formed.

Incidentally, the damson, a member of the plum family received its name from the Damastine, grown in Damascus since pre-christian times. The local damsons are generally believed to have been brought from Turkey to be used for their dye in the days when the woollen trade was prevalent in the area. Other suggestions are that the trees were brought back by the Crusaders or were introduced even earlier by the Romans.

Dan Becks alongside the B5286 [360006].

Dancing Gate situated in the triangle of land between the A591 and the road to Millbeck [245264] ...Danson Place in the 16th century. Posibly personal name.

Darling Fell locally Durling Fell. Steep fell rising above the N shore of Loweswater 391m (1283ft) [128225].

Darling How farm off the B5292 and near Spout Force on Aiken Beck [183258].

Darling How Lorton Fells. Between Brown How and Whinlatter Top [192249].

Darling How Wythop valley. W Wythop Hall [196284].

Darling How Plantation Thornthwaite Forest [184173].

Davies, Edward Hunter author, broadcaster, publisher. Born 1936, married Margaret Forster, author, 1960. Residence: Loweswater.

Daw's Pond Barton [480261] ...named after the local family of Dawes. Dr Lancelot Dawes was vicar of Barton and Lord of the Manor, in the 17th century. He built the parsonage, now Glebe Farm, in 1637.

Dawson Pike WSW White Pike [242953].

Dawsonground Crags Eskdale. E Stony Tarn, W Scale Gill. Rise to 397m (1302ft) [204027] ...probably a connection with Dawson Place which was later succeeded by the Woolpack Inn.

Dead Beck rises between Great and Little Calva at 285313 and joins the River Caldew at 284296.

Dead Pike see **Steel Fell**.

Decoy Hag on summit of ridge running NNW-SSE Lowther Park [536225] ...'decoy' in the 'newly planted clearing'.

Decoy Hag Pond Lowther Park [533230].

Decoy Pond Decoy Hag, Lowther Park [531226] ...Large artificial pond used to decoy waterfowl.

Decoy Pond Muncaster [094961] ...see above.

Deep Gill Little Dale. See **Scope Beck**.

Deep Gill farthest tributary rises W Great Scoat Fell at 149113. Joins with Silvercove Beck at 132134 to become Woundell Beck which enters the River Liza at 134140. A footbridge over the beck near its confluence with Silvercove Beck was donated by the Ramblers Association and is on the Nine Becks Walk route made in 1974.

Deep Slack deep 'hollow' down which the infant Mere Beck flows [291096].

Deepdale deep, wild and lonely lateral valley running roughly SW from Patterdale. Down it flows Deepdale Beck. In his *Guide to the Lakes* Wordsworth says of Deepdale "It was terminated by a cove, a craggy and gloomy abyss, with precipitous sides ..." An apt description. The valley is a classic example of glaciation with the characteristic hanging valley of Link Cove, several moraines, and a fine Roche Moutonee ('sheep rock'), a bedrock, or protuberance, that has been shaped by glacier overriding. The side facing the oncoming ice is smooth and formed by glacial abrasion while the side away from the moving ice is steep and rough and is considered to be the result of the plucking action of the glacier. The cliffs of Greenhow End bifurcate the head of the dale, the left arm rising to Link Cove, Hartsop Above How and Hart Crag while to the right are the crags of Fairfield and Cofa Pike. A barely discernible path winds its way up to Deepdale Hause where it joins the well-trodden path, Fairfield-Cofa Pike-St Sunday Crag [391133].

Deepdale steep-sided valley down which flows Aira Beck. Its head is ringed by Hart Side, Stybarrow Dodd, Watson's Dodd, and Great Dodd [355203].

Deepdale Beck its farthest headstream rises below Fairfield at 360119. Another rises at the head of Link Cove. On its way down Deepdale joined by Dry Gill, Blackshaw Sike, Coldcove Gill, and Sand Gill, before it meets Goldrill Beck at 403150.

Deepdale Bridge Bridgend. Carries A592 over Deepdale Beck [399144].

Deepdale Common large area of former common land N Deepdale Beck [380137].

Deepdale Crag Stybarrow Dodd [345190].

Deepdale Hall farm alongside track from A592 to Wall End, Deepdale [396141].

Deepdale Hause head of Deepdale. Col connecting Cofa Pike to St Sunday Crag [361125].

Deepdale Park wooded parkland landscape similar to Glenamara Park. Bounded by Wall End, Deepdale Beck, and lower section of Hartsop Above How [397137].

Deepdale Slack rises Hart Side at 360104. Flows down between Glencoyne Head and Scot Crag to meet Wintergroove Gill and The Nick at 366187. Then becomes Glencoyne Beck.

Deer in the Lake District these are principally red and roe with occasional intrusion of fallow, sika and muntjac. The red deer occurs particularly in the Martindale deer forest, Gowbarrow Park, Grizedale Forest park and the Furness woodlands while the roe in wooded areas, particularly Grizedale Forest, and also scrub areas. Incidentally, do you know the proper name for red deer, male and female, at different ages? If so, ignore the following. If not, I feel sure that you will find the following extract from an old book interesting: "A male Red in its first year is a Calf; second year a Brockett; third year a Staggard; fourth year a Stag; fifth year a Stag at All Points; sixth year Stag; seventh year Hart and eighth year Hart of Greafe. A female Red in its first year is a calf; second year Brockett's Sister; third year a Heinuse and fourth year a Hind."

Deer Bield Crag impressive rock buttress overlooking Far Easedale. Frequented by climbers [305095] ...see **Deer Bields** below.

Deer Bields between Tarn Crag and Deer Bield Crag on the ridge separating Easedale and Far Easedale [303095] ...a natural shelter (bield) for deer in a cleft between two rocky outcrops.

Deer Enclosures Wet Sleddale. Ancient stone-walled deer enclosures alongside Sleddale Beck between Tonguerigg Gill and Sherry Gill [536106].

Deer Hows S Fox How/Fox How Farm [364047] ...hills frequented by deer.

Deerclose Cottage alongside Great Wood, Borrowdale [273218].

Deergarth Gill see **Launchy Gill**.

Deergarth How Island one of the two islands in Thirlmere. Prior to flooding was a rocky knoll called Deergarth How [310163].

Delicars alongside the A5084, Torver to Sunny Bank road [287928] ...land on which the dill grows.

Demming Crag Birker Fell. Possesses several rock climbs. Spot-height at 525m (1722ft) [222002].

Denehead Bridge carries First Moss Lane over Underbarrow Pool [468906].

Dennyhill farm just W Walmgate Foot and alongside Bampton to Haweswater road. [517174].

Derwent, River see **River Derwent**.

Derwent Bank Holiday Fellowship property on the W shore of Derwent Water near its foot [253230].

Derwent Bay Derwent Water [252215].

Derwent Bay property alongside Derwent Bay, Derwent Water [251215].

Derwent Bay Bears bears sculptured by chainsaw at Derwent Bay Sawmill, Derwent Bay, Portinscale [251215].

Derwent Bridge carries the B5289 over the River Derwent [251240].

Derwent Fells name given to fell area W of the head of Bassenthwaite Lake [215269] and also to area of fells W of Derwent Water [215198].

DERWENTFOLDS

Derwent Foot here the River Derwent enters Bassenthwaite Lake [231274].

Derwent Hill Portinscale 90m (295ft) [255235].

Derwent House Victorian property, Borrowdale. A guest house [257178].

Derwent Isle see **Derwent Water**.

Derwent Water shown as two words, Derwent Water, on the OS map and in several other works but many other books and guides give the name as one word, Derwentwater. Although the lake with a length of 4.6kms (nearly 3 miles) only ranks as the 8th longest in the Lake District being just over a quarter that of Windermere it equals the latter as the widest at 2kms (1.25 miles) and it certainly ranks as one of the most attractive and beautiful. With a maximum depth of 11m (72ft) it is relatively shallow in relation to many other lakes. Wastwater is nearly 3.5 times deeper and Windermere nearly 3 times deeper. Similar to Buttermere and Crummock Water, Derwentwater and Bassenthwaite Lake were once one large lake but became separated by huge amounts of silt and gravel washed down by mountain streams and a river, the Greta. Both lakes are roughly the same maximum depth and contain a very rare and ancient whitefish, the vendace along with perch, pike and trout.

The OS map shows eight islands of which the largest are well-wooded, better known and most notable. These are Derwent, Lord's, Rampsholme and St. Herbert's. The first named is the only one to be inhabited. Known by the Vikings as Hestholme (stallion/horse island) it became Vicar's Island in the 12th century. In the 16th century it was occupied by German miners who had been brought over to this country to work mines in the area. Subsequently came into the ownership of the Earls of Derwentwater and later occupied by the eccentric Joseph Pocklington who made considerable embellishments to house and grounds not appreciated by many including William Wordsworth. Then known as Pocklington's Island. Today, it is titled Derwent Island and the manor house, set in 7 acres of woodland and built in 1780 is a Grade II listed building. The house and island have been owned by the NT since 1951. Lord's Island, so called because it and its manor house (remains can still be seen) were owned by the Earls of Derwentwater. James the second Earl was beheaded for treason in 1715 and his younger brother, Charles, captured in 1745, was also beheaded. Rampsholme, the smallest of the four major islands, is the island on which the wild garlic grows or possibly Hrafn's summer pasture.

In the 7th century St. Herbert is said to have built a hermitage or cell on an island which later took the title, St. Herbert's Island. He died in 687AD and, for many centuries afterwards the island became a mecca for pilgrims. Owned by the NT since 1951. Another island appears periodically at the head of the lake. Known as the Floating Island it has often been the subject of myths and superstitions but actually it comprises a mass of rotting vegetation brought to the surface of the lake by gases. The other tiny named islands are Lingholme, Otter, Otterbield and Scarf Stones. On the shore of the lake between Calf Close Bay and Broomhill Point stands a unique sculpture known as the 'Hundred Year Stone'. This has been in its position since December 1995, and marks the centenary year of the NT in the Lake District. From a distance the sculpture looks like a split boulder but on close examination the two faces reveal intricate carvings. These refer numerically to the centenary of the Trust and consist of 10 concentric circles divided into 10 segments referring to the past and future of the organisation. The work is that of Devon based sculptor Peter Randall Page.

The Keswick and Derwentwater Launch Co. Ltd. operates a ferry service around the lake daily throughout the year (except Christmas Day) between seven boatlandings. There is, however, a reduced service from December to February. The company also hires out self-drive motor boats and rowing boats. Canoes, dinghies, windsurfers and rowing boats can be launched from the shore or islands owned by the NT. Also at the foot of the lake are the Derwentwater Boat Club, Nicol End Marina, a Canoe Centre and the Lakeside Holiday Park with its own private lake frontage, launching and mooring facilities, boat hire and private fishing.

Derwent Water possessses several named bays - Abbot's, Barrow, Brandelhow, Calfclose, Copperheap, Derwent, Galemire, Great, Isthmus, Kitchen, Myrtle, Otterbield, Strandshag, Victoria and Withesike. Fishing for perch, pike, salmon and trout is by permit. For the most recent boating and fishing information consult Keswick Launch and NT leaflets or Tourist Information Offices [260210] ...the lake through which the river flows (the Derwent) that abounds with oak trees.

Derwentfolds NW Wescoe. E Lonscale [298255].

Derwentwater see **Derwent Water**.

Derwentwater Boat Club foot of Derwent Water [253232].

Derwentwater Canoe Centre see **Canoe Centre**.

Derwentwater Marina marina complex with facilities for canoeing, windsurfing, sailing and rowing.

Devil's Chimney one of several delightful little headlands E shore upper reach Ullswater. Other notables are Silver Point, Purse Point, and Blowick. The shore path from Patterdale to Sandwick passes close by [394178].

Devil's Gallop alongside the Hawkshead-Newby Bridge road just S of Esthwaite Water [363946]. Good examples of hearths and pitsteads used in charcoal making are to be found here ...local superstition.

Devil's Punchbowl see **Watendlath Beck**.

Devoke Water largest Lakeland tarn in isolated position W of the Ulpha to Eskdale fell road and usually approached by footpaths or bridleway from that road or bridleway from the A595 ENE Waberthwaite. Surrounded principally by Rough Crag, Water Crag, Stord's Hill and Seat How. Possesses a two-storey boathouse on Washfold Point. The tarn is owned by the Muncaster Estates. It contains red trout which, it is said, were originally introduced from Italy by the Monks of Furness Abbey. Served by several small streams on its S side including Rigg and Hall Becks and is the source of Linbeck Gill which joins the River Esk.

That early man occupied this area is emphasised by the considerable number of stone circles, ancient cairns and enclosures which have beeen discovered in the vicinity. At an alt. of C240m (C787ft) it has a maximum depth of 14m (46ft) [158969] ...either the 'dark' water or a Celtic name similar to that of Divock of Moor Divock in the former Westmorland.

Dewpot Holes see **Moor Divock**.

Dikey Hill near Bramley. Rises to 242m (794ft) to the E of Bramley Seat [113239].

Dixon Ground Coniston. One of the many old 'grounds' in the Lake District. In this case named after an early Dixon family [299976].

Dixon Scrow W Dixon Ground. Coniston [291978] ...for the definition of scrow see **Glossary** in Reference Section.

Dob Gill W Thirlmere. Ravine down which flows Dob Gill out of Harrop Tarn at 312136. The stream drops down by substantial and impressive cataracts. The track from Wythburn to Watendlath crosses the gill where it emerges from Harrop Tarn and passes to the right of the latter through dense spruce and larch to reach the open fell. The stream used to join the Wyth Burn but now enters Thirlmere direct at 317140.

Dobbies Lakeland's naughty, mischievous spirits similar to leprechauns.

Dobbin Wood N bank of middle reaches of Ullswater. Alongside A592 [418206]

...fairy/sprite wood.

Dobby Lane Crook [460950] ...lane haunted by a dobby (sprite or apparition).

Dobby Shaw Seathwaite, Duddon valley [228955] ...wood haunted by spirits/goblins/apparitions. Gobling Beck nearby.

Dobgill Bridge carries the road around the W side Thirlmere over Dob Gill [317139].

Dobson Bottom Lowther Park [539208].

Dobson, Tommy founder of the Eskdale and Ennerdale Foxhouds and its Master for 53 years. He died in 1910 aged 83 and his tombstone is in St. Catherine's Churchyard, Eskdale.

Dobson's Bridge Scales-Guardhouse road. Crosses the River Glenderamackin at 350265.

Dock Tarn Watendlath Fell. Attractive tarn set amongst heather clad slopes and knolls. Possesses an island, bays and promontories. A popular walk from either Watendlath or Stonethwaite C410m (C1345ft) [274144] ...dock/water lily tarn.

Docker Nook Longsleddale [505013] ...possibly the surname Docker and meaning dairy farm in the hollow or derived from the docker plant.

Dockernook Crag above Docker Nook and Dockernook Wood, Longsleddale [503015].

Dockernook Gill rises Sleddale Forest at 483014. Joined by Black Beck at 494009 and meets the River Sprint, Longsleddale, at 509015 ...see **Docker Nook**.

Dockernook Wood below Dockernook Crag and above Docker Nook, Longsleddale [504016].

Dockey Tarn small tarn WNW of the cairn on the summit of Nab Scar. SE Alcock Tarn. Lies at an altitude of C380m (C1247ft) [353073] ...from the local Dockray family.

Dockray hamlet on A5091 between Matterdale End and the A592. Aira Beck flows through it on its way from Deepdale over High Force and Aira Force to Ullswater and an old track called the Old Coach Road begins W of the village and runs across the moors below Wolf Crags and Clough Head to St John's in the Vale [393216] ...dock/sorrel.

Dockray Nook NW Felldyke from which it is approached by a lane [088201] ...nook or corner overgrown with dock/sorrel.

Doctor(s) Bridge an old packhorse bridge over the River Esk carrying the road and track to Penny Hill Farm. Called after Dr Edward Tyson who had it widened in 1734 to allow his carriage to pass over it. Subsequently, it was strengthened and restored by the NT in 1955 [190008].

Dod Hill between Wansfell summit and the A592, 451m (1480ft) [411053] ...rounded hill.

Dod Knott Birker Fell [211004].

Dod Pike WNW Cockley Beck [240021].

Dodd subsidiary summit of Red Pike (Buttermere). Joined to Red Pike by The Saddle 641m (2103ft) [164158].

Dodd small hill on the slope of High Seat and to the N of Ashness Fell [278189].

Dodd N Whiteside. Between Hope Gill and Cold Gill 454m (1489ft) [169231].

Dodd sometimes referred to as Skiddaw Dodd. Rounded hill on the slope of Skiddaw 502m (1647ft). In 2002 conifers on the summit were removed leaving an excellent viewpoint particularly to the N [244274].

Dodd Beck rises slope of Loadpot Hill at 461185 and joins Heltondale Beck at 472191.

Dodd Bottom at the head of Swindale and at the foot of High and Low Blake Dodd [502116].

Dodd Crag Sale Fell [189294].

Dodd Crag Castlerigg Fell. Towers above Shoulthwaite Glen/Gill with spot-height above lengthy crags at 460m (1509ft) [291206].

Dodd Gill rises W slope Loadpot Hill at 451177 and joins Fusedale Beck at 445186.

Dodd, The see **The Dodd**.

Dodd Wood Dodd/Skiddaw Dodd. See also **Ospreys**.

Doddick NE Threlkeld on A66. Overlooked by Doddick Fell, Blencathra [336265].

Doddick Farm Doddick [335265].

Doddick Fell slope of Blencathra between Doddick Gill and Scaley Beck. Doddick Fell Top 682m (2238ft) [332279].

Doddick Gill descends from Blencathra ridge below Hallsfell Top [326277]. Becomes Doddickgill Beck which joins River Glenderamackin at 335258.

Doddickgill Beck see **Doddick Gill**.

Dodds (The Dodds) sometimes called The Dods. Refers to the four major Helvellyn ridge Dodds - Little, Watson's, Stybarrow and Great.

Dodds Howe Crosthwaite [437916] ...former local family of Dodd

Dodgson Wood E side Coniston Water [303930].

Dodknott Gill rises Birker Fell at 214004 and flows S and then W of Dod Knott to join the Esk at 216009.

Dodsgill Beck rises Starling Dodd (hence the first element) at 145155 and enters Ennerdale Water at 137138.

Doe Green SE Sandwick [426192].

Doe House Gill rises W Great Carrs at 266010 and joins the River Duddon at 259021.

Dog Crag E Swindale, below Outlaw Crag [511125].

Dog Hill SSW Tailbert [532141].

Dog How SE High Stonythwaite. W Wallowbarrow Crag [216966].

Dog Nab slight projection E shore Windermere [385916].

Dollywaggon Pike most southerly mountain on the Helvellyn ridge and the 8th highest of its major peaks. Origin of this unusual name is not known but W G Collingwood in his *The Lake Counties* (1902) believes that it may be derived from ON, dolgr, meaning a giant and veginn, lifted. This explanation is reiterated by W H Cooper in his *The Tarns of Lakeland* 858m (2815) [346131].

Don Bottom Askham [503235].

Dora's Field next to Rydal Churchyard. Originally known as The Rashfield it is famous for its daffodils. Wordsworth purchased it in 1826 with the intention of building a house on the land. This never materialised and subsequently the field was given by him to his daughter Dora (d.1847) and renamed Dora's Field. Owned by the National Trust since 1933 [364062].

Dore Head col between Yewbarrow and the Red Pike ridge and at the junction of paths to and from Yewbarrow, Red Pike, Wastwater and Mosedale (the latter via Dorehead Screes) C490 (C1608ft) [175095] ...earlier Door Head. The door/opening between Yewbarrow and the Red Pike ridge. There is also a Great Door at the southern end of Yewbarrow.

Dorehead Screes steep scree slope leading up from Mosedale to Dore Head [177097].

Doup Crag line of crags running N-S on E slope Park Fell Head [420092] ...doup is a North Country dialect word meaning buttocks which in turn comes from ON 'rounded cavity'.

Doups N Millbeck [256267] ...see **Doup Crag** above.

Dove Cottage Town End, Grasmere. Believed to be early 17th century and at one time was an inn, The Dove and Olive Branch, on the old road from Ambleside over White Moss to Keswick. Acquired by William Wordsworth in 1799 and was his, and his sister Dorothy's home (and his wife Mary from 1802), until 1808 when they all moved to Allan Bank across the vale which in those days was simply called Town End. From 1809 Thomas de Quincey of *Confessions of a Lotus Eater* fame lived there until he moved to Fox Ghyll in 1820. The property was acquired by the Wordsworth Trust in 1890 and since then the name Dove Cottage has come into common parlance. The cottage and adjoining Grasmere and Wordsworth Museum and craft/book shop are open to the public. A small car park adjoins the museum but the principal one is alongside the present Ambleside-Keswick road (A591) as is the Wordsworth Restaurant and snack bar. In April 2003, the first foundations for a new centre, the Jerwood Centre, were laid in the grounds of Dove Cottage and the building was expected to open a year later. This will house the Wordsworth Trust's constantly growing literary collection, improved research facilities, a conservation area and a space for poetry readings [342070].

Dove Crag precipitous crag at the head of Dovedale and on the principal Fairfield Horseshoe route. There are several rock climbs on its steep face. Climbed by Alfred Wainwright on 9 November 1952, and on his return he wrote the first pages of *Book 1 - The Eastern Fells* (1955). Hart Crag is 1.2kms (3/4 mile) NE and Fairfield a further 1.6kms (1 mile) NW then W, 792m (2598ft) [375104] ...crag frequented by doves/pigeons. See also **Priest's Hole**.

Dove Crags rim of crags on the N face of Grasmoor towering above a grassy ampitheatre and Gasgale Gill [178207].

Dove Nest today called The Samling. N of Low Wood and off the A591. Situated in 47 acres of ground. Built as a cottage in the 18th century with gables added in the 19th century. Felicity Hemans (1793-1835), poetess and hymn writer, spent several summers here. Today she is probably best remembered for the lines "the boy stood on the burning deck, whence all but he had fled ..." and "The stately homes of England/How beautiful they stand ..." At one time it was a management training and development centre. Today, a retreat or hideaway for individuals or where groups can gather to share ideas, do their own particular things or plan for the future away from day-to-day pressures. In 1996 an 80-seat theatre was opened in a converted barn. Renamed The Samling, 'samlings' being an old Cumbrian word for gatherings of people [384025].

Dove Nest Wood National Trust woodland above Dove Nest [384027].

Dovecote Wood Muncaster Castle grounds [101961].

Dovedale scenic wild valley which runs from Hartsop to Dove Crag. In a similar way that upper Deepdale is divided at its head by Greenhow End so Dovedale is split at its head by Stangs/Stang Crags. One branch leads to Huntsett Cove, another up Hogget Gill and Sales. Down the principal valley flows Dovedale Beck (frequently referred to as Hartsop Beck). At its foot is Hartsop Hall, a former manor house; site of ancient settlements; and a long-disused mine. Believed to be the scene of Wordsworth's *Lucy* - "She dwelt among the untrodden ways/Beside the springs of Dove ..." Owned by the National Trust [390116] ...dale frequented by doves/pigeons or the dark valley.

Dovedale Beck also referred to as Hartsop Beck. Principal headstream rises between Hart Crag and Dove Crag at the head of Houndshope Cove at 372111. Flows down Dovedale and on its way to Brothers Water is joined by Hogget Gill and Kirkstone Beck. Joins Brothers Water at [401125].

Dovenest Crag massive crag overlooking The Coombe and on the W slope of Rosthwaite

Cam. Possesses several caves and is frequented by rock climbers who sometimes combine their climbing expertise with cave exploration [253116].

Dow Bank between Huntingstile Crag and Raven and Spedding Crag [330056] ...more than likely pigeon/dove bank.

Dow Crag buttress SE slope of Scafell Pike and overlooking upper Eskdale. Frequently referred to as Esk Buttress by climbers to differentiate it from other Dow Crags particularly that near Coniston. Several climbing routes including Central Pillar [222065] ...possibly the black crag or the crag frequented by deer or doves.

Dow Crag across Spothow Gill from Harter Fell 404m (1325ft) [204994] ...see below.

Dow Crag highest point in a ridge running from Brown Pike, above the Walna Scar road, over Buck Pike and down to Goat's Hawse. It shows a huge precipitous face to the E and its buttresses and gullies are a mecca for rock climbers. From its summit at 778m (2552ft) there is a near perpendicular drop of 275m (902ft) to Goat's Water [263978] ...either the crag frequented by doves/pigeons/deer or the black crag.

Down in the Dale Wasdale. Centuries ago possessed six small farms which were eventually amalgamated into one. The last house here was demolished during the Second World War and the last surviving building is a barn [185082].

Down in the Dale Bridge carries the road to Wasdale Head over Mosedale Beck [184082].

Dowthwaite Crag overlooks Dowthwaitehead [370210].

Dowthwaite Gill rises W Thirlmere at 301178 and enters the reservoir at 306179.

Dowthwaitehead hamlet 2 miles from Dockray [370208]. In 1942 a Hurricane crashed near Dowthwaitehead Farm ...'Dufa' or 'Dufe's' (feminine name literally meaning dove) clearing at or near the head of the valley.

Dowthwaitehead Moss WNW Dowthwaitehead [361211].

Driedley Gill rises Glaramara at 245098 and joins Langstrath Beck at 254093.

Drigg Point southern point of Drigg sited SW Ravenglass [071952] ...Drigg - a place where boats had to be carried or dragged over a section of land or shallow water.

Droomer Windermere. Not very long ago School Knott could be approached by foot from Windermere Station by pleasant by-ways and the three major properties hereabouts were Droomer Farm, Old Droomer and Old Heathwaite. Today urbanisation has taken place and the large Droomer [416983] and Heathwaite [416979] housing estates sprawl across the area and surround the old properties ...Droomer most likely a surname; Heathwaite is a high clearing.

Dropping Crag Scafell Pike [215074] ...possibly the dripping crag.

Dropping Crag Yewbarrow [169076].

Dropping Crag below Harter Fell and WNW Birks [225994].

Dropping Crag Torver High Common [259954].

Dropping Crag on the N arete of Mellbreak [144199].

Drum House see **Honister Quarries and Mines**.

Drumlins smooth hillocks or mounds usually elongated which have been formed from debris deposited by receding glaciers. Principally found in lowland areas of the Lake District or its environs. A considerable number exist in the Heversham, Hincaster, Stainton and Sedgwick area; the Eden Valley and around Skelsmergh. Other areas include the Cunsey Beck valley and the Esthwaite valley (the 'Ees') ...'druin' - a ridge or back and 'lin' an abbreviation of ling and meaning small or little. Hence little ridge.

Drunken Duck Inn, The Barngates. A 16th century inn at one time called Barngates Inn.

Situated at the meeting of the Outgate-Skelwith Bridge road and that from Hawkshead-Pull Wyke. The inn changed its name in Victorian times. The story goes that the then landlady found her ducks lying apparently dead in the road. She began to pluck and prepare them for dinner, an action which quickly awoke the birds. A beer barrel had apparently leaked into their feeding trough and they were, in effect, drunk and for a time 'out to the world'. The landlady is said to have knitted them woollen jackets until their feathers grew again [351013]. A micro brewery commenced brewing at the Drunken Duck in 1997.

Drunken Duck Tarn see **Barngates Tarn**.

Dry Cove Bottom far from dry. Several streams including Henfoot Beck and Swallow Scar Beck flow into it to form Tilberthwaite Beck which becomes Yewdale Beck. The old Tilberthwaite copper mine nearby re-opened about 1850 and was last worked in the 1940s [297011].

Dry Beck Ennerdale. Rises 120156 and enters Ennerdale Water at 118148 ...in its leaflet *Ennerdale Forest* the Forestry Commission notes that "at most times of the year water can be seen at this point (where the Smithy Beck Trail crosses the beck) but most of it percolates between the rocks and is lost to sight. Nearer the edge of the lake no water can be seen and the beck looks, but does not sound, completely dry. Hence the name."

Dry Gill drops down from region of Helvellyn Screes at 328154. Normally a dry gully in its upper reaches but becomes a watercourse lower down. This enters Thirlmere at 321152.

Dry Gill rarely dry. As a stream rises at 389124 and joins Deepdale Beck at 388130.

Dry Gill rises The Band at 260059 and shortly after disappears before re-appearing to join Buscoe Sike below Whorneyside Force at 262054.

Dry Grove Gill normally belies its name. Stream rises in marshy area to E of Swindale at 512121 and joins Swindale Beck at 508123.

Dry Hall alongside the Broughton Mills to Seathwaite fell road [220918].

Dry Howe farm, Bannisdale [527021] ...'dry hill'. Presumably takes its name from the hill at its rear, Whiteside (the 'dry, open hillside').

Dry Scale Gill Longside Wood [239284].

Dry Tarn alongside the popular route (Breast Route) up Great Gable from Sty Head. Usually dry [216099] .

Drybarrows NNE Pinnacle Howe and WSW Winder Hill [498170] ...dry hills.

Drygrove Gill substantial ravine W slope The Knowe. Extreme upper gill usually dry. Stream commences 457087 and joins Lingmell Gill at 447085.

Dryhowe Bridge crosses Bannisdale Beck [531018].

Dryhowe Gill rises between Todd Fell and Dryhowe Pasture at 515023 and joins Bannisdale Beck at 527023.

Dryhowe Pasture Bannisdale. NW Dry Howe [518025].

Dryhurst off the Cleator Moor to Ennerdale Bridge road [056154].

Dub Beck rises N Fangs Brow at 106233. Flows into Loweswater and out again to ultimately become Park Beck which flows through Loweswater village before entering Crummock Water at 152206.

Dub Hill alongside Heltondale Beck [502210] ...pool by the hill.

Dub How Farm above Out Dubs Tarn [368949].

Dub Ings Bannisdale [519032] ...pool in, or alongside, the meadow.

Dub Ings Wood Bannisdale. S Blackcrag Plantation and above Dub Ings [514032].

Dubbs Beck rises Applethwaite Common at 422026 and flows down through Dubbs

Reservoir to join Borrans Reservoir at 429009 ...see **Dubbs Reservoir**.

Dubbs Reservoir/Tarn alongside Dubbs Road. Constructed originally to supply Windermere but today is simply an adjunct to the Thirlmere Aqueduct. Stocked with brown and rainbow trout. Permits for fishing available from the WADAA, 228m (748ft) [421017] ...dubb, a pool.

Dubbs Road from Moor Howe on the Ings-Troutbeck road to the Garburn Road. Dubbs Reservoir alongside [424006-421031] ...see **Dubbs Reservoir**.

Dubhow property in ruins alongside track E Goldrill Beck from Patterdale to Hartsop. Foot of Dubhow Beck and Dubhow Gill [406143] ...pool by the hill.

Dubhow Beck rises in cleft below Stony Rigg at 411149 and flows down between Dubhow Crag and Dubhow Brow to be joined by Dubhow Gill and subsequently meets Angletarn Beck at 407141.

Dubhow Brow E Dubhow Beck. WSW Angletarn Pikes [411147].

Dubhow Crag N of and overlooking Dubhow Beck [409148].

Dubhow Gill rises 410144 and joins Dubhow Beck just above Dubhow at 406144. There are disused copper mine workings just S of the gill.

Dubs, The see **The Dubs**.

Dubs Bottom Fleetwith. Below Dubs Quarry. A wet area [211131] ...'dub' - a pool. See also **Dubs Quarry** and **Moses Rigg**.

Dub's Quarry Ennerdale [185128].

Dubs Quarry Fleetwith. Worked from about 1750 until 1932. Moses Rigg of whisky smuggling fame or notoriety and who gave his name to Moses Trod is said to have lived at the quarry where he had a whisky still. The bog water hereabouts was claimed to be perfect for the manufacture of whisky [210135].

Dudderwick W of the head of Haweswater. Prior to flooding of the valley it was the highest habitation in Mardale but is now submerged under the waters of the reservoir. Today only the name shown on the fellside remains to remind us of the dwelling and its environs [467110].

Duddon Grains head of Wrynose Pass. Several streams combine here to form the River Duddon [274029] ...'grein', a fork of a river or valley.

Duddon, River see **River Duddon**.

Duddon Valley valley through which flows the River Duddon from its source to the sea ...see **River Duddon**.

Dudmancombe Gill rises Red Gill at 204173 and joins Keskadale Beck at 208186.

Dumbarton Wood alongside the road from Near Sawrey to the Hawkshead-Newby Bridge road [372943].

Dun Crag Longsleddale. Foot of Shipman Knotts [480064] ...either hill crag or grey crag.

Dungeon Ghyll rises NE Pike o'Stickle at 278078 and flows down over Dungeon Ghyll Force to join Great Langdale Beck at 291062. Centuries ago it was called Pedder Ghyll (pedlars' ghyll). There is a Pedder Stone not far distant on the E section of the Wrynose Pass ...the stream flows through a narrow valley which gives the impression of a cavern. Dorothy Wordsworth in her *Journals* notes that dungeon refers "to those fissures or caverns, which in the language of the country are called dungeons."

Dungeon Ghyll Force impressive waterfall, one of several on Dungeon Ghyll. Has an approximate 18m (60ft) drop. In Victorian times it was approached by guard rails and a proper path. Today, the path from behind the New Dungeon Ghyll Hotel needs care and attention from those walkers or scramblers who wish to view the falls [290066].

Dungeon Ghyll New Hotel dated 1862 and, like its rival higher up the dale, the inn was originally an old farmhouse [295065] ...see **Dungeon Ghyll**.

Dungeon Ghyll Old Hotel Great Langdale. Affectionately known as the ODG. The hotel, formerly a second farm at Middlefell Place and later a farm and inn (the oldest part, the public bar, was a 16th century cow byre, and the W wing was a barn) was presented to the NT by Prof. G M Trevellyn in 1929 but continued to work as a farm until 1948 when the tenancy of it passed to Sid Cross (see also **Langdale and Ambleside Mountain Rescue Team**). He created the public bar out of the cow byre. Over the ensuing years many famous climbers have stayed at the ODG and its predecessor and even an Emperor of Japan stayed there in 1915 and climbed in the area [286061] ...see **Dungeon Ghyll**.

Dunmail Raise summit of the pass of Dunmail Raise, the highest point on the A591 between Grasmere and Keswick, and formerly the boundary between Cumberland and Westmorland. Known in Wordsworth's days as the 'The Rays'. A large pile of stones at the summit, earlier called a tumulus, is said to cover the remains of Dunmail, a Cumbrian leader, killed during a battle fought hereabouts in 940AD. This is not true, however, as Dunmail actually died many years later on a pilgrimage to Rome. The heap of stones possibly commemorates Dunmail's stand and leadership or a later battle and as a consequence of this and the age of the cairn it has been scheduled as an Ancient Monument. There is a strong belief today that this battle actually took place a few miles down the road at Orrest Head. A century and a half later another battle is believed to have been fought on Dunmail Raise. In this case between the rebel leader Earl Boethar and his men and a strong force of Normans. The victory went to Boethar. See also **Butharlyp How** and **Butter Crag**.

The former counties of Cumberland and Westmorland met at the summit. Just S of the col the main road crosses Raise Beck. The latter bifurcates nearby, one arm flowing down to Thirlmere and the other flowing S to become the River Rothay. In 1971 the A591 was straightened and widened to three lanes on the S side and a dual carriageway constructed over the summit. Just below the summit on the S side of the Raise and on the right-hand side of the road travelling up from Grasmere is a stone building which, originally an isolation hospital, has been used for decades as a club walking and climbing centre. There are many drumlins to the W of the road S of the summit. The view from the summit down to Grasmere is quite spectacular and was described by Thomas Gray in his journal of 1769 as "one of the sweetest landscapes that art ever attempted to imitate." A substantial tunnel nearly 3 miles long and well below the Raise carries the water from Thirlmere on its first stage to Manchester. It is often said that the weather can differ considerably on either side of the Raise and on my many journeys over it I find that there appears to be some justification for such a statement, 238m (781ft) [327117] ...Dunmail's cairn.

Dunmallard Hill also referred to as Dunmallet. To the W of Pooley Bridge across the River Eamont. A tree clad eminence on top of which is an ancient British hill fort, the latter being scheduled as an Ancient Monument [468246] ...'hill of the slaughter'.

Dunmallet see **Dunmallard Hill**.

Dunnerdale another name for the Duddon Valley and one which has been around for at least 7 centuries. W G Collingwood notes that the name is derived from Duddenerdale while Eckwall says that "Dunnerdale does not now denote the Duddon Valley but the district E of the river." Noted author Hunter Davies in his *A Walk Around the Lakes* refers frequently to the Duddon Valley while other authors and guide book writers mention one or the other and, at times, both. The OS shows the Duddon Valley as Dunnerdale and the civil parish is Dunnerdale-with-Seathwaite. That doyen of fell walkers and Lake District writer, Alfred Wainwright, in his *Wainwright and the Valleys of Lakeland* chooses to refer to the valley as the Duddon Valley although pointing out that it is increasingly known as Dunnerdale "a name not to my liking and which I prefer not to use." He suggests that the true Dunnerdale is the valley down which Dunnerdale Beck flows en route to join the River Lickle. Obviously the reader has the choice but I, like Wainwright and others, prefer the title Duddon Valley and only refer to Dunnerdale in Dunnerdale Beck, Forest, Fells or Hall Dunnerdale.

Dunnerdale Beck rises from a spring E Park Head road and near Stainton Ground Quarries at 220935. Subsequently joined by Hare Hall Beck and Red Moss Beck before entering the River Lickle at 224908. In his *The Outlying Fells of Lakeland* (1973) Alfred Wainwright notes that geographically speaking the Dunnerdale Beck valley is the true Dunnerdale and not the Duddon Valley.

Dunnerdale Forest large afforested area W of the River Duddon [230988].

Dunney Beck rises SSE Alcock Tarn at 351076 and joins the River Rothay at 349064 ...dun (brownish-grey) coloured stream.

Dyke farm off the A595 2.4kms (1.5 miles) N Waberthwaite [115951]. On the escarpment NE of Dyke (not NNE as shown on the OS map) there is a monument which was apparently erected as a navigation guide for ships entering the port of Ravenglass.

Dyke Nook alongside the A591 [235299].

E

Eagle Crag alongside Riggindale Scar [463113].

Eagle Crag overlooks Easedale and is a continuation of Blea Crag [298083].

Eagle Crag prominent buttress looking down Grisedale. Eagle Crag Mine hereabouts was closed in 1877 [357141].

Eagle Crag impressive crag rising above the confluence of Langstrath Beck and Greenup Gill. Its N and W faces are frequented by rock climbers 521m (1709ft) [276121].

Eagle Crag above Burtness (Birkness) Comb [172145].

Eagle Crag Mine see **Eagle Crag**, Grisedale.

Eagles with the names of many Eagle and Heron Crags in the Lake District there is ample evidence that the golden eagle and the sea eagle were at one time very abundant here. However, well over a century ago they disappeared but a pair of golden eagles returned to nest in the Haweswater area in 1969. Since then there has been a succession of pairs. Today, these are the only regular pair of nesting golden eagles in England. In May 1996 the pair hatched a chick which made its maiden flight the following August. For the previous three years the eagles had been unsuccessful in raising a chick. They were also unsuccessful in 1997 and 1998. The eagles are strongly protected by law and watched over diligently by RSPB volunteers.

Earing Crag The Band [256062] ...possibly an echoing crag similar to Gouter Crag, Swindale, or Speaking Crag alongside Haweswater.

Earl Henry's Drive a carriage drive, 4kms (2.5 miles) in length, from the A6 near Eamont Bridge through Lowther Park to Lowther Castle [525276]. It was conceived and constructed by Henry Lowther, third Earl, who died shortly before its completion. Another drive, from the S, is known as Emperor's Drive to commemorate the visit of Kaiser Wilhelm II.

Earthworks

Loweswater	[139203]
Allen Knott	[415011]
Dacre Castle	[461266]
NE Measand Bridge	[490156]
Setterah Park	[514212]
Scarside Plantation	[530913]
W-WNW Shap Abbey	[542154]
SW Shap Abbey	[545147]

Easedale from Grasmere Easedale runs NW and then W for approximately 4.8kms (3 miles) to the foot of the High Raise plateau below Sergeant Man. In the Wordsworths first year at Town End and not knowing the name of the valley they called it 'The Black Quarter' because when viewed from Town End it appeared on many occasions that clouds and storms seemed to gather there and also it was in shadow late in the day. Down the valley flows Easedale Beck on its way to join the River Rothay. On its course tourists are provided with two principal attractions, the impressive Sourmilk Gill waterfall and Easedale Tarn [325083] ...Asi's valley or valley of the river referring to Easedale Beck.

Easedale Beck farthest headstream rises at the head of Easedale at 292087 and flows down Easedale between Belles Knott and Eagle Crag. Shortly afterwards it is met by another stream which flows in and out of Codale Tarn having risen between Codale Head and Tarn Crag at 294092. On through Easedale Tarn, down Sourmilk Gill and over the well-known Sourmilk Gill Force. Met by Little Brinhowe Gill, Blindtarn Gill, Far Easedale Gill where, on the 1:25000 map it is shown as Easedale Beck, and finally Coal Beck before flowing into the River Rothay at 336080.

Easedale Road road which leaves Grasmere village opposite Sam Read's bookshop and heads up Easedale [334080].

Easedale Tarn large tarn very popular with tourists being just 1.6kms (1 mile) from Easedale Road, Grasmere. Alongside a well-trodden path from Grasmere to either Sergeant Man/High Raise, Borrowdale or Langdale. One of the deepest tarns with a maximum depth of 21m (69ft). However, this seems shallow compared with the deepest tarn, Blea Water, which has a depth of 68m (223ft). The tarn forms part of the Lonsdale Commons which includes Near and Far Easedale and the Langdale Pikes and were leased to the National Trust by Lord Lonsdale in 1961. Free fishing is available at the tarn for brown trout, eels and perch, 290m (951ft) [308087].

Near the tarn's outflow a large boulder, a pile of stones and a battered iron seat are the last vestiges of a hut erected in the 19th century and in its early days a shelter and refuge for riders and their ponies. Even earlier it may have been a shepherd's hut. In the second half of the 19th century Robert Hayton of Grasmere began serving refreshments to tourists and also hired out a boat. After his death his son-in-law, William (Swanny) Wilson, carried on the enterprise and served lunches and teas and a much sought after meal of bacon and eggs. Photographs in existence show that the interior in its hey day was kept exceptionally tidy and clean. After he retired in 1914 other members of the family carried on the tradition and, in the 1920s, supplies were carried up to the hut on the back of a pony. W H Cooper in his *The Tarns of Lakeland* (1960) records that "during the 1930s an Irishman, Michael O'Brien, sold mineral waters there..." For over 50 years it catered in the summer months for the needs of travellers and walkers but by the 1940s it was a ruined building and over the years since vandalism and the weather have completely obliterated the structure known in its heyday as The Tourists Rest.

East Chockstone Gully St Sunday Crag [367137].

East View near Potter Fell Road and Garnett Bridge. Looks E over the River Sprint and the A6 [521989]. There is a West View alongside the A6 at Selside.

East/West Park lie to the NW [476271] and SW [474265] respectively of Dalemain.

Eastern Fells (between Shap and Longsleddale) see Reference Section: **Heights**.

Easthwaite S River Irt. SW Wastwater [137034] ...the east clearing.

Eastward farm, E Littlewater Tarn. W Walmgate [512170].

Easy Gully see **Pavey Ark**.

Ecclerigg Crag crag on promontory N White Cross Bay. On the promontory and in adjoining Crag Wood and alongside White Cross Bay, many flat rocks can still be found inscribed with names, political messages, phrases, etc. One large rock reads "National Debt £800,000,000. Save My Country Heaven, George & William Pitt." Some are now covered by weeds. All were, however, carved by 'John Longmire, Engraver', an Ambleside eccentric who spent years over the 1830s and 40s creating them [389005] ...surname or eller (alder).

Ecclerigg Farm off the A591 between White Cross Bay and the Brockhole Visitor Centre [392009].

Ecton Crag overlooks the confluence of Easedale Beck and Far Easedale Gill [319089].

Eddy Grave Stake between High Tove and High Seat [290170].

Eddy Scale [276957] ...Eddy's hill pasture.

Eden Beck rises between Lingy Crag and Cat Crag at 413140 and joins Angletarn Beck at 404143 near the latter's confluence with Goldrill Beck.

Eel Beck rises slightly NE of Eelbeck Bridge, Eskdale, and joins the River Esk at 173004.

Eel Crag rocky buttresss between Coledale Hause and Sail C800m (C2625ft) [190207]. See also **Crag Hill** ...see **Eel Crags** below.

Eel Crags lengthy precipitous W face of High Spy. Frequented by rock climbers [233165] ...nothing to do with eels but means the steep bad crags (bad in this case meaning difficult and no doubt many rock climbers could testify to this!)

Eel House near Eel House Bridge over Cunsey Beck [369939] ...eels trapped on Cunsey Beck were taken to the Eel House for preparation.

Eel House Bridge carries the Near Sawrey to Hawkshead-Newby Bridge road over Cunsey Beck [369941].

Eel House Intake E Hawkshead-Newby Bridge road near Eel House [359945].

Eel Tarn Eskdale. Contains small brown trout, C210m (C689ft) [189019] ...either 'evil' implying a ghostly tarn (the area is subject to wraithes of methane gas), or 'steep' tarn.

Eelbeck Bridge Boot, Eskdale. Carries the road up Eskdale over Eel Beck [177009].

Eerin Crag NNE Levers Water [283997].

Ees a promontory E shore Esthwaite Water [363956] ...an unusual name with several possible derivations. Two concern the 'Es' of Esthwaite Water and therefore refer to either East or ash tree while another refers to the shape of the two principal promontories alongside the water. These are ear-shaped and the name could suggest a corruption of 'ears'. Another suggestion is that it originates from the ON 'ey' meaning an island. Ees and Strickland Ees were, at one time, most likely surrounded by water and consequently the Ees were the islands (the Eys) today, the Ees. The most likely meaning, however, is promontory or headland with Ees being a contraction of the OE 'Nes' (nose/headland) with its elongated 'ee' sound. Collins New Naturalist Series *The Lake District* referring to drumlins (page 50) says "These form characteristic projecting promontories called 'Ees' in Esthwaite Water."

Ees Bridge carries minor road from Near Sawrey to the Hawkshead-Newby Bridge road over Cunsey Beck [366952].

Ees Hows S shore Esthwaite Water [364951].

Ees Wyke bay immediately N of Ees, Esthwaite Water [363957] ...creek/bay alongside Ees.

Ees Wyke Country House Hotel Near Sawrey. Former large Georgian house once the holiday home of Beatrix Potter and in those days known as Lakefield.

Egremont Crab Fair held since 1267. An annual country fair held on the third Saturday in September and which is in celebration of the crab apple and not the crab. In the evening of the fair the World Gurning Championship is held. See also **Gurning**.

Elba Monument see **Plumgarth Roundabout**.

Elder Beck rises Moor Divock at 482220 and joins Aik Beck at 469235. This joins Ullswater at 467238 ...alder (tree)stream.

Elder Coppice W Esthwaite Lodge [349967].

Elder Cottage alongside the minor road from Brandlingill to Low Lorton [140267] ...alder cottage.

Elderbeck off the Pooley Bridge to Howtown road and alongside Elder Beck [473236].

Elf Howe Over Staveley [468001] ...fairy hill.

Ellas Crag Rowling End [232208].

Eller Beck rises at 166241 and joins Whit Beck at 159251.

Eller Dubs pools on the infant River Duddon alongside Wrynose Pass [268024] ...alder trees by the pools.

Eller How Eskdale Moor. Former isolated dwelling here. Now very much in ruins [184033] ...alder hill.

Elleray Windermere [411989]. The original Elleray was built in 1808 by Professor John

Wilson, poet, Edinburgh professor and later 'Christopher North' of *Blackwoods Magazine*. He died in 1854 and 12 years later the house passed into the hands of Henry Heywood, a Manchester banker. Mr Heywood demolished the old mansion and built in its place a new Elleray which was completed in 1871. This is now the Windermere Preparatory School for Boys and Girls, part of St Anne's School.

Elleray Bank alongside track from Windermere to the A592 [410993].

Ellerbeck Birkby. Off the minor road from the A595 to Eskdale Green [117962].

Ellerbeck Bridge carries the track from Birkerthwaite to Low Ground over Highford Beck [177986].

Ellerbeck Farm Crook [463948] ...alder by the stream.

Ellergarth Great Langdale [316063] ...alder enclosure.

Ellerhow Moss Eskdale Moor [182034].

Ellers former farm E Little Loughrigg Tarn and alongside minor road from the A593 to the B5343 [348039] ...alders.

Ellers Great Langdale [311064]. Early this century a property called Ellars was dismantled and Ellergarth built on the site.

Ellers off the Grange-in-Borrowdale to Manesty road [248179] ...place overgrown with alder trees.

Ellers Beck see **Greenup Sikes**.

Ellers Bridge Underbarrow. Carries Grigg Hall Lane over Underbarrow Pool [466915] ...bridge by the alders.

Ellerwood alongside the A592 [398948] ...alder trees wood.

Elliptical Crag slope of Pillar near Wind Gap. Overlooks the head of Mosedale [170117].

Elmhow farm in Grisedale [372150].

Elmhow Crag adjoining Birks Crag, Birks. Overlooks Grisedale [379150].

Elmhow Plantation one of three plantations in close proximity to each other in Grisedale. Provides protection from the elements for Elmhow Farm [372150].

Elter Holme E shore Esthwaite Water [364960] ...a promontory practically an island therefore called Elter (swan) Holme.

Elter Water shallow reedy lake in Great Langdale which gives its name to the nearby village. Usually takes the form of three small waters joined together with a total length of 0.8kms (0.5 mile) and at its widest 0.4kms (0.25 mile). However, in the distant past there was obviously a much larger lake hereabouts but infilling, particularly by the deltas of Great Langdale Beck and the Brathay, has shrunk this and, at some time in the future Elter Water will, like several other former valley lakes, disappear altogether. W G Collingwood called it "a true Lake of the Lakes," but it is often not listed as a lake owing to its fluctuating size and unusual symmetry and is downgraded to a tarn and replaced in the order of things by Brothers Water. Situated at an altitude of C60m (C197ft) it is normally shallow but in time of considerable rainfall both size and depth can vary considerably. The privately owned water has trout, pike and perch [332042] ...swan lake. Swans, particularly whooper, still frequent the waters in winter.

Eltermere Elterwater. Country hotel set in 3 acres of landscaped gardens overlooking Elter Water. Erected 17th century with later additions. It was the original Elterwater Hall before the present one was built in the 19th century. A sister hotel to the Three Shires Inn, Little Langdale [328045].

Elterwater village at the head of Elter Water from which its takes its name. Contains

several 17th century houses one of which, Neaum Crag, was the birthplace of the St Martin's Langdale Linen Industry, the brainchild of Canon Rawnsley but set up by John Ruskin in 1883 to provide work for Langdale cottagers. Later the industry was centred at Tilberthwaite and spread to Keswick, Troutbeck Bridge and The Spinnery, Bowness. Thrived until after the First World War when cheap foreign products undercut prices. The village green flanked by the Britannia Inn has in its centre a maple tree planted in 1936. Many of the cottages were quarry workers' cottages built for those who worked in the large quarries thereabouts particularly Elterwater Quarry. The post office and village store faces a bowling green and nearby there is an art gallery, formerly the Gig House Gallery but since Easter 1998, renamed the Judy Boyes Studio. A holiday village/timeshare has been erected on the site of the former Elterwater Gunpowder Works. The single-arched bridge over Langdale Beck dates from 1702. To the S of the bridge there is a Youth Hostel [328048]. See also **Elter Water**.

Elterwater Common large common to the N and E of Elterwater. Part owned by the National Trust with small National Trust car park on it [332048].

Elterwater Gunpowder Works established in 1824, 60 years after the first gunpowder mill in the north of England had been built at Sedgwick. Later taken over by ICI and closed in 1931. The site of the works started as a holiday village in the 1930s and today is a substantial timeshare estate complete with a hotel and country club [326030]. A ghost of a man in old fashioned clothing has been seen on several occasions. Believed to be one of four men killed in an explosion at the works in 1916.

Elterwater Hall built in the 19th century and replaced the previous Elterwater Hall which was renamed Eltermere. Today the hall is part of the Langdale Timeshare complex [327044].

Elterwater Quarry one of the few remaining working quarries in the Lake District [324051].

Elterwater Youth Hostel Elterwater. A converted farmhouse and barn [327046].

Emblesteads Gill rises on the slope of High Seat at 282175 and joins Watendlath Beck at 272171 ...possibly a personal name + stede (place/site).

Embleton village and scattered parish in valley to the E of Cockermouth. Its church is dedicated to St. Cuthbert and is erected on a site where, it is reputed, St. Cuthbert's body was rested on its long journey from Lindisfarne. In the mid-19th century an iron sword (the Embleton Sword), believed to date from the first century AD, was discovered hereabouts. Main occupation is farming ...more than likely Eambald's farmstead but there is a suggestion that it could be derived from OE 'emel' meaning caterpillar.

Embleton High Common SW Ling Fell N Kirk Fell. Spot height at 294m (964ft) [169281].

Emerald Bank Newlands valley. Foot of Rowling End [234203].

Emperor's Drive a carriage drive through Lowther Park from the S named in commemoration of the visit of Kaiser Wilhelm II.

Enclosures

In Fell	[060061]
Corney	[110919]
Brantrake Moss, N Black	[151980]
Little Crag, Birker Moor	[184977]
Between The Pike and Hesk Fell	[185942]
Near Crosbythwaite Bridge	[186948]
Torver High Common	[267950]
Banishead	[285967]

End of Borrowdale as its name implies, the end of Borrowdale, east Lakeland [515063].

English Lakes Hotels see **Low Wood Hotel**.

Ennerdale remote valley containing Ennerdale Water and down which flows the River Liza from its source below Windy Gap, through Ennerdale Forest (planting of which began in the 1920s) to enter Ennerdale Water. All vehicles, apart from those authorised, must be left at Bowness Knott car park near the foot of the lake. From there it is a 12.8 kms (8 miles) walk to the source of the Liza and the only habitations are Low Gillerthwaite Field Centre; Ennerdale YH at 3.6 kms (2.25 miles); High Gillerthwaite Farm (of which noted local author and writer Bob Orrell was a tenant from 1977-1996). Today it is a camping barn; Black Sail YH is 9.6 kms (6 miles) up the valley. Ennerdale is the only lake valley which has no proper road running along its length of lake. The Side, on the S slope of the valley, was part of a large deer park under the auspices of the Monks of Furness Abbey and originally established in 1338. There are high mountains to its N, E and S with the best known being the climbers' mecca Pillar Rock on Pillar approached by a footbridge across the River Liza erected by the county council with costs shared by the Fell and Rock Climbing Club and which stands as a memorial to those members of the club who lost their lives in the Second World War. The present structure replaced an earlier one and was opened in 1960. The other major and very well-known mountain is Great Gable above the head of the valley. Principal passes from the dale are Floutern, Scarth Gap and Black Sail to Crummock Water, Buttermere and Wasdale respectively.

At the foot of the lake stood the Boat House Inn. This burned down in 1911. Rebuilt and modernised and renamed the Anglers Inn, later Anglers Hotel, it was demolished in the late

1970s when there was a threat to raise the water level of the lake. The scheme was subsequently rejected after a public inquiry in 1980. The site of the former hostelry is now part of the present-day car park below How Hall Farm. In 1884 a plan to run a railway line up the valley was also defeated. There are three major low level walks in the valley - the Smithy Beck Forest Trail 5.4 kms (3.4 miles), the Liza Path which, combined with a return along the Nine Becks Walk, is 14 kms (8.8 miles) and the Nine Becks Walk 15.5 kms (9.7 miles). A leaflet on these walks with other information and titled *Ennerdale Forest* has been issued by the Forestry Commission.

Australia has its wild dog, the dingo, and in 1810 Ennerdale had its own wild dog, a large and savage beast, which nightly for months ravaged sheep in the area and evaded capture by its speed and guile. Eventually, after being shot in the leg and a 16 kms (10 mile) flight, it was finally shot and killed in the River Ehen. Upon subsequently being weighed it tipped the scales at 8 Imperial stones or 112lbs and for a time afterwards the 'Wild Dog of Ennerdale' was displayed in Keswick [110153] ...Anund's valley or the valley of the River Ehen, the latter flowing out of Ennerdale Water.

Ennerdale Bridge small picturesque village built around a bridge which spans the River Ehen. The former 16th century church of St. Mary, with its 'homely' priest and its churchyard, provided the setting for Wordsworth's lengthy poem *The Brothers*. However, the church that Wordsworth knew was replaced in the mid 19th century. Ennerdale Bridge provides a starting point for walkers and climbers up Ennerdale and to the peaks alongside and at its head. It is also on the popular Coast to Coast Walk [070159] ...bridge over the Ehen or possibly the bridge by Anund's valley.

Ennerdale Fell fell area to the S of Ennerdale rising to its highest point, Iron Crag, at 640m (2100ft) [125128].

Ennerdale Fell Plantations afforested area, Ennerdale [165132].

Ennerdale Forest large afforested area on both sides of the Ennerdale valley [155137].

Ennerdale Water Ennerdale. 4 kms (2.5 miles) in length with a maximum breadth of 1.4 kms (0.87 of a mile) at its foot where it widens considerably. Consequent on this broadening the lake was earlier called Broadwater. It has a depth of 42m (138ft) and a height above sea level of 112m (367ft). Provides a water supply for West Cumbria. No boats are allowed on the lake and fishing is by permit. Ennerdale Water contains brown trout and it is one of the few Lakeland waters which contains char [107150]. See also **Ennerdale**.

Ennerdale (Gillerthwaite) YH 3.6 kms (2.25 miles) from Bowness Knott car park. Converted from two forest cottages [142141].

Epley Point promontory the northern projection of High Wray Bay, Windermere [377006].

Erne Crag E Heron Pike, Great Rigg ridge and overlooking Rydal Beck [360087]. Summit at the rear is 621m (2037ft) ...eagle crag. The heron of nearby Heron Pike will also refer to the eagle and not the heron.

Erne Nest Crag some maps show it as Earnest Crag as does Wainwright in his *The Eastern Fells*. Overlooks Deepdale and faces Greenhow End across the entrance to Link Cove [375120] ...eagles' nest crag.

Esk, River see **River Esk**.

Esk Buttress see **Dow Crag**.

Esk Falls one of several spectacular waterfalls on the upper Esk. In this case that which drops down in a narrow channel near the confluence of the Esk and Lingcove Beck [226037].

Esk Hause depression between Esk Pike and Great End. It is not the highest pass in the Lake District. Others situated higher include Mickledore between Scafell and Scafell Pike and Ore Gap but it is considered to be the highest pass in regular use. Well-trodden paths from the Scafell range, Bowfell/Esk Pike, Eskdale, Glaramara/Allen Crags meet here. A nearby but lower meeting of tracks at the highest point on the Sty Head to Rossett Gill route is often incorrectly considered by many to be Esk Hause. The Hause is 759m (2490ft) above sea level at 233080 ...'pass at the head of the Esk'. The latter has its source slightly S of the Hause.

Esk Pike rocky mountain between Ore Gap and Esk Hause. Although ranked as 14th in the hierarchy of Lakeland mountains it was not named as such until 1870 and not named on OS maps until the 1960s. Centuries ago it is said to have been called Tongue Fell because of its position overlooking Tongue Head between Angletarn Gill and Allencrags Gill 885m (2903ft) [237075] ...given its present title because it overlooks the upper Esk.

Esk View Farm Boot, Eskdale [176005].

Eskdale Fell crags and fell area to the E of Burnmoor Tarn. Highest point is Great How with its trig. point at 522m (1713ft) [192038]. In the region of Great How/Raven Crag are several unnamed small tarns with more sited further E on Quagrigg Moss.

Eskdale Green village principally between the Rivers Mite and Esk. To its N a road from Ravenglass meets that from Santon Bridge and this area is served by the Irton Road Station on the Ravenglass to Eskdale Railway. To its S the road from the Hardknott Pass meets that from Ulpha over Birker Moor and nearby is The Green Station, the penultimate on the line before Dalegarth, Boot. One of the two Lakeland Outward Bound Schools is sited at Eskdale Green. The church is dedicated to St. Bega and the village possesses two hostelries, the Bower House Inn, originally known as the Hound Inn, and the King George IV, earlier the King of Prussia but renamed at the start of the First World War. This pub was also, at one time, called the Tatiegarth Inn (potato enclosure/place where potatoes are collected) [143999].

Eskdale Green Station see **The Green Station**.

Eskdale Green Tarn private tarn in the grounds of the Eskdale Outward Bound School [145001].

Eskdale Mill Boot, Eskdale. Approached by an old packhorse bridge over Whillan Beck. The 'Bank' Corn Mill is reputed to have been in existence since the 13th century but documentary evidence only dates from 1578. Corn milling ceased in the 1920s but the mill wheel continued to provide electricity until 1955. The old mill was then locked and left derelict. In 1972 Cumberland County Council bought the mill, renovated much of it, and established a museum/exhibition of milling which shows and explains the mill's working of the old machinery. The mill is open to the public in the season [176012].

Eskdale Moor S Burnmoor Tarn [184036].

Eskdale Needle NW Hard Knott. Frequently referred to as The Steeple but not to be confused with its taller namesake W of Pillar, Ennerdale. It is an isolated rock which, on the side facing Eskdale is approximately 15m (50ft) high [228024].

Eskdale Outward Bound School formerly part of the Gate House Estate. The mansion was the former home of Lord Rea. Opened in 1950 it was the country's first Outward Bound mountain school as opposed to the first Outward Bound Centre, the sea school at Aberdovey in North Wales, which was opened in 1941. One of its early wardens was Eric Shipton famous mountaineer of Himalayan fame. The other Outward Bound School in the Lake District is at Hallsteads, Ullswater [143002].

Eskdale YH purpose built hostel sited 0.4 kms (1/4 mile) up Eskdale from the Woolpack Inn [195011].

Eskholme Marsh Muncaster. Alongside the River Esk [109966].

Eskin alongside the minor road from Wythop Mill to Wythop Hall [185291] ...ash tree.

Eskmeals large sandy area between Bootle and the Esk estuary. Listed as a Danger Area as it comprises a Ministry of Defence proving gunnery range [081935].

Eskmeals House off the road from the A595 (Holmrook) to the Eskmeals coast road [091935].

Eskmeals Viaduct carries the railway line over the lower Esk [088944].

Esp Ford off Mill Lane, Crosthwaite [444907] ...'aspen tree' ford, the latter being that across the River Gilpin.

Esps Farm Embleton [146293] ...farm by the aspen trees.

Esthwaite Coppice across the Hawkshead-Newby Bridge road from Esthwaite Hall [355960].

Esthwaite Hall W Esthwaite Water and alongside the Hawkshead-Newby Bridge road. The original hall was built by the de Sandes family about 1400 and held by them for centuries. Part of this hall still stands adjoining the present 18th century farmhouse. There have been many notable members of the Sandes/Sandys family but one of the best known and possibly the most famous was Edwin, born at the hall in the early 16th century. He subsequently became Archbishop of York [358959].

Esthwaite Hall Beck rises Grizedale Forest Park at 346955 and flows down under Esthwaite Hall Bridge and alongside Esthwaite Hall to join Esthwaite Water at 360959.

Esthwaite Hall Bridge carries the Hawkshead to Newby Bridge road over Esthwaite Hall Beck [357957].

Esthwaite How Farm near Sawrey [368956].

Esthwaite Intake SW Esthwaite Hall [363953].

Esthwaite Lodge Regency mansion overlooking Esthwaite Water from its W. Once the home of novelist Francis Brett Young. Today a Youth Hostel [354967].

Esthwaite Water 0.8kms (0.5 mile) SE Hawkshead. A pretty lake, 2.4kms (1.5 miles) in length and 0.6kms (0.37 mile) at its widest point. Beatrix Potter thought it "the most beautiful of the Lakes" and it was a favourite of Wordsworth during his schooldays at Hawkshead. Possesses one island and four major promontories three of which resemble ears (see **Ees**). Depending on the particular work consulted its depth varies between 14m (46ft) and 24m (79ft) but the erudite *Depth Charts of the Cumbrian Lakes* published by the Freshwater Biological Association provides a figure of 15.5m (51ft) and a height above sea level of 65.4m (214.5ft) [360970]. Mainly fished for trout but there is also a considerable pike population. See also **Hawkshead Trout Farm** and **Fishing** ...water beside the clearing in the ash-trees or water by the eastern clearing.

Ether Knott Grange Fell possesess three main summits, Brund Fell, the highest, Ether Knott to its E and King's How overlooking Borrowdale [268172].

Eusemere large house and estate, Pooley Bridge. Former home of Thomas Clarkson (1760-1846), a life-long campaigner for the abolition of slavery and to whom William Wordsworth wrote a sonnet on the final passing of the Bill for the Abolition of the Slave Trade in 1807. Wordsworth first visited Eusemere with Coleridge in 1799 and until the Clarksons left in 1804 William, Dorothy, and Mary, were frequent visitors to the house. Even afterwards they were guests of the new tenants and later of William's cousin John and his wife until John's death there in 1819 [470241] ...most likely the marsh at the lake outlet.

Evening Bank Wood alongside the A592. Between Dalemain and Stainton [483273] ...a delightful sounding name but its origin is obscure. 'Evening' may be a corruption of a personal name.

Ewe Close E of the head of Swindale and The Knott [509119].

Ewe Crag Beda Fell. Overlooks Thrang Crag and Howe Grain [433173].

Ewe Crag see **Loughrigg Fell**.

Ewe Crag Birkby [122965].

Ewe Crags N Crabtree Brow, Kentmere [447047].

Ewe How W Latrigg. The Cumbria Way from Keswick passes alongside [271248].

Eycott Farm E Eycott Hill. W of A66-Haltcliff Bridge-Hesket Newmarket road [399297].

Eycott Hill E from Souther Fell across Glenderamackin valley and Naddles Beck 345m (1132ft) [387295].

F

Fair How Dockray [388215].

Fairbank Farm Nether Staveley [454980]. Not to be confused with High Fairbank Farm 1.2kms (0.75 mile) to its W.

Fairfield at one time known as Rydal Head but the latter is now the area below it at the head of the Rydal Beck valley. Highest mountain of the Fairfield range. Separated from Dollywaggon Pike on the Helvellyn range by Grisedale Pass and Tarn 873m (2864) [359118] ...its extensive flat-topped summit suggests a 'fair' or 'pleasant fell' but could also be derived from the ON 'faer' meaning sheep.

Fairfield between Great Carrs and Grey Friar. Not as high as its namesake in the Eastern Fells 695m (2280ft) [266007]

Fairfield Lorton Vale. Off the B5292 [154268].

Fairfield Brow WSW/SW slope below Fairfield [356115]

Fairfield Horseshoe there are several Fairfield Horseshoes or Rounds but the most popular starts from Ambleside via Low or High Sweden Bridge, over Low Pike, High Pike, Dove Crag, Hart Crag, Fairfield, Great Rigg, Heron Pike, Nab Scar, down to Rydal, through Rydal Park and back to Ambleside (or vice versa). Others commence either at Patterdale, Cow Bridge, Bridgend or Ambleside, the latter returning via the Red Screes ridge. There is also an excellent Horseshoe from the Kirkstone Pass Inn via Red Screes but this usually requires transport back from Patterdale to avoid the long slog back up Kirkstone Pass.

Fairfield Range see Reference Section: **Heights**.

Fairholme Green alongside the A5084. N Lake Bank [286902].

Fairies the last fairies in Westmorland are reputed to have been seen by a man walking home over Sandwick Rigg, Martindale. See also **Boggles**, **Dobbies**.

Fairy Ark between the River Lickle and minor road from Broughton Mills [237923].

Fairy Crag W of and overlooking Swindale Beck [535160].

Falcon Crag ESE Dollywaggon Pike. Adjoining Tarn Crag [352128].

Falcon Crag precipitous craggy face overlooking Derwent Water and situated across Cat Gill from Walla Crag. Frequented by rock climbers [272206].

Fall Crag N Lingy Crag. Separated from the latter by Angletarn Beck and its ravine [409143].

Fall Crag E Crummock Water and the B5289 [163196].

Fallen Yew farm, Underbarrow [468922].

Fangs Brow brow on the Loweswater to Mockerkin road [107229].

Fangs Brow Farm top of Fangs Brow and just inside the NP boundary [106228].

Far Bank off the A595 (Waberthwaite) [107926].

Far Broadgill rises E slope Narrow Moor at 235176 and, according to the OS map, ends at 230176 which suggests that it disappears underground before reappearing at Newlands Beck.

Far Easedale valley down which Far Easedale Gill flows from its source to its meeting with Easedale Beck. Separated from the Greenburn valley by the long ridge, Helm Crag to Calf Crag. Leased to the National Trust in 1961 as part of the Lonsdale Commons [316097].

Far Easedale Gill two principal streams rise at 295100 and 296102 respectively and combine at 298100 to become Far Easedale Gill. This flows down Far Easedale to join Easedale Beck at 321086 and the combined watercourse joins the River Rothay at 336080.

Far End community N end of Coniston and off the A593 [303982].

Far Gill rises N Goat's Hawse at 265984 and joins Tarn Head Beck at 263992.

Far Grain rises slope of Sale How at 274288 and joins the River Caldew at 276296 ...the far river/valley fork.

Far Hill between Little Worm Crag and White How [200972].

Far Hill Crag E Seathwaite Tarn [259989].

Far Howe E A66-Mungrisdale road. Approached from A66 [378287].

Far Kiln Bank Duddon valley (212940).

Far Kiln Bank Park between High Kiln Bank and Low Kiln Bank Parks [209936].

Far Moorend Ennerdale Bridge. Low Moorend nearby [078154].

Far Orrest farm NE Near Orrest and S Allen Knott [413008] ...see **Orrest Head**.

Far Ruddy Beck flows down Ling Comb and joins Crummock Water at 164170 ...Both Far Ruddy and Near Ruddy Becks are so called from the red colour of their stones. See also **Red Pike**.

Far Sawrey village approximately 0.8kms (0.5mile) E of Near Sawrey at the junction of the B5285 and the minor road to High Cunsey. The 18th century Sawrey Hotel has two bars, one with the unusual name, Claife Crier Bar (see **Crier of Claife**). St Peter's Church was built in 1869. Track and footpath lead on to and over Claife Heights.

Far Southerfell alongside the old road, Scales-Mungrisedale [361282].

Far Swan Beck flows through Glencoyne Park from 382200 and enters Ullswater at 392193.

Far Swine Crag alongside Groove Beck. WNW High Pike and N Near Swine Crag [368090].

Far Tongue Gill rises below Hindscarth Crags at 217159 and joins Newlands Beck at 227164.

Farm Uzzicar/Uzzicar Farm just off the Braithwaite to Buttermere road and at the foot of Barrow [234218] ...Uzzicar - the house/farmstead in the cultivated land/field - from the OE 'hus' and OE 'aecer'. Incidentally, 'aecer' has now become acre and a specific area of land 4046.81 sq. metres (4840 sq. yards). In the 12th century Uzzicar was Huseker/Husaker. A shallow lake hereabouts was drained about this time and the area became the Neulandes (1318), the newly acquired cultivated land which today is Newlands and the Newlands valley.

Farmery W Ponsonby Fell, alongside Birrel Sike [075071] ...Nothing to do with farming. More than likely from the OF and referring to an infirmary for sick monks. Calder

Abbey is nearby.

Farra Grain farthest headstream rises W Carron Crag at 324944. Joined by Farra Grain Gill at 328926 and joins Grizedale Beck at 337923 ...'four branches'.

Farra Grain Gill rises Grizedale Forest Park at 316928 and joins Farra Grain at 328926. Crossed by two packhorse bridges which carried the old route before the present forest road was built.

Farra Grain Heights above Farra Grain Gill, Grizedale Forest Park [322931].

Farthwaite property W River Calder [062104] ...far clearing.

Fawe Park property W shore Derwent Water. Fawe Park alongside [254227].

Fawe Park parkland W shore Derwent Water [251226].

Fawcett Forest wild area which in days long gone by principally covered the district between Longsleddale and Tebay and included Bannisdale and Borrowdale. Anciently 'Fauside'. Shown on the OS map at 530033. Little of the afforested area now remains. Similar to Wet Sleddale which was owned by Shap Abbey and Grange-in-Borrowdale which was owned at one time by Furness Abbey in that it was once owned by an abbey, that of Byland, Yorkshire, to whom it was given in the 12th century by William de Lancastre. Part of the area, lying between Bannisdale and Borrowdale is simply called 'The Forest' and is spot-heighted at 528m (1732ft) at 528036 ...'variegated hillside'.

Fawn Crag slope of Base Brown overlooking Seathwaite [231117].

Fell Edge off the Underbarrow-Crosthwaite road [451914] ...the edge of Crosthwaite Fell.

Fell End end of a fell which drops down from Tarn Hows Intake to the B5285 [320987].

Fell End Eskdale [149007].

Fell End near Ennerdale Bridge [068149].

Fell Foot farm at the head of Little Langdale. Its history has been traced back to the early 17th century but a property probably occupied the site previously. Once an inn serving travellers going to and coming from Wrynose and Hardknott Passes. Purchased by the National Trust in 1958 from the le Fleming family who had owned it for 250 years. At the rear is a terrace classed as a 'thing' mount, a Viking moot, where the Norsemen met either as a parliament or to administer justice. Nearby, a road branches off the main pass route and heads for Great Langdale [299032].

Fell Foot Bridge crosses the River Brathay near Fell Foot, Little Langdale [300032].

Fell Foot Park a popular recreational and picnic area 1.6kms (1 mile) N of Newby Bridge on the A592 and between the road and the lake. The house in the grounds was demolished early last century but the country estate was acquired by the NT in 1948. There is considerable parking, picnic areas, bathing, fishing from the beach alongside the shore, a café, information centre and gift shop. Boat launching facilities are available and there is a touring caravan site and 19 self-catering holiday chalets. During the season a ferry operates between the park jetty and Lakeside [382870].

Fell Gate farm off Crook Road opposite Bonning Gate [480946].

Fell Lane track from A595 at the start of the traverse of Muncaster Fell [104973].

Fell Lane Initial section of ancient track from Waberthwaite over Waberthwaite Fell to Ulpha [120938].

Fell Plain Crook. Alongside the B5284, Crook-Borwick Fold road. Dales Way passes by [453964].

Fell Racing also known as Guides Racing. Popular at Lakeland sports meetings where the contestants race up a steep slope through bracken and over rocks to a flag on the summit of a fell and return at breakneck speed.

Fell Running running great distances over Lakeland fells against the clock. See also **Bob Graham Round: Bowderdale**.

Fell Side off the A5074 [446900].

Fell Walking Lakeland possesses both high and low level walks to suit all tastes and all degrees of fitness. Guide books proliferate and leaflets covering walks are obtainable from the Lake District Visitor Centre at Brockhole, LDNP Information Centres and Tourist Information Offices. Alfred Wainwright details routes up 214 fells, the lowest being Castle Crag in Borrowdale, in his 7-volume *A Pictorial Guide to the Lakeland Fells* with another 111summits in his *Outlying Fells of Lakeland* while Bill Birkett in his *Complete Lakeland Fells* provides 129 circular walks encompassing 541 fell tops over 305m (1000ft). The Fell and Rock Climbing Club in its *The Lakeland Fells*, a complete illustrated guide for walkers (not rock climbers) describes every fell over 300m (984ft) within the Lake District National Park. Many more works cover all aspects of walking in the Lake District from particular areas, walks for motorists, naturalists, family walks, walks with children and even pub to pub walks. Before venturing on the fells for the first time read *Enjoying the Fells in Safety* obtainable from the LDNP Offices or the section 'Safety on the Fells' incorporated in the section on **Mountain Rescues and Turnouts** at the rear of this work. Always remember that, although the valleys may be sunny and warm, conditions on the fells, and particularly on the high fells can be totally different. Be prepared and take care at all times.

Fellbarrow although Fellbarrow gives its name to the group of fells which comprise the most northerly of the western fells Fellbarrow itself, surmounted by a trig. point and lying at the centre of the group, is not the highest. This honour goes to the obviously inappropriately named Low Fell which is some 7m (23ft) higher. Fellbarrow is 416m (1365ft) [132242].

Fellbarrow group of fells see **Reference Section: Heights**.

Fellborough W shore Windermere near Sandy Nab [383944].

Felldyke community alongside the Croasdale to Lamplugh road [085198].

Fellend near Ennerdale Bridge [068149].

Fellfield property off the Knipe Fold-B5286 road [347996].

Fellfoot farm alongside Broadfoot Lane, Staveley [464998].

Fence Wood head of Wasdale, alongside Wasdale Head Hall Farm [182066].

Fellside Manesty [249190].

Fellside Farm Mosser [123250].

Fenton Keswick [277233] ...homestead/village on the marshy land.

Ferney Green area and property, the latter erected in the first half of the 19th century, S Bowness and alongside the A5074 [405962].

Ferngill Crag S of the head of Far Easedale, SE Broadstones Head [298097].

Fernwood High Lorton. Off the B5292 [159262].

Ferry House, The W shore Windermere. The building began its life as the Ferry Hotel in 1879 having replaced an earlier Ferry Inn. During the Second World War a girls' private boarding school from the south coast was moved into the premises. At the end of the war it became an hotel again but only for a short period. The building was sold to the Freshwater Biological Association who moved into it from Wray Castle in 1951 [390957].

Ferry View angled between the A 5074 and the B5284 and near the Windermere ferry [405956].

Fewling Stones Swindale Common, SSW Beastman's Crag [513118] ...rocks where wildfowling took place.

Fickle Crag W River Duddon and above the track to Grassguards [228977].

Fickle Steps stepping stones below Fickle Crag which continue the Walna Scar Road and the path from the Coniston ridge via Seathwaite Tarn over the River Duddon to Eskdale via Grassguards. Not recommended as a means of crossing the river when the latter is high. There is a footbridge nearby [228976].

Field Close off the Staveley to Crook road and alongside the Dales Way [467976].

Field End E Scothall Plantation, S Kemplerigg [088020].

Field Gate Bampton Grange. Alongside the road from the former to Shap [529181] ...'Bampton Field' gate or opening.

Field Head N A66 [378277].

Field Head Eskdale. Alongside the Eskdale to Ulpha road [153990].

Field Head House Near Sawrey to the Hawkshead-Newby Bridge road [368919].

Field Head House Outgate. Originally two cottages believed to be of 17th century origin. Became one property late 19th century and two again in 1951. Returned to one country house in the 1970s [349000].

Field House Borrowdale. Off the B5289 [259180].

Field Systems (areas showing signs of early land cultivation)

Stockdale Moor	[098078]
Stockdale Moor	[098087]
Birker Moor	[163987]
E Birker Moor Road	[190957]

Field Tenement Crook [449955] ...surname Feild's or Field's holding.

Fieldside outskirts of Keswick. High Fieldside nearby [284236].

Films & Filming in the Lake District over the years the Lake District and adjoining areas have provided the settings for many films and TV series and the following are some of them. Burneside Hall, Burneside, was the setting in 1923 of the movie *Owd Bob* starring Ralph Forbes while in 1946 the Langdale Chase Hotel was the setting for Alfred Hitchcock's *The Paradine Case* starring Gregory Peck and Ann Todd. In the same year but just over the Cumbrian border in Lancashire Carnforth Station was used for the film *Brief Encounter* starring Celia Johnson and Trevor Howard. Grizedale was part of the setting for the 1958 film *The One That Got Away* the story of POW escapee, Franz von Werra (1914-41). Hardy Kruger played the part of von Werra. In May/June 1973, *Swallows and Amazons* was filmed at Bank Ground Farm and around Coniston, Coniston Water and Derwentwater. The film was released in 1974. The cast included Virginia McKenna, Ronald Fraser, Brenda Bruce, Suzanna Hamilton, Sophie Neville, Simon West and John Franklyn-Roberts. *Tommy*, 1974, with its stars Roger Daltry and Elton John, was filmed in Borrowdale. Eskdale Outward Bound School provided the setting in 1984 for *She'll Be Wearing Silk Pyjamas* starring Julie Walters. *Withnail and I* starring Richard Grant, Paul McGann and Richard Griffiths was filmed at Sleddale Hall near Penrith (released 1986), and Peter Capaldi's 1992 film *Soft Top Hard Shoulder* was partly shot at Sandside.

An episode of *Hercules Poirot* starring David Suchet was filmed at Windermere in 1994. Since then there have been *Jane Eyre* at Dalemain; *The Tenant of Wildfell Hall* at Appleby; *Bloomin' Marvellous* at Newby Bridge; *Hetty Wainthrop Investigates* at Kendal. The ITV comedy *Neville's Island* was shot at Windermere and Derwentwater in October 1997, and shown in June 1998 and *The Lakes*, on and around Ullswater, was shown on BBC1 in Sept/Oct 1997. Another series was shown Jan-March 1999. A film *The Darkest Light* was filmed at Sedbergh in 1998. A science fiction film *Alien Blood* was shot in the Rusland valley and Skelwith Force in October 1998, and in March 1999, Levens Hall and its topiary gardens provided the setting for a four-part BBC TV serial *Wives and Daughters* starring Michael Gambon and Penelope Wilton. In April 2000, the short film *Mavis & the Mermaid*, filmed around Barrow and Furness, had its premiere. The film starred Eric Sykes and Sylvia Syms. *Pandemonium* starring John Hannah as William Wordsworth and Linus Roach as Samuel Taylor Coleridge, filmed in Bristol, the Lake District and London, was premiered in November 2000. A three-part romantic comedy *Ted and Alice* set in the Lake District and starring Dawn French as a tourist officer and Stephen Tomkinson as an alien was shown on BBC TV during April 2002. For three days in April 2002, Levens Hall was the scene of mainly exterior shots for an adaptation of *The Hound of the Baskervilles* shown later on BBC1. This starred Richard E Grant (Stapleton), Richard Roxburgh (Sherlock Holmes), Ian Hart (Watson) and Matt Day (Sir Henry Baskerville). Filming began at Ambleside in November 2002, with later shots at Derwent Water and Windermere Station, for a comedy-drama *Cheeky*. Cast members included Trudie Styler, Johnny Vegas, Ian Hart, Lesley Sharp and Sean Wood. The film was due to be released in 2003. On 10 December 2002, the BBC film *Tomorrow La Scala* was shown on BBC2. The cast included Jessica Stevenson and Shaun Dingwall and was shot at Haverigg Prison (renamed for the programme HMP Seaworth) with inmates as extras. Also, in December *If Only* starring Jennifer Love and Paul Nicholls was shot in the Lake District. *Killing Mr Softly* with Heather Graham was also Lakeland based. It was announced in the first half of 2003 that Cate Blanchett was to play Beatrix Potter in a forthcoming film *Miss Potter*.

Finsthwaite although lying inside the LDNP Finsthwaite is not covered by the appropriate map. However, I have included it as I consider it particularly worthy of inclusion. The

charming village lies 1.6 kms (1 mile) N of Newby Bidge on the back road to Hawkshead. Its sturdy church dates from the 17th century and was last restored in 1896. In the church yard there is a cross, erected in 1913, to mark the grave of the Finsthwaite Princess, Clementina Johannes Sobasky Douglas, who was buried there in 1771. There are several romantic stories surrounding her one of which is that she is reputed to be an illegitimate daughter of Bonnie Prince Charles (the Young Pretender). To the E of the village of Summer House Knott is Finsthwaite Tower built in 1799 as a memorial to the men of the Royal Navy. To the W are the Low and High Dams, the latter much the larger and in a beautiful setting. It was enlarged from Finsthwaite Tarn in 1835 to provide power for Stott Park Bobbin Mill (see under **Thurs Gill Mill**) [368878] ...Finn's/Finnr's clearing.

Fir Island northernmost of Coniston Water's two islands. The other is Peel Island. Formerly known as Knott Island after an earlier owner. Owned by the National Trust [306942].

First, Second & Third Moss Lanes three lanes radiating westwards over Underbarrow Pool to low lying pastures on the other side [468906], [470904], [473903].

Fish & Fishing possibility of pike, perch, char, eels, brown trout, rainbow trout, sea trout, schelly, vendace and even salmon, in various combinations in the lakes, tarns, rivers and becks in the area. Of the lakes, Brotherswater possesses trout, perch, and possibly schelly; Haweswater has trout, perch, char, and schelly; Thirlmere contains perch, trout, char and pike; Ullswater has trout, perch, pike, schelly, some salmon which enter from the Eamont, and possibly char. Some fishing is free ie Brothers Water, Ullswater, Windermere and tarns like Blea Water, Grisedale, Harrop, Red and Small Water. Coniston has some free fishing while Thirlmere is free to holders of United Utilities rod licences. Other waters may be fished by permit, while the rights to some waters are held by private fishing clubs or associations ie Esthwaite Water requires permit from Hawkshead Trout Farm to fish on its western shore and by boat; Hayeswater's trout and perch are fished by members of the Penrith Angling Association and Grasmere and Rydal (pike, perch and eels) require permission of WADAA. In some cases fishing may be prohibited altogether ie Elter Water and Little Langdale Tarn.

This is only a synopsis of what fishing is or is not available and from whom permits need to be obtained. For more information on where to fish and what type of fish to expect initially consult the appropraite lake or tarn in the gazetteer section and the information sheet covering facilities available to fishermen issued by the Lake District National Park information service and the National Trust leaflet *Boating and Fishing on National Trust Waters in the Lake District*. There is also a booklet issued by the Rivers Authority titled *Fishing in the North West* and an excellent compact book published by the *Westmorland Gazette* called the *Anglers Guide to the Lake District* which details over 100 lakes, tarns, rivers and other waters and notes what species of fish are present, if fishing is free, a NRL is needed or permits are required and, if so, from where. Information on fishing can also be obtained from the National Park Visitor Centre at Brockhole, individual National Park information offices and Tourist Information Offices. Don Blair in his *Exploring Lakeland Tarns* (1993) has a useful 7-page section on angling in Lakeland and further information is available in *The Fisherman's Guide to South Lakeland* compiled and edited by Chris Sodo and *Fishing in Lakeland* a guide to the waters controlled by the WADAA. Another source of reference is the 240-page *Lake District Anglers' Guide* by Laurence Tetley (1999).

Fish Ladder outflow of Crummock Water [151208].

Fisher Crag imposing crag W Thirlmere under Armboth Fell and facing Deergarth How

Island. The 'Ghimmer Crag' of Wordsworth's *The Waggoner* [306163].

Fisher Gate on the Eskdale to Ulpha fell road [157991].

Fisher Gill rises Armboth Fells at 293159 and enters Thirlmere at Armboth [307171]. A path to Watendlath via High Tove follows the line of the gill in its early stages before traversing the boggy Armboth Fells. There is a Fisherplace Gill on the opposite side of Thirlmere.

Fisher High Blawith Fells. N Beacon Tarn [273910].

Fisher Place habitations to E of A591 at Dale Head (see also **Dale Head**). Interesting waterfalls on Fisherplace Gill above it and the Bartholomews 1 inch map shows properties on the N side of the gill as being called 'Brotto'. Sir Hall Caine wrote about the area in his novel *Shadow of a Crime* [318184] ...presumably named after a family called Fisher. Not far distant there is a Fisher Crag and E of the B5322 which runs through St John's in the Vale we have a Fisher's Wife's Rake.

Fisher Quarry N Honister Hause. Worked from 1839 and re-activated in 1901 [224144].

Fisher, Vivian see **Low Strutta**.

Fisher's Wife's Rake steep grassy rake starting below Walthwaite Crags and leading to Sandbed Gill. WSW Clough Head and a scramblers route to that summit [323211]. An intriguing aspect is that Fisher's Wife's Rake leads up to a Jim's Fold (sheepfold). What was the connection between Fisher's Wife and Jim? Who was she? Who was he?

Fisher Wood Wythop Mill [182294].

Fishercrag Plantation W Thirlmere between Fisher Gill and Fisher Crag [304166].

Fisherground Farm Eskdale. Alongside Fisher Ground, a halt on the Ravenglass to Eskdale Railway [152002].

Fisherplace Gill becomes this after the confluence of Sticks Gill and Brund Gill at 328180. These rise near summit of Sticks Pass and slope of Raise respectively. Interesting waterfalls above Fisher Place. Originally flowed into How Beck but on construction of water race/leat in the 19th century it was diverted by gravity to Thirlmere to enter at a point WSW of Station Coppice car park. Incidentally, there is a Fisher Gill on the other side of Thirlmere.

Fisherty How small hill W of and overlooking Windermere [374018] ...'hill near where fish are caught'.

Fishgarths Wood N A593 behind Nanny Brow [362037] ...surname Fish/Fisher + 'enclosed' wood.

Fitts Turnhole Borrowdale. W B5289 [257183].

Fitz Bridge bridge which carries the Felldyke to Lamplugh road over Wisenholme Beck [084206] ...bridge by the (water) meadow.

Fitz Museum see **Keswick**.

Fitz Park Keswick. Alongside the N bank of the River Greta. Spacious play area for children, bowls, putting, tennis and a cricket ground [268238] ...park on or by the water meadow.

Flag Pots small ponds between Lonscale Fell and Jenkin Hill [280273].

Flakenhowe Crags W Haweswater. Between it and Band End [471123].

Flask Brow above Torver Bottom (270959) ...brow of the hill above the marsh. Torver Bottom below with many streams flowing through it is very marshy.

Flaska a large tufted grass area W Trout Beck and E Mosedale Beck [370250] ...the flat wood from flasshe meaning a pool/swampy/marshy area.

Flass swampy/marshy area alongside Flass Tarn [127034] ...from 'flasshe' meaning a pool/swampy/marshy area.

Flass Knotts Lingmell NE ridge [211087] ...swampy area by the rocky hills.

Flass Tarn small tarn frequently dry near the foot of the track which commences at Nether Wasdale and traverses Irton Fell, Miterdale Forest and Across Miterdale to Eskdale 60m (197ft) [130035] ...see **Flass**.

Flass Wood Loweswater. Alongside Green Wood [143203].

Flat Bield shelter W Hole Rake [291991].

Flat Crags E face Bowfell. The great slab of Flat Crags is, as its name suggests, a huge flattish slab of rock well-inclined and used by rock climbers and experienced scramblers [249065].

Flat Fell W Nannycatch Beck 272m (892ft) [052137].

Flatfell Screes E slope Flat Fell dropping down to Nannycatch Beck [056136].

Flatts Cop near Calder Bridge and alongside the Calder Bridge to Ennerdale Bridge road [052075] ...flat hill-top.

Flatts Farm Bootle [095901].

Fleet Gutter Ennerdale. Rises at 100170 and joins Croasdale Beck at 087170 ...Fleet refers to a creek or stream.

Fleetwith area between Fleetwith Pike and Grey Knotts [216133] ...possibly either ford over a sheet of water or, as Robert Gambles suggests the wooded area or bog from which water flows. Both Warnscale and Gatesgarth Becks rise in the vicinity.

Fleetwith Edge see **Fleetwith Pike**.

Fleetwith Gully gully leading up from Warnscale Bottom to the summit of Fleetwith Pike [204141].

Fleetwith Pike from Buttermere Fleetwith Pike is seen as a steep cone-shaped mountain with the road up Gatesgarthdale to its N and E and Warnscale Bottom to its W. It is fringed on three sides by crags, one of which, Honister Crag, drops over 305m (1000ft) to the Honister Pass road. Normally climbed from Honister Hause there is, however, a steep ascent from Gatesgarth along Fleetwith Edge [202144]. This rises over 500m (1640ft) in approximately 1.1 kms (0.7 mile). Near its foot at 197148 is a white cross, a memorial "erected by friends of Fanny Mercer accidentally killed 1887." Fanny was a maid who, while descending with another maid and a butler, fell to her death 648m (2126ft) [205142] ...peak above Fleetwith. See **Fleetwith**.

Fleming Tranearth former farmstead now a climbing hut (281956) ...Fleming's ground frequented by cranes.

Fleming Wood W shore Windermere. S Belle Grange [386987].

Flesh Crags E Scandale Beck [385072] ...flat crags.

Fletcher's Wood woodland W of the Elterwater-Colwith road. Bequeathed to the NT in 1944 [326038].

Flew Scar Longsleddale. Above Wellfoot Wood and Hollin Root [490034].

Flinty Grave Fairfield Crags. A scree shoot [361117].

Flock Inn Yew Tree Farm, Rosthwaite.

Flora of Lakeland Geoffrey Halliday in his work of 611 pages titled *A Flora of Cumbria*, published by the N-W Regional Studies, University of Lancaster (1997), refers to the presence of 1373 species of flora in Cumbria. See also **Flora & Fauna** in Reference Section.

Florence Mine Egremont, see Reference Section - **Mines**.

Floshgate between Brackenrigg and Pooley Bridge alongside the A592 [457239] ...pool or watery place. Usually, and particularly in Lancashire, known as a 'flash'.

Flour Gill one of many streams which rise below Greenup Edge and High Raise and eventually become Wyth Burn. Flour Gill rises just below Greenup Edge at 287104. Subsequently joins a combined Birks Gill and Mere Beck before becoming Wyth Burn and flowing into Thirlmere at 322131 ...flowery stream.

Floutern Crag overlooks Floutern Tarn [124169].

Floutern Kop viewpoint slightly N of Floutern Tarn and the summit of Floutern Pass 451m (1480ft) [122174].

Floutern Pass path between Crummock Water and Ennerdale which crosses the summit of the pass near Floutern Tarn at C410m (C1345ft) [121172].

Floutern Tarn elongated tarn with Great Borne towering to its S and the summit of of the Floutern Pass slightly to its N. The source of Mosedale Beck C380m (C1247ft) [125170] ...appropriately named, tarn in a boggy area.

Flusco Hill between Dacre Beck and the R Eamont and overlooking the A592, 177m (581ft) [472259] ...most likely the flat wood hill.

Foegill Crag slope Middle Fell below Goat Crag [155065].

Fog Mire Wasdale Head. Alongside Fogmire Beck [190091] ...coarse grass or swampy /marshy ground.

Fogmire Beck rises Wasdale Fell at 197094 and joins Mosedale Beck at 188090.

Fold End Gallery Boot, Eskdale. Established 1973.

Fold Gate alongside the Hawkshead-Newby Bridge road. Near Hawkshead YH [356965].

Fold Gate Corney [119919] ...foul/dirty gate.

Folds off the Duddon Bridge to Ulpha road W of the Duddon [178911].

Folly Bridge footbridge over the River Derwent. Built in 1791 [250139].

Foot & Mouth Disease foot and mouth disease struck Cumbria in 1967. However, a far more serious outbreak occurred in February 2001, and between then and the end of September when the last case was confirmed some 2827 farms in the county were subjected to culls. The county was finally declared disease free in January 2002. Altogether more than one million sheep and 250,000 cattle were slaughtered.

Footmoorgate Gill rises SW slope Ullscarf at 287116 and joins Greenup Gill at 281120.

Footpaths there are approximately 2682 paths and bridleways in the Lake District National Park. Today, the cost of repairing one metre (3.3ft) can be between £10 and £45.

Force Beck Grizedale Beck drops over Force Falls and becomes Force Beck. Subsequently met by Ashes Beck/Dale Park Beck and Bell Beck near Rusland and takes the name Rusland Pool. This joins the River Leven near Haverthwaite.

Force Crag overlooking Measand Beck [469159].

Force Crag head of the Coledale valley [197214].

Force Crag Mine head of the Coledale valley. Mining for silver and lead was carried out in the 16th century. Since the 1860s, however, mining has principally been for barytes with, over the years, intermittent working. Today the Force Crag Mine is owned by the NT which is carrying out a conservation programme of industrial and archaeological heritage at the site. In 2002 the mine was scheduled as an Ancient Monument. Force Crag was the last working mine in the Lake District National Park and its ore-processing equipment remains in-situ. Workings at High Force [193214] and Low Force [200216].

Force Falls waterfalls at Force Mills. Here Grizedale Beck drops over the falls and becomes Force Beck. Water from the falls used to power a mill a short distance downstream [340911].

Force Forge/Mills head of the Rusland valley and at the foot of the Grizedale valley. Force Mills [340911] lies alongside Force Falls from which it takes its name. Force Forge [336907] is sited lower down Force Beck. Force Mills was the site of bobbin mills and bloomeries while Force Forge was the site of an 18th century bloomsmithy and bobbin and corn mills.

Force Hole below waterfall on Howes Beck [501177].

Force Jump waterfall on the River Kent at Kentmere [460044]

Force Knott ENE Force Mills [343916] ...the rocky hillock which overlooks the Force ie Force Falls, Force Mills.

Force Mills see **Force Forge/Mills**.

Forces Falls also referred to as Swindale Falls. Spectacular falls where Mosedale Beck drops down into Swindale [509114].

Forces, The see **The Forces**.

Fordingdale Bottom hanging valley through which flows Measand Beck [478158].

Fordingdale Force waterfall on Measand Beck below Force Crag [470158].

Fore Hawthorn Riggs between the Hawkshead-Newby Bridge road and the connecting road from Far Sawrey [375931] ...The front Hawthorn Riggs as opposed to nearby back Hawthorn Riggs.

Forest Bridge carries the Nether Wasdale-Santon Bridge road over the River Irt [128037].

Forest Hall farm alongside the A6 between Bannisdale Low Bridge and Kidshowe Bridge. Formerly the ancient manor house of Fawcett Forest [547012].

Forest Side Grasmere E A591. Once the edge of a considerable forest but today more like a sizeable plantation as exemplified by the nearby Forestside Plantation [345082]. A large building of the same name is, like several other properties hereabouts (see *Wordsworth & The Lake District* by David McCracken 1984, page 39), claimed to be the site of the cottage of Michael, the shepherd, in Wordsworth's poem *Michael*. Owned by Countrywide Holidays Association [342081] ...name dates back to the 14th century when Thomas de Foresta held land hereabouts.

Foresthow Eskdale Green [137996].

Forestry Commission manages 40 woodlands covering over 20,000 acres in Cumbria. The largest are Grizedale and Whinlatter Forests.

Forests (Medieval) in medieval times large 'forest' areas covered considerable portions of the Lake District. These particular areas were not completely afforested but were subject to Forest Laws which were used to protect the interests of their owners for the purpose of hunting game such as deer, wolves and wild boar. Apart from the gigantic royal forest of Inglewood there were private forests such as Copeland, Derwent, Fawcett, Grisedale, Grizedale, Millom, Skiddaw and Sleddale. Over the succeeding centuries, as the population increased, much of the 'forest' land was acquired for agricultural use ie the grazing of sheep and cattle, or denuded for the making of charcoal. Today's principal forests, albeit some covering areas once occupied by those of medieval times, are of comparatively recent origin - planting at Thornthwaite by the Forestry Commission began in 1919, Ennerdale in 1927 and the Grizedale woodland was acquired in the 1930s and has been increased, modified and developed since then.

Forestside Plantation see **Forest Side**.

Forge, The see **The Forge**.

Forge Bridge carries the Eskdale to Ulpha fell road over the R. Esk. Forge House nearby. Centuries ago called Auesthaitbrig. Land thereabouts owned by the Stanley family of

Auestwait (now Dalegarth Hall) for centuries [149995].

Forge Brow above the bank of the River Greta [282242].

Forge Hills across the Esk from Forge House 47m (154ft) [142991].

Forge House alongside the Eskdale to Ulpha fell road [147992]. The Eskdale and Ennerdale foxhounds are kenneled here.

Forge Wood Ulpha [192927].

Forked How Troutal Fell. S Looking How [244993].

Fornside farm and holiday cottages off the B5322 [321206] ...'Forni's hill pasture'.

Forts the largest in Cumbria was the five acre Carrock Fell which is also the only mountain fort in the county. Others in the area covered by this work are:-

Allen Knott alongside the Troutbeck valley	[415011]
Castle Crag, Borrowdale	[249159]
Castle Crag (Shoulthwaite Castle) above Thirlmere	[300188]
Castle Crag, W Haweswater Reservoir	[469128]
Dunmallard Hill, foot of Ullswater	[468246]
Hardknott Castle Roman Fort	[219015]
Maiden Castle, Burn Moor	[186054]
Maiden Castle, Soulby Fell	[451244]

Forts (Roman) N A66 near Troutbeck [384272]; Galava, Ambleside [373034]; Hardknott Castle [219015].

Foss How alongside Tarn Beck and above the cascade of Thrang/Throng Force on the beck [241986] ...hill above the force/waterfall.

Foster Beds alongside Red Pike (Wasdale) ridge [162104] ...Foresterbedd 14th century and Forster Bed in the 16th century.

Fother Gill ravine and watercourse. Two streams rise on Lamplugh Fell at 110191 and 110192 respectively. Combine to form Fother Gill which joins Cogra Moss at 099193.

Fothergill Head read of the Comb Gill ravine. Comb Gill, the farthest headstream of Croasdale Beck, rises here [114189].

Foul Mart N head of Seathwaite Tarn [257997] ...polecat.

Foul Scrow NNW Dixon Ground, Coniston [293979] ...for derivation of scrow see **Glossary**.

Foule Crag Blencathra 845m (2772ft) [324283].

Foulshaw Moss raised bog just inside the National Park boundary and alongside the River Kent. It is Cumbria's largest single peat bog. The biggest peatland restoration project ever carried out in this country began in September 2001, and was the first stage of a three-year programme to clear 75% of the trees on the site to create 190 hectares of open lowland.

Foulsyke Loweswater. Alongside the Loweswater via Thackthwaite to Low Lorton road [142215] ...dirty small stream.

Foumart Gill alongside the Croasdale to Lamplugh road. Stream which flows down it eventually joins with others to enter the River Marron [087194] ...gill/ravine frequented by polecats.

Four Stones Hill E Burnbanks. Probably named after Standing Stones only two of which, looking like gate posts, remain near the summit and are scheduled, along with a nearby settlement, as Ancient Monuments 415m (1362ft) [492162].

Four Stones Tarn shown but not named on the OS map. Just below the Standing Stones near the summit of Four Stones Hill. Sited at an altitude of C400m (C1312ft) [491163].

Fox, George (1624-91) itinerant preacher who, from Swarthmoor Hall in 1652, founded the Society of Friends (Quakers) and converted many to that religion over the years following. Quaker Meeting Houses were established throughout the area that is now Cumbria and descriptions and history of 53 are given in *Quaker Meeting Houses of the Lake Counties* by David M Butler (1978). George Fox toured and preached constantly. He died in 1691 and is buried in London. His wife of 22 years, Margaret Fell, survived him by 11 years and is buried at Sunbrick.

Fox Bield Broad End, Skiddaw [260282].

Fox Bield Foxbield Moss, Birker Moor [190987].

Fox Crag NE Low Ludderburn [407913].

Fox Crag Plantation alongside minor road, Birks Bridge-Ludderburn [407915].

Fox Crags S Stainton Pike. NW Whitfell [154936].

Fox Fold W of the path from Honister Hause to Dale Head [224139].

Fox Ghyll off the minor road from Pelter Bridge, Rydal, to Rothay Bridge, Ambleside. Originally built in the 17th century. Home of Thomas de Quincey (1785-1859) and his wife, Margaret, from 1820-25. During this period he had his *Confessions of an English Opium-Eater* published in the *London Magazine* and this appeared in book form the following year. Earlier he was editor of the *Westmorland Gazette*. The house was enlarged and the grounds landscaped by Letitia Luff, friend of Dorothy Wordsworth. Later it became the home of W E Forster, Irish Secretary from 1880-82. Today, it is a guest house [363051].

Fox Haw between Long Mire and Park Head Road 385m (1263ft) [223936] ...hill frequented by foxes.

Fox How alongside minor road from Pelter Bridge, Rydal, to Rothay Bridge, Ambleside. Built in 1833 by Thomas Arnold, headmaster of Rugby School, with much advice from William Wordsworth concerning its architecture. Used as a holiday home by Dr Arnold until his death in 1842 and this tradition carried on by son, Matthew, poet and critic. Mrs Humphrey Ward, novelist and Thomas's grand-daughter spent part of her childhood at Fox How [365049].

Fox How Farm across the minor road, Pelter Bridge-Rothay Bridge, from Fox How [365049].

Fox Hunting traditional Lakeland sport but by reason of the difficult mountainous terrain encountered differs from fox hunting in other flatter areas. The hounds are usually followed on foot and not on horseback. Five packs of hounds - Blencathra, Coniston (founded about 1825), Eskdale and Ennerdale (founded 1857), Melbreak (assembled 1807) and Ullswater (formed by the amalgamation in 1873 of the Matterdale and Patterdale packs) - cover the highest ground of the Lake District. Two others, Lunesdale and North Lonsdale, operate alongside or over the Lake District borders. Each meets frequently between September and May. Over the years each pack has had its noted huntsmen. The best known and best remembered was the legendary John Peel (1776-1854) immortalised in the song *D'Ye Ken John Peel*, words by John Woodcock Graves, and sung to the familiar tune arranged by William Metcalfe. Other famous huntsmen include Joe Bowman and Joe Wear of the Ullswater Pack, Anthony Chapman of the Coniston Pack, John Crozier of the Blencathra Hunt and Tommy Dobson and Bill Porter of the Eskdale and Ennerdale Hunt.

Fox Trap see **Goose Bield**.

Foxbield Moss Birker Moor [192990].

Foxbield Wood S Gatterigghow [109036].

Foxes Tarn sometimes referred to as just Fox Tarn. Small tarn high up on Scafell. A path to the summit of that mountain from Eskdale passes by the tarn. Considered to be the second highest tarn in Lakeland after Broadcrag Tarn 820-830m (2690-2723) [209064] (see also **Broadcrag Tarn**).

Foxhole Bank near Foxhole Wood [432926].

Foxhole Wood between the A5074 and Back Lane [430928].

Foxwell adjoining Scar Foot alongside the Kendal to Underbarrow road. Used to be called Scarfoot Cottage but name changed in the 1980s [481922] ...water pumped from adjacent well and foxes are often seen thereabouts.

Frank Tranearth Torver (275954) ...Frank's ground frequented by cranes.

Freeze Beck rises at 413150. After being joined by Blue Gill at 413160 the combination of the two becomes Boredale Beck.

Freeze Beck rises Birker Moor at 192964 and joins with Woodend Pool and shortly afterwards Ulgra Beck to become Crosby Gill at 184956.

Freshwater Biological Association founded in 1929 to foster research on the biology of freshwaters. Previously its headquarters was Wray Castle but is now Ferry House, W shore Windermere. The latter was built as the Ferry Hotel in 1879. Ferry House houses a library, workshops, etc and laboratories. See **Ferry House**.

Friar Gill rises at 056100 and joins the River Calder at 064101 ...see **Monks Bridge**.

Friar Well a spring W River Calder [057100].

Friar's Crag Derwent Water. A craggy headland a short walk from Keswick and just S of the boat landing stages. The crag provides an excellent viewpoint up the lake to the Jaws of Borrowdale and of the encircling fells. Acquired by the NT in 1921 as a memorial to Canon Rawnsley (1851-1920), Vicar of Crosthwaite (1883-1917) and a founder of the NT. A memorial plaque nearby records "that he set his great love of the fair things of nature and art... to the service of God and man." Another memorial nearby is to John Ruskin and was placed there in 1900. Ruskin first visited Friar's Crag at the age of five and later he described the view from it as "one of the three most beautiful scenes in Europe" [264228] ...Traditionally the place where monks embarked for St. Herbert's Island and where St. Cuthbert parted from St. Herbert.

Friday Point promontory on bend of lower Esk ESE Muncaster Castle [107958].

Friends of the Lake District organisation formed in 1934. An association which, in their own words, 'continues to work to protect the natural beauty of the area to ensure that they leave to future generations the outstanding landscape that we now enjoy.'

Frith S Hawkshead Hill [339983] ...frith is from the OE 'fyrhoe' and means wood.

Frith Beck rises below Whelpsty How at 179915. Joins with other streams slightly W of Bleabeck Bridge at 188919 to become Blea Beck. This joins the River Duddon at 195920.

Frith Crag overlooks Frith Wood and Woodnook Gill [517156].

Frith Gill rises Puddingstone Bank at 267157 and joins the River Derwent at 255159.

Frith Hall the gaunt remains of Frith Hall appear on the skyline W of the River Duddon looking like something out of Wuthering Heights. The ruin lies alongside a track and subsequently footpath and bridleway between Beckstones and Millbrow, Ulpha. The hall was once a hunting lodge of the Huddlestons of Millom and later an inn of some repute [189916] ...hall in the wood.

Frith Plantation SW Hawkshead Hill. Nearby is Frith [335983] ...see **Frith**.

Frith Shed between Millplace Coppice and High Frith Gill [108008] ...see **Frith** + shed/building.

Frith Wood S Haweswater Beck and alongside waterworks private road from A66 to

Haweswater [517158] ...'wood' wood.

Frith Wood E High Rosthwaite [248900].

Frith Wood Borrowdale. Above Frith Gill [259155].

Frost Hole in a side valley off the Staveley to Bowston and Garnett Bridge road [486989] ...'frosty hollow'.

Froswick peak on the Yoke-Ill Bell-High Street ridge. Roman road to, and over, High Street traverses along its W slope which is grassy except for the deep cleft of Blue Gill. To the E Froswick shows a steep and craggy face dropping down to the River Kent 720m (2362ft) [435085] ...originally the name given to a cove to the E of the summit but now given to the peak itself. May have meant the cold dairy farm. On the other hand, Fros may have been part of a surname.

Froth Pot deep pool in the River Duddon upstream from Birks Bridge [236996] ...the EPNS refers to a Froth Hall in 1774 from which the 'pot' obviously took its name. Froth, either a surname or a corruption of 'frith' meaning wood and so in the latter case the pool by the hall in the wood.

Fulling Mills early mills in which cloth, etc was fulled by being made heavier and more compact through beating with wooden mallets or treading with the feet. The latter process provided another name, walk mills. On the introduction of water power, the material was pressed between rollers. Subsequently it was cleaned before being stretched out on tenter hooks to dry. Research suggests that Cumbria possessed at least 500 such mills. One of the earliest was established at Troutbeck Bridge in the 13th century. It later became a corn mill then a paper mill before ending its mill days as a bobbin mill. Today, it houses a firm of monumental masons.

Furness originally the name signified the promontory of Rampside Point but later was applied to all that area north of the sands (the former Lancashire) between the Duddon and the Leven W-E and the R Brathay to the N. To its E between the Leven and the Winster valley lies the district of Cartmel including Cartmel Fell ...Futh's headland (ON 'nes').

Furness Fells in its wider meaning the title Furness Fells applies to all those fells in the area called Furness (see **Furness**). However, although shown on the OS map as a considerable portion of fell area between the Coniston Fells and Wetherlam at 295000 the Furness Fells today are generally deemed to comprise the low fell area between Coniston Water and Windermere.

Fusedale one of the five valleys included in the area of Martindale. The other four are Boredale, Bannerdale, Howe Grain, and Ramps Gill. Down it flows Fusedale Beck on its way to join Ullswater alongside Howtown Pier [445183] ...valley with a cattle shed.

Fusedale Beck rises Wether Hill at 453166. Joined by Groove Gill, Dodd Gill, and enters Ullswater alongside Howtown Pier at 443199.

Fusethwaite Yeat alongside Moorhowe Road, Troutbeck [412013] ...cattle shed in the clearing by the gate or opening to the fell.

G

Gable Beck rises Beck Head at 205106 and joins Lingmell Beck at 199092.

Gable Crag northern precipitous face of Great Gable. Possesses several rock climbs [212105].

Gable Gill rises Long Side, Carl Side, at 249279 and joins Skill Beck at 246277. Meets Wath Beck and ultimately joins the River Derwent at 243260.

Gait Kirk below the summit of Ponsonby Fell and on the edge of Blengdale Forest [089070] ...'kirk' could possibly refer to a circle of stones.

Gaitkins Cold Pike [259033] ...'small goats'.

Gaitscale farm, long since abandoned, near Gaitscale Gill and the River Duddon [256023] ...W Green in his *Tourists' New Guide* (1819) calls it Great Scale which means the 'great hut or shelter' but more than likely it is the hut/shelter or summer pasture frequented by goats.

Gaitscale Close enclosed fell area near Gaitscale [250022].

Gaitscale Gill rises near Stonesty Pike Tarns at 252042 and joins the River Duddon at Wrynose Bottom at 258020.

Galava Roman Fort head of Windermere on the alluvial plain at Borran's Field (National Trust), Waterhead. An interim fort between that at Hardknott and the route over High Street to Brougham. Built to replace an earlier smaller fort and manned until the late 4th or early 5th century. Excavations can be seen [373034].

Gale Bay Ullswater [465235] ...the bay by the bog-myrtle/gale/sweet gale.

Gale Crag on Hartsop above How ridge 512m (1680ft) [392124].

Gale Fell N Starling Dodd, E Great Borne 518m (1699ft) [134164] ...probably the fell above the ravine. There are several clefts/ravines in its vicinity.

Gale Gill rises Mallen Dodd at 279252 and, according to the OS map, ends by the roundabout at the junction of the A66 and the A591 ...stream in a ravine.

Gale Naze Crag head of Windermere [371029] ... 'crag at the end of the narrow promontory'.

Galeforth Brow Longsleddale. Down it flows Galeforth Gill on its way from Greycrag Tarn to the River Sprint [486066] ... 'the waterfall in the ravine'.

Galeforth Gill rises Greycrag Tarn at 492076 and drops down over Galeforth Brow to meet the River Sprint in Longsleddale at 482065.

Galemire Bay Derwent Water [255226] ...Bay by the gale/bog myrtle on the mire/swampy ground.

Gales see **Winds**.

Galesyke Nether Wasdale. Off the Nether Wasdale to Wastwater road [133039] ...possibly the stream in the ravine or the stream by which the gale (bog myrtle) grows.

Galleny Force waterfall on Stonethwaite Beck just after the confluence of Langstrath Beck and Greenup Gill [272131] ...possibly from galena/lead ore.

Gallows Hill Gosforth. E A595. Even though it is only 67m (220ft) in height it is the highest point for some distance around. Bears a trig. point [076023] ...similar to Hanging How in that it was at one time a place of execution.

Galloway Farm Thackthwaite, Lorton Vale [148236].

Galls Tarn small private tarn S Holehird and sited in the grounds of St Anne's School,

Troutbeck Bridge C140m (C459ft) [409003].

Gamblesmire Lane S Cunswick Hall [484930] ...the lane across Gamall's bog.

Gambling Crag E Willy Winder Hill. ENE Seat Robert [532117].

Gambling Moss between Hallmoss Hill and Gambling Crag. Gambling Well and source of Peathill Gill here [534115].

Gambling Well S Gambling Crag. Source of Peathill Gill [532115].

Gamlin End steep and mainly scree slope leading down from High Crag to Seat [182138].

Gap, The see **The Gap**.

Garburn/Garburn Nook/Garburn Road/Garburn Pass Garburn itself is shown on the map as being from the summit of Garburn Pass to Buck Crag [437047]. Garburn Nook is at 435043. Garburn Pass in its entirety begins at the Troutbeck valley and covers 6.5kms (4 miles) over the fells to Kentmere rising to a height of 447m (1467ft) at 436044. On the Troutbeck side of the pass Garburn Road [422034], a rutty track, passes Applethwaite Quarry on its way to the summit of the pass while on the Kentmere side the track descends along Crabtree Brow [445045]. In earlier times this was a prominent drove road linking one from Ambleside and one from Longsleddale. From the summit of the pass the Garburn Peat Road headed N to the peat allotments alongside Yoke and below Star Crag ...stream (burna) in the gore - 'gore' or nook being the triangular projection of land into Kentmere. Presumably the stream mentioned is Hall Gill which follows much of the track down into Kentmere.

Gargill head of tributary of Wasdale Beck [544066] ...possibly from 'gara' meaning a triangular piece of land.

Gargill Pike W Gargill, overlooking Wasdale Mouth [540066].

Garner Bank NNW Rough Crag 244m (800ft) [158986].

Garnett Bridge hamlet alongside a bridge over the River Sprint at the entrance to Longsleddale and alongside the road up the valley. Once possessed two working mills [524992] ...named after the local Garnett family. Garnett House is in Strickland Ketel just outside Burneside.

Garnett Bridge Wood at the rear of Garnett Bridge [520994].

Garnett Wood S Castle Wood [373946].

Gars Brow WSW summit of Steel Fell [315110].

Garth Close E River Duddon. SE Hinning House [241997] ...a tautology as both garth and close mean enclosure.

Garth Heads Boredale, opposite Housesteadbrow farm [428186] ...enclosure at the end of a ridge.

Garth Row Lane Underbarrow. Garthrow to Underbarrow road (B5284) [478916].

Garthrow Underbarrow. Small community on side road off the Underbarrow to Brigsteer road [477912] ...enclosure with row of houses nearby.

Gasgale Crags precipitous crags above Gasgale Gill. Summit at 719m (2359ft) [175221] ...see **Gasgale Gill** below.

Gasgale Gill narrow ravine down which flows Liza Beck. A path up it leads to Coledale Hause and the high summit of Grasmoor [176216] ...the ravine where the goat huts are situated.

Gasketh situated alongside the track between Moorgate and Miteside [099986].

Gate Crag W shore Haweswater. Across an inlet from The Rigg [470120].

Gate Crag Birker Moor 283m (928ft) [184997].

Gate Crags W Ullswater. Overlook Hagg Wood [426223].

Gate Gill rises between Middle Tongue and Hall's Fell, Blencathra, at 322275. Drops down through Gategill and Threlkeld to join the R Glenderamackin at 324251.

Gate House Outward Bound School see **Eskdale Outward Bound School**.

Gate House Tarn see **Eskdale Green Tarn**.

Gategill farm at the foot of Gategill Fell, Blencathra. The Blencathra foxhounds are kennelled here [325261].

Gategill Fell below Gategill Fell Top. S face of Blencathra overlooking Threlkeld [319268].

Gategill Fell Top Blencathra 851m (2792ft) [318273].

Gaterigghow Bridge carries the track from the Nether Wasdale to Gosforth road over the River Irt to Gat(t)erigg How [108041] ...see **Gatterigghow**.

Gatescarth alongside the River Irt at Santon Bridge [109020] ...the gap or pass through which the goats go.

Gatescarth Beck rises in marshy area near the summit of the Gatescarth Pass at 474094 and joins Haweswater Reservoir at 469109.

Gatescarth Pass Mardale Head to Sadgill, Longsleddale, approximately 5.6kms (3.5miles). From Mardale Head at the head of Haweswater the Pass, 6th highest in the Lake District, and formerly a pack-horse route and drove road zig zags to its summit at 594m (1949ft) [474092] between Branstree and Harter Fell. Both are climbed quite easily from here. It then drops down to meet the former drove road coming up Mosedale and shortly afterwards it becomes a quarry road from Wrengill Quarry. Down the valley it meets another drove road, this time from Kentmere to Sadgill, at the Sadgill packhorse bridge, and the present surfaced road down Longsleddale [469107-484057] ...either the pass frequented by goats or simply the road pass.

Gatesgarth Cottage alongside the B5289 at the head of Buttermere and the foot of the Honister Pass [195149].

Gatesgarth Farm farm alongside the B5289 at the head of Buttermere and the foot of the Honister Pass. Each succeeding tenant holds the title of Lord of the Manor of Scales [194150].

Gatesgarthdale Beck rises Fleetwith at 221133 and flows down Gatesgarthdale to meet Buttermere at 190152 ...the stream which flows along a valley with a pass through a gap (Honister Hause) or, similar to Gatescarth, Mardale and that at Santon Bridge and meaning either 'the pass frequented by goats' or simply 'road pass'.

Gateway Inn off the B5284, near Plumgarths roundabout at the end of the Kendal by-pass [485948] ...gateway to the lakes.

Gatherstone Beck rises Black Sail Pass at 191114 and joins Mosedale Beck at 179105.

Gatherstone Head overlooks Gatherstone Beck near its confluence with Mosedale Beck [183109].

Gatterigghow former farm now let as a cottage. Gaterigg How on OS 1:63360 (1 inch to 1 mile) map of 1947. Alongside the track S from the Nether Wasdale to Gosforth road. The track crosses the River Irt by Gaterigghow Bridge. The property came to the NT in 1965 as part of the Wrigley Estate [108039] ...goat ridge hill.

Gavel ESE Seat Sandal overlooking Grisedale Pass [348113] ...gable end.

Gavel Crag E High Street Roman Road, SW Bleathwaite Crag and W Hall Cove [437097] ...crag having the appearance of a gable end.

Gavel Crag ESE Seat Sandal. Overlooks Gavel and Grisedale Pass. Wainwright describes it as 'a miniature Pillar Rock' [346113].

Gavel Fell between White Oak and Fothergill Head 526m (1726ft) [117184]. A subsidiary summit to its NW is called High Nook and is 488m (1601ft) in height ...gable fell.

Gavel Moss below Gavel Pike. Coldcove Gill rises here [377138].

Gavel Neese steep SW slope of Great Gable initially grass then scree up to the Gable Traverse [204097] ...gable's nose.

Gavel Pike peak E shoulder St Sunday Crag. Pyramidical when seen from the A592 784m (2572ft) [373134] ...'gable-like pointed hill'.

Gaze Stone How ESE Cockley Beck 395m (1296ft) [255014].

Geology principally, the northern part of this area is comprised of the Borrowdale Volcanic Series with intrusions of granite in the Threlkeld area (one of which until 1982 was mined via the Threlkeld Quarry), several intrusions in the Skiddaw Forest and an area of Shap Granite on the eastern boundary. To the far E there is a large area of carboniferous limestone and a section of Skiddaw Slate runs roughly each side of Ullswater from its foot to its middle reach while another area lies at the foot of Haweswater. Blencathra, and to its E, N, and W, is comprised of Skiddaw Slate and S of the whole region is an extensive area of Silurian rocks known to geologists as the Windermere Group. The central section provides a buffer between the Borrowdale Volcanic Series to the N and the Silurian (Stockdale Shales and Coniston Flags, etc) to the S. The dividing line is a thin band of Coniston Limestone running from Duddon Bridge, above the head of Coniston Water, across the head of Windermere and over Longsleddale to the Shap Fells. Intrusions occur in small areas.

Geordie Greathead Crag overlooking the head of Swindale [499113] ...an unknown

George Greathead. There is also a Geordie's Crag, E Ullswater. Maybe this commemorates the same person?

Geordie's Crag E shore Ullswater 1.2kms (0.75 mile) from Howtown. On promontory overlooking middle reaches of Ullswater. From near Geordie's Crag across to Skelly Nab is the lake's narrowest point and between the crag and nab fishermen used to stretch nets to catch the schelly or skelly [435204] ...'Geordie' is a pet form of George. Who George was is not known. Perhaps the George Greathead whose name is given to a crag overlooking the head of Swindale.

Ghosts, Apparitions, Spectres, etc. over the centuries Cumbria and its Lake District has seen or heard its share of ghosts, apparitions and the like and several books have been written on the folklore and legends surrounding these unique happenings. This work contains several references to local spirits, bogles, etc., but probably the most extraordinary sitings of recent years and covering a time span of at least 70 years has been the experience of many fell walkers. During their perambulations on the high fells they have witnessed an immaculately dressed city gent type complete with bowler hat, dark suit, rolled umbrella, brief case and wearing polished town shoes (recorded on occasions as unscratched and not mudded even in wet, boggy conditions) striding past them with not a glance to left or right. In 1931 such a person was seen heading from Rhossett Gill to Angle Tarn, in 1940 on the track to Watendlath from Ashness Bridge. Likewise, in the late 1940s on Green Gable, on the summit of Helvellyn in the 1960s, and Styhead Pass in 1991. A similarly dressed person has also been observed on Scafell Pike on more than one occasion, on the summit of High Street and Mosedale at the head of Wasdale.

Certainly people have walked the fells in all kinds of non-fellwalking garb and in some instances no garb at all. Writing in *Cumbria* magazine in November 2000, a correspondent noted that in the early 1940s a colleague used to walk the fell tops always in a dark suit and ordinary black shoes but not wearing a bowler hat or carrying a rolled umbrella. The author suggests that this was a possible origin of what he termed 'the myth'. However, the first sightings of the office-dressed man was well before this date and during the time span since, over 70 years, observers have, to a man or woman, agreed as to his identical dress and general attitude.

Ghyll see **Applethwaite**.

Ghyll Bank Over Staveley. Gill Bank on Bartholomew 1 inch map [476003].

Ghyll Bank Newlands valley [237205].

Ghyll Farm alongside Sleven Beck, a tributary of the River Calder [064110].

Ghyll Foot on earlier OS maps Gill Foot. N Grasmere village alongside the minor road, Mill Bridge (A591)-Town Head (A591). Old bridge here carries the road over the Green Burn [332095].

Ghyll Head Fish Pond earlier Rosthwaite Tarn. Across Ghyll Head Road from Ghyll Head Reservoir. Privately owned [397927].

Ghyll Head Outdoor Education Centre Ghyllhead (see **Ghyllhead** below). Manchester City Council's outdoor activities centre. Celebrated its 25th anniversary in 1992 [394927].

Ghyll Head Reservoir alongside Ghyll Head Road. Reserve reservoir for water supply to Windermere and district. Trout fishing (brown and rainbow) controlled by the WADAA [398923].

Ghyll Head Road connects the A592 at Ghyll Head with Birks Road [400920].

Ghyll Pool Potter Fell. On the outflow from Potter Tarn. Dammed in 1934 to provide a reservoir for the Burneside paper works. Lies at an altitude of 220m (722ft) [497984] ...pool in the ravine.

Ghyllhead area and property just off the A592, Newby Bridge-Bowness road and at the start of the fell road (Ghyll Head Road) from the A592 to Ludderburn [394928].

Giant Tree of Thirlmere see **Trees**.

Gibb Hill Farm Ponsonby [065055].

Gibbet Moss not named on OS map. Between Priest Pot and the B5285. Many years ago during drainage operations part of what was believed to have been a gibbet was dug up [358979]. Not far distant Gallabarrow was without doubt also the site of a gallows.

Gibraltar Sleddale Forest. Between White Moss and Staveley Head Fell [476018] ...uncertain origin. One suggestion is that from a certain angle it has the appearance of a miniature rock of Gibraltar arising out of the landscape.

Gibraltar Crag N Skiddaw Man[260294] ...someone obviously had a fondness for Gibraltar.

Gibson Knott rocky outcrop on the long ridge which stretches from Helm Crag over Gibson Knott and Moment Crag to Calf Crag 420m (1379ft) [321099] ...surname + rocky outcrop.

Gig House Gallery art gallery, Elterwater. Now the Judy Boyce Gallery. Takes its former first two names from the original use of the building as housing for small horse-drawn vehicles which belonged to the former Elterwater Gunpowder Company [329048].

Gill former small farm off the Gosforth to Wastwater high road [130053] ...see also **Buckbarrow** (farm).

Gill property alongside Mill Beck [421981].

Gill Bank Boot, Eskdale. Farm alongside Whillan Beck. Owned by the NT. The old corpse route from Wasdale Head to Boot passes nearby [181018]. A wool-carding mill once existed at Gill Bank.

Gill Beck rises NW Carhullan at 487185 and flows down past Gillhead and Butterwick to be joined by Pow Beck at 513197. Enters the River Lowther at 515200.

Gill Beck rises Cold Well, Nether Wasdale Common, at 133067 and flows past Gill to meet Cinderdale Beck and join the River Irt at 127038.

Gill Beck rises 128014 and joins the River Mite.

Gill Beck rises 118171 and joins Ennerdale Water at 101160.

Gill Brow Mosser Mains [116251].

Gill Cove cove on the E face of Brim Fell through which flows Cove Beck [273993].

Gill Cove Crag below Brim Fell and overlooking Levers Water [275990].

Gill Crag Hartsop above How. The latter is known by locals as Gill Crag which, according to Wainwright is "a more satisfactory name for the fell" [384120].

Gill Dubbs pools in Haweswater Beck below Haweswater Reservoir dam [506158].

Gill Edge near Dockray [388217].

Gill Foot (Ambleside), see **Ghyll Foot**.

Gill Foot on earlier maps Ghyll Foot. N Grasmere village alongside minor road, Mill Bridge (A591) to Town Head (A591) [332095].

Gill Force waterfall on the River Esk near Boot village [179002].

Gill Force waterfall on the River Calder at 067112.

Gill Grains Lingmoor Fell [303037] ...'grein' a fork of a river/stream/valley. Two gills meet here.

Gill Head Farm off minor road, Troutbeck-Wallthwaite [380269].

Gill House off the Santon Bridge to Nether Wasdale road. Mecklin Beck alongside [116022].

Gill Wood Nether Wasdale. Black Beck flows down its N boundary [126045].

Gillbank property approximately 500m (1/3 mile) N Colthouse alongside the Colthouse-High Wray road [360987].

Gillbrae Farm Lorton. Off the B5292. High Gillbrae nearby. The latter is shown on the Bartholomew map as Gill Brow [157269].

Gillbrow Keskadale. Off the Newlands Pass road [224195].

Gillercombe hanging valley to the W of Base Brown and along which flows Sourmilk Gill [224120].

Gillercombe Buttress see **Raven Crag, GreyKnotts**.

Gillercombe Head head of Gillercombe between Green Gable and Brandreth [215114].

Gillerthwaite Loweswater [144210].

Gillerthwaite Field Centre see **Low Gillerthwaite**, Ennerdale.

Gillerthwaite YH Ennerdale. 3.6kms (2.25 miles) from Bowness Knott car park. Converted from two forest cottages [142141].

Gillflinter Beck rises on slope between Little Dodd and Red Pike at 153153 and joins the River Liza at 147139 ...the stream in the ravine of Finnporr (ON personal name).

Gillfoot Corney [116918].

Gillhead farm, Butterwick [505191].

Gillriggs between the Askham-Bampton Grange road and the R Lowther [518228] ...ravine at the foot of the ridge.

Gillriggs Cover woodlands alongside the Askham-Bampton Grange road [517228].

Gillside farm, Glenridding. Up lane from Rattlebeck Bridge. Camping and caravan site adjoining [379168].

Gillsrow alongside the minor road, Troutbeck-Wallthwaite [373266].

Gilpin Farm off the B5284, Crook-Bowness road [436951] ...see **River Gilpin**.

Gilpin Lodge adjoining Gilpinpark Plantation. 3.2 kms (2 miles) from Windermere alongside the B5284. Bowness-Crook road. Today it is an award winning Country House Hotel [429959].

Gilpin Mill Crook. Former fulling and later bobbin mill sited alongside the River Gilpin. Its last owners were the Fell family who moved to Troutbeck Bridge to start the firm of W H Fell Ltd. (see **Troutbeck Bridge**) [434943].

Gilpin, River see **River Gilpin**.

Gilpinpark Plantation alongside the B5284, Crook-Bowness road. A headstream of the River Gilpin runs through it while another runs alongside it [434958] ...see **River Gilpin**.

Gimmer Crag S face of Loft Crag, Great Langdale. Well-known to climbers through routes which include Amen Corner, Asterisk, Bracket and Slab, Crack, Joas and Kipling Groove [277069] ...'gimmer', a female yearling sheep.

Glade How lesser summit of Seatallan above Buckbarrow. Possesses substantial cairns C430 (C1411ft) [134064].

Gladstone Knott first crinkle from the E of Crinkle Crags [255045].

Glaramara bulky mountain between Grains Gill and Langstrath. Possesses two principal summits. With its accolades, Rosthwaite, Stonethwaite and Thornythwaite Fells, it provides a huge fell area to the S of of Rosthwaite, Borrowdale. The first peak approached from the N is the highest at 783m (2569ft) [246105] and is ascended either by an easy approach contouring around the crags to the W or directly up an interesting but easy 6m (20ft) rock scramble. The second summit S across a small shallow ravine is slightly lower at 775m (2543ft) [246102]. There is the site of a minor neolithic stone-axe factory just below the summit ...an interesting name which in the early 13th century was Hovedgleurmerke much later corrupted to its present form. It means the mountain with the shieling/hut at the head of the ravines. The bulk of Glaramara has several ravines including the impressive upper reaches of Comb Gill.

Glaramara Seatoller, Borrowdale. An adventure centre [247138].

Glassy Crag Wetherlam [290011].

Glebe Farm Barton. See **Barton**.

Glebe House Lowther Park, alongside the New Road [534241] ...a glebe house refers to a manse.

Glebe House NE Waberthwaite. Off the A595 [109940].

Glebe, The see **Bowness-on-Windermere**.

Glede Howe N Willy Winder Hill. SE Black Crag 476m (1562ft) [521120] ...'hill of the kite'.

Glen Mary see **Tom Gill**.

Glen Mary Bridge carries the A593 over Tom Gill (gill valley also has the name Glen Mary) [322999] ...see **Tom Gill**.

Glen Rothay Hotel Rydal. Built originally in the 17th century and bears a 1624 datestone. Became known as Ivy Cottage or Tillbrooke's Cottage. Once the home of Edward Quillinan who married Dora Wordsworth, second child of William and Mary. In the 1830s greatly enlarged and renamed Glen Rothay. Dubbed by Wordsworth 'the Botched Ivy Cottage'. Later became David's Inn and ultimately the Glen Rothay Hotel. Part of the main building and facing the A591 is the Badger Bar [363062].

Glen, The see **The Glen**.

Glenamara Park Patterdale. On 1 inch Bartholomew it is named Glemarah and by Wainwright 'Glemara'. Well-wooded parkland landscape (similar to Deepdale Park) bounded by Thornhow End, Home Farm, Oxford Crag, Arnison Crag and Trough Head [390151] ...possibly means the glen-like park of a person unidentified.

Glencoyne or **Glencoindale** formerly called Linkdale. A lateral dale running W from Ullswater to a hanging glaciated valley below precipitous crags. From this upper valley Glencoyne Beck drops down a deep ravine and the amphitheatre from which it flows is practically encircled by Glencoyne Head, Hart Side, and Sheffield Pike. The lower reaches of the dale open up between Glencoyne Park and Glencoyne Wood and at its foot stands the old farm of Glencoyne [385187] built in 1629 and extended in 1700. A typical and unspoilt Lakeland farm. The Glencoyne Estate including the farm was gifted to the National Trust in 1948. Glencoyne's beech woods are impressive [385186] ...possibly 'reed valley'.

Glencoyne farm, see **Glencoyne**.

Glencoyne Bay 1.6 kms (1 mile) N of Glenridding on the A592. Public launching for light craft here.

Glencoyne Beck head streams, The Nick, Deepdale Slack and Wintergroove Gill, join forces at 366187 and become Glencoyne Beck which flows down the dale to join Ullswater at 387188.

Glencoyne Bridge carries the A592 over Glencoyne Beck [387188].

Glencoyne Brow overlooking Glencoyne and Ullswater [377190].

Glencoyne Head impressive cliffs at head of Glencoyne [359190].

Glencoyne Park large area W A5091 and N Ullswater and A592. Separated from

Glencoyne Wood by Glencoyne Beck. There is a settlement in the park at 390199 [393199].

Glencoyne Wood mixed deciduous wood S Glencoyne. Summit cairn on crags at rear 451m (1480ft). Bought for the National Trust by public subscription having earlier been earmarked for building development [379180].

Glendermackin, River see **River Glendermackin**.

Glenderaterra Beck short stream which rises at 294286. Joined by Sinen Gill at 296278 and Roughton Gill at 296274 before entering the River Greta at 299247. In his *In the Valleys of Lakeland* Wainwright inadvertently refers to it as the River Glenderaterra ...similar to Glenderamackin in that the name is of unknown origin.

Glenderaterra Valley between Lonscale Fell and Blease Fell and down which flows Glenderaterra Beck.

Glenridding a dale and a village. The lateral dale of Glenridding [370172] starts at the village of the same name on the shore of Ullswater and heads W towards the Helvellyn ridge. Just over l.6kms (l mile) up the dale at the top of Greenside Road is the now sealed Greenside Mine, several former mine buildings and an extensive spoil area. Over the years many spoil heaps have been stabilised, landscaped and turfed ...glen + clearing or bracken valley.

The village of Glenridding [387168], at the head of Ullswater and on the picturesque A592, Penrith to Newby Bridge road over Kirkstone Pass, began principally as a mining village. Today it is a stop on the Lake District tourists' route itinerary and the starting point for many mountain walks, the most popular being up the dale to the Helvellyn ridge. In the season two steamers run a regular service from Glenridding Pier to Pooley Bridge via Howtown and back (see **Ullswater**). In November 1992, a hydro-electric generating scheme built by Norweb was opened on the beck above the village. From a small dam near the former Greenside Mine water is piped to a turbine house lower down the dale. This generates enough power to supply about 500 homes in the surrounding area. This replaced an earlier scheme the leat of which is shown at 367172.

Glenridding Beck principal headstream rises just below the summit of Helvellyn Lower Man at 340156 and flows down through Brown Cove and Keppel Cove. Subsequently joined by Red Tarn Beck and on its way down Glenridding by Swarth Beck, Bleacove Beck and Mires Beck, before flowing through the village of Glenridding to join Ullswater at 39017. In May 2002, a 10-year-old boy was drowned after jumping into a pool in the beck (see also **Glenridding**).

Glenridding Bridge Glenridding. Carries the A592 over Glenridding Beck [387169].

Glenridding Common some 2500 acres including most of the former Greenside Mine site, upper reaches of Glenridding and the summit of Raise [350170].

Glenridding Dodd rounded height between Glenridding and Mossdale Beck with excellent view from its summit over Glenridding and the upper reaches of Ullswater and beyond 442m (1450ft) [381176].

Glenridding Hotel (Ratchers Tavern) Glenridding. Since 1996 has housed a library and display to Donald Campbell. Next to the hotel is the Kilner Coffee House originally owned by a Tom Kilner [387169].

Glenridding House Glenridding [387173].

Glenridding Sailing School The Spit, Glenridding [390171].

Glenridding Screes large scree area stretching from S Sheffield Pike to E Glenridding Dodd [370175].

Glenwood off the A595 2.8kms (1.75 miles) N Waberthwaite [110950].

Glow Worm Rock see **White Moss Common & Baneriggs**.

Goat Crag Eskdale. N Whahouse Bridge [204018].

Goat Crag Middle Fell. Above Foegill Crag [154066].

Goat Crag overlooking Seathwaite Tarn [254994].

Goat Crag E Goat's Water [268975].

Goat Crag W Caw (225944).

Goat Crag on the escarpment E slope High Spy overlooking Borrowdale [245162].

Goat Crag precipitious face below Buttermere Moss. Goat Gills drop down spectacular ravines to its E [189164].

Goat Crag line of crags ENE of the summit of Bleaberry Fell and overlooking Shoulthwaite Gill [293199].

Goat Crags S slope Scales Fell. Overlook Scaley Beck and A66 [338271].

Goat Crags Lingmell [204079].

Goat Crags E side Watendlath valley between Raise Gill and Emblesteads Gill [277170].

Goat Gill rises alongside Goat Crag, Middle Fell, at 152067 and joins Wastwater at 158060.

Goat Gill rises Heckbarley at 078143 and drops down ravine.

Goat Gills streams which rise above Goat Crag and flow down spectacular ravines to combine and subsequently meet Hassnesshow Beck at 190162.

Goat House Scar Kentmere. Above Crabtree Brow. Spot height at 407m (1335ft) [450046] ...as its name implies 'the goat house/building' on the scar.

Goat Scar N Shipman Knotts. Steep and craggy hillside which towers above and drops down to Longsleddale. Path from Shipman Knotts to Kentmere Pike passes over spot-height at 626m (2054ft) [473069] ...believed to originate in this case from ON goltr 'wild boar' and not the goat.

Goat's Crag overlooks Yewdale Beck and faces Raven Crag across the valley [307002].

Goat's Hawse col above Goat's Water and between Dow Crag and Coniston Old Man. Traversed by walkers' routes from Goat's Water to Seathwaite Tarn and the Duddon valley and from Dow Crag to the Coniston Old Man ridge. Its summit stands at 649m (2129ft) [266983] ...see **Goat's Water**.

Goat's Water in deep hollow between the impressive precipices of Dow Crag and the principally grassy slope of Coniston Old Man. Contains trout and some char. Altitude is 503m (1650ft) and has a depth of 13m (43ft) [266976] ...earlier Gaits Water. Water frequented by goats.

Goatfoot Crags S Goat's Water (266965).

Gobling Beck rises below Green Pike at 240950 and joins Tarn Beck at 225960 ...as it adjoins Dobby Shaw the name obviously signifies an area haunted by spirits/goblins or apparitions.

Godferhead (Godfred) Loweswater. Off the Loweswater to the B5289 road [146214].

Godmond Hall alongside Potter Fell Road. The site of the ancient Godmond Hall was later occupied by a farmhouse and part of the old hall's walls have been incorporated in the building [500978] ...named after local family Godmond/Godmund.

Godworth ENE Kelton Fell 365m (1197ft) [101183].

Goldrill Beck flows out of Brothers Water at 402132 and on its way to join Ullswater at 393166 is swollen by Pasture Beck/Hayeswater Gill, Eden Beck, Angletarn Beck, Deepdale Beck, Stonebarrow Gill, Rooking Gill and Grisedale Beck ...'the stream where the marsh marigold (kingcup) grows'. There is also a Gold Rill Beck at Grasmere.

Goldrill Country House Hotel alongside Red Bank Road. Takes its name from the Gold Rill, a stream thereabouts [335073].

Goldrill House Patterdale. Became a Youth Hostel. Demolished in 1970 and a purpose-built hostel opened on the site in 1971 [399156].

Goldscope Mine Scope End, Newlands valley. A lead and copper mine possibly first basically mined as far back as the 13th century. However, large scale mining began in 1564 when German miners were brought in to work for the Company of Mines Royal. In the 1590s the mine closed but reopened in the 17th century and from then work continued intermittently until the mid-19th century during which there was a more prosperous period. In 1864 the mine eventually closed and, although there have been attempts since to work the mine, to all intents and purposes it closed in the 19th century [226185/230184] ...although a small amount of gold was mined the name is a corruption of that given by the German miners to the rich vein discovered - 'Gottes Gab' - God's Gift.

Goldsworthy, Andy (sculpture and author) Andy Goldsworthy planned 'to locate the remains of 100 sheepfolds from maps and rebuild them by the year 2000 in such a way that they become a piece or contained a piece of sculpture'. Books include *Andy Goldsworthy*, *Stone*, *Wood*, *Time* and *Arch*.

Golf Keswick - off the A66 at Threlkeld. Windermere - alongside the B5284, Bowness-Crook road. These are the only 18 hole courses in the Lake District National Park.

Goodcroft slightly SSW confluence of Swindale Beck and the River Lowther [534161] ...Gode's croft.

Goody Bridge carries Easedale Road over Easedale Beck [333081] ...similar to nearby Goody Bridge Farm in that it is named after a person called Goody or Guddy.

Goose Bield rounded stone structure with overhanging stones as the top layer in which a dead goose, etc., was suspended from a plank precariously balanced on the wall. The fox walked along the plank towards the bait, the plank tipped up and the fox fell into the hole and was unable to escape because of the overhanging stones. Found on several locations in the Lake District including above Levers Water, above Seathwaite Tarn, Great Borne and The Benn.

Goose Crag just N Gambling Crag [532118].

Goose Howe property alongside Browfoot Lane, Kentmere [461001] ...goose 'hill'.

Goosegreeen WSW Little Mell Fell. Adjacent minor road, Matterdale Rigg-A592 [411235].

Goosewell farm Alongside minor road near Castlerigg Stone Circle [295238].

Goosey Foot Tarn Grizedale Forest Park. A tarn once a reservoir for Hawkshead. As it is sited near Guinea Hill it is also known as Guinea Hill Tarn [338970] ...said to resemble the web foot of a waterfowl.

Gosforth large village on the A595 4.8kms (3 miles) SE of Seascale and at the meeting of roads from Seascale, Eskdale and Wasdale. Way back in time it was a Viking settlement and many people today visit Gosforth to see the famous Gosforth Cross, a sandstone monolith of approx. 4.5 metres (14.5ft) which stands in the churchyard and is deemed to date from the 10th or 11th century. Also, the hogback tombs and Viking 'Fishing Stone' in the church. The church itself was rebuilt in the 19th century but a church had existed on the site since the 12th century. One of the oldest buildings in Gosforth dates from 1628 and today part of it houses the library. Gosforth Hall was built in the mid-17th century and is now a popular hotel and restaurant. A Viking connection lies just outside the village where are to be found the remains of an early Viking homestead known locally as Danes Camp ...Gosford in 1160, 'goose ford'.

Gosforth Crag between Low Tarn and Great Knott [167094] ...goose/geese ford crag.

Gosforth Crag Moss SE Gosforth Crag [170090].

Gosforth Hall Hotel Gosforth. Gosforth Hall was erected in the mid 17th century. Today the hall, which still contains many of the original features, is a popular hotel and restaurant [072036].

Gosforth Hall Plantation [106052].

Gouther Crag E of and overlooking Swindale [514126] ...echoing crag. There is another named echoing crag, Speaking Crag, at the head of Haweswater.

Gouthercrag Gill begins life as Haskew Beck which issues from Haskew Tarn at 521113. Becomes Gouthercrag Gill near Gouther Crag at 518128 before entering Swindale Beck at 514131.

Gowan Bank Farm off minor road from Ings to B5284 at Crook. Today separated from the River Gowan by the Kendal-Windermere railway line [447980].

Gowan, River see **River Gowan**.

Gowbarrow Fell in National Trust Gowbarrow Park 481m (1578ft) [408218] ...probably 'windy hill' but also suggested 'hill of the cuckoo' (the gawk).

Gowbarrow Hall farm, Ullswater. Off the A592 [433214].

Gowbarrow Park acquired by the National Trust in 1906 for £12,800. N Ullswater and the A592. Encloses Aira Force, High Force, Airy Crag, Gowbarrow Fell, Collier Hagg, Dobbin Wood, Yew Crag, Green Hill, Bernard Pike and Hind Crag. Hereabouts, near the water's edge between Stybarrow Crag and Glencoyne Beck, William and Dorothy Wordsworth saw the daffodils immortalised in William's poem *The Daffodils* (not as many people believe alongside Rydal Water) best remembered by the first verse:

I wandered Lonely as a Cloud,
That floats on high o'er vales and hills,
When all at once I saw a crowd,
A host of golden daffodils
Beside the lake, beneath the trees,
Fluttering and dancing in the breeze.

Excluding the highest point, Gowbarrow Fell, the area rises to 464m (1522ft). The café alongside Aira Beck was rebuilt by the National Trust in 1970 [408214].

Gowder Barrow W slope Muncaster Fell [123984] ...echoing hill.

Gowder Crag S Haycock [145104] ...possibly, similar to Gowder Crag, Borrowdale, and Gouther Crag, Swindale, in that the name signifies an 'echoing' crag.

Gowder Crag huge cliff towering over Lodore and the Lodore Falls [266187] ...echoing crag. In days gone by a cannon was kept in front of the Lodore Hotel. For a monetary payment persons could have the cannon discharged to hear its echoes from the surrounding hills and particularly Gowder and Shepherd Crags.

Gowder Dub Jaws of Borrowdale [251166] ...'gowder' usually signifies echoing but why a pool/widening of the river should echo is not clear. There is, however, a Gowder Crag lower down the valley near Lodore and in an early guide book reference is made to the notable echos from Gowder and nearby Shepherd Crag.

Gowk Hill E Ramps Gill and W Wether Hill. Spot height shown at 469m (1539ft) but contour at 470m (1542ft) [445167] ...'cuckoo' hill.

Gowther Barrow E Hutton [206903].

Graham Scottish hill between 610m (2000ft) and 762m (2499ft). Lakeland mountains in this height range are often referred to by the same name.

Graham Starkey Hut Patterdale. Named in memory of Graham Starkey, a British Associate Member of the Swiss Alpine Club.

Grain Gill Rises Whiteoak Moss at 120177 and combines with Comb Gill, Ill Gill and High Bridge Gill to become Croasdale Beck. This joins the River Ehen at Ennerdale Bridge.

Grain Moor N Hummer Lane. S Broughton Moor Quarry [256935] ...grein is a fork of a river or valley.

Grains area alongside Grains Gill [235102] ...'shieling/hut near the fork in a valley'. The fork in this case is the meeting of Styhead Gill and Grains Gill.

Grains Gill the upper reach of Grains Gill is called Ruddy Gill. The latter begins its life just below Allen Crags at 235084 and flows in a deep channel initially NW before abruptly changing direction to flow NNE through an area of haematite and therefore looking exceedingly red. This provides the stream's name. Shortly after emerging from its chasm Ruddy Gill becomes a more substantial Grains Gill which, on being joined by Styhead Gill, becomes the River Derwent near Stockly Bridge at 234111.

Grains Gill rises W Heron Pike-Great Rigg ridge at 355088 and joins Greenhead Gill at 350087 ...'river/valley fork'.

Grandsire large imposing fell to the E of School Knott and School Knott Tarn. Its rocky summit outcrop stands at 251m (823ft) but is not quite the highest point in this group of fells. This honour goes to an unnamed summit 2kms (1.25 miles) SE of Grandsire which is 5m (16ft) higher [432973] ...Grandsire, an archaic word for grandfather.

Grange off Fell Lane, Waberthwaite [123940].

Grange Crags N face Grange Fell [258176].

Grange Fell undulating fell area E of the Jaws of Borrowdale and SE Grange. Highest summit is Brund Fell 415m (1362ft) [264162]. See also **King's How**.

Grange Hotel, The see **The Grange Hotel**.

Grange House Bampton Grange [525184].

Grange-in-Borrowdale as opposed to Grange-over-Sands alongside Morecambe Bay. Attractive hamlet at the N end of the Jaws of Borrowdale. Off the B5289 and across the River Derwent. Consists of two churches, one C of E and early 19th century and the other a former Wesleyan Chapel (datestoned 1849) now a Methodist church, a farm with campsite, cottages, choice of accommodation ranging from B&B to country house hotel, places where refreshments can be obtained, a PO and toilets. The starting point for several walks including the High Spy-Maiden Moor-Cat Bells ridge, Grange Fell (including King's How) and a pleasant stroll along the Derwent. Both the Cumbria Way and the Allerdale Ramble pass close by. Nearby is Castle Crag (believed to have given Borrowdale its name), the Bowder Stone (a large boulder weighing nearly 2000 tons), the Lodore Falls (described succinctly by Southey in his poem *The Cascades of Lodore*). At Grange itself there is an attractive centuries old double arched bridge over the Derwent (much photographed and the subject of many paintings) with nearby roche moutonees (striated rocks worn smooth on one side and rough on the other as the result of glacial movement).

Grange received its own water supply in 1912 but it was another 44 years before it had its first grid-supplied electricity [252175] ...grange/granary/farm which many centuries ago belonged to Furness Abbey. Grange-over-Sands has the same meaning but in this case it belonged to Cartmel Priory.

Grange Lane connects the Loweswater to Mockerkin road with that from Loweswater to Mosser [118229].

Grasmere this charming village, encircled by hills and mountains is a mecca for tourists and fellwalkers. It lies in central Lakeland on the B5287 which leaves the Ambleside-Keswick road (A591) near Dove Cottage and returns to it opposite the Swan Hotel. William Wordsworth lived here from 1799-1813 and associations with him abound. Dove Cottage, his first home, Allan Bank his second, and the Old Rectory his last home in Grasmere before the family moved to Rydal Mount. Several other properties were the houses of friends and many are referred to in his poems or by Dorothy Wordsworth in her diary. The present Church of St Oswald (dedicated to a King of Northumbria) is believed to have been built on the site of a previous church. The oldest part dates from the 13th century and the churchyard contains the graves of William, Dorothy and Mary Wordsworth, other members of the Wordsworth family, and Hartley Coleridge (see also **St Oswald's**). Sarah Nelson's celebrated Grasmere Gingerbread Shop, built in 1687 as a schoolroom and in which Wordsworth taught, has been selling gingerbread continuously for over 150 years. At the Heaton Cooper Studio originals and prints by famous local artist, W Heaton Cooper (died 1995 aged 91), his father A H Cooper, and other members of this artistic family, can be viewed and purchased. There is a LDNP Information Centre (opened 1986) alongside Red Bank Road. Two traditional events held annually at Grasmere are the Grasmere Sports (see **Grasmere Sports**), and the Rushbearing Festival (see **Rushbearing**) [337075].

In 1953 a Fairy Firefly crash-landed on the sports field. Principal hotels are the Bridge House, Dale Lodge (Tweedies Bar), Goldrill Country House, Harwood, How Foot, Lancrigg Vegetarian Country House, Moss Grove (at one time Baldry's 'temperance hotel'), Oak Bank, Prince of Wales, Red Lion, Rothay Bank, Rothay Garden, Swan, Traveller's Rest, White Moss House and Wordsworth Hotel ...the village takes its name from the nearby lake. Several sources suggest that this was originally the 'water where swine (grise) drank', but both Ekwall and the EPNS state that the origin is 'the lake with the grassy shore'.

Grasmere Lake the picturesque lake, which gives its name to the adjoining village, is roughly 1.6kms (1 mile) in length and has a maximum breadth of just over 0.8kms (0.5 mile). It is situated at an altitude of 62m (203ft) and has a maximum depth of 21.5m (71ft). On its only island, where the Wordsworth family and friends often picnicked, stands an old barn restored by the National Trust. No power boats are allowed on the water but sailing is permitted and rowing boats can be hired at Wellfoot Boat Landing. This business, which includes a café, was begun in 1957 and was operated by Mr and Mrs Allonby for 43 years until its sale in 2000. Coarse fishing for pike, perch and eels is by permit from the WADAA. Judging by its change of name over the centuries Grasmere has risen in status. Called a 'pool' in the 14th century, it became a 'tarn' in the 16th and early 17th centuries, a 'water' in the late 17th and early 18th centuries and today full-bodied Grasmere, a lake [340065].

Grasmere Rushbearing see **Rushbearing**.

Grasmere Sports it is said that the sports were moved from the Ferry Inn, Bowness, Windermere, to Grasmere c1861 but that Grasmere already had its sports many centuries before then. However, as a continuous annual event Grasmere Sports is deemed to celebrate its centenary in 1952 and at least the date provides an anchor and a specific time to work from. The third move in Grasmere was to its present site after the Second World War.

Until 1998 the sports were held on the third Thursday after the first Monday in August. From 1998 the sports day was held on a Sunday, the Sunday following the third Thursday after the first Monday in August. To coincide with the 150th anniversary of the sports in 2002 a book, *Grasmere Sports - the first 150 years - a Compilation of Fact, Photographs, Documents and Opinion* by Roy Lomas, was published.

Grasmere Tea Gardens the Tea Gardens situated across the river from the church are still as popular in the season as they obviously were way back in 1905 when Fothergill of Grasmere took a photograph of them with their then clientelle [338073].

Grasmere Youth Hostels 1) Butterlip How. Large Victorian house sited alongside Easedale Road [337079]. 2) Thorney How. Originally a Lakeland farmhouse [332084].

Grasmere, Vale of see **Vale of Grasmere**.

Grasmoor large bulky imposing mountain to the E of Crummock Water. Highest summit in the group of fells between the Whinlatter and Newlands passes 852m (2795ft) [175203] ...although its plateau-like summit is grassy and certainly the fell name appears to describe it as such the present generally accepted interpretation is the gris(z)e moor or the wild boar moor.

Grasmoor End craggy end of Grasmoor overlooking Crummock Water [165202].

Grasmoor group of fells see Reference Section: **Heights**.

Grass Holme small island in Windermere [382925].

Grass Paddocks part of a 6.4kms (4 miles) wooded area owned by the NT along the E side of Coniston Water. The area also includes Crab Haws, part of Anna's Wood, Dales Wood, Dodgson Wood and Bailiff Wood. There are five car parks alongside the minor road [298913].

Grass Skiing a grass ski slope was in operation at Limefitt Caravan Park for many years but is not now in operation.

Grassgarth Ings with Hugill. A farm and beer shop in the early 19th century [442996] ...the grass 'enclosure'. The name Grassgarth dates from about the 10th century when a 'grass', an in-field area of approximately 8 acres, was deemed sufficient grazing pasture to support a horse and colt, three cows, 17 sheep and 20 geese. For its needs a small farm would possess 8 or 10 'grasses'.

Grassgarth Coppice Buttermere [176165].

Grassguards earlier Grass Gars. Isolated occupied farm approached by track from the Duddon valley. It is said that a dwelling had existed on its site for 700 years and for approximately 400 of them it had been inhabited by the Sawrey family. In his best seller *Plague Dogs* (1977) Richard Adams mentions it as the place where Rowf eventually caught up with Snitter. At that time he referred to it as 'a dead place now solitary, untenanted these many years' [224981]. Hereabouts 6,000 native trees and shrubs were formally planted in about 15 acres of land in 2002 by the Forestry Commission. Eventually 100 acres will generate itself and the wood will also be called Grassguards ...see **Grassgarth** above.

Grassguards Gill rises between Green Crag and Long Crag at 202985 and flows down past Grassguards to join the River Duddon at 228975.

Grassthwaite Howe cottages WSW Patterdale Hall. A large mansion which used to stand behind the present-day cottages was home for generations of the Dobson family who, at one time, owned most of Grisedale. Home of the Ullswater Foxhounds huntsman and the foxhounds are kennelled here [384160].

Grave Gill rises at the foot of Loft Crag, Great Langdale, at 280068 and joins Mickleden Beck at 275060. Along with nearby Skull Gill suggests a connection with death in one form or another.

Gray Beck rises between Harrot and Embleton High Common at 163277 but, according to the OS map, ceases at 145275 before reaching the River Cocker?

Gray Borrans ancient cairns WNW Gray Crag [122063].

Gray Bull a 2.7m (9ft) high granite boulder NNE Wasdale Pike and ESE Sleddale Pike. [540092] ...'bull' signifies a large sized boulder.

Gray Crag a long narrow ridge running 2kms (1.25 miles) NNW from Thornthwaite Crag culminates in Gray Crag and a steep descent by path to the Hayeswater track above Wath Bridge near Hartsop. Overlooks Threshthwaite Cove and Pasture Beck to the W and Hayeswater Gill and Hayeswater to the E with precipitous descents on both flanks. Two summits, the lower one near the N end of the ridge is 699m (2293ft) [428117], and the higher one, mid-way between that and Thornthwaite Crag, is 710m (2329ft) [430110].

Gray Crag S slope Lank Rigg below Boat How [088100].

Gray Crag W summit of Buckbarrow on the Seatallan ridge [125062].

Gray Stone S Green Crag [198978].

Graymains alongside the A595 2.8kms (1.75 miles) N Waberthwaite [113957].

Grayson Side off the B5292 near its junction with the A66 [134290].

Graystones peak in the Lord's Seat Group. E Kirk Fell. Two summits shown, one at 456m (1496ft) [178264] and the other slightly N at 454m (1489ft) [178266].

Graythwaite off the Loweswater to Mockerkin road [116232].

Graythwaite Hall W Windermere, alongside the Newby Bridge-Hawkshead road. Sometimes referred to as High Hall to differentiate it from nearby Low Graythwaite Hall. An Elizabethan building built by the Sandys family and home of the family for four centuries and still a Sandy residence. Considerable alterations in the 19th century. The house is not open to the public but the garden, designed initially by Thomas Mawson, is open during the season [371913].

Graythwaite Old Hall see Low Graythwaite Hall.

Graythwaite Wood ENE Graythwaite alongside Whittern Gill [119233].

Great Arming How Birker Moor. Little Arming How to its SW [184993].

Great Bank prominent crags SE Irton Fell ridge and overlooking Miterdale 329m (1079ft) [144019].

Great Barn E minor road, A66-Matterdale End. Alongside Nabend-Lowthwaite road [413244].

Great Barrow Boot, Eskdale. Spot height at 232m (761ft) [187017].

Great Bay head of Derwentwater [258190].

Great Birkhouse Hill/Little Birkhouse Hill Great Birkhouse Hill is WNW Haweswater Dam at 493163 and Little Birkhouse Hill to the N of Great Birkhouse Hill at 494165. According to the OS map Great Birkhouse is lower than Little Birkhouse, the former being C380m (1247ft) and the latter C400m (C1312ft) ...obviously size is the governing factor.

Great Borne mountain N of Ennerdale Water and above Floutern Tarn and Pass. Trig. point at 616m (2021ft) [124164] ...possibly the fell above the great stream this being the River Liza/Ennerdale Water. See also **Herdus**.

Great Brathay alongside the Drunken Duck Inn-B5286 road [355015].

Great Carrs mountain a short distance by path from Swirl How on the Coniston Old Man ridge but as the crow flies divided by the deep hollow of Broad Slack. In October 1944, a Halifax bomber LL505 'S' for Sugar, on a training flight from RAF Topcliffe, York, crashed on Great Carrs killing all 8 crew members. Part of the wreckage can still be seen in Broad Slack. Two engines were recovered in 1997 and as a temporary measure before installation in a new village museum in Coniston, one was placed in Coniston churchyard. Another was taken to a museum down south. A simple wooden cross built into a cairn comprising parts of the wrecked aircraft provides a memorial to the tragedy 785m (2575ft) [270009] ...Carr from 'kjarr' can refer to either a wood or swamp/marsh and both Great and Little Carrs do lie above Wet Side Edge. However, according to W G Collingwood the 'Carrs' cannot be explained as Norse 'kjarr' but being castle-like rock may be from the Welsh 'caer'.

Great Castle How WNW Little Castle How [308079] ...rocky knoll which appears to resemble a collapsed castle or fortification.

Great Castle How Tarns two attractive shallow tarns alongside the path at the foot of Great Castle How [305077/306077].

Great Cobble lies slightly N of Black Crag, Black Fell ...great summit [341018].

Great Coppice Grizedale Forest Park [352962].

Great Coppice S River Irt. High and Low Coppice nearby [120035].

Great Cove ESE Long Top, Crinkle Crags [254046].

Great Cove below Little Gowder Crag and Tewit How. Through it flows the infant Deep Gill on its journey down to Ennerdale [143115].

Great Crosthwaite see **Crosthwaite**.

Great Crag Birker Moor C320 (C1050ft) [187978].

Great Crag E Rosthwaite. WNW head of Dock Tarn [268147].

Great Dodd Helvellyn range. N Sticks Pass. NNE Watson's Dodd, ESE Calfhow Pike and SSE Clough Head. Principally a grassy summit with some summit rocks and a three-sided stone shelter. Highest of the four Helvellyn Dodds 857m (2812ft). In August 1943, an Avro Anson crashed near its summit killing its pilot. In 1783 was just Dod Fell [342206] ...the great bare rounded summit.

Great Door the path from Overbeck Bridge to the summit of Yewbarrow passes between Dropping Crag and Bell Rib before entering a huge cleft (Great Door) prior to attaining the ridge. There is also a Dore Head to the N of Yewbarrow [171078].

Great End the great northern end of the Scafell massif but also a mountain in its own right. Its near precipitous face overlooks Sty Head/Styhead Tarn, Sprinkling Tarn and Ruddy and Grains Gills. This impressive buttress is riven by several gullies of varying degrees of difficulty for walkers and scramblers and, in winter, ice climbers. Those gullies named are Central, Cust's, Skew Gill and South East Gully (formerly Robinson's Gully) while to the W are the ravines of Grainy Gills, Greta Gill and Piers Gill. From its domed summit Scafell Pike is only 2kms (1.25 miles) initially S then SW. In 1959 a minor neolithic axe factory was discovered on the summit 910m (2986ft) [227085].

Great Gable affectionally known as just 'Gable'. An impressive mountain at the head of Wasdale and NW Sty Head. Extremely popular with walkers, scramblers and climbers. The latter are particularly well catered for by the Great Napes including Napes Needle, Kern Knotts and Gable Crag. Usually approached by walkers via the Tourist Route (known as the Breast Route). In 1996 the NT received the Upland Path Award for its repair work on this badly-eroded path. There are, however, several other routes to its summit. In 1923 the Fell and Rock Climbing Club purchased Great Gable as part of 1184 acres of land thereabouts. Subsequently they gave the land to the NT as a memorial to club members killed in the First World War. The following year a bronze memorial was unveiled to the 20 members killed and each Remembrance Sunday a well-attended simple service is held on the summit and wreathes and poppies are placed at the foot of the memorial. Great Gable is the central feature of the Lake District National Park logo. Its summit just fails by 15.5m (51ft) to achieve 914m (3000ft) like its near neighbours Scafell, Scafell Pike, Broad Crag and Ill Crag 899m (2949ft) [211103] ...Mykelgavel in the l4th century. The present name has the same meaning and is an appropriate description of it as seen from certain viewpoints - the great gable (end).

Great Gable rocky outcrop NE Dale Head. Much lower and smaller than its namesake at the head of Wasdale [226157].

Great Gable group of fells see Reference Section: **Heights**.

Great Gill rises Hardknott Tarns at 234029 and joins the River Esk at 225030.

Great Gill rises Cockley Moss at 167951. Joined by Little Gill before entering Woodend Pool at 173966.

Great Gill Head Crag head of Great Gill, Hardknott [230030].

Great Grain Gill rises E slope Branstree at 483100 and joins Mosedale Beck at 499095 ...the great river fork gill. Two lengthy streams combine to form the gill.

Great Grain Gill rises Whin Rigg at 156036 and joins Robin Gill at 162031.

Great Green Hows Tarn see **Green Hows Tarn/Great Green Hows Tarn**.

Great Hartbarrow Cartmel Fell. Before Arthur Ransome and his wife moved to Low Ludderburn they lodged at Great Hartbarrow [408906].

Great Hill above Rigg Wood, E side Coniston Water [307922].

Great Hollow Rosthwaite Fell. Holds several small tarns [258116].

Great Horse Crag Wrynose Fell. Below Little Horse Crag and overlooking the road over Wrynose Pass [285035] ...Great and Little obviously refer to the actual size of the crags.

Great How S Little Langdale, W A593, Skelwith Bridge-Coniston road 211m (692ft) [322026] ...great hill. Other noted Great How(e)s are Great How, Eskdale Fell 522m (1713ft), Great Howe above Longsleddale 494m (1621ft) and Great How, overlooking Thirlmere 335m (1099ft). See below.

Great How well-wooded knoll and excellent viewpoint to the W of the A591 and E Thirlmere. Faces the impressive Falcon Crag across the foot of the reservoir 335m (l099ft) [314188].

Great How Eskdale. Trig. point at 522m (1713ft) [197040].

Great How Crags a subsidiary height on the Swirl How ridge with its steep craggy face overlooking Levers Water [276999].

Great How Tarns see **Eskdale Fell**.

Great Howe Longsleddale. Grey Crag lies to its NE. Spot height at 494m (1621ft) [489064]. A Manchester Corporation Waterworks survey post here and another nearby on Brock Crag, see also **Pillars** ...great hill.

Great Intake area of 'intake land' WNW Beacon Tarn between the A593 and Yewdale Fell Side [312996].

Great Intake large intake area to the E of the Grizedale-Satterthwaite road [343938].

Great Intake Low Fell 397m (1302ft) [302022].

Great Intake adjoining Little Intake. Two principal heights, one at 89m (292ft) and the higher at 102m (335ft) [253907].

Great Knott Satterthwaite. SSE Little Knott [334917].

Great Knott W Pike o'Blisco. N Cold Pike 696m (2283ft) [260043].

Great Knott Bassenthwaite Common 445m (1460ft) [248299].

Great Knott E Low Tarn, SW Dore Head [170093].

Great Lad Crag large crag overlooking Nether Beck from the W. Little Lad Crag is 0.8kms (0.5 mile) higher up the valley [148093].

Great Ladstones/Little Ladstones Great Ladstones is just N of Bleak Hill and Little Ladstones lies to the NE Great Ladstones. Great Ladstones C440 (1444ft) [532124], Little Ladstones C390 (C1280ft) [535126] ...Lad (and sometimes Boy) is often given to particular stones or boulders eg Lambert Lad (a boundary stone), Ladthwaite, Lad Crags.

Great Langdale Great, as opposed to its southerly and shorter neighbour Little Langdale.

Claimed to be the most popular valley in the Lake District. Motorists can complete an impressive round by travelling to the head of the valley and taking the road by Blea Tarn over to Little Langdale and then back to Ambleside. Walkers and scramblers routes abound and climbers are well catered for by the buttresses of the Langdale Pikes, Gimmer Crag, the huge cliff of Pavey Ark, Raven Crag and Scout Crag. From Skelwith Bridge where the road from Ambleside divides, one road going to Coniston and the other, the B5343, up Great Langdale, the road passes the two villages of Elterwater and Chapel Stile. Shortly after leaving Chapel Stile the road bears left and the Langdale Pikes and Pavey Ark suddenly and dramatically appear; a popular viewpoint for both artists and photographers. At the head of the valley high up above Mickleden and alongside the steep scree slope descending from Pike o' Stickle, Neolithic man established a stone axe factory. To the archaeologist a major find but surprisingly considering the fact that it had been there for thousands of years it was not discovered until 1947 [312055] ...the great long valley.

Great Langdale Beck from the confluence of two substantial headstreams, Oxendale and Mickleden Becks, at 280060 Great Langdale Beck flows on down the valley to join Elter Water. On its journey it is swelled by Redacre Gill, Dungeon Ghyll, Stickle Gill (Mill Gill), Scale Gill, Robin Gill, Baysbrown Pool and Megs Gill.

Great Meldrum W Ullswater. WNW Swinburn's Park over Kirksty Brow 437m (1434ft) [415223].

Great Mell Fell isolated well-rounded hill showing its steepest side to the NNW and NW and partly clothed by trees. Lies between the A5091 and the minor road, A66-Matterdale End. Here the rocks have formed a conglomerate (coarse-grained sedimentary rock consisting of rounded fragments of rock embedded in a finer matrix, in this case, sand). The conglomerate beds in both Great Mell and Little Mell are 244-274m (800-900ft) thick. At its foot there is a disused rifle range 537m (1762ft). Given to the National Trust by the Treasury in 1968 [397254] ...the great 'bare hill'. Great Mell Fell and Little Mell Fell can be classed as outlying sentinels of the Helvellyn range.

Great Moss between the River Esk and High/Low Gait Crags. Once occupied by a shallow lake and now an extremely marshy area [223053].

Greatmoss Tarn Great Moss [224055].

Great Napes large rocky tower on the S slope of Great Gable between Little Hell Gate and Great Hell Gate. Several gullies, ridges and Napes Needle for climbers to hone their skills [210100].

Great Oaks Wood W shore Windermere [375902].

Great Ore Gate alongside Cunsey Beck [373937]. See also **The Forge**.

Great Paddy Crag just S of Buck Barrow 532m (1745ft) [150909].

Great Rigg on ridge SSW Fairfield. Usually climbed as part of the Fairfield Horseshoe. Actual summit is called Greatrigg Man 766m (2513ft) [356104].

Great Round How crags between Hay Stacks and Grey Knotts. Little Round How to their N, 554m (1818ft) [207128].

Great Saddle Crag Shap Fells. N Little Saddle Crag, WNW Wasdale Pike C560 (C1837) [526087].

Great Scoat Fell see **Scoat Fell**.

Great Spring afforested area at the foot of Underbarrow (Scout) Scar [483912] ...great plantation.

Great Spring E Dale Park valley [357927].

Great Spring Wood between Gowan Bank Farm and Fairbank Farm [449980].

Great Stickle Dunnerdale Fells. Trig. point at 305m (1001ft) at 212916. Not to be confused with the higher Stickle Pike to its N or the even higher Pike of Stickle, Langdale.

Great Stone of Blakeley large boulder E of Kinniside Stone Circle and alongside the upper reach of Mere Beck [065141].

Great Tongue tongue of land between Little Tongue Gill and Tongue Gill [343103].

Great Tower Plantation alongside the A592. N Birks Road. Extensive woodland area presented to the Boy Scouts Association in 1936 and subsequently opened as a national Scouts camping ground with wood and lake frontage [392915].

Great Whinscale rocky outcrop, Birker Fell, 425m (1394ft) [198990] ...shelter in the whin/gorse.

Great Wood alongside Bleaberry Hill. W High Dale Park [351934].

Great Wood Duddon valley. Path from Birks Bridge passes through the wood to Birks where one route traverses Dunnerdale Forest to Grassguards while another ascends to Harter Fell [233992].

Great Wood Waberthwaite. W A595 [102928].

Great Wood Buttermere [171176].

Great Wood extensive afforested area between Walla Crag and Derwent Water and alongside the Borrowdale Road. Acquired by the NT in 1969 and there is a substantial car park here. Cat Gill flows alongside its S boundary [271213].

Great Worm Crag Birker Fell, 427m (1401ft) [194969].

Great Yarlside head of Wasdale and near Little Yarlside which is 69m (226ft) lower. The trig. point alongside the summit is unusual in that it is a circular metal plate set into the ground as opposed to being inserted into the top of a pillar. Similar ones are to be found on Branstree, Seat Robert and on Hallsfell Top, Blencathra. Spot-height at 585m (1919ft) but contour nearby at C590m (C1936ft) [524077] ...Great Earl's seat.

Greatbank Coppice Miterdale. Below Great Bank [147016].

Greatend Crag precipitous N face of King's How, Grange Fell [259170].

Greathall Gill rises in deep gully below Whin Rigg at the SW end of the ridge and screes at 144031. Drops steeply down to join the River Irt at 143038 near its outflow from Wastwater ...the great hall is Wasdale Hall near the foot of the gill.

Greathead Crag above Easedale Tarn [310092].

Greathow Wood slopes Great How [314188]

Greatrigg Mann see **Great Rigg**.

Greaves off the minor road from Dacre to Sparket [445260].

Greaves Beck rises 435239 and joins Dacre Beck at 448263. 200 years ago it was Greeves Beck.

Greaves Ground off the A593, SW Torver [265923].

Green alongside B5322 0.8kms (0.5 mile) N of junction with A591 [319197].

Green, George & Sarah, tragedy see **Blea Rigg**.

Green Bank Broughton Mills [220908].

Green Bank Borrowdale. At the entrance to Troutdale [261180].

Green Burn farthest headstream rises at 306108. Flows down through Greenburn Bottom and Greenburn valley to meet Raise Beck at 332096 and become the River Rothay. Similar to nearby Wyth Burn in that it appears to have what is unusual for Lakeland streams, a Scottish derivation. However, this is not so as the 'burn' is from the OE 'burna'. Similarly, there are four apparent Scottish glens alongside and near Ullswater:- Glenamara, Glencoyne, Glenridding and Caiston Glen. The derivation of these, according to the English

Place Name Society, is from the Welsh 'glyn'.

Green Close alongside the minor road from Hutton to A66-Matterdale End road [425265].

Green Comb ravine down which flows Cat Gills [294117].

Green Combe S Dock Tarn [274141].

Green Cove W Looking Stead. Alongside the ridge to Pillar [184119].

Green Crag alongside the upper Esk [224044].

Green Crag W face Ill Crag overlooking the head of Little Narrowcove [219074].

Green Crag Wrynose Fell [279033].

Green Crag highest of several serrated peaks on Birker Fell and a fine viewpoint, 489m (1604ft) [200983].

Green Crag Hay Stacks ridge 528m (1732ft) [202131].

Green Crags E Little Scoat Fell. Overlook the head of Mosedale [167114].

Green Crook between Pow Beck and the R Lowther [514195].

Green Farm Wet Sleddale [551120].

Green Gable separated from its taller neighbour Great Gable by the col, Windy Gap, at the top of Aaron Slack. Principally green as its name implies but with much scree on the slope facing Great Gable. In 1943 an Avro Anson crashed on Green Gable killing its 2 crew members, 801m (2628ft) [215017].

Green Haw Top Seathwaite Fells. W slope Dow Crag [256978].

Green Hill between Smithy Hill and Ghyll Head Road, 161m (528ft) [405920].

Green Hill in National Trust Gowbarrow Park. Overlooks Ullswater [410208].

Green Hill W Staveley to Crook road [466955].

Green Hill E Bassenthwaite Lake [229293].

Green Hole alongside the confluence of Lingcove Beck and Yeastyrigg Gill [238056].

Green Hole between Shelter Crags and Buscoe Sike [256055].

Green House Rosgill. E bank River Lowther [535166].

Green How alongside Dockray-Dowthwaitehead road [388219].

Green How E Low Close, Dunnerdale and W Sheep Crag [248001].

Green How SE Cockley Beck [257008].

Green How W Scafell. On grassy slope above Rakehead Crag. A path up Scafell from the head of Wastwater passes alongside it. This particular route was much favoured by the Victorians because it was principally over grass. Today the path is not as popular and considered tame although tedious [196067].

Green How W River Duddon (204958).

Green How Torver Low Common, 185m (607ft) [272924].

Green How Birker Moor. SW Stanley Force 200m (656ft) [172992].

Green How Birker Moor. E Ellerbeck and Whincop Bridges, C270m (C886ft) [184988].

Green Howe Great Langdale [301067].

Green Hows Tarn/Great Green Hows Tarn Two artificial waters on the Graythwaite Estate. Green Hows, also known as High Tarn, lies just off the Graythwaite-Thwaite Head road [362906]. Great Green Hows Tarn lies approximately 0.5kms (0.3 mile) S of Green Hows Tarn and 0.8kms (0.5mile) N of Finsthwaite High Dam [360900]. Both are private and there is no public access.

Green Lonning lane (lonning) connecting Wythop Mill with Embleton [172290].

Green Mire marshy area head of Bassenthwaite Lake. Spot height at 69m (226ft) [230264].

Green Owlett between lower reaches of Tailbert Gill and Swindale Beck [531152] ...possibly the grassy area frequented by owls or young owls (owlets).

Green Pikes NNW Pikes (236951).

Green Quarter during the Border wars with Scotland Kentmere was subjected to Border tenure. It was divided into Quarters namely Crag, Green, Hallowbank and West Wr(e)ay each further divided into holdings. From each holding a fighting man was to be provided to defend against the Scots. Green Quarter lies to the E of Kentmere village [468036].

Green Quarter Fell grassy height overlooking Kentmere from the E. Bridleways from Staveley and Kentmere to Longsleddale, traverse it and nearby Cocklaw Fell. Skeggles Water nearby [474036]. See also **Hollow Moor**.

Green Rigg alongside the A593 [268931].

Green Rigg Bank N Hummer Lane and Green Rigg [269936].

Green Side steep grassy slope and crags overlooking Sticks Pass and Gill and leading to the summit of White Stones (see also White Stones). The nearby former Greenside Mine took its name from it [352185].

Green Tongue E Bowfell. Grassy tongue of land between Rossett Gill and Grunting Gill and dropping down to Mickleden Beck [258068].

Green Trees alongside the Abbeygate Bridge to the A5086 road. Coppice nearby [126278].

Green Tuft Island Windermere [374020].

Green Wood Loweswater. Adjoining Flass Wood [145201].

Green Yew Winster [418933].

Greenah E minor road, A66-Matterdale End. Off minor road, Nabend-Lowthwaite [414249] ...green hill.

Greenah Crag Farm N A66. Adjacent Greenah Moss [397284].

Greenah Moss N A66. NNE Troutbeck [394281].

Greenbank farm, Little Langdale. Former home of Lanty Slee, notorious whisky smuggler. He died there in 1878 [320032].

Greenbank N slope Gowbarrow Fell. Alongside minor road connecting A5091 with Matterdale Rigg-A592 road [409227].

Greenbank Farm alongside track from A592 to Wall End, Deepdale [398147].

Greenbank Farm between the A5074 and minor road, A5074-Crosthwaite [424923].

Greenbank Farm off the A5091 at Troutbeck [386257].

Greenburn valley down which flows Greenburn Beck [288023]. Up the valley is Greenburn Reservoir/Tarn (now disused) but constructed to provide water power for the copper mine lower down the valley. This, Greenburn Mine, also known as Coniston or Great Coniston Mine, mainly dates from around 1845 and finally closed in 1917. Several ruined buildings including the waterwheel pit and engine house and spoil heaps can still be seen at 290022. A wooden bridge enabling walkers to cross Greenburn Beck even when the latter is in spate was constructed in the summer of 1998.

Greenburn Beck farthest headstream rises just below top of Broad Slack at 273008 and flows down through Greenburn Reservoir and subsequently into Little Langdale Tarn. On its journey it is joined by named streams, High Keld Gill, Low Keld Gill and Birk Fell Gill.

Greenburn Beck rises Broad Slack below Great Carrs at 272008 and flows down Greenburn to enter Little Langdale Tarn at 307031. See also **Greenburn**.

Greenburn Bottom part of the valley through which the Green Burn flows [317106]. The OS suggests that alongside the valley at 315110 lies the centre of the Lake District.

Wainwright, however, suggests that the central point is slightly WNW on Ullscarf.

Greenburn Mine see **Greenburn**.

Greenburn Reservoir/Tarn see **Greenburn**.

Greenburn Valley narrow valley which drops down from Greenburn Bottom between the ridge terminating in Helm Crag and that of Steel Fell. Through it flows the Green Burn on its way to join Raise Beck and become the start of the River Rothay.

Greencombe Breast steep slope SE Ullscarf and overlooking the Wyth Burn [299116].

Greencove Wyke SE of the summit of Scafell. From its head one arm of How Beck drops down to join the Esk [211060].

Greendale community near the foot of Greendale Gill [144056].

Greendale Gill rises Greendale Tarn at 147073. Bifurcates near Greendale Farm at 143056 from where Cinderdale Beck drops down to join the River Irt 127038 and Countess Beck joins Wastwater at 152054.

Greendale Tarn sizeable tarn in glaciated hanging valley between the crags of Middle Fell and the slope of Seatallan. Contains brown trout, C410m (C1345ft) [147074].

Greengable Crag NW Green Gable summit [213109].

Greengarth Hall W of Irton Church and on the boundary of the LDNP. For many years housed the Cumbria Directorate of NIREX and was a hostel for workers at Sellafield. Today the Greengarth Business Park [080006].

Greengate near Haweswater Beck and alongside minor road, Bampton Grange to Walmgate Foot [520177].

Greengate Wood alongside the Santon Bridge to Nether Wasdale road [112023].

Greengill Tongue tongue of land between Comb Beck and Stinking Gill [076133].

Greengrove Folds two sheepfolds below Lingmell End and alongside Lingmell Gill [449090].

Greenhead Kentmere [455045].

Greenhead WSW Little Mell Fell. Off minor road, Matterdale Rigg-A592 [413236].

Greenhead Gill rises Great Rigg at 354098. Joined by Grains Gill and Rowantree Gill before meeting the River Rothay at 339080. Here "Besides the boisterous brook of Greenhead Ghyll" was the sheepfold where Wordsworth spent some time composing his lengthy poem *Michael*. Even in Wordsworth's time Dorothy recorded that the "sheepfold is falling away." Traditionally it is said to be ruins alongside the right bank of the gill after the aqueduct and just round a substantial left hand bend. However, the exact location has not been ascertained with any degree of certainty. The gill is of great interest to the mining antiquarian for up it are the remains of an Elizabethan lead mine closed in 1573. This is scheduled as an ancient monument and is also classed as one of the few relatively-undisturbed 16th century lead mines in Britain.

Greenhole Crags above Green Hole [235058].

Greenhow Crags overlook Green Combe and Cat Gills from the W [294114].

Greenhow End precipitous projection into the head of Deepdale which in effect splits the dale into two with Link Cove and Hart Crag to the S and Cawk Cove, Sleet Cove, Fairfield Crags, and Cofa Pike to the N. More craggy than its name suggests [371121].

Greenhow Gill rises Ullscarf at 292120. Joined by Mere Gill at 281121 and the combined watercourse joins Greenup Gill at 280122.

Greenhow Knott on the N slope of Seathwaite Fell near Stockley Bridge [231108].

Greenlands off the minor road from the A595 to Santon [090011].

Greenriggs just S of the Kendal to Underbarrow road and on the outskirts of

Underbarrow village. At one time called Thorns Villa (still shown as such on the OS map), and earlier Thorns or Thornes. At least 360 years old. Between 1970 and 1989 adopted the name Greenriggs (the name Thorns Villa is still on the metal garden gate) and became a country house hotel and restaurant. Recently turned into several dwellings. New Field House, detached property alongside, was originally designed as staff accommodation and built early 1980s, High and Low Greenriggs nearby [475918].

Greenriggs Head Plantation southern end of Lowther Park. Nearby is West Greenriggs Plantation and Back Greenriggs [544202]

Greenriggs Sike rises southern end of Lowther Park at 540205. Becomes Bessy Gill at 543220 and this joins the R Leith at 552217.

Greenrow E of the minor road, A66-Matterdale End. Alongside Nabend-Lowthwaite road [413244].

Greenside Mine Glenridding. Originally one of the largest lead mines in England and the largest in the Lake district. Probably discovered in the middle of the 17th century although mining to a smaller degree could have taken place centuries earlier. Began what can be termed modern-day production with the formation of the Greenside Mining Co in 1820. This firm continued extracting lead, and to a much lesser degree silver, until 1962 when the mine, which went over l.6kms (l mile) into the mountainside and reached a maximum depth of 427m (1400ft), was closed and sealed. At one time the company employed 150 men and owned 50 cottages in and around Glenridding. In July 1952, four men were killed in a fire at the mine. Much has been done over the years to stabilise, landscape and turf the spoil heaps. Several of the old mine buildings have been put to good use, one as a YHA Hostel and others as hostels. A pony track and paths from Glenridding village to the summit of Helvellyn pass the former mine building and workings. Acquired by the LDNP Authority in 1963 and scheduled as an ancient monument [363178].

Greenside Road former miners' road from Glenridding village to Greenside Mine. [377172].

Greenthwaite adjoining Coldfell Road [065145].

Greenup slope of Narrow Moor to the N of Blea Crag [239173].

Greenup Edge lowest section of a high level ridge between High Raise and Ullscarf and at the head of Wythburn and Far Easedale valleys and Greenup Gill. A popular walkers path between Borrowdale and Grasmere traverses the col as does the well-known Coast-to-Coast route C610 (C2001ft) [286106] ...the edge/ridge above the green valley, the latter being the valley down which flows Greenup Gill.

Greenup Gill its farthest tributary rises just below Greenup Edge at 283104. Subsequently Black Gills and several unnamed streams combine to become Greenup Gill which is enlarged by Footmoorgate Gill at 281120 and the combined Greenhow and Mere Gills at 280122. Joins with Langstrath Beck at 274130 to become Stonethwaite Beck.

Greenup Sikes several streams rise on Greenup with principal ones at 241175 and 241173. All combine and are joined by other streams to become Ellers Beck which joins the River Derwent at 257183.

Greta Bank Farm Keswick. Near Windebrowe and Calvert's Bridge [272241].

Greta Gill farthest headstream rises between Great End and Broad Crag at 224081 and joins Piers Gill at 214087 to become Lingmell Beck ...earlier shown as Girta Gill possibly because its waterfall is 'girter' (greater) than falls on nearby streams.

Greta Hall Keswick. Remodelled by William Johnson, a wealthy carrier, as a mansion in 1799-1800. A three-storey building which bears two plaques one recording that Samuel

Taylor Coleridge lived here from 1800-3 (before he upped and left his family and went off on his wanderings) and the other that Robert Southey and family were resident from 1805-43. Several tenants later it was purchased by Canon Rawnsley in 1909 who rented it to Keswick School. Purchased by the school governors in 1921 and today used as part of Keswick School [265237].

Greta Hamlet Keswick. Principally consists of a built-up area, Greta Hall and the Cumberland Pencil Co. works and museum [265238].

Greta, River see **River Greta**.

Grey Crag E Deepdale Hause [363126].

Grey Crag E of Grasmere and slightly W of Alcock Tarn which it overlooks, 350m (1150ft) [348076].

Grey Crag highest point of Sleddale Fell and, along with nearby Harrop Pike, the most easterly of the Lakeland mountains. Grey Crag is 638m (2093ft) [497072].

Grey Crag lower Whelp Side overlooking Thirlmere [329145].

Grey Crag Place Fell. Overlooks Ullswater [400172].

Grey Crag Coniston Fells. Above Levers Water Beck [282987].

Grey Crag High Stile. Summit at 807m (2648ft) [170148].

Grey Crags Little Man, Skiddaw [264274].

Grey Friar bulky dome-like mountain with its allegance to the Duddon. Approximately 1.6kms (1 mile) via Fairfield from Swirl How. A rock on its summit is shaped like the Matterhorn and is appropriately titled 'Matterhorn Rock' 770m (2526ft) [260004] ...Ekwall in his *The Place Names of Lancashire* simply states "Grey Friar is self-explaining". Possibly this means that it takes its name from the grey summit rocks which look like a selection of Grey Friar monks.

Grey Knotts on the Honister Hause-Brandreth-Green Gable ridge 697m (2287ft) [217126].

Grey Stone large glacial boulder alongside Mere Beck, Torver Low Common [277922].

Grey Stones Hindscarth [218166].

Greycrag Tarn today consists of several shallow pools on a very marshy col between Tarn Crag and Grey Crag (Sleddale Fell). At one time called Braban Tarn after the Kendal Parish family of Brab(b)an. Galeforth Gill and Little Mosedale Beck both rise in this marshy area, the former flowing SSW to meet the River Sprint in Longsleddale, and the latter flowing initially NE before joining Mosedale Beck, 595m (1952ft) [492076].

Griddle How between the A593 and the old road from Hawkshead-High Cross [328014] ...flat-topped like an oven griddle.

Grigg Hall Lane Underbarrow. Connects Brigsteer to Underbarrow road with that from Underbarrow to Crosthwaite (B5284) [468913] ...from local surname Grigg. Alongside are High and Low Gregg Halls.

Grigghall Bridge carries the Underbarrow-Crosthwaite road over Chapel Beck near the latter's confluence with Underbarrow Beck [465918] ...named from the local family of Grigg. Nearby are High and Low Gregg Halls. According to the EPNS in their *Place Names of Westmorland* Gregg in this case is a corruption of Grigg.

Grigghall Lane Underbarrow. Track running SW from Low Gregg Hall [462911].

Grike fell SSW of the foot of Ennerdale Water and between Crag Fell and Heckbarley. A very large cairn on its summit has provided the local name for the fell, Stone Man. Deep ravines split its N face 488m (1601ft) [085141] ...'grike'is a northern dialect word for cleft/deep ravine.

Grike Ennerdale [081155] ...see previous entry.

Grim Crag/Grimcrag E Birker Fell road and Birkhouse Farm. 44 acres acquired by the NT in 1956 and a further 11 acres purchased through Lake District Funds in 1986. Grimcrag Farm is now a ruin [197947].

Grimcrag Bridge carries the track from the Birker Fell road to Brighouse Farm over Crosby Gill (196944).

Grime Pit alongside the bridleway, Low Dale Park-Hazel Seat [353916].

Grisedale scenic dale running SW from the head of Ullswater to Grisedale Hause. In its middle and upper reaches impressive rock scenery of St Sunday Crag, Cofa Pike and Fairfield on the SE and Striding Edge, Falcon Crag, Eagle Crag, Tarn Crag and Dollywaggon Pike to the NW. Traversed by a former pony track linking Patterdale to Grasmere [370150]. In Broomhill Plantation is the site of an ancient settlement [367149] ...valley of the wild boar/pig.

Grisedale Beck rises Grisedale Tarn at 352122. Joined by Ruthwaite Beck, Nethermostcove Beck and Hag Beck before meeting Goldrill Beck at 395164 shortly before the latter joins Ullswater.

Grisedale Bridge Patterdale. Carries the A592 over Grisedale Beck [390160].

Grisedale Brow overlooks Grisedale [365153].

Grisedale Forest Grisedale, SW Ullswater. Not to be confused with Grizedale Forest, E Coniston Water. Today it is a forest in name only but in medieval times it was a considerable afforested area belonging to the Barony of Kendal. Grisedale means the dale of the wild boar/pig and the hunting of this provided much sport in those days. The forest was subsequently cut down to provide more grazing for sheep, fuel, building material or charcoal, and the cleared land ultimately passed into the hands of tenants or settlers who established farmsteads [356135].

Grisedale Gill Whinlatter. Rises below Grisedale Pike at 202227. Joined by Sanderson Gill at 208242. Flows under Comb Bridge which carries the B5292 over Comb Beck then under Chapelbeck Bridge and becomes Chapel Beck which flows past the church (chapel) of St Mary and enters Newlands Beck at 232260.

Grisedale Hause see **Grisedale Pass**.

Grisedale Pass from Grasmere to Patterdale 11.3kms (7 miles). Rises to Grisedale Hause [349117], the col linking Seat Sandal with Fairfield. The summit of the pass is 588m (1929ft).

Grisedale Pike graceful triangular peak, the highest summit on the Whiteside, Hopegill Head, Grisedale Pike, Sleet How, Kinn ridge. Although usually climbed from Braithwaite over Kinn and Sleet How the most direct route is from the car park in Hospital Plantation and over Hobcarten End. The pike's S face overlooking Coledale is steep and craggy with the Force Crag Mine at its foot 791m (2595ft) [199226] ...peak above the valley where pigs were grazed.

Grisedale Tarn N of Grisedale Hause and W of the Grisedale Pass path between Grasmere and Patterdale. Situated at a height of 539m (1768ft) it is one of the deepest tarns with a maximum depth of 35m (115ft). Free fishing for trout, perch, and eels. Legend has it that the crown of Dunmail, King of Strathclyde, was thrown into the waters where it lies to this day. A short distance below its foot and within yards of where the Grisedale Pass path meets the start of the zig zag path up the Dollywaggon screes stands the Brothers Parting Stone [353123]. This commemorates the last meeting of William Wordsworth and his brother John in 1800. Years later John's ship sank with no survivors. The rock was inscribed in 1888 at the behest of Canon Rawnsley, co-founder of the National Trust, and on it are 8 lines of the *Elegiac Verses, In Memory of My Brother, John Wordsworth* written by William after the loss of his brother [350120]. Both William Wordsworth and his brother John often fished for trout in Grisedale Tarn.

Grizedale a narrow valley traversed by the road from Hawkshead through Satterthwaite to Ulverston. Also, hamlet in the dale approximately 4.8kms (3 miles) from Hawkshead. Grizedale Forest Park Visitor and Wildlife Centre, former Theatre in the Forest and Grizedale Lodge Hotel (restaurant in the forest) here [336943] ...valley of the pigs.

Grizedale Beck rises High Man Tarn, Grizedale Forest, at 329965. Becomes Force Beck after dropping over Force Falls, Force Mills. Met by Ashes Beck/Dale Park Beck and Bell Beck near Rusland and takes the name Rusland Pool. This joins the River Leven near Haverthwaite.

Grizedale Forest Park a large forest area lying between Coniston Water on its W and the Hawkshead-Newby Bridge road on its E, and the B5285 N and Force Forge S. Not to be confused with Grisedale near Patterdale. Before the 12th century the woodland hereabouts became the property of the monks of Furness Abbey and in 1516 much of the area was made into a deer park. This covered a circumference of 8kms (5 miles). Today, deer are still prominent in the life of the forest, between 300 and 400 of them but they are now protected. The woodland was acquired by the Forestry Commission in the 1930s and has been increased, modified and developed since. The forest has been open to the public since 1961 and many footpaths and trails have been waymarked for walkers ranging from the Bogle Crag Yellow Walk 1.2kms (0.75 mile) to the Silurian Way 15.3kms (9.5 miles). There is also nearly 16kms (10 miles) of track waymarked for cyclists. A unique feature of the park is the many sculptures, some 80, set in various situations. Highest point is Carron Crag 314m (1030ft), an excellent viewpoint. The Forest Visitor and Wildlife Centre occupies stables attached to the former Grizedale Hall (see **Grizedale Hall**). Across the road from the visitor centre at Grizedale the Theatre in the Forest opened in 1970 but closed several years ago. Just N of the theatre the Restaurant in the Forest at the Grizedale Lodge Hotel (earlier Ormandy Hotel) opened in 1976. Basic information on the forest park is contained in leaflet *Grizedale Forest Park: A Forest Enterprise Guide Map* but more detailed information can be obtained from the Forest Park Visitor Centre. In 1996 Grizedale Forest received a top award, the Centre of Excellence Award [336943] ...see **Grizedale**.

Grizedale Hall erected by Harold Brocklebank, shipping magnate, in 1904 it replaced an earlier Grizedale Hall. Acquired by the Forestry Commission in 1936 it was demolished in the 1950s. Today, the stables attached to the hall, house the Forest Visitor and Wildlife Centre and there is a Caravan and Camping Club site on the hall's grounds. During the Second World War the hall was used as a POW camp for German officers and on 7 October 1940, Luftwaffe pilot, Oberleutnant Franz von Werra (1914-1941) escaped from the camp but was captured on Hesk Fell above Ulpha five days later. An evening escape from another camp in the Midlands in December resulted in recapture at Hucknall Aerodrome the following morning. He finally escaped from Canada to Germany the following year. However, in October 1941, while on a routine patrol his ME 109 plunged into the sea. Neither the aircraft nor von Werra were ever traced. His exploits were first published in book form in 1956 under the title *The One That Got Away* and later became the subject of a film of the same title with Hardy Kruger in the title role. Another escapee Bernard Berndt, a U-boat commander, was shot on the fells by members of the Home Guard.

Grizedale Lodge Hotel Grizedale. Earlier the Ormandy Hotel (see **Ormandy Intakes**). The Restaurant in the Forest opened in the hotel in 1976 and provides meals and, up to the theatre's demise, dinners for theatregoers to the Theatre in the Forest [335950].

Grizedale Moor One of four 'moors', the others being Hawkshead, Monk Coniston and Satterthwaite, which comprise much of the western half of Grizedale Forest Park [327962].

Grizedale Tarn approximately 1km (2/3 mile) due E of Grizedale Visitor Centre. Actually comprises three tarns a fairly large one and two much smaller. The large one lies alongside the Grizedale Tarn Walk 5kms (3.25mile) which starts and finishes at the Grizedale Visitor Centre. There is a viewpoint by the tarn. Grizedale Tarn was used as an emergency water supply for the now demolished Grizedale Hall, C210m (C689ft) [346944].

Groove Beck rises at 372095 and joins Rydal Beck at 364087.

Groove Beck rises Matterdale Common at 357214. Joins Blake Sike at 377224 and becomes Thornsgill Beck which ultimately becomes Trout Beck.

Groove Beck Fold sheepfold [373221].

Groove Gill head of Groovegill Beck [393205].

Groove Gill rises W High Street ridge at 454173 and joins Fusedale Beck at 446174. This enters Ullswater alongside Howtown Pier at 443199.

Groove Gill rises E Wastwater at 194063 and joins Hollow Gill at 184066.

Groovegill Beck flows from 388205 down through Groove Gill and Glencoyne Park to enter Ullswater at 399198.

Grounds mainly in the High Furness area and principally from the end of the 15th century to the first half of the 16th century many tenants particularly of Furness Abbey were allowed to enclose small areas of land no larger than 1.5 acres and on which a farmhouse could be built. These small holdings were known locally as 'grounds' and are still referred to as such today although most have increased in size over the centuries. Writing in 1774 Father West, one of the earliest writers of Lake District guides, noted that, "inclosures were called the grounds of the person that first enclosed them and some retain the same name at present." Many are still called by the name of their original tenants ie Atkinson, Bank, Bolton, Dixon, Dodgson, Holme, Keen, Knipe, Rawlinson, Roger, Sawrey, Stephenson, Thompson, Walker and Waterson Ground.

Grove farm off the A591 below Banner Rigg [423991] ...there is a grove/copse nearby.

Grove Farm Hartsop. Acquired by the National Trust in 1992 [409131].

Grove Gill rises lower slope of Broad End at 404070 and passes under the A592 near Woundale Raise. Joins Stock Ghyll at 397064 ...the stream which passes through or alongside the wood.

Grovefoot Farm S Sparket. Off the minor road, Nabend-Dacre [432250].

Grubbings Wood continuation of Yewbarrow Wood and Bowers Wood, Longsleddale [507021] ...cleared land.

Grubbins Point promontory W shore Windermere [379915] ...grubbin/grubbings is land cleared by digging up roots, etc.

Grunting Gill two tributaries rise at 254062 and 260060 respectively. Joins Mickleden Beck at 266069.

Guardhouse three quarters of a mile SE Doddick. On minor road, A66-Scales (A66) [340259] ...house in the enclosure.

Guardhouse Bridge Guardhouse. Crosses R Glenderamackin at [340260].

Guards End Gosforth [089047] ...see **Guards Head**.

Guards Head Gosforth. At one time nicknamed Sheepshanks' Hall and said to have been a smithy ...enclosure at the head as opposed to Guards End which is the enclosure at the end.

Guards Wood Coniston [311982] ...wood in or by the enclosure (garth).

Gubbergill alongside minor road from the A595 to Santon Bridge [084994] ...Gubbergillhead in the mid-17th century.

Guerness Gill rises E Haweswater at 491127. Joined by Moss Gill and enters Haweswater at 481134. See also **Guerness Wood**.

Guerness Wood E shore Haweswater. A remnant of the former extensive Naddle Forest. Prior to flooding to make the present-day reservoir there was, in the region of Guerness Gill and Wood, a prominent headland jutting into the lake. Here in the vicinity of Guerness Nib, the promontory which now lies under the waters, there was a copper mine [487144] ...the unusual name 'Guerness' probably means fishing-trap headland. Indeed, in times of yore, seine netting was practised hereabouts. Apart from Haweswater itself which boasts trout, perch, schelly (skelly) and char the area immediately E of the reservoir has a considerable piscatorial association. Near Guerness there is Pod Net (eel trap), Eel Coop, on Haweswater Beck, and one possible meaning of Naddle could be a fish name.

Guide Books to the Lake District see **Lake District Guide Books**.

Guide Crag Buck Barrow [152912].

Guide Stone alongside the Cumbria Way on the W side of the Glenderaterra valley [292279].

Guinea Hill Hawkshead Moor, Grizedale Forest Park 243m (797ft) [336967] ...see China Plantation.

Guinea Hill Tarn see **Goosey Foot Tarn**.

Gunson Knott most northerly of the Crinkle Crags [250051]. In June 1937, a plane crashed below Gunson Knott killing its crew of two ...Gunson's Knott.

Gurnal Dubbs largest of the eight named tarns on Potter Fell. Originally plural hence the 'dubs' (pools) but subsequently dammed to provide a reservoir for the Burneside paper mill. Also known as Fothergill Tarn after previous owners, the Fothergill family of Lowbridge House, Bannisdale, who originally erected the substantial stone boat house there. A lovely tree-clad island adds to the beauty of this large tarn. Contains brown and rainbow trout to which fishing rights are held by the Kent Angling Association. Maximum depth of 4.5m (15ft) and altitude C290m (C951ft) [502992] ...similar to Gurnal Bridge over the River Sprint and Gurnal Wood, Crook, in that it takes its name from the Gurna(e)l family of Kendal.

Gurning traditional 'sport' where the head is placed through a braffin (a horse-collar) and the person who pulls the ugliest face is deemed the winner. The World Gurning Championship is held annually at the Egremont Crab Fair ...dialect word from girn/grin.

Gutherscale W Derwent Water off the Portinscale to Grange road [245211] ...Godric's shieling/hut.

H

H P Plantation E Staveley-Kentmere road [459016] ...H P stands for Henry Pattinson of the Windermere building firm. He acquired the land and built a plantation on it. By judicious planting of different trees the initials H P could be read when looking down on the plantation from heights above.

H Ram St John's in the Vale. E B5322 and W Hilltop Quarries ...not an animal, the name of a farm, or a degree of computer memory. It simply stands for hydraulic ram. In this case one of many throughout the country installed at the turn of the century to pump water from natural water supplies. With the advent of mains supply a considerable number were left dry and derelict [319231].

H Ram W Crowmire off the Troutbeck Bridge-Town End road [400007] ...similar to one sited in St John's in the Vale. The name simply means 'hydraulic ram', see **H Ram** above.

Haber Hill near Askham [504232] ...hill where hay was grown.

Haber Tarn partially overgrown. Situated in Mirebank Plantation, NNW Helton [501224].

Hacket, High/Low see **High/Low Hacket**.

Hackney Holes curious rock formations on S slope of Robinson [201164].

Hackthorpe High Plantation Lowther Park. S Hackthorpe and on the boundary of the National Park [543222].

Hag Beck rises Trough Head at 387143 and flows through Glenamara Park to meet Grisedale Beck at 390161.

Hag End alongside Dales Way near Outrun Nook [433970] ...end of clearing.

Hag Stones several large stones on Moor Divock [492226].

Hag Wood Lingmoor Fell [312049] ...clearing in the wood.

Hagg W Bassenthwaite Lake and Woodend Brow [207276] ...'hogg' - clearing.

Hagg Beck rises slope of Lord's Seat at 206268, flows by Hagg and eventually becomes Beck Wythop which joins Bassenthwaite Lake at 216285.

Hagg Bridge carries track to Troutbeck Park Farm and footpath to Threshthwaite Mouth over Hagg Gill [421054].

Hagg Gill its farthest headstream, Blue Gill, rises on Froswick at 434085. This flows down a deep chasm and at its foot becomes Hagg Gill which joins Trout Beck alongside Hagg Bridge at 421054 ...hagg is either derived from the ON 'clearing' or Modern English dialect 'copse, plantation'. In either case, along with nearby High and Low Mere Greave (the high 'boundary copse' and the low 'boundary copse') and Hird Wood, the name reminds us of a time when Troutbeck Park was obviously a far more wooded area than it is today.

Hagg Pond Claife Heights. Actually two tiny tarns in Hagg Wood linked by a small stream. Sometimes referred to as Hagg Wood Tarns, 190m (623ft) [367982] ...pond by or in the clearing.

Hagg Wood Claife Heights. Incorporates two tarns [367981], see above.

Hagg Wood E Swinburn's Park. Rises to 342m (1122ft) [428220] ...clearing + wood.

Hagg Wood Tarns see **Hagg Pond**.

Haggs Park between Muncaster Castle and the River Esk [107962].

Haggs Wood W Irton Hall [095006] ...hagg in very early form meant clearing but in more modern dialect refers to copse/plantation.

Hailhead Well between Threlkeld Hall and the A66 [330259].

Hale Beck two lengthy tributaries rise at 074038 and 066030 respectively. The beck joins the River Bleng at 090033.

Halfmoon Wood W of the middle reaches of Ullswater and the A592. Certainly resembles its name [423208].

Halhead Hall alongside the B5284, Plumgarths to Crook road [489948] ...possibly the hall is named from the surname of Sir Henry Halled of Kendal.

Halhead Nab S Halhead Hall. Projection at the N end of Cunswick Scar [489944].

Hall Bank near Aldby Farm [460276].

Hall Bank steep craggy slope between Keldas and the A592 at Glenridding. Takes its name from the nearby Patterdale Hall [387165].

Hall Bank Embleton. Spot height at 138m (453ft) [158295].

Hall Beck Skeggleswater Dike which drains Skeggles Water becomes Hall Beck on entering the narrow valley alongside Staveley Head at approximately 470017. It joins the River Kent between Scroggs Bridge and Barley Bridge at 469991 ...named after Staveley Hall which is no longer in existence and, in fact, was a ruin well over 300 years ago.

Hall Beck rises 161957 and joins Devoke Water at 160969.

Hall Bolton Gosforth. Old manor house approached either from the Gosforth to Nether Wasdale road across Hallbolton Bridge or from the Gosforth to Santon Bridge road [089031] ...the word hall was added at a later date. For the origin of Bolton see **Bolton Head**.

Hall Bridge near Hawkshead Hall. Carries the B5286 over Black Beck [350987].

Hall Bridge also known as Hall Dunnerdale Bridge. Bridge which carries the road up the Duddon valley over the River Duddon (213953).

Hall Carleton Carleton. At the head of minor road off the A595 [071979].

Hall Cove combe at the head of the Kentmere valley. Bounded by Gavel Crag, Bleathwaite Crag and the Mardale Ill Bell-Lingmell End ridge. Down it flows the infant River Kent [442097] ...'cove above the hall'.

Hall Dunnerdale farm and properties by the River Duddon [215955]. Alongside Hall Dunnerdale an extremely large salmon weighing 26lbs was hooked by John Dawson, a local man.

Hall Dunnerdale Bridge see **Hall Bridge**.

Hall Flatt off the Santon to Santon Bridge road [104013].

Hall Gill rises N slope Sallows at 438042. Flows alongside the Garburn Pass, past

Kentmere Hall and joins the River Kent at 455036.

Hall Hill alongside Troutbeck Park Farm in a triangle of land formed by the farm, Trout Beck and Hagg Gill [422056].

Hall Lane from Staveley via Barley Bridge to Park House and Staveley Head [474998] ...a field nearby was known in the 19th century as 'Hall Field' and Hall Beck flows down from alongside Staveley Head to meet the River Kent near Scroggs Bridge. The hall, however, disappeared long since and was, in fact, a ruin at the end of the 17th century.

Hall Stanton hamlet ESE Santon. The prefix 'hall' was added at a later date [101013].

Hall Waberthwaite end of minor road which leaves the A595 just over 0.8 kms (0.5 mile) NE Waberthwaite [110950], (see also **Waberthwaite**).

Hall Wood Grizedale Forest Park. Near the former Grizedale Hall [331933].

Hall Wood S Kentmere Hall [452036].

Hall's Fell between Gate Gill and Doddick Gill, Blencathra. Leads to Hallsfell Top, the highest peak of Blencathra. Named after Threlkeld Hall which it overlooks [326270].

Hall's Fell Ridge Hall's Fell to Hallsfell Top, Blencathra [325274].

Hallbolton Bridge carries the track from the Nether Wasdale to Gosforth road to the Gosforth to Santon Bridge road over the River Bleng [089033].

Hallgarth off the Braithwaite to Thornthwaite roaed [225248].

Hallgarth Beck rises 232249. Joined by Masmill Beck and the combined watercourse enters Newlands Beck near Chapel Beck at 232259.

Hallin Bank ESE Sandwick. SSW slope Hallin Fell [430193].

Hallin Fell overlooks middle reaches of Ullswater. E Sandwick, W Howtown. Summit surmounted by exceptionally well-built 12ft obelisk, sundry cairns, and, according to *The English Lake District* by Ward Lock & Co (19th edition), "on the summit... is a monument to Lord Brougham." This would be the 1st Lord Brougham (1778-1868), of Brougham Hall, near Penrith, lawyer, Chancellor of the Exchequer 1830-34, noted orator, and inventor of the Brougham carriage. Whether the obelisk itself is the monument referred to or there is another thereabouts I have not been able to establish. The large obelisk has two softer stones inserted in it on which are inscribed initials and numbers. These are weathering away but still decipherable is the word and number 'Built 1864'. 388m (1273ft) [433198] ...obscure origin.

Hallinhagg Wood E shore Ullswater between Sandwick Bay and Kailpot Crag [430201].

Hallmoss Hill W Wet Sleddale Reservoir and Sleddale Hall [533114].

Hallow Bank Kentmere [465054] ...Bartholomew and Wainwright quote it as Hollowbank but the EPNS *Place Names of Westmorland* shows the place as having been Hallowbank(e) since the early 17th century and that the name means Hall hill.

Hallow Bank Quarter Kentmere. During the Border Wars with Scotland Kentmere was subjected to Border tenure. It was divided into Quarters - Crag, Green, Hallow Bank and West Wr(e)ay - each further divided into holdings. From these a fighting man was to be provided to defend against the Scots [460070].

Hallsfell Top highest peak on Blencathra, 868m (2848ft) [323277]. Possesses a sunken trig. point. Other similar trig. points are sited on Branstree, Great Yarlside and Seat Robert.

Hallsteads between the A592 and Skelly Neb, Ullswater. House built in 1815 by John Marshall. The latter and his wife, Jane Pollard, a close friend of Dorothy Wordsworth, were frequently visited by the Wordsworths. It was John's eldest son, William, who acquired Patterdale Hall from the Mounsey family in 1824. Hallsteads later became a private hotel but since 1985 the hall and its 18 acres of woodland and over 0.8kms (0.5 mile) of private lake shore, has been one of the two Lakeland bases (the other is in Eskdale) of the Outward Bound School. Mountain Rescue Post here [438211] ...site of a hall.

Hammer Hole alongside the High Cunsey-Graythwaite road. According to W G Collingwood Hammer Hole was the landing place for raw materials for the nearby Forge [381927] ...hammer from the ON 'hamarr' meaning a 'steep rock or cliff'.

Hammerscar Plantation slightly W of the col at the head of Red Bank Road [338055]. Behind it and further W is the craggy knoll of Hammerscar of whose summit Thomas West said in 1778 "it was the most advantage station to view this romantic vale (Grasmere) from" ...hammer from the ON 'hamarr' meaning a steep rock or cliff.

Hanging Haystack Rosthwaite Fell. NE Bessyfoot [263130].

Hanging How Santon [095018] ...a place of execution similar to the not far distant Gallows Hill.

Hanging Knott end of a spur of Bowfell overlooking Angle Tarn [244075].

Hanging Stone stands between Caw Fell and Haycock at 131105 ...from the OE 'hangende' meaning steep/overhanging.

Hanging Stone N slope Base Brown. Large boulder perched precariously on the rim of a crag [227118].

Hanging Stone W Ullock Pike. Block of stone attached to the top of a small crag and which from below appears to be hanging from it [241288].

Hanging Stones W Haweswater. Between Whelter Crags and Birks Crag [465131].

Hannah Crag W Swindale. Above Truss Gap [510132] ...personal name? + crag.

Hannakin Hawkshead. Alongside the Hawkshead-Newby Bridge road [353977] ...Ekwall suggests a personal name possibly Anny's/Annie's kin.

Hard Crags Bowfell. Above Green Tongue [250068].

Hard Hill S slope The Pike [186927].

Hard Knott Summit of Hardknott 549m (1801ft) [232024] ...from ON 'haror' meaning difficult + rocky peak.

Hard Rigg ridge W Hardrigg Gill and NNE Burnmoor Tarn [191057] ...possibly the ridge frequented by hares.

Hard Tarn very small tarn situated at an altitude of 716m (C2297ft) on ledge above Ruthwaite Cove. SE Nethermost Pike and below Nethermost Crag [346138] ...possibly similar to Hard Knott in that hard is from the ON 'haror' meaning difficult and the tarn is certainly difficult to access and hard to find.

Hardknott triangular fell area bounded by the River Esk/Lingcove Gill, Mosedale and the Hardknott Pass. Its highest point is Hard Knott at 232024 ...see **Hard Knott**.

Hardknott Castle Roman Fort the Roman 'Mediobogdum' is the fort sited in the middle of the curve. Nearby the Esk bends from the NE to flow W along Eskdale. Situated at a height of 244m (800ft) by the road which rises over the Hardknott Pass and the old Roman road from Ambleside to Ravenglass. Built 117-138 in the reign of Emperor Hadrian and practically destroyed in 196-7. It was not recognised as a Roman site until the late 17th century. The square-shaped fort comprised a defensive wall crowned by battlements and with a tower at each corner. Four gates to the NW, SE, SW and NE the latter leading to a large parade ground and that to the SE to a bath-house. Buildings inside the wall were the headquarters, the commander's house, the granary and barrack accommodation [219015].

Hardknott Gill there are two Hardknott Gills, one flowing E and one W. Both rise on the slope of Hardknott, the former at 229020 before flowing under the pass road, down to the N of Black Hall farm and on to join the River Duddon at 249010. The latter rises near the summit of the pass at 230015 and flows down a ravine below and parallel to the pass road before joing the River Esk at 212013.

Hardknott Pass pass which links Eskdale with Dunnerdale and the Wrynose Pass. Its original name was 'Wainscarth' meaning 'the gap through which a waggon could go'. The Roman road from Ambleside to Ravenglass used the gap. Second highest road pass in the Lake District after Kirkstone but with its 33.3% (1 in 3) gradient a tougher test for both man and machine. Improvements were made to the track over the pass in the 19th century but the road remained unmetalled until the 1930s. During the Second World War the pass was used by the Ministry of Defence. Rises to 393m (1289ft) at 231015.

Hardknott Tarns shown but not named on the OS map. Two tarns NNE Hard Knott. The source of Great Gill [234029].

Hardrigg Gill rises W slope Scafell at 198062. Joined by Long Gill and Oliver Gill and the combined watercourses join Whillan Beck at 188044.

Hardriggs Crosthwaite [436918] ...the ridge/hill difficult to till.

Hare Bennett between Place Fell summit and Grey Crag. Nearby, to the N, is Hare Shaw [403170] ...possibly the grassy place frequented by hares.

Hare Crag Eskdale. N Wha House Farm [201012].

Hare Crag Skiddaw Forest. NW Skiddaw House 538m (1765ft) [277299].

Hare Crags Torver (280950) ...from the ON 'horg' meaning a heap of stones or simply the crags frequented by hares.

Hare Gill Birker Moor. Stream rises 160983 and joins with Black Beck at 165988 to become Red Gill.

Hare Gill see **Leaps Beck**.

Hare Hall large property off the Broughton Mills to Seathwaite fell road [206922].

Hare Hall Beck flows out of Stickle Tarn and joins Dunnerdale Beck at 218919.

Hare Raise WSW Burn Moor [144922].

Hare Shaw a high point on the ridge between the head of the Naddle valley, of which it provides a good viewpoint, and Branstree, 503m (1650ft) [498131]. Wainwright points out that the two cairns on Hare Shaw and the one on Harper Hills were erected by Mark Richards in March 1973 ...hare copse or small wood.

Hare Shaw SSW Birk Fell summit, Place Fell and WNW The Knight. Nearby, to the S, is Hare Bennett [401178].

Harper Hills between Naddle Beck and Mere Sike. A small reservoir here receives water from Blea Tarn and Haweswater pumping station and supplies water to the Swindale Water Treatment Works. Wainwright notes that the cairn on Harper Hills was erected by a Mark Richards in March 1973, 419m (1375ft) [508143].

Harris Side SW slope of Murton Fell [089187].

Harrison Combe WNW Harrison Stickle [276077] ...Harrison's valley.

Harrison Crag N slope Birks. Overlooks Grisedale and Braesteads [381151] ...named from a former local family called Harryson.

Harrison Stickle highest of the Langdale Pikes and, like its near neighbour Pike o' Stickle, it provides an outline recognisable over long and short distances for tourists in the area and is a mecca for fell walkers, 736m (2415ft) [282074] ...along with former Harrison Place and Harry Place, Great Langdale, it is named after a local family of Harrison and therefore is Harrison's 'steep peak'.

Harrop Pike overlooking Little Mosedale 637m (2090ft) [501078] Harrop Pike and nearby Grey Crag are the most easterly mountains of the Lake District National Park ...pointed hill overlooking the craggy valley (the latter is presumably the head of Little Mosedale).

Harrop Tarn W Thirlmere. At the head of Dob Gill and NE Tarn Crags. Very reedy and surrounded by afforestation. Fed principally by Mosshause Gill and Ullscarf Gill. Free fishing for brown trout and perch. Reputed to be haunted by a headless spectre. Maximum depth is 6m (20ft) and its altitude is 290m (951ft) [311136] ...either boundary or hare valley.

Harrot most westerly summit of the Lord Seat Group 292m (958ft) [160275] ...rocks above a valley. On its S slope Scarf Crag overlooks a valley.

Harrow Head/Harrowhead farm alongside the Gosforth to Wastwater high road. Acquired by the NT in 1977 along with nearby Buckbarrow, Broadgap and Gill [125055].

Harrow Head Wood S of the Gosforth to Wastwater high road. W Tosh Tarn [125052].

Harrow Slack W shore Windermere near Coatlap Point [388962] ...possibly Harry's hollow.

Harrowhead Farm see **Harrow Head/Harrowhead**.

Harry Bank hill slope leading up to Penny Bank and Bethecar Moor [325906].

Harry Guards Wood alongside Yew Tree Tarn [320005] ...is Harry still guarding his wood? Actually Guards/Garth means an enclosure.

Harry Hodgson's Well slope Blakeley alongside Coldfell Road. Stream flowing from it flows into Nannycatch Beck [063134].

Harry Intake Grizedale Forest Park [324932].

Harry Place Farm Great Langdale [313061] ...Furness and adjoining areas have their 'grounds'. Great Langdale has its 'places' - Harry, Middlefell, Robinson. Given to the National Trust in 1944 by Prof. G M Trevelyan ...Harry, like Harrison Stickle, is derived from a local Harrison family.

Hart Crag Crag Quarter, Kentmere [452057].

Hart Crag crags alongside the ridge from Caudale Moor over Pike How to Broad End [413083].

Hart Crag NNE of the summit of Place Fell [408173].

Hart Crag NNW Hart Side summit. Overlooks Matterdale's Deepdale [358199].

Hart Crag rough summit midway between Dove Crag and Fairfield on the principal Fairfield Horseshoe route. Hartsop above How ridge descends from it, 822m (2697ft) [368113].

Hart Head Farm Rydal [364064].

Hart Hill ENE Loadpot Hill [463183].

Hart How Bow Fell [243062].

Hart Howe E Back Lane [437937] ...hart hill.

Hart Side W Ullswater. Looks across Deepdale to Stybarrow Dodd, Great Dodd and Matterdale Common. Part of high level route E to Brown Hills and ridge route SW and W to Stybarrow Dodd, 756m (2480ft) [359197].

Harter Fell between Eskdale and Dunnerdale. A pyramical mountain easily recognised over short and long distances. Of the three Harter Fells in or near the Lake District this is the middle one in height. On its E and S slopes there is considerable afforestation of which planting began in the mid-1930s. An OS triangulation column sited at 649m (2129ft) is not the highest point. The latter, a rocky outcrop slightly NE, is 653m (2142ft) [219997] ...see below.

Harter Fell from the head of Haweswater Mardale's Harter Fell presents an enormous craggy face. Its summit, however, is a grassy dome and its summit cairn a collection of old iron fence posts and railings set into a mound of stones. These provide a weird and spectral scene especially when approached through mist. Harter Fell has three subsidiary summits, the Knowe C760m (C2493ft), Little Harter Fell C670m (C2198ft) and Adam Seat 666m (2185ft). Two major passes traverse close by, the Nan Bield to the W and Gatescarth to the E both providing the basis for principal routes to the summit, 778m (2553ft) [460093] ...'hill of the hart'. There are two other well-known but lower Harter Fells, one between Eskdale and Dunnerdale 653 m (2142ft) and the other in the Howgill Fells 522m (1713ft).

Harter Fell Gully through crags ENE Harter Fell summit and NNW Little Harter Fell [469097].

Hartley Beck rises slope Robinson at 196162 and joins Gatesgarth Beck at 195150 ...possibly the stream by the deer meadow.

Hartley Crag Birker Moor [183995].

Hartley Wife rocky islet, Windermere [398968] ...surname Hartley?

Hartrigg Kentmere. Large farm, the highest in Kentmere [456060]. Countless walkers will recall Lucille, the tame red deer, adopted by the farmer as a babe and who lived at Hartrigg for 16 years until her death in 1995. A particular favourite of children she had a penchant for Mars bars and Polo mints. In 1999, as part of the Kentmere Hall & Hartrigg estate along with Kentmere Hall and the farmhouses of Rook Howe and Scales, came up for sale by private treaty ...hart ridge.

Hartsop Low Hartsop. Of ancient origin being mentioned as far back as 1184 when it was Herteshop(e). Many motorists hurrying along the A592 bound to or from the Kirkstone Pass are unaware of this secluded hamlet lying just to the E of the main road, 3.2kms (2 miles) SSE Patterdale and near Brothers Water. Yet it is a delightful, interesting, and peaceful settlement nestling at the foot of Pasture Beck/Hayeswater Gill and between the heights of Hartsop Dodd to the S and Brock Crags to the ENE. Nearly 200 years ago Wordsworth referred to it as "the decaying hamlet of Hartsop, remarkable for its cottage architecture." Today, there is still a small amount of decay around Hartsop but at the same time there is

much beauty and neatness to be seen in and around many of its cottages. Most of these date from the 17th century. There are remains of a corn mill, drying kiln and old mine workings; cottages with spinning galleries; a former inn; two farms; old barns; and something to catch the eye at each turn of the only road through the hamlet such as an old oven set in a wall as a repository for deliveries. The road ends in a decent-sized car park from which paths head up the valley to Hayeswater, Caudale Moor and the High Street range. To the W of the A592 the former 15th century Hartsop Hall, now a farm, was given to the National Trust by the Treasury in 1947. The latter had accepted it in lieu of death duties. It was actually the first property acquired by the Trust in this way. Grove Farm, Hartsop, was acquired by the National Trust in 1992 and consequently the last remaining area of freehold fell not already owned by that body at the head of the Ullswater valley came into its possession [409131] ...valley of the hart.

Hartsop above How summit which is better known by locals as Gill Crag. Hartsop above How is actually a long curving ridge dividing Deepdale from Dovedale and running from Hart Crag to drop between Deepdale Park and Low Wood to the A592. Part of an often traversed Fairfield Horseshoe. Its summit lies 2.4kms (1.5 miles) ENE Hart Crag, 570m (1870ft) [385121].

Hartsop Beck see **Dovedale Beck**.

Hartsop Dodd sometimes called Low Hartsop Dodd. End of an arm of Caudale Moor which follows the E side of Kirkstone Pass. Faces High Hartsop Dodd across the pass but is 99m (325ft) higher than it but 36m (118ft) lower than Middle Dodd. 'High', 'low' and 'middle' refer to geographical locations. Hartsop Dodd (Low Hartsop Dodd) is situated lower down the side of the valley than High Hartsop Dodd while Middle Dodd occupies a central position between the two, 618m (2028ft) [411118].

Hartsop Hall 15th century manor house which is now a farm. Passed from the de Lancaster family to Sir John Lowther (afterwards Viscount Lonsdale). Subsequently, the Hartsop estate was acquired by the Treasury in lieu of death duties and given to the National Trust in 1947. It was the first property acquired by the Trust in this way [398120].

Hartsop Hall Mine see **Hartsop Mine**.

Hartsop Mine also known as Hartsop Hall Mine. Disused mine about 0.4kms (0.25 mile) W of Hartsop Hall. Originally opened late 16th or early 17th century. Reopened 19th century and closed about 1860. Reopened in 1931 and finally closed in 1942, [395119].

Harwood Hotel Grasmere village. Originally built in the 1850s as a tea and coffee house and reading room. Much later became a guest house known for many years as the Temperance Guest House.

Haskett Buttress Great Scoat Fell [155115].

Haskew Beck rises Haskew Tarn, W Seat Robert, S Willy Winder Hill at 521113. Becomes Gouthercrag Gill at 518128 and this flows into Swindale Beck at 514131.

Haskew Tarn isolated shallow tarn on ridge between Swindale and Wet Sleddale. W Seat Robert and S Willy Winder Hill. Source of Haskew Beck, C470 (C1542ft) [521113] ...named from the family of a John Askew.

Hassness property E side of Buttermere (lake) off the B5289 [187158].

Hassness Tunnel A rock-hewn tunnel, 35m (115ft) in length and on the popular walk along the E shore of Buttermere. Thought to have been cut by local miners in the 19th century. It was closed in 1995 for repairs but was reopened in May 1997.

Hassnesshow Beck rises 195163 and after being joined by Goat Gills joins Buttermere at 186158.

Hatteringill isolated property between Hatteringill Head and Broadmoor Hill approached by a track from the Low Lorton to Mosser fell road [138247].

Hatteringill Head above Hatteringill. The summit of Whin Fell in the Fellbarrow Group 385m (1263ft) [134248].

Hause SW spur Caw Fell [116090] ...a hause is a pass or col or a connecting ridge.

Hause, The see **The Hause** ...see above.

Hause Crag ENE Boredale Hause. Overlooks the head of Boredale [412158].

Hause Crag overlooks the head of Riggindale [444116].

Hause End below The Hause on lower slope of spur from Low Kop to Cawdale Beck and between Cawdale and Willdale [490176].

Hause Farm ESE Sandwick alongside the minor road from Howtown [434191].

Hause Foot habitation, Crookdale. As its name implies it is situated at the foot of a hause (pass). The latter was on the old Kendal-Shap road superseded by the present A6 in the 1820s. The old road still continues up Crookdale to Hause Foot from where it proceeds as an extremely wide footpath up the hillside and over the hause (much earlier referred to as Crookdale Hause) to cross the A6 slightly N of its summit [550056].

Hause Gap see **Grisedale Tarn**.

Hause Gate col between crags on the route from Manesty to Cat Bells ridge [245192].

Hause Gill rises W Thirlmere at 309150 and joins the reservoir at 317150.

Hause Gill farthest tributary rises slightly E of the former Yewcrag Quarries and the path from Honister Hause to Dale Head at 227144. The gill joins the Derwent near Seatoller Bridge at 246136.

Hause Moss S Hause Gap. Tongue Gill rises here [350114].

Hause Point W shore Thirlmere. Apart from its head and foot the reservoir is at its narrowest here. The road around the W side of Thirlmere cuts through rocks by New Nick which after construction of the reservoir replaced the previous Nick. The rock on the shore side has steps cut into it and a seat on top provides an excellent viewpoint [317152].

Hause Riggs SSE Seat Sandal. Between the head of Little Tongue Gill and Tongue Gill [346110] ...the ridges by the head of the pass/col.

Hause Well a spring which issues from a crevice just S of the Old Coach Road, St John's in the Vale-Dockray [339235].

Hausegreen Crag above Greendale [150058].

Hausewell Brow section of Old Coach Road, St John's in the Vale-Dockray [335235].

Haverigg Holme off the A593 [261918] ...oats ridge on the isolated piece of land or water meadow.

Haw Ulpha [196935].

Hawes E Bridge End. NW Climb Stile [256902].

Hawes ENE Pickthall Ground [213906].

Hawes End W Derwent Water. Off the Portinscale to Grange road [249213].

Hawes How Island one of the two islands in Thirlmere. Prior to flooding of the valley it was a rocky knoll known as Hawes How [314157].

Haweswater and Mardale Haweswater was originally a lake just over one third the size of the present reservoir, 3.7kms (2.25 miles) in length, and with a maximum depth of 28m (92ft). It was practically cut in two by the Measand Beck delta. The upper section was appropriately called High Water and the lower, Low Water, and the two were connected by the Straits. A road around the W side of the lake passed through Measand and terminated just beyond the village of Mardale Green, Mardale. The dale ran from the head of the lake to Blea Tarn and Small Water. Over the years Mardale was threatened by a railway tunnel under Branstree and a road along Longsleddale, over the Gatescarth Pass, and through the valley to Penrith. Neither of these two ideas came to fruition but Manchester Corporation Waterworks obtained the Haweswater Act in 1919 which enabled it to acquire the lake and construct a large reservoir. Subsequently, a high dam was built at Burnbanks, the Mardale Tunnel was bored under Branstree to Stockdale in Longsleddale and from there an underground pipeline follows the valley to the Watchgate Water Treatment Works at Selside. Incidentally, a second Haweswater-Watchgate aqueduct via Shap is a pumped transfer.

By 1941 the reservoir level had been raised by 29m (95ft) submerging the remains of farms - Chapel Hill, Dudderwick, Flake How, Goosemire, Grove Brae, Measand, Measand Beck, Riggingdale and Whelter - cottages at Mardale Green and Measand, Measand Beck Hall, a 17th century church and the famous 17th century Dun Bull Inn. Measand Grammar School, founded in 1713, was dismantled and rebuilt as a private residence at Walmgate Head. Wood Howe, Haweswater Reservoir's only island was, prior to flooding, a tree-topped knoll, a projection of the Rigg. A new road was built on the E side of the reservoir and today the only property above the dam and standing alongside this road, is the Haweswater Hotel, built in 1937, to replace the old Dun Bull.

The drought of 1984 caused the foundations and some walls of the Mardale Green properties, Chapel Bridge, and trackways to and from the former properties to reappear. Many thousands of people flocked to see this. So many, in fact, that police were needed to control the traffic along the road to the head of the dale. For some considerable time afterwards many people were seen wearing teeshirts bearing the logo 'I've Seen Mardale'. Previously, the village had re-emerged in 1976 and recently in 1989, 1995 and 2003.

In the mid-19th century Mardale Green was a thriving little community which each week sent 3,000lbs of butter to Manchester. Like Patterdale, Mardale had its 'Kings', in this case the Holmes, direct descendants of one Hugh Holme who fled from King John in the 13th century, took shelter in a cave on the N side of Rough Crag, Riggindale Scar (shown as Hugh's Cave on the 2.5 inch OS map at 456115). He became the first King of Mardale and the last of the male line who succeeded to that title was Hugh Parker Holmes who died in 1885.

Eagles bred in the Lake District until the 19th century but disappeared until 1969 when a pair returned to the Riggindale area. Today a pair still have their eyrie there. The eagles are strongly protected by law and watched over diligently by RSPB volunteers.

Similar to Brotherswater (commemorated by name) and Windermere by a memorial Haweswater also has a memorial to two young men who drowned there. This comprises two boulders and a memorial stone on the north shore. The stone reads "These stones in their original position on the shore of the lake and 25 yards south of this point marked the place near which Robert Noble Wilkinson, aged 15 years, of Wet Sleddale, and George Ashworth, aged 19 years, of Manchester, were drowned while bathing in the lake on July 10th 1874."

The present lake is 6.9kms (4.25 miles) in length with a surface level of 240m (787ft) making it the highest of the lakes. Its maximum depth is 57m (187ft) [480140]. Contains char, schelly and trout ...Haefer's or Hafr's water. A tarn in Silverdale, Lancashire, is also called Haweswater.

Haweswater Beck commences at the outflow of Haweswater Reservoir [503158]. Flows under Naddle Bridge where it is joined by Naddle Beck, then over Thornthwaite Force. Subsequently joined by Woodnook Gill and Howes Beck (diverted into Haweswater in

1959) before meeting the River Lowther at 519182.

Haweswater Hotel Alongside road E Haweswater. Built in 1937 to replace the old Dun Bull Inn, Mardale Green, which was submerged with the village when the valley was flooded for the present reservoir [483139].

Hawk, The see **The Hawk**.

Hawk Bridge carries minor road over the River Lickle [239920].

Hawk Crag Place Fell. Overlooks head of Boredale [414168].

Hawk Rigg N Blake Rigg and Tilberthwaite Gill [301014] ...ridge frequented by hawks.

Hawkbarrow Cottage Gosforth [103042] ...cottage by the hill frequented by hawks.

Hawkbarrow Farm Gosforth. Off the Gosforth to Nether Wasdale road [100040].

Hawkearth Bank between minor road, Winster-Birks Bridge and the A5074 [418923] ...land frequented by hawks.

Hawkrigg Farm Far Sawrey [382950].

Hawkshead quaint and picturesque small town nestled in the High Furness fells between Grizedale Forest and Claife Heights. Formerly in Lancashire. An old rhyme reads:-

A quaint old town is Hawkshead, and an ancient look it wears,
Its church, its school, its dwellings, its streets, its lanes, its squares,
With pent-houses and gables and over archway, lanes and nooks.

Earliest known mention is at the beginning of the 13th century in the Coucher Book of Furness Abbey. From the early 17th century until the 19th it was a principal centre of the woollen industry and pack horse trains from Hawkshead crossed Windermere by ferry and headed for Kendal and beyond. Today, tourists and tourism are the principal mainstays. A

by-pass road constructed in 1974 relieved traffic congestion through its narrow streets and squares. The old grammar school, closed in 1909, was attended by William Wordsworth from 1779-1787. It now houses a museum and library open to the public from April to October. The present St Michael and All Angel's Church dates from about the end of the 15th century. The building was rough-cast until 1875. Hawkshead Methodist Chapel dates from 1862. The town boasts four hostelries, the King's Arms, the Queen's Head, the Red Lion and the Sun - all four are centuries old.

Two particular notables, apart from Wordsworth, associated with Hawkshead and district were Edwin Sandys who became Archbishop of York in the 16th century. He was born at nearby Esthwaite Hall. Beatrix Potter, famous illustrator, authoress and later farmer, lived for many years at Hill Top, Near Sawrey, now owned by the National Trust and open to the public, and later Castle Cottage [352981] ...Haukr/Houkr's shieling/summer pasture.

Hawkshead Courthouse 0.8kms (0.5 mile) NNW Hawkshead alongside the B5286, Hawkshead-Clappersgate road. This, substantially 15th century building, comprising a single room spanning an archway to private property, is all that remains of the original Hawkshead Hall, the Manor House of monks from Furness Abbey. Here the Abbot or his representative would collect tenants' dues and hold court. In the early 16th century the hall ceased to be used by the monks and over the ensuing years became the home of several notable families including the Kendalls and Nicholsons before its demolition. The Courthouse was given to the National Trust in 1932 and now houses a museum of rural life. It is open to the public seasonally [350988].

Hawkshead Flat SE Near Sawrey, SW Far Sawrey [376953].

Hawkshead Hall Hawkshead [350988].

Hawkshead Hall Farm N Hawkshead alongside the B5286, Hawkshead-Clappersgate road [350988].

Hawkshead Hall Park large afforested area in the N of Grizedale Forest Park [334979].

Hawkshead Hill principally a cottage hamlet on the B5285, Coniston-Hawkshead road. The approach to Tarn Hows branches off the main road here. The Baptist Chapel dates from 1678 [338987].

Hawkshead Moor SW Hawkshead. Large area of Grizedale Forest Park [340967].

Hawkshead Trout Farm Esthwaite Water. 3kms (2 miles) S of Hawkshead off the Hawkshead-Newby Bridge road. Permits obtainable for rainbow trout fishing ('any method' according to brochure) whether from a rowing boat on the water or a line from the shore. For the less sporting but with the certainty of a 'catch' the farm also sells fresh trout [360955]

Haws craggy hill area above Jackson Ground [231930].

Haws Bank area to the S of Coniston village and next to Bowmanstead [301966].

Haws Wood between the A592 and Windermere (lake). Contains a caravan site [384905].

Hay Stacks sometimes Haystacks. A fell of peaks, tarns (of which Innominate, Blackbeck and Haystacks are the best known), crags, screes and other varieties of landscape, between Warnscale Bottom and Ennerdale. A favourite of Alfred Wainwright who classed it as the best fell-top of all and his ashes were scattered on or around Innominate Tarn, 597m (1959ft) [193132] ...if one accepts the single word Haystacks the derivation could come from the resemblance of tors on the summit to stacks of hay. However, the dual word Hay Stacks is believed to be the true title of the fell and in this case it means high rocks or possibly a personal name and therefore 'Heggr's rocks'.

Haycock on the Caw Fell, Little Gowder Crag, Great Scoat Fell, Little Scoat Fell ridge to Pillar. The most westerly of the fells over 762m (2500ft) at 797m (2615ft) [145107]. Not to be confused with the much lower Haystacks between Warnscale Bottom and Ennerdale ...possibly named from its shape which suggests a huge lump or a heap.

Haycote Farm alongside the Winster-Bowland Bridge road [416900] ...hay shed farm.

Hayes Garden World Ambleside. One of the largest garden centres in the N of England with expertise of the Hayes family in landscaping and horticulture in the Lake District going back over 200 years. Began in Ambleside in 1908 and grew steadily over the succeeding years. A large new building opened in 1972 and a large plant house in 1987 [377036].

Hayeswater lies ESE Hartsop in a deep U-shaped valley between Gray Crag and The Knott. Sixth largest of the tarns within the LDNP ranking after Devoke Water, Seathwaite Tarn, Burnmoor Tarn, Over Water and Blea Water. Its waters are used to supply the needs of the people of Penrith and its trout and perch are fished for by members of Penrith Angling Association, 422m (1385ft) with a maximum depth of 17m (56ft) [432122] ...possibly 'Eith's Lake', 'Hayes Lake', or means 'a deep hollow in a fell which provides a route between two settlements'.

Hayeswater Gill centuries ago the valley down which it flows was known as Aisdale. The gill rises at the head of Thornthwaite slightly NE of the summit of Thornthwaite Crag at 434102. Flows through Hayeswater and is joined by the unusual named Sulphury Gill and Prison Gill and the more prosaic sounding Calfgate Gill before meeting Pasture Beck at 416127. This joins Goldrill Beck at 402133.

Hazel Bank end of Lord's Seat-Robin Hood-High House Bank ridge. Overlooks the old road to Shap and Crookdale Beck [549052].

Hazel Bank N Wasdale, SW Wasdale Head 427m (1401ft) [545077].

Hazel Bank Hotel see **Rosthwaite**.

Hazel Hall off the A593 [271930].

Hazel Head farm off the Birker Fell road. Acquired by the NT in 1950 (196941).

Hazel Holme alongside the Cleator Moor to Ennerdale Bridge road [036147].

Hazel Lodge see **Black Sail Hut**.

Hazel Seat Wood W Field Head House. SSW Hazelseat [364918].

Hazel Shaw W Swindale Beck [532158] ...hazel 'copse'.

Hazelhow End between Thornsgill Beck and Cockley Moor [378226].

Hazelhurst alongside old road, Scales-Mungrisdale [362289].

Hazelseat property alongside the Hawkshead-Newby Bridge road [368925].

Head Lane Crosthwaite. Leads from the A5074 to Hubbersty Head [429915].

Head of Heltondale Beck NE slope Loadpot Hill. Heltondale Beck rises here and flows down through Heltondale on its way to originally join the R Lowther but is now tunnelled into Haweswater [463186].

Head of Riggindale see **Riggindale Beck**.

Heaf/Heft Herdwick sheep are let along with the farm and are known as hefted sheep. A heaf is a portion of fell which is grazed by a flock of sheep. The latter have a strong homing instinct, passed down through generations, for their own heaf.

Heald between Broom Bank and Stanegarth [498176] ...slope.

Heald Brow E side Coniston Water [310941] ...slope on the brow of the hill.

Heald Brow Pasture above Heald Brow [316943].

Heald Wood The Heald, Claife Heights [386976] ...wood on the slope.

Heald, The see **The Heald**.

Heaning Farm alongside the Mislet-A591 (Bannerrigg) road. Farmhouse dates back to

1681 and is now divided into two residences [432991] ...farm on, or by, the enclosed land.

Heathwaite Coniston [296969) ...possibly the high clearing.

Heathwaite (Windermere) see **Droomer**.

Heathwaite Manor off Lickbarrow Road [418969].

Heavy Sides W Braithwaite [222238].

Hebs Crag Howe Grain, Martindale. Alongside minor road up to Dale Head, Bannerdale, and near the old Martindale Church [435185].

Heck Beck rises Heckbeck Head at 419152 and flows down past site of a settlement [423154], now scheduled as an Ancient Monument, to join Bannerdale Beck at 427153 ...'heck' is a dialect expression meaning hatch.

Heck Cove above Bannerdale. Between Heck Crag and Heckbeck Head [418151].

Heck Crag line of crags overlooking the head of Bannerdale. E of north summit of Angletarn Pikes [420148].

Heckbarley fell area W Grike. Rises to 390m (1279ft) [076142].

Heckbeck Head head of Heck Beck [418152].

Heel Toe Hill E Top O Selside. Extensive view from summit [313919] ...sounds like a destination for a speedy walker!

Hegdale this little community lies NW of Rosgill. On the moors behind it stands Mary's Pillar [539176], erected by Thomas Castley, a member of a centuries-old local family, in memory of his daughter Mary, who died aged 24. From the Pillar there are splendid views of part of Mardale and Haweswater and the mountains and hills surrounding. Two wells are shown at Hegdale [534171] ...bird cherry, hagberry, hegberry or heckberry tree + dale.

Height House alongside minor road near Broughton Mills [231906].

Heining Bank NNE Askham. Wooded slope leading down to the R Lowther [517246] ...enclosure + bank (slope).

Heining Wood NNE Askham alongside the River Lowther and containing Heining Bank [517248].

Hell Gill Buscoe Sike passes through the deep ravine of Hell Gill before dropping over the spectacular Whorneyside Force [259055] ...'the stream which flows through the cavern-like ravine'.

Hell Gill rises Little Carrs at 268014 and joins the River Duddon at 264022 ...see **Hell Gill** above.

Hell Gill Force see **Whorneyside Force**.

Hell Gill Pike above the source of Hell Gill and on the Great/Little Carrs and Wet Side ridge, 692m (2270ft) [270014].

Helm Crag also known as The Helm. N of Grasmere village and to the W of the A591. Probably the best-known fell in Lakeland and over the years countless coach drivers and car drivers have pointed out to their passengers the resemblance of certain rocks on the summit ridge to people or animals. At the SE end, as seen from near the Swan Hotel, the lion towers over the lamb or, as Benjamin saw the rocks in Wordsworth's *The Waggoner*, 'the Astrologer and the Ancient Woman', 229m (250 yards) NW another group of rocks are said to resemble either a lion couchant, another lion and the lamb, an old woman playing the organ, or 'the Howitzer' depending on the particular viewpoint. Actually Helm Crag is not an individual fell but the end of a 3.6kms (2 miles) ridge which curves alongside Far Easedale. Its boulder strewn summit certainly made an impression on Thomas West in 1778 when he described it as "a curious Pyramidal mountain that exhibits an immense mass of antediluvian ruins." These words were echoed but not with quite the degree of eloquence by a writer in 1792 who noted that "the summit is covered with pieces of rock that gave it the features of a grand ruin, occasioned by an earthquake, or a number of stones jumbled together after the mystical manner of the Druids." Earlier, in 1769, Thomas Gray had remarked on its "strange broken outline on its top, like some gigantic building demolished, and the stones that comprised it flung across each other in wild confusion." The OS point is at 398m (1306ft) [327093] but the highest point is at 405m (1329ft) [326093] ...'the crag on the hilltop above the scar' or, as seen from certain angles the fell has the appearance of a helmet. In this case the name may have originated as the 'hill which looks like a helmet (helm)'.

Helm Farm Bowness-on-Windermere. Shown on OS map as an 'antiquity' [413970] ...helm from the ON means either hilltop or shelter. The farm is situated alongside a fell top. The EPNS gives its derivation as 'cattle shelter'.

Helmside N Grasmere village. Foot of Helm Crag and alongside the Green Burn. Old bridge here carries the Low Bridge-Town Head road over the Raise Beck just before the latter's confluence with Green Burn [331097].

Helppot Helpott in the 16th century and Hellpot in the 18th century. Today a farm but tradition has it that at one time it was an inn alongside the old packhorse/turnpike route from Kendal to Ulverston [480926] ...hellpit or deep hole/cavity.

Helsfell farm between the Kendal by-pass and Cunswick Fell [498939] ...see **Helsfell Nab**.

Helsfell Nab ridge WNW Kendal on which is part of Kendal Golf Club course [501936] ...hill of the cave. There is a cave on the Nab.

Helsgarth shown but not named on the OS map. 17th century cottage property just S of Stool End Farm, Great Langdale. As an habitation it fell into disuse many years ago and was utilised as a barn before extension in the mid-1930s. Since then it has been used as a holiday cottage [277056] ...possibly the enclosure near the Hell Gill, a deep cavern-like gorge through which runs Buscoe Sike.

Helton village 1.6kms (1 mile) S of Askham on the Askham-Bampton road. Centuries ago it was known variously as Helton Morvill or Helton Flecket (family names) to distinguish it from Helton (today Hilton) near Appleby [511221] ...farmstead on the slope.

Helton Fell WSW Helton. N upper reaches of Heltondale Beck. Encompasses Whitestone Moor [478203].

Heltondale property alongside Heltondale Beck and the start of the unfenced road via Rough Hill to the Bampton to Carhullan road [504207].

Heltondale valley which commences S of Helton and down which flows Heltondale Beck on its way to originally join the River Lowther but is now tunnelled into Haweswater. The dale is fairly wide as far as Dalehead 3.2kms (2 miles) but narrows as Heltondale Beck continues up the valley for another 2kms (1.25 miles) to the head of Heltondale Beck. A 2.74kms (3000 yards) long tunnel from Ullswater to Heltondale deep under Tarn Moor was opened in the late 1960s and carries water from the lake en route to Manchester [493205].

Heltondale Beck rises at the head of Heltondale, NE slope of Loadpot Hill, at 463186. As it travels down Heltondale it is joined by Dodd Beck, Red Gutter, Inkern Beck, Brown Beck, Blaika Sike, Mossy Beck and Setterah Sike, before originally joining the River Lowther at 515202. However, in October 1959, the waters of Heltondale and Howes Becks were diverted and tunnelled into Haweswater alongside the dam. Two bridges over the beck, one 168m (550ft) S of Widewath [502208] and the other 229m (750ft) SSW of Widewath at 501208 are both scheduled as Ancient Monuments.

Heltonhead Helton [503218].

Helvellyn A conjectural name. Some suggest that it was once a sacred hill to early inhabitants and called the Hill of Baal, or El-Velin, and so the present-day Helvellyn. Several centuries ago it was called Lauvellin, and presumed to be a hill belonging to a person possibly Vellin or Willan. The present name, however could be derived from 'hel' - hill; 'gwal' - wall; 'lyn' - a lake and the whole meaning 'the hill that walls the lake (Red Tarn)' or from 'helfa' - place where fish are caught or animals hunted and 'lyn' - a lake. The latter being Red Tarn. On the other hand it could simply be a corruption of Lauvellin, the 'hel' being a pronunciation of the capital L. Apparently, one pays one's money and takes one's choice. What is definitely known is that Helvellyn is situated W Patterdale and E Thirlmere. Highest part of the Helvellyn ridge it is also the third highest of the Lake District peaks after Scafell Pike and Scafell and was Westmorland's only peak over 914.4m (3000ft). Undoubtedly the most popular mountain for fell walkers and there are 14 generally accepted routes to its summit covering various degrees of difficulty for walkers and scramblers. Three monuments are to be found in the vicinity of the summit - 1) a small stone tablet just S of it commemorates the landing and take-off of the first aeroplane to land on a British mountain, in 1926; 2) on the summit edge the Gough memorial records the death of Charles Gough in 1805 and the faithful dog which kept vigil by his body for three months. The tragedy is told by Wordsworth in his poem *Fidelity* and by Sir W Scott in *Helvellyn*; 3) on Striding Edge, overlooking Nethermost Cove, stands the iron Dixon memorial to a huntsman who fell from the spot in 1858. On the E of the summit is Brownrigg Well from which originates Whelpside Gill. Gilpin in 1772 pointed to Helvellyn's "superior grandeur, stretching, near a league and a half in one vast concave ridge" 950m (3117ft) [342151].

Helvellyn Range see Reference Section: **Heights**.

Helvellyn Gill rises between Helvellyn Lower Man and White Side at 336162. The major portion joins the Thirlmere Leat and subsequently Thirlmere. That which escapes the leat meets How Beck and joins St John's Beck near Smaithwaite Bridge at 316195.

Helvellyn Lower Man 0.8kms (1/2 mile) NW Helvellyn. Only 25m lower than Helvellyn 925m (3035ft) [337155].

Helvellyn Screes large scree area WNW to SW of Helvellyn Lower Man [328156].

Helvellyn Youth Hostel Greenside, Glenridding. In a building formerly associated with the now defunct Greenside Mine [366173].

Hemp Rake W Broom Lane [452917] ...rough path through the hemp.

Hempgarth Wood/Plantation NNE Dacre and S of A66(T), [467276] ...the enclosure in which hemp was grown + wood/plantation.

Hen Comb between the upper reaches of Mosedale and Whiteoak Beck the grassy dome of Hen Comb is situated at the end of a ridge rising from Loweswater and which is marked on the OS map as Loweswater Fell. There is evidence of early mining activity to the NE of its summit above Mosedale Beck. From the E its summit is approached by a very steep and unpathed grassy slope 509m (1670ft) [132181] ...hill above the comb/valley frequented by water hens. Both Mosedale, Floutern Moss and upper Whiteoak Beck are boggy with many streams.

Hen Crag Wetherlam S ridge [290008] ...possibly, along with Hen Tor and Henfoot Beck, a reference to there having been water hens in the vicinity.

Hen Holme islet in Windermere close to Lady Holme [397974] ...island frequented by water hens (moorhens).

Hen Rock Windermere [396955] ...rock frequented by water hens.

Hen Tor Wetherlam S ridge [291009]. The word 'tor' is usually associated with rocky outcrops in South West England and the description here is unusual in the Lake District.

Henfoot Beck rises below Hen Tor, Wetherlam, at 292008. It is joined by its major tributary Swallow Scar Beck at 296010 and eventually combines with other streams to become Yewdale Beck.

Henhow cottage in Martindale long since in ruins. In the late 18th to late 19th century associated with a murder and subsequent haunting [434177] ...hen/water hen hill.

Hepworth Air Filtration Kentmere. Works near Kentmere Tarn [456020], see also **Kentmere Tarn**.

Herdus N of Ennerdale and Ennerdale Water and W Great Borne. The name Herdus is somewhat controversial. Some map makers ignore its existence while others suggest that it is Great Borne and writer Alfred Wainwright is emphatic as to its position when he says "Great Borne is... locally and correctly known as Herdus." Even the EPNS does not mention Herdus but suggests that Great Borne is identical with a hill called Hardeanut in the 13th century (Herdus a corruption?). W G Collingwood writing over a hundred years ago says that Herdus is a corruption of Herdhouse and other writers suggest Herdhause. However, the present OS map and other guide books definitely show Herdus as a separate entity slightly W of Great Borne and with a lower height of 562m (1844ft) [118163].

Herdwick Sheep see **Sheep**.

Hermons Hill Gosforth [104042]. Three centuries ago was said to be Hagworm's Hill therefore probably adder/viper hill.

Heron Crag Riggindale Scar [465113]. The title 'heron' refers in this case to the golden eagle or sea eagle.

Heron Crag W of the River Esk facing Great Gill Head Crag across the valley. Here the Esk valley begins to narrow [221030] ...crag frequented by eagles.

Heron Crag precipitous crag W Eagle Crag summit [274121] ...see above.

Heron Crag E of and above Stonethwaite Beck [265143] ...see above.

Heron Island larger of Rydal Water's two islands [356062] ...in most cases heron refers to the 'erne', the eagle, but in this case it does mean the heron.

Heron Pike on Nab Scar-Great Rigg-Fairfield ridge 612m (2008ft) 356083 ...owing to its height heron refers to the eagle rather than the heron. Erne (Eagle) Crag is nearby. Incidentally, given that a mountain is generally deemed to start at 610m (2000ft), Heron Pike is certainly one of the smallest mountains in the Lake District.

Heron Pike SE Sheffield Pike and S Black Crag. Overlooks Mossdale Beck and Ullswater [374178].

Heron Stones boulders below Heron Crag, Eskdale [222039].

Hesk Fell sometimes Hest Fell. Large grassy flat-topped hill between Ulpha and Devoke Water and prominent particularly from the Birker Moor Road 477m (1565ft) [176947] ...horse hill.

Hesket Farm off the Dacre to Sparket road [445261] ...ash tree headland + farm. Similar to 'Hesket' in Hesket Newmarket.

Hesket Wood alongside Dacre Beck [442266] ...ash tree headland + wood.

Hesketh Hall Broughton Mills [223908].

Heugh Scar crags at the northern extremity of Heughscar Hill [487237] ...end of the hill ridge.

Heughscar Hill W-WSW Askham from which it is easily ascended. Summit is bracken and grass covered with a limestone outcrop along the top. Ancient boundary stone on summit. Along its W flank runs the High Street Roman Road C370 (C1214ft) [488231].

Hewrigg Farm Irton. Between the A595 and the minor road from the A595 to Santon [083010].

Hewthwaite on slope leading up to Bonscale Pike [448200] ...either high clearing or ridge end.

HF Holidays Ltd Two centres in the Lake District - Derwent Bank, Portinscale, and Monk Coniston, Coniston.

High Abbey Wythop Mill. Low Abbey nearby [174294] ...unknown origin.

High Adam Crag above The Screes, Wasdale, and above Low Adam Crag [156045].

High Armaside alongside minor road from the B5292 to Hundith Hill Road [152276].

High Arnside farm E High Cross off the A593. Owned by the National Trust to whom it was given by Sir Samuel Scott in memory of his son who died in the Second World War. This fact is commemorated on a stone below the farm [332017].

High Arnside Tarn E of the old road, now mainly a track, from Knipe Fold to High Cross. Below Arnside Intake. Like nearby Tarn Hows it was artificially created by James Marshall. Fishing for rainbow trout is controlled by the WADAA, 168m (551ft) [331011].

High Bakestones above Scandale Head and S of the ridge route from Dove Crag to Little Hart Crag. Surmounted by a large column, a work of art, C710m (C2329ft) [379099] ...the high 'baking stones' as opposed to Low Bakestones the place where these stones were obtained. A considerable walk and climb was obviously necessary to obtain such stones, see also **Bakestones Moss**.

High Bank adjoining High Frith [170997].

High Bank below Low Snockrigg [185165].

High Bank Low Lorton. Low Bank Farm nearby [146259].

High Barn alongside track between Hawkshead-Grizedale road and Hawkshead-Newby Bridge road [345969].

High Barn alongside track from Kirkstone Road through Seathwaite to Roundhill Farm [384048].

High Barn Longsleddale. Near Stockdale Bridge [491047].

High Beck rises head of Windgap Cove at 165121 and joins the River Liza at 157138. Low Beck to its W.

High Beckside near Mungrisdale [366299].

High Bield cottage, Little Langdale [302037] ...high shelter/hut/dwelling.

High Birchclose E minor road, A66-Matterdale End. Adjacent minor road, Nabend-Dacre [414252].

High Birk Grizedale Forest Park [314933].

High Birk Howe farm, Little Langdale. Believed to be the oldest house in Little Langdale with Fell Foot probably the second. Purchased by the National Trust in 1948 [314033].

High Birkhow foot of Wastwater and across the minor road from Wasdale Hall YH, 124m (407ft) [142045].

High Birkin Knott overlooks Swindale. Nearby is Low Birkin Knott [497120].

High Birks off the A5074 Tarnside-Bowland Bridge Road [428906].

High Blake Dodd overlooks the head of Swindale. Nearby is Low Blake Dodd [495118]

High Bleaberry Knott Above Whorney Side and Low Bleaberry Knott [255052] ...the high bilberry peak.

High Blind How highest point on Claife Heights. Trig. point at 270m (886ft) [382973].

High Boonwood Gosforth [069045] ...boon ON 'bon' meaning request, favour, plea.

High Borrans hamlet with several old properties at the end of a lane which leads off the A591-A592 road [433009]. Nearby is an ancient settlement, Hugill British Settlement, a Celtic farming village. Although the hutments have long since disappeared the earthworks, footways and ancient boundary are still discernible. The site is on private land. Nearby is Borrans Reservoir whose outflow is the principal source of the River Gowan. A large outdoor centre here is operated by North Tyneside Council [433009] ...'Borran(s)' signifies a burial ground, an ancient pile of stones or a ruin. The name Borran combined with earthworks at Allen Knott, the settlement at High Borrans and two in Kentmere suggest a sizeable celtic population hereabouts.

High Borrow Bridge carries the former Kendal-Shap road over Borrow Beck. This route was replaced in the 1820s by the present line of the A6 and a new bridge, Huck's Bridge, built over the beck [550040].

High Bowkerstead Farm see **Bowkerstead Farm**.

High Bridge carries the Dacre to Sparket road over Dacre Beck. A deep pool nearby, known locally as The Wash Dub was, in days gone by, used by farmers to wash their sheep prior to shearing. Low Bridge nearer Dacre carries the road from the A592 to Dacre over Dacre Beck [452261].

High Bridge Gill rises Banna Fell at 108180 and combines with Comb Gill, Ill Gill and Grain Gill to become Croasdale Beck which enters the River Ehen at Ennerdale Bridge.

High Bridge Petton Gosforth [069031] ...see **Bridge Petton**.

High Broadrayne alongside the A591 N Grasmere village. Once a parsonage and the home of the Rev Joseph Simpson, Vicar of Wythburn Chapel for over 50 years, and a dear friend of William and Dorothy Wordsworth [335094].

High Brock Crag Beda Fell. Overlooks Boredale. Brock Crag and Low Brock Crags are also alongside the same ridge [418161].

High Brock Crags E of Scandale Beck. Low Brock Crags below [376072].

High Brow alongside minor road from the B5320 to Askham. Nearby is Low Brow [490254].

High Brow N Dowthwaite Crag 575m (1887ft) [368214].

High Brundrigg farm alongside the B5284, Plumgarths to Crook road [484950]. Across the road from Low Brundrigg ...more than likely the high burnt ridge.

High Buck How on Borrowdale Fells and the ridge leading up to Glaramara. Low Buck How to its NNW [257133].

High Bull Crag above Low Bull Crag. SSW Stony Cove Pike [415094] ...the word bull usually signifies a large boulder or crag.

High Buzzard Knott Stonethwaite Fell. Above Low Buzzard Knott [252099] ...'the high peak frequented by buzzards'.

High Cat Crag S bank River Greta [312248].

High Cat Crag W Windermere. Low Cat Crag to its ENE [373915].

High Close estate and building situated alongside the col on the road between Elterwater and Grasmere. In early life the building was both a shop and inn but in the 19th century it was rebuilt by a member of the influential Balme family who also constructed a lengthy drive and planted many of the trees thereabouts. The High Close estate was acquired by the National Trust in 1953 and the house is now a Youth Hostel. The gardens and woodland are open to the public [338052].

High Close Grange-in-Borrowdale [248177].

High Close Youth Hostel see **High Close**.

High Coledale between Coledale Beck and Barrow Gill and adjoining the path from Stile End and Barrow Door to Braithwaite [226228].

High/Low Colwith farms alongside the Little Langdale to Elterwater road [330031] [331033] ...the high and low places in the wood by the col or ridge.

High Coppice above the Santon Bridge to Nether Wasdale road. Nearby are Low and Great Coppices [115030].

High Coppice Eskdale. Across minor road from Low Coppice [140979].

High Corney E of the minor road from the A595 S to Corney [123928].

High Cove Seathwaite Fells. Head of The Cove [256973].

High Crag between Nethermost Pike and Dollywaggon Pike. Overlooks to the E Ruthwaite Cove 885m (2900ft) 343137].

High Crag between the Drunken Duck Inn-Outgate road and the B5286. Belies its name being only 158m (518ft) high [355009].

High Crag Crook. Above Low Crag [462942].

High Crag S Cockley Beck. Slightly E of and above Low Crag [247008].

High Crag third highest of the three principal summits on the Red Pike-High Stile-High Crag ridge, 744m (2441ft) [180140].

High Crag S Dock Tarn. Overlooks Stonethwaite Beck [274140].

High Crag Buttress precipitous N face of High Crag [181145].

High Craghall alongside the Duddon Bridge to Ulpha road W of the Duddon. Low Craghall faces across the road 225m (738ft) [180917] ...high crag hill.

High Crags on the Hindscarth-Scope End ridge 529m (1736ft) [217175].

High Crags SSE Little Town, Newlands valley 412m (1352ft) [237190].

High Crags W Nethermost Pike [339141].

High Cross highest point on the B5285 between Hawkshead and Coniston and where a road leaves the former for Knipe Fold [332986].

High Cross The 'new' road (A591) from Coniston-Ambleside, the old road from Hawkshead-Ambleside, W of Arnside Plantation, and a track from Tilberthwaite all meet hereabouts 158m (518ft) [328017].

High Cross Castle Windermere Youth Hostel. Prominent large white painted house 1.2kms (0.75 mile) up Bridge Lane from Troutbeck Bridge [405013].

High Cross Tarn see **Wharton Tarn**.

High Cross Youth Hostel see **High Cross Castle**.

High Cunsey hamlet on the road from Far Sawrey to the Hawkshead-Newby Bridge road. Centuries ago a busy and populous place with the nearby Forge, Cunsey Bridge furnace and later bobbin works and many charcoal burners in the woods thereabouts [381942].

High Dale Park farm, Dale Park [354932].

High Dale Park Plantation Dale Park [362935].

High Doat Borrowdale. With Johnny Wood on its E slope it was acquired by the NT in 1964, 283m (928ft) [247144] ...doat/dote is a dialect word meaning 'share of an open field, common land, etc.'

High Dodd subsidiary summit of Place Fell. NNE Low Moss, 501m (1644ft) [416182].

High Dyke alongside minor road from Mosser to Eaglesfield [109266].

High Dyke Wood W Dyke off the A595 [119952].

High End near the end of the ridge from Great Carrs and Little Carrs and Wet Side Edge which drops down to Greenburn. Spot height nearby at 488m (1601ft) [281024].

High Eskholme foot of the S slope of Muncaster Fell. ENE Low Eskholme [119979].

High Fairbank farm off minor road, Ings-Crook [442978]. Not to be confused with Fairbank Farm 1.2kms (0.75 mile) to its E.

High Falls Rydal, see **Rydal Falls**.

High Farm Penruddock [424275].

High Farm see The High Farm.

High Fell S ridge Black Sails [283000].

High Fell S Low Tarn [163088].

High Fell overlooks Low Water from its S. Brimful Beck flows to its E. Spot height at 532m (1745ft) [162091].

High Fells W slope Watson's Dodd. E Castle Rock [330196].

High Fieldside outskirts of Keswick. Fieldside nearby [286237].

High Fold Troutbeck [408028].

High Force waterfall upon Aira Beck [400209].

High Force crag at the head of the Coledale valley below which Pudding Beck drops down over High Force (waterfall) and shortly afterwards Low Force before it joins Coledale Beck [192214].

High Force waterfall at the head of Coledale on Pudding Beck below the crags of High Force.

High Forest see Naddle Forest.

High Frith between the R Esk and Whis Gill. Adjoins Low Frith [165997] ...high wood.

High Frith Gill Irton Park. Down the gill flows Stony Beck [112007] ...the high wooded narrow valley.

High Gait Crags [229057] ...the high crags frequented by goats.

High Gillbrae Lorton. Off the B5292. Gillbrae Farm nearby. Shown as Gill Brow on Bartholomew map [158269].

High Gillerthwaite Farm Ennerdale. Its history can be traced back to the 14th century. Saved from ruin by noted author Bob Orrell who wrote *Saddle Tramp in the Lake District* and for many years a regular contributar to *Cumbria* magazine. He lived there from 1977-1996. Today it is a camping barn [143141].

High Goat Gill rises W Powley's Hill at 501136 and joins Naddle Beck at 500142.

High Great Knott W Trout Beck and E Woundale. Low Great Knott lies to its S [415070].

High Green Troutbeck [412036].

High Greens NNW Green Pikes. S Gobling Beck (235953).

High Gregg Hall Underbarrow. Across the Underbarrow-Crosthwaite road from Low Gregg Hall [464915] ...Gregg is a corruption of local surname 'Grigg'. Hence nearby there are Grigg Hall Lane, Grigghall Bridge and Grigghall Lane.

High Ground alongside the A593, Torver to Coniston road. Spot height at 105m (344ft) [295953].

High Ground off Birker Moor fell road. S Low Ground [173981].

High Ground Manesty [249189].

High Grove along with Low Grove Farm that at High Grove has long since disappeared from the old road/track from Ambleside to Kirkstone Pass. Today, a track traverses along the side of the valley to Middle Grove Farm then a semblance of track to High Grove. The remaining section of track which met with what later became the A592 has been taken over by nature and only a walker's path continues to join the Struggle near Pet's Bridge. Grove Gill nearby [400066].

High Guards Coniston. Above Back Guards Plantation [309982] ...high enclosure.

High/Low Hacket Two farms above and between Fletcher's Wood and approached from the Langdale to Colwith road. The Wordsworths and their children stayed at High Hacket in October 1810, on a recuperative holiday, [324036] and [324034] ...the high and low piece of cleared ground. In the 17th century it is recorded that all the trees on Hacket Ground were bought for use in charcoal making.

High Hartsop Dodd end of ridge running NE from Little Hart Crag. Pyramidical in shape and with the appearance of a separate fell when viewed from Hartsop Hall or Brothers Water. High Hartsop Dodd is actually 99m (325ft) lower than Hartsop Dodd (Low Hartsop Dodd). The 'high' and 'low' refer to geographical positions alongside the pass between them, 519m (1703ft) [394107].

High Hay Wood slightly E of the A592 [411995].

High Hill Keswick. Bounded on three sides by a loop of the River Greta [263239].

High Hole Beck rises below Robinson Crags at 200173 and joins Keskadale Beck at 197177.

High Hollin Bank head of Coniston Water. Off the B5285 [321982].

High Hollins Brackenthwaite. Off the B5289 and the road from Hopebeck to the B5289. Low Hollins nearby [159228].

High Hollows W Mosedale Beck [356249].

High House foot of Knipescar Common. Approached by lane and track from the Bampton Grange-Rosgill Head-Shap road [538185].

High House alongside Potter Fell Road [502979].

High House Borrowdale. High House Bank towers above it [537048].

High House Butterwick [502194].

High House Crook [440941].

High House Seathwaite, Borrowdale. Last property in the dale. The 18th century High House subsequently became a ruin but was later rebuilt as the K-Fellwalkers base (K standing for K Shoes, Kendal) [236119].

High House Hugill. 16th century yeoman's residence later converted into farmhouse and cottage. The farm was purchased in 1994 and the following year refurbished and split into two residences, High House and High House Cottage. Hugill British Settlement nearby [438005].

High House Longsleddale. Low House is slightly lower down the valley [507019].

High House Over Staveley [475010].

High House Watermillock. Farm off minor road from A592 to Matterdale End (A5091) [434229].

High House Winster [411936].

High House practically opposite the driveway to Greengarth Hall [082006].

High House Bank above High House, Borrowdale 495m (1624ft) [543048].

High House Crag Buttermere [175173].

High House Fell between Lord's Seat and Crookdale Beck [522068].

High House Tarn largest of the Lincomb Tarns on the Glaramara to Allen Crags ridge and the only one actually named on the OS map [241093]. Above it to the S on a rocky shelf lies a delightful unnamed tarn practically enclosed by rock faces. Wainwright in his *The Southern Fells*, 'Allen Crags 7' provides an illustration of this and refers to it as "a perfect mountain tarn."

High How High Lorton [167258].

High How Hill E of the unfenced road from Heltondale to Scalegate and Scales Farm [493209].

High Howe sheepfold [468178].

High Hows Lamplugh. Between Cogra Moss and Wisenholme Beck 313m (1027ft) [096202].

High Hows Quarry Castle Crag, Borrowdale. Shown but not named on the OS map [251160], see also **Dalton, Millican**.

High Hows Wood Castle Crag, Borrowdale [252158].

High Hurst Duddon valley (206941).

High Iron Crag on slope of Illgill Head above Low Iron Crag [164053].

High Katelade above Trussgap Brow, Swindale [524133].

High Keld Gill rises Keld Gill Head, Wetherlam, at 282012 and joins Greenburn Beck at 279018 ...the high spring gill. Low Keld Gill joins Greenburn Beck lower down the valley.

High Kid Crag lower slope of Grasmoor above the B5289. Low Kid Crag nearby [163204].

High Kiln Bank Farm Duddon valley. Once a hostel but ceased as such after a devastating fire in the 1980s (212942).

High Kiln Bank Park above Kiln Bank and traversed by the Broughton Mills to Seathwaite fell road [213938].

High Kinmont ENE Middle Kinmont [123907] ...'Kinmont' - place either at the head or end of a moor/mountain.

High Knipe Knipe. Farm between Low Knipe and Knipe Scar [520197].

High Knott northernmost point of the low lying ridge W of the Kentmere valley and commencing at Reston Scar. The whole ridge is often referred to as Hugill Fell but the fell has its own summit between Reston Scar and High Knott. High Knott rises to C270m (C886ft) [454001]. Its summit is crowned by a well-built cairn in which is incorporated a plaque inscribed "In Memory of Thomas Williamson of Height, in Hugill, Gent, who died Feb 13th 1797. Aged 66 years. Erected in 1803." The cairn was originally constructed by the Rev T Williamson in memory of his father who, it is said, used to climb up High Knott every day before breakfast. However, it was restored along with the plaque in 1962. The summit is popularly known as the Williamson Monument/Memorial but this is no relation to that grandiose structure of the same title in Ashton Park, Lancaster.

High Knott Place Fell. E Scalehow Beck [414189].

High Knott Rosthwaite Fell. N Bessyfoot [257128].

High Kop E Keasgill Head [459160].

High Lane Kentmere. Road which connects Green Quarter with Brockstones and Hallow Bank and off which a track continues to Overend [463048].

High Lanshaw northern extremity of Lanshaw Hill [539146] ...the high long copse.

High Latterhead alongside the minor road from Loweswater via Thackthwaite to Low Lorton. Latterhead nearby [149228] ...see **Latterhead**.

High Level Route to Pillar & Pillar Rock path from near Looking Stead which traverses the Ennerdale flank of the ridge and goes by Robinson's Cairn and up to the summit of Pillar and also to the base of Pillar Rock. Used by experienced walkers and climbers [180121].

High Leys Crook. Off the track leading from the Crook-Underbarrow road [452939]

...high clearing.

High Lickbarrow old farm Lickbarrow Road [419973] ...high burial mound hill. No trace today of such a burial place.

High Light Haw Bethecar Moor 263m (863ft) [303905].

High Ling Crag above Crummock Water and Low Ling Crag [154182].

High Liza Bridge carries the B5289 over Liza Beck [156224].

High Lodore Borrowdale. Behind the Borrowdale Hotel. Here are the High Lodore Falls on Watendlath Beck [263183].

High Longthwaite Watermillock. Off minor road from the A592 to Matterdale End and the A5091 [436230].

High Lorton see **Lorton**.

High Loup Mardale Banks, E Haweswater [480120]. Nearby is Low Loup ...high leap.

High Ludderburn property across minor road from Low Ludderburn [404912].

High Man Grizedale Forest Park 282m (925ft) [328965].

High Man see **Skiddaw Man**.

High Man Tarn shown but not named on the OS map. Slightly E of the summit of High Man, Grizedale Forest Park. Grizedale Beck rises here, C260m (C853ft) [329965].

High Mere Greave High Mere Greave and Low Mere Greave are on slopes to NW [435071] and SW [434065] respectively of the summit of Yoke. Once large copses but today only the names remain to remind us that they were the high boundary copse and the low boundary copse.

High Merebeck off the Cleator Moor to Ennerdale Bridge road [038145].

High Mill former corn mill alongside the River Winster. In the 19th century Winster possessed 3 mills including a High and Low Mill [414942].

High Mill one of the mills which once operated at Lorton. Situated alongside Whit Beck and Highmill Bridge [160252].

High Moorside Irton. E A595. Low Moorside and Moorside Wood nearby [078015].

High Moss SW Outerside [209211].

High Mosser Mosser [118244].

High Nest off the A591 at Nest Brow. Low Nest nearby [291228].

High Nook not named on the OS map. Subsidiary summit of Gavel Fell 488m (1601ft) [120189].

High Nook Farm Loweswater. Part dates from the 16th century. Acquired by the NT in 1976 [129205] ...farm in a high sheltered place.

High Nook Tarn now named on the OS map. Nestled in comb SW High Nook Farm from which it takes its name, C220m (C722ft) [124199] ...see **High Nook Farm**.

High Over Park Torver [283946].

High Oxen Fell approached by track off the A593, Skelwith Bridge-Coniston road. Track also serves Low Oxen Fell [323019].

High Park above Rydal Park [371067].

High Park farm, Little Langdale [323029] ...see **Birk Rigg Park**.

High Park Hawkshead Hall Park, Grizedale Forest [333977].

High Park Plantation Grizedale Forest Park [332982].

High Parkamoor above Low Parkamoor, E side Coniston Water. Farm now in ruins [310926] ...see **Parkamoor**.

High Pate Crag Claife Heights. WSW High Blind How and above Low Pate Crag [381970] ...pate is a northern name for a badger and this is most likely the origin of the place name.

High Peat Stock above Low Peat Stock, Cockley Beck Fell. N Grey Friar [258011].

High Pen Lamplugh Fell 475m (1558ft) [110189].

High Pike between Low Pike and Dove Crag on the Low Pike-Fairfield ridge 656m (2152ft) [374088]. Besides the High Pike below there is another such, the most northerly of the Lake District mountains, in the Caldbeck Fells.

High Pike WNW Grey Friar [255006].

High Pike Haw Torver High Common 354m (1161ft) [264949].

High Pikehow S Haycock and below Gouder Crag 574m (1883ft) [144100].

High Pool Bridge carries Second Moss Lane over Underbarrow Pool [470902].

High Prior Scales NE of Low Prior Scales [063074] ...the Prior's higher shepherd's hut. Calder Abbey is nearby.

High Raise, Eastern Fells

High Raise considered by many to be the centre of the Lake District fells and certainly the highest of the central fells. High Raise is a large plateau area which commences at the Langdale Pikes and ends above Greenup Edge. It includes Sergeant Man, Thunacar Knott and High White Stones. The latter is a collection of grey/white stones (hence the name). The trig. point surmounting the stones is the highest point of High Raise and again many point out that High White Stones is the real name of the highest point and not High Raise, 762m (2500ft) [281095]. Another High Raise on the High Street ridge is slightly higher at 802m (2631ft).

High Raise on the High Street ridge and on the line of the Roman road. NE Rampsgill Head. Of the fells to the E of Ullswater it is second in height only to High Street, 802m (2631ft) [448134]. Not to be confused with High Raise 762m (2500ft), the highest point of the central fells or Raise 883m (2897ft) on the Helvellyn ridge.

High Rannerdale N Squat Beck, Rannerdale [172186].

High Raven Crag ESE slope Helm Crag. Low Raven Crag nearby [330092].

High Raven Crag on the slope of Fleetwith Pike N of Fleetwith Edge [201146].

High Reston Farm just off the A591 near Reston Hall [455987].

High Rigg also referred to as Naddle Fell or St John's Fell. Between Naddle Valley and St John's in the Vale. N top - 357m (1171ft) [309220]; Central top 343m (1125ft) [308215]; S top 311m (1020ft) [316201]; E top 307m (1007ft) [311211].

High Rogerscale alongside minor road from Low Lorton to Brandlingill [146265] ...Roger's high shieling.

High Rosthwaite E of the A593 [242901] ...the high clearing marked by a cairn or heap of stones.

High Row alongside the Dockray to Dowthwaitehead road [385218].

High Row Farm foot of Blease Fell, W slope of Blencathra [312256].

High Saddle Coldbarrow Fell. Low Saddle to its N 675m (2215ft) [289129].

High Saltcoates Farm near the end of minor road off the A595 [079970].

High Scarf Crag S shoulder of Scafell. Rises in tiers to 487m (1598ft) [215044] ...crag by the 'skaro', gap/mountain pass.

High Scawdel large buttress of Dale Head to the latter's ESE. Its extensive plateau-like summit holds several small tarns the largest being Launchy and High Scawdel [238147] ...bare hill at the head of the dale/valley.

High Scawdel Tarn a peat moss tarn on High Scawdel. Shown but not named on the OS map. Slightly SW of Launchy Tarn C550m (C1804ft) [231147].

High Seat highest point on the ridge between Castlerigg and Coldbarrow Fell and practically equidistant between Bleaberry Fell and High Tove. Its rocky summit outcrop is a welcome haven from the surrounding heather and bog. With a trig. point height of 608m (1995ft) it just misses becoming a mountain [287180].

High Seat Man High Seat [288171].

High Side Embleton. Section of N slope of Long Fell [164287].

High Side High Lorton. Off the B5292 [161264].

High Side Embleton [163286].

High Skelghyll National Trust farm alongside the old track from Ambleside through Skelghyll Wood to Troutbeck [390029] ...see **Skelghyll Wood**.

High Snab between Keskadale Beck and Scope Beck. Neighbour of Low High Snab [222190] ...see **Low Snab**.

High Snab Bank end of Robinson-Blea Crags ridge and above Scope Beck and High Snab and Low High Snab [215184].

High Snockrigg prominent hill overlooking Buttermere from the E. A lower summit on the slope of Robinson 526m (1726ft) [187169].

High Spy highest point on Scawdel Fell. E of the upper Newlands valley. Sometimes referred to as Lobstone Band (although this is lower to the summit's E) or Eel Crags (particularly by the rock climbing fraternity), the precipitous W wall of High Spy, 653m (2142ft) [234162] ...high lookout or viewpoint.

High Spying How Striding Edge. Overlooks Nethermost Cove and Beck [351149].

High Stanger Farm see **Stanger**.

High Steel Knott on the escarpment E slope High Spy overlooking Borrowdale [245164].

High Stile Torver [290942].

High Stile highest summit on the Red Pike-High Stile-High Crag ridge. Possesses two summits, one at 806m (2644ft) at 168148 and the other nearby, the summit of Grey Crag, at 807m (2648ft) at 170148.

High Stile ridge (Herdus-Seat). See Reference Section: **Heights**.

High Stile Wood Seatoller. Low Stile Wood adjoining [242136].

High Stock Bridge bridge across the River Derwent. Low Stock Bridge lower down the river [243260].

High Stonythwaite W Wallowbarrow Crag. SE Iron Crag [216968].

High Street principally a lengthy ridge running S to N with a very extensive plateau-like grassy summit capped by a triangulation point. The Romans used its high ridge as a connecting 'road' between their forts at Ambleside and Brougham, near Penrith. This traversed High Street itself, High Raise, Loadpot Hill and Heughscar Hill. The route was later referred to in the 13th century as 'Brethstreet' (the paved way of the Britons) while the more recent name for the ridge and summit, High Street, recalls what must have been the highest 'street' in the country. Up to the 19th century surrounding shepherds and farmers held their annual meets and fair days on the summit area where there was much carousing, feasting, and horseracing. The summit is still called Racecourse Hill. The mind boggles at the energy expounded on getting themselves, their horses, food, and large quantities of ale, up to the summit and then to participate in all the jollification associated with such an event. The 'meet' was subsequently transferred to Mardale and held there until flooding of the valley. Today it is held annually at Bampton. Major routes of ascent are from Hartsop (via Caudale Moor or the Knott), Kirkstone Pass Inn (via Caudale Moor), Mardale (via the Nan Bield Pass; Rough Crag/Long Stile; or Kidsty Pike), Patterdale (via Angle Tarn) and Troutbeck (via Troutbeck Park/Head and Threshthwaite Mouth) and Kentmere (via Nan Bield Pass or Hall Cove), 828m (2717ft) [441110].

High Street Range see Reference Section: **Heights**.

High Street Roman Road Ambleside to Brougham via Allen Knott, Scots Rake, or by Grandsire, Yoke, Ill Bell, Froswick, to High Street then via High Raise, Loadpot Hill and Heughscar Hill.

High Strutta above Low Strutta and Strutta Wood. E of the road to Watendlath [272195].

High Sweden Bridge ancient packhorse bridge which carries a path from the Low Sweden Bridge-Low Pike path across Scandale Beck to join the track up Scandale and over the Scandale Pass [379067] ...Sweden (Swithen) land cleared by burning.

High Sweden Coppice alongside Scandale Beck. Low Sweden Coppice below [378061] ...see **High Sweden Bridge**.

High Swinklebank Farm Longsleddale [494043] ...swinklebank means the spring on the hill slope where swine drank.

High Swinside Farm Foot of Swinside. Off the road from the B5292 to Hopebeck [169246].

High Taggleshaw Tarn see **Taggleshaw Tarns**.

High Tarn see Green Hows Tarn/Great Green Hows Tarn.

High Teighton How Wrynose Fell. Above Low Teighton How and the summit of Wrynose Pass [275033].

High Thistleton Gosforth. Low Thistleton nearby [098047] ...the high dwelling by the thistles.

High Thrushbank just off the Loweswater to Mockerkin road. Thrushbank nearby [133215].

High Tilberthwaite see **Tilberthwaite**.

High Tock How Tock How Farm, High Wray. Off the High Wray-Colthouse road. One of the many farms bequeathed to the National Trust by Mr W Heelis (husband of Beatrix Potter) in 1945. Nearby, alongside the aforementioned road is a well/horse trough and drinking fountain erected in 1891 by a member of the Richardson family of nearby Balla Wray in memory of her husband. The inscription reads "In Memory of Happy Days," [363998] ...personal name + hill.

High Tongue on tongue of land between Tarn Beck and the River Duddon [233977].

High Top E Keasgill Head [459160].

High Torver Park Torver. Large detached property dating from 1850 on the edge of the village [283946].

High Tove summit on the ridge between Watendlath and Armboth. An exceedingly wet area 515m (1690ft) [289165] ...possibly tove is a dialect word for 'tuft' and refers to the hill's heathery, tufty summit.

High Wallowbarrow Farm S Wallowbarrow Crag. Sold to the NT in 1974 by the Lake District Farm Estates [221963].

High Water Head area at the head of Coniston Water [314982].

High Waterside alongside the Cleator Moor to Ennerdale Bridge road. Low Waterside to its WSW [050156].

High Wax Knott W of Scarth Gap Pass. Low Wax Knott to the E of the Pass [187140].

High Wether Crag Black Sails [284006] ...'wether' - castrated ram.

High Wether Howe E Mosedale, N Scam Matthew, 531m (1742ft) [515109] ...high hill of the wethers (castrated rams).

High Whineray Ground Duddon valley. Low Whineray Ground nearby [202903] ...the high whin/gorse ground.

High Whitbeck Bridge carries the minor road from Hopebeck N to the B5289 over Whit Beck [158250].

High White Rake steep and rough passage (rake) through the escarpment below Blea Crag and leading from Greenup to ampitheatre at the rear of Nitting Haws and Goat Crag. Low White Rake to its ESE [240171].

High White Stones see **High Raise**.

High Winder S Winder Hall Farm. At one time the latter was called Low Winder [493239] ...high wind-swept shieling offering shelter from the wind.

High Wood Nether Wasdale [123046].

High Wood E bank of the foot of Crummock Water [158203].

High Wray see **Wray**.

High Wray Bay Windermere [377005] ...see **Wray**.

High Wray Farm see **Wray**.

High Wythow Yewdale Fells [302991] ...the high white hill, an area principally dry, open.

High Yewdale farm alongside the A593 NNE Coniston. Bequeathed by Beatrix Potter to the National Trust [315997].

Highcross Loweswater. Off the Loweswater to Mockerkin road [137213].

Highcross Wood Lowther Park [530240].

Higher Peel Near promontory Coniston Water near Peel Island [295917].

Higher Thorny Slack Satterthwaite Moor. Above Thorny Slack [329911].

Highfield Crag overlooks Naddle Beck [506148].

Highfield House off the B5285 [345986].

Highfield Plantation W Askham, E Heughscar Hill [497235].

Highfield Wood E Bassenthwaite Lake. W Sand Hill. Section of the Allerdale Ramble passes along two sides of it [229288].

Highford Beck lengthy stream which rises Birker Moor between White Crag and Far Hill. Joined by Little and Smallstone Becks and subsequently Arminghow Gill whence it becomes Birker Beck. This flows over Stanley Force into the deep wooded ravine of Stanley Gill where it takes the name Stanleygill Beck. Meets the R Esk at 173002.

Highgate off lane S Troutbeck-Wallthwaite road [358258].

Highgate Farm on the northern edge of the Lake District National Park off the A66(T) [445275].

Highgateclose end of lane S Troutbeck-Wallthwaite road [358255].

Highlands Wood S Holehird SW Far Orrest [411006].

Highlow Tarns see **Tarn Hows**.

Highmill Bridge carries the minor road to Low Swinside over Whit Beck [159251].

Highnook Beck rises at 116190 and joins Whiteoak Beck at 130206.

Highnose Head slope of Kirk Fell overlooking Mosedale [189100].

Highpark Loweswater. Lowpark nearby [145203].

Highpark Buildings S of Lowpark Buildings in parkland adjoining Thornthwaite Hall [523162].

Highpark Wood alongside A591 E Thirlmere and NNW the Swirls [317167].

Highs Moss Claife Heights [377981].

Highs Moss Tarn Highs Moss, Claife Heights. Overgrown tarn alongside footpath from Near Sawrey past Moss Eccles Tarn and Wise Een Tarn to Belle Grange, C220m (C722ft) [375980].

Highside Farm Embleton [168288].

Hill down lane off minor road Scales-Guardhouse [351256].

Hill W Little Mell Fell. Off minor road, Matterdale Rigg-A592 [410238].

Hill, The see **The Hill**.

Hill Cottage Longsleddale [489046].

Hill Farm Ings [443988].

Hill Farm off the minor road from Aikbank Mill via Brandlingill to Randle Cross [121266].

Hill Fell S Tarn Hows and alongside the road from Hawkshead Hill to Tarn Hows [329991].

Hill Fell Plantation adjoining Hill Fell S Tarn Hows [325989].

Hill Forts see **Forts (Iron Age)**.

Hill of Oaks see **Windermere** (lake).

Hill Plantation Lowther Park [529205].

Hill Top Crosthwaite [429917].

Hill Top Near Sawrey, see **Near Sawrey**.

Hill Top Farm off B5322 St John's in the Vale [317230].

Hill Top Farm off minor road, A66-Matterdale End [418272].

Hilltop Quarries disused. St John's in the Vale, E B5322 [321231].

Hind Cove alongside the high level route to Pillar and Pillar Rock via Robinson's Cairn [178122].

Hind Crag Glaramara [239110].

Hind Crag in NT Gowbarrow Park overlooking Ullswater [405206].

Hind Crag NW slope Glaramara and overlooking the confluence of Styhead and Grains Gills [239112].

Hind Gill rises below Coombe Head at 248108 and joins the River Derwent at 235116.

Hind Side Glaramara [240103].

Hindle Crag in NT land alongside the road from Loweswater to the B5289 at Brackenthwaite [151219].

Hindscarth highest summit on the Scope End-High Crags-Hindscarth ridge. Faces its slightly taller 'twin' Robinson across Little Dale 727m (2385ft) [216165] ...pass/gap frequented by deer.

Hindscarth Crags E face Hindscarth overlooking the Newlands valley [216162].

Hindscarth Edge ridge connecting Dale Head to Hindscarth [216157].

Hinning House Duddon valley [240999] ...'hegning' - enclosed land.

Hinning House Eskdale [124973] ...see above.

Hinning House Bridge Eskdale. Bridge carrying track to and from Hinning House [121973].

Hinning House Close Duddon valley. SW Hinning House [237994].

Hinning House Fell W Great Carrs, N Grey Friar and above Hinning House in the Duddon valley [260009].

Hird House Troutbeck Park. Similar to Hird Wood and Holehird in that it was named from members of the local Hird family. One of them Hugh Hird, also known as the Troutbeck Giant or the Cork Lad of Kentmere, was a legendary giant of a man who lived with his mother in the Troutbeck valley in a house and land granted by the King who was impressed by Hugh's prowess. Legend has it that he routed a party of marauding Scots at Threshthwaite Cove by firing rails at them from his bow of a bough of a large yew tree. Also, while workmen were constructing Kentmere Hall he single-handedly lifted into place a 9 metres (30ft) beam which 10 men could not move. He is also said to have eaten a whole sheep at one sitting. Apparently his strength killed him. He died as a result of injuries sustained by pulling up trees by the roots [419058], see also **Holehird**.

Hird Wood Troutbeck Park [417060] ...see **Hird House**.

Hird, Hugh see **Hird House/Holehird**.

Hirst Park Muncaster Castle grounds [107965].

Hirst Lodge alongside the A595 at the entrance to Hirst Park, Muncaster [110968].

Hirst Plantation Muncaster Castle grounds [017968].

Hoathwaite Beck rises at spring alongside the A593 at 289948 and joins Coniston Water at 303953 ...stream in the hollow clearing.

Hoathwaite Farm Torver. Acquired by the NT in 1977 [296949] ...farm in the hollow clearing.

Hoathwaite Landing W shore Coniston Water near Coniston Hall. At its rear is Hoathwaite Farm National Trust property [302951] ...landing by the hollow clearing.

Hob Gill rises on Satterthwaite Moor at 317919. Flows into and out of Wood Moss Tarn and joins Grizedale Beck at 338915.

Hob Gill Plantation Satterthwaite. Alongside Hob Gill [332917].

Hobcarton valley and ridge S of the Whinlatter Pass [192233] ...of uncertain origin. Possibly either Cartan/Kjartan's valley (hop) or hill/mound (lobbe).

Hobcarton Crag impressive line of crags rising to over 152m (500ft) at the head of the Hobcarton valley [190220].

Hobcarton End above Black Crag on the N ridge of Grisedale Pike 634m (2080ft) [195235]. Alongside the ridge between Black Crag and Hobcarton End an Avro Anson crashed in February 1943, killing four crew members.

Hobcarton Pike see **Hopegill Head**.

Hobcarton Plantation alongside the Whinlatter Pass road, the B5292 [192243].

Hobgrumble Gill rises between Captain Whelter Bog and Howes at 493106 and falls between Nabs Crag and Geordie Greathead Crag to join Mosedale Beck at 504120. The confluence becomes Swindale Beck ...hob is either hobgoblin or refers to the small hanging valley above the gill; 'grumble' is rumble or noisy and certainly the stream descends the narrow ravine in long, steep and at times noisy falls.

Hobkin Ground alongside minor road from Broughton Mills to Torver [228908].

Hodge Close small community [317018] with a small white-washed cottage bearing the name Hodge Close near the large Hodge Close Quarry (also called the Lagoon) [317017]. Possibly the latter was once two quarries which eventually joined to form one. Very impressive when viewed from above but very deep and a magnet for divers, climbers and abseilers. Work ceased in the 1950s. Water now fills the quarry to approximately two thirds of its original depth. It is extremely dangerous and over the years has claimed several lives.

Hodge Close Quarries see **Hodge Close**.

Hodge How Eskdale. Near Doctor(s) Bridge 101m (331ft) [187007].

Hodge Wife Gill ravine down which Strands Beck flows [267905].

Hodgehowe property off the A591 near Calgarth Hall [402996] ...personal name + nook of land.

Hodgehowe Wood alongside the A591 near its junction with the A592 [404995]. Small hill alongside rises to 79m (259ft).

Hodgson Hill E shore Ullswater [465233] ...local family of Hodgson or Hod(I)son.

Hodgson How Portinscale 99m (325ft) [245237].

Hodgson's Leap Underbarrow Scar (Scout Scar) [486915] ...Hodgson made a bet that he would blindfold his horse and the pair of them would leap from the scar. This they did and presumably he never picked up any winnings. One certainly feels sorry for the poor horse.

Hodson's Tarn unnamed on OS map. Slightly NNE of Robinson's Tarn C200m (C656ft) [369982].

Hog Bank Oxen Fell [324017].

Hog Gill rises under Hoggill Brow, Hartsop above How, at 387125 and joins Deepdale Beck at 387129.

Hog Hole Fairfield Crags. A long narrow scree shoot [365120].

Hog House Beck rises as a spring E Drunken Duck Inn at 353011 and joins Blelham Beck at 372014 ...in British dialect a 'hog' is a young sheep (lamb) that has yet to be sheared and therefore the whole name refers to the shed which houses sheep by the stream.

Hogg Park between Wythop Hall and Ladies Table [207287].

Hogget Gill rises SE Dove Crag at 379102 and joins Dovedale Beck at 390114 ...named from the family of Richard Hoggard.

Hoggill Brow Hartsop above How. Between summit and Gale Crag [388122].

Hogs Earth behind Gowder Crag, Borrowdale [267186] ...land where lambs pastured.

Hol Beck farthest headstream rises at 400044 and the beck drops down through a deep and wooded chasm and under the A591 to join Windermere at 385019 ...stream which flows down a deep cavity.

Holbeck Ghyll Hotel off Holbeck Lane. A 19th century house formerly a hunting lodge of Lord Lonsdale. Today it is a country house hotel [392022] ...named after Hol Beck, see above.

Holbeck Lane leaves the A591, Windermere-Ambleside road, S of the Lowwood Hotel and joins the Troutbeck Bridge-Troutbeck road at Town End [389019].

Holbeck Lane Cottage Holbeck Lane. Built in 1866 and originally the residence of the groomsman for nearby Briery Close [391019].

Hole Beck farthest headstream rises at 255928 and the beck joins Steers Pool (Lord's Gill) at 251911.

Hole Beck property alongside Hole Beck and the A593 [252917].

Hole Gill rises Lank Rigg at 092118 and is one of several tributaries including Short Grain, Red Gill, Long Grain and Bleaberry Gill which combine to become Worm Gill.

Hole House Farm alongside the R Eamont NNE Pooley Bridge [474251] ..house/farm in a hollow.

Hole-in-the Wall formerly a hole in the wall but today a well used stile over which passes the path from Glenridding and Patterdale to Striding Edge, Helvellyn [359115].

Hole in T'Wall Inn see **New Hall Inn**.

Hole Mire High Lorton. Alongside the B5292 [162260].

Hole Rake passage and track between Above Beck Fells (Coniston Fells) and the Yewdale Fells. A major tributary of Crook Beck rises nearby [293991].

Holehird mansion and gardens off the A592, Windermere. Holehird certainly existed as a farm centuries ago when the property was owned by a Thomas Hird. There is also a possible connection with Hugh Hird, the Troutbeck Giant (see **Hird House**). Later it became a country house which was extended by a Mr Lingard, a Manchester industrialist, over the 1850s and early 60s. Bought by another Manchester industrialist, John McMillan Dunlop (d 1878) in 1865, he made considerable alterations and extensions to the house and gardens over the succeeding four years. These more than likely included the construction of the present walled garden. An inscription over the main entrance to the mansion bears the initials 'JMcD 1869.' In 1897 the house was acquired by William Groves of the Salford brewing firm of Groves and Whitnall for the sum of £18,675. (Incidentally, Groves and Whitnall Ltd were taken over by Greenall Whitley & Co Ltd of Warrington in 1961 and brewing ceased in 1972). The house and gardens were bequeathed in 1945 by Edward Leigh Groves to the people of Westmorland for "the purpose of the better development of the health and social welfare services of the County." Subsequently acquired as a Cheshire Home and still serves this purpose. The grounds are open to the general public.

Approximately 3.5 acres including a walled garden and three national collections, hydrangeas, astilbes and ferns are managed by the Lakeland Horticultural Society (formed in 1969) and is looked after by volunteers. These gardens are open to the general public [410009] ...the holding of Hird.

Holehird Tarn Troutbeck Bridge. Artificial tarn in the grounds of Holehird Cheshire Home off the A592. Coarse fishing available by ticket from adjoining Lakeland Horticultural Society office, C120m (C394ft) [408008].

Holehouse Ulpha. Up the valley of Holehouse Gill. Actually three houses [181930] ...house in the hollow.

Holehouse Bridge bridge across Holehouse Gill near Holehouse [181932].

Holehouse Gill rises Holehouse Tarn at 155940. Joined by Storthes Gill at 169938 and Tongue Gill at 183926 then on past Holehouse (from which it takes its name) and through a wooded valley to join the River Duddon at 194924. A reservoir alongside, sometimes erroneously called Holehouse Tarn, was used to supply power to the Ulpha bobbin mill.

Holehouse Tarn a peat moss tarn below Stainton Pike. The source of Holehouse Gill, C470m (C1542ft) [154940].

Holghyll near Hutton. Contains Skitwath Beck [429273].

Hollens Farmhouse Grasmere. Approached through an impressive archway off the A591. Hollins Cottage is next door and the Hollins further on up a private track [343074].

Hollin alongside Heltondale Beck, Heltondale [491200] ...holly tree.

Hollin Band Plantation Claife Heights [375982] ...plantation by or on the holly ridge.

Hollin Bank E of the A593, Skelwith Bridge-Coniston road [331022] ...holly bank.

Hollin Bank Underbarrow. Alongside the Underbarrow-Crosthwaite road [458913] ...holly bank.

Hollin Crag between the River Brathay and Greenburn Beck. End of the ridge from Great Carrs over Little Carrs and Wet Side Edge [296027].

Hollin Crag slightly N of the eastern section of Wrynose Pass [289033] ...holly crag.

Hollin Crag W Potter Fell Road [517983] ...holly crag.

Hollin Head Cottage Eskdale. Alongside the road up the valley. S Hollinghead Crag [158002].

Hollin House Haw E Seathwaite Bridge [235968].

Hollin House Tongue cross the River Duddon from Wallowbarrow Crag. Its summit is Pen [227969].

Hollin How NW Dockray [390219].

Hollin How Eskdale [148001].

Hollin How N Wallowbarrow Crag [222971] ...holly hill.

Hollin Howe Staveley Head Fell [472018] ...holly hill.

Hollin Root Longsleddale [493035] ...holly root.

Hollin Root off minor road, B5322-A66 [309239].

Hollin Slack alongside Hollin Crag N of Wrynose Pass [291033] ...holly hollow.

Hollinghead Bank W Boot [167008] ...holly at the head of the bank.

Hollinghead Crag Eskdale. N Hollin Head Cottage [157007].

Hollinhow Gill rises Low Moss, Place Fell, at 416178 and drops down ravine to join Boredale Beck at 421176.

Hollins farm, Dockray [394217].

Hollins, The Grasmere. Off the A591. Large mansion of which the coach-house and stables have been claimed as the site of Michael's cottage, the home of Michael the shepherd of Wordsworth's *Michael.* (For other claimants see *Wordsworth & the Lake District* by David McCracken, 1984, page 39) and Michael's Fold. Originally a farm but enlarged in the mid 19th century and became the Hollins and Lowther Hotel. Later the home of a Mr Alcock who dammed and stocked with trout the tarn which subsequently took the name Alcock Tarn. Some 50 years ago was an approved riding school and guest house and during part of the Second World War 20 Women's Timber Corps girls were billeted in the building. Later the property occupied by a National Trust Regional Office [343076].

Hollins Boot, Eskdale [179011].

Hollins near the confluence of the Rivers Bleng and Irt [108031].

Hollins Bridge carries the track to Hollins over the River Irt [103029].

Hollinthwaite E Pooley Bridge to Howtown road. Alongside Elder Beck [476232] ...holly clearing. Obviously in what was once a part of a much wooded area as emphasised by nearby names such as Aik (Oak) Beck, Elder Beck, Barton Park (in the mid-17th century 'full of eller (elder) and hazell') and Woodside.

Hollow Clough Gill rises S Lord's Lot at 445922 and joins the River Gilpin at 438912.

Hollow Gill rises E Wastwater at 191064. Joined by Groove Gill at 184066 and then flows through Fence Wood and by Wasdale Head Hall Farm to join Wastwater at 179068.

Hollow Moor highest point of Green Quarter Fell rising to 426m (1398ft) at 469040. Excellent viewpoint for crags and mountains which encircle the head of Kentmere.

Hollow Moor in Forestry Commission area E River Bleng and W Kid Beck [109059].

Hollow Moss Beck rises Dunnerdale Fells at 208923 and joins the River Duddon at 204937.

Hollow Stone just S of the lower reach of Hopgill Beck and near the road along the E side of Haweswater [481117].

Hollow Stone below Goat Crag E slope of High Spy [247162] ...see **Hollow Stones** below.

Hollow Stones SE Tarn Hill. Trig. point at 188m (617ft) [450919].

Hollow Stones boulders below Pikes Crag, Scafell Pike, and crossed by a route to the latter from Wasdale via Brown Tongue [206074] ...not hollow stones but stones in a hollow/basin.

Hollowgate alongside the A6 [549031] ...a track started from here crossed Breast High (Breasthigh Road), N of Borrowdale, and continued to Tebay. This is thought to have been called Hollowgate 'the hollow way'.

Hollows W A5091. SSW Matterdale End. A one-time wayside inn 392228.

Hollows Farm Grange-in-Borrowdale. Former YH. Camping site [247171].

Hollowstones near Irton Road Station [136999].

Holly Crag N Hartsop above How ridge. Overlooks Deepdale Beck [383123].

Holly How Youth Hostel Far End, Coniston [302980].

Holmcrag Wood Grange-in-Borrowdale [251170].

Holme Beck rises between Carling Knott and Burnbank Fell at 112204 and flows into Loweswater at 123217.

Holme Bridge old packhorse bridge across the R. Irt between Carleton and Drigg Holme [077987].

Holme Brow WNW Pull Wyke [358204].

Holme Crag E shore head of Windermere [378025] ...crag on an island or on land nearly surrounded by water. In this case the latter. It does, however, overlook a tiny islet.

Holme Fell to the W of the A593 and Yew Tree Tarn. Ivy Crag on the heathery plateau possesses a very large cairn which many assume to be the summit of the fell. This actually lies some 183m (200 yards) to its W at 317m (1040ft). Given to the National Trust in 1930 [315006].

Holme Force series of attractive waterfalls on Holme Beck [119214].

Holme Ground farm alongside the road from the A593 to Hodge Close. Bequeathed to the National Trust by Beatrix Potter. In the early 20th century figured prominently in the Langdale Linen Industry (see also **Elterwater** and **Tilberthwaite**).

Holme Ground Tarns two former reservoirs constructed from a natural tarn to supply water to the nearby slate quarries, 230m (755ft) [215011/216011].

Holme Islands Crummock Water [165172].

Holme Well Wood W shore Windermere [379926].

Holme Wood alongside Loweswater. Through it flows Holme Beck over Holme Force and there are several attractive paths and tracks through the wood. Purchased by the NT in 1937 [123212].

Holmes Head Farm approached by track off the minor road, Outgate-Skelwith Fold [350022] (see also **Holmes Head Tarn**).

Holmes Head Tarn private tarn (not named on the OS map) alongside track to Holmes

Head Farm, C110m (C361ft) [350023].

Holmes Wood W Underbarrow Moss [460903] ...local family of Holme.

Holmesdale Green Bridge crosses Birkside Gill at 326124.

Holmeside alongside track off minor road from the A595 (Holmrook) to Santon Bridge [091992].

Holmgill Knotts S slope Kirk Fell [198099].

Holmrook small village alongside a bend of the River Irt and alongside the A595. On the W boundary of the LDNP. Within its confines are the Lutwidge Arms [079999] which stands on the site of Holmrook Hall home farm; the remains of Holmrook Hall of which the shape and extent of the former Victorian garden can still be seen under vegetation. The hall was the seat of the Lutwidge family for many years. One of the family, Skeffington Lutwidge, became an admiral. However, the name is probably best remembered through Charles Lutwidge Dodgson (author and artist Lewis Carroll), a cousin of the family and who frequently visited the hall. The village also possesses an ancient well with a fine sandstone surround but the rear wall has been rebuilt and the spout bears the date 1988 [079996] ...'holm' from the ON holmr is an islet or a piece of land partly surrounded by a stream (the River Irt) and 'rook' is suggested as being from krokr meaning a crook or bend (again the River Irt).

Holy Trinity Church Brathay, see **Brathay Church**.

Holy Well Gosforth. At one time it was surrounded by a medieval chapel [073041].

Holywath Coniston [299979] ...'wath' - a ford.

Home Farm Bowness-on-Windermere. NNW Matson Ground [415968].

Home Farm Graythwaite. W Graythwaite Hall [367914].

Home Farm Newtown, Lowther Park [528242].

Home Farm Patterdale. Sited off minor road from A592 to Grisedale [390158].

Home Farm Muncaster [096966].

Homesteads (ancient habitations):

Tongue How	[070099]
NW Gosforth Hall Plantation	[104054]
Waberthwaite Fell. Alongside Whitrow Beck	[134939]
Ennerdale	[152139]
Lanthwaite Green	[160210]
E shore Buttermere	[191156]
Alongside Torver Beck	[277961]
Torver	[279950]
Alongside Scrow Beck and near Bell Cottage	[288976]
W Burnbanks	[500160]

Honeybee Wood below Underbarrow Scar (Scout Scar) [482904].

Honister Crag large impressive precipitous crag on the N face of Fleetwith Pike. Towers for 305m (1000ft) above the Honister Pass road. Disused quarries in its vicinity [211142].

Honister Hause summit of Honister Pass between Borrowdale and Buttermere C360m (C1181ft) [225136].

Honister Pass pass over Honister Hause between Borrowdale and Buttermere. Up to 80 years ago the road, as such, over Honister was exceptionally stony and steep. So much so that the then owners of the quarries constructed their own road. In 1922 it was recorded that 'there is now a toll road from Seatoller to the summit of the Pass.' This was free to vehicles on quarry business but for other vehicles a toll of 2d for cycles and ls for motor vehicles was charged. Even then the road had five gates which had to be opened. The charge for motor vehicles had risen to 2s 6d in the 1930s. The present surfaced road, a section of the B5289, was built in the l930s [220141].

Honister Quarries & Mines the quarrying of green slate is believed to have begun in a small degree at Honister in 1643 and on a larger scale in the 1750s with considerable expansion from 1833. Of the principal sites in the region of Honister Hause Dubs Quarry was worked from about 1750 until 1932; Quey Foot opened in 1898 but had a very short life; Sam New and Fisher began about 1839; Yewcrag from 1848; Ash Gill from about 1820 and Hopper mainly between the 1960s and 1985. The former horse-powered Dubs Incline which led from Dubs Quarry to the Hause and which today is trod by countless walkers usually as far as the remains of the old winding house (Drum House) at its highest point, was constructed in 1891. The Honister Quarry mountain rescue team was the only rescue group then operating in the central lakes area and was in existence long before the Keswick Mountain Rescue Team which was formed as far back as 1947. Slate mining and quarrying ceased altogether at Honister in 1986. In 1987, however, two local men took over the lease of the former Buttermere Green Slate Co. and, on a much smaller scale to previous years, slate from mines and old waste heaps, is now being worked again. Buildings alongside the Hause are in use and one houses a visitors centre where the Honister experience can be seen and information on the history of Honister and refreshments can be obtained [220130] ...Honister - Huni's/Unnis summer pasture or place.

Further information on quarrying at Honister can be obtained from the LDNP/Royal Commission on the Historic Monuments of England leaflet *Honister Slate Mines and Quarries*; *Honister Slate* by I Tyler (1994) and *Slate from Honister* by the Cumbria Amenity Trust Mining Society.

Honister Youth Hostel Honister Hause [225136].

Hooker Crag summit of Muncaster Fell. Trig. point at 231m (758ft) [112983].

Hooker Moss Muncaster Fell. Below Hooker Crag [113985].

Hope, The see **The Hope**.

Hope Beck rises at the head of Hope Gill at 184224. Flows down Hope Gill and joins the River Cocker at [155237].

Hope Gill ravine down which Hope Beck flows [173232].

Hope Park Keswick. Floral displays, miniature golf course, obstacle golf and putting green [265232].

Hopebeck at the junction of the minor road from the Whinlatter Pass road (B5292) with that from the B5289 to Cross Gates and Low Lorton [163240].

Hopebeck Bridge carries the B5289 over Hope Beck [157237].

Hopegill Head central summit on the Whiteside-Grisedale Pike ridge and second highest peak to Grisedale Pike. Hope Gill is to its NE, Whiteside to its W, Grisedale Pike to its E, Ladyside Pike to its N and Crag Hill to its S, 770m (2526ft) [186222]. The north face of Hopegill Head is locally called Hobcarton Pike ...head of the narrow ravine (hop) + gill.

Hopgill Beck rises 483103. Joined by Captain Whelter Beck and Rowantreethwaite Beck before entering Haweswater at 479118.

Hopper Quarry Fleetwith. Mainly operated between the l960s and l985 [213137].

Horn Crag Far Easedale [317098] ...see below.

Horn Crag SE face of Slight Side [211048] ...shaped like a horn or possibly a hunting connection with nearby Foxes Tarn.

Horrock Wood Farm Watermillock. Off the A592 [443220].

Horrockwood Watermillock. Alongside the A592 [443219] ...a heap or confused mass (loose stones or rubbish) in or alongside the wood.

Horse Close W shore Buttermere. Acquired by the NT from Prof. G M Trevelyan in 1940 [183153].

Horse Crag promontory overlooking a bend in Yewdale Beck and Low Tilberthwaite [306009].

Horse How Seathwaite Fells. Nearby is Stallion Head [250979].

Horse Parks Eskdale. Near Muncaster Head [136988].

Horse Pasture Wood Thwaite Head [355908].

Horseclose Wood Irton Park [113004].

Horseholme Wood Lowther Park. E bank R Lowther [523254] ...horse + water meadow + wood.

Horsehow Crags S Hardknott Pass. NNE Demming Crag 433m (1421ft) 225009].

Horseman Bridge carries the A592 over Pasture Beck [406132].

Horsemire Head W Dockray-Dowthwaitehead road. Between Little Pike and Low How [376217].

Hoses farm alongside the Broughton Mills to Seathwaite fell road [217927].

Hospital Plantation across the B5292 from the Whinlatter Visitor Centre. The first planting of trees by the Forestry Commission began here in 1919 [214238].

Hotels & Guest Houses certain major hotels are listed in the general text but there are obviously a considerable number not included. Many of these are to be found in *Cumbria: the Lake District*, an annual booklet issued by the Cumbria Tourist Board and obtainable from any Cumbria Tourist Board Information Office. This also lists other types of accommodation as well as information on other topics. The information offices also offer a free local booking service to personal callers and most operate the nationwide 'Book-a-Bed-Ahead' service.

Hound Trailing popular sport in Cumbria. Rags made of wool are soaked in an official mixture of aniseed and paraffin. Two trail rags are then dragged over a mountainous circuit one for a senior trail and the other for a junior. The hounds are unleashed and follow the scented trail at great speed to the finishing line where 'photo finishes' are frequent. The first six hounds receive prize money. Betting on individual dogs can be considerable. The Hound Trailing Association which regulates the sport was founded in 1906.

Houndshope Cove E of and below Hart Crag [375113].

Hounslow Bank Dodd/Skiddaw Dodd [250270].

House Holm see **Norfolk Island**.

Hovel Knott shapely peak S of Great and Little Stickles [211912].

How Ambleside [379043].

How Watendlath Fell. W of the foot of Blea Tarn [284144].

How alongside How Farm. Hill rises to 94m (308ft) [248243].

How Beck a section of Helvellyn Gill joins How Beck below Great How at 317186 and this enters St John's Beck at 316195.

How Beck one arm rises Greencove Wyke, slope of Scafell, at 211060. This meets another stream which emerges from Foxes Tarn at 215060 and the combined watercourse, How Beck, joins the Esk at 221057. On its lower section is the well-known Cam Spout.

How Beck rises Grizedale Forest at 341972 and joins Esthwaite Water at 356972.

How End off the minor road from the A595 S to Corney [117926].

How Farm off minor road from Mosser to Eaglesfield [117264].

How Farm alongside How and the River Derwent [247244].

How Foot Hotel Town End, Grasmere. Former holiday home of the Rev William Spooner (1844-1930) who gave his name to 'Spoonerisms', transpositions such as 'blushing crow' (crushing blow), 'half warmed fish' (half formed wish) and 'Let Us Drink to the Queer Old Dean' (Dear Old Queen).

How Gill two headstreams rise at 271272 and 273270 respectively. The gill flows trough Applethwaite where it becomes Applethwaite Gill and shortly afterwards is joined by Burr Gill at 260250. Subsequently meets Wath Beck which enters the River Derwent at 243260 ...hill stream.

How Green farm, Hartsop [409131].

How Hall Farm Ennerdale. Below it stood the Anglers Inn its site now part of a car park below the farm.

How Head cottage E side Coniston Water. 18th century property now a guest house with two self catering units [318973].

How Head Plantation Monk Coniston Moor, E side Coniston Water [322969].

How Intake alongside the Hawkshead-Grizedale road [345969].

How Scale Haw between Old Park Beck and Banking Hows [222952].

How Top Grasmere [344068]. In her diary for 4 September 1800, Dorothy Wordsworth describes attending a funeral at John Dawson's How Top "about 10 men and 4 women. Bread, cheese and ale..."

How Top SE Mungrisdale 277m (909ft) [377285].

How, The see **The How**.

Howbank Eskdale. Off the minor road from the A595 to Eskdale Green [119966].

Howe earlier High Howe to differentiate it from nearby Low Howe. Off the unfenced road, track, and ultimately path from Heltondale to Carhullan [490191].

Howe Banks Lingmoor Fell [317041].

Howe Banks Quarry Lingmoor Fell [318041].

Howe Farm W Esthwaite Water. Off the Hawkshead-Newby Bridge road [352971].

Howe Farm Winster [420933].

Howe Gill near Askham [502231] ...ravine in a hollow.

Howe Gill rises on Shap Fells slightly NE of Wasdale Pike at 538086 and joins the R Lowther near its source at the outflow from Wet Sleddale Reservoir at 554117.

Howe Grain rises SSE of the summit of Loadpot Hill at 459176 and joins Atkinson's Grain at 471175 which is subsequently joined by Sealhole Grain to become Cawdale Beck. This becomes Howes Beck before flowing into Haweswater Beck at 518180 and shortly afterwards joins the R Lowther ...grain means fork of a river or meeting of streams.

Howe Grain valley, Martindale, along which flows the lower reaches of Rampsgill Beck and Bannerdale Beck which unite in Howe Grain to become Howegrain Beck [435177].

Howe Hill near Crosses Farm. Spot-height at 177m (581ft) [413003] ...surname + hill or simply 'hill' hill.

Howe Hill off the Pooley Bridge to Howtown road. There is a large caravan and camping site hereabouts [478241].

Howe, The see **The Howe**.

Howebill House E How Hill and between Heltondale Beck and the unfenced road from Heltondale to Scales Farm [497210].

Howegrain Beck Bannerdale Beck and Rampsgill Beck combine to become Howegrain Beck ('grain' means the fork of a stream or river) at 436177. This flows down Howe Grain and is joined by Boredale Beck at 426194 to become Sandwick Beck which enters Ullswater slightly N of the hamlet of Sandwick at 423200.

Howes actually only a subsidiary summit of Branstree. Not spot-heighted but contour at C580m (C1903ft) [499104]. A lower cairned summit is noted at 544m (1785ft) [503105]. Several small cairns in the vicinity ...most likely from the local family of Howe.

Howes Beck Cawdale Beck becomes Howes Beck in its lower reach below the Howes at approximately 505177. Originally joined Haweswater Beck at 518180 but in October 1959, it was diverted and tunnelled into Haweswater alongside the dam. This joins Haweswater Beck at 518180.

Howestead Brow N Beda Fell ridge [429183].

Howesteadbrow farm, Boredale, Martindale. Believed to date from the 17th century. Across the road is Garth Heads [428185] ...'site of a building (possibly a hall) at the foot of a brow'. From here a short steep path climbs up to and over a brow (Howestead Brow).

Howgate St John's in the Vale. E St John's Beck [313227]

Howgate Foot Knipe [520194] ...'road or way at the foot of the hill'.

Howgill Tongue tongue of land above How Gill [272269].

Howgill Wood Lamplugh [092205].

Howgraves S of Tarn Hows [330996] ...suggests a burial site or sites on the hill.

Hows Boot, Eskdale [180013].

Hows, The see **The Hows**.

Hows Wood Boot, Eskdale. Planted with conifers in the 1960s. Purchased from the Forestry Commission by the Friends of the Lake District in the 1980s and has recently been replaced with native broadleafed trees [180007].

Howside Ennerdale [093167] ...property on the side of a hill. The hill in question rises to 212m (695ft).

Howtown hamlet S shore Ullswater at the foot of Fusedale and approximately 5.6kms (3.5 miles) from Pooley Bridge. Minor roads continue to Sandwick, to Martindale and up Boredale to Boredale Head and up Bannerdale to Dale Head. One of the most scenic low level Lakeland walks 9.7kms (6 miles) starts from Howtown and goes via Sandwick and the shore of Ullswater to Patterdale. There are also excellent walks up the nearby dales and alongside the Martindale Deer Forest where there is always the chance of seeing the large herd of red deer. For boating enthusiasts there is a public launching site for light craft up to a maximum of 20ft but there is a 10 mph speed limit on the lake. During the season two steamers ply daily between Glenridding Pier, Howtown Pier and Pooley Bridge Pier and vice versa. A mountain rescue post here [443196] ...village alongside a hill.

Howtown Hotel Howtown [443196].

Howtown Pier Howtown Wyke, Ullswater [443199].

Howtown Wyke bay on Ullswater at Howtown [442200] ...Howtown creek.

Hubbersty Head hamlet just over 1.2kms (0.75 mile) E of Crosthwaite and 0.4kms (0.25 mile) off the A5074. The hill/headland to its N rises to 103m (338ft) [427916] ...local surname Hub(b)er or similar + path to the headland/hill.

Huck's Bridge built in the 1820s to carry the present A6 over Borrow Beck. Slightly to its W is High Borrow Bridge carrying the old Kendal-Shap road over the same beck. An adjacent cottage was formerly the Bay Horse Inn [553040]. Alongside the Shap road at the top of the rise S of Huck's Bridge there stood for many years a large clock, the Leyland Clock. This was later removed to the Brewery, Kendal ...from the local family of Huck(e).

Huddlestone's Shop heap of stones overlooking Stonethwaite Beck and Stonethwaite

[268140] ...of unknown origin. Perhaps a frequent resting place of a person called Huddlestone. Today, a seat or plaque would be placed here in his or her honour.

Hudson Place one of the three 'Places' in the Loweswater area which take their names from the original inhabitants. The others are Iredale and Jenkinson Places [115222].

Hugh's Cave see **Haweswater & Mardale**.

Hugh's Garden section of large garden at the rear of Lowther Castle [526235].

Hugh's Laithes Pike Naddle Low Forest. Overlooks the foot of Haweswater Reservoir. Under its summit cairn is said to be the last resting place of Sir James Lowther (also known as the Bad Earl or Wicked Jimmy) who broke his neck after falling from a horse while considerably inebriated. Buried in the family grave he apparently could not rest and his 'wanderings' upset the villagers. All efforts to lay his ghost came to nothing. Eventually his body was dug up and buried on Hugh's Laithes Pike where, as far as is known, he now rests in peace although walkers have claimed to see a figure hereabouts at dusk. Also under the hill, but at a much deeper level, is the Haweswater to Swindale water supply tunnel, 426m (1397ft) [502152] ...said to be named after Hugh Holme of Mardale + barn + pointed hill.

Hugill see **Ings with Hugill**.

Hugill British Settlement see High Borrans.

Hugill Fell summit to the W of the Kentmere valley on the low ridge (more often than not given the name Hugill Fell) between Reston Scar and High Knott. A substantial cairn on a central summit is spot-heighted at 273m (896ft) [459931] ...for Hugill see **Ings with Hugill**.

Hugill Hall Ings with Hugill. Also known as Ings Hall. 17th century and the birthplace of noted naturalist and celebrated antiquarian, Peter Collisson [450996] ...see **Ings with Hugill**.

Hullary Wood Lorton Vale [155245].

Hullockhowe on minor road from Bampton to Carhullan [503184] ...'hill where the wolves play' or personal name + hill.

Hummer Bridge carries Hummer Lane over Lord's Gill [263934] ...see **The Hummers**.

Hummer Lane minor road which meets the A593 2kms (1.25 miles) SW Torver [265934] ...see **The Hummers**.

Hummers see **The Hummers**.

Humphrey's Crags SW Low Pike and E Rydal Beck [370075] ...surname Humphrey + crags.

Hundhowe off Staveley/Bowston/Garnett Bridge road [495978] ...hill frequented by hounds or where hounds were kept.

Hundith Hill off the Hundith Hill Road [144286].

Hundith Hill Hotel country house hotel off the B5292 and Hundith Hill Road [141289].

Hundith Hill Road Strawberry How Road to the B5292 [144288].

Hundred Year Stone see **Derwent Water**.

Hundreds Road drove road [398028] leading to Troutbeck Hundreds (see **Troutbeck**).

Hundreds, The see **Troutbeck**.

Hunger Hill alongside Walmgate Foot to Littlewater road [514174] ...'poor land' hill.

Hunsett Cove NE Dove Crag. W Stand Crags. Littered by huge boulders [381109].

Hunting Stile off Red Bank Road, Grasmere. A former substantial residence which many years ago was converted into four residences [335062].

Huntingstile Crag above Hunting Stile and alongside path from the B5343 to Red Bank

Road. This path, a packhorse route, was also a corpse road by which people from Langdale were brought for burial in Grasmere until 1845 [335055] ...from 'sty' meaning a steep path.

Huntpot Dub small stream which rises at 267919 and joins Lord's Gill at 261921 ...literally - Hunter's deep hole pool.

Hurlbarrow Bleng Fell [071057] ...possibly circular/round hill referring to Bleng Fell.

Hurst Side Duddon valley. Alongside the Ulpha to Seathwaite road [202939] ...wood side.

Hursthole Point promontory W shore Bassenthwaite Lake [220276]. Parking and picnic site across the A66 nearby.

Hussey Well Beck rises Bursting Stone Quarry at 280971. Joined by small tributary from Boo Tarn. Subsequently meets Summers Cove Beck at 282961 and the combination joins Torver Beck at 282958.

Hutaple Crag on craggy spur from Fairfield to Greenhow End [367121].

Hutch Head WNW Hutton. Off minor road, A66-Hutton [431268].

Hutching's How slope of Lingmell [194084] ...surname + hill.

Hutton hamlet 0.8km (0.5 mile) S A66 [435267] ...homestead/village on the hill.

Hutton ESE High Whineray Ground [204902].

Hutton John not to be confused with the stately home of Hutton-in-the-Forest. The manor was first mentioned over 700 years ago and mansion owned by the Huttons from the 14th to the 16th century and since then by the Huddlestones. Hall built around a pele tower, one of several large peles in the area including Blencow, Catterlen, Dacre, Dalemain, Greenthwaite and Johnby. Features alongside are a dovecote and St Mary's Well. Much different today than it obviously was in 1802 when Dorothy Wordsworth remarked that "the valley, which is subject to the decaying mansion that stands at its head, seems to join its testimony to that of the house to the falling away of the family greatness." In a note to his poem *The Horn of Egremont Castle* Wordsworth points out that the story was actually related to Hutton John [440270] ...homestead or village on a projecting ridge of land + an unidentified John. Maybe the unidentified John of nearby Johnby?

Huton Moor End property and farm alongside the minor road, Scales-A66 [365271].

Huyton Hill mansion built late 19th century W shore Windermere near Pull Wyke. A preparatory school for boys from after 1935 until 1969. Author Arthur Ransome used the grounds as Beckfoot and the nearby Pull Beck was the Amazon River in his *Swallows and Amazons* [368020].

Hycemoor Side Farm between the Bootle to Eskmeals road and that from Corney to the former [088904] ...possibly water-plant moor.

I

Ian's Wood S slope Muncaster Fell [114979].

Idle Hill between Wansfell summit and Woundale Raise [406059] ...hill formerly owned by a local Idle family.

Ill Bell peak on the Garburn Pass-Yoke-Froswick-High Street ridge usually climbed as part of the Kentmere Horseshoe. Its summit is cone or bell-shaped and the latter provides its name - the hill shaped like a bell. Walkers will find three large cairns on the summit (one was demolished but has since been replaced). Mainly grassy slopes to the W but precipitous crags to the E, 757m (2484ft) [436077]. Not to be confused with Mardale Ill Bell across Kentmere.

Ill Crag although it is usually given a single name Scafell Pike was formerly Scafell Pikes or the Pikes and comprised the three principal summits of Scafell Pike, Broad Crag and Ill Crag, all above 914m (3000ft). The latter, situated slightly E of the path from Esk Hause to Scafell Pike, shows an extremely craggy face to the head of Eskdale. In 1947 a Spitfire crashed near its summit killing its pilot, 935m (3068ft) [223073] ...'crag on the hill'.

Ill Crag Newlands Hause-Ard Crags ridge, see **Ill Gill**.

Ill Gill rises Steel Fell at 320115 and joins Wyth Burn at 315120 ...'evil gill'.

Ill Gill rises on slope of Lingmell at 201083 and joins Lingmell Beck at 196090 ...ravine/narrow valley on a hill, steep ravine or possibly evil ravine.

Ill Gill rises Kirk Fell at 199105 and joins Gable Beck at 201098 ...see **Ill Gill** above.

Ill Gill rises slope Seatallan at 134081 and joins the upper River Bleng at 125086.

Ill Gill rises between Knott Rigg and Ill Crag at 200190 - the latter not named on the OS map but spot-heighted at 546m (1791ft) [200192]. Joined by Ard Gill before joining Keskadale Beck at 214192.

Ill Gill short stream which rises on the slope of Gavel Fell at 113184. Joins Comb Gill at 109182. This combines with Grain Gill and High Bridge Gill to become Croasdale Beck which joins the River Ehen at Ennerdale Bridge.

Illgill Head Kirk Fell. Overlooks the head of Ill Gill [199103] ...see **Ill Gill** above.

Illgill Head on high ridge above the Wastwater Screes. Trig. point at 603m (1978ft), spot height nearby at 604m (1982ft) but actual summit slightly ENE 609m (1998ft) [169049]. A Cherokee crashed on its steep face in March 1973. Four persons were killed ...see **Ill Gill** above.

In Fell between Ponsonby and Scargreen Beck. Infell Wood at its foot and an 'enclosure' on its summit area [060060].

In Scar the nearer part of Knipe Scar/Knipescar Common in Bampton [536194].

Infell Wood see **In Fell**.

Ing Troutbeck valley [421046] ...meadow/pasture. There is also an Ings alongside the A591 and one near Threlkeld.

Ing Bridge old bridge which carries Ing Lane over Trout Beck [419048].

Ing Lane leaves Town Head, Troutbeck, and crosses over Ing Bridge to Troutbeck Park Farm [418044].

Ings between Threlkeld and Wescoe ...the name means 'pasture' or 'meadow land' [310252]. There is another Ings alongside the A591 between Kendal and Windermere and an Ing in the Troutbeck Valley.

Ings with Hugill straddles the A591 to its N and S. W of Kendal. Bulmer's *History, Topography and Directory of Westmorland, Etc.* (1885) notes that "Ings Chapelry includes within its jurisdiction the greater portion of the township of Hugill, and a part of Nether Staveley comprising an area of 3250 acres with a population of 204" while Hugill "...contains the small hamlets of Heights, Grassgarth, Ings, Reston, and Ulthwaite" with a rateable area of 2750 acres and 392 inhabitants. At that time residents were chiefly employed in agriculture (several farms are still in existence) or bobbin turning (none today). Ings Church, dedicated to St Anne, was built in 1743 by wealthy merchant Robert Bateman (see Reston Hall), refurbished in 1842 and extended 1877/8. It possesses a floor of Italian marble. Ings garage and filling station began in a small way in the early 1930s; the Little Chef adjoining opened in 1979; the Watermill Inn, opened in 1991, was a sawmill and joiners shop for over 250 years until 1960. Became the Mill Holme Country Hotel before acquisition by Alan Coulthwaite who turned it into a popular real ale oasis. In late 1999 the hotel was named as joint second prizewinner out of 60,000 pubs in CAMRA's National Pub of the Year Competition and in 2000 was voted Beer Pub of the Year in *The Good Pub Guide 2001*; Meadowcroft Country Hotel is well-established and posseses 10 bedrooms. Ings Caravan Park opened in 1960. For more information consult booklet *Ings With Hugill: A Westmorland Village* (1993) or *The Chapelry of Hugil or Ings, in the Ancient Parish of Kendal* by G E P Reade (1916) [446986] ...ing - meadow/water meadow/outlying pasture; hugill - high ravine or high path.

Ingshead Hole W of the B5289 and the River Derwent [257181].

Inkern Beck rises SE of the Head of Heltondale Beck at 467184 and joins Heltondale Beck at 479194.

Inking Knott Torver Low Common [278927].

Inmans Intake W Force Mills. NW Force Forge [332910].

Inn on the Lake Glenridding. Large hotel set within 20 acres of ground on the edge of

Ullswater. Built in 1840 and considerably renovated and modernised during the 1970s. Featured prominently in the 4-part BBC drama *The Lakes* (Sept/Oct 1997). Earlier the Ullswater Hotel but recently after a substantial refit and refurbishment re-named the Inn on the Lake. Has a separate ramblers' bar for walkers [387171].

Innominate Tarn Hay Stacks. A more recent name for Loaf Tarn. The earlier name is said to be derived from the mushroom-like peat clumps resembling risen dough. Innominate means unnamed/not named and it was suggested that it should be called Wainwright's Tarn after the late Alfred Wainwright who loved Hay Stacks. This was decided against and even Wainwright said that he liked the name 'Innominate' and that it should remain as such. His ashes were scattered on and around the tarn, 525m (1722ft) [197129].

Inscar Plantation see **Knipe Scar & Knipescar Common**.

Intack Sike rises WSW Drybarrows at 496168. Joins Willdale Beck at 495176. This meets Cawdale Beck at 497177 ...'piece of enclosed land' + 'small stream'.

Intake Land part of the common fell 'taken in' and usually enclosed by stone walls by yeoman farmers in order to create new pastures, etc. Most intake lands date from the enclosure of common lands by the 1784 Act of Parliament but some are more ancient.

Intake Wood E of High Close on slope of Loughrigg [343052] ...'intake' refers to a piece of land taken in from waste and enclosed.

Iredale Place one of three 'Places' in the Loweswater area which takes their names from the original inhabitants. The others are Hudson and Jenkinson Places [111227].

Ireland Wood Bampton 244m (800ft) [511179] ...wood named after Ireland.

Iron Crag ESE summit of Middle Fell overlooking the foot of Nether Beck [156069].

Iron Crag W Wallowbarrow Heald 408m (1339ft) [211972].

Iron Crag Bethecar Moor [317911].

Iron Crag vertical cliff at the foot of Bleaberry Fell and overlooking Shoulthwaite Gill and Glen [297193].

Iron Crag line of crags at the summit of Ennerdale Fell and W Silvercove Beck. Cairn at 640m (2100ft) [123119].

Iron Gate former gate at the foot of Cockley Beck Fell. Legend says that three kings now lie buried with their golden crowns in cairns by the Iron Gate [258020].

Iron Groves source of Red Gill. Redgill Head here [143928] ...presumably the name like that of Red Gill, refers to the nature and colour of the earth hereabouts.

Iron Keld Arnside Heights [338011] ...either a corruption of Arni's spring/keld, a surname which figures prominently hereabouts, or possibly the spring which emerges through the iron deposits.

Iron Keld Plantation large conifer plantation principally S and SE of Iron Keld [338008].

Iron Stone rock in Crummock Water [154190].

Irt, River see **River Irt**.

Irton the parish of Irton with Santon covers approximately 3.2kms (2 miles) in length and 2.8kms (1.5 miles) wide and lies between the Rivers Irt and Mite. It includes the hamlets of Santon, Hall Santon, the larger Santon Bridge and a part of Holmrook ...the farmstead on the Irt.

Irton Church dedicated to St Paul. Present church rebuilt in 1857 and possesses a peal of 8 bells. However, a church has existed on the site since the 13th century. In the churchyard stands a 10ft high sandstone Celtic cross believed to be of 9th century origin. It is carved with interlacing and intricate knot-work [092005].

Irton Fell ridge of approximately 2.8kms (1.75 miles) which commences W of Greathall Gill and runs SW to Irton Pike. On the ridge below the pike there is an ancient cairn and circle. Rises to 395m (1296ft) [144026].

Irton Hall Irton. Alongside the Holmrook to Santon Bridge road. The home of the Irton family for centuries. Originally built around a 14th century embattled pele tower it still encompasses other remains of the 14th and 16th centuries. Has been extensively modernised. Housed a special school for many years but now consists of cottages, apartments, a 'petting' zoo, a restaurant and tea room and other attractions set in 40 acres of parkland. It is said that after a defeat in 1464 Henry VI took refuge under a oak tree in the hall grounds. The huge tree is still there. However, this event is also credited to Chapel Hill, Muncaster Fell, where a tall 3-tier monument commemorates it [105006].

Irton Park Irton. Extensive parkland created by the early owners of nearby Irton Hall [120007].

Irton Pike SW end of the Irton Fell ridge. Well-forested slopes. Its top has been deforested and is now a much better viewpoint C220 (C722) [121016].

Irton Road Station on the Ravenglass to Eskdale Railway [138000].

Isa Crag Deepdale [372128].

Isaac Gill rises below Gladstone Knott at 258047 and joins Browney Gill at 265051 ...Isaac's stream.

Isthmus Bay Derwent Water [260227].

Iving Howe small farm property renovated and extended many times. Little Langdale [321032] ...ivy hill.

Ivy Crag High Dale Park Plantation [361933].

Ivy Crag Holme Fell [318005].

Ivy Crag slope Dodd/Skiddaw Dodd [243268].

Ivy Crag see **Loughrigg Fell**.

Ivy Knott alongside White Crags W Langstrath Beck [265117].

J

Jack Croft Pond in Lowther Castle garden adjoining Hugh's Garden and Peg Huck Well [524235].

Jack Gap Plantation Grizedale Forest Park. Adjoining Jack Gap Wood [331958].

Jack Gap Wood Grizedale Forest Park [333956].

Jackdaw Crag below White Crag and overlooking Easedale [324088].

Jack's Rake see **Pavey Ark**.

Jackson Ground farm off a minor road from Broughton Mills [232929] ...see **Stephenson Ground**.

Jackson's Fold sheepfold alongside Stile Gill [276282].

James's Quarry WNW Grasmere [325079].

Jeanie Brewster's Well isolated well/spring rising between Whitestone Moor and Knotts and alongside Annas ('Agnes') Sike which its waters join. Jeanie would seem to have to travel some distance to obtain water from her well! [479205].

Jeffy Knotts Wood alongside Bog Lane [358033] ...surname + 'rocky hilltop' + wood.

Jemmy Crag W shore Windermere [388951] ...Jimmy's? crag.

Jenkin Embleton [160283].

Jenkin Hill Skiddaw group. Between Skiddaw Little Man and Lonscale Fell C730m (C2395ft) [274275].

Jenkin Hill Farm Thornthwaite [224257].

Jenkin's Crag see **Jenkyn's Crag**.

Jenkinson Place one of the three 'Places' in the Loweswater area which takes their names from the original inhabitants. The others are Iredale and Hudson Places [112225].

Jenkyn's Crag variously spelt Jenkin/Jenkin's Crag. In Skelghyll Wood and an excellent viewpoint for Windermere and the mountains to the W. Approached by paths from Ambleside, Waterhead and Troutbeck. Owned by the National Trust since 1957 when it came to it as part of the Wansfell Estates [384029] ...obviously named after a person called Jenkyn or Jenkin but unfortunately neither I nor the National Trust have any information as to the actual identity of the person.

Jenny Dam private water lying in hollow on Green Hill above Crook. Consequently has alternative name, Green Hill Tarn [462955].

Jenny Greenteeth Tarn see **Wharton Tarn**.

Jennyhill off minor road connecting the A5091 with minor road, Matterdale Rigg-A592 [406236].

Jim's Fold sheepfold [326221].

Jobson Close foot of Loughrigg Fell [356059] ...surname + enclosure.

Joe Bank's Fold sheepfold, E Minum Crag, High Spy [239166].

John Bell's Banner Caudale Moor is often referred to as this but on the OS map John Bell's Banner is the slope WSW Stony Cove Pike facing Middle Dodd across Kirkstone Pass [412098] ...'banner' refers to a boundary mark but who was John Bell? One source suggests a local huntsman but it was most likely named after the Rev John Bell (1585-1630), Curate of Ambleside for many years, who is said to have placed a banner on Caudale Moor as a boundary marker to attempt to resolve a long-standing dispute.

John's Grove see **White Moss & Baneriggs**.

Johnny House alongside Langstrath Beck [271127].

Johnny Wood Borrowdale, see Rosthwaite.

Jopplety How see Joppletyhow Moss.

Joppletyhow Moss Brund Fell, Grange Fell [267165] ...Jopplety How [264163] is a crag on Brund Fell but its immediate area is a jumble (Jopplety could suggest this) of crags, heather and marsh.

Jordan's Crag in afforested area E River Lickle [244939].

Jubilee Bridge bridge across Hardknott Gill near its confluence with the River Esk [213011].

Julian Holme Gosforth. Off the Gosforth to Nether Wasdale road [094037] ...Juliansholm in the 14th century, Gillianholme in the 17th century.

Jungle Cafe the cafe stood on a bend of the A6 alongside Wolfhowe Gill. Now a caravan sales site. Lorry drivers and others who traversed the A6 will recall the small cafe, an important stopping place particular on the journey northwards. Opened in the 1920s. A petrol filling station was added after the Second World War. The cafe and filling station's death knell was the opening of the M6 motorway in 1970. Subsequently, the building became the Wayfarer and opened for meals and functions then it became an artist's studio and today the original cafe building is offices and reception room for the caravan business [547025] ...why the Jungle Cafe? Lorry drivers christened the area thereabouts, the jungle, because it was thickly wooded with overhanging branches. Consequently on opening the cafe the proprietor called it the Jungle Cafe.

Juniper Tarn not named on the OS map but shown and named on the Grizedale Forest Park Guide, C200m (C656ft) [340964].

K

Kail Pot widening of the River Esk near its confluence with Scale Gill [217024] 'cabbage pot', a large circular cavity which resembles a pot or boiler used to boil cabbage of the like.

Kailpot Crag E shore Ullswater near Howtown. From the water can be seen a carved inscription to the memory of Lord Birkett which simply but concisely reads: "He loved Ullswater. He strove to maintain its beauty for all to enjoy" [433204] ...'cabbage-pot' crag - a large circular cavity in the rock resembles a pot or boiler. Local legend says that the fairies boiled their kail here.

Keasgill Head head of Keasgill Sike and alongside the High Street ridge between Red Crag and Wether Hill [455159].

Keasgill Sike rises Keasgill Head alongside High Street ridge at 455159. Joins Longgrain Beck at 460151 and subsequently becomes Measand Beck which flows into Haweswater Reservoir at 487154 ...'recess' - gill - small stream.

Keen Ground Georgian mansion, Hawkshead [347983] ...see **Grounds**.

Kelbarrow Grasmere. House on hillside near a principal track from Red Bank road alongside Silver How and over to Chapel Stile in Great Langdale [331071] ...'hill with a spring'. Two wells are shown on OS map on the hill slope.

Keld hamlet just over the National Park boundary. On the E bank of the R Lowther 1.6kms (1 mile) SW of Shap by road. The small chapel, now owned by the National Trust, is early 16th century and, for the first time since the Reformation, mass was held in it in September 1995. The old Butter Market building is now occupied by a craft shop. In days long gone by, the old corpse road from Mardale to Shap passed through Keld. In March 1849, seven skeletons of men were dug up in a field at Keld and it is surmised that they were buried as a result of a battle fought there [553144] ...'spring'. The Place Names of Westmorland suggest that this was W of the village.

Keld Dub pool in the River Lowther at Keld [554143].

Keld Gill rises as Mealhowe Gill alongside path from Wet Sleddale to Truss Gap, Swindale, at 528120 and becomes Keld Gill at approximately 531127. Joins the R Lowther at 551143 ...'spring' gill.

Keld Gill Head above High and Low Keld Gills [282010].

Keldas delighful pine-topped height which is actually the eastern extremity of Birkhouse Moor. Shows steep and craggy face over Hall Bank to the A592. Excellent views of upper reaches of Ullswater and the mountains around 311m (1020ft) [385163].

Keldhead Heltondale [488197] ...spring head.

Keldron Spring near Helton. Between the Askham to Helton road and the Askham to Bampton Grange road [516225] ...'spring in the thicket.'

Kelly Hall Tarn small tarn on Torver Back Common just off the A5084, C120m (C394ft) [289933] ...named after a nearby house now demolished.

Kelswick farm, Wythop valley. Nearby are the remains of an ancient chapel [192292] ...spring by the farm.

Kelton Fell N Croasdale 311m (1021ft) [095182]. Not to be confused with Keltonfell Top which is slightly lower and just outside the National Park. There are several former haematite mine workings on its slopes ...more than likely refers to the fell with the spring by the homestead. A spring on its lower slope is the source of a small tributary of Croasdale Beck.

Kemp Tarn Staveley. E of the summit of Reston Scar. Lies at a height of C220m (C722ft) 464989 ...Kemp's Tarn.

Kemplerigg off the Gosforth to Santon Bridge road [088023].

Kendal although not quite in the LDNP Kendal, the 'Auld Grey Town', formerly Kirkby Kendal or Kirkby-in-Kendal, is worthy of inclusion here because it is the 'Gateway to the Lakes' from the E and S respectively and, until 1974, was the largest town and administrative centre for Westmorland. Today it is the administrative centre for S Lakeland. A weekly market was granted by Richard I in the late 12th century and for centuries wool was the dominant industry and particularly Kendal Green cloth in which the famous Kendal bowmen were clad. Present major industries include agriculture, carpets, engineering, shoes and the world famous Kendal Mint Cake. Kendal Castle above the E bank of the R Kent lies in ruin. Dating from the late 12th or early 13th centuries it is said that at one time it was the birthplace and childhood home of Katherine Parr, last of Henry VIII's wives. On the southern outskirts of the town, at Watercrook, is the site of a Roman fort (Alavna). Kendal Parish Church (Holy Trinity) stands on the site of an earlier building and dates from the 13th century. One of the largest churches in England it has five aisles and is only 0.9m (3ft) narrower than York Minster. Also of interest in the town itself are the many 'yards' around which houses are grouped. Some of these yards have very narrow entrances. Noted attributes to the Kendal scene are the Abbot Hall Art Gallery, the Brewery Arts Centre, three museums, and a large leisure complex. There is a Tourist Information Centre in Highgate.

Kendal By-Pass part of the A591 from the junction with the old A6 to the roundabout at Plumgarths opened in 1971 [507900-497945].

Kendal Mountain Search and Rescue Team founded in 1953. Based at Busher Walk. Their premises were completed in 1980 and an improved version in September 1999. Adopted its current title in 1959.

Kendal Racecourse former old-established racecourse alongside Brigsteer Road. Used particularly for steeplechasing from the early 1820s. Later trotting races from around 1920 and harness racing for a short time at the beginning of the 1990s [500916].

Kendal-Windermere Railway opened in 1847. The last steam train to Windermere pulled by the locomotive Oliver Cromwell ran along the line in April 1968.

Kennel Crag ESE Levers Water [285990] ...possibly from 'krenal', a battlement.

Kent, River see **River Kent**.

Kentdale the River Kent rises just below High Street and flows down through Kentmere Reservoir, Kentmere Village, through Kentmere Tarn and onwards to Kendal and beyond. The section of Kentdale between the source of the Kent and Staveley is commonly called Kentmere after the original mere.

Kentmere small scattered village at the head of Kentmere, Kentdale, and at the end of a 6.4kms (4 miles) stretch of road from Staveley. Its church, dedicated to St Cuthbert, is ancient but how ancient is open to conjecture. Some say it dates from Saxon times while others quote the Norman era. It does, however, possess 16th century roof beams but has been considerably restored over the years with major reconstruction work and a new tower in 1866. Other notable buildings are the Village Institute, opened in 1926, and re-opened after re-furbishment in 1993 and Kentmere Hall. Kentmere Reservoir lies to the N of the village and Kentmere Tarn to its S. At Kentmere two drove roads meet, one over the Garburn Pass from the W and the other over Stile End from Longsleddale from the E. A

packhorse track, today a principal walker's route, leads up to and over Nan Bield [456041]. Settlements at 440090, 452069 and 461025. Suggested reading, *A Lakeland Valley Through Time: A History of Staveley, Kentmere and Ings* published by the Staveley and District History Society (1955).

Kentmere Common between Kentmere Reservoir and Lingmell End [445090].

Kentmere Hall Kentmere. Hall built on to a 14th century pele tower. The home for many years of the Gilpin family one of whom Richard is claimed to have killed the last wild boar in England and another famous Gilpin, the Rev Bernard, became known as the 'Apostle of the North'. Today the hall is a farm and, in 1999, as part of the Kentmere Hall & Hartrigg Estate came up for sale along with Hartrigg Farm and Rook How and Scales Farmhouses [451042].

Kentmere Hall Plantation Kentmere. W bank R Kent. S of Kentmere Hall [455023].

Kentmere Horseshoe like the Fairfield Horseshoe it is a round high-level route. Starting from the village of Kentmere it takes in the Garburn Pass, Yoke, Ill Bell, Froswick, part of High Street and Mardale Ill Bell. It then crosses the Nan Bield Pass, over Harter Fell, Kentmere Pike, Shipman Knotts and back to Kentmere via Green Quarter or Stile End.

Kentmere Park large area to the W and S of Kentmere Hall. Bounded principally by Park Beck, Garburn Pass, Hall Gill and the River Kent. Its highest point is Sallows [440036].

Kentmere Pike equidistant on ridge between Harter Fell and Shipman Knotts and usually ascended on the ridge walk to Harter Fell or as part of the Kentmere Horseshoe. A trig. point on the E side of the wall is hidden from the view of walkers who follow the recognised path to the W of the wall 730m (2395ft) [465078].

Kentmere Pottery see **Sawmill Cottage**.

Kentmere Reservoir originally Kentmere Head Reservoir. An Act of Parliament in 1845 authorised the construction of impounding reservoirs on the Kent, Mint and Sprint. Five reservoirs were planned but, due to cost, only Kentmere Reservoir was built (1845/6) to regulate the supply of water to mills on the River Kent. It is situated at an altitude of 290m (951ft) [445080]. During 1995/6 the reservoir remained empty after faults were found in the outflow pipe and also water was disappearing into the clay core of the reservoir. However, repair work, including leakage prevention and pipe repairs was completed in September 1996. Not to be confused with Kentmere Tarn S of the village of Kentmere.

Kentmere Tarn Not to be confused with Kentmere Reservoir above. The original larger Kentmere Lake was drained over 150 years ago to provide new pasture land. Later it was discovered that the bed contained deposits of diatomite (see also **Skeggles Water**) (minute vegetable organisms which form deposits with external casing of silica) used in abrasives, fillers, filtering mediums, insulation, paints and varnishes. Consequently, some 60 years ago the diatomite was initially extracted on a small scale and later more commercially from another tarn which had formed owing to the excavations. The production of diatomite reached 10,000 tonnes a year in the late 1940s. Work continued until the mid-1980s when extraction ceased because it was more economic to import diatomite or use alternative materials. An 'aerial ropeway' shown on the OS map carried buckets of material dredged from the tarn down to the processing plant. A small side lake has been stocked with rainbow and brown trout and the large lake through which the Kent flows contains brown trout. Fishing is private. The former diatomite works nearby is now owned by Hepworth Air Filtration but from 1942 until 1974 it was operated by Cape Asbestos. During excavations in 1955 two canoe-type boats, thought to be Viking or Saxon were unearthed. One was given to the National Maritime Museum and the fragments of the other to the Kendal Museum. The tarn lies at an altitude of C150m (C492ft) [455030].

Kentmere Valley see **Kentdale**.

Keppel Cove comb at the head of the Glenridding valley. Embraced on three sides by Red Screes, the E face of the Helvellyn ridge and Catstye Cam crags. The former Keppel Cove Tarn within its confines is now a marshy area but at one time it was a reservoir for the Greenside Mine. In 1927 a cloudburst caused its banks to burst and flood waters swept down to Glenridding causing considerable damage but fortunately no loss of life. A few years later the company built a high dam below the moraine but this was breached in 1931 and never repaired. Much of the dam wall of the latter still stands C550m (C1804ft) [345165].

Keppel Cove Tarn see **Kepple Cove**.

Kepple Crag S slope Harter Fell (219989) ...possible crag frequented by horses.

Kepple Crag Birker Fell 328m (1076ft) [199999].

Kern Knotts Great Gable. Comprises Kern Knotts and Lower Kern Knotts. Situated alongside the Gable Girdle, a high level path from Sty Head which circumvents Great Gable. Rock climbs for both novices and experts [216096].

Kerris Hill between the Crook (B5284)-Borwick Fold road and the Crook Road 230m (755ft) [460963] ...the Place Names of Westmorland suggests a variant of Carus Hill, named from a local family called Cayrous. There is also a Carus Green N of Kentrigg and E of the Kendal-Burneside road.

Keskadale valley off the Newlands valley. Down it flows Keskadale Beck and on its N slope is the road over the Newlands Pass to Buttermere. See also **Keskadale Beck** ...W G Collingwood says that the name is a corruption of Gatesgarthdale while the *Place Names of Cumberland* (EPNS) refers to it as the valley by Ketil's shieling.

Keskadale Beck Moss Beck (rising on Buttermere Moss) and High Hole Beck (rising below Robinson Crags) combine at 197177 and from there Keskadale Beck flows down the dale, is joined by Dudmancombe Gill and Ill Gill, and continues past Keskadale Farm to join Newlands Beck by Little Town at 232196. Alongside the valley are the Keskadale Oaks which, according to *The Lake District* (Collins Naturalist Series) are "fragments of almost pure sessile oakwood... lie at an altitude of 1000-1400ft." Alongside the beck but at a higher level is the Newlands Pass road to and from Buttermere.

Keskadale Farm Keskadale. Last inhabited property in the dale before Buttermere [210913].

Keswick Keswick is the major town in the north of the Lake District often referred to as the 'Queen of the Lakes' due to its unique position ringed by high mountains and fells with the delights of Borrowdale immediately S, the picturesque Derwent Water adjoining and Bassenthwaite Lake nearby. A market town situated between Skiddaw to its N and Derwentwater/Borrowdale to its S. W are the passes of Newlands and Whinlatter to Buttermere and E the trunk road to Penrith. Its history dates back not only centuries but milleniums. Castlerigg Stone Circle is at least 3000 years old and the name Kesewick was evident c1240. The town received its Market Charter in the 13th century. St. Kentigern's Church at Crosthwaite is said to have been founded in the 6th century rebuilt in the 12th and rebuilt and enlarged in 1844. Keswick's development really began in the mid 16th century when German miners were brought in to mine the copper and lead thereabouts. The Penrith to Keswick section of the Penrith-Whitehaven railway opened in 1864 but closed in March 1972.

The Keswick of today boasts many interesting buildings including the Moot Hall, famous town centre landmark dating from at least the 16th century. Rebuilt in the 17th century the present structure dates from 1813. Over the years, the building has been a store, a court house, a market, a prison, a museum and today a National Park Information Centre with an upper community room. Other features are Greta Hall, former home of Coleridge and later Robert Southey, St. John's Church, built in 1838, and the Theatre by the Lake. There is also a cinema, opened in 1914, an excellent museum and art gallery [268237], a pencil works and museum, a tea pottery, Cars of the Stars Museum, a leisure pool, shops, eating places, tourist accommodation and several parks. Friar's Crag overlooking Derwent Water and the mountains beyond is a famous viewpoint [267234]. For more information read *Keswick The Story of a Lake District Town* by George Bott (1994). See also **Castlerigg Stone Circle**, **Crosthwaite Church**, **Friar's Crag**, **Greta Hall**, **Keswick Pencil Factory & Museum**, **Pencil Manufacture**, **Theatre by the Lake**. ...the name means cheese farm.

Keswick Golf Club Threlkeld 6.4kms (4 miles) E Keswick. Course lies between the R Glenderamackin and the former Keswick-Penrith railway line [333253].

Keswick Landing Stages see **Keswick Launch**.

Keswick Launch Keswick. Launches sail, weather permiting, all year except Christmas Day. For times of sailing consult Keswick Launch office or *Keswick Launch on Derwentwater* leaflet. Launches sail around the lake stopping at Ashness Gate, Lodore, High Brandelhow, Low Brandelhow, Hawse End and Nicole End Marina. Also, from the landing stages, self-drive motor boats and rowing boats can be hired [264228].

Keswick Mountain Rescue Team formed shortly after Wilfred Noyce, later a member of John Hunt's successful Everest team, had been badly injured while climbing on Great Gable in April 1946. For more information see *Call Out: The First 50 Years* by George Bott.

Keswick Pencil Factory & Museum the Southey Works is now the only surviving pencil factory in Keswick. The museum attached to it traces the history of pencil making from the discovery of graphite (wad) in the 16th century to modern production methods [263238], see also **Coledale Inn**.

Keswick to Penrith Railway part of the Cockermouth-Penrith line. Opened in 1864 and closed in March 1972. From Keswick several miles of the former track bed now provide a scenic footpath. At the time of writing plans were afoot to possibly reopen the line.

Keswick School Crosthwaite [260243]. See also **Greta Hall**.

Ketley Gate tumuli on Moor Divock near the junction of the track from Heltondale-Pooley Bridge and that from Howtown-Askham [488223].

Kettle Cove W slope Scafell between between Hardrigg Gill and Long Gill [196058].

Kettle Crag between Brown Beck and Heltondale Beck [478198] ...possibly, like the 'kettle' of Kettle Crag in Langdale, means kettle or cauldron and refers to a bubbling spring hereabouts.

Kettle Crag above Wall End Farm, Great Langdale, and on the slope of Pike ofBlisco [279050] ...see **Kettle Crag** above.

Keyhow Eskdale Green. Alongside the River Mite [133003].

Keyhow Coppice NW Keyhow [131006].

Kid Beck farthest headstream rises Thorn How, Nether Wasdale Common. Flows through the unusual named Turdypack Gill and joins the River Irt at 112043. The old boundary between Gosforth and Nether Wasdale.

Kid Moor S Heltondale Beck and Keldhead [486191] ...young goat's moor.

Kidbeck Bridge carries the Gosforth to Nether Wasdale road over Kid Beck [115046].

Kidbeck Farm Nether Wasdale. Alongside the Nether Wasdale to Gosforth road and near Kid Beck and Kidbeck Bridge [115045].

Kidbeck How Nether Wasdale [118045].

Kidbeck Moss Nether Wasdale. E Kid Beck and N River Irt [117042].

Kidmoor Edge edge of Kidmoor dropping down to Heltondale Beck [481194].

Kids Howe SE Wolf Howe and alongside the A6 [547020] ...Kits Howe in the 18th and 19th centuries. Possibly a personal name but could also be 'the hillside where kids (goats) where grazed'.

Kidshowe Beck rises 534029 and flows under the A6 to join Ashstead Beck at 551019.

Kidshowe Bridge carries the A6 over Kidshowe Beck [547019].

Kidson How W Swirl How ridge and overlooking the upper reach of Tarn Head Beck [269999].

Kidsty Howes craggy extremity of spur E from High Street ridge over Kidsty Pike [463125].

Kidsty Pike distinctive sharp pointed summit towering above Riggindale and on a spur running E from the High Street ridge to Kidsty Howes. The highest point reached on Wainwright's Coast to Coast Walk. An unusual occurrence concerning lightning and a spring which took place on the pike in the early 19th century is chronicled in Wordsworth's *The Brothers* - lines 139-145, and in *Prose of Lakeland* compiled by B L Thompson (1954) - page 96, 780m (2559ft). Noted author and antiquary William Camden (1551-1623) was taught as a child that 'Kidftowpike, Catfycam, Helvellyn and Skiddaw-man, Are the highest hills ever clumb by Englifhmen' [447126] ...'kid's steep path'.

Kilbert How Place Fell. Overlooks Ullswater [407188] ...'Ketilbert's Hill'.

Kill Gill rises slope Hollow Moor, Kentmere, at 468038 and joins the R Kent at 459041.

Kiln Bank Duddon valley [211941].

Kiln Bank Cross stretch of the Broughton Mills to Seathwaite fell road by its summit at 259m (850ft) and where the bridleway from Ulpha to Long Mire and on to the Walna Scar Road crosses. Name suggests that in earlier times a cross was sited here [215933].

Kiln How near the head of Bassenthwaite Lake. Alongside the A591 [235275].

Kiln Potts N Ullock Pike and the Edge. A section of the Allerdale Ramble passes by [241296].

Kilnhow Beck see **Blease Gill**.

Kilnhow Crag Irton Fell [137032] ...kiln 'hill' crag.

Kilnshaw Chimney scree gully on Red Screes and usually climbed as part of the steep path from the Kirkstone Pass Inn to the summit of Red Screes [398086].

Kilnstones Longsleddale. Former farmhouse now a family residence. Dating from the 16th century. A previous property on the site was once owned by Shap Abbey and inhabited by monks. It was also a halt for travellers of all kinds [502021].

Kilnstones Wood adjoining Dockernook Wood, Longsleddale (502018).

King's Head Hotel Thirlspot. At the foot of Helvellyn on the A591 Keswick to Grasmere road. Former 17th century coaching inn [307178].

King's How subsidiary summit of Grange Fell. Grange Fell, including King's How, was purchased by public subscription for the NT in 1908. The name was given by Princess Louise who dedicated it to her brother, King Edward VII, 392m (1286ft) [258167].

King's Wood S of the settlement of Beck Wythop and alongside the A66 [214281].

Kinmont Beck rises Corney Fell at 137902. Joined by Buckbarrow Beck at 133901 and joins the River Annas at Bootle at 108897 ...for derivation of Kinmont see **High Kinmont**.

Kinmont Buckbarrow W Buck Barrow 535m (1755ft) [147910] ...for derivation of Kinmont see **High Kinmont**.

Kinn slope above Braithwaite [223233] ...possibly from the ON 'kinn' meaning slope. There is another suggestion that as in German 'kinn' means chin it was given this name by German miners in the 16th century.

Kinney How ENE Blakeley Raise [074137] ...possibly similar to Kinmont and meaning 'head of the hill'.

Kinniside grassy hump on Kinniside Common rising to 375m (1230ft) [078116] ...Cyne's valley head or head of the hill.

Kinniside Common large and mainly grassy area between the River Calder and Worm Gill. Its highest point is Lank Rigg at 541m (1775ft) [085119].

Kinniside Cop small hill E Cleator Moor and W Meadley Reservoir 180m (590ft) [041146].

Kinniside Stone Circle see **Blakeley Raise Stone Circle**.

Kirby Quay W shore Coniston Water (313976).

Kirk Close bounded on the S by the B5289 and on the W and N by Hassnesshow Beck [189159].

Kirk Fell in his gazetteer in *The Lake Counties* (1902) W G Collingwood simply acknowledges Kirk Fell as being the W buttress of Great Gable. Be this as it may the fell is a mountain in its own right and separated from Gable by the col of Beck Head. The latter is 180m (591ft) below the summit of Kirk Fell and 277m (909ft) below Great Gable's summit. It is claimed that the path straight up Kirk Fell from Wasdale Head to the summit is the straightest and steepest for walkers in Lakeland. In fact, from Mosedale Beck to the summit cairn there is 712m (2336ft) of strenous walking in 1.6kms (l mile). This means a gradient of 41.2%. Kirk Fell possesses two summits one at 787m (2582ft) and the other, at the head of the slope overlooking Wasdale Head, at 802m (2631ft) [195105] ...'the fell above the church', the latter being St. Olaf's, Wasdale Head, or possibly similar to the first definition of Kirk Fell below.

Kirk Fell fell to the W of the Lord's Seat Group. Two summits, the highest at 438m (1437ft) at 173266 and the other due S at 420m (1378ft) at 173264 ...either circle fell (from the OE 'circul') and referring to its conical shape or the fell above the church, the latter being Lorton Church.

Kirk Howe Great Langdale. Between Rossett and Dungeon Ghyll Old Hotel [290063].

Kirk Stone see **Kirkstone Pass**.

Kirkbarrow Barton. Alongside the B5320 [490262] ...'hill above the church'

Kirkby House Underbarrow [464920] ...local family Kirk(e)by.

Kirkfell Crags Kirk Fell [193111].

Kirkfell House High Lorton [164259].

Kirkfell Tarn actually two tarns in a hollow between the two summits of Kirk Fell [197106].

Kirkgate Farm Loweswater [140207] ...farm by the way to the church.

Kirkgill Wood Loweswater [137209].

Kirkhead Loweswater [140208].

Kirklands Farm Irton. Nearby is the kirk (Irton Church) [089002].

Kirkstile Inn Loweswater. This 16th century inn was originally a brew farm. A micro brewery (Loweswater Brewery) was established at the inn in the summer of 2003. This revived a brewing tradition which was carried on there until the 1830s. At the time of writing the brewed beer was Melbreak Bitter but further beers are to be available in 2004 [141209].

Kirkstone Beck rises alongside the summit of Kirkstone Pass at 403083 and flows down the pass. Joined by Caudale Beck and Caiston Beck before it meets Dovedale Beck at 399118 and subsequently enters Brothers Water at 401125.

Kirkstone Foot Ambleside. Country house hotel of 17th century origin. Self-catering studio apartments and cottages within its grounds [380046].

Kirkstone Galleries see **Touchstone Interiors**.

Kirkstone Pass from the S two roads wind their ways upwards to meet near the summit of the pass, the A592 from Windermere via Troutbeck and a steeper minor road 'The Struggle' from Ambleside. In June 2002, a coach travelling down the Struggle went out of control at its foot, ploughed through a wall, down a steep slope and ended up on its side in a garden. Fortunately, no passengers were killed but many were injured. The summit of the pass at 455m (1493ft) [401082] is the highest in the Lake District crossed by a motor road and over it the A592 drops down to Brothers Water and on to Patterdale. This section of road was declared a main road in 1880 but only received its first coat of tarmac in 1930. Just below the summit on the S side is the Kirkstone Pass Inn and just below the summit on the N side and to the left of the road is a boulder, not very large, but when viewed from the N is shaped like the gable end of a kirk (church). It is generally accepted as giving the pass its name and to this a certain degree of credence is given initially by the noted antiquarian, the Rev Thomas Machel, who, in his journal of 1692, gave the Kirk Stone as the origin of the name Kirkstone Fell, and later by William Wordsworth in his *Pass of Kirkstone* when, of the stone he says "... and whose church-like frame/Gave to this savage Pass its name." In *The Place Names of Cumbria* Joan Lee suggests that the name is actually stone circle pass, derived from OE 'circul' (circle) and OE 'stan' (stone) hence the possibility that at one time there there could have been stone circles thereabouts that have been destroyed. To the left of the road as it heads down the pass and running parallel with it but at a slightly higher level is a possible Roman road. Snow covers the summit of the pass on an average of about 50 days a year. This cover is not always suitable for skiing but when conditions are right a small area of the fellside just N of the inn and to the right of the road is used for this recreation, particularly by beginners to the sport (see also **Kirkstone Pass Inn** following).

Kirkstone Pass Inn stands just S of the summit of Kirkstone Pass. Apparently possesses an intriguing and confusing history. A sign on it reads 'Kirkstone Pass Inn - 1496-1500 feet above sea level' and in *Inns of Character in the Lake District* it is recorded that "in the 1500s the hotel was only a workman's hut, then became a roadhouse before finally a coaching inn." However, other sources suggest that before a Parson Sewell built the inn in 1840 there was no building on its site or thereabouts. De Quincey in his *An Excursion over Kirkstone Pass* (1807) states that the only two objects on the summit of the pass "... were a guide post and the Kirk Stone." Furthermore, Wordsworth, a frequent traveller over the road, notes in his ode *The Pass of Kirkstone* (1817) that "save the rugged road we find no apponage of human hands" and in a later stanza "Though habitations none appear." What is certainly known is that at C450m (C1476ft) it is the highest inn in the Lake District and one of the highest in England. The highest is the Tan Hill Inn - 528.9 metres (1732 feet) above sea level, alongside the North Yorkshire/Durham boundary. A low whitewashed building some 60 years ago, the Kirkstone Pass Inn has since been extensively enlarged and modernised. Used to be called the Traveller's Rest but after much confusion with the Traveller's Rest at Grasmere and that at Glenridding the name was changed to its present title [401080].

Kirkstone Quarries head office based at Skelwith Bridge. Kirkstone Quarry was reopened in 1949 after being closed for 20 years . A move to new premises near Milnthorpe in 2004 freed space at Skelwith Bridge for the expansion of production facilities.

Kirkstone Road Ambleside to Kirkstone Pass. The highest and steepest portion is called the Struggle [383049].

Kirkstonefoot area at the foot of the N section of the Kirkstone Pass. The Brotherswater Inn was previously known as the Kirkstone Foot Inn [404119].

Kirksty Brow SE slope Great Meldrum [416221].

Kirkstyle Gill rises northern extremity of Gowbarrow Park at 409220 and joins Parkhouse Gill at 425211.

Kitbain Gill rises near Black Crag at 279275 and joins the watercourse formed by the meeting of Pike Sike and Stile Gill at 281281 to become Salehow Beck.

Kitchen Bay Derwent Water [252213].

Kitchen Ground off a track off the minor road from Holmrook (A595) to Santon Bridge [106995] ...centuries ago the ground/land of a John Kitchen.

Kitt How S Woodend [167961] ...possibly hill frequented by kites (birds).

Kitty Crag ESE Hole Rake [296990] ...as above.

Knicklethorns sometimes just Nickles. Howe Grain [433182] ...knobbly rocks or rounded hill by a wood.

Knight, The see **The Knight**.

Knipe scattered hamlet, SSE Helton, in the parish of Bampton. Principally comprises Howgate Foot, High Knipe, Low Knipe and Knipe Hall ...takes its name from the Knipe of Knipe Scar which means steep rock/overhanging rock.

Knipe Fold community NW Hawkshead alongside the Barngates to High Cross road

[343997] ...Knipe has been adopted as a surname but its derivative is steep or overhanging rocks.

Knipe Hall Knipe. Dates chiefly from the 16/17th centuries [519195].

Knipe Moor below Knipe Scar. The road from Askham to Bampton Grange crosses it [522191.]

Knipe Scar & Knipescar Common NE Bampton Grange. Knipescar Common is a relatively flat-topped green sward with limestone outcrops and boulders and three substantial tree plantations, Scarside (in which there is an earthwork scheduled as an Ancient Monument), Inscar and Scar, atop a roughly 1.6kms (1 mile) ridge called Knipe Scar. The latter name is actually given on the map to the steep, craggy, northern end of the ridge. The highest point of the common is 342m (1122ft) [536191]. The scar and common overlook the River Lowther to the W and the Lowther parkland to the N and provide impressive views of the High Street range, Blencathra and the Pennines. Much evidence of early man in the form of a stone circle, an enclosure [530193], scheduled as an Ancient Monument, tumuli, and of former industry represented by disused quarries and an old lime kiln. The latter at [540183] is an early 19th century example of a small farm kiln ...Knipe means steep rock/overhanging rock ie the craggy end of the scar.

Knipe Tarn due E of Stonehills Tarn. Privately owned. Surplus water flows down to join the River Gilpin C150m (C492ft) [427944] ...Knipe is a prominent local surname derived from steep rock/peak or overhanging rock.

Knock Murton see **Murton Fell**.

Knoll, The see **The Knoll**.

Knott farm, Underbarrow. N Knott Hill and in the 16th century referred to as Nether (Lower) Knott or Overknote [474930].

Knott, The (Swindale and High Street) see **The Knott**.

Knott, The (near Broughton Mills) see **The Knott**.

Knott Coppice alongside the Hawkshead-Grizedale road [337948].

Knott End end of the Knott [225916].

Knott End Eskdale. Alongside minor road, A595 to Eskdale Green. Since 1989 has housed the Centre for Complementary Care, a healing centre [134976].

Knott End between High Crags and Looking Crag E Newlands valley [234192].

Knott Ends S Low Tarn and between Nether Beck and Over Beck [160083].

Knott Halloo jagged rocky outcrop on Gategill Fell, Blencathra [320267].

Knott Head SW Little Langdale Tarn [304026].

Knott Head alongside the Braithwaite to Whinlatter road (B5292) [221245].

Knott Hill Underbarrow. Craggy hill N B5284 [476924].

Knott Hill W Rather Heath and Ratherheath Tarn. Rises to 136m (446ft) [472959] ...rocky hill.

Knott House Farm Grasmere. To the E of the A591. Sole survivor of several properties built on the site of a mansion of which "the Pillars of the Gateway in front of the mansion remained when we first took up our abode at Grasmere" according to Wordsworth [339087] ... a knott usually refers to a rocky hilltop. However, the *Place Names of Westmorland* suggests that in this case the title could be from either a local surname Knot mentioned in the 14th century or Knott in the 17th century. Considering Wordsworth's observations on the remaining gateposts it is more than likely the latter.

Knott Rigg a summit on the ridge leading from Newlands Hause to Ard Crags. Of the three principal summits on the ridge Knott Rigg is the lowest at 556m (1824ft) [197189].

Knotts alongside the A592 [407002] ...rocky hillocks.

Knotts hamlet 1.2kms (3/4 mile) SW Watermillock and alongside minor road off the A592 [436213].

Knotts Low (Tilberthwaite) Fell. N High Tilberthwaite. Spot height at 234m (768ft) [309021].

Knotts on S slope Souther Fell above Mousthwaite Comb [350277].

Knotts rocky outcrop on Helton Fell alongside Annas Sike [482204].

Knotts W A5091. WNW Thornythwaite [391225].

Knotts NE head of Seathwaite Tarn (263996).

Knotts rocky hilly area W Dock Tarn [267144].

Knotts Ullister Hill [208258].

Knotts crags overlooking Tarbarrel Moss [203252].

Knotts of the Tongue rocky outcrops on the Tongue between the upper reach of the Esk and Calfcove Gill [231078].

Knotts, The see **The Knotts**.

Knowe Crags W end Blencathra ridge 804m (2638ft) [312270], see also **Blease Fell**.

Knowe, The see **The Knowe**.

Kokoarrah rocky islet in the Irish sea just off the Ravenglass dunes [044969].

Kye Wood E side Coniston Water [315962] ...possibly the wood in which the cows grazed.

L

Labrynth, The see **The Labrynth**.

Lacet W Hutton. Alongside minor road to Hutton from minor road, A66-Matterdale End [431268] ...'Lased' in the first half of the 18th century.

Lacet Hill W Lacet [428268].

Laconby N Santon. NW Santon Bridge [097027] ...possibly a surname similar to Lachan or Lochan + dwelling.

Laconby Wood [093028].

Lad Crag E face Helvellyn ridge between Striding Edge and Nethermost Pike [344147] ...lad is frequently applied to individual boulders and crags ie Great Ladstones, Lad Crags/Knott, Lad Stones Bield, Ladstones and Lambert Lad. Derived from 'hlaed' meaning pile.

Lad Crag see **Loughrigg Fell**.

Lad Crags W Haweswater [478151].

Lad How Duddon valley [213961].

Lad Hows spot-heighted at 426m (1398ft) [172193] but its ridge continues up to the summit of Grassmoor.

Lad Knott alongside Ladknott Gill. Overlooks St John's in the Vale [323201].

Lad Stones Bield sheepfold Wetherlam S ridge [296998] ...see **Lad Crag**.

Ladcrag Beck rises alongside Great Lad Crag at 146093 and joins Nether Beck at 149088.

Ladder Brow steep slope behind the Borrowdale Hotel up which a zig zag path ascends to the High Lodore Falls and the road to Watendlath [265182].

Ladies in the Lakes bodies of three women found in three different lakes. See **Coniston**

Water, **Crummock Water** and **Wastwater**.

Ladies Table W Bassenthwaite Lake and the A66. NE Wythop Hall 296m (971ft) [209288].

Ladknott Gill rises St John's Common at 328204 and joins Mill Gill at 320198.

Ladstock Country House Hotel Thornthwaite. A former country residence dating back over 200 years. Set in 7 acres of woodland and lawns [223255].

Lady Holme island in Windermere owned by the National Trust. Formerly Chapel Island or St Mary's Holme. In the 13th century the then Lord of the Manor of Windermere established a small chantry chapel, one of over 2000 chantries which existed in England at the time of the dissolution of the monasteries by Henry VIII in the 16th century. (A chantry chapel was one endowed for the singing of masses for its founder after his/her death and for the dead generally). From the 16th century the chapel quickly fell into disrepair. Only steps cut into the rocks on the N side of the island and the previous name St Mary Holme and at one time Lady Holme remain to remind us that for 300 years a chapel existed on the island [398975].

Lady Well spring between Askham Hall and the R Lowther [517240].

Lady's Rake see **Walla Crag**.

Ladyside Pike earlier Lady's Seat. Conical summit on the Swinside to Hopegill Head ridge 703m (2306ft) [185227].

Lady's Seat W Haweswater S Castle Crag. Named after Lady de Morvill whose husband Hugh de Morvill was granted the barony of Westmorland by Henry II, [469126].

Lag Bank in afforested area E River Lickle 393m (1289ft) [247943].

Lagget alongside Lagget Beck [057126].

Lagget Beck rises from springs at 065130 and flows down to meet Nannycatch Beck at 053126.

Lags Coppice alongside the lane leading from the B5285 to Tarn Hows Cottage and Tarn Hows [318989].

Lags Wood E Coniston Water [325979].

Lair Beck rises alongside the roundabout at the junction of the A66 and the A591 at 264245 and joins the River Derwent at 249249 ...muddy stream.

Lairfold Rigg Nether Wasdale Common [123071].

Lake Bank E shore Esthwaite Water [364966].

Lake District Farm Estates see **Browside**.

Lake District Guide Books although the Lake District or aspects of it had been written about earlier the first real guide to the Lake District was probably that of Celia Fiennes who wrote of the area during her 'Great Journey' of 1698. In the first half of the following century Daniel Defoe incorporated the Lake District in his *A Tour Through the Whole Island of Great Britain*. The poet Thomas Gray wrote his *Journal of the Lakes* in 1769 and several years later the Rev William Gilpin wrote his *Tour in the Mountains and Lakes of Cumberland and Westmorland*. Thomas West wrote a *Guide to the Lakes* in 1778. In this he took his readers to various 'stations' or viewpoints. Land Surveyor, James Clarke, completed his *Survey of the Lakes of Cumberland, Westmorland...* in 1789 and in 1819 William Green produced his *Tourist's New Guide* followed four years later by Jonathan Otley with his *Pocket Guide...* In 1834 Edward Baines' *Companion to the Lakes* appeared and the following year William Wordsworth produced his *Guide Through the District of the Lakes*. From 1841 onwards A & C Black, publishers, produced a series of guide books while in 1853 Miss Harriett Martineau of Ambleside produced her influential guide to the Lake

District. This was illustrated by the well-known artist William Aspland. Murray's *Handbook for Westmorland, Cumberland and the Lakes* arrived in 1867 and M J B Baddeley's *The English Lake District* was published in 1886. Watercolourist, historian and archaeologist, W G Collingwood, issued his *The Lake Counties* in 1902. This was updated and re-released in 1988.

More recently there have appeared works by The Little Guides, W T Palmer, H H Symonds, Norman Nicholson, Penguin Books, Ward Lock publishers, Geographia, Arthur Mee, the Ordnance Survey, Hunter Davies, Melvyn Bragg, Frank Welsh, the inimitable Alfred Wainwright, the Fell and Rock Climbing Club, Bill Birkett and many others. Today there are countless guides to all aspects of the Lake District from walkers' and climbers' guides, geological and natural history to tea shop and pub guides and even walks on the level for the less energetic or disabled. The Armitt Library, Ambleside, is acknowledged as holding one of the nation's foremost collection of old guides.

Lake District National Park the largest National Park in England and Wales. Established in 1951 it covers 2292sq kms. of which 104,979ha. is moorland, 28,931ha. woodlands and 76,815ha. farmland. The National Park Authority owns 4% of the park, more than half is owned privately, and the National Trust owns 25%. There are 10 National Park Information Centres - Bowness Bay, Broughton-in-Furness, Coniston, Glenridding, Grasmere, Hawkshead, Keswick, Pooley Bridge, Seatoller Barn (Borrowdale) and Waterhead and, at the time of writing, there were 10 Local Information Points (LIPs) in the National Park sited at Post Offices at High Lorton, Ennerdale Bridge, St. Bees (outside the park but along with Ennerdale Bridge adjacent to the the Coast to Coast walk), Ulpha (sub-office), Gosforth, Far Sawrey, Elterwater also at Forest Spinners (Rusland), Barn Door out-door clothing shop (Wasdale Head) and the terminus of the Ravenglass & Eskdale Railway at Ravenglass. The National Park Visitor Centre is located at Brockhole on the A591 between Windermere and Ambleside. In 1999 a list compiled by staff at the National Geographic Traveller Magazine named the Lake District as one of the top 50 places of the world to visit.

Lake District National Park Authority see **National Park Authority**.

Lake District Planning Board see **National Park Authority**.

Lakeland Birds see **Birds in the Lake District**.

Lakeland Flora see **Flora of Lakeland**.

Lakeland Horticultural Society see **Holehird**.

Lakeland Mammals over the years several books have been written concerning Lake District mammals including the detailed *Lakeland Mammals: a Visitor's Handbook* by W R Mitchell and Peter Delap (1974). Of those referred to in this work the pine marten is possibly on the increase, otter hunting was outlawed in the Lake District in 1977 and today the population is increasing substantially. Unfortunaely the red squirrel is being ousted by its grey counterpart although, at the time of writing, a campaign has been launched to help protect red squirrels particularly by creating squirrel refuges. However, it would seem that one animal must be added to the list, a large black cat (thought to be a panther) of which, up to July 2002, there had been reports in the *Westmorland Gazette* of sightings from over 20 different areas in the Lake District particularly southern Lakeland and there have been many sitings since then including two at the same time.

Lakeland Ski Club a ski club was established in the Lake District in 1936 on Raise towards the northern end of the Helvellyn range. A tow and an engine house were installed in 1989 and a new hut was constructed in 1999, see also **Skiing**.

Lakeland View property alongside the B5292 [212244].

Lakes for grid references see **Lakes** section. For more information see under the particular lake.

Lakes School Troutbeck Bridge. Opened October 1965, [402001].

Lakeside & Haverthwaite Railway Haverthwaite Station is sited alongside the A590 near Newby Bridge. The line was originally owned by British Railways and the branch line from the main Carnforth to Barrow line carried pasengers and freight from Ulverston to Lakeside. Closed by British Rail in 1967. Subsequently acquired as a preservation line in 1972. Unfortunately with the construction of the Haverthwaite by-pass the only section now remaining , albeit a beautiful one through the Leven valley, is the (4.6 kms) 3.5 miles section from Haverthwaite to Lakeside on Windermere. Steam trains run daily at Easter and from May to the end of October.

Lakeside YMCA Centre celebrated its Golden Jubilee in 2002.

Lamb Bridge Scales-Hutton Moor End-A66 road. Crosses R Glenderamackin at 354268 ...personal name or lamb (sheep).

Lamb Howe property S Lambhowe Hill [421918] ...lamb hill.

Lamb Pasture E Dry Howe, Bannisdale. Spot-height at 367m (1204ft) [534021].

Lambert Lad boundary stone N Loadpot Hill and alongside the High Street Roman road ...the name 'lad' is often applied to individual boulders and crags and in this case it is the 'lad' which denotes the boundary of Lambert's land [458189].

Lambfoot Dub small tarn above the Corridor Route from Sty Head to Scafell Pike [221084] ...'dub', a pool, which resembles a lamb's foot.

Lambford Bridge footbridge across Whillan Beck near Burnmoor Tarn [188038].

Lambground Corney [121916].

Lambhowe Hill W A5074. N Lamb Howe [421920] ...lamb 'hill hill'.

Lambhowe Plantation SW Lamb Howe [419914].

Lambing Knott lower slope Robindon. Above the B5289 [193155].

Lamper Knott on the High Raise to Sergeant's Man ridge. WSW Sergeant's Crag [270111].

Lamplugh village and large parish alongside the NP boundary. Old established with records dating back to the middle of the 12th century. St Michael's Church was restored, enlarged and modified in 1870 but there are traces of an ancient structure some 600 years old. Formerly there were several iron ore and coal mines in the area but these have disappeared and today agriculture is the main industry. Similar to a saying by former Wythburnians that a squirrel might have gone from Wythburn Chapel to Keswick without alighting on the ground a couplet referring to the earlier countryside around Lamplugh reads:

a squirrel could hop from tree to tree,
from Lamplugh Fells to Moresby.

Lamplugh is famed for its Lamplugh pudding, toast or biscuit soaked in warm ale with rum and spices to taste [089208] ...the EPNS suggests that the first element is the OB 'landa' meaning enclosure with an unrecognised second element. Another suggestion is the church of the parish.

Lamplugh Fell fell area to the SE of Lamplugh [106192].

Lamplugh Hall the old hall, now a farmstead has, at its entrance, an archway which bears the Lamplugh family crest and the date 1595 [088207].

Lancrigg Grasmere. This imposing white-fronted building at the foot of Helm Crag looks out over Easedale. Originally a farmstead it was much extended in the 1840s with, it is said, advice from William Wordsworth who specified the present chimneys. On a terrace in the grounds, known as Lancrigg Terrace or Wordsworth's Terrace, the poet composed much of *The Prelude* and an inscribed tablet set on a rock bears a Latin inscription commemorating the fact that Dorothy Wordsworth sat there and wrote down her brother's compositions while he walked on the terrace. For many years until his death in 1865 Sir John Richardson, Arctic explorer, physician, surgeon, writer and naturalist, lived at Lancrigg. His grave is in Grasmere churchyard. Today, the building, set in 27 acres, is a vegetarian country house hotel [330085] ...so called because of its site at the end of a long ridge (lancrigg) which curves round Far Easedale and over Helm Crag.

Landing Stages, Keswick see **Keswick Launch**.

Lands Point promontory W shore Coniston Water near Coniston Hall [306962].

Lane End at the junction of the Croglinhurst to Broughton Mills road and that from Broughton-in-Furness to Broughton Mills [220900].

Lane End Waberthwaite [107934].

Lane End Farm Waberthwaite [107935].

Lane Ends ENE Little Mell Fell [433245].

Lane Head alongside track from A592 to Wall End and at top of track from Deepdale Bridge to the above [397144].

Lane Head head of lane leading to Tarn Hows [325996].

Lane Head S A66 [375270].

Lane Head Coppice W Tarn Hows. E of and alongside the A593 [324999].

Lanefoot alongside the Cold Fell Road [063153].

Lanefoot Farm off minor road Brandlingill to Low Lorton [139265].

Lanefoot Farm alongside the minor road from Braithwaite which connects with the Braithwaite-Thornthwaite road [228246].

Lanehead Nabend. Alongside minor road from Nabend to Dacre [433256].

Lanehead S of How Head on the E side of Coniston Water. Not named on the OS map. Built in 1848 on the site of an earlier alehouse it later became the home of W G Collingwood (1854-1932), painter, historian, archaeologist and author. Particularly well-known for his *The Lake Counties* (1902) and the historical novel *Thorstein of the Mere*. He was, for many years, secretary to John Ruskin at Brantwood and for 32 years editor of the *Transactions of the Cumberland and Westmorland Antiquarian and Archaeological Society*. His son, Robin G (1889-1943), also lived here for a time. He became an eminent philosopher and archaeologist and professor of metaphysical philosophy at Oxford. The Collingwood family lived at Lanehead for 76 years until 1967. Lanehead was to provide the principal setting for 'Beckfoot' in Arthur Ransome's *Swallows and Amazons* fame. Today it houses an Outdoor Education Centre run by Cleveland County Education Committee.

Lang Crag lengthy frontage of crags, hence the name which means long, to the N of Codale Tarn [296092].

Lang How between Brigstone Moss and Swinescar Pike 414m (1358ft) [318071] ...long hill.

Lang How Tarn see **Youdell Tarn**.

Langdale & Ambleside Mountain Rescue Team during the 1950s the late Sid Cross, then proprietor of the Old Dungeon Ghyll Hotel, Great Langdale, organised a voluntary mountain rescue team, the Langdale Rescue Team. In 1969 this amalgamated with the Ambleside Rescue Team, a founder member of which, Stewart Hulse, stepped down as team leader of the Langdale & Ambleside Mountain Rescue Team in March 2000, after 21 years

in that position. Towards the end of 2002 work commenced on a new centre at Ambleside and a new base on the old site was opened in January 2004.

Langdale Chase Hotel E shore Windermere. Mansion built in 1891 as a private residence for a Manchester businessman. In the early 1930s converted into a country house hotel. Exceptional views of lake and mountains from its dining room and terrace. Set in five acres of gardens [387017].

Langdale Combe source of Stake Gill and just below the summit of the Stake Pass. A boggy area with many glaciated moraine mounds [262085] ...a 'combe'is a short valley or deep holllow.

Langdale Fell fell area overlooking Mickleden [273068].

Langdale Pikes the best known and most commonly referred to as the Langdale Pikes are Pike of Stickle 709m (2326ft) and Harrison Stickle 736m (2415ft) overlooking the head of Great Langdale. These are actually the end of a long ridge with High Raise (High White Stones) 762m (2500ft) as its highest point. Among the excellent viewpoints from which the two Stickles can be seen are - the Lowwood Hotel, alongside the A591; the road up Great Langdale after Chapel Stile; Skelwith Fold; Blea Tarn and the highest point of the road between Little Langdale and the head of Great Langdale and the summits of Lingmoor Fell and Side Pike. As a region the Langdale Pikes is deemed to incorporate Loft Crag (with its southern bastion Gimmer Crag) C670m (C2198ft), Pavey Ark 700m (2297ft) and lesser heights Thorn Crag and Pike Howe. Some sources even suggest that Thunacar Knott 723m (2372ft) and Pike of Blisco, N and S respectively of the head of Great Langdale, should be added to the list. In 1998 the Langdale Pikes were designated as a Site of Special Scientific Interest by English Nature because of their special rock formation [278073].

Langdale Timeshare Development principally on the site of the former Elterwater

Gunpowder Works. The complex incorporates the Chapel Stile Timeshare apartments and Langdale lodges, the Langdale Hotel and Country Club (incorporating Purdey's Restaurant and Wainwright's Inn) and Elterwater Hall [326030].

Langfield Banks slope overlooking Dacre Beck. Rises to 173m (568ft) [468261].

Langfield Wood foot of Langfield Banks alongside Dacre Beck [472265].

Langhowe Pike ESE Swindale Foot [528135].

Langley Corney. Off the minor road from the A595 to the Bootle to Eskmeals road [097912] ...female personal name + shieling/hill pasture.

Langley Park off the minor road from the A595 to the Eskmeals coast road. Just over 1.6 kms (1 mile) N Langley. W Great Wood [097930].

Langstrath as its name suggests it is a long valley and certainly one of the longest uninhabited valleys in the Lake District. Starts approximately 1.6kms (1 mile) SE Stonethwaite and ends alongside Tongue Head near Angle Tarn and alongside the path from Rossett Gill to Sty Head. Once exceptionally wooded but most of the woodland was cut down centuries ago to provide fuel for the bloomery at Smithymire Island near the foot of the valley. At the head of the valley there is an impressive waterfall on Allencrags Gill [260095].

Langstrath Beck Allencrags Gill and Angletarn Gill join forces at 248088 to become Langstrath Beck. This flows down Langstrath to meet Greenup Gill at 274130 and become Stonethwaite Beck which joins the River Derwent at 253154.

Langstrath Country Inn see **Stonethwaite**.

Lank Rigg once called Long Fell. A remote and extensive grassy fell the highest point of Kinniside Common. Bounded on the N by Whoap Beck and Red Gill, on the S by Worm Gill, on the E by Worm Gill and its tributaries and on the W by the River Calder. A small tarn lies in a hollow SW of the summit. Nearby there is a tumulus and on its S slope a homestead, ancient cairns and a settlement which suggest the fell was better known in prehistoric times than it is today. Trig. point at 541m (1775ft) [092120] ...long ridge.

Lank Rigg Tarn see **Lank Rigg**.

Lankrigg Moss WNW of the summit of Lank Rigg. N of the confluence of Long Gill and Ya Gill [077126].

Lanshaw Hill Ralfland Forest WSW Keld. High Lanshaw is at its northern extremity. [544140] ...long copse + hill.

Lanshaw Sike tributary of the R Lowther. Rises at 539139 and joins the Lowther at 548146.

Lanthwaite Cottage alongside the B5289 [158206].

Lanthwaite Gate ruined farm and modern property. The gate across the road here has long since disappeared [158211].

Lanthwaite Green area to the E of the foot of Crummock Water. Once a British settlement and there is a 'homestead' shown at 160210. A parking place alongside the B5289 provides access to several walks particularly that across the grassy green and up Gasgale Gill to Coledale Hause and Grasmoor or that up Whiteside and on to Hopegill Head and Grisedale. Adjectively Lanthwaites in the area are Lanthwaite Hill (now Brackenthwaite Hows)/Gate/Green Farm/Cottage/Wood [160209].

Lanthwaite Green Farm Lanthwaite Green. Alongside the B5289 [159208].

Lanthwaite Hill see **Brackenthwaite Hows**.

Lanthwaite Wood foot of Crummock Water. Acquired by the NT in 1937 [154209].

Lanty Crag S Heltondale Beck, W unfenced road from Heltondale to Rough Hill. At its rear at 273m (896ft) there is a tumulus [500202].

Lanty Scar see **Loughrigg Fell**.

Lanty Slee see **Slee, Lanty**.

Lanty Tarn Martindale. Above St Peter's Church and near both road and path between Martindale and Howtown. To all intents and purposes it is now dried up [435190].

Lanty Well a spring on the ridge between Kinn and Sleet How [211229].

Lanty's Tarn named after Lancelot Dobson whose family at one time owned most of Grisedale and who, for generations, lived at Grassthwaite Howe, Patterdale, a mansion which once stood behind the present-day cottages. The tarn was subsequently enlarged and nurtured by the Marshalls of Patterdale Hall who fished there in summer and collected ice from it in winter, 276m (906ft) [384163].

Larch alongside a tributary of Meregill Beck [139241].

Lassie Crag W Thirlmere adjoining Low Bank [304181].

Latrigg smooth grassy fell the southernmost summit of Skiddaw with the River Greta flowing along its foot. There is a smaller Latrigg to its N near Over Water 368m (1207ft) [279247] ...animal's lair on the hill.

Latrigg Tarn between Longmire Road and Dubbs Road and below Dubbs Reservoir. A small private fish pond. Not to be confused with the much larger Overwater at the foot of Lattrigg, northern Lakeland, 245m (804ft) [417018] ...tarn by the animal's lair on the ridge.

Latter Barrow Birkby, 166m (545ft) [129966] ...see **Latterbarrow** below.

Latter Barrow a subsidiary summit on Kinniside Common overlooking the River Calder and Latterbarrow Beck 354m (1161ft) [074115].

Latterbarrow National Trust fell at the N end of Claife Heights and to the E of the Colthouse-High Wray road. Its summit provides an excellent viewpoint and is surmounted by a tall well-built cairn known as Latterbarrow Man. At 244m (804ft) [367991] it is not the highest summit of Claife Heights. This honour goes to High Blind How with its trig. point at 270m (886ft) [367991] ...there are several Latterbarrows in Cumbria and they all refer to the animal's lair on the hill.

Latterbarrow summit to the W of Irton Fell. Well wooded. Overlooks Nether Wasdale to the N. Crags to the S of its summit C200m (C656ft) [127027] ...see **Latterbarrow** above.

Latterbarrow afforested hill on the slope of Ennerdale rising to 273m (896ft) [130147].

Latterbarrow Beck rises Lank Rigg at 087111 and joins the River Calder at 066109 ...stream by the hill where animals have their lair.

Latterbarrow Crags to the S of the summit of Latterbarrow, W Irton Fell [127027].

Latterbarrow Moss Kinniside Common. N Latter Barrow [076120].

Latterhaw Crag overlooks Deepdale from its N slope [388133] ...hill with a lair upon it + crag.

Latterhead alongside the road from Loweswater via Thackthwaite to Low Lorton. High Latterhead nearby [149226] ...possibly animal's lair but the EPNS suggests that from its early form 'Laterhead' it means hill/slope head. To its immediate W the land rises substantially to 423m (1388ft).

Launchy Gill (Lancelot's Gill). Sometimes referred to as Deergarth Gill. Stream rises high on fells W Thirlmere in the region of 292158 and flows through Launchy Tarn into Thirlmere which it joins at 310158. Two spectacular converging waterfalls plunge to form smaller falls. The famous Cop Stone, Armboth's equivalent to Borrowdale's Bowder Stone, stands above Launchy Tarn and the Web Stone (sometimes referred to as the Justice Stone) where, during the 1665 plague, traders met locals to purchase webs and yarns the latter had manufactured, stands alongside the gill. Also, alongside the gill is a large precariously placed boulder known as the Tottling Stone ('tottle' means liable to topple over or look very unsteady). The water authority has provided a short nature trail which commences from the road at the foot of the gill. Launchy Gill is an outstanding example of upland oak and birch woodland and is a Site of Special Scientific Interest (SSSI).

Launchy Tarn on Launchy Gill and, to differentiate it from Launchy Tarn below, often referred to as Launchy Gill Tarn. Not so much a tarn as a widening of the beck [302150].

Launchy Tarn There are three principal tarns below Dale Head, Dalehead, Launchy and High Scawdel. Launchy can be termed the middle one. A peat moss tarn it lies to the SE of Dalehead and NE of High Scawdel C550m (C1804ft) [233150].

Laurel Bank Embleton [164288].

Laverock How WSW slope Ponsonby Fell, NE Stargreen Beck, ESE Birrel Sike [067064] ...possibly lord's hill.

Lavery Gill rises E slope High Spy at 241160 and joins Tongue Gill at 248152.

Lawrence Scar Wood W Dale Park valley and below Brock Crag [348927].

Lawson Park former farm on the edge of woods and alongside a bridleway from the road along the E side of Coniston Water. Just below the property there is an excellent viewpoint over Coniston Water and Coniston to the Old Man. Similar to nearby Parkamoor in that in much earlier times it was a small sheep farm belonging to Furness Abbey. Remained a sheep farm until acquisition by the Forestry Commission. The site of the fictitious Animal Research, Scientific and Experimental (ARSE) in Richard Adams' *The Plague Dogs* [317951] ...'park' in this case refers to an enclosure wrested from the woodlands.

Lawyer's Brow Shap Fells. W Great Yarlside [518076] ...not a place to hold a lawyer's convention! Did it obtain its name because it was at one time the subject of a legal battle, was it once owned by a lawyer or did members of the legal profession pass this way en route to clients or courts elsewhere?

Layburn Dyke rises NW corner of Aynums Wood and joins Main Drain which drains the various 'mosses' to the W of the Underbarrow and Helsington Pools. In days gone by peat from these mosses was cut by local inhabitants and after drying was taken to Kendal where it was sold at 8 portions for 1d, [462967].

Laythwaite Crags W of and overlooking Haweswater [473147] ...track-bridge clearing + crags. The bridge presumably crossed Laythwaite Sike but the old track was submerged when the level of Haweswater was raised.

Laythwaite Sike rises 474145 and joins Haweswater at 477143.

Lea, The see **The Lea**.

Lead Pike SW of the foot of Seathwaite Tarn (246982).

Leads Howe hill to the W of Kentmere Reservoir [441081].

Leady Moss S Sosgill. W Bramley [103237].

Leagate old settlement alongside the A6 [540006] ...cleared woodland opening.

Leaps Beck begins life as Hare Gill on Sadler's Knott at 104186. Name changes to Leaps Beck between Murton Fell and Kelton Fell. Subsequently Smaithwaite Beck and finally Smithy Beck before becoming one of the many tributaries of the River Marron. The latter subsequently joins the River Derwent.

Lease Knott Birkby [124964] ...probably the rocky hill above the pasture/meadow.

Leathside Dub in the River Derwent between Grange and Derwentwater [257179].

Lee Haw Gutter rises between Red Gill Beck and Low Long Crag at 263960 and joins the former at 265956.

Leeming Cottage alongside minor road, A592-Matterdale Rigg [433219].

Leeming Farm Watermillock. Off the A592 [439219].

Leeming House Hotel country house hotel, Watermillock. Approached down lane off the A592. House built in 1847 [442216].

Legburthwaite one of four settlements which make up the village of Thirlmere. Alongside the B5322 0.4kms (0.25 mile) N of its junction with the A591 [319193]. There is a car park and picnic area just W of the B5322 and a youth hostel alongside ...probably Leggr's hill clearing.

Leghorn Hall see **Reston Hall**.

Lesketh How hillock W of the A591 and Scandale Beck [370050] ...in 1772 'Lascalehow' and this suggests 'skali' (shieling) and the whole name being the hill/mound with a hut on or alongside.

Levers Hawse depression in the ridge between Brim Fell and Swirl How. A stony steep path descends from the Hawse to Levers Water C680m (C2231ft) [271994].

Levers Moss Scrow W Levers Water Beck (287983), see 'scrow' in **Glossary**.

Levers Water Coniston Fells. Reservoir, previously a corrie tarn which was dammed to provide power for the many former copper mines in the valley below. Copper is no longer mined thereabouts but Levers Water still provides an essential service. In the 1970s a water treatment plant was built below the dam. This now provides drinking water for Coniston and area. With a depth of 38m (125ft) it is the second deepest tarn in the Lake District after Blea Water. Contains trout [279993] ...choice of three derivations - an ancient personal name, rushy/reedy or noisy (a spectacular waterfall just below the tarn is particular noisy when in spate).

Levers Water Beck its source is Levers Water at 282992. Subsequently joined by Low Water Beck it later becomes Church Beck which flows into Coniston Water at 308969.

Levers Water Bottom valley bottom through which Swirl Hawse Beck flows en route to Levers Water [278084].

Levers Waterfall a spectacular waterfall on Levers Water Beck just below its outfall from Levers Water [282991].

Lewthwaite Gill rises E slope High Crags at 221176 and joins Newlands Beck at 229179.

Leyland Clock this large clock bearing the advertising slogan 'Leyland Motors For All Time' was situated alongside the A6, on the rise above Hucks Bridge, from 1931-1970. Since 1973, however, it has stood outside the Brewery Arts Centre in Kendal but only in 1996 was it restored to its former working glory.

Lickbarrow Road links the B5284 with Thornbarrow Road, Windermere [412959].

Lickle, River see **River Lickle**.

Light Water rises Whiteside at 522013 and flows under the A6, alongside Selside and under Bowthwaite Bridge to meet the River Mint at 554984 ...the light, bright, stream.

Lightbeck Underbarrow. Below Knott Hill [478923] ...takes its name from the beck alongside, a light, bright stream.

Lilies of the Valley two islands in Windermere W of Belle Isle [390967/391967] ...where lilies of the valley grow in profusion. In *The Prelude* (Book II lines 58-61) Wordsworth refers to boating on Windermere and to the islands:

Was now an Island musical with birds
That sang for ever; now a Sister Isle
Beneath the oaks' umbrageous covert, sown
With lilies of the valley, like a field:

Lily Fell low fell SW Staveley, 182m (597ft) [464977] ...possibly the personal name Lily or simply means the little fell.

Lily Hall Ennerdale Bridge [073158].

Lily Pond Claife Heights. Alongside the Colthouse-Belle Grange track. Few lilies now remain, C200m (C656ft) [368983].

Lily Tarn below Todd Crag, Loughrigg Fell. Largest of the many small tarns on the fell. At one time it was stocked with golden carp, 200m (656ft) [364040] ...Lily's (surname) tarn or possibly the little tarn.

Lily Wood Duddon valley [215960] ...either a personal name or little wood.

Limefitt House Limefitt Park, Troutbeck [417030].

Limefitt Park caravan park which began in the 1950s as a small camping site. Over the succeeding years enlarged and granted permanent status in the 1970s. Now covers over 100 acres and has over 200 caravan pitches. At one time possessed a grass ski run. Today there is a substantial shop and a pub (the Haybarn Inn) on the site [417032] ...its original spelling was Limethwaite and refers to the clearing or water meadow on which flax is grown.

Lime Kilns there are many old lime kilns in the LDNP. Most date from the 18th century and a considerable number are listed buildings. Some are specifically mentioned in this work but the LDNP Authority has published a leaflet *Lime Kilns in the Lake District* which traces the history of eight of the best surviving examples in the area.

Limekiln Plantation NNW Askham [500241].

Limestone Haws Little Arrow Moor [278969].

Limestone Hill E Torver Intake. W Knipe Fold to The Drunken Duck Inn road [340045].

Linbeck alongside the A595 to Eskdale Green road [140981] ...lime tree stream.

Linbeck Bridge carries the A595 to Eskdale Green road over Linbeck Gill [140982].

Linbeck Gill rises Devoke Water and shortly afterwards drops over a 8m (26ft) fall before being joined by Black Beck at 148978. Enters the R Esk at 140983.

Lincomb Tarns name given to several tarns on the Glaramara to Allen Crags ridge and sited just below a rocky summit. Spot-heighted at 684m (2244ft) [241094] ...tarns in the comb/valley where the lime trees grow, see also **High House Tarn**.

Lind End off a minor road from Broughton Mills [231912].

Lindend Bridge carries the path from Lind End to Carter Ground and beyond across the River Lickle [230913].

Lindeth Farm off Lindeth Lane [411952] ...lime tree hill farm.

Lindeth Fell Country House Hotel former Edwardian country house, Lyth Valley road, Bowness-on-Windermere [505953] ...lime tree hill.

Lindeth Howe Country House Hotel Storrs Park, Bowness. House built in the 1870s by a wealthy mill owner. Purchased by Beatrix Potter in 1919 and her mother came to live here. She died at Lindeth Howe in December 1932. The hotel is set in five acres of garden ...lime tree hill hill.

Lindeth Lane from the B5284-A5074 [412952] ...lane by the lime tree hill.

Lindeth Tarn off Lindeth Lane. Now disappeared and its site is a refuse dump [412947] ...lime tree hill tarn.

Lindreth Brow Underbarrow [468937] ...brow of the lime tree hill or possibly a surname derived from this.

Ling Comb deep hollow/valley below Red Pike, Buttermere. Down it flows Far Ruddy Beck [159161].

Ling Fell overlooks Wythop Dale, Wythop Beck and Wythop Mill. Trig. point at 373m

(1224ft). On its N slope there is an old corpse road [180286] ...the rounded heather-clad hill.

Ling Holm small island in Windermere [386936] ...ling/heather island.

Ling How Bassenthwaite [241300].

Ling Mell Plantations Ennerdale [142135].

Lingcomb Edge rocky edge above Ling Comb [156161].

Lingcove Beck rises WSW Three Tarns at 243059. Joined by Yeastyrigg Gill at 238056 and joins the River Esk near Lingcove Bridge at 227036. Possesses spectacular waterfalls. In days gone by the Lingcove valley was a popular packhorse route from Eskdale to Borrowdale ...W G Collingwood says that Lingcove means 'cove of a torrent' but the EPNS states the more obvious cove with the ling/heather.

Lingcove Bridge ancient single-arched packhorse bridge across Lingcove Beck. Sometimes referred to as Throstle Garth Bridge. On a walkers' route to upper Eskdale and Scafell Pike. Nearby are Esk Falls on the River Esk and Throstlegarth Fall on Lingcove Beck [228037].

Lingholm W shore Derwent Water 1.8 kms (1 mile) S of Portinscale off the Portinscale to Grange road. At Lingholm Squirrel Nutkin and other Beatrix Potter stories were written. Lingholm Gardens, renowned particularly for their rhododendrons and azaleas, were developed in the early 1900s by Lord Rochdale and were subsequently open to the public until 1997 when they closed completely [254222].

Lingholm Islands three islets, Derwent Water. Lingholm is on the shore nearby [256224].

Lingmell Ennerdale. Spot-heighted at 435m (1427ft) [142130].

Lingmell outlier of the Scafell range and linked to the main ridge by a narrow col, Lingmell Col. Along with Broad Crag, Great Gable and other land hereabouts it was given to the NT by the Fell and Rock Climbing Club in 1923, 800m (2625ft) [209082] ...ling/heather hill.

Lingmell Col col between Lingmell and Scafell Pike [211079].

Lingmell Crag N Face Lingmell [208084].

Lingmell End end of the ridge from High Street over Mardale Ill Bell. Rises steeply over Kentmere Common. At its foot is a former settlement C660m (C2165ft) [446092] ...heather end to the ridge.

Lingmell Gill a major headstream rises below Lingmell Col at 208079 while another rises below Black Crag at 202072. Both meet at the foot of Brown Tongue from where the gill drops down to join Wastwater at 181072. At one time the stream continued across the flat alluvial plain at the head of Wastwater to join Lingmell Beck but during the First World War German Prisoners of War re-routed it directly into Wastwater and at the same time constructed a concrete bridge across the gill.

Lingmell Gill rises below Nan Bield Pass col at 451094. Joined by many small streams which flow down from the eastern fellside before the gill enters Kentmere Reservoir at 445084.

Lingmell Scars rocky foot of bank alongside Lingmell Gill [197075].

Lingmoor Fell often just referred to as Lingmoor. Large fell area between Great and Little Langdale. Its summit, Brown How, is 469m (1539ft) [303046] ...heather moor fell.

Lingmoor Quarry Lingmoor Fell [309043].

Lingmoor Tarn Lingmoor Fell. Picturesque tarn containing three islands C390m (C1280ft) [301051].

Lingy Acre Portinscale [251232].

Lingy Bank N Tongue Gill. W River Derwent [248153].

Lingy Crag WNW Brock Crags. Above Patterdale (valley) and Calf Close [410138] ...heather crag.

Lingy End end of a ridge overlooking Willygrass Gill [270138] ...heather/ling end.

Lingy Hill S Thornship, WSW Steps Hall C250m (C820ft) [558135].

Lingy Holm one of Ullswater's four islands. In low water conditions two separate rocky outcrops [394181] ...heather island.

Lingy Stone Seathwaite Fells (249977) ...stone in the ling/heather.

Lining Crag between Langstrath and the Stake Pass and NW Langdale Combe [256089] ...possibly the crag with ling/heather growing by or upon it.

Lining Crag alongside the bridleway between Greenup Edge and Stonethwaite Beck [283112] ...see **Lining Crag** above.

Link Cove at the head of Deepdale. A fine example of a glaciated hanging valley. Practically encircled by crags - Erne Nest Crag, Hart Crag, Scrubby Crag and Greenhow End [372117]. Over the years has been the scene of many accidents to fellwalkers resulting in call-outs by mountain rescue groups.

Link Hause col between Hart Crag and Fairfield [367114]

Linkrigg Gill rises Sillathwaite Wood at 064123. Joined by Lagget Beck before entering Nannycatch Beck at 053126.

Linsty Hall Wood Force Forge [328903].

Linthwaite House Hotel Crook Road, Bowness. Its 14 acres of garden include a substantial tarn which can be fished by guests staying at the hotel [407954] ...clearing in the lime trees.

Linthwaite House Tarn see **Linthwaite House Hotel**.

Lisco Farm off cul de sac extension minor road, Scales-A66, [370272].

Literary Lakeland writings concerning the Lake District really began with the early guide books writers and has been continued by many authors of the present day, see *Lake District Guide Books*. The Wordsworth circle, predominently comprising Samuel Taylor Coleridge, Robert Southey, Charles and Mary Lamb, John Keats, Hartley Coleridge, Thomas de Quincey and Walter Scott (later Sir Walter), enthused about the area in their writings. Other notable writers/poets, not in any strict order, include Dr. Thomas Arnold, Matthew Arnold, Canon H D Rawnsley, Percy Bysshe Shelley, Hugh Walpole (later Sir Hugh), Graham Sutton, Hall Caine, Nicolas Size, James Spedding, Alfred Tennyson, W G Collingwood and John Ruskin. Then, bringing the story up to date, we have Norman Nicholson, Richard Adams, Arthur Ransome, Melvyn Bragg (now Sir Melvyn), Alfred Wainwright, John Wyatt, Chris Bonnington (now Sir Chris), Hunter Davies and Margaret Forster and many others too numerous to mention.

For more detailed information consult *Clouds and Stones, Lakeland's Literary Heritage* by Bob Matthews, *A Literary Guide to the Lake District* by Grevel Lindop (1993) and the **Bibliography** section at the end of the Reference Section.

Little Arming How Birker Fell 244m (800ft). Great Arming How to its NE [182992].

Little Arrow farm and other properties alongside the A593, Torver to Coniston road [290950]. Arrowfield at Little Arrow, a country guest house dating from 1896 ...see **Little Arrow Moor**.

Little Arrow Intake NW Little Arrow. Alongside Torver Beck [284959].

Little Arrow Moor area to the S of Coniston Old Man and traversed by the Walna Scar Road. In February 1954, on the moor above Little Arrow Farm a 'flying saucer' was first photograpahed by 13-year-old Stephen Darbyshire [275969] ...possibly, hill slope or hill pasture or little shieling on the moor.

Little Barrow Boot, Eskdale. Below Great Barrow [184015].

Little Baswicks W shore Windermere. Alongside the High Cunsey-Graythwaite road. [381923] ...see Baswicks.

Little Beck rises Birker Moor at 169974 and joins Highford Beck at 175982.

Little Birkhouse Hill see **Great Birkhouse Hill**.

Little Blake Rigg NW foot of Seathwaite Tarn [243991].

Little Braithwaite 0.8 kms (0.5 mile) SE Braithwaite [238230].

Little Brinhowe Gill rises between Great and Little Castle Hows at 309076 and joins Sourmilk Gill at 319087.

Little Carrs N Great Carrs 692m (2270ft) [270015] ...see **Great Carrs**.

Little Castle How ESE Great Castle How [312077] ...see **Great Castle How**.

Little Cove Mires Beck flows down through the cove on its way to join Glenridding Beck [374164].

Little Cove alongside Bleaberry Gill, Seathwaite Fells (255981).

Little Crag Birker Moor C280m (C919ft) [184977].

Little Crosthwaite E Bassenthwaite Lake. Alongside the A591 [234276].

Little Dale valley between Hindscarth and Robinson down which flows Scope Beck on its way to join Newlands Beck. A tarn in its middle reaches was man-made to supply water to the former Goldscope Mines [212170]. Littledale Edge links Hindscarth and Robinson at the head of the valley [210160].

Little Dodd WSW Great Dodd C780m (C2559) [337204].

Little Dodd between Starling Dodd and Red Pike. Lowest of the three neighbouring Dodds at 590m (1936ft) [149155]. Starling Dodd is 633m (2077ft) and Dodd, below Red Pike, is 641m (2103ft).

Little Dodd Loweswater Fell. N Hen Comb [132191].

Little Ellers Portinscale [249235].

Little Fell S Stang End, Little Langdale. W Great How [319025].

Little Gatesgarthdale section of the Honister Pass as the latter descends to Seatoller. The present road, the old road and Hause Gill pass through it [235139] ...see **Gatesgarthdale Beck**.

Little Gill rises Littlegill Head on the Rossett Pike to Mansey Pike ridge at 254080 and joins Stake Gill and Rossett Gill at 262073 to become Mickleden Beck.

Little Gill rises Cockley Moss at 166958. Joins Great Gill at 171962. This joins Woodend Pool at 173966.

Little Gowder Crag NW Haycock [140110]. Gowder Crag is S of Haycock ...see **Gowder Crag**.

Little Grain Gill headstreams rise 159039, 164043 and 165043 and the gill joins Robin Gill at 163033.

Little Grain Gill rises Whin Rigg ridge at 161042 and 159039 respectively and joins Robin Gill at 163033.

Little Green Hows S Green Hows Tarn [362905].

Little Hart Crag stands on guard at the head of Scandale and N of the summit of the pass. 0.8kms (0.5 mile) SW of High Hartsop Dodd. Summit comprises double rocky outcrops. A wall of crags, Black Brow, runs NW-NNE of it 637m (2090ft) [387100].

Little Hart Crag Tarn see **Scandale Tarn**.

Little Hartbarrow Cartmel Fell [408907].

Little Harter Fell subsidiary summit of Harter Fell, Mardale, between Adam Seat and the summit of Harter Fell C670 (C2198ft) [470093].

Little Horse Crag Wrynose Fell. Above Great Horse Crag and overlooking the Wrynose Pass [284036] ...great and little obviously refer to the actual size of the crags.

Little How ENE Thirlmere Dam. Between A591 and minor road W Thirlmere [315193].

Little How Crags between Levers Hawse and Great How Crags at the S end of the Swirl How ridge [274997].

Little Intake at the rear of Bridge End and adjoining Great Intake [247906].

Little Isle the smaller of Rydal Water's two islands [356061].

Little Knott Satterthwaite, NNE Great Knott [332921].

Little Lad Crag overlooks Nether Beck from the W. The larger Great Lad Crag is situated 0.8kms (0.5 mile) lower down the valley [151101].

Little Ladstones see **Great Ladstones**.

Little Langdale from its source alongside Wrynose Pass the River Brathay flows through Little Langdale before turning to Elter Water. Today Little Langdale is principally a peaceful valley with many farms and cottages scattered along the valley bottom. In the summer months, however, this peace is somewhat shattered by the number of cars threading their way along, and at times blocking, the narrow road leading to and from Wrynose and Hardknott Passes. The old Roman road from Ambleside to Ravenglass traversed the valley and in more recent times the seclusion of Little Langdale provided much opportunity for smugglers and illicit distillers to ply their trade and transport their wares over the fells. The most notorious was Lanty Slee who had illicit stills and storage places on the surrounding fells. More than likely many of these have not as yet been discovered. Born in 1802 Lanty died at his home, Greenbank Farm, Little Langdale, in 1878. Places of interest are Colwith Force; Little Langdale Tarn; Slaters Bridge over the River Brathay and the 19th century Three Shires Inn. At the head of the dale Fell Foot Farm, once an inn, is deemed to possess a 'thing'mount', a Viking moot, upon which the Vikings met either as a parliament or to administer justice [315034] ...little long valley. See also **Slater(s) Bridge**.

Little Langdale Tarn Little Langdale. Presented to the NT in 1985 by the Friends of the Lake District in commemoration of their 50th anniversary. The River Brathay and Greenburn Beck flow into this valley bottom tarn and the River Brathay emerges from the outflow 102m (335ft) [309032]. Private fishing for trout, pike and perch.

Little Loughrigg knoll between Loughrigg Tarn and Skelwith Bridge C150m (C492ft) [344040].

Little Man see **Skiddaw**.

Little Meldrum NE Great Meldrum. Spot heights at 404m (1325ft) [422228] and 424m (1391ft) [425233].

Little Mell Fell isolated hill E minor road, A66-Matterdale End. S Thackthwaite. Here the rocks have formed a conglomerate (coarse-grained sedimentary rocks consisting of rounded fragments of rock embedded in a finer matrix - in this case, sand). The conglomerate beds in both Little Mell and Great Mell are 244-274m (800-900ft) thick, 505m (1657ft) [423240]. Little Mell Fell can be considered an outlying sentinel of the Helvellyn range.

Little Mine Crag E Newlands valley. Mining for copper was tried on the side of the crag [233191].

Little Moor Santon Bridge [104021].

Little Mosedale valley off Mosedale down which Little Mosedale Beck flows. Overlooking at its head is Harrop Pike [506086] ...the little boggy valley.

Little Mosedale Beck rises between Tarn Crag and Harrop Pike at 496078 and joins

Mosedale Beck at 506100.

Little Moss Side off the minor road from the Underbarrow-Crosthwaite road to the A5074 [449906].

Little Mossy Beck rises Whitestone Moor at 478209 and joins Mossy Beck at 487213.

Little Narrowcove deep gully rising to scree shoot from the River Esk to the col between Broad Crag/Ill Crag and Scafell Pike. The stream which flows down it rises at 220072 and flows down to join the Esk at 228066.

Little Ore Gate S Great Ore Gate [370932] ...the gate/way by which iron ore was transported to the Forge alongside Cunsey Beck.

Little Paddy Crag below Great Paddy Crag [151906].

Little Pie Eskdale. Hill above Eel Tarn and to its W [187019].

Little Pike W Dockray-Dowthwaitehead road [378218].

Little Pikes above Far Gill [265987].

Little Round How N Great Round How 494m (1621ft) [207132].

Little Saddle Crag Shap Fells. S Great Saddle Crag, W Wasdale Pike C570 (C1870) [527083].

Little Sandy Beck rises in marshy area just outside the NP at 109261 and joins the River Cocker at the Rake at 130281.

Little Scoat Fell see **Scoat Fell**.

Little Spring alongside the road through the Dale Park valley [354925] ...little plantation.

Little Stand on the ridge S from Crinkle Crags to Gaitscale Close 727m (2385ft) [251032].

Little Stanger Gill rises High Knott at 259130 and joins Stonethwaite Beck near Big Stanger Gill at 266134 ...stanger, a pole, usually denoting a boundary.

Little Stickle below Great Stickle, Dunnerdale Fells [211914].

Little Tongue W Little Tongue Gill [342108].

Little Tongue Gill rises below Hause Riggs at 344109 and joins Tongue Gill at 340098.

Little Town Newlands valley. Not a town by any stretch of the imagination but a pretty little hamlet consisting of farms and cottages and a church/chapel, the latter dating from the 16th century or even earlier, but since rebuilt. Adjoining it is a schoolroom closed in the 1960s. Little Town and nearby Cat Bells are immortalised in Beatrix Potter's *The Tale of Mrs Tiggy-Winkle* [234196].

Little Walls Wetherlam. Rocky outcrops on summit [278012].

Little Worm Crag Birker Moor C400m (C1312ft) [193971] ...from the OE 'wyrm' meaning snake.

Little Yarlside between Crookdale Beck and Wasdale Beck and near Great Yarlside which is 69m (226ft) higher 516m (1693ft) [532072] ...the little earl's seat.

Littlecell Bottom NW Buck Barrow [146918].

Littledale Crags E Little Dale and below the Hindscarth-High Crags ridge [215175].

Littledale Edge see **Little Dale**.

Littlegill Head head of Little Gill [254080].

Littlethwaite alongside the Lorton-Thackthwaite-Loweswater road [150246].

Littlewater hamlet directly N of Burnbanks village. Approached by minor road from Walmgate Foot. Littlewater Tarn to E [507170].

Littlewater Tarn E Littlewater on private land 259m (850ft) [509170].

Littlewood Farm off the back road from Staveley to Hall Lane [480993].

Liza, River see **River Liza**.

Liza Beck formerly Gasgale Gill. Flows down Gasgale Gill via Coledale Hause from its source at 187205 and joins the River Cocker at 152224 ...light stream.

Liza Path Ennerdale. Constructed and waymarked in 1985 on the S bank of the River Liza. The full round from the Bowness Knott car park returning via the N section of the Nine Becks Walk is 14 kms (8.8 miles).

Loadpot Hill last principal northern summit of the High Street range with extensive slope and subsidiary heights continuing northwards to drop down by easy gradient to Pooley Bridge, Bampton, and Askham. The Roman road detours slightly W of its summit. The latter is the meeting place of several parish boundaries represented by boundary stones and posts and there is a stone circle at the head of Swarthbeck Gill. Until the early 1970s a prominent landmark just S of the summit cairn was a tall stone chimney stack and fireplace, all that remained of Lowther House, a former shooting lodge. About that time the ravages of Lakeland weather took their toll and the structure finally collapsed into a heap of stones 672m (2205ft) [457181] ...presumably 'the hill with a hole where ore was worked'. Wainwright points out that the remains of a haematite mine may still be seen near the summit. This is sited at 455206.

Loadpot Hole shallow depress N slope of Loadpot Hill. Faces due N and consequently many a time holds snow until the spring [459187].

Loanthwaite alongside Loanthwaite Lane [355991]. High and Low Loanthwaite farms were part of Beatrix Potter's (Mrs Heelis') bequest to the National Trust ...Ekwall suggests that the first element may be 'calm' or 'lane'. More than likely it is the latter being derived from the OE 'laning' or ME 'lonning'.

Loanthwaite Lane connects the B5286 to the High Wray-Colthouse road [356991] ...see **Loanthwaite**.

Lobbs E Mosedale Beck. Approached by lane and track off minor road, Troutbeck-Wallthwaite [360247].

Lobstone Band E slope High Spy [240161] ...'lob/lobb' is a mining term one meaning of which refers to an irregular vein of ore resembling a flight of steps. In days gone by mining was much in evidence in the vicinity.

Lobstone Band Door Lobstone Band, Low Scawdel [242161].

Lock Bank E Ullswater. Slope leading up from Sharrow Mire to White Knott [465218] ...pen or fold on a slope.

Lodge, The see **The Lodge**.

Lodge Head Tarn see **Tent Lodge Tarn**.

Lodore means the low door or gap. See **High Lodore, Lodore Falls, Lodore Hotel, Lodore Wood**.

Lodore Falls behind the Lodore Hotel, Borrowdale are the High Lodore Falls and the more famous Lodore Falls or Cascades. The latter fall precipitously down a cleft between Gowder and Shepherds Crags. In times of drought the falls are the merest trickle but after heavy rain the several drops are exceedingly noticeable and noisy. It is said that when conditions are favourable the falls can be seen and heard from Friars Crag [265187]. In his poem *Cataract of Lodore* (1820) Robert Southey aptly describes the falls after rain:

Collecting, projecting,
Receeding and speeding.
And shocking and rocking,
And darting and parting,
And threading and spreading,
And whizzing and hissing...
All at once and all o'er with a mighty roar

Lodore Hotel In 1789 described as a 'neat and commodious little inn'. Now, principally Victorian with later additions, it is now called the Hilton Lodore Hotel but earlier was the Stakis Keswick Lodore Swiss Hotel [264189], see also **Gowder Crag**.

Lodore Wood rear of the Lodore Hotel [267189].

Loft Crag Great Langdale. W Thorn Crag. Its S face, Gimmer Crag, incorporates famous rock climbs (see **Gimmer Crag**) C670m (C2198ft) [277072].

Loft Rigg How WNW foot of Seathwaite Tarn [246991].

Loftbarrow subsidiary height in the Fellbarrow Group C350 (C1148) [131231].

Loftshaw Hill N A66 and Troutbeck 312m (1024ft) [387278].

Logan Beck farthest headstream rises E slope Burn Moor at 155925. Subsequently met by Bowscale Beck before entering the River Duddon at 196898 ...stream in the little hollow.

Logan Beck Bridge carries the Duddon Bridge to Ulpha road W of the Duddon over Logan Beck. Datestoned 1962 [184903].

Loganbeck alongside the Duddon Bridge to Ulpha road W of the Duddon [183905].

London Head Santon Bridge. Off the Santon Bridge to Eskdale Green road [117017].

Long Band ridge on High Rigg running SE from Cowrake Head towards Wren Crag [314205].

Long Band lengthy line of crags W Ullscarf and overlooking Stonethwaite Beck [281126].

Long Brow W and NW slope leading up to Mungrisdale Common. Overlooks Scalehow Beck and R Caldew [303295].

Long Close Farm Alongside the A591 [240267].

Long Comb valley off the head of the Coledale valley. Source of Birkthwaite Beck [204208].

Long Crag Bannisdale Fell 493m (1617ft) [516052].

Long Crag between the River Esk and Lingcove Beck [230050].

Long Crag buttress of Holme Fell [318004].

Long Crag Kentmere Park [443036].

Long Crag line of crags W Barton Fell and overlooking Ullswater [462213].

Long Crag on N slope Low Birk Fell [408193] ...over 200 years ago it was 'New Crag'.

Long Crag Tilberthwaite High Fells [286015].

Long Crag W Greenup Edge [279104].

Long Crag Wrynose Fell [280040].

Long Crag crags along the W slope Yewbarrow [172083].

Long Crag Middle Fell. S of the summit and facing Goat Crag across Goat Gill [151065].

Long Crag Buckbarrow [135057].

Long Crag Dunnerdale Forest (230982).

Long Crag above Mouldry Bank Beck (298982).

Long Crag above Hinning House Close, Duddon valley [238993].

Long Crag W Duddon Valley and Dunnerdale Forest C410m (C1345ft) [204989].

Long Crag Grange Fell [256171].

Long Crag alongside spur leading down from Steeple to Ennerdale [156111].

Long Crag Buttermere [182165].

Long Crag head of Coledale Valley and above Force Crag Mine [198219].

Long Crags below Helvellyn Screes [326155].

Long Crags N Arnsbarrow Hill, Bethecar Moor [313914].

Long Doors Dodd/Skiddaw Dodd [248274].

Long Fell Shap Fells. Runs parallel with the A6 between Wasdale Crag and Longfell Gill. Surmounted by tall mast at its highest point. Spot heights at 452m (1483ft) [557085] and 424m (1391ft) [558091].

Long Fell Embleton. Spot height at N end at 276m (905ft) [164282]. Two others at 313m (1027ft) [166277] and 319m (1047ft) [167275] before a continual rise to the summit of Kirk Fell at 438m (1437ft).

Long Garth alongside the Duddon Bridge to Ulpha road W of the Duddon [181920].

Long Gill rises W of the summit of Lank Rigg at 087120. Joined by Ya Gill at 077123 and meets the River Calder at 073124.

Long Gill rises W Long Green, Scafell ridge, at 203056 and joins Hardrigg Gill at 194055.

Long Grain part of long sloping ridge from High Raise to Measand Beck [463146].

Long Grain rises 118120. Meets Bleaberry Gill at 102113 and with combined watercourses of Short Grain, Red Gill and Hole Gill becomes Worm Gill.

Long Green Scafell S slope [209058].

Long Green Head alongside track from Moorhowe Road past Limefitt Park and ultimately to Threshthwaite Mouth [421043] ...reference to the long green valley hereabouts and further emphasised by the name 'ing' nearby (meadow/pasture).

Long Greenriggs Plantation Lowther Park. N of West Greenriggs Plantation [537217].

Long Gutter rises near Moorgate at 096991 and flows down to meet unnamed stream at 090985. This subsequently joins the R Mite.

Long Haws Banishead/Baniside [289964].

Long Height Claife Heights [377986].

Long Hill overlooks Yewdale Moss from the SSW [299994].

Long Hill Birker Moor [190974].

Long House former farmhouse. Great Langdale [306067].

Long House foot of Seathwaite Fells. E Tarn Beck. Farm purchased by the NT in 1983 (238970).

Long House Close Seathwaite Fells. E Long House. N Long House Gill (248971).

Long House Gill rises Seathwaite Fells at 257974 and flows through the Cove and alongside Long House before joining Tarn Beck at 235973.

Long Houses off the Staveley-Kentmere road. 18th century houses their length exaggerated by attached barns [459031].

Long How W Great Carrs [262010].

Long How Buttermere [170172].

Long Mire lengthy valley, Dunnerdale Fells, down which flows Long Mire Beck [228938].

Long Mire Beck rises Long Mire at 226941. Joined by Broadslack Beck at 231933 and meets the River Lickle at 237925.

Long Moss Watendlath Fell. Unnamed tarn here [294145].

Long Moss E of and below King's How [260167].

Long Moss Tarn long and narrow tarn on Torver Back Common C130m (C426ft) [291936].

Long Parrock SW High Cunsey. W High Cunsey-Low Cunsey road [379939] ...long paddock.

Long Pike Great End [224082].

Long Rigg ridge leading down from Powley's Hill to Swindale Foot Crag [509137].

Long Scar Wrynose Fell. SSE Pike of Stickle [273036].

Long Scars Blawith Fells. Above the A5084 [285903].

Long Side highest point of Longside Edge, see **Longside Edge**.

Long Side fell side below Longside Edge [245284].

Long Slack W Hawkshead-Newby Bridge road. NW Eel House [366942] ...long hollow.

Long Stile rocky arete leading up from Caspel Gate to High Street [445113] ...'stile' - steep.

Long Tongue promontory W shore Windermere [377906].

Long Top second 'crinkle' of Crinkle Crags from the S and the highest point of Crinkle Crags 859m (2818ft) [249049].

Long Wood behind Cappelrigg off Capplerigg Lane [476944] ...long 'hollow'.

Longfell Gill rises on Shap Fells at 549090. Flows under the A6 and becomes Blea Beck at 569100. This is joined by Wasdale Beck at 579096 and the enlarged stream becomes Birk Beck which ultimately flows into the River Lune at Tebay.

Longgrain Beck rises NE High Raise and E Low Raise at 452138. Joined by Keasgill Sike at 460151 and becomes Measand Beck which joins Haweswater at 487154.

Longlands off Coldfell Road [057145].

Longlands Road through Rayrigg Wood to Birthwaite Road [404978].

Longmire, Low Longmire, Longmire Road the first two are properties off the A592 and Moorhowe Road respectively and sited at 414020 and 413016. The latter, a track from Moorhowe Road to Troutbeck Park [415019] ...Longmire simply means the long mere/bog but Longmire was also the name of an earlier Troutbeck family and Longmires lived at Longmire for over 300 years and for some considerable time at Low Longmire.

Longmire Road see **Longmire**.

Longmire Wood E A595. ESE Carleton Hall [087986].

Longmire Yeat Troutbeck [409031] ...surname + gate/way. The latter one of several which led from the valley to the common pastures above. Another property owned for many years by a branch of the Longmire 'clan' of Troutbeck.

Longmoor just off the Cleator Moor to Ennerdale Bridge road [059156].

Longside Edge ridge between Carlside Col and Ullock Pike. Its highest point is Long Side at 734m (2408ft) [249284].

Longside Wood below Longside Edge and Long Side [244280].

Longsleddale of the 6 valleys which radiate like spokes of a wheel westwards from the A6 between Kendal and Shap, Longsleddale is by far the most populous and certainly the most popular. Having said this, Longsleddale is a valley that most motorists pass by without realising as they head to or from Shap. For this the rest of us must be thankful. It is a lovely valley with scenery varying from rounded hills and green pastures at its foot and middle to steep and craggy mountains shutting in its higher reach beyond Sadgill. From the A6 a road proceeds to the last three habitations at Sadgill. From here it is 3.2kms (2 miles), initially by a wide track to Wrengill Quarry and then a footpath to the summit of Gatescarth Pass. The river, which keeps in close proximity to the road and track for most of its length, is the Sprint which ultimately joins the Kent at Burneside. Between Buckbarrow Crag and Garnett Bridge glaciation caused the valley to be divided into 4 lakes. None of these exists today but there is evidence of a terminal moraine cut through by the river above Sadgill and rock bars and moraines lower down the valley.

At the head of the dale the Wrengill Slate Quarry was possibly the earliest or at least one of the earliest in the Lake District. Slate was quarried here until just after the Second World War when the Italian prisoners of war working it were sent home. Sadgill was once the 'Piccadilly' of drove roads. One came over from Kentmere to meet a route along Longsleddale. The latter crossed the Sprint at Wads Howe packhorse bridge, followed the left bank of the river and re-crossed at the Sadgill packhorse bridge. It then travelled northwards to the head of Mosedale where one drove road went down Swindale and another along Wet Sleddale. A packhorse route continued to Mardale.

Over the centuries Longsleddale's beauty and tranquillity has been nearly defiled on three occasions. In 1840 a scheme was projected to lay a railway line through the valley, by a tunnel under Gatescarth, down Mardale and on to Penrith. Fortunately, at the last moment the route over Shap was the one chosen. Five years later the valley pastures above Sadgill were scheduled to be the site of a reservoir but the exorbitant cost of such a scheme precluded its inception. One hundred years later a scheme to reopen the Wrengill Quarry and link an aerial ropeway on steel pylons with Sadgill also came to nothing as did a later idea to take the M6 motorway through the valley. One scheme, however, did come into being. Consequent on the flooding of Mardale in the 1930s a tunnel was drilled under Branstree to Stockdale (where evidence of tunnelling can still be seen). From here a pipe carries water to the Watchgate Water Treatment Plant at Selside and subsequently to Manchester. Fortunately, after much initial spoilation, the pipe rests unseen below the valley floor. The church near the middle of the valley is dedicated to St Mary. Rebuilt in 1863 it is the third building, the first probably erected in the 13th century. A compliment to the local residents are the toilets opposite the church. Cared for by volunteers they surely must be the neatest and cleanest in the Lake District. The oldest structure in the dale is the pele tower incorporated in Yewbarrow Hall. Longsleddale is the 'Long Whindale' of *Robert Elsmere* by Mrs Humphrey Ward and it also inspired the 'Greendale Village' of the Postman Pat books [494038] ...the long valley valley.

Longsleddale Lime Kiln see **Stockdale**.

Longtail Hill steep section of the B5284, Bowness-Crook road, rising from the A5074 [406957].

Longthwaite Watermillock. Alongside minor road from the A592 to Matterdale End and the A5091 [439228].

Longthwaite old cottages and farm S Rosthwaite. The farm was given to the NT in 1977 and the nearby Longthwaite YH was completed in 1939 [255144].

Longthwaite Beck rises from a spring near Cove [432237] and meets Pencilmill Beck at 445227. This joins Ullswater at Castlehows Point at 451226.

Longthwaite Youth Hostel Borrowdale. Completed in 1939 [285142].

Lonscale below Lonscale Fell [292254].

Lonscale Crags line of crags E face of Lonscale Fell [293265].

Lonscale Fell Skiddaw group. Its curved summit is grassy but to its E it shows a 1.6kms (1 mile) line of crags culminating in a lesser but sharp-pointed peak 703m (2306ft) overlooking the Glenderaterra valley and beck. To the fell's N the ridge continues over Burnt Horse to Salehow Beck and the River Caldew, to its W a grassy walk to Jenkin Hill and Skiddaw Little Man while to its S lies Latrigg and the River Greta 715m (2346ft) [286271] ...the long fell with a shepherd's summer hut.

Lonsties alongside the A591, Keswick [280232] ...unknown origin. Possibly steep lane(s). 'Lon' an abbreviation of lonnin (lane) and 'sty' (steep).

Looking Crag overlooking Little Town and the Newlands valley [234194].

Looking How Cartmel Fell 164m (538ft) [403906] ... possibly similar to Spy Crag (Staveley), Spying Howe (Patterdale) and Looking Howe (Grasmere) in that it means look-out hill.

Looking How prominent crag overlooking Easedale [309081] ...look-out hill.

Looking How above the River Duddon and Hinning House [244998] ...look-out hill.

Looking Stead a summit on the Black Sail Pass to Pillar ridge. An excellent viewpoint hence its name. The High Level route to Pillar via Robinson's Cairn starts here 627m (2057ft) [186118].

Looking Steads Glaramara [244103] ...a looking out place/site.

Looking Stone W Thirlmere between Thrang Gill and Middlesteads Gill [302174] ...look-out + stone.

Lord Cove E Nab Scar-Heron Pike ridge. Lord Crag above [357076] ...see **Lord Crag**.

Lord Crag on Nab Scar-Heron Pike ridge. Above Lord Cove [355075] ...similar to other Lord Crags (Lord(s) Seat), Hugh's Seat or Simon Seat in that the lord here could refer to either Hugh or Simon de Morville early Barons of Westmorland. May also be the name of another local family.

Lord Lonsdale's Commons comprises 16,842 acres and all the high land from Seat Sandal to the Head of Great Langdale and including the bed of Grasmere (lake) and part of Rydal Water, White Moss, Near and Far Easedale, the bed of Easedale Tarn and the Langdale Pikes. Leased to the National Trust at a peppercorn rent in 1961.

Lord's Bridge Crosthwaite. Carries the Crosthwaite-A5074 road across the River Gilpin [436914] ...see **Lord's Lot**.

Lord's Gill Bull Haw Moss Beck and Lord's Gill practically meet in the vicinity of Plattocks but the former flows NE to ultimately meet Torver Beck. The latter heads S via Steers Pool and Kirkby Pool to be met by many small watercourses before entering the River Duddon estuary at Kirkby-in-Furness [226826].

Lord's High Allotment S slope White Maiden [254952].

Lord's How W of the head of Blea Tarn (Watendlath) [283140].

Lord's Island see **Derwent Water**.

Lord's Lot Crosthwaite. Rises to 209m (686ft) [446929] ...possibly from Adam Le Lauerd mentioned in Lay Subsidy Rolls (1332), see also **Lord's Bridge**. 'Lot', abbreviation of allotment (of land).

Lord's Low Allotment Broughton Moor. S Lord's High Allotment [258939].

Lord's Rake Lord's Rake is the only experienced walkers' or scramblers' route to the summit of Scafell from the N. Beginning as a wide scree gully it continues as a straight steep ascent and at times descent with considerable loose stones makes walking hazardous. Care should be taken at all times. At the commencement of the Rake proper there is a cross carved into the wall of rock marking the death of four men in 1903. However, those intent on following the Rake need not worry. They were not killed attempting that route but fell from the Pinnacle above it. A substantial rock fall in 2003 blocked the traverse and made it exceedingly dangerous [207069].

Lord's Seat between the End of Borrowdale and High House Fell 524m (1719ft) [519066] ...similar to place names Hugh Seat, Simon Seat, Lord Seat and nearby Yarlside all of which are most likely named after the de Morville family, early Barons of Westmorland.

Lord's Seat E Howtown. On High Street ridge alongside the Roman Road [460192] ...named after a member of the de Morville family who succeeded to the Barony of Westmorland.

Lord's Seat rocky outcrop below Gavel Pike. Overlooks Coldcove Gill and Deepdale [379135].

Lord's Seat highest summit in the NW fells. To its S and W lies afforested area but the final approach to the summit is by heather to a grassy shoulder 552m (1811ft) [204266] ...of medieval origin from 'hlaford' meaning lord and it certainly 'lord's it' over its many neighbours. An Avro Anson crashed on its slope in April 1943, and five crew were killed.

Lord's Seat group of fells, see Reference Section: **Heights**.

Lord's Wood alongside Lord's Gill [263928].

Lorton Large chapelry in Lorton Vale 8kms (5 miles) from Cockermouth. Of ancient origin being firstly called Loretona, secondly Loretuna and subsequently Lortun(a) and Lorton(e) in the 12th century. Divided into High [163257] and Low Lorton [152261] with the latter principally W of the B5289. Today, farming and tourism are the main industries but in years gone by there were mills and a brewery with power provided primarily by Whit Beck. Lorton Church, dedicated to St. Cuthbert, is early 19th century but a chapel/church has occupied the same site for over 800 years. In an earlier building the imposter John Hatfield, the self-styled Hon. Alexander Augustine Hope MP, was married to Mary Robinson, known as the 'Beauty of Buttermere' in October 1802 (he was later executed for forgery at Carlisle). For more information on this consult Melvyn Bragg's *The Maid of Buttermere*.

At the Methodist Chapel John Wesley preached in the mid-18th century. Lorton Hall in Low Lorton was built around a 15th century pele tower. Behind the village hall, appropriately named Yew Tree Hall, stands a fine yew tree, believed to be over 1000 years old. Under the tree, of which Wordsworth wrote in 1803:

A Yew tree, pride of Lorton Vale
Which to this day stands single, in the midst
Of its own darkness as it stood of yore

George Fox preached in 1652 when the tree was so full of people that he recorded: "I feared they would shake it down." Although the tree is still of vast circumference the elements and mutilation have taken their toll. The notable Jennings Brewery, established at Cockermouth in 1874, began its life in Lorton in 1828 in what is now the village hall ...'Hlora's farmstead' or the farm by the roaring stream, the latter being Whit Beck.

Lorton Church [155260] see **Lorton**.

Lorton Church Vicarage [155262].

Lorton Fells part of the Lord's Seat Group of fells. N of the Whinlatter Pass. Highest point is Whinlatter Top at 525m (1722ft) [197249] joint second highest of the Lord's Seat group.

Lorton Gully Grasmoor [166204].

Lorton Hall Low Lorton. Built around a 15th century pele tower [153258].

Lorton Low Bridge Low Lorton. Carries a minor road over the River Cocker [152257].

Lorton Park High Lorton [158257].

Lorton Vale lush and wide valley stretching from Cockermouth, encompassing High and Low Lorton, and ending at Crummock Water. Along it flows the River Cocker [154244].

Losca wooded area W Gosforth Hall Plantation [101051] ...the EPNS suggests that it is probably loft in the wood.

Lothwaite a summit in the Lord's Seat group 345m (1132ft) [203297] ...possibly loft in the clearing.

Lothwaite Side SE Lothwaite [205294].

Loudon Hill between Dacre and Park House [464269] ...possibly named after a John de Louden mentioned in a document of 1332.

Loughrigg Brow Ambleside. Off the Pelter Bridge-Rothay Bridge road. Built in the mid-19th century it later became the home of the Lancaster Storeys and later, for 50 years until November 1997, it was a CHA guest house. Having been purchased by a property developer it was, at the time of writing, intended to turn it into ten luxury apartments. [369044].

Loughrigg Cave see **Loughrigg Terrace**.

Loughrigg Fell often affectionately known as just Loughrigg. An extensive area of undulations, crags, bracken covered slopes, woodlands, many small tarns and two named, Lily and Loughrigg. To its N are Grasmere and Rydal Water, to the S the Brathay valley, to the E the Rothay valley and to the W the Grasmere to Langdale road. Above the several woodlands on its perimeter are named crags Ewe [348056], Ivy [353042], Lad [347049], Todd [360040] as well as Black Mire [355046], Lanty Scar ('Lancelot's rocky outcrop') [362055] and Scartufts (possibly 'the tufted rocky outcrop') [353052]. The summit of Loughrigg Fell is marked by an OS trig. point at 335m (1099ft) [347051] ...ridge above the lake, the latter being Loughrigg Tarn.

Loughrigg Fold property W Loughrigg Tarn. Acquired by the NT in 1952 [342043].

Loughrigg Holme alongside minor road from Pelter Bridge, Rydal, to Rothay Bridge, Ambleside. The home of Edward Quillinan, poet and translator, and Dora, Wordsworth's daughter, after their marriage in 1841. She died in 1847 and he in 1851 [364053].

Loughrigg Quarries see **Loughrigg Terrace**.

Loughrigg Tarn nearly circular tarn nestled at the foot of Loughrigg Fell and Little Loughrigg. Called by Wordsworth 'Diana's Looking-glass'. Fishing by permit is principally for roach, perch and pike with some trout. The tarn gives Loughrigg/Loughrigg Fell its name ie ridge above the lake. It is situated at a height of 94m (308ft) [345044].

Loughrigg Terrace popular terraced path, NW slope of Loughrigg Fell and high above the foot of Grasmere (lake). Excellent views of the lake, Grasmere village, the vale and over to the Fairfield range. In order that walkers can appreciate the view several seats have been positioned along the terrace walk [345058]. Above the path from Rydal and Pelter Bridge to the Terrace there is a huge cave, Rydal Cave, which looks natural but actually is the result of quarrying at the long-since disused Loughrigg Quarries.

Loup Knott crag W Barton Fell and overlooking Auterstone Crag and Ullswater [461211] ...leap + knott.

Louper Weir E shore Windermere [392931] ...weir over which the fish leap.

Lover's Walk Plantation plantation S of A66(T) and NW Dalemain [470277].

Low Abbey Wythop Mill. High Abbey nearby [172294] ...unknown origin.

Low Adam Crag the Screes, Wasdale. Below High Adam Crag [157048].

Low Arnside E High Cross off the A593 and near High Arnside Farm [334019]

Low Bakestones below High Bakestones and due W of the Scandale Pass col [381096] ...place where baking stones are found, see also **Bakestones Moss**.

Low Bank on the Rannerdale Knotts ridge [171181].

Low Bank W Thirlmere. Lower slope High Seat [303182].

Low Bank Farm Low Lorton. High Bank nearby [147260].

Low Bank Ground property E side Coniston Water. Today an Outdoor Education Centre operated by Wigan Municipal Borough Council [316969].

Low Beck rises Mirklin Cove at 152116 and joins the River Liza at 151139.

Low Beckside near Mungrisdale [366298]. Nearby at [363302], there is a late 18th century lime kiln.

Low Birchclose Off minor road, A66-Matterdale End. Alongside Thackthwaite Beck [415257].

Low Birk Fell E of and overlooking Ullswater. NNE Birk Fell, a northern spur of Place Fell [411190].

Low Birker farm, Eskdale [188004].

Low Birker Pool several streams combine to become Low Birker Pool but the two farthest tributaries rise near Fox Bield and below Crook Crag at 189986 and 195987 respectively. Subsequently the stream flows over Birker Force before entering the River Esk at 184003 ...similar to several other pools the name does not refer to a pool or pond but derives from the ME 'poll' and means stream.

Low Birker Tarn Birker Moor. Pear-shaped tarn below Tarn Crag. From its outlet a small stream joins Low Birker Pool [190995].

Low Birkin Knott overlooks Swindale. Nearby is High Birkin Knott [499123].

Low Birks off Woodside Road [428900].

Low Blake Dodd overlooks the head of Swindale. Between Black Bells and High Blake Dodd [496116].

Low Bleaberry Knott above Whorney Side and below High Bleaberry Knott [257052] ...the low stony peak on which, or by which, the bilberry grows.

Low Blind How Claife Heights. Below High Blind How [384974].

Low Boonwood Gosforth. Below Middle and High Boonwood [064045] ...boon, from the ON 'bon' meaning request, favour, plea.

Low Bowkerstead between Force Mills and Satterthwaite [337913].

Low Bridge carries the road from the A592 to Dacre over Dacre Beck. High Bridge, higher up Dacre Beck, carries the Dacre to Sparket road over Dacre Beck [460263].

Low Bridge Kentmere. Carries the Staveley-Kentmere road over the River Kent. Alongside it stood the Low Bridge Inn which lost its licence in 1887 [458040].

Low Bridge Beck rises NE Pikes at 240950 and joins Tarn Beck at 230963.

Low Bridge End Farm W B5322 across St John's Beck [318205].

Low Bridge Inn (Kentmere) see **Low Bridge** (Kentmere).

Low Brigham see Brigham.

Low Brock Crags Beda Fell. High Brock Crag and Brock Crag are also alongside the same ridge [428176].

Low Brock Crags E Scandale Beck. High Brock Crags above [377072].

Low Brow off minor road from the B5320 to Askham. Nearby is High Brow [487254].

Low Brundrigg farm alongside the B5284, Plumgarths to Crook road and opposite High Brundrigg [484950] ...most likely the low burnt ridge.

Low Buck How N end of the Borrowdale Fells on ridge leading up to Glaramara. High Buck How to its SSE [258136].

Low Bull Crag SSW Stony Cove Pike. Below High Bull Crag [414091] ...bull signifies a very large boulder or crag.

Low Burthwaite Wood E Ling Fell. Alongside the minor road from Old Scales to Wythop Mill [189288].

Low Buzzard Knott Stonethwaite Fell. Below High Buzzard Knott [251097] ...the low peak frequented by buzzards.

Low Cat Crag S bank R Greta [310247].

Low Cat Crag W shore Windermere. W Crag Holme. High Cat Crag to WSW [377918].

Low Close Dunnerdale [243001].

Low Cock How off Coldfell Road [057143].

Low Colwith see **High/Low Colwith**.

Low Coppice National Trust land alongside the road from the A593 to Hodge Close [308009].

Low Coppice between High and Great Coppice [117033].

Low Coppice Eskdale. Alongside the A595 to Eskdale Green road [137980].

Low Crag Butterwick [507195].

Low Crag S Cockley Beck. High Crag above [245008].

Low Crag S ridge Wallowbarrow Crag [223966].

Low Crag Buttermere Fell. Below High Crag Buttress [185148].

Low Cragg Crook. Below High Cragg. Foot of Crag Hills [461941].

Low Craghall alongside the Duddon Bridge to Ulpha road W of the Duddon. Faces High Craghall across the road [182915] ...low crag hill.

Low Cunsey Farm S Cunsey Bridge and alongside the road from Far Sawrey-Graythwaite [380932].

Low Dale Park farm near the foot of Dale Park valley [350917].

Low Dale Park Plantation Dale Park. E Low Dale Park [355916].

Low Deer Park Plantation Lowther Park. Alongside the R Lowther [520226].

Low Dodd N High Dodd, Place Fell [416185].

Low Elfhowe Over Staveley [469998] ...Elf Howe, the 'Fairy Hill' is nearby.

Low Eskholme on plain between Muncaster Fell and the R Esk. WSW High Eskholme [116971].

Low Eskholme Tarn an overgrown tarn NW Low Eskholme, 9m (29ft). The OS map shows two tarns, Low Eskholme is the larger [114973].

Low Fell Low (Tilberthwaite) Fell as opposed to Tilberthwaite High Fells. Between Tilberthwaite and Little Langdale. The area possesses many former quarries, caves, tunnels and levels. These are interesting to see but can be extremely dangerous to explore. In one of them is a cave once used as an illicit still by the notorious smuggler, Lanty Slee. It is now walled up. Spot height at 397m (1302ft) [302021].

Low Fell property alongside the A5074-Great Hartbarrow road [421910].

Low Fell Shap Fells. W Shap Blue Quarry, 349m (1145ft) [560107].

Low Fell Low Fell is actually the highest summit of the Fellbarrow group at 423m (1388ft) [137226], see also Loweswater Fell.

Low Fell Plantation alongside the A5074-Hartbarrow road [420907].

Low Fold Crook. SW High Leys [450936].

Low Fold Over Staveley [469003].

Low Fold Troutbeck [408027].

Low Force waterfall on Aira Beck [399206].

Low Force waterfall on Pudding Beck as it drops down through Force Crag.

Low Forest see **Naddle Forest**.

Low Frith Eskdale. Adjoining High Frith [162998] ...low wood.

Low Gait Crags E Great Moss, N Long Crag, S High Gait Crags [231053] ...the low crags frequented by goats.

Low Gardens Bridge across the R Lowther between Lowther Park and Yanwath Wood [521250].

Low Gillerthwaite Ennerdale. A field centre run by the Leeds College of Education [139141].

Low Goat Gill rises SW Harper Hills at 507140 and joins Naddle Beck at 504143.

Low Graythwaite Hall also known as Graythwaite Old Hall. S Graythwaite Hall. Originally owned by the Sawrey family in the 16th century and later for several centuries by the Rawlinson family [372909].

Low Great Knott W Trout Beck and E Woundale Beck. High Great Knott lies to its N [414066].

Low Greenriggs farm, Underbarrow, off Grigg Hall Lane. High Greenriggs nearby [470912].

Low Gregg Hall farm, Underbarrow [465915] ...Gregg is a corruption of Grigg, a local surname. Hence Grigg Hall Lane, Grigghall Lane and Grigghall Bridge.

Low Ground approached by track off the Birker Moor fell road [175988].

Low Grounds Point W shore Windermere. End of arm of Pull Wyke facing Sandy Wyke across bay [368021].

Low Grove former farm alongside the old route from Ambleside to Kirkstone Pass [390052], see also **High Grove**.

Low Grove Farm between Applethwaite and Millbeck [258259].

Low Hacket see **High/Low Hacket**.

Low Hall Duddon valley [214951].

Low Hall S Green Trees. N Mirk Lane [126273].

Low Hall Garth Little Langdale. Former small farm, now a climbing hut [310029].

Low Hartsop see Hartsop Dodd.

Low Hartsop Mine see **Myers Head Mine**.

Low Hen Croft off the A593. S Baskell [237901].

Low High Snab neighbour to High Snab [222189] ...see **Low Snab**.

Low Hollins Brackenthwaite. Off the B5289 and the road from Hopebeck to the B5289. High Hollins nearby [158226].

Low Hollows adjacent minor road, A66-Guardhouse [334261].

Low Holme alongside the track between Miterdale and Eskdale Green [143007].

Low House Ings with Hugill [451993].

Low House Longsleddale [512013]. High House is 0.8kms (0.5 mile) further up the valley.

Low House Brackenthwaite. Alongside the B5289 [156225].

Low House Crag on slope of Todd Fell behind Low House, Longsleddale [513015].

Low House Farm sometimes called Low Cleabarrow. Off subsidiary road from B5284-Lickbarrow Road [420964].

Low House Farm Thackthwaite [423254].

Low House Farm alongside Scope Beck [227191].

Low How E of the head of the path alongside Ruddy Gill [233090].

Low How W Dockray-Dowthwaitehead road, 497m (1631ft) [374215].

Low Hows Wood N side Castle Crag, Borrowdale. High Hows Wood on the S side [252164].

Low Iron Crag slope Illgill Head. Below High Iron Crag [165056].

Low Katelade between Swindale Beck and Trussgap Brow [522133].

Low Keld Gill rises below Keld Gill Head, Wetherlam, at 284012 and joins Greenburn Beck at Greenburn Reservoir at 284021 ...the low spring gill.

Low Kid Crag lower slope of Grasmoor overlooking the B5289. High Kid Crag nearby [162201].

Low Kiln Bank Park WSW High Kiln Bank and Far Kiln Bank Parks [206934].

Low Knipe community, Knipe, alongside the R Lowther. High Knipe is between it and Knipe Scar [516200].

Low Kop hill to the N of Measand Beck and on path from Bampton over High Street ridge to Howtown 572m (1877ft) [474165].

Low Lane track below High Lane, Kentmere. From Green Quarter to Overend [461046].

Low Light Haw Bethecar Moor [301901].

Low Lindeth Undermillbeck Common [416953] ...the low lime tree hill.

Low Ling Crag on a peninsular which juts out into Crummock Water 104m (341ft) [157183]. High Ling Crag above.

Low Liza Bridge carries the road from the B5289 through Scales to Loweswater over Liza Beck [154224].

Low Long Crag Torver High Common [267960].

Low Longmire see **Longmire**.

Low Longrigg E River Mite [172029].

Low Lorton see **Lorton**.

Low Loup alongside confluence of Rowantreethwaite Beck and Hopgill Beck [481118]. Nearby is High Loup ...low leap.

Low Ludderburn Ludderburn, Cartmel Fell. Home of Arthur Ransome and his wife from 1925-35. Here he wrote five books including his best-known *Swallows and Amazons* (1930) [406912], see also **Ransome, Arthur**.

Low Ludderburn Tarn Ludderburn, Cartmel Fell. Alternative name Peer How Tarn. Shallow tarn lying between Cote Hill and Peer How. Stream from it joins the River Winster

C130m (C426ft) [404916].

Low Man see **Skiddaw**.

Low Mere Greave see **High Mere Greave**.

Low Mill Bridge carries the minor road from Mill Bridge (A591) to Town Head (A591) over the River Rothay. The old mill nearby is now a private residence [334091].

Low Mill House Underbarrow. Alongside Underbarrow Pool. Formerly the mill was a bobbin mill known as Underbarrow Mill [465916].

Low Millerground Windermere was at one time crossed by two ferries, the present one and one from Belle Grange to Miller Ground Landing by Low Millerground. The 17th century Low Millerground Cottage at the foot of Queen Adelaide's Hill was the ferry house and still possesses a bell turret which housed the bell to summon the ferry [403988] ...named from the family of Milner, Mylner.

Low Moorend Ennerdale Bridge. Far Moorend nearby [075155].

Low Moorside Irton. High Moorside and Moorside Wood nearby [079017].

Low Moss Place Fell. NE of the summit. SSW High Dodd. Source of Low Moss and Hollinhow Gills [415179].

Low Moss col between Stile End and Outerside [217218].

Low Moss NNW Bleaberry Fell [280207].

Low Moss Close between Wash Dub Beck and Stephead Gill [240959].

Low Moss Gill rises Low Moss, Place Fell, at 413180 and joins Scalehow Beck at 411184.

Low Nest off the A591 at Nest Brow. High Nest nearby [291226].

Low Over Park Torver [282945].

Low Oxen Fell property off the A593, Skelwith Bridge-Coniston road. Track to it continues to High Oxen Fell [326021].

Low Park E Penn [194905].

Low Park Colwith [333032] ...see **Birk Rigg Park**.

Low Park E High Park, Grizedale Forest [341978].

Low Parkamoor see **Parkamoor**.

Low Pate Crag Claife Heights. Below High Pate Crag [385970].

Low Peat Stock Cockley Beck. Below High Peat Stock [257016].

Low Peel Near small promontory S High Peel Near, Coniston Water [296914].

Low Pen Lamplugh Fell. W of High Pen [103189].

Low Pike S of High Pike on the ridge of the major Fairfield Horseshoe 508m (1667ft) [374078].

Low Pike Haw across Seal Gill from Bleaberry Haws. High Pike Haw to its NE [261946].

Low Place farm, Miterdale [154018] ...on a wall nearby a notice to walkers reads 'Hod Reet Fur Eshdel' (head right for Eskdale).

Low Plain farm off the Brigsteer to Underbarrow road. A farm park of particular appeal to children [474900].

Low Plumgarths Plumgarths [496946] ...low plum tree enclosure.

Low Pool Bridge carries Third Moss Lane over Underbarrow Pool/Beck [471900].

Low Prior Scales E of the River Calder. SW High Prior Scales [059073] ...the prior's lower shepherd's hut. Calder Abbey nearby.

Low Raise ENE of High Raise 754m (2474ft) [456137].

Low Raven Crag E slope Helm Crag. Overlooks the River Rothay and the A591 [330093].

Low Raven Crag near the foot of Fleetwith Edge, High Raven Crag nearby [197147].

Low Red Pike below Red Pike, Wasdale [167106].

Low Rigg between Naddle Vale and St. John's in the Vale. N High Rigg, 277m (909ft) [303227].

Low Rogerscale Farm alongside minor road from Brandlingill to Low Lorton. High Rogerscale to its ESE [140267] ...Roger's shieling.

Low Saddle Coldbarrow Fell, Ullscarf ridge. High Saddle to its S, 656m (2152ft) [288133].

Low Saltcotes end of a minor road off the A595. Saltcotes Caravan Park here [080969].

Low Scar Wood W Dale Park Beck [353938].

Low Scarside ENE Bampton Grange. Below Knipescar Common [536185].

Low Scawdel subsidiary summit of High Spy and N High Scawdel 521m (1709ft) [242162].

Low Skelghyll farm alongside Skelghyll Lane and below High Skelghyll [393026] ...see **Skelghyll Wood**.

Low Snab farm at the foot of Scope End [229187] ...snab is a dialect word for steep place/point of land.

Low Snockrigg Buttermere. Between the B5289 and High Snockrigg [184167].

Low Spying How ENE High Spying How. S of the path from the Hole-in-the-Wall to Striding Edge. Overlooks Grisedale [355151].

Low Stanger Farm see **Stanger**.

Low Stile Wood Seatoller, Borrowdale. High Stile Wood adjoining [243135].

Low Stock Bridge bridge over the River Derwent near Derwent Foot, Bassenthwaite Lake. High Stock Bridge upstream [236268].

Low Stonythwaite E High Stonythwaite [220969].

Low Strutta Borrowdale. Adjoining Strutta Wood and between the road to Watendlath and the B5289 [269199]. For years pre-Second World War and for many years afterwards a real Lakeland character, Vivian Fisher, manned a gate (Low Strutta Gate) across the Watendlath road below Watendlath Bridge. This he would open for walkers, etc. from whom he expected a small recompense. Vivian would chatter to all, recite poetry and sing songs. He lived in a makeshift hut nearby. Much later he went to live in Keswick where he died ...see Strutta Wood.

Low Sweden Bridge carries the path from Ambleside to Low and High Pike over Scandale Beck [375055] ...Sweden (swithen) - land cleared by burning.

Low Sweden Coppice alongside Scandale Beck. High Sweden Coppice above [377058) ...see **Low Sweden Bridge** above.

Low Swinklebank Longsleddale [496039] ...'swinklebank' means the spring on the hill slope where swine drank.

Low Swinside Lorton Vale. High Swinside Farm nearby [166247].

Low Taggleshaw Tarn see **Taggleshaw Tarns**.

Low Tarn below Red Pike. Scoat Tarn is to its N and Greendale Tarn to its SW, C520m (C1706ft) [162093].

Low Teighton How above the summit of the Wrynose Pass and the Three Shire Stone [278029].

Low Thistleton Gosforth. High Thistleton nearby [095045] ...low dwelling by the thistles.

Low Tilberthwaite see **Tilberthwaite**.

Low Todrigg off minor road to Hutton from minor road, A66 to Matteredale End [419268].

Low Wallowbarrow SW High Wallowbarrow, Duddon valley [219962].

Low Water tarn which rather belies its name as it is situated at 544m (1785ft) on the E slope of a high ridge with the summits of Coniston Old Man and Brim Fell towering above it. At one time it supplied water to power the machinery for the huge quarry below. 14m (46ft) deep and contains trout. The source of Low Water Beck which falls in impressive cascades before joining Levers Water Beck [275983].

Low Water Beck its source is Low Water at 276983 and it cascades down to meet Levers Water at 285986.

Low Waterside off the Cleator Moor to Ennerdale Bridge road. High Waterside to its NE [044153].

Low Wax Knott E Scarth Gap Pass. High Wax Knott to the W of the pass [188140].

Low Wether Crag alongside the S ridge of Black Sails [284002].

Low Whinery Ground Duddon valley. High Whinery Ground nearby [201904] ...the low whin/gorse ground.

Low White Rake see **Nitting Haws**.

Low White Stones below **High White Stones** [282101].

Low Wood adjoins Dalegarth Hall, Eskdale [167000].

Low Wood principally an oak, ash and hazel woodlands which sweeps down to Brothers Water and to a section of Goldrill Beck. Designated a SSSI by the Nature Conservancy Council [401135].

Low Wood SSW High Close [337050].

Low Wood foot of Wastwater [144041].

Low Wood alongside the road up the Duddon valley and opposite the Low [204944].

Low Wood Hall Strands, Nether Wasdale [123042].

Low Wood Hotel Deemed to celebrate its tri-centenary in 2002. Originally an old small coaching inn and mentioned by Thomas West in his *Guide to the Lakes* (1778) as possessing a fine view of the lake - which it still does. Ruskin originally described it as "little more than a country cottage." Greatly expanded in the 1850s and on his return in 1867 Ruskin then noted that it was "too noisy and fashionable - Manchester fashion." Further enlargements over the years, and 1989 saw the completion of a conference centre, a leisure complex and restaurant coupled with a complete refurbishment. Across the A591 is the Lowwood Water Ski Centre. At the old inn in 1847 notables including William Wordsworth met to formulate their opposition to the proposed extension of the railway line from Windermere to Low Wood. This opposition was to be successful and the line ended, as it does today, at Windermere. The hotel is now owned by English Lakes Hotels, a group which also includes the Wild Boar Hotel at Crook, the Waterhead Hotel at Waterhead and the Storrs Hall Hotel, Windermere [386217].

Low Wray see **Wray**.

Low Wray Bay Windermere [377013].

Low Wray Bridge carries the road from the B5286 to High Wray over Blelham Beck [371010].

Low Wythow Yewdale Fells. High Wythow to its SW [304993] ...the low white hill meaning an area principally dry, open. White Gill rises nearby.

Low Yewdale 311991. Nearby at [309988] there is an 18th century lime kiln made of local slate and owned by the NT.

Low Yews alongside the A5074 [428911].

Lowbank Crags Seatoller Fell. Overlooks the Seathwaite Valley [237131].

Lowbridge House Bannisdale. Erected in 1837 and enlarged since [537011].

Lowclose off the Askham to Yanwath road [514252].

Lowcrag Wood between the road to Watendlath and the B5289. S of Strutta Wood [268195].

Lowcray above the River Bleng and Lowcray Bank [082059].

Lowcray Bank above the River Bleng and below Lowcray [084059].

Lower Fall Rydal, see **Rydal Falls**.

Lower Gatesgarth head of Buttermere (lake). Alongside the B5289. Built in 1909 as a cottage for climbers and walkers [192154].

Lower Hows Furness Fells [289005] ...the lower hills.

Lower Kern Knotts see **Kern Knotts**.

Lower Man see **Helvellyn Lower Man**.

Lower Routen Beck Tarn on Routen Beck, Potter Fell. Occupied by several small islands, C250m (C820ft) [514991].

Loweswater scattered village and lake of the same name. The village centre lies alongside Park Beck and halfway between the lake and Crummock Water. An ancient site with an 'earthwork' at 139203 while a promontory on the W bank of Crummock Water is suggested as having once been a place of refuge. Also, not far distant, at Lanthwaite Green there is a 'homestead'. Records date from the beginning of the 13th century when Loweswater was a chapel to St. Bees Abbey. In fact, before the 17th century coffins were carried on horseback from the parish over a track which cuts across the breast of Carling Knott to Lamplugh and ultimately to St. Bees. The present church, dedicated to St. Bartholomew, was erected in 1827, remodelled in 1884, and is adjacent to the Kirkstile Inn. Mellbreak towers above the village to its S. The Mellbreak Foxhounds are kennelled nearby at Lorton but one of its famous huntsmen, Jonathon Banks, lived all his life at Loweswater and, until his death in 1928, he accounted for 1800 foxes [141209].

The lake lies WNW of the village. One of the smallest lakes being only 1.8 kms (1.12 miles) in length and 0.5 kms (0.3 miles wide). From its outflow Park Beck, initially named as Dub Beck, flows through the village to Crummock Water. Fishing for brown trout and coarse fish including perch and occasionally pike is by permit. No private craft are allowed but rowing boats can be hired. The lake appears as somewhat of an oddity. It is the only lake whose outflow water runs centrally and both the eye and mind suggest that its water is flowing away from Crummock Water and that its foot is its head and its head its foot. In his *The Lakes ABC* by David Scott, MA (1955), the author notes that "there is some excuse for this confusion, as many geologists are of the opinion that the head was once its foot." The lake and adjoining Holme Wood are owned by the NT. Lies at an altitude of 121m (398ft) [125217] ...leafy lake.

Loweswater Fell shown on the OS map as that from Loweswater rising to Hen Comb [134190].

Loweswater Fell S summit of the Fellbarrow range 412m (1352ft) [136223].

Loweswater Fells large fell area to the S of Loweswater bounded on the N by Loweswater, on the S by the Floutern Pass, on the W by the Croasdale-Fangs Brow road and on the E by Crummock Water. Highest point is Blake Fell at 573m (1880ft) 110197.

Loweswater Fell/Blake Fell range of fells (for area covered see **Loweswater Fells** above), see Reference Section: **Heights**.

Loweswater Hall alongside the Loweswater to Mockerkin road [120224].

Lowfield E bank of the River Cocker. Off the Roundclose Hill to Southwaite Bridge road [131282].

Lowfield Lane Kentmere. From the Staveley-Kentmere road to Green Quarter. Low Field Foot in 1836 [459038].

Lowhouse Beck property between Neds Low Wood and Smithy Hill. The beck alongside flows down to join the River Winster [410924].

Lowpark Loweswater. Highpark nearby [144204].

Lowpark Buildings N of Highpark Buidings in parkland adjoining Thornthwaite Hall [523165].

Lowside off the A66 [356271].

Lowther, River see **River Lowther**.

Lowther Brow E Hagg Gill, Troutbeck Park [426055] ...from a member of an early Lowther family.

Lowther House Butterwick [502196].

Lowther Park situated on the NE boundary of the National Park it comprises much of the Parish of Lowther which contains within its boundaries the villages of Lowther, Newtown, Hackthorpe, Melkinthorpe and Whale. For centuries the park has been held by the Lonsdale/Lowther family. Principally, apart from parkland and plantations, Lowther Park possesses Lowther Castle, Newtown, Lowther, St. Michael's Church and mausoleum, Lowther Leisure Park and Lowther Caravan Park.

Lowther Castle, now merely a turreted and towered facade, was originally designed by Sir Robert Smirke and erected at the beginning of the 19th century on the site of an old hall destroyed by fire in 1726. Described as a 'princely' and 'majestic' mansion, Wordsworth wrote a sonnet in 1833 which began: "Lowther, in thy majestic Pile are seen/ Cathedral pomp and grace, in apt accord/ With the baronial castle's sterner mien" and ended very appropriately as it turned out with: "Fall if ye must, ye Tower of Pinnacles/ With what ye symbolise; authentic Story/ Will say, Ye disappeared with England's Glory." It, or most of it, 'fell' in 1957 when the interior was demolished. In late 2003 the facade was being stablilised and after completion there are possible plans and options for other additions to the castle to be included.

Lowther (Newton) was constructed c1693 by Sir John Lowther to replace the old village of Lowther (demolished 1692) which stood in front of Lowther Hall (later the site of Lowther Castle) and so obstructed the view from the latter. Lowther Village, designed by the Adam Brothers, was erected nearly a century later, c1765-1773, as a model village for estate workers. It was never fully completed and today, modernisation has reduced the number of houses.

St. Michael's Church near the castle was rebuilt and enlarged in the latter half of the 17th century on the site of a much earlier building and was restored in 1857. A large mausoleum, erected in the latter year, stands in the churchyard. Several of the Lowther family are buried within its vaults. Norse hog back gravestones were found alongside the entrance to the churchyard and are now exhibited in the church porch.

Lowther Horse Driving Trials and Country Fair - the trials commenced in 1972 and the country fair three years later. The Duke of Edinburgh is a frequent entrant to the trials.

Lowther Leisure Park - (synonymous with Lowther Park) offered a day out and adventure playground for both young and old. Closed during the foot and mouth epidemic and not reopened.

Probably the most famous of the Earls of Lonsdale was the 5th Earl, Hugh Cecil (1857-1944). Known as the Yellow Earl (the Lowther colour is yellow) he was a prominent sporting figure and bequeathed boxing's Lonsdale Belts. He was also the first president of the Automobile Association and even today yellow is the colour of the association.

For up to date information consult current leaflet or contact Lowther Parklands, Hackthorpe, Penrith, Cumbria, CA10 2HG.

Lowther Street Waberthwaite. Connects the A595 with the minor road to Corney [113939].

Lowthwaite WSW Little Mell Fell [416237].

Lowthwaite Beck rises N slope of Little Meldrum. Flows through Lowthwaite and ultimately feeds into Blackdike Beck at 408236.

Lowthwaite Crag E Low Snab across the Newlands Beck [233186].

Lowthwaite Farm off the B5322 [319226].

Lowwood Hotel see **Low Wood Hotel**.

Lowwood Water Ski Centre Windermere. Across the A591 from the Lowwood Hotel [385019].

Lucy's Tongue above Swart Beck. WSW of the summit of Sheffield Pike [363179].

Ludderburn area principally comprising High Ludderburn, Ludderburn Hill, Ludderburn Moss, Low Ludderburn Tarn and Low Ludderburn ...clear, pure stream.

Ludderburn Hill above High and Low Ludderburn [403913].

Ludderburn Moss owned by the NPA. Comprises 22 hectares of fell, woodland and bog. A wildlife and picnic area with some fine views.

Lumholme Broughton Mills [219904].

Lunch House S of the upper Wet Sleddale Reservoir. A substantial wooden hut near many shooting butts [546100].

Lund Bridge across the River Irt [142039] ...the small wood by the bridge.

Lunsty Howe Kentmere. Tumulus here [453036].

Lunthwaite Dowthwaite Head [375206].

Lurge Crag overlooks Deepdale. Between Lurge Gill and Browndale Beck [352202].

Lurge Gill rises ENE slope Great Dodd. Joins Aira Beck at 355204.

Lurgegill Head ENE Great Dodd. Head of Lurge Gill [346208].

Lyth Gallery see **Town Yeat**.

Lyth Valley also known as damson valley because of the prepondarence of damson trees in it. Runs from Gilpin Bridge to Crosthwaite and through it runs a section of the A5704, see also **Damsons**.

Lyulph's Tower off the A592 and below the NT Gowbarrow Park. Believed to have derived its name from L'Ulf, L'Ulph or Ulf, a former Baron of Greystoke, whose castle is said to have stood on the site. The present structure was erected in the late 18th century [404202].

Lyzzick Hall Hotel country house hotel, Underskiddaw, alongside the minor road Applethwaite-Millbeck-A591 [249263] ...'lyzzick' - bright, shiny oak.

Lyzzick Wood SE slope Dodd/Skiddaw Dodd [251269].

M

M6 motorway, only passes through approximately 0.8kms (0.5 mile) of the Lake District National Park on its E boundary [550207-548218].

Machell Coppice E side Coniston Water below Lawson Park [310949] ...personal name + small wood.

Maggie's Bridge across Dub Beck/Park Beck, Loweswater [134210]. The track from the bridge to High Nook Farm is known as Maggie's Lonnin (Lane).

Maiden Castle also Caerthanoc or Caer/Thannock, Soulby Fell. An ancient fort [451244] ...the Welsh interpretation means 'fortified place' plus personal name. The present title is echoed several times throughout the country, six others in Cumbria, one on Burnmoor, one on Soulby Fell and another the name of an habitation alongside it, one below Harter Fell summit, one at Stainmore and another at Kirkby Thore. There is much conjecture as to the origin of the name. It could be 'virgins' fortress' signifying one so strong that it could be defended by girls or may refer to a place where girls took part in activities such as sport or possibly the fort on the stones moor derived from the Celtic 'meini stones'.

Maiden Castle habitation W Soulby Fell alongside minor road [446247] ...see **Maiden Castle** above.

Maiden Castle rocky outcrop well below the summit of Harter Fell [222993].

Maiden Castle N of Burnmoor Tarn and shown on the OS map as Maiden Castle Cairn at 186054. According to the EPNS "there is no obvious trace of any earthwork which might have given rise to the name." However, reference is made in old works and guide books to earthworks with a diameter of 6.5m (21ft) alongside the old corpse road from Wasdale Head to Eskdale and which were named as such over 400 years ago [186054].

Maiden Holme islet in Windermere near Coatlap Point. Possesses one stunted oak tree and a few bushes. Believed to be the smallest property owned by the NT in this country [391960].

Maiden Moor mainly grassy summit on the ridge between Cat Bells and High Spy with line of steep crags to its W and crags and steep slopes to its E. Usually approached along the ridge from either Cat Bells or High Spy or from Manesty and Grange 576m (1890ft) [237182].

Maiden Stone Gatesgarthdale. Alongside the road over Honister Pass [218144].

Mains Farm Pooley Bridge. Alongside the B5320 [476246] ...Pooley demain (demesne) lands farm. The dictionary definition of demesne is 'land surrounding a house or manor: a region or district'.

Mainsgate alongside the minor road from the A595 (Holmrook) to Santon Bridge [097998] ...see above.

Mallen Dodd slightly N of the summit of Latrigg [278251].

Man Crag Oxen Fell [325014] ...usually signifies a height just below the summit of the fell eg. Little Man, Skiddaw; Helvellyn Lower Man and Benn Man.

Manesty hamlet and farmhouse [250185] at the head of Derwentwater. Famous author Hugh Walpole (later knighted) purchased Brackenburn (built 1909) [249912] in 1923 and here he wrote most of his works. He died at Brackenburn in 1941. Brandelhow Woods [252194] was the first Lake District acquisition by the NT in 1902 while the large Manesty Park to its S [253191] was bought by the Trust, mainly in 1908, just before the area was about to be sold for building plots. In one corner of the park the Caravan Club of Great Britain has a site. An ancient salt well, shown on the OS map at 252185 was credited with curative powers (see **Salt Well**). Alongside Brandelhow Bay an old lead mine was abandoned in 1891 [250196] ...Mani's path.

Manesty Band below Black Crag [247186].

Mansey Pike W Langdale Combe [259095].

Marble Stone prominent rock with iron fence post embeded in it on lower Gamlin End between Seat and High Crag [183137].

Marchbank Beck rises Threlkeld Common. Joins the River Glenderamackin at 330253.

Marchbank Wood S bank River Glenderamackin. Alongside Keswick Golf Club course [335255].

Mardale see **Haweswater & Mardale**.

Mardale Banks bank/slope E Haweswater Reservoir [481126].

Mardale Beck takes this name after the confluence of Small Water Beck and Blea Water Beck at 463106 and joins Haweswater at 468109.

Mardale Common W to N of Selside Pike. Traversed by part of the Old Corpse Road [485115].

Mardale Head end of the minor road along the E side of Haweswater. Here is a car parking area and the start of the Nan Bield and Gatescarth passes and fells to the N [469107].

Mardale Ill Bell rocky lump on the ridge from High Street which drops down to the Nan Bield Pass. Not to be confused with the Ill Bell viewed SSW across the head of the Kentmere valley. Impressive views to Blea Tarn/Long Stile and Small Water from top of crags N and E respectively. Normally climbed as part of the Kentmere Horseshoe or on the ascent of High Street from the Nan Bield Pass summit C760m (C2493ft) [448101] ...hill shaped like a bell above Mardale.

Mardale Waters Blea Water, Small Water and the streams serving them and between them are known collectively as Mardale Waters [456106].

Mariel Bridge carries the Old Coach Road, St. John's in the Vale to Dockray, over Mosedale Beck [350227].

Mark Gate Great Langdale. Path from the New Dungeon Ghyll Hotel passes through Mark Gate and the foot of Loft Crag to the Langdale Pikes [286066] ...Mark's way (to higher pastures).

Mark's Well Helton [511221] ...local family of Marks.

Markeems rocky area slightly E of Browney Gill [266049].

Marron, River see **Leaps Beck**.

Marshside off the Bootle to Eskmeals minor road [081905].

Mart Bield near the summit of Cat Bells [243196] ...shelter of the pine marten.

Mart Crag overlooks Hell Gill and Wrynose Bottom [268016] ...crag frequented by pine martens.

Mart Crag E slope Clough Head. Overlooks Mosedale Beck [346225].

Mart Crag High Rigg W St. John's in the Vale [310206].

Mart Crag crags SW of Martcrag Moor [265079].

Mart Crag Lingmoor Fell [301041].

Mart Crag below Greenhow End and overlooking Mossydale, Deepdale [372124].

Mart Crag Yewdale Fells 318m (1043ft) [304990].

Mart Crags Dunnerdale Forest [225991] ...see initial **Mart Crag** above.

Mart Fold sheepfold [347225].

Mart Knott Ennerdale Fell. W Silvercove Beck [127134].

Martcrag Moor dreary and usually boggy moorland above Mart Crag. Traversed by footpath between Stake Pass and Pike of Stickle. Two minor stone-axe factories have been discovered here. Rises to 547m (1795ft) [268083].

Martcrag Moor Tarn shown but not named on the OS map. A pretty tarn amid dreary moorland, C540m (C1772ft) [267081].

Martindale E Ullswater. Comprises a parish and area to the S of Hallin Fell-Sandwick, the Hause, Boredale, Howegrain, Rampsgill, Bannerdale and Fusedale. Part of it is occupied by the Martindale Deer Forest (see **The Nab**). Martindale boasts two churches. The old church, dedicated to St. Martin, stands alongside the road leading along Howegrain and on to Dale Head, Bannerdale. Built in 1633 on the site of a previous church it was, until 1881, the Parish Church of Martindale. On the day of the actual consecration of the nearby St. Peter's Church, 6 January 1882, there was a terrible storm which took the roof of the old church. Restored in 1883. The pulpit bears the date 1634 and the baptismal font is believed to be of Roman origin and was probably found in the vicinity of High Street. A single yew tree in the churchyard is believed to be 2000 years old. The new church near the Hause, is one of the loneliest churches in the country. It succeeded the old church in 1881 and is dedicated to St. Peter.

200 people lived in the dale from the 16-18th century. However, by 1900 the population had fallen to 123 and today the normal resident population is below 80 [435186] ...St. Martin's valley. Before 1266 a cross dedicated to St. Martin stood in the valley.

Martindale Deer Forest see **The Nab**.

Martindale Forest on the E slopes of Bannerdale and alongside Howe Grain and Ramps Gill are clusters of woodland, the last surviving relics of the huge forest which covered the Martindale area centuries ago. Mainly of alder such areas of woodland would, according to *The Lake District* (Collins New Naturalist series) "be left standing to provide shelter for the deer, and within them, on suitable soils, alder would come to dominate the wood as browsing by the deer prevented the regeneration of other trees." [440170].

Martineau, Harriet see **The Knoll**.

Mary Mount Hotel Borrowdale. Alongside the B5289 [266192].

Mary Point see **White Moss & Baneriggs**.

Mary's Pillar see **Hegdale**.

Masmill Beck rises NE Sleet How and W Kinn at 216232. Subsequently met by

Hallgarth Beck and enters Newlands Beck at 232259.

Mason, Charlotte see **Charlotte Mason College of Education**.

Matson Ground Bowness-on-Windermere. Off Lickbarrow Road. 17th century origin. One of many 'grounds' established in the 16th and 17th centuries (see **Grounds**). Today a substantial property and farm [416967].

Matterdale valley running between Troutbeck (A66) and Ullswater (A592) and served by the A5091. Comprises two villages, Matterdale End and Dockray ...madder valley. Takes its name from the madder plant (a member of the bedstraw family) from whose root a reddish dye was obtained.

Matterdale Beck a principal headstream of Dacre Beck. Rises alongside New Road which links the B5091 to Dockray at 386224. Flows through Matterdale End to join Cooper Beck at 400234 to become, as suggested, Dacre Beck.

Matterdale Beck rises alongside the New Road which links the B5091 to Dockray. Flows through Matterdale End to join Cooper Beck at 400234.

Matterdale Common large grass and moss area NE Great Dodd [349214] ...'Le Common' in the 15th century.

Matterdale End village alongside, and adjacent to, the A5091. Situated between Troutbeck and Dockray. Matterdale Church, half way between Dockray and Matterdale End, was built in the 16th century, extensively altered in the 18th century and restored in the 19th century [394234].

Matterdale Rigg minor road from A66-Matterdale End crosses Matterdale Rigg at 281m (921ft) [402239].

Matthew Tranearth Torver. Adjoining Frank Tranearth [274951] ...Matthew's ground frequented by cranes.

Matty Benn's Bridge see **Monks Bridge**.

May Crag below the Hindscarth-High Crags ridge and NW Squat Knotts [218172].

Mayor of Troutbeck see **Queen's Head Hotel**.

Meadley Reservoir E Cleator Moor. Fed by Mere Beck [051146].

Meadowplatt Plantation alongside Park Beck, Kentmere [449021].

Mealhowe Gill Ralfland Forest. Rises 528120. Becomes Keld Gill at approximately 531127 and this joins the R Lowther at 551143 ...'meal' possibly means either coloured, variegated, or middle.

Measand the hamlet of Measand which included Measand Beck Hall, Measand Grammar School, cottages and farms, stood near the outlet of Measand Beck into Haweswater and alongside the road around the W side of the lake. All except Measand School were submerged under the water of the enlarged reservoir over 50 years ago. The school was dismantled and rebuilt as a private residence at Walmgate Head. It was often said that at Measand "they sowed in Latin and reaped in Greek." Apart from possessing an early grammar school Measand can claim a place in history in that it was the first place to have a library of books lent free of charge to all callers. There is the site of earthworks 201m (660 yards) NE of Measand Bridge [490156]. These are scheduled as an Ancient Monument ...marsh, sand bank.

Measand Beck Keasgill Sike and Longgrain Beck rise at Keasgill Head and NE High Raise summit respectively and join forces at 460151 to become Measand Beck. This flows down over Fordingdale Force, through the hanging valley of Fordingdale Bottom and spectacularly over the Forces to join Haweswater Reservoir at 487154. Before the making of the present reservoir the Measand delta practically cut Haweswater in two but both this and the cluster of properties at Measand near the delta were submerged when the water level was raised by 29m (95ft) [475160].

Measand End end of ridge dropping down from High Raise to lower reaches of Measand Beck [479154].

Mecklin Beck rises below Kilnhow Crag at 135030 and joins the River Irt near Mecklin Bridge at 111019.

Mecklin Bridge carries the Santon Bridge to Nether Wasdale road over Mecklin Beck [112020].

Mecklin Park Irton Fell [128023].

Mecklin Wood WNW Irton Pike [118024].

Media principal coverage of the Lake District, Cumbria or parts of Cumbria is by *The Advertiser, Bay Radio, BBC North West, BBC Radio Cumbria, Border Television, CFM Radio, Cumberland & Westmorland Herald (*east Cumbria area including Alston, Appleby, Keswick, Kirkby Stephen, Penrith), *Cumberland News* (north Cumbria including Carlisle and Penrith), *Cumbria magazine, Cumbria & Lake District Life, Cumbrian Gazette, Evening News & Star* (Carlisle, Cockermouth, Keswick, Maryport, Penrith, Whitehaven, Workington), *Granada Television, Keswick Reminder, Lake District Life, Lakeland Echo, Lakeland Radio, Lakeland Walker, Lancashire Evening Post, Lancaster Guardian, Lancashire Life & Lake District Life, North West Evening Mail* (Furness area including Barrow), *Times & Star* (Workington), *Westmorland Gazette* (south Cumbria including Ambleside and Kendal), *Westmorland Messenger* (Appleby and Kirkby Stephen), *Whitehaven News* (Copeland area including Cleator Moor, Egremont, Millon and Whitehaven).

Meethop Dub on St John's Beck at the foot of the Thirlmere overflow [309192] ...either middle valley pool or pool in the sandy valley.

Meeting Hill Birker Moor. Below Broad Crag [193978].

Megs Gill rises below Silver How at 323065 and flows down to meet Great Langdale Beck at 323052.

Mell Beck rises SE Gowk Hill at 447165 and joins Rampsgill Beck at 438162 ...sand bank stream.

Mell Fell Wood W slope Great Mell Fell [390253].

Mellbreak locally Mellbreak. An attractive fell. Viewed from the E shore of Crummock Water Mellbreak has a slight resemblance to the Wastwater Screes dropping as it does steeply to the lake and like the path below the Screes there is a low level path alongside Crummock Water. From the Kirkstile Inn Mellbreak appears as a huge steep pinnacle with what appears to be a very narrow crest. Its summit is actually a broad plateau with a North Top at 509m (1670ft) [143195] linked by a saddle to a South Top at 512m (1680ft) [149186] ...obscure origin. It has been suggested that the first participal is similar to the 'mell' of Great and Little Mell Fells in that it refers to a bare hill while the second is from the ON 'brekka' meaning a slope particularly one dropping steeply to a lake.

Mellfell Beck rises Binks Moss at 390241 and flows below Great Mell Fell to join Dacre Beck at 411250.

Mellfell House E Little Mell Fell. Off minor road to Bennethead [430238].

Mellguards Howtown. In the mid-19th century it was 'Millguards' [446195].

Meolbank Gosforth [081025] ...sandy bank.

Meolbank Plantation [108052] ...plantation on, or by, the sand bank.

Mere Beck rises E High Raise at 287094. Joined by Birks Gill, Flour Gill and Cat Gills to become the Wyth Burn which joins Thirlmere at 322131.

Mere Beck rises WNW Keasgill Head and below the High Street ridge at 451160. Flows down to meet Rampsgill Beck at 439160.

Mere Beck rises between Miterdale and Eskdale Green at 142005 and joins the River Esk at 144993.

Mere Beck rises below Pool Scar at 262911 and flows through Torver Low Common to join Torver Beck at 287927. For centuries it has formed the border between the parishes of Blawith and Torver.

Mere Beck two tributaries rise from springs at 068140 and 062141 respectively and the beck flows into Meadley Reservoir.

Mere Crag Shap Fells. Between Sleddale Fell and Borrowdale Moss [504065].

Mere Gill rises NNE of the summit of High Seat at 290185 and joins Shoulthwaite Gill at 299189.

Mere Gill rises Ullscarf at 289124. Joins Greenhead Gill at 281121 and the combined watercourse joins Greenup Gill at 280122.

Mere Moss Torver Low Common. Mere Beck flows through it [272919].

Mere Sike rises between Powley's Hill and Harper Hills at 509139 and joins Swindale Beck at 522143.

Merebeck Gill rises at Caddy Well, a spring, at 144023 and joins the River Mite at 147012.

Meregarth property E shore Windermere near Calgarth Hall [399994] ...enclosure by the mere (Windermere).

Meregill Beck rises Owsen Fell at 104212. Joined by Black Beck at 098222. Subsequently becomes Snary Beck which joins the River Marron.

Meregill Beck twin tributaries rise at 135239 and 136238 respectively and the beck is joined by Thackthwaite Beck at 152243. The combined watercourse meets the River Cocker at 151252.

Merewood country house hotel alongside Mirk Lane [392013].

Merklins alongside the Grizedale-Satterthwaite road [338937] ...unknown origin but the 'mer' may be mere or marsh and 'lins' possibly lime trees.

Michael's Fold off a minor road E of the A591. Another suggested site for the home of Michael, the shepherd of Wordsworth's poem *Michael.* Today, a much reduced 'Clipping Tree', under which Michael and others sheared their sheep, is claimed to still stand in the grounds. The present large house is now divided into three apartments [342083].

Michael's Nook Grasmere. Alongside a minor road E of the A591. Formerly a country house hotel and restaurant but in 2002 approval was given to convert it into four residential units. Another sizeable property which is claimed to be on the site of Michael's cottage, the shepherd of Wordsworth's poem *Michael* [341086]. (For other claimants see *Wordsworth & The Lake District* by David McCracken (1984) and **Michael's Fold**.)

Mickle Door wide and steep scree run between Long Top and the third crinkle of Crinkle Crags [250049] ...similar to Mickledore between Scafell and Scafell Pike in that it means the great opening in a ridge between walls of rock.

Mickle Moss ENE High Borrans. Spot-height at 232m (761ft) [444014] ...'large bog'.

Mickleden valley continuing from the head of Great Langdale to the foot of the Stake Pass and the Rossett Gill Pass. A fine example of a glaciated valley with many hummocks of moraine at its head. Several cairns in the valley bottom have been suggested as implying that there was once a settlement here [266067] ...the big valley.

Mickleden Beck Rossett Gill, Little Gill and Stake Gill combine in the region of 262073 to become Mickleden Beck. This meets Oxendale Beck at 280060 and becomes Great Langdale Beck.

Mickledore col/pass between (Scafell Pike) and Scafell. Considered to be the highest named pass in the Lake District C840 (C2756ft) [210069] ...similar to Mickle Door, Crinkle Crags, in that it means the great opening between walls of rock.

Middale Longsleddale [496034] ...name obvious.

Middle Bank Corney. Near Bank to its SE. Far Bank to its NNE [103917].

Middle Boonwood Gosforth. Between Low and High Boonwood [065044].

Middle Crag S High Tove C480m (C1575ft) [288158].

Middle Dale Park large property, Dale Park. Believed to be about a century old and formerly a farmhouse and granary [352923].

Middle Dale Park Plantation E Dale Park Beck and ENE Middle Dale Park [359925].

Middle Dodd northern extension of Red Screes. Very prominent when viewed from the foot of Kirkstone Pass. Higher than either nearby High Hartsop Dodd or Hartsop Dodd (Low Hartsop Dodd). The 'middle' refers to its geographical location between the two 654m (2146ft) [397095].

Middle Elfhowe Over Staveley [469999] ...Elf Howe, the Fairy Hill nearby.

Middle Fairbank Tarn ESE High Fairbank. SW Fairbank Farm. At one time a reservoir (Stewart's Reservoir) created out of a small tarn by the building of a dam at its E end. This provided water power for the bobbin mill at Staveley. The mill has long since ceased to exist and the water has been stocked with trout for private fishing. A relatively large tarn and some idea of its size can be gleaned from the fact that it is slightly larger in area than the well-known Watendlath Tarn [450973].

Middle Fell craggy fell between Nether Beck and Greendale Gill/Tarn 582m (1909ft) [151072].

Middle Fell Lamplugh Fell [104193].

Middle Fell Farm Great Langdale. Much earlier known as Middlefell Place. Present homestead dates from the 17th century but documents for 1332 mention a settlement hereabouts and a Charles Mithelfell. Members of the Middlefell family occupied the farmstead in the 17th and 18th centuries. Bought by the NT in 1938 [285061].

Middle Grove farm, the only one left of Low, Middle and High Grove, on the old route from Ambleside to Kirkstone Pass [392054] ...see also **High Grove**.

Middle How E Hawkshead-Newby Bridge road [371922].

Middle How overlooks the head of the Wyth Burn valley 483m (1585ft) [296110].

Middle Kinmont off the minor road S from Corney to the A595 (Cross House). High Kinmont to its ENE [117905] ...see **High Kinmont**.

Middle Park Duddon valley [196913].

Middle Row Farm foot of Blease Fell, Blencathra. Adjacent to Blencathra Centre [305255].

Middle Swan Beck flows through Glencoyne Park from 383191 and enters Ullswater at 389191.

Middle Swinklebank now shown on OS map. Property midway between High and Low Swinklebank, Longsleddale. Former YHA hostel.

Middle Taggleshaw see **Taggleshaw Tarns**.

Middle Tongue between Browndale Beck and Aira Beck [351196].

Middle Tongue between Whelpside Gill and Comb Gill [334139].

Middle Tongue descends from Blencathra ridge between Gategill Fell Top and Hall's Fell Top to Gate Gill [321272].

Middle Top see **Skiddaw**.

Middlebank Wood E A595. Adjacent Borrowdale Wood [103921].

Middleboot Knotts between Piers Gill and Greta Gill and overlooking the former [213082].

Middlerigg Tarn private artificial tarn including small island alongside Wain Lane 84m (276ft) [397011].

Middlesteads Bank W Thirlmere. Lower slope High Seat between Dowthwaite Gill and Middlesteads Gill [302177].

Middlesteads Gill rises Armboth Fell at 295172 and joins Thirlmere at 306172 ...presumably the gill in the middle. In this case between Fisher Gill and Thrang Gill.

Middleton Place on the minor road off the A595 to the Eskmeals coast road [097922].

Middleton Place Crossing carries the minor road from the A595 by Middleton Place over the railway line [090921].

Mile Crags NNE of confluence of Measand Beck and Haweswater [490161] ...possibly named because the crags are one mile from Burnbanks or overlook the one mile point on the former road from Burnbanks along the W side of Haweswater.

Miles Gill rises near the summit of the Garburn Pass at 433045 and joins Trout Beck at 420046 ...surname? + stream.

Milkingstead Eskdale [154997].

Milkingstead Wood Eskdale [153996].

Mill Underbarrow. Alongside Chapel Beck. Originally one of several which flourished in the Crook, Crosthwaite and Underbarrow areas [463923].

Mill Ulpha [190926].

Mill, The see **The Mill**.

Mill Beck rises from several springs in Schoolknott Plantation at 428978/430975 and flows N and then W under the railway line before ultimately passing St John's Church, Windermere and on through woods where it is accompanied by a path called Sherriff's Walk. Joins Windermere S Rayrigg Wyke at 402977 ...from a very early corn mill which stood alongside 'Mulnebec' in the 13th century. This also gives its name to Undermillbeck.

Mill Beck rises as Sail Beck below Sail at 200196. This is joined by Addacomb Beck, Third Gill, Ramps Gill and Swinside Gill before taking the name of Mill Beck at Buttermere. Enters Crummock Water at 167173 ...from the old corn mill (now the Bridge Hotel) alongside the beck.

Mill Beck flows through the village of Millbeck. At one time dammed and provided water power for a now disused woollen mill. For its source and continuation see **Tongues Beck**.

Mill Bridge carries A591 over Tongue Gill [336091] ...from a former corn mill hereabouts.

Mill Bridge crosses R Glenderamackin at 326250.

Mill Bridge bridge across Torver Beck approx. 1.3kms (0.8 mile) from the beck's confluence with Coniston Water [285932] ...Torver High Mill nearby is now a private residence.

Mill Brow farm on hillside above Skelwith Bridge. Breeds pedigree Limousin cattle [347037] ...brow above the mill. A mill stood hereabouts centuries ago.

Mill Crags situated behind the former old corn mill at Bampton. *The Cumbria Village Book* (1991) notes "that the mill was bought by a local lady... who ran the village shop and post office for over 20 years" [512182].

Mill Farm Calder Bridge [042061].

Mill Gill flows down from Millgill Head at 341202 to join leat (water race) at 320197.

Mill Gill rises slope Blea Rigg at 294076 and joins Stickle Ghyll/Gill at 295066. The combined watercourse meets Great Langdale Beck at 298064 ...see **Millbeck**.

Mill Gill Great Langdale, see **Stickle Ghyll/Gill**.

Mill Gill Waberthwaite, see **Rowantree Gill**, **Samgarth** and **Stainton Becks**.

Mill Hill former farm, Loweswater [135205].

Mill House Farm alongside minor road from the A595 (Holmrook)-Santon Bridge road to Eskdale [118000].

Mill How Sandwick Beck. Only the name remains to remind us of a corn mill closed in the mid-19th century.

Mill Lane Crosthwaite. Connects the Underbarrow-Crosthwaite road with the A5074. Alongside it stood a former corn mill now a private residence [445909].

Mill Moor S Pooley Mill from which it takes its name 176m (577ft) [479255].

Mill Place SW Santon Bridge. Slightly E of the River Irt [106011].

Mill Place Nether Wasdale [130042].

Mill Plantation alongside B5322 NNE Green [320198].

Millbeck Great Langdale. Near the foot of Mill Gill. Earlier Low Millbeck to differentiate it from High Millbeck (now known as Stickle Cottage) higher up the valley. A very early mill, possibly corn and later fulling, is believed to have stood hereabouts. Millbeck was given to the NT in 1944 by Prof. G M Trevellyn [295066].

Millbeck alongside the minor road from Hopebeck S to the B5289 [163236] ...appertaining to an Adam de Milnebeck (recorded 13th century).

Millbeck village which takes its name from a woollen mill in operation from the 1700s. This was converted at the beginning of the 20th century into a dwelling house. The mill was served by the beck which flows through the village. Millbeck Hall is a 15th century pele tower with 16th century additions built by Nicolas Williamson. Later it was owned by the Brownrigg family. The Allerdale Ramble passes through the village and the latter is the start of an alternative route via Carl Side to the top of Skiddaw [256261].

Millbeck Farm Millbeck [255261].

Millbrow steep section of the minor road which drops down to the old mill at Ulpha [188924].

Millcrags farm, Bampton. Near the former Bampton Mill and with crags on the Howes at the rear [511182].

Milldam Crook. Farm which takes its name from a former dam which served a medieval fulling mill located nearby [442946]

Miller Bridge Ambleside. Packhorse bridge across the River Rothay from Pelter Bridge-Rothay Bridge road to Rothay Park [371045] ...possibly like Miller Ground from the surname Milner or Mylner.

Miller Bridge House Ambleside. Near Miller Bridge. In the early 19th century it was a school [370043].

Miller Brow W Brow Head Farm, Ambleside [376045].

Miller Crag overlooks Stickle Ghyll from its W and positioned just below Pike Howe [290068] ...from the Mylner family or the miller of the former ancient mill situated in the area, see also **Millbeck**, **Stickle Ghyll/Gill**.

Miller Crag near Muncaster Mill [095974].

Miller Hill off the Bootle to Eskmeals minor road. A hill in name only. The road nearby actually rises to 14m (46ft) [085902].

Miller Howe Hotel hotel and restaurant on Rayrigg Road, Windermere. The main house was built in 1916. Millar Howe was purchased by chef John Tovey in 1971 and over the succeeding years he made it one of the Lake District's most prestigious hotels. He became a celebrity chef and made regular appearances on TV and wrote many cookery books. John Tovey retired in 1998 and subsequently the hotel was taken over by former newspaper editor, Charles Garside.

Miller Place off the minor road S from Hopebeck to the B5289 [162232].

Miller Stands Wrynose Fell E [289035].

Millerground Landing see **Low Millerground**.

Millgate alongside the junction of the A595 and minor road S to Corney. Near Mill Gill [115945].

Millgill Head SSW Great Dodd [341202].

Millkeld Sike rises from spring at 514216 and joins the R Lowther at 516215 ...a former mill (referred to in the 14th, 15th and 16th centuries) by the spring alongside the stream.

Millrigg name given to an ancient British settlement on a terrace to the E of the River Kent and Kentmere Tarn [461025].

Millrigg Knott above and to the E of the Staveley to Kentmere road. Spot height at 300m (984ft) on the ridge at the rear [461013].

Millriggs property alongside the Staveley to Kentmere road. Ancient British settlement above. Nearby is Saw Mill Cottage earlier, as the name suggests, associated with a saw mill [458023].

Mills the many rivers and streams of South Westmorland and adjacent Lancashire provided power for hundreds of mills centuries ago. A considerable number are mentioned in this work but many more are itemised in *Water-Power Mills of South Westmorland on the Kent, Bela and Gilpin and their Tributaries* by John Somervell (1930). This actually lists and describes 101 mills. Another work is the *Watermills of Cumbria: a close look at corn mills with over 50 plans and diagrams* by Mike Davies-Shiel (1978).

Millses Dockray [397217].

Miners Crag the W face of High Spy overlooking Newlands Beck comprises a lengthy precipice called Eel Crags. The most southerly of these crags, Miners Crag, overlooks disused mine workings while at its rear are the former Rigghead Quarries [231158].

Mint, River see **River Mint**.

Minum Crag High Spy [236166].

Mire House off the B5322 [315239].

Mire House Cottage E Bassenthwaite Lake. Alongside the A591. Mirehouse slightly to its N [234278].

Mire Side Hill SSE Skelwith Fold 124m (407ft) [352025].

Mirebank Plantation NNW Helton [501225].

Mirefoot alongside Potter Fell Road [499977] ...foot of the bog or bog at the foot.

Mireground Corney [117912].

Mirehouse N of Keswick off the A591 and near the head of Bassenthwaite Lake. Built in 1666 and owned by the Spedding family since the beginning of the 19th century. Many famous writers including Carlyle, Southey, Tennyson and Wordsworth were entertained here. An early Spedding spent years writing the classic *The Life and Letters of Frances Bacon* in 14 volumes and it was while staying at Mirehouse in 1835 and sitting on the shore of Bassenthwaite Lake near St. Bega's Church that Tennyson wrote his famous *Morte d'Arthur*. House opening times are limited but the grounds and tearoom are open daily [232284].

Mires Beck rises E slope Birkhouse Moor and joins Glenridding Beck at 380169.

Miresbeck Glenridding. Alongside Mires Beck [378167].

Mireside alongside the A5074 [437907] ...side of the marsh/mere.

Mireside Ennerdale [104160].

Miresyke Loweswater. Between the Loweswater to Mockerkin road and that to Mosser [122225].

Mirethwaite barn alongside Sleddale Beck [538109].

Mirk Gill rises WNW Little Ladstones. Joins Peathill Gill at 543128. The latter becomes Thornship Gill before joining the River Lowther at Thornship at 556141 ...murky (gloomy dark, muddy) stream.

Mirk Cove below the summit of Little Scoat Fell [161116].

Mirk Hill [434917] ...the dark (murky) hill.

Mirk Lane connects the A591 at Brockhole to Holbeck Lane [393014] ...dark/muddy lane.

Mirk Lane section of minor road from Brandlingill to Low Lorton [129269].

Mirklin Cove deep cove W Steeple [152117] ...the first element is 'dark'.

Mirkside E Naddle valley [511148].

Mislet small community including a farm alongside a minor road between the Ings to Troutbeck road and the A591. Once a Quaker stronghold and there is an old Quaker burial ground here. A Quaker Meeting House was opened at the beginning of the 18th century and closed in 1821. Subsequently converted to cottage property. A Quaker School was once established here. Mislet was bequeathed as part of the Crosthwaite Estate to the NT in 1986 [432996] ...possibly Michel's/Mitchell's sheiling (summer pasture).

Mislet Plantation small copse W Borrans Lane [428007].

Mitchell Cove below Green Gable. The source of Mitchell Gill [218108] ...the EPNS suggests that the name is probably associated with the family of Thomas Mitchell referred to in the Crosthwaite Parish Register of 1718.

Mitchell Gill rises Mitchell Cove below Green Gable at 218108 and joins Styhead Gill at 226106.

Mitchell Knotts NE Far Sawrey [384959].

Mitchelland a traditional old Westmorland farmhouse considerably modernised. Situated alongside the B5284 to Winster road [434951]. The rounded hill opposite Mitchelland is a classic example of a drumlin (see **Drumlin**) ...land of the old established family of Michel/Mitchell.

Mitchelland Plantation alongside the B5284 [433954].

Mite, River see **River Mite**.

Mite Houses off the minor road, A595 to Saltcoats. Near the River Mite [081975].

Mitebank Marsh alongside the River Mite [088973].

Miterdale the valley of the River Mite. In its upper reaches a pleasant, secluded and unfrequented valley with the Mite flowing from its source high on the slope of Illgill Head. At the valley head the infant river drops over a spectacular ampitheatre of cliffs and crags. Today, the upper valley possesses several ruined farmsteads, an outdoor pursuits centre, a farm, much woodland and buildings which once housed a large bobbin mill and the pond which served the mill [152015].

Miterdale Forest Forestry Commission land, Miterdale [137015].

Miterdale Head ruined farmstead, Miterdale [161025].

Miterdale Head Moss between Miterdale and Boot. Possesses an unnamed tarn [167017].

Miteside as its name suggests it is situated alongside the River Mite. Below Muncaster Fell [101984].

Moasdale Beck Stonesty Gill and an unnamed stream combine at 240033 to become Moasdale Beck. This is joined by Clemety Sike at 246018 before entering the River Duddon near Cockley Beck Bridge at 247017 ...see **Mosedale** below.

Molds below Hindscarth Edge [216154].

Moment Brow below Moment Crag, Far Easedale [312101].

Moment Crag on ridge N Far Easedale [311102].

Monk Coniston Hall large mansion at the head of Coniston Water. Home for many years of a branch of the notable landowning Marshall family one of whom was responsible for damming and, in effect, making the present High Arnside Tarn, Tarn Hows and Yew Tree Tarn. The last family to own Monk Coniston as a private residence were the grandparents of noted pastel artist, Christopher Assheton-Stones. The hall was given anonymously to the NT in 1945 a year after the large Monk Coniston Estate was acquired by the Trust. Subsequently, the building was let to the Holiday Fellowship today known as HF Holidays [318983] ...the land was once owned by the monks of Furness Abbey.

Monk Coniston Moor E side Coniston Water in the Grizedale Forest Park [324970].

Monk Coniston Tarns see **Tarn Hows**.

Monk Moors off the A595 to the coast road alongside Eskmeals [091926] ...possible connection with the monks of Furness or Calder Abbey.

Monks Bridge known locally as Matty Benn's Bridge. Attractive old packhorse bridge over the upper River Calder [064102] ...the name implies a former connection with Calder Abbey and, in fact, the area of the Calder Valley between Calder Bridge and Monks Bridge provides several place names with obvious religious connections.

Moor alongside the A591 [283230].

Moor Divock Moor Divock is part of Askham Fell and lies to the W of Halton and to the E of the High Street Roman Road. It is of particular interest to both the antiquarian and the archaeologist for it is the site of many tumuli of which a large number are now covered by bracken. Over 100 years ago M W Taylor wrote in the *Transactions of the Cumberland and Westmorland Antiquarian Society* (Original Series) that in a distance of just over 1km (0.75 mile) there were 9 bronze age stone circles. Today only one is recognisable and there is possibly the remains of a second. Nearby, alongside the course of the Roman Road there is another stone circle called 'The Cockpit' [483222] which was more than likely used as a pit for cockfighting. To the NNE of the moor and to the W of the track from Askham there is an ancient British settlement site with a nearby tumulus. There is also a megalithic Cop Stone (Top Stone) [496216] which may have been one of another circle of stones and a Threepow Raise [482219], a disputed boundary marked by a tumulus. There are also numerous Shake Holes, Wofa (wolf) Holes, Pulpit Holes (circular holes), Dewpot Holes, small tarns and a disused quarry to trap the unwary walker. Where the path from Askham to Howtown crosses Moor Divock it does so by an exceedingly wet area which Alfred Wainwright describes in his *Far Eastern Fells* as "Possibly the worst bog on any regular Lakeland path" [490220] ...similar to Devoke Water but in this case it could mean the dark moor or the name of a person who owned it or lived near it.

Moor End ESE Gubbergill. Off a track from the A595 to Santon Bridge [088991].

Moor Farm Torver [282937].

Moor Gill flows out of Long Moss Tarn and joins Coniston Water at Moor Gill Foot [297939].

Moor Gill Foot foot of Moor Gill where the latter enters Coniston Water [297939].

Moor Head head of Applethwaite Common [429039].

Moor House Duddon valley [209952].

Moor How E Red Dell Beck [288993].

Moor How E Birks Road. N Moor How Park. Rises to 229m (751ft) [397911].

Moor How Crag Duddon valley [218958].

Moor How Park S Moor How [396903].

Moor How Plantation alongside Birks Road [394912].

Moor Howe hilly area near the junction of Moorhowe Road and Dubbs Road [425006].

Moor Lane Satterthwaite. Bridleway between Satterthwaite and Grizedale [331923].

Moor Moss boggy area at the head of Far Easedale [299101].

Moor Side lower NNE slope Birkhouse Moor looking across Glenridding Beck to Glenridding Screes [366170].

Moorahill Farm W Bampton, E Carhullan and N Cawdale Beck [494182] ...moorland hill farm.

Moorend between Pooley Bridge and Barton off the B5320 [479254].

Moorend Farm off the minor road connecting the A5091 with the minor road, Matterdale Rigg to the A592 [405231].

Moorgate NW Gasketh. Long Gutter alongside [095990].

Moorhowe Road Moor Howe/Dubbs Road down to the A592 [420008].

Moorside Corney [111916].

Moorside Wood Irton. High and Low Moorside nearby [081017].

Morris Brow Lowther Park above Burtree Scar [527226] ...moor hills brow.

Morris Dancing popular in Cumbria and other rural areas of the country. Believed to originate from the ancient ritual dances with the name Morris derived from 'morisco' meaning Moorish. Cecil Sharp (1859-1924) whose recordings of several dances prevented them from extinction suggested that the name may have arisen from the fact that some of the participants blackened their faces which was suggestive of the African Moors. Of the several troupes of dancers in Cumbria there springs to mind the Belfagan Women's Morris Dancers, the Carlisle Sword, Cumberland Morris Men, Morris & Clog and Westmorland Step and Garland.

Mortal Man Hotel Troutbeck. At the N end of the village. Originally the White House Inn when it was erected in the second half of the 17th century. Renamed in the early 18th century and in the 1880s the old building was incorporated into a much larger building. Takes its name from the original sign painted by artist and customer, Julius Caesar Ibbotson (1759-1817) about 1800. This disappeared years ago but, like its modern replica, depicted two locals, one fat and one lean, and with the following words issuing from their mouths:

Thou mortal man that liveth by bread
How come thy nose to be so red?
Thou silly ass that looks so pale
It is by drinking Sally Birkett's ale.

Sally Birkett was an early landlady.

Mortar Crag Place Fell. NNE of the summit [409180].

Mortimere private artificial tarn in the grounds of Brathay Hall. Created from a small existing pond by Mike Mortimer, one time director of studies at the hall. He died in 1983 but his name lives on as a lasting memorial in the name of the tarn 55m (180ft) [364029].

Mosedale a continuation of Swindale. Centuries ago it was part of a major drove road from Ambleside to Appleby via the Garburn Pass to Kentmere then on to Sadgill and up Longsleddale to Mosedale. Here one route went down Swindale and one along Wet Sleddale to join principal drove roads to Appleby and Lancashire. The now derelict Mosedale Cottage was presumably associated at one time with the former substantial Mosedale Quarry and its satellites. Over the years since it has, like Skiddaw House, been used as a shelter for shepherds and occasionally by climbing and fell-walking groups. [498095] ...the valley of the mosses or peat bogs.

Mosedale valley down which Moasdale Beck flows on its way to join the River Duddon at Cockley Beck. On earlier maps the valley is often called Moasdale which is unusual considering that the other two 'mossy/boggy valleys', in the Lake District are listed under Mosedale as are five other Mosedale Becks. In the 13th century Moasdale was Mosedale. Wainwright considers that the spelling Moasdale is "probably an aberration" [239032].

Mosedale impressive valley running NW from Wasdale Head to the col between Pillar and Red Pike. Down it flows Mosedale Beck [179101].

Mosedale lengthy valley down which flows Mosedale Beck from its source at Floutern Tarn to Park Beck, Loweswater. To its W is the ridge culminating in Hen Comb and to its E is Mellbreak [140184].

Mosedale Beck rises slope Great Dodd. Joined by Rowantree Gill, Rowantree Beck, Mother Sike, Caral Beck and joins the River Glenderamackin at 350264.

Mosedale Beck rises on watershed beyond the head of Mosedale at 486089. Joined by Great Grain Gill, Little Mosedale Beck and Swine Gill on its way down Mosedale. Drops over the spectacular Forces into Swindale where it is met by Hobgrumble Gill at 504120 and becomes Swindale Beck. This eventually joins the R Lowther.

Mosedale Beck Rowantree Beck rises on N slope of Great Dodd at 342210. Joined by Rowantree Gill and several other unnamed streams it becomes Mosedale Beck just below Mariel Bridge at 350227. Subsequently joined by Mother Sike and Caral Beck it flows onwards to join the R Glenderamackin at 350264.

Mosedale Beck rises Black Combe below Little Scoat Fell at 165112. Joined by Gatherstone Beck at 179105 and flows down Mosedale to Wasdale Head where it is joined by Fogmire Beck at 188090. Meets Lingmell Beck at 184077 and the combined watercourse enters Wastwater at 179074. On its lower reach is Ritson's Force, a waterfall named in memory of Will Ritson of Wasdale Head, (see also **Wasdale Head**).

Mosedale Beck rises Floutern Tarn and descends Mosedale to join Park Beck at 137209.

Mosedale Cottage see **Mosedale** (below Swindale).

Mosedale Crags W slope Kirk Fell overlooking Mosedale [186104].

Mosedale Holly Tree A solitary tree named on the OS map in Mosedale, Loweswater Fells [142183].

Mosedale Quarry disused large quarry sited alongside Mosedale and behind Mosedale Cottage [494097].

Mosedale Viaduct carries the former Keswick-Penrith railway line over Mosedale Beck [355258].

Mosedalebeck Fold sheepfold [354229].

Mosergh Farm NNE of Garnett Bridge [526999] ...probably from the Mosergh family whose name is derived from 'hill pasture in the bog'.

Moses Trod sometimes referred to as Moses Sledgate although the rocky and at times narrow trod/path in question was obviously most unsuitable for sledges. Perhaps the name was a corruption of Slategate meaning the way by which slate was transported from the Honister Quarries to Wasdale and West Cumberland by packhorse. Legend has it that a Honister quarryman by the name of Moses Rigg used the route to smuggle illicit whisky and more than likely valuable wadd/graphite. From the Drum House on the old tramway from Honister Pass the Trod passes along the slope of Grey Knotts, the W slopes of Brandreth and Green Gable and through Stone Cove. High up on nearby Great Gable there are still remains of a hut believed to have been one of Moses' many secret stores and also claimed to be the highest place ever chosen for a building in England. The route then passes through Beck Head, the col between Great Gable and Kirk Fell, from where it drops down above and to the E of Gable Beck to Lingmell Beck which it follows to Wasdale Head. The Trod was last used commercially in the mid-19th century.

Moss Beck two tributaries rise on Buttermere Moss at 191169 and 197168 respectively and join forces at 193173 to become Moss Beck which flows over Moss Force before joining Keskadale Beck at 197177.

Moss Cottage Loweswater [146216].

Moss Crag Glencoyne Wood. Overlooks the foot of Glencoyne and Ullswater [385183].

Moss Crag High Rigg, W St John's in the Vale [309212].

Moss Crag between Quarry Gutter and Wash Dub Beck [241963].

Moss Crag large boulder alongside the road over Honister Pass. Much photographed and and the subject of many paintings [213147].

Moss Dikes between minor road, B5322-A66, and minor road, Threlkeld Bridge-Naddle Bridge-A66 [311240].

Moss Dub Ennerdale. Shallow pool near the River Liza. The Liza Path passes alongside [146137].

Moss Eccles Tarn second largest of the Claife Heights tarns. Owned by the National Trust and a Site of Special Scientific Interest. Situated alongside the bridleways from Near and Far Sawrey to High Wray and Belle Grange. A favourite place of Beatrix Potter and she and her husband stocked it with brown trout, built a boathouse and spent many happy hours in a small rowing boat on the tarn. This, recovered from the bed of the tarn, is now on display at the Windermere Steamboat Museum. With nearby Esthwaite Water, Moss Eccles Tarn provides the setting for Beatrix's *Tale of Jeremy Fisher*. Fishing is for brown trout by permit from the WADAA. Permits are obtainable from the Tower Bank Arms, Near Sawrey, C170m (C558ft) [372968].

Moss End Wood W shore Windermere between High Cunsey-Graythwaite road and the Hawkshead-Newby Bridge road [375922].

Moss Force spectacular waterfall on Moss Beck [193174].

Moss Gill rises E Haweswater and Brown Howe at 488124 and joins Guerness Gill at 488130. This joins Haweswater at 481134.

Moss Mire between Comb Crags and Watendlath Beck [268179].

Moss Plantation Eskdale. S High Eskholme [119976].

Moss Rigg Quarry Moss Rigg Wood [312024].

Moss Rigg Wood alongside the track from High Tilberthwaite to Little Langdale [314025].

Moss Side in the triangle of land formed by the Staveley by-pass, Crook Road and the railway line. Alongside the Dales Way long-distance walking route [471977].

Moss Side off minor road from the Underbarrow-Crosthwaite road to the A5074. Little Moss Side across the road [451906].

Moss Side S Ratherheath Lane [485955].

Moss Side Tarn shown but not named on the OS map. Shallow tarn with little open water. Between Ratherheath Lane and Moss Side 105m (344ft) [483956].

Moss Wood E bank Bassenthwaite Lake [220300].

Mossdale Bay Ullswater [388181].

Mossdale Beck rises below Heron Pike at 377178 and joins Ullswater at 388180.

Mosser centuries ago it was Mosergh(e). The village of Mosser is situated on either side of the road from Sosgill to Eaglesfield and Lorton. Before the Dissolution, Mosser possessed a chantry [114248]. Centuries ago the road from Lamplugh via Sosgill through Mosser to Cockermouth was an old drove road and at times would have been far busier than it is today ...shieling in the moss.

Mosser Beck two major tributaries rise at 132239 and 132235. Met by Cat Gill at 117260. Subsequently becomes Sandy Gill which enters the River Cocker at 137271.

Mosser Fell in the Fellbarrow Group. Its summit is Fellbarrow at 416m (1365ft) [132242].

Mosser Mains Mosser [115251] ...see **Mains** in Reference Section.

Mossergate Farm Mosser [117246].

Mosshause Gill rises high on fell W Thirlmere at 298136 and joins Harrop Tarn at 311137.

Mossmire Coppice E High Lodore. W Watendlath Beck [267182].

Mossy Beck rises 483217. Joined by Nesgillhow Beck and Little Mossy Beck before entering Heltondale Beck at 495206.

Mossydale boggy area below Mart Crag, Deepdale, and between the two major head streams which join in upper Deepdale to form a substantial Deepdale Beck [375124].

Mother Sike rises Wolfcrag Moss 359225 and joins Mosedale Beck at 353229.

Mothersike Brow section of Old Coach Road, St John's in the Vale-Dockray [355227].

Motor Vessels - Swan, Swift, Teal & Tern on Windermere, see under the particular name.

Mould Rigg Kentmere Park [447033] ...hill top on the ridge.

Mouldry Bank above Miners Bridge, Coniston (296982) ...possibly from molda/moldi meaning crown or hilltop.

Mouldry Bank Beck rises 297987 and joins Church Beck at 299978.

Mount Barrow between Calgarth Hall and Calgarth Park [400999] ...the EPNS suggests that this is possibly the modern form of the long lost Monkbarrow (Monk hill) which took its name from being part of the endowment of the chapel of Lady Holme.

Mountain Biking the mountain bike or ATB (all-terrain bike) with its multiple gears and thicker more rugged tyres than the conventional cycle has provided a relatively new sport. Love it or hate it the sport has developed in the hilly and mountainous areas of the Lake District and mountain bike racing has recently become a feature in the famous Grasmere Sports. Biking on public footpaths is prohibited but there are rights of way on bridleways (must give way to walkers and horseriders) and byeways. These are designated cycle routes and there are several long distance routes. Bikes can be hired and there are guides available from book sellers, information offices or cycle dealers.

Mountain Goat Company Windermere-based Mountain Goat Co operates daily tours and excursions, package holidays and private hire. It began its life as a scheduled service operator and celebrated its Silver Jubilee in 1977. At the time of writing the company operates seven 16-seat minibuses.

Mountain Pinfold sheepfold adjoining Scalderskew Wood and near Worm Gill [090090] ...pound/enclosure on the fell.

Mountain Rescue one of the earliest mountain rescue teams was that comprised of workers from the Honister Quarries. This was in operation long before the Keswick Mountain Rescue Team was formed in 1947. Today, mountain rescue in the Lake District is covered by the Lake District Search and Mountain Rescue Association. This umbrella organisation consists of the mountain rescue teams of Cockermouth, Furness, Keswick, Langdale & Ambleside, Millom Fell, Patterdale, Penrith, Wasdale; the Cumbria Ore Mines Unit; Kendal Mountain Search and Rescue Team; Kirkby Stephen Search and Mountain Rescue Team; Search and Rescue Dog Association (SARDA) (Lakes), and many other organisations on call through the police. See **Mountain Rescues /Safety on the Fells** sections at rear of the work.

Mountain View E Holmrook. Alongside track off minor road from A595 to Santon Bridge [088994].

Mountain View cottages, Borrowdale, originally built for quarry workers, alongside Strands Bridge over the River Derwent. Originally called Leconfield Terrace [251137].

Mountjoy off the Crook-Underbarrow road [462932] ...'hill of joy'.

Mountjoy Wood alongside the Crook-Underbarrow road [460931].

Mousthwaite Comb steep-sided hollow between Scales Fell and Souther Fell [347276] ...mouse enclosure or Musi's enclosure.

Muddock Crags E Buttermere (lake) and above the B5289. Foot of Robinson [191158].

Muddy Brow slightly W of the A6 between Forest Hall and Kidshowe Bridge 279m (915ft) [547015]

Muddy Brow Plantation across the A6 from Forest Hall Farm [546014].

Mullender alongside Swindale Lane, Swindale [518134] ...from family of John Mullinder.

Muncaster area and hamlet to the E of Ravenglass principally comprising Muncaster Castle and its grounds, Muncaster Mill and Muncaster Fell ...Mula/Muli's fort or fort on a headland/promontory.

Muncaster Bridge carries the A595 over the River Esk [113964].

Muncaster Castle, Garden & Owl Centre alongside the A595 and 1.6kms (1 mile) E of Ravenglass. The castle has been the home of the Pennington family since the early 13th century. A pele tower stands on Roman foundations and has been extended over the centuries to become today's castle. Some paranormal investigators claim it as the most haunted castle in Britain and it was featured in a series called *Strange but True* on ITV in September 1995. Its 77 acres woodland gardens are particularly noted for their rhododendrons, camellias, azaleas and rare and exotic trees and shrubs. The owl centre has one of the finest collection of owls in the world and is the headquarters of the British Owl Breeding and Release Scheme (BOBARS).

All three are open to the public. For times of opening consult current leaflet or Tourist Information Offices [103964]. See also **Chapel Hill**.

Muncaster Chase Muncaster Castle grounds [104968] ...a 'chase' comprised a small unenclosed deer forest. In this case one held by and used by earlier Pennington families.

Muncaster Fell ridge running NE from Muncaster Castle to Muncaster Head and Eskdale Green. Highest point is Hooker Crag at 231m (758ft) [112983]. Two crew were killed when an Avro Anson crashed near Muncaster Head in September 1942.

Muncaster Head below the head of Muncaster Fell [140990].

Muncaster House Loweswater [147210].

Muncaster Mill see **Muncaster Water Mill**.

Muncaster Mill Bridge near Muncaster Mill. Carries the A595 over the River Mite [094977].

Muncaster Tarn also known as Chapel Hill Tarn. Artificial tarn made by the Penningtons of Muncaster Castle presumably for fishing. Contains three islands. Situated on Chapel Hill, hence its other title, and positioned alongside the path, continuation of Fell Lane, over Muncaster Fell C160m (C525ft) [106978].

Muncaster Water Mill NE Ravenglass and alongside a station on the Ravenglass and Eskdale Railway. One of the few working water-powered corn mills in the country. A mill has occupied the site for over 500 years. However, the present building dates from about 1700. Ceased milling in 1961 but restarted in the 1970s and produces stoneground products [096977]. Open to the public. For times of opening consult current leaflet or Tourist Information Office.

Mungrisdale Common grassy area principally bounded by Scalehow Beck, R Caldew, Blackhazel Beck and Roughton Gill 633m (2077ft) [312292] ...'church dedicated to St Mungo (St Kentigern) in the valley of pigs' + common land.

Munro a Scottish mountain over 914m (3000ft). The handful in the Lake District over this height are often referred to by this title.

Murf Nether Wasdale [131040] ...murf/murth - moor.

Murl Rigg Slope Pillar overlooking Mosedale [180115].

Murthwaite farm, Longsleddale [515007] ...moorland clearing.

Murthwaite Bridge carries track across the River Mite [115996] ...bridge by the moorland clearing.

Murthwaite Knott Longsleddale. On fellside behind Murthwaite [518008].

Murthwaite Moor Wood [097035] ...the wood on/by the moor clearing.

Murton Fell fell to the SE of Murton and E of the Croasdale to Lamplugh road. Its summit is the conical Knock Murton at 447m (1467ft) [095191]. There is considerable mining evidence on its lower slope ...Murton is the habitation/farmstead/village on the moor and Knock Murton is hillock by Murton.

Mustard Hill Grizedale Forest Park 263m (863ft) [320935].

Myers Head Mine (Low Hartsop Mine) Confluence of Pasture Beck and Hayeswater Gill. Drilling completed in 1868 and the mine finally abandoned because of flooding c1878. Scheduled as an Ancient Monument in 1998 and by mid-1999 work was completed on Phase 1 of a project to conserve the mine and improve public access to its site [416126]. There is a smaller mine lower down the stream at 412129.

Myrtle Bay Derwentwater [255192] ...the bay alongside which the bog myrtle/sweet gale grows.

N

Nab projection into Esthwaite Water [358972].

Nab, The see **The Nab**.

Nab Cottage Rydal. Alongside the A591. Before the present road was constructed the drive in front of the cottage was part of the old road. The building was erected in 1702 and was at that time Nab Farm. In the early 19th century it was owned by John Simpson and during this time his daughter Margaret was courted by Thomas de Quincey. He married her in 1817. For four years from 1829 de Quincey owned the property. Later, Hartley Coleridge, son of Samuel Taylor Coleridge, lived here for 11 years, until his death in 1849. Today it is a guest house and also provides English language courses for overseas visitors [355062] ...takes its name from Nab Scar which towers above it.

Nab Crag NE of summit of Birkhouse Moor. Overlooks Blea Cove and Beck [366165] ...from 'nabbi', a projecting peak.

Nab End end of ridge overlooking the A6 from its W [548034].

Nab End rocky outcrops N of the summit of the Nab. Overlooks Bannerdale and Rampsgill Becks and head of Howe Grain [433156].

Nab Gill Mine see **Boot**.

Nab Scar escarpment which towers above Rydal Water. Normally climbed as the start of the Fairfield Horseshoe and is the end of a long ridge which sweeps down from Fairfield over Great Rigg and Heron Pike. The summit cairn, set well back from the edge of the escarpment, is at C450m (C1476ft) [356072]. Between the summit cairn and Heron Pike the path follows for a time the tumbled-down remains of one of the Lake District's earliest stone walls. This was erected in 1277 by Roger de Lancastre to delineate a deer park between the two spurs of high land on each side of Rydal Beck. Thirlmere aqueduct runs through a tunnel under the scar. The commanding position of the fell provides an excellent view point particularly for looking down to Rydal Water and the Rothay Valley ...projecting craggy peak at the end of the ridge.

Nabend E minor road, A66-Matterdale End. Adjacent minor road to Dacre [414251].

Nabs Crag overlooking head of Swindale and Swindale Head [502112].

Nabs Hill [454903] ...'nabbi' - projecting peak.

Nabs Moor W Mosedale. Between Nabs Crag and Howes [502110].

Naddle alongside the A591 between Dale Bottom and Shaw Bank [299216] ...see **Naddle Forest**.

Naddle Beck in its upper reaches called Shoulthwaite Beck but takes the name of Naddle Beck after flowing under Rough How Bridge (Shoulthwaite Bridge) at 300206. Subsequently joined by Brown Beck and William's Beck before entering the R Greta at 303246.

Naddle Beck rises Naddle Forest at 495135 and on its way down through the Naddle valley or glen is joined by High Goat Gill. Meets Haweswater Beck alongside Naddle Bridge at 510160.

Naddle Bridge carries minor road, A66-Threlkeld Bridge-A66, over Naddle Beck [300238].

Naddle Bridge carries the road from Bampton to Haweswater across Haweswater Beck. Thornthwaite Force nearby. SW of the bridge there is a settlement scheduled as an Ancient Monument [510160].

Naddle Bridge bridge carrying the old Keswick-Penrith road over Naddle Beck [300238] ...for possible derivation see **Naddle Forest**.

Naddle Farm the centuries-old Naddle House, now Naddle Farm, is situated at the entrance to the Naddle valley/glen [510153].

Naddle Fell see **High Rigg**.

Naddle Forest comparatively little now remains of the once extensive afforested area which covered Naddle High [495143] and Low Forest [503150] and surrounding areas. Principally, it was the charcoal burners plying their trade who led to the demise of all but a token relic woodland. Other factors were tree felling for burning generally or building, while the inevitable deer and sheep have not helped. It is also hard to believe that the remaining woodland and scrub harbours the remains of many old dwellings most of them built in the late 17th or early 18th centuries and which lasted for upwards of 150 years. The prominent Wallow Crag, overlooking the road alongside Haweswater and the foot of the reservoir, was once the favourite haunt of eagles. To the E of Naddle Forest is the quiet little Naddle valley or glen not as well known as the Naddle Valley across, and along part of which, runs the A591 Grasmere to Keswick road. The area is reputed to have its ghost, a White Lady, who haunts the Bewcastle Crag-Harper Hills-Naddle valley area. However, to the best of my knowledge she has not been seen for some considerable time ...point or sharp end of a ridge or hill or a slight possibility that it means snake forest being derived from the ON 'naor' meaning adder.

Naddle Gate alongside the Bampton to Haweswater road near Burnbanks. Several wooden bungalows, built originally by Manchester Corporation Waterworks to house workers constructing the nearby dam, are now in private ownership [510162].

Naddles Beck rises from spring alongside marshy area to the E of Eycott Hill at 395293 and flows around Greenah Crag Farm and on to join Barrow Beck at 378297.

Naddles Crags NE side of Eycott Hill [388296].

Nag's Head Wythburn, see **Wythburn**.

Nan Bield Pass Kentmere to Mardale Head. Approximately 8kms (5 miles). Part of a once prominent route from Kendal via Kentmere to Mardale and ultimately Penrith before that over Shap took precedence. From the foot of the Garburn Pass the Nan Bield Pass crosses to the E of the River Kent then past Overend, to the right of Tongue Scar, by Smallthwaite Knott, and ultimately zig zags its way to the col. Here there is a roofless stone shelter (Nan's Bield). The route then undertakes a rocky descent to Small Water where it passes three small stone shelters presumably built for earlier 'small' wayfarers. Continues down to Mardale Head where it is met by the Gatescarth Pass. Rises to 640m (2100ft) at 453096 and is the third highest of the major Lakeland passes [456041-469107] ...the pass alongside Nan's hut or shelter or from the Gaelic 'na-n' meaning 'of the or with the' therefore the the pass of the shelter or the pass with the shelter.

Nanny Brow Clappersgate. Country house hotel and restaurant. Built in 1908 as a private residence and converted into a hotel in the 1950s [362035] ...the story goes that before the house was built 'nanny' goats used to graze on the brow and this subsequently gave the building its name.

Nanny Lane drove road/track from Troutbeck to the Hundreds and higher slopes of Wansfell [403040] ...Nan's Lane or Nanny Goat Lane.

Nannycatch Beck rises Blakeley Moss at 062141 and subsequently, after being joined by Lagget Beck, flows down Uldale where it becomes Kirk Beck which continues down to Egremont. It is interesting to note that from the same grid reference Nannycatch Beck flows

S while water from a spring joins Rowland Beck which flows N to meet the River Ehen.

Nannycatch Gate footbridge here across Nannycatch Beck [056129].

Napes Needle outstanding rock pinnacle on the Great Napes, Great Gable. First climbed in 1886 by W P Haskett-Smith, noted British climber. Scramblers and experienced walkers can view its climbers from the Southern Traverse (Gable Girdle) or the nearby 'Dress Circle'.

Narrow Moor section of ridge which connects Maiden Moor with High Spy [237175].

National Park Authority when the Lake District National Park was established in 1951 its governing body was the Lake District Special Planning Board. Since April 1997, responsibility for the park officially came under the control of the National Park Authority comprising 26 members. The NPA actually owns only a small proportion of the land in the park.

National Trust charity founded in 1895. The largest landowner in the Lake District with nearly a third of the National Park under its direct control. This includes over 90 hill farms, thousands of acres of woodland, many beauty spots, several lakes and waterfalls, over 1500 vernacular buildings, and 2000 miles of dry stone walls. A considerable number of National Trust properties are referred to in this work but for more details and other properties, etc. consult Bruce Thompson's *The Lake District and the National Trust: 1895-1946* and *Guardian of the Lakes: A History of the NT in the Lake District from 1946* by Elizabeth Battrick (1987). See also the Hundred Year Stone under **Derwent Water**.

Natty Bridge wooden bridge over Yewry Sike [243945].

Naylor, Jos, MBE see **Bowderdale**.

Near Bank Corney. Middle Bank to its NW [106915].

Near Birkett Bank approached by lane off B5322 [320236].

Near Birkettbank approached by lane off B5322 [322239].

Near Broadgill rises E slope Narrow Moor at 235178 and, according to the OS map, ends abruptly at 230178.

Near Gill rises below Dow Crag at 260981 and joins Tarn Head Beck at 262993.

Near Hill Crag E Seathwaite Tarn. Above Near Gill [257986].

Near Howe Mungrisedale. Off the A66 to Mungrisedale road [374288].

Near Orrest farm at the side of the road between Ings-Troutbeck road and Troutbeck Bridge [419002]. Alongside the line of part of the old Kendal-Windermere road which ran from Ings via Mislet, Mislet Moors and Near Orrest to Troutbeck Bridge. It is suggested that even earlier a Roman road passed nearby.

Near Ruddy Beck rises slope of Red Pike/Dodd at 161160 and joins Buttermere Dubs at 165169.

Near Sawrey village on the B5285 between Windermere (lake) and Hawkshead. Approximately 0.8kms (0.5 mile) W of Far Sawrey. Famous as the home for many years of illustrator and authoress Beatrix Potter who lived at Hill Top and later Castle Cottage. The latter is now split into four private dwellings. The principally early 17th century Hill Top is now owned by the National Trust and open to the public. In 1997 a 4.8kms (3 mile) path called the 'hilltop to the lake path' was opened from Hill Top to the ferry terminal at Windermere. The Tower Bank Arms adjacent to Hill Top has been owned by the National Trust since 1976. Originally a beer shop it later became the Albion Inn before taking its present title. Like its neighbour and other places in and around Near Sawrey the hostelry features in Beatrix's works [370956] ...'near' refers to the fact that the village lies nearer Hawkshead than Far Sawrey. 'Sawrey' wet/muddy place. Both Sawreys are situated in a low lying valley between Esthwaite Water and Windermere. At one time this was a very wet

and muddy area and there are records of a causeway being built hereabouts to enable the pack horse trains and other wayfarers to travel with less difficulty to the Windermere ferry.

Near Swallowhurst Corney. Alongside the A595 [101906] ...near swallow wooded hill.

Near Swan Beck flows through Glencoyne Park and enters Ullswater at 388190.

Near Swine Crag S Far Swine Crag on W slope High Pike [369086].

Near Thwaites W Coldfell Road and E Nannycatch Beck [060129].

Near Tongue Gill rises below Hindscarth Crags at 218160 and joins Newlands Beck at 227166.

Neaum Crag alongside the B5343 [340038]. The birthplace of the St Martin's Langdale Linen Industry (see **Elterwater**). There are timber chalets for self caterers in woodland adjoining ...the north country dialect word 'neam' means uncle. Neaum is also one of three types of slate found in local quarries - London, Country and Neaum (Neam) Tom.

Neaum Wood below Little Loughrigg [344037] ...see **Neaum Crag**.

Neds Low Wood E Podnet Tarn, 120m (394ft) [408925].

Needless Gill rises Stords, Swainson Knott, at 076083 and joins the River Calder at 066085.

Neile Stove crag, Bethecar Moor [311915].

Nelly's Wood ESE Setterah Park and slightly E of the R Lowther [518207] ...Nelly who?

Nesgillhow Beck rises Whitestone Moor at 470205. Joins Mossy Beck at 484216 and this enters Heltondale Beck at 495206 ...hill with a new shieling beside the stream.

Nest Brow brow on the A591 between Causeway Foot and Moor. The properties of High and Low Nest are approached off the A591 here [289226].

Nether Beck one major tributary rises Scoat Tarn at 158103 and another E Haycock at

150107. Joined by Waver Beck, Ladcrag Beck, Ash Gill, Standy Gill and Black Beck before entering Wastwater at 163065. In the 14th century it was called le Blakecombek ...nether meaning lower.

Nether End alongside the A593 between Tarn House Cottage and High Yewdale [317996] ...lower end.

Nether House Farm Longsleddale [514003] ...nether meaning lower.

Nether How Buttermere [168171].

Nether Place Keswick [279237].

Nether Stainton off the A595 [114954] ...the lower stony farmstead.

Nether Wasdale area E of Gosforth and near the foot of Wastwater. Principally comprises farms and cottages. The charming village of Strands close by the River Irt is often referred to as Nether Wasdale and the OS map continues this practice. To the S of Strands and the area of Nether Wasdale lies the River Irt and Irton, Wastwater is to the E and the high fells of Buckbarrow, Nether Wasdale Common and Seatallan rise to the N. The tiny parish church at Strands was once a chapel in the medieval parish of St Bees. Two old hostelries sited directly across from one another vie for custom [126041] ...nether means lower and therefore Lower Wasdale as opposed to Wasdale Head.

Nether Wasdale Common large area above Nether Wasdale and on the SW slope of Seatallan [136079].

Netherbeck Bridge carries the road along Wastwater over Nether Beck [161066].

Netherclose Loweswater [147217].

Nethermost Cove deep and impressive combe E Helvellyn ridge. Overlooked on the N by Striding Edge and WSW by Nethermost Pike [349145].

Nethermost Crag between Nethermost Pike and High Crag overlooking immediate E Hard Tarn and Ruthwaite Cove [345139].

Nethermost Pike third highest peak of the Helvellyn range. Overlooks Nethermost Cove 891m (2923ft) [344142].

Nethermostcove Beck rises head of Nethermost Cove at 347146 and joins Grisedale Beck at 363145

Nettle Cove on E slope Rydal Fell near Rydal Head [360111].

Nettle Crag Little Arrow Moor [275967].

Nettle Slack W Wet Side Edge [270020] nettle 'hollow'.

Nettlehowe Crag overlooking confluence of Rampsgill Beck and Bannerdale Beck [439178] ...the crag on the hill covered with nettles.

Nettleslack former 17th century farmstead in Boredale [423182] ...nettle 'hollow'.

New Bridge across Great Langdale Beck at Chapel Stile [317053].

New Bridge over Easedale Beck near Brimmer Head Farm [328082].

New Bridge across the River Derwent at Rosthwaite [252151].

New Close adjoining Newfield Close [224955].

New Close Ulpha, Duddon valley [202935].

New Close piggery off the A591 [256255].

New England Hotel Bowness-on-Windermere. Built 1859.

New Field House see **Greenriggs**.

New Hall Nether Staveley. Dales Way passes close by [463971] ...not so new. It was so called in the 18th century.

New Hall Inn Bowness-on-Windermere. Centuries old inn commonly known as 'Hole in't Wall' because at one time ale was served through a hole in the wall to the adjoining smithy. The latter has been absorbed into a dining area for the inn. A famous landlord was the former Cumbrian wrestler, Thomas Longmire, and a famous guest, Charles Dickens.

New Ing former farm now in ruins, Wet Sleddale [546111].

New Intake Banishead/Baniside [288961].

New Nick see Hause Point.

New Plantation Ulpha Park [191911].

New Road across Lowther Park from the A6 [535241].

New Road minor road connecting A5091 to Dockray. Highest point C430m (C1411ft) [384222].

New South Wales Plantation Grizedale Forest Park [346935] ...see **China Plantation**.

Newbiggin community on minor road to Eskmeals from Waberthwaite [096991] ...new building. Biggin is a dialect word for building.

Newbiggin Marsh N Newbiggin and adjoining Waberthwaite Marsh [094943].

Newclose Wood adjoining Oakthorpen Wood [392015].

Newfield Inn Seathwaite, Duddon valley. Not so new! William and Dorothy Wordsworth stayed at the farmhouse/inn in 1804 and Dorothy records that supper, overnight, breakfast, horse and ale cost 4s 6d (22p in current coinage). In July 1904, a group of workers from the nearby Seathwaite Tarn project who had been drinking heavily were ordered out of the hostelry by the landlord. Before they left they smashed windows and all the inn furniture. They then seized anything and everything drinkable before leaving to vent their anger on the church, vicarage and schoolhouse breaking 92 panes of glass. Returning to the inn they marched on the landlord, barman and a waterworks engineer. The three men stood their ground and were armed. The mob, undeterred by the weaponry, continued to advance. Consequently, the landlord and his two companions fired into the crowd resulting in the death of one man and injury of two, one serious. Police reinforcements subsequently arrived. The landlord and his two stalwarts were charged with one death and unlawful wounding but were released [226960].

Newfield Wood near the Newfield Inn, Seathwaite, Duddon valley [225958].

Newhouse Farm Lorton Vale. Alongside the B5289 [156240].

Newhouse Gill rises Seatoller Fell alongside the old plumbago mine at 230128 and joins the River Derwent at 234124.

Newlands Newlands valley [239207] ...see **Newlands** below and **Farm Uzzicar**.

Newlands area covered by the Newlands valley. Centuries ago a shallow lake or tarn, Husaker or Uzzicar, in what is today the lower Newlands valley was drained in order to reclaim agricultural land. Consequently this newly acquired land was called 'the new land' (Neulandes in 1318).

Newlands Beck rises SE Dale Head at 229147 and eventually joins Bassenthwaite Lake at 227266.

Newlands Beck Bridge bridge over Newlands Beck between Braithwaite and Portinscale [241237].

Newlands Hause summit of the Newlands Pass between Newlands and Buttermere. Sometimes erroneously called Buttermere Hause. The latter was actually on the old road between Hause Point, Crummock Water and Rannerdale Knotts. From Newlands Hause there are excellent views of Moss Force when in spate and of Buttermere at the foot of a steep descent 333m (1092ft) [192177].

Newlands Valley the valley is that of Newlands Beck which flows into Bassenthwaite Lake. However, two entrances to the valley are considered to be Braithwaite and

Portinscale both lying just off the A66. From here the valley passes Swinside, Stair and Little Town before entering its higher reaches between the Cat Bells-Maiden Moor-High Spy ridge to its W with the precipitous Eel Crags, Castlenook headland and other towering cliffs and to its E the prominent Hindscarth Crag and Squat Knotts. This section of the valley was extensively mined in days gone by and of particular interest are the Goldscope Mines and Castlenook Mine. The valley head is appropriately called Dale Head.

Newsham SE Threlkeld [331247].

Newspapers see **Media**.

Newtown Muncaster. It was Newton in the early 16th century [093956].

Newtown see **Lowther Park**.

Newtown Knott Muncaster. Beacon on its summit [095954].

Nichol Dub pool in the River Derwent at Seatoller [245135].

Nichol End W shore Derwent Water. A marina here [254229] ...possibly the end of the rounded hill top that being to its immediate SW.

Nicholson, Norman OBE born at Millom in 1914. Died there in 1987. Author and Lakeland poet. He won the Queen's Medal for poetry in 1977 and was awarded an Hon DLitt by Liverpool University in 1980. A plaque on the front of 14 St. George's Terrace, Millom, commemorates him.

Nick, The see **The Nick**.

Nick Head col between Sheffield Pike and Glencoyne Head. Crossed by the Glencoyne arm of the Sticks Pass route. The Nick rises here [363183].

Nickles Beda Fell [431179] ...either rounded hill top or knobbly rocks.

Nigh Hill 'Night' Hill on earlier maps. E Lord's Lot [448926].

Night Hill see **Nigh Hill**.

Nine Becks Walk Ennerdale. A walk of nearly 15.8 kms (9.7 miles) crossing the River Liza, Silvercove Beck, Deep Gill, unnamed stream, Low Beck, High Beck, River Liza, Gillflinter Beck and Dodsgill Beck.

Nitting Haws rocky outcrop on escarpment NE High Spy. Above the steep Low White Rake by which sheep were driven either up or down or to and from the hollow at the rear of the Haws and Goat Crag [243169].

Nook Wythburn. Former habitation off the road around W side Thirlmere [319129].

Nook near Hall Bridge, Duddon valley [211954].

Nook End Farm end of the road from Ambleside to Low Sweden Bridge. Track and then footpath continues over the bridge to Low Pike and also to High Sweden Bridge [375054].

Nook Farm Underbarrow [466925].

Nook Sike rises near Laythwaite Crags at 473149 and joins Haweswater at 479145.

Nook, The see **The Nook**.

Nor Moss Claife Heights [376992] ...moss to the north ie the N end of Claife Heights.

Noran Bank Farm also referred to as Norenbank or Norman Bank. Alongside A592 S Patterdale [398151].

Norfolk Island earlier House Holm. The largest of Ullswater's four islands [392185] ...named after an earlier Duke of Norfolk.

Norman Crags E A5091 and NE Dockray [398221].

North Lonsdale Foxhounds founded in 1947.

Normoss between the A595 (Waberthwaite) and the minor road S to Corney [109928] ...north moss.

North Top see **Skiddaw**.

Nunnery Beck rises on the slope of Hollow Moor, above Green Quarter, Kentmere, at 470042 and joins the R Kent at 460043 ...obscure.

Nursery Lowther Park [531237].

Nuttera Beck rises Green Quarter, Kentmere, at 466032 and joins Kentmere Tarn at 456027 ...stream by the nut tree.

Nutty Sheepfold S of the summit of Beacon Fell, Blawith Fells [278905].

O

Oak Bank off minor road from the Underbarrow-Crosthwaite road to the A5074 [449908]

Oak Hill High Lorton [159260].

Oak Howe locally 'Yak' Howe. Old property in Great Langdale below Oakhowe Crag [309058].

Oak Howe Needle detached pinnacle of rock on Oakhowe Crag, Lingmoor Fell [304057].

Oak Isle small islet adjoining Park Nab, E side Coniston Water [291902].

Oakbank off the B5284, Plumgarths to Crook road [472954].

Oakbank alongside the minor road from Loweswater via Thackthwaite to Low Lorton [147222].

Oakhowe Crag extensive crag, Lingmoor Fell, overlooking Great Langdale. Spot height at rear 417m (1368ft), 52m (171ft) below the summit of Lingmoor Fell [305055].

Oakland Windermere. Off the A591 [409991].

Oaks former farm alongside the Red Bank-Skelwith Bridge road and near Loughrigg Tarn. Along with the High Close estate it was acquired by the NT in 1953 [342047].

Oaks N slope Burthwaite Heights [189285].

Oaks, The see **The Oaks**.

Oakthorpen Wood alongside the A591 near Brockhole [390014] ...settlement in the oak wood.

Oatmeal Crag N of Near Sawrey. A favourite Sunday afternoon spot for Beatrix Potter. Its lower slopes provided the setting for *The Tale of Mr Tod* [368963] ...meal is a bare headland or hill and possibly oat is 'out' the whole being the 'outer bare hill'.

Occupation Wood NW Soulby Fell Farm. Practically adjoining Big Wood [453254].

Old Brandelhow W shore Derwent Water and off the Portinscale to Grange road [250206].

Old Brathay see **Brathay Farm**.

Old Burtness on the fell slope W shore Buttermere [172159] ...old birch tree headland.

Old Church Bay Ullswater [443213].

Old Church Hotel W shore Ullswater, off the A592. A country house hotel. House built in 1754 and owned at one time by the Marshall family (see also **Patterdale Hall** and **Hallsteads**). Takes its name from an ancient church which occupied a site hereabouts. A 'new' church was consecrated in the 16th century and this was replaced in the second half of the 19th century by the present All Saints Church, Watermillock [442212].

Old Close walled tree area alongside the A593 below Tom Heights [326010].

Old Close near Cockley Beck [246010].

Old Close Coppice adjoining Old Close, below Tom Heights [325008].

Old Close Coppice S Bog Lane [354032].

Old Coach Road a track of approximately 10kms (6 miles) running from Wanthwaite (B5322), below Threlkeld Knotts, Clough Head and Wolf Crags to Dockray. Highest point

C440m (C1443ft). Begins at 316231 and ends 393216. Regardless of its name, doubts have been expressed as to whether the Old Coach Road was regularly traversed by former coaches. However, considering the present 'good' state of the 'road' there does not seem to be any apparent reason why coaches should not have used it regularly in the past. It was certainly used for the transportation of peat and as a pack horse route and cart track. Just to its N and between it and the former Threlkeld Quarry are the remains of an ancient British village.

Old Corpse Road before the church at Mardale Green (see **Haweswater & Mardale**) was granted a burial ground in 1728, bodies had to be transported on horseback to Shap for burial and this particular route was used principally for this purpose. From Mardale Green it zig zags to Mardale Common, passes just below Ritchie Crag and over and down to Swindale Head then down Swindale and over the moors to Shap. The last recorded use of the track as a corpse road was in 1736 but it was certainly used for other purposes for a considerable time after that date and today is much used by fell walkers. It is said that on one occasion while a cortege was working its way along the highest section of the track there occurred a terrific thunderstorm which caused the pony carrying coffin and body to bolt. Three weeks later, still with the load upon its back, the pony was found and the journey completed. What condition the corpse and coffin were in is not recorded. A similar story is told of a corpse being transported from Wasdale Head to Eskdale. In this case the horse bolted and was never seen again except on wild nights when the horse carrying its load is said to gallop over the moors [493122].

Old Elleray the Elleray Cottage in which John Wilson (later Prof Wilson) lived from the time he purchased the Elleray Estate in 1807 until completion of the large mansion, Elleray, the following year. He frequently lived in it for some considerable time afterwards. As a consequence of his pseudonym in Blackwoods Magazine (Christopher North) the house became known as Christopher North's Cottage. In 1966 the 'Cottage' was converted into two houses named Christopher North's Cottage and Old Elleray respectively. The former was bought by St Anne's School in 1982 for boarders [411991].

Old Heathwaite Bowness, see **Droomer**.

Old Hall Farm Ulpha. Alongside it and the minor road from Duddon Bridge or Bootle and W of the Duddon are the ruins of Ulpha Old Hall, a 16th century pele tower mentioned in one of Wordsworth's Duddon Sonnets as "that embattled House, whose massy Keep... fallen and diffused into a shapeless heap." Legend tells of a lady of the hall who fled from a wolf and was drowned in Holehouse Gill. Consequently a pool in the nearby gill is known as Lady's Dub [182924].

Old Intake Claife Heights [371988].

Old Man Breast S slope Coniston Old [274975].

Old Man of Coniston see **Coniston Old Man**.

Old Park S Lowthwaite. Off the minor road from Lowthwaite to Todgill, Ullcat Row and the A5091 [417231].

Old Park Beck rises slope of Caw at 228943 and meets the River Duddon at 219959.

Old Parrock small enclosure (paddock), Bethecar Moor [319901].

Old Parrock Hill above Old Parrock, Bethecar Moor [317903].

Old Plantation alongside the A591 between Sandbeck and Dry Scale Gills [235286].

Old Rake steep end of Hummer Lane [270934] ...old rough path or track.

Old Rectory, The see **The Old Rectory**.

Old Scales Wythop valley. Alongside the road from Wythop Mill to Wythop Hall [194286] ...'skali' - shepherd's summer hut.

Old Windebrowe see **Windebrowe**, Calvert Trust.

Oliver Gill twin headstreams rise Quagrigg Moss at 201046 and 200044 respectively and the gill meets the combination of Long Gill and Hardrigg Gill at 189048 from where the stream continues to meet Whillan Beck at 188044 ...Oliver's Gill - named as such over four centuries ago.

Ore Gap variously spelt Ure or Ewer. N Bowfell summit. Takes its name from the iron ore which, centuries ago, was mined hereabouts and taken down Langstrath to the bloomery lower down that valley. The Gap is the summit of an ancient route from Eskdale to Langstrath and Borrowdale and its highest point is C770m (C2526ft) at 240072.

Ormandy Hotel see **Grizedale Lodge Hotel**.

Ormandy Intakes Grizedale [340952] ...probably similar to other Ormandys in the former Westmorland in that it refers to the manorial name Ormond.

Ormathwaite hamlet in the parish of Underskiddaw. Nordmanthwait in the 12th century and Northmanethwait in the 13th [268254] ...clearing of the Northmen or Norse. Also, possibly derived from a personal name ie. Noromann or Moromaor.

Ormathwaite Hall Ormathwaite. Sometimes confused with Armathwaite Hall at the foot of Bassenthwaite Lake. The hall was the ancestral home of the Brownrigg family from 1677-1800 of which its best known inhabitant was Dr William Brownrigg (1711-1800), a leading scientist of his day [268253].

Orrell, Bob author and writer. See **High Gillerthwaite Farm**.

Orrest Head a pleasant walk of approximately 0.8kms (0.5 mile) from the A591 alongside the Windermere Hotel takes one up to the top of Orrest Head, an excellent all-round viewpoint, and, like Alfred Wainwright, many people's first introduction to the real Lake District. On its 238m (781ft) summit there is a view-indicator and seating accommodation. Orrest Head, like nearby Elleray Woods, is owned by Windermere Parish Council having been presented by the family of Arthur Heywood of nearby Elleray to his memory in 1902. In 2002 a new plaque was unveiled on the summit [414994] ...headland/hill on which a battle was fought. The actual battle is not known but by its commemoration in the name it must have been a substantial skirmish. There is a strong belief that the battle supposed to have taken place at Dunmail Raise may have been fought around Orrest Head.

Ospreys In June 2001, news was released that since April of that year a pair of ospreys had arrived alongside Bassenthwaite Lake at a special nest platform built by the Forestry Commission. These were the first ospreys to successfully nest in England for 150 years and, in June, a chick hatched out. A special observation area was set up in Dodd Wood and this was much frequented by visitors. Two birds returned in April 2002, and weeks later eggs were laid and two chicks hatched out. The open-air viewing centre at Dodd Wood is 4.8 kms (3 miles) north of Keswick off the A591. Live pictures from the nest are beamed onto screens at the Whinlatter Visitor Centre. The birds returned in 2003 and produced three eggs and in June it was confirmed that at least two chicks had hatched.

Otter Bank E bank Swindale Beck near its confluence with the River Lowther [537161].

Otter Hunting a Lake District tradition for centuries until it was outlawed in 1977.

Otter Island Derwent Water [253194].

Otterbield Bay Derwent Water [252210].

Otterbield Island Derwent Water [254211].

Otters otter hunting was outlawed in the Lake District in 1977. A report issued in 1999 noted that the otter was making a comeback in the country generally and in North Cumbria the population was close to its maximum sustainable level while in South Cumbria, although not up to the same degree, the population was increasing.

Out Dubs Tarn S of Esthwaite Water and actually a large pond ('dub') on Cunsey Beck. Situated at an altitude of approximately 65m (213ft) [366948].

Out Scar southern end of Knipe Scar and Knipescar Common. The farthest point of Knipe Scar in Bampton [547187].

Outerside fell to the NW of Causey Pike and showing a steep face to Coledale 568m (1863ft) [211215].

Outgang Farm Helton [506219] ...the way out by which cattle were taken to pasture.

Outgate hamlet just over 0.8kms (1 mile) N of Hawkshead on the B5286. At its centre is the popular Outgate Inn and from opposite the inn a road leads past the Drunken Duck Inn to Skelwith Fold and Skelwith Bridge [355998] ...the 'gate' or way out from the valley fields to the enclosed fell land.

Outlaw Crag E Swindale, above Dog Crag [512124] ...not far distant is Thiefstead. The two names suggest an area at one time wild and dangerous to travellers.

Outrun Nook alongside the Dales Way [435969] ...much earlier Towtron. Took its name from a tarn nearby, now a boggy area, which was originally 'Tofi's lake'.

Outward Bound Centres see **Eskdale** and **Hallsteads**, Ullswater.

Over Beck farthest headstream rises Dore Heal at 169097 and joins Wastwater at 168068 ...'Overboutherdalebek' in the 14th century. Bowderdale Farm is near its foot.

Over Cove E Ill Bell-Froswick ridge [437081].

Over Staveley the township of Over Staveley, the word over meaning 'upper' as opposed to Nether Staveley ('Lower' Staveley) covers approximately 2,500 acres principally N and E of the River Kent and including most of the village of Staveley [474006].

Overbeck Bridge carries the road alongside Wastwater over Over Beck. Walks to Dore Head, Red Pike and Yewbarrow commence here [168068].

Overend farm and property, Kentmere. Alongside the path to Nan Bield [464058].

Overside Wood W of Derwent Water. N Derwent Bay [249220].

Owlet Wood E Outrun Nook. W Borwick Fold Tarn. Rises to 212m (695ft) [440969] ...wood frequented by owls.

Owsen Fell E Lamplugh. Rounded fell rising to 409m (1342ft) [101210].

Ox Pike between Iron Crag and Wallowbarrow Heald [213972].

Oxen Fell fell area alongside the A593, Skelwith Bridge-Coniston road, including High and Low Oxen Fell, Hog Bank and Man Crag. Spot height at 228m (748ft) [326017]. There is tell of the Oxenfell Dobby, spectre or hobgoblin, which haunts the Oxenfell road at night. The name is also that of property alongside the A593 at the foot of the fell [329018].

Oxen House Bay W side Coniston Water near Oxen House farm [291921].

Oxendale valley radiating SW from the head of Great Langdale. Along it flows Oxendale Beck [274053] ...dale of the oxen.

Oxendale Beck flows along Oxendale. Three major streams combine at 264052 to form the enlarged Beck - Buscoe Sike, Crinkle Gill and Browney Gill. Oxendale Beck meets Mickleden Beck at 280060 to form Great Langdale Beck. The lower of the two wooden bridges across Oxendale Beck possesses two metal plaques. One 'In Memory of Simon Alexander 1942-62 Who Ascended Scafell Pike on 3rd August 1961 On One Leg and Crutches'. The other 'In Memory of Hugh Grandfield (a cross here) Mount Aconcagua, The Andes, March 1980, age 23'.

Oxenstone Beck rises below Scarny Brow, Coldfell Road, at 061145 and joins Rowland Beck at 067153. This subsequently enters the River Ehen.

Oxford Crag N Arnison Crag [393154].

P

Paddle Beck rises at 107276 and joins the River Cocker at the Rake at 130281.

Paddle School alongside the A 5086 and Paddle Beck [109279].

Paddock Crag Barf [217266].

Paddock Wray Eskdale [183012] ...toad corner.

Painting the Lake District Since William Bellers published his engravings of the Lake District in the mid-18th century many notable artists have represented the area in all its moods and attempted to show its inherent beauty. Included among these (in alphabetical and not chronological order) were:- Sir George Beaumont, W G Collingwood, John Constable, A Heaton Cooper, A W Cooper, Joseph Farrington, Thomas Gainsborough, William Green, Robert Hills, J C Ibbotson, Edward Lear, Paul Nash, Ben Nicholson, Beatrix Potter, John Ruskin, Francis Towne, J M W Turner and Peter de Wint. Since then countless members of art societies and other individuals have followed in the footsteps of the masters. For information on more early artists and other details consult *The Discovery of the Lake District: A Northern Arcadia and its uses* published by the Victoria and Albert Museum (1984).

Palace How off the minor road from from Aikbank Mill to Eaglesfield [109271].

Palacehow Brackenthwaite. Off the Loweswater to the B5289 road [152220].

Pan Holes old mine workings Scope End [226186].

Panthers seen in Lakeland, see **Black Cat Sightings**.

Paper Moss High Rigg, W St John's in the Vale [307216].

Parish Crag Bridge below Parish Crag. Carries path from Abbey Bridge-Shap Abbey and one from Rayside over Swindale Beck [535159].

Park of French origin the word more often than not refers to an enclosed piece of ground for pasture, or arable farming ie. Barton Park, Park Foot Farm. Exceptions are the large created parks such as Lowther and Greystoke and the former deer park of Troutbeck and the present one of Martindale.

Park Bank steep slope W Swindale between Truss Gap and Swindale Head [507130].

Park Beck farthest headstream rises Sallows at 434038. Flows alongside Kentmere Park from which it takes its name. Joined by many tributaries including Black Beck before entering the R Kent at 454016.

Park Beck Loweswater. Commences at the outflow of the lake as Dub Beck. Subsequently, as Park Beck, joined by Whiteoak Beck at 135210 and Mosedale Beck at 137209 before entering Crummock Water at 152206.

Park Breast Irton Park [119004].

Park Bridge crosses Haweswater Beck below Thornthwaite Hall [515161].

Park Bridge bridge which carries the road from Highpark and Lowpark over Park Beck [145205].

Park Brow alongside A5091 and adjoining Glencoyne Park [398207].

Park Cliffe Farm Birks Road off the A592. Moor How Park to its SE. Park Cliffe Caravan and Camping Estate adjoining [390909].

Park Coppice adjoining Coniston Hall Park [298956].

Park Crags The Park, E side Coniston Water [310936].

Park Farm Colwith. Alongside the Cumbria Way [335032] ...see **Birk Rigg Park**.

Park Fell part of extensive fell area between Outgate-Skelwith Fold road and the A593. Rises to 284m (932ft) at 339024.

Park Fell the fell near the head of Troutbeck Park [430090].

Park Fell Head head of Troutbeck Park and below Threshthwaite Mouth. Principal head stream of Trout Beck rises just below the Mouth, flows down Park Fell Head and on through Troutbeck and Troutbeck Bridge to join Windermere near Calgarth Hall [426094].

Park Foot E Ullswater. Off the Pooley Bridge to Howtown road [470231].

Park Foot Farm E Ullswater below Barton Park and off the Pooley Bridge to Howtown road. A trekking centre. Also caravan and camping park adjoining [470231].

Park Gate at the entrance to Coniston Hall Park [298963].

Park Ground between Torver Brow and Torver Beck [283934].

Park Head Road earlier a track between Seathwaite and the fell road from Broughton Mills to Seathwaite which served the former major quarries of Caw and Stainton Ground and mine levels. Today it is principally a footpath [218936].

Park Hill small hill alongside the minor road from the A595 to Eskdale Green [125975].

Park House Barton Park, E Ullswater. Called Barton Park House in 1823 [471228].

Park House farm on hillside slightly NNW of Dalemain. Frequently visited by Wordsworth in the early 19th century when it was the home from 1804-8 of Mary's brother, Tom Hutchinson [470271].

Park House Lowther Park [532220].

Park House Over Staveley. Bridleways to Longsleddale across Sleddale Forest and over Green Quarter and Cocklaw Fells commence here [470008] ...named after Staveley Park mentioned as early as the 14th century.

Park Moss Ulpha Park [184910].

Park Nab promontory E side Coniston Water. Water Park at its rear [291903].

Park Neb promontory, Great Bay, Derwent Water [257189].

Park Nook Waberthwaite [107930].

Park Plantation Grizedale Forest Park [328952].

Park Plantation S Mecklin Park between Ainhouse Plantation and Miterdale Forest [130018].

Park Quarry Troutbeck valley [427063].

Park, The see **The Park**.

Parkamoor Low Parkamoor below High Parkamoor, E side Coniston Water. In much earlier times it was a small sheep farm belonging to Furness Abbey and remained a sheep farm until acquisition by the National Trust in 1968. Today it is let as a private residence [307926] ...'park' in this context means an enclosure wrested from the woodland.

Parkbreast Coppice below Park Breast, Irton Park [120003].

Parkgate gate house at the SW entrance to Irton Park [113002].

Parkgate Farm SE Dockray. Off A5091 [396213].

Parkgate Tarn Irton Park. Once an ornamental fish pond created out of a smaller tarn by the owners of nearby Irton Hall [118006].

Parkgate Wood alongside Parkgate at the SW entrance to Irton Park [115003].

Parkhouse Gill farthest headstream rises from spring on Little Meldrum at 423226. Flows through Swinburn's Park. Joined by Kirkstyle Gill and enters Ullswater at 426207.

Parkhouse Moss Eskdale [129983].

Parkhouse Plantation Lowther Park, adjoining Park House [531221].

Parknook Gosforth. House mentioned in 1575 [081032].

Parknook Wood Gosforth. NE Parknook [084035].

Parrocks Gill rises 234188 and joins Newlands Beck at 231189 ...stream by the paddock.

Parks Underbarrow. Off the Brigsteer to Underbarrow road [470911].

Parsonage Farm Irton [093003].

Parkspring Wood W southern section of Cunswick Scar [487928] ...'spring' here refers to 'copse'.

Pass of Dunmail Raise see **Dunmail Raise**.

Pasture Beck rises Threshthwaite Cove at 424106 and runs down through Pasture Bottom (Threshwaite Mouth Glen) to meet Hayeswater Gill at 416127 and alongside Hartsop to join Goldrill Beck at 402133.

Pasture Bottom also called Threshthwaite Mouth Glen. Foot of Hartsop Dodd (Low Hartsop Dodd) and alongside Pasture Beck [418120].

Pate Bield near Far End, N Coniston village [300982] ...'pate' is a northern name for the badger and this is most likely the origin of the name - badger's shelter/den. Other bields associated with animals include deer, fox, goose and otter.

Patterdale village on the A592 1.6kms (1 mile) S Glenridding and just past the head of Ullswater. Tradition has it that it is named after St Patrick who, after his ship foundered on the Duddon Sands in AD 540, walked over the mountains to this lonely spot. It is more likely, however, that a later landowner, Patrick or Patric, gave his name to the area. In the 12th century it was Patrichesdale and in the 13th century Patricdale. The village certainly had a 'King'. Centuries ago the first to receive the local hereditary title, King of Patterdale, was one John Mounsey who was instrumental in organising a small force of locals that rebuffed a Scots raiding party on the narrow track over Stybarrow Crag. The Mounsey dynasty continued until 1824 when Patterdale Hall, the last 'palace' of the 'Kings', was sold to the Marshall family, public benefactors, who provided much work locally and planted rare trees

on the estate and elsewhere, (see also **Patterdale Hall**). Patterdale Church dates from 1853 replacing a much earlier medieval chapel. Like Glenridding, Patterdale is an excellent centre for dale and mountain walking. The name Patterdale is also given to the stretch of valley from the village to the foot of Kirkstone Pass [397159].

Patterdale Common two areas are designated Patterdale Common. One, a large area of fellside NW/WNW Grisedale [363152]. The other is on the slope of Place Fell overlooking Patterdale [403166]. The word 'common', as in nearby Glenridding Common and Deepdale Common, reminds us of a time when, before they were enclosed under the Parliamentary Enclosures Acts, considerable areas of high and low fell and parts of valleys were common grazing lands principally without 'stint' - ie there being no restriction upon the number of animals or birds that could be grazed upon them.

Patterdale Hall Patterdale. Originally built by a Mounsey, King of Patterdale, in 1796. Dorothy Wordsworth voiced her opinion that the hall was unsuitable to the valley and she so strongly objected to its colour that the latter was changed the following summer. In 1824 the hall passed into the hands of the Marshall family. The present building, considerably altered and extended, is a residential outdoor activities centre catering for schools and other groups [389161].

Patterdale Hotel an old coaching inn which has obviously been considerably altered since Clark in his *Survey of the Lakes* (1787) referred to it as "the little alehouse called Nell-House." At one time called the King's Arms. Wordsworth and Sir Walter Scott slept here prior to climbing Helvellyn the following day. It was shortly after this visit that Wordsworth wrote his poem *Fidelity*, the story of the ill-fated Charles Gough and his faithful dog, and Scott wrote his *Helvellyn* [396159].

Patterdale Mountain Rescue Team formed in 1964 and in June 1996 mounted its 1000th rescue operation. From its inception its base had been Deer Howe but initial work started on a new rescue centre in July 1998, and this was opened in August 1999.

Patterdale Youth Hostel see **Goldrill House**.

Pattersons Fold sheepfold alongside Styhead Gill [223103] ...the EPNS suggests that the name is possibly associated with the family of Mary Paterson referred to in the Crosthwaite Parish Register of 1768.

Pavey Ark Pavey Ark is actually the cliff edge of Thunacar Knott and is reputed to be the highest sheer cliff in Lakeland. A favourite of rock climbers with climbs like Gwynne's Chimney and Rake End Chimney. Walkers can approach its summit by grass and scree from the dam at Stickle Tarn or by North Rake while scramblers can join North Rake by Easy Gully. For more experienced scramblers there is the exhilarating Jack's Rake, classified as an easy rock climb and used by climbers to reach the start of climbs. This route climbs diagonally across the cliff face. Wainwright in his *Central Fells* provides a detailed description of the Rake 700m (2297ft) [285079] ...possibly Pavia's (feminine name) shieling/shelter. In 1280 the monks of St Bees Priory recorded a 'Pavia filia Willelmi'. Maybe this is the person commemorated in the name.

Peagill just off the Nether Wasdale to Gosforth road [106044]

Pearl Fishing for over two millennia the rivers Ehen and Irt have been fished for their freshwater pearl mussels and even today these elusive and rare moluscs still exist but are protected by Statute.

Pearson's Fold sheepfold alongside Cawfell Beck [112096].

Peat Hill overlooks Wet Sleddale [541121].

Peat Hills [248999].

Peat Howe old cottages S Rosthwaite and across the River Derwent from Longthwaite [256144].

Peat Pot tarn off the minor road from Santon to the A595. Altitude approximately 45m (148ft) [093016] ...peaty hole/hollow.

Peathill Crag S Hardknott Pass [226013].

Peathill Gill rises Gambling Well at 532115. Flows between Bleak Hill and Peat Hill. Subsequently joined by Mirk Gill and before entering the R Lowther at 556141 becomes Thornship Gill.

Peatslack Hill between Brown Beck and Heltondale Beck [471193].

Pedder Stone large stone alongside Wrynose Pass E [289032] ...a resting place for pedlars.

Peel promontory W shore Crummock Water. There are remains of a pele tower here which is believed to have been at one time a place of refuge [151203].

Peel Crag between the River Duddon and Tarn Beck [230966].

Peel Island southernmost of Coniston Water's two islands and principally the 'Wildcat Island' of Arthur Ransome's *Swallows and Amazons* with its 'secret harbour'. At one time it is believed to have had a pele tower (hence its name) or a rude fortress on it. There is evidence of what is believed to have been a fortification hidden under vegetation and it is also considered to have housed a bloomery or the like [215919].

Peel Place off the B5289 at Lanthwaite [160213].

Peel Wood east of the track from Ambleside up Scandale [381058].

Peelplace Noddle SW Stony Tarn. Surmounted by a rocky knoll [197022] ...an unusual name which over the centuries has been Pyle Place, Peelplace or Peopleplace. Noddle obviously refers to a head.

Peer How Hill above minor road, Birks Bridge-Ludderburn. Between it and Cote Hill to its W lies Ludderburn Tarn [406917].

Peg Crag S Buck Barrow [151902].

Peg Huck Well in the garden of Lowther Castle adjoining Jack Croft Pond [524234] ...there is mention of two Margaret Huckes, one in 1544-6 and the other in 1598.

Peggy's Bridge footbridge over Warnscale Beck [190148].

Pelter Bridge carries the minor road from the A591 to Rothay Bridge, Ambleside, over the River Rothay [366060] ...pelter's bridge.

Pen rocky summit of Hollin House Tongue [228967].

Pen SE slope of Scafell Pike. Its rocky summit provides a delightful panorama over upper Eskdale 768m (2520ft) [220069] ...pen means hill.

Pen End ENE the Pen. End of slope leading down from Loadpot Hill over the Pen towards Heltondale [487188].

Pen Intake small intake above Kye Wood, E side Coniston Water [317961].

Pen, The (N Cawdale), see **The Pen**.

Pencil Crag overlooking Thornsgill Beck [377236].

Pencil Manufacture names such as Pencil Mill and Pencilmill Beck serve to remind us that the manufacture of pencils was, and in fact, still is, a prominent Lakeland industry. The world's first pencil factory was actually opened in Keswick in the 16th century using graphite found in Borrowdale and today the Rexel company (the Cumberland Pencil Co) still has a large factory in the town although the graphite used in present-day production is imported. A museum alongside the factory traces the history of the Cumberland Pencil Co from its humble beginnings over 400 years ago through to the present day, the more sophisticated methods of production, and the finished product. Around the beginning of the 16th century shepherds accidentally found graphite (then locally referred to as wadd, a term still used today) under tree roots at Seathwaite, Borrowdale. They discovered that it was good for marking sheep. One old person later cut off a splinter and positioned it in the groove of a piece of wood and then sharpened the point. The pencil was born. The museum is open to the public and each year up to 100,000 visitors pass through its doors.

Pencil Mill alongside Pencilmill Beck and off the minor road from Knotts (A592) to Matterdale End and the A5091 [435222].

Pencilmill Beck emanates from various springs on or around Little Meldrum principally those at 426226, 427229, 427231 and 428226. Flows under Pencilmill Bridge and past Pencil Mill. Meets Longthwaite Beck at 445227 and joins Ullswater at Castlehows Point [451226].

Pencilmill Bridge NNW Knotts (A592). Carries minor road over Pencilmill Beck [433223].

Pengennet Kentmere. Above Rams Slack [453051] ...obscure origin but possibly hill + a surname.

Penn craggy hill S Ulpha Park. E Loganbeck 244m (800ft) [189905] ...hill top.

Penn slope Whiteside C550m (C1804ft) [168224] ...see above.

Pennington Height between Satterthwaite and Low Dale Park [344922].

Pennington Intake Bethecar Moor [319904].

Penny Bank Bethecar Moor. Above Harry Bank [320907].

Penny Crag Wood W Broughton Mills to Seathwaite fell road. S Scrithwaite Farm [222911].

Penny Hill Farm Eskdale. Bequeathed to the NT by Beatrix Potter on her death in 1943. At one time it was the Pyet's Nest (magpie's nest) an inn serving travellers on the old packhorse route up and down Eskdale [194008] ...local surname.

Penny Rigg S Tilberthwaite Gill [303003].

Pennybridge Dub widening of the River Derwent slightly N of its confluence with the Crook (Stonethwaite Beck) [253156]. Other dubs in the area are Gowder, Stang and Wilkinson.

Penrith Does not quite lie within the LDNP but as Kendal is the gateway to the Lakes from the SE, so Penrith is the gateway to the lakes from the NE. With easy access to Keswick and its surrounding fells and the northern fells via the A66 and to the delights of Ullswater and adjoining areas to its SW. Whereas Kendal is the 'old grey town' so Penrith is 'the old red town' because of the colour of the sandstone used in the construction of many of its buildings. A prominent market town, its charter to hold a market and annual fair was granted by Henry III in 1223. The town has many narrow streets and passages to explore and possesses several ancient buildings including the castle, dating from the last years of the 14th century and St Andrew's Church which dates from 1720. Of its many prominent hostelries the Gloucester Arms, the Two Lions and the George have particular historical connections. The town is proud of its links with the Wordsworths. William and Dorothy lived here for a time, attended school here and later William spent summer holidays in the town. In close proximity to Penrith are Brougham Castle, Dacre Castle, Dalemain House, Hutton-in-the-Forest, Mayburgh Henge, King Arthur's Round Table, Long Meg and her Daughters (the last three all ancient stone circles), Penrith Beacon, Ullswater, Haweswater and, of far more recent origin, Rheged Discovery Centre, Europe's largest grass covered building, whose attractions are extremely popular to visitors ...several possible meanings - princially the red hill (from the underlying sandstone outcrop of which many of its buildings are constructed, or chief ford (referring to that over the River Eamont), or chief seat (it was, and still is a major town).

Penrith-Keswick Railway part of the Cockermouth-Penrith line. Opened in 1864 and closed in March 1972. There were intermediate stations at Blencowe, Penruddock, Troutbeck and Threlkeld. Several miles of the former track bed from Keswick now provide a scenic footpath.

Penrose Beck rises Grizedale Forest at 333974 and joins Black Beck at 351987.

Penruddock village 0.4 kms (0.25 mile) N of the A66 and formerly the second of 4 stations between Penrith and Keswick on the now defunct railway line [427277] ...either similar to Penrith meaning head/top end + ford or alternatively hill + red the latter referring to the colour of the soil thereabouts.

Pens End SW of the Screes, Wastwater [148035] ...end of the hill or ridge.

Perch, The see **The Perch**.

Peregrine Falcons in 1967 the number of pairs in the Lake District had fallen to seven. However, by 2001 the total had risen to 100 pairs.

Perlings Bethecar Moor [304909].

Pets Brae below Snarker Pike and W of the Struggle [392078] ...see **Pets Quarry**.

Pets Bridge carries the Struggle, part of the Ambleside-Kirkstone Pass Inn road, over the upper reaches of Stock Ghyll Ghyll [398076] ...see **Pets Quarry**.

Pets Quarry also called Kirkstone Quarry. Stone quarry below Snarker Pike and to the W of the Struggle [393072]. Similar to Pets Brae and Pets Bridge in that it takes its name from a person called Pet or Pett who possibly centuries ago started a small slate quarry here. This was subsequently abandoned and over many years, to all intents and purposes, it merged into the landscape. However, the quarry was reopened in 1950 and from humble beginnings it has been extended over the succeeding years to become the prominent workings seen particularly from the Struggle or the upper reaches of the A592 S of the Kirkstone

Pass Inn. Its head office is based at Skelwith Bridge. In December 1994, permission was granted by the Lake District Planning Board to Kirkstone Quarries Ltd to extend the quarry and allow digging for another 10 years and in January 2000 permission was granted to extract green slate for a further 15 years.

Pewits, The see **The Pewits**.

Pheasant Inn situated on a loop road off the A66 near the foot of Bassenthwaite Lake. Award winning hotel which began life as a farmhouse in the 16th century later becoming a farm brew house. It has been run as a hotel since 1826 (200307].

Philipson's Wood Kentmere. Named after a member of an early local family of that name [458018].

Pianet Knott Lingcove Beck [234046] ...not known. A French surname perhaps? There is another obvious French connection slightly N in the form of Pike de Bield.

Pickett Howe Brackenthwaite [155220] ...piked/peaked hill.

Pickle Coppice Miterdale [152019] ...coppice in the small field or enclosure.

Pickthall Ground WSW Hawes. NW Wood House [210905].

Pierce How Beck rises Low Fell at 306017 and practically circumvents High Tilberthwaite before flowing NNE to join the River Brathay at 317028.

Piers Gill two headstreams rise at 216076 and 213075 respectively and join at 213079 to take the name Piers Gill. This then flows through a deep ravine (Piers Gill), between the W slope of Great End and Lingmell, before joining with Greta Gill at 214087 to become Lingmell Beck. The ravine is very impressive particularly from the Corridor route or the path along its eastern edge. However, its bed is no place for walkers or scramblers as one of the latter found out earlier last century. He fell and broke both ankles and lay at the bottom for l8 days. Fortunately he landed beside a pool of water and was found alive by a party who had decided to attempt to climb the gill while it was in an exceedingly dry condition. Near the top of Piers Gill a Piper Cherokee crashed in 1978. Its three occupants were also very lucky - although injured they all survived.

Pike N end of the Castlerigg Fell ridge. Overlooks Castlerigg and the A591 C360m (C1181ft) [286218].

Pike Crag Buckbarrow [136057].

Pike Crag Seathwaite Fells [254978].

Pike de Bield between the upper reach of the Esk and Yeastyrigg Gill 810m (2657ft) [236068]

Pike de Bield Moss S Pike de Bield [233062].

Pike How subsidiary summit of Caudale Moor to the SW of Stony Cove Pike [411090].

Pike How Duddon valley. Above Pike How Close (239994).

Pike How Birker Moor. E Rough Crag [168979].

Pike How Close E River Duddon. S Hinning House (239996).

Pike Howe above Miller Crag and Stickle Ghyll/Gill. Sometimes referred to as one of the Langdale Pikes [290068]. See also **Langdale Pikes**.

Pike Howe cairned subsidiary summit of Caudale Moor to the SW of Stony Cove Pike [411090].

Pike of Blisco also called Pike o'Blisco. Overlooks Oxendale and the head of Great Langdale. Sometimes included as one of the Langdale Pikes 705m (2313ft) [271042] ...origin unknown but the late W H Cooper suggested that it could be named after Buscoe/Buscoe Sike which it overlooks to its NW. Certainly a similar sounding name.

Pike of Carrs above Carrs, Far Easedale [306103] ...presumably the pike above the swampy/marshy area.

Pike of Stickle also called Pike o'Stickle or Sugar Loaf. One of the well-known Langdale Pikes. A cave alongside the steep scree slope W of the pike and high above Mickleden was possibly connected with a major neolithic stone axe factory which remained undiscovered until 1947, 709m (2326ft) [274074) ...steep pointed hill.

Pike Rigg E shore Buttermere below the B5289 [180164].

Pike Side farm, Duddon valley. Along with Beckstones, Brighouse, Hazel Head and Thrang Farms, was acquired by the NT in 1950 [184932].

Pike, The see **The Pike**.

Pike Sike rises E of Skiddaw Little Man at 272279 and combines with Stile Gill at 277281. The watercourse joins Kitbain Gill at 281281 to become Scalehow Beck which joins the River Caldew.

Pikeawassa summit and southerly top of the narrow ridge of Steel Knotts which runs roughly S from Howtown between Fusedale and Howe Grain 432m (1417ft) [440181] ...pike above the marsh or wet area.

Piked How E Bursting Stone Quarry and between it and the quarry road (281973).

Piked Howe farm below Spy Crag and off the back road from Staveley to Hall Lane [480989].

Piked Howes N Crabtree Brow, Kentmere [446049] ...pointed hills.

Pikes ENE Caw 469m (1539ft) [238947].

Pikes Crag W gullied buttress of Scafell Pike with its highest point being Pulpit Rock, a prominent viewpoint. The crag, or more to the point crags, possess several rock climbs 877m (2877ft) [210072].

Piketoe Knott W slope White Side overlooking Helvellyn Gill and start of Swirls Forest Trail [323168].

Pillar highest of the fells S of Ennerdale and particularly famous for its huge Pillar Rock on its Ennerdale side. Although craggy and precipitous to its N the summit is a grassy plateau with a trig. point, rough shelters and cairns 892m (2926ft) [171121] ...takes its name from its Pillar Rock.

Pillar Cove grassy and stony hollow below Pillar Rock [174123].

Pillar High Level Route see **High Level Route to Pillar**.

Pillar Rock earlier Pillar Stone. Its actual summit is called High Man. Huge pillar-like precipitous crag N of the summit of Pillar. Famous for its rock climbs. First climbed in July 1826, by a local shepherd, John Atkinson. In his poem *The Brothers* Wordsworth describes a tragic event concerning a young shepherd which occurred on Proud Knott. Wordsworth substituted Proud Knott for Pillar Rock [172125].

Pillars large stone survey posts l) E Branstree/Artlecrag Pike and 2), 3) and 4) on Tarn Crag, Great Howe and Brock Crag respectively. Erected in the 1930s by Manchester Corporation Waterworks during construction of the Mardale-Stockdale tunnel which carries water from Haweswater under Branstree to Stockdale from where an underground pipeline follows Longsleddale and on to the Watchgate Water Treatment Plant at Selside. By looking through the raised arms of each pillar in turn to the next pillar the line of the tunnel, many hundreds of feet below the surface, can be plotted.

There are also three pillars, two on the southern slopes of Wansfell and one alongside Robin Lane. These are observation posts along the line of the Thirlmere aqueduct.

Pillow Mounds near Cunswick Hall and Tarn [487939] ...pillow-shaped, flat-topped and rectangular they are claimed to have been identified as man-made warren earthworks used for farming rabbits dating from the medieval period. There are also several pillow mounds sited alongside Scandal Beck N of Ravenstonedale.

Pinch Cove below Snarker Moss [384080] ...surname + cove.

Pinch Crags above Pinch Cove and overlooking Scandale from the E [383078].

Pine Martens rare but not extinct in the Lake District and possibly on the increase now that they are not hunted for their pelts. They avoid humans and are not often seen in daylight seeking their prey, small mammals and small birds, by night.

Pinethwaite Lickbarrow Road [420972].

Pinfold alongside Loweswater (lake) and adjoining the road from Loweswater to Mockerkin [129217] ...pound/enclosure enclosed by stones.

Pinnacle Bield Stonethwaite Fell [249098] ...shelter by the pinnacle.

Pinnacle Howe N of the foot of Haweswater. SSW Drybarrows [497167].

Pinnacle Ridge arete on St Sunday Crag [367139].

Pinstones Point W shore Windermere between Balla Wray and Belle Grange [383998] ...pund stones meaning a pound or enclosure of stones.

Piot Crag on small ridge from Mardale Ill Bell which juts out between Blea Water and Small Water [452103] ...magpie crag.

Pipehead Wood near Irton Hall [102003]

Piperwife Wood Corney [106911].

Place Fell E of the head of Ullswater. An earlier name is said to have been Blaise Fell after St Blaise one of the most popular medieval saints and the patron saint of throat sufferers and wild animals. However, the 13th century version of the present name - Plescefel - suggests an open, marshy area and even today the plateau-like summit possesses many small tarns and much marsh to the N and E of it. The fell appears as a huge rugged mass rising steeply from the lake shore and belies its relatively inferior height. Possesses several subsidiary summits including Round How, The Knight, Birk Fell and High Dodd. Walkers generally ascend Place Fell from Boredale Hause. Wordsworth noted that the last wild goats in the country disappeared from here in 1805. Occasionally, many deer from the Martindale Deer Forest traverse its summit and slopes 657m (2156ft) [406170].

Plain Riggs Torver Low Common. Above Torver Tarn [280928].

Plantation Bridge carries Winter Lane which joins the A591 with Burneside over the Kendal-Windermere railway line [482969].

Plantation Tarn see **Rose Castle Tarn**.

Plattocks Torver High Common [266942].

Plough Farm alongside road to Bannisdale and the old road to Shap. Behind the former Plough Inn on the A6 [532001].

Plough Fell between Buck Barrow and the minor road between Duddon Bridge and Ulpha W of the Duddon 448m (1470ft) [162912].

Plough Inn Selside. Hostelry situated alongside the A6 8kms (5 miles) N of Kendal. Not as old as many Lake District hostelries, about 130 years. At its rear a building which was the Old Plough stands alongside the old road from Kendal-Shap [534000].

Plum Dub pool in the River Esk [135980].

Plumbago Mines Borrowdale, see **Seathwaite**.

Plumgarth SE Irton Park. Off the minor road from the A595-Santon Bridge road to Eskdale Green [124004] ...plum tree enclosure.

Plumgarths hamlet and farm property off the A591 and alongside the B5284 [493947]. A century ago there was a noted hydropathic establishment here. In those days patients occupying first class bedrooms paid £2.50 per week and those in second class rooms £2.20 per week. Plumgarths Farm is now Plumgarths Food Park and Farm Shop. This was visited by Prince Charles on 12 March 2003. Plumgarths was also the site of a toll bar on the Kendal-Windermere turnpike ...plum enclosures.

Plumgarths Roundabout sometimes referred to as the Crook roundabout. Situated at the N end of the Kendal by-pass, A591, where the latter meets the B5284 to Bowness via Crook road and the Windermere Road, A5284, from Kendal. In a field nearby in the angle formed by the junction of Hollins Lane and the A591 stands a tall obelisk shown on the OS map as the Elba Monument. This is a memorial to William Pitt and is inscribed "In honour of William Pitt, the Pilot that weathered the storm, Elba." James Bateman of Tolson Hall intended to inscribe these words on this monument when he built it in 1814. However, owing to Napoleon's escape from Elba the inscription was not engraved. A century later the tablet was placed here in 1914 by Charles Cropper of Ellergreen.

Pod Net on stream E Haweswater [485135] ...eel trap.

Podnet Tarn also known as Birket Houses Tarn or Podnet Moss Tarn. Not named on the OS map. Lies between Birkett Houses Allotment and Neds Low Wood and to its W Ghyll Head Road. Private fishing. Altitude 130m (426ft). Designated a Site of Special Scientific Interest [405925] ...modern English 'pod-net', a particular net used to catch eels.

Poltsgill Sike rises between Measand End and Sandhill Knotts at 481154 and joins Haweswater at 483150.

Ponsonby small community approached by minor road from the A595. In the 12th century known as Puncumesbi [055055] ...Puncun's homestead.

Ponsonby Fell rounded grassy fell to the W of the River Bleng and Blengdale Forest and some 3kms (2 miles) from the small community of Ponsonby. In October 1955 two people were killed when a Canberra crashed on the fell and in January 1993, two died when a light aircraft crashed and its wreckage was strewn over a wide area C310m (C1017ft) [082071].

Ponsonby Old Hall farm. Originally the Home Farm of Ponsonby Hall which was built in the 17th century for the Stanley family. At the time of writing the Stanley family still operate the farm and have diversified into the Ponsonby Farm Park which is open from Easter to the end of September [056051].

Pool Scar E Staveley to Kentmere road [460008] ...scar above the pool. No obvious pool but possibly refers to a widening of the river hereabouts.

Pool Scar E Steers Pool (Lord's Gill) [263914] ...rocky outcrop above the poll/pol ie pool or stream. Mere Beck and its tributaries have their sources below the scar.

Poolscar Wood E A593. S Huntpot Dub [265918].

Pooley Bridge ancient 3-arched bridge which carries the B5320 over the River Eamont. Earlier the bridge and the Eamont hereabouts provided part of the boundary between Cumberland and Westmorland [470244].

Pooley Bridge village at the foot of Ullswater and alongside the River Eamont. Takes its name from the bridge which carries the B5320 over the Eamont. The bridge part of the name was not added until about 1793 although the bridge was erected much earlier. St Paul's Church dates from 1868. The village boasts three public houses - the Crown Hotel, the Sun Hotel, a 16th century coaching inn, and the Pooley Bridge Inn (formerly the Swiss Chalet Inn). To the W across the River Eamont is Dunmallard Hill and to the N, alongside the A592, the mansion of Dalemain. In the season two steamers leave the pier at Ullswater for Howtown and Glenridding and vice versa [471244] ...Pooley, in 1252 Pulhou(e), means the hill by a pool. The latter may have been on the Eamont below the bridge.

Pooley Mill former old mill alongside the River Eamont NNE Pooley Bridge [477260]

...Powley Milne in 1578.

Poor Hag Wet Sleddale [545109] ...poor clearing.

Poorhag Gill rises Shap Fells at 547102 and joins Wet Sleddale Reservoir at 546112.

Porterthwaite Miterdale 143011] ...possibly associated with the family of a George Porter mentioned in the 16th century.

Portinscale village just off the A66 and 1.6 kms (1 mile) W of Keswick. At one time the village housed many of the workers who were employed in the mines and quarries thereabouts but today tourism and farming mainly provide the village's employment. The largest of the three hotels, the Derwent Water, began its life as the Black Dog Inn then became the Blucher Arms and much later took its present title. The Tower Hotel was originally built in 1860 and the other hostelry is the Farmers' Arms. Slightly S on Derwent Water are two marinas, the Derwentwater Marina and Nicol End. At the beginning of the last century a hoard of stone tools and weapons of Neolithic man were found at Portinscale [250237] ...an OE name meaning either townswomens' or harlots' (prostitutes') hut.

Post Knott Bowness-on-Windermere. E of the A5074 and S Brant Fell Road. Area acquired by the National Trust in 1929. Excellent viewpoint from its craggy summit overlooking Bowness Bay and up and down Windermere C130m (C426ft) [406964] ...it is said that the Kendal postman used to sound his horn to inform locals of his impending arrival.

Postlethwaite Allotment in afforested area E River Lickle [248939].

Postman Pat Books while based as a teacher at Castle Park School, Kendal, John Cunliffe first wrote a series for the BBC using a fictitional Lakeland town as his inspiration. The post office in the series was based on that at Beast Banks, Kendal, and Longsleddale became Greendale. The post office at Beast Banks closed in 2003. To date Mr Cunliffe has written more than 100 Postman Pat books and scripts for two 13-episode TV series.

Potato Peg Plantation Grizedale [343944] ...nickname?

Potherilt Hill SW Pickthall Ground [208903].

Pots of Ashness small pools SW Great Lad Crag [145091] ...pools by the ash tree headland.

Potter Fell the land mass of Potter Fell across Kentdale provides the first view of the Lake District as seen by the motorist speeding down the Kendal by-pass (A591) to the roundabout at Plumgarths. A hillocky and hollowy landscape rising to 395m (1296ft) to the WNW of Potter Tarn at 490998. Contains eight named tarns - Ghyll Pool, Gurnal Dubbs, Potter Tarn, Routen Beck Tarns (Lower and Upper) and Taggleshaw Tarns (High, Low and Middle) ...surname Potter derived from deep hole on the hill pasture.

Potter Fell Road links Burneside with Garnett Bridge and follows the lower slope of Potter Fell [505978].

Potter Tarn Potter Fell. Originally dammed to provide a water supply for the Burneside paper mill. Lies at an altitude of C250m (C820ft) [494989].

Potter, Beatrix (1866-1943). Illustrator, writer and sheep farmer. Beatrix Potter began drawing at an early age. Her first book *The Tale of Peter Rabbit* was privately printed in December 1901, and subsequently published by Frederick Warne in October 1902. Since then countless children (and adults) have been entertained by her many works. She purchased a farm, Hill Top, Near Sawrey, in 1905 and lived there until her marriage to William Heelis, solicitor, in October 1913, when they moved to Castle Cottage, Near Sawrey (acquired by her in 1903). Even after that date she received visitors at Hill Top and still did all her drawing work and kept her valuable furniture, pottery and china there. With her royalties from her many books she bought farm property and estates in the Lake District and over the years became an authority on Herdwick sheep.

Beatrix Potter died in December 1943, was cremated at Blackpool, and her ashes scattered on her beloved fells at Near Sawrey. In her will she bequeathed over 4,000 acres in the Lake District to the National Trust. These included 15 farms and numerous cottages. William Heelis died in August 1945. Hill Top was opened to the public by the National Trust in 1946. There are three permanent Beatrix Potter exhibitions in the Lake District - Beatrix Potter Gallery, Hawkshead; World of Beatrix Potter Attraction, Bowness-on-Windermere and Beatrix Potter's Lake District, Keswick. There are several books concerning her life and works but two in particular are *Beatrix Potter: Artist, Storyteller and Countrywoman* by Judy Taylor (1986) and *Beatrix Potter 1866-1943: The Artist and Her World* by F Warne (publisher) and the National Trust (1987).

Pottergill off the Loweswater via Thackwaite to Low Lorton road [143224].

Poukes Moss boggy area on Kinniside Common E Kinniside [081117] ...possibly the moss frequented by goblins.

Pound Farm off the B5284, Plumgarths to Crook road [471953] ...farm in the enclosure.

Pounder Sike rises W Round How at 391208 Joins Aira Beck at 391215.

Pounsey Crag E of the summit of Eagle Crag [279120].

Pouterhow Pike more a lump than a pike W of the summit of High Seat [282179].

Pow Beck rises as Toddle Gutter at 512187 and joins Gill Beck at 513197. This meets the R Lowther at 515201.

Pow Beck lengthy stream which rises from a spring near Skelgill and flows windingly along the Newlands valley where it is joined by many watercourses before it enters Newlands Beck near the latter's entry into Bassenthwaite Lake at 230260.

Pow How overlooks Pow Beck. SW Ullock [243228].

Powley's Hill ENE Hare Shaw. WNW Truss Gap, Swindale 465m (1526ft) [505135] ...from the local family of Powley or Pulley.

Powter How small community alongside the minor road from Braithwaite via Thornthwaite to the A66 [221263].

Powterhow Wood N Powter How and between the A66 and the minor road from Thornthwaite to the A66 [222268].

Priest Gill rises 533030 and drops down to Bannisdale Beck which it meets at 528023.

Priest Pot tarn slightly N of Esthwaite Water. Originally part of the latter but became isolated by deposits from nearby Black Beck. It is said that it took its name because it holds the measure a thirsty priest could drink if it were filled with ale. More than likely, however, its name is derived from its having been fished by monks of Furness Abbey and later by occupants of Hawkshead Hall (at one time the Manor house of monks from Furness Abbey) 66m (216ft) [357978].

Priest Wood Grizedale [339942]. The Ridding Wood Walk, one of the shorter Grizedale Forest walks, passes through Priest Wood ...the monks of Furness Abbey acquired woodlands hereabouts and held them for centuries.

Priest's Crag SSE Little Mell Fell. Summit on rear fell 424m (1391ft) [424233]. All Saints Church, Watermillock, is just below it. The story goes that at one time the local minister objected strongly to the noise made by people hunting in the woods near the church and consequently the Bishop of Carlisle ordered the wood to be cut down. Hence the name Priest's Crag.

Priest's Hole cave on Dove Crag. Roughly 3m (10ft) in depth. At one time a priest's hole or hideaway. Today it serves as a shelter or bivouac for climbers [376109].

Prince of Wales Hotel see **Thistle Grasmere Hotel**.

Prior Bank between Buckbarrow Beck and Kinmont Buckbarrow [143909].

Prior Park between Buckbarrow Beck and Kinmont Buckbarrow [143909] ...possibly a connection with former priory at Seaton.

Priorling near Stakes Bridge which crosses the River Calder [059068].

Prison, The see **The Prison**.

Prison Band steep shoulder between Swirl How and Swirl Hawse [276006] ...'prison' possibly refers to something imprisoned, enclosed or hemmed in. In this case Prison Band provides a barrier between the valley down which Swirl Hawse Beck flows and Greenburn.

Prison Crag overlooks Hayeswater Gill. Prison Gill flows down deep ravine alongside it [423132] ...see the above definition of 'prison'.

Prison Crag S Prison Band on E slope Swirl Band [275004].

Prison Gill rises slope of Rest Dodd at 428136 and drops down ravine below Prison Crag to join Hayeswater Gill at 423130.

Proud Knott on Pillar ridge overlooking Ennerdale. The site of a tragedy involving a young shepherd, the story of which Wordsworth adapted in his poem the *Brothers*. He changed the location to Pillar Rock [182121].

Pudding Beck This unusually named stream rises above the crags of High Force at 191217 and drops down over High and Low Forces to join Coledale Beck at 200215.

Pudding Stone see **Boulder Valley**.

Puddingstone Bank alongside the track from Rosthwaite to Watendlath [268158] ...see **Boulder Valley** (Pudding Stone).

Pull Beck the waters from two springs, one above Pull Scar at 343018 and the other below Black Crag at 343015, join together at 344016 to form Pull Beck. This drops down alongside Pull Scar to reach Windermere at Pull Wyke (364021) ...depending on its actual derivation either from OE, ON or early Welsh pull means a pool, a pond or slow running stream.

Each is applicable in this case. On its course it passes through a substantial pool or pond and enters Windermere at the extremely large pool of Pull Wyke. Also, in its lower reaches it travels leisurely down to Pull Wyke.

Pull Garth Wood NE Pull Wyke [363025] ...for derivation of 'pull' see **Pull Beck**. Garth is an enclosure.

Pull Scar escarpment E Great Cobble [345018] ...see **Pull Beck**.

Pull Woods between the B5286 and the W shore Windermere. S Pull Wyke Bay [366018].

Pull Wyke bay at the head of Windermere. Along with Sandy Wyke it is classed as a Wildlife Refuge. From its innermost recess across to Low Wood is 2kms (1.25 miles), the widest section of Windermere [365021] ...for derivation of pull see **Pull Beck**. Wyke is a creek or bay.

Pull Wyke community alongside the B5286, Clappersgate-Hawkshead road, and 1.6kms (1 mile) S of Clappersgate [362023].

Pullscar Plantation S Pull Scar [345013].

Pulpit Rock see **Pikes Crag**.

Pump House W shore Crummock Water [151205].

Punch Bowl Inn Crosthwaite. A 16th century coaching inn which began life as a corn mill, then became a farmhouse/smithy and finally an ale house [446912].

Punch Bowl Inn Underbarrow. Last of three inns at Underbarrow which used to serve travellers on the old Kendal to Ulverston road [468922].

Purse Bay between Blowick Bay and Purse Point, Ullswater [394175].

Purse Point narrow wooded promontory E shore upper reach Ullswater N Blowick Bay and Purse Bay [393175] ...no doubt so called because it and Purse Bay resemble in shape a purse.

Pye Howe Great Langdale. Former old farmhouse now a cottage [308065] ...magpie hill or possibly surname pye/pie.

Pyet's Nest Inn see **Penny Hill Farm**.

Q

Quagrigg Moss marshy area between Eskdale Fell and Slight Side. Possesses several small tarns and feeders of Oliver Gill and Catcove and Cowcove Becks [203043].

Quarries see **Quarries** in Reference Section.

Quarry Brow below Ill Bell, E Hagg Gill and NNE of large disused quarry [432074].

Quarry Garth country house hotel & restaurant. Set in 8 acres of gardens and woodland off the A591 at Windermere [396008] ...takes its name from a disused quarry nearby.

Quarry Gutter rises near Walna Scar Quarries at 246959 and joins Tarn Beck at 231964.

Quayfoot Quarry long-since disused quarry also called Rainspot Quarry because some of the slate quarried here had dark spots similar to raindrops. The latter were due to angular pieces of volcanic material blown from the vent along with finer ash [253167].

Queen Adelaide's Hill Windermere. In 1840 Queen Adelaide, Dowager Queen of King William IV (the 'Sailor King') who had died three years earlier, stepped ashore at Low Millerground on a visit to Windermere. She ascended nearby Rayrigg Bank/Oakbank (one of West's Stations) to admire the view. The hill was renamed Queen Adelaide's Hill in honour of the occasion. Acquired by the National Trust in 1913 82m (269ft) [404987].

Queen's Head Hotel Town Head, Troutbeck. Alongside the A592. A 17th century coaching inn recently extensively restored. The centuries-old tradition of electing a hunting Mayor of Troutbeck is held annually at the Queen's Head. This is followed by the mayor's hunt. An original Elizabethan four poster covers part of the bar area [414038].

Queen's Hotel Ambleside. One of the oldest Lakeland inns and one which over the centuries has had various names - the Black Cock, the Cock, the Bishop and the Commercial. More recently the building was a youth hostel.

Quey Foot Quarry N Honister Hause. Small quarry opened in 1898 but which had a relatively short life [223145].

Quakers (Society of Friends), see **Fox, George** (1624-91).

R

Rabbit Cat How W Ravenglass [072966].

Rabbit How Eskdale Green. End of Muncaster Fell [138993].

Rabbit Warren alongside the A591 [236293].

Racecourse see **Kendal Racecourse**.

Racecourse Hill see **High Street**.

Racom Bands Rosthwaite Fell. Band of crags rising to 541m (1775ft) [261123].

Racy Cottage S slope Great Mell Fell. Approached from minor road, A66 to Matterdale End, or by forest track from A5091 [396247] ...pasture marked by a cairn + cottage.

Radio see **Media**.

Raikes SW Great Stickle [208912].

Railways Carnforth-Carlisle coast line - first major section from Maryport to Carlisle opened in 1845 and the whole route in 1857. Subsequently several detour lines or branch lines opened from the main line including: the Workington-Cockermouth-Keswick-Penrith line of which the Workington-Cockermouth section opened in 1847 and closed in 1966. The Cockermouth-Keswick-Penrith section opened in 1864 for mineral traffic and 1865 for passengers. The Workington-Keswick line closed in 1966 and the Keswick-Penrith in 1972. The Coniston line opened in 1859 and closed to passengers in 1958 and to freight in 1962.

The Haverthwaite-Lakeside line originally opened in 1869. Passenger traffic ceased in 1965 and goods traffic in 1967. It was acquired by a preservation society in 1972. The 11km (7 mile) Ravenglass & Eskdale Railway (La'al Ratty) opened in 1875 with a 914mm (3ft) guage. The line closed in 1913 and was converted in 1915 to a 381mm (15ins) guage. Closed to all intents and purposes in 1953 but taken over by a preservation society in 1960 and has provided a passenger service since that date. The Oxenholme-Kendal-Windermere line opened in 1847 from the principal Lancaster-Carlisle line and the last steam train to Windermere ran along the line in April 1968 and was then replaced by diesels.

A dramatic accident, but fortunately one without loss of life, occurred on the Furness line at Lindal in September 1892. A goods engine was shunting wagons when suddenly the ground beneath the track gave way. As the engine and tender fell into the gaping hole the crew managed to jump clear. The tender was recovered but the engine sank an estimated 61m (200ft) below the ground surface and is still there to this day.

Rainors off the Gosforth to Nether Wasdale road [091039].

Rainsborrow Cove NW Rainsbarrow Crag and E of the ridge between Yoke and Ill Bell. Precipitous on three sides [440073].

Rainsborrow Crag Kentmere. Impressive precipice E slope Yoke [444068]. There is an unnamed tarn on a shelf behind the crag at 442068. Why not Rainsborrow Tarn? ...more than likely raven's hill crag.

Rainsborrow Wood Ulpha. Below the Pike [190930] ...raven hill wood.

Raise fifth highest peak of the Helvellyn range. Situated between Sticks Pass and White Side. A ski tow on its NNE slope is operated, in appropriate weather conditions, by the Lake District Ski Club, 883m (2897ft) [343174].

Raise Beck rises Dollywaggon Pike at 343128. Bifurcates at Dunmail Raise, from which it takes its name, the principal arm flowing N to join Thirlmere at 323131 and the other S to become the River Rothay at the confluence with Green Burn at 332096.

Raise Gill rises alongside the ridge between High Seat and High Tove at 287172 and joins Watendlath Beck near Watendlath Tarn outflow at 275163.

Raised Fold sheepfold [377244].

Raises E Coniston Water. W Arnsbarrow Hill [305914].

Rake between Slate Knott and Dod Pike, Hardknott [238019].

Rake Beck rises NW Hollin How at 220973 and joins the River Duddon at 217960.

Rake Beck rises between Herdus and Great Borne at 120163 and enters Ennerdale Water at 106157.

Rake Cottages former miners' cottages alongside Greenside Road, Glenridding. At the foot of the Rake [379172].

Rake Crag S Boredale Hause and E path between there and Angletarn Pikes [407154].

Rake Crags facing Black Crag across Blackcrag Gill 506m (1660ft) [313113].

Rake How NE of N top High Rigg [311222].

Rake, The see **The Rake**.

Rakefoot Castlerigg. Foot of Pike [284221].

Rakegill Beck originally arose high up on Lamplugh Fell but was dammed in the 19th century to provide a water supply for Arlecdon. Today the beck commences at the Cogra Moss (Arlecdon Reservoir) outflow and subsequently becomes Wood Beck which helps to swell the River Marron.

Rakegill Wood alongside Rakegill Beck [090197].

Rakehead Crag Scafell. Overlooks Lingmell Gill [194068].

Rakerigg above Blea Tarn [288046].

Ralfland Forest today a forest in name only. It was in medieval times one of several forests in the eastern Lake District. Others included Fawcett Forest, Grisedale Forest, Sleddale Forest and Thornthwaite Forest. Ralfland Forest roughly covered the area between Wet Sleddale and Rayside [538132] ...Ralf, Ralph, Ranulf's land + forest. At the beginning of the 12th century a Ranulf de Briquessart (de Meschines) was the first recorded holder of the Barony of Westmorland having been granted the district by Henry I as a reward for services rendered.

Ramp Holme wooded island in Windermere. At one time called Roger Holme and later Berkshire Island after its then owner the 18th Earl of Suffolk and Berkshire. Given by Mr O R Bagot of Levens Hall to the National Trust in 1971 [394953]. There is also a Rampsholme Island in Derwent Water ...ramp - wild garlic.

Ramps Beck rises 446243 and joins Ullswater at 456235 ...the EPNS presumes 'Hrafn's' Beck or much earlier 'Hrafn's gil', see also **Ramps Gill**.

Ramps Gill valley, major portion of which is in the Martindale Deer Forest. Runs down from Rampsgill Head to meet Bannerdale and become Howe Grain. Down it flows Rampsgill Beck [441153] ...'ramps' here has four possible meanings - l) ramsons, 2) ravens, 3) rams or 4) a personal name Hrafn.

Ramps Gill rises W slope Knott Rigg at 194186 and joins Sail Beck at 190186 ...see **Rampshaw Beck**.

Rampsbeck Hotel NE Watermillock. Off the A592 and standing in parkland between the road and Ullswater with an extensive frontage on the latter [452232].

Rampsgill Beck flows down Ramps Gill from Rampsgill Head at 439128. Joined by Bannerdale Beck at 436177 to become Howe Grain Beck. Subsequently Sandwick Beck which enters Ullswater at 423200.

Rampsgill Head on earlier OS maps and Bartholomews shown as Ramsgill Head. Equidistant between the Knott to the W and Kidsty Pike to the ESE. Its summit is grassy but between the NNE and WNW it shows a craggy, boulder strewn and scree face which looks down Ramps Gill and over a considerable portion of the Martindale Deer Forest 792m (2598ft) [443128].

Rampshaw Beck rises Ashness Fell at 276188 and joins Cat Gill at 270193. The latter enters Derwent Water at 267195 ...stream by the copse where the wild garlic grows or the copse by the beck frequented by ravens. Ramp may also be from the personal name Hrafn.

Rampsholme Island see **Derwent Water**.

Rams Beck rises 280245 and flows down to the A66 embankment.

Rams Slack Kentmere. Between Birk Rigg, Pengenet and Raven Crag [455052] ...ram's hollow

Ramshaw Beck rises SSE Boat How at 178031 and joins Whillan Beck at 184022 ...ram's copse/wood by the stream.

Ramsteads off the Outgate-the Drunken Duck Inn road [351002] ...ram's place/site.

Randale Beck rises between Kidsty Pike and High Raise at 448129 and joins Haweswater at 469118

Randel Crag Bassenthwaite Common. Below Gibraltar Crag [253295]. In September 1943, just below Randel Crag at the head of Barkbethdale a Flying Fortress crashed killing its crew of 10.

Randerside NE Great Dodd C720m (C2362ft) [349211] ...Randolf's mountain pasture/shieling.

Randerside Fold sheepfold [355207].

Randle Cross here the minor road from Brandlingill meets that from Abbeygate Bridge to the A5086 [118278].

Randy Pike alongside the B5286 S Pull Wyke [364010] ...possibly a diminutive of Randolph. On the other hand maybe from 'rani', a projecting tongue of a hill or 'randy', a dialect term for rough.

Range House near Eskmeals and the gunnery range [091924].

Rannerdale little valley running from Crummock Water and the B5289 alongside Rannerdale Knotts. Down it flows Squat Beck and Rannerdale Beck. In its lower reaches there was once a medieval settlement with its own chapel. The valley is said to have been the scene of a battle in the 11th century between the Saxons and the Normans and the setting for a novel *The Secret Valley* by Nicholas Size [166188] ...raven valley.

Rannerdale Beck lengthy stream which rises Wandope at 185200. Joined by Squat Beck at 169186 and enters Crummock Water at 162191.

Rannerdale Bridge carries the B 5289 over Rannerdale Beck [163191].

Rannerdale Farm at the entrance to Rannerdale and alongside the B5289. The farmhouse was built in 1865 and it and its land were acquired by the NT in 1980 [163187].

Rannerdale Knotts low ridge between Buttermere and Rannerdale Farm and running parallel with the head of Crummock Water and the B5289 355m (1165ft) [167182].

Ransome, Arthur author. Born Headingley, Leeds in 1884. His first home in the Lake District was Low Ludderburn from 1925-35 and here he wrote the first of 14 children's classic stories, and his most popular work, *Swallows and Amazons*. Previously, while waiting to move into Low Ludderburn he and his wife lodged at nearby Great Hartbarrow. Subsequently he lived at the Heald, Coniston (1940-45), Lowick Hall (1947-50) and Hill Top, Haverthwaite (1963-65). He died in 1967 and is buried in Rusland churchyard. There are numerous works about him and a leaflet issued by the Arthur Ransome Society *Arthur Ransome's Swallows and Amazons in the Lake District* lists other sources, suggests further reading and shows Ransome sites in the Lake District.

Rascal How end of the S ridge of Wetherlam. Between Mouldry Bank Beck and Levers Water Beck [295984].

Rashfield see **Dora's Field**.

Rasp Howe Green Quarter, Kentmere [467033].

Rather Heath alongside Ashes Lane off the A591, Kendal to Windermere road, and N of Ratherheath Lane which connects the A591 with the B5284. It was on Rather Heath in the early 17th century that Kendalian yeomen and locals met and as the result of a subsequent petition maintained their ancient rights and independence which James I had tried to abolish [483961] ...head of the ridge or personal name + headland.

Ratherheath Farm off Ratherheath Lane [477956]

Ratherheath Lane from the A591 to the B5284. Ratherheath Tarn alongside and also caravan and camping sites [484957].

Ratherheath Plantation Rather Heath [478962].

Ratherheath Tarn large tarn alongside Ratherheath Lane. Surrounded by woodland with two peninsulas practically meeting in the middle making, in effect, a double-shaped tarn. Owned by the Cropper family but coarse fishing is controlled by the WADAA, 106m (348ft) [484959]. Slightly N is the smaller Scream Point Tarn while on the other side of the path from Ashes Lane to Ratherheath Lane at 482960 there is an unnamed tarn slightly smaller than Scream Point.

Rattan Haw ESE summit of Yew Bank [267908] ...possibly the hill frequented by rats.

Rattle Gill Ambleside, see **Stock Ghyll**.

Rattlebeck Bridge Glenridding. Over Glenridding Beck [380169].

Raven largest bird of the crow family. A bird of the high fells. Prolific in much earlier years as emphasised by 30 Raven(s) Crags in the Lake District. Today it is said that there are possibly somewhere in the region of just under 100 nesting pairs in Cumbria.

Raven Crag above Walthwaite and alongside the path from there to Silver How or Grasmere [325057].

Raven Crag crag overlooking screes E of the Red Screes ridge and facing Kirkstone Pass. SSW Red Screes summit [395083].

Raven Crag E slope Kentmere Pike overlooking Longsleddale [473078] ...crag of the raven.

Raven Crag Great Gable. Above Kern Knotts [214098].

Raven Crag Great Langdale. Behind the Old Dungeon Ghyll Hotel. A favourite of rock climbers [285064].

Raven Crag Hardknott. Overlooks the road near the summit of the pass [229016].

Raven Crag high precipitous crag towering nearly 274m (900ft) above the foot of Thirlmere and the road around the W side of the reservoir. A striking landmark and possibly the best known, if not always by name, of the many Lakeland Raven Crags. Popular with rock climbers. Excellent viewpoint down Thirlmere and over to the Helvellyn range 461m (1512ft) [304188].

Raven Crag Holme Fell [312003].

Raven Crag impressive line of crags SE Hartsop Dodd (Low Hartsop Dodd) and overlooking Pasture Beck and Threshthwaite Cove [420112].

Raven Crag Kentmere [455050].

Raven Crag N Allen Crag, Beda Fell, and overlooking Henhow and Howe Grain [431177].

Raven Crag N Chimney Crag, Troutbeck. W A591 [415048].

Raven Crag overlooking Swarthbeck Gill [455205].

Raven Crag overlooks Dale Park Beck [351932].

Raven Crag Eskdale Fell [193042].

Raven Crag overlooks the R Bleng and Ill Gill [128085].

Raven Crag below Brantrake Crags [145983].

Raven Crag Muncaster Fell. Overlooks the Ravenglass & Eskdale Railway [120992].

Raven Crag Birkby 199m (653ft) [133969].

Raven Crag Thorneythwaite Fell. Overlooks the Coombe [249114].

Raven Crag Ennerdale ENE summit of Pillar. Overlooks Ennerdale [179125].

Raven Crag E craggy face of Grey Knotts. Known to climbers as Gillercomb Buttress [223125].

Raven Crag alongside the N arete of Mellbreak [142200].

Raven Crag E steep face of Low Fell [138227].

Raven Crag E A591. Below the Edge [239295].

Raven's Crag E of the fell road between Seathwaite and Broughton Mills [223925].

Raven's Crag overlooking the River Duddon and the Duddon Bridge to Ulpha road [203907].

Raven Crag Tarn small tarn on Raven Crag. Not named on the OS map [230017].

Raven Crag Tarns see **Eskdale Fell**.

Raven's Crag Tarn in hollow E Raven's Crag summit [204907].

Raven Howe alongside the High Street Roman Road between High Raise and Red Crag C710m (C2329) [450146].

Raven's Nest craggy escarpment W Gaitscale Gill [254027].

Raven Nest How craggy hill overlooking the head of Seathwaite Tarn (258990).

Raven Tor high crag ENE Brim Fell summit (276989).

Raven Villa Ravenglass [085967].

Ravencragg off the Pooley Bridge to Howtown road. Used as a training ship for sea cadets during the war years [452212].

Ravenglass village on the W coast at the confluence of the Rivers Esk, Irt and Mite and one of the first Lakeland villages to be made a conservation area [084964]. Of ancient origin. The Romans built a fort (Glannovente) here about AD130 on the site of an earlier fortlet. This remained in use until the end of the 4th century. There is now very little to be seen of the fort particularly due to the construction of the railway in the 19th century which cut through it and obliterated much of it. However, a short walk from the village are the walls of an old Roman bathhouse known as Walls Castle [089957]. Excavation of this was carried out in 1881. Today, some of its high walls still stand but time and weather have obviously taken their toll over the centuries. Alongside the walls there is not only a description of the former bathhouse but also a description and illustration of how the old fort must have looked.

Ravenglass was granted a market charter in 1208. As a major port for centuries it flourished until the Industrial Revolution but by the 1880s port trade had declined and today the estuary is silted-up. Impossible for large boats but a boon to the sailing fraternity and also to seabirds. Ravenglass Gullery and Nature Reserve [070960] is home to thousands of sea birds and has the largest nesting site in England for black-headed gulls. It also houses the rare and protected natterjack toad. Ravenglass is the start of the narrow-guage Ravenglass and Eskdale Railway and nearby is Muncaster Castle and Muncaster Mill ...generally accepted as meaning the land of a person called Glas. Other suggestions are promontories by a stream or boundary stream. See also **Muncaster Castle** and **Muncaster Water Mill**.

Ravenglass & Eskdale Railway narrow guage steam railway which runs for 11 kms (7 miles) up Eskdale from Ravenglass to Dalegarth, a short walk from Boot village. Known affectionately as 'T'laal Ratty' and at least one work states that it is named after an early contractor called Ratcliffe although most people consider that it takes its name, and an appropriate one at that, from the rattling of the engine and carriages as they progress along the track. Opened in 1875 as a 914mm (3ft) guage track initially to carry iron ore from the Eskdale mines, particularly Nab Gill Mine, Boot, to the coast. The following year it began to carry passengers. Closed in 1913 due to mine closures. Purchased by model engineer, Mr Bassett Lowke in 1915, and he converted the track to a 381mm (15") guage. Granite quarries and passengers provided its livelihood until the quarries closed in 1953. Taken over in 1960 by a preservation society and today it is operated by the Ravenglass & Eskdale Railway Co. Ltd. There are intermediate halts at Muncaster Mill, Irton Road, Eskdale Green, Fisherground and Beckfoot. Frequent services in the spring and summer months but a reduced service in winter.

Ravenglass Gullery & Nature Reserve see **Ravenglass**.

Ravenoaks Watermillock. W of A592 [444222].

Ravenscar Plantation Over Staveley [467989].

Raw Crag Ian's Wood, S slope Muncaster Fell [115978].

Raw Ghyll farm, Ings with Hugill [453990] ...row of houses by the ravine.

Raw Head former farm, Great Langdale [304067] ...head of a row of houses.

Raw Pike NNE Raw Head, Great Langdale. S Great Castle How [308074].

Rawfoot alongside minor road from Rosgill to Bampton via Bomby [530171] ...'row' as per hedgerow, or possibly the surname Raw.

Rawhead W of unfenced road from Bampton/Bampton Grange or Rosgill to Swindale [527163] ...see **Rawfoot**.

Rawlinson Nab promontory W shore Windermere. One of West's Stations [386931] ...over the centuries Rawlinsons were prominent landowners in the Furness area particularly the Rawlinsons of nearby Low Graythwaite Hall (Graythwaite Old Hall), Grizedale Hall and Rusland Hall.

Rawlinson's Intake S Low Graythwaite Hall [372904] ...Low Graythwaite Hall (Graythwaite Old Hall) was occupied for centuries by the Rawlinson family.

Rawlinson's Wood Close WSW Low Graythwaite Hall [366907] ...see **Rawlinson's Intake**.

Ray Crag WNW Stonesty Pike [244041] ...crag frequented by deer.

Rayrigg Bank see **Queen Adelaide's Hill**.

Rayrigg Hall Windermere. Occupied by the Phillipson family and subsequently the Flemings and for several years the holiday home of William Wilberforce (1759-1833) MP and leading figure in this country to campaign against the slave trade. The hall has been much altered since the 17th century and even to the extent of adding a S front and orientating the house from facing away from the lake to overlooking it [403981] ...roe-buck or roe-deer.

Rayrigg Wood E Rayrigg Wyke [405978].

Rayrigg Wyke Bay E shore Windermere. S Rayrigg Hall. A protected wildlife area [402978].

Rayside earlier Racet(t). Small community 4kms (2.5 miles) from Shap. It is the northern boundary of the former Ralfland Forest. A spring, known as Kilhow Well, has a local reputation for curing rheumatism [536155] ...roe-buck shieling/pasture.

Reamer Bank S Brown Hill, SW Steps Hall [553131] ...no derivation in *Place Names of Westmorland* but as it lies between two mires, Channel and Tewfit, reed mire is suggested.

Rectory foot of Priest's Crag [430229].

Rectory, The see **The Rectory**.

Rectory Farm see **The Rectory**.

Red Bank Pit today the site of a car park and viewpoint to the left of the road down Kirkstone Pass N.

Red Beck rises Glaramara at 243099 in the vicinity of several small tarns and meets Grains Gill at 235103.

Red Beck rises SW Hanging Stone and below Red Crag at 128102 and flows into swampy area adjoining the River Bleng at 129092.

Red Beck rises between the Side and Crag Fell, Ennerdale, at 104137 and joins Ennerdale Water at 110143.

Red Brow on the B5289 at the S end of the Jaws of Borrowdale [256159].

Red Brow near Ferry House, W shore Windermere [386955].

Red Crag alongside High Street ridge between Raven Howe and Keasgill Head. Just below is Redcrag Tarn 711m (2333ft) [450152].

Red Crag Shap Fells. NW End of Borrowdale, ENE Mere Crag 539m (1768ft) [508067].

Red Crag above Thornthwaite [220255].

Red Crag S Hanging Stone and between Red Beck and Tongue Gill [130099].

Red Crag crag on the precipitous Eel Crags on the W face of High Spy [232161].

Red Crags SSE slope of Capple Howe [438019].

Red Dell valley down which Red Dell Beck flows [285995]. Alongside the Dell are several old copper mine workings one of which, the Triddle Mine, takes its name from the Dell (T'Red Del).

Red Dell Beck rises Red Dell Moss at 287008. Flows through Red Dell and joins Levers Water Beck/Church Beck at 293983.

Red Dell Head Moss head of Red Dell Beck [286009].

Red Dell Head Workings E Red Dell Beck. Old copper mine workings, part of the former extensive Coniston Mining Field [284003].

Red Gill farthest headstream rises just below the Walna Scar Road at 263963 and Red Gill joins Ash Gill Beck at 274950.

Red Gill rises Red Gill Head Moss at 290000 and joins Red Dell Beck at 286997.

Red Gill Black Beck rises below Wonder Hill, Birker Moor, at 173985. Subsequently becomes Red Gill which is joined by Whis Gill at 158992.

Red Gill shown but not named on the OS map. Rises N slope of Grike at 085145 and drops down to near Crag House Farm at 084150.

Red Gill rises Redgill Head, Iron Groves, at 143927 and joins Whitrow Beck at 138939.

Red Gill source of Dudmancombe Gill [205174].

Red Gill rises 096123 between Lank Rigg and Whoap and combines with other tributaries including Short and Long Grains, Hole Gill and Bleaberry Gill to become Worm Gill.

Red Gill tributary of Mosedale Beck. Rises at 130166 and joins Mosedale Beck at 130171. A small mining level on its W bank has not been worked for 130 years.

Red Gill in its upper reaches a long steep scree run descending from Grasmoor End and Grasmoor. No stream marked in its upper reaches but one commences in marshy area lower down. This joins Crummock Water. A path from the foot of the gill ascends alongside the stream and the scree slope [169201] ...named after its scree colour.

Red Gill Beck rises below Walna Scar and Walna Scar Road at 260963. Joined by Lee Haw Gutter at 265956 to become Ash Gill Beck.

Red Gill Head Moss S Wetherlam. Source of Red Gill [291001].

Red Gutter rises at 471186 and joins Heltondale Beck at 473191.

Red House Hotel former Victorian country house, Underskiddaw [252263].

Red How W Gaitscale Gill [254029].

Red Knott E slope of the Hindscarth-High Crags-Scope End ridge overlooking the Newlands valley [223178].

Red Lion Hotel Grasmere village. Former coaching inn opened about the beginning of the 19th century by a Robert Newton on his removal from an inn which today houses the National Trust shop and gallery. The Red Lion's former stables are now the Lamb Inn and Buttery. Nearly 140 years ago Harriet Martineau noted that the "traveller's choice is usually between ham and eggs, and eggs and ham." A far cry from today's extensive menu.

Red Moss Cockley Moor [379221].

Red Moss W upper Stinking Gill. Below Kinney How [077138].

Red Moss Beck rises Dunnerdale Fells at 212921 and joins Dunnerdale Beck at 221916.

Red Nab W shore Windermere. Between Pinstones Point and Belle Grange. Car park nearby at the end of track from High Wray [385995].

Red Pike second highest peak on the Red Pike-High Stile-High Crag- Seat ridge 755m (2477ft) [161154] ...named from its rock colouring particularly seen in the screes in the vicinity of Bleaberry Tarn, the path on the E side of Scale Force and the stones in and alongside Near and Far Ruddy Becks. In June 1944, a Wellington bomber crashed on the Pike killing 8 crew. Nearly three years earlier an Hawker Hector had crashed on its N face killing its pilot.

Red Pike on the ridge from Steeple over Little Scoat Fell to Dore Head. Its summit is 826m (2710ft) at 165106 but there is a lower summit to the S above Black Crag at 801m (2628ft).

Red Scar Beda Fell. Blue Gill rises just below it [415157].

Red Scar W Great Worm Crag [188969].

Red Screes mountain with its summit to the W of the Kirkstone Pass and separated from the Fairfield range by Scandale Pass. At one time called Kilnshaw Chimney after the chimney on its E slope. The Red Screes ridge runs northwards from Ambleside via Snarker Pike/Moss culminating at a trig. point at 776m (2546ft) [396088]. The shortest, but steepest, route to the summit is from the Kirkstone Pass Inn and up Kilnshaw Chimney. Other longer routes are from Ambleside via Scandale or along the Red Screes ridge ...from the red screes particularly noticeable in the combe below Raven Crag to the S of the summit.

Red Screes N Keppel Cove on lower slope Raise [343168].

Red Screes NW-N slope Clough Head [333227].

Red Screes Tarn on the summit of Red Screes just below the cairn and trig. point. At an altitude of 774m (2539ft), it is the third highest of the generally accepted tarns after Broad Crag and Fox [396087].

Red Sike rises Flaska at 371254 and joins Trout Beck at 366270.

Red Syke Farm off minor road, A5091 to Walthwaite [363264].

Red Tarn between Pike of Blisco and Cold Pike and the source of Browney Gill. Nearby, the Red Tarn Mine had a short life before its closure in 1875 but evidence of workings and slag still remains C530m (C1739ft) [268037] ...so called because of the red colour of the surrounding subsoil and rocks.

Red Tarn Helvellyn towers 244m (800ft) above it to the immediate W and its two encompassing arms on the N and S respectively are Swirral Edge and Striding Edge. At 718m (2356ft) it is the sixth highest of the generally accepted Lakeland tarns after Broadcrag, Fox, Red Screes, Kirkfell and Sergeant Man. Maximum depth is 25m (82ft). Free fishing for trout and the unique schelly, the latter few and far between and so far only confirmed to be found in England at Ullswater, Haweswater and Brothers Water but with the possibility of it existing in two or three other lakes and tarns. The schelly is classed as a rare fish and it is illegal to take any away. Wordsworth is said to have fished the tarn. The highest tarn in the Lake District which supports brown trout. In the 1860s a low boulder dam was constructed to provide a water supply for the Greenside Mine, Glenridding, and this was still in use until the closure of the mine in 1962 [349152].

Red Tarn Beck flows from Red Tarn at 350153 and meets Glenridding Beck at 358169.

Red Tarn Moss ESE Red Tarn [271035].

Redacre Gill farthest headstream rises Wrynose Fell at 277038. Joined by many tributaries before entering Mickleden Beck at 292061.

Redbank Wood Ambleside. W slope Wansfell ridge [384039].

Redbrow Bank adjoining Stackers Brow and overlooking Whis Gill 162m (531ft) [161995].

Redcrag Tarn the larger of two small tarns just below Red Crag on the High Street ridge 700m (2298ft) [451150].

Redgate Gill rises Redgate Head, Place Fell, at 409166 and joins Freeze Beck/Boredale Beck at 415163.

Redgate Head below Round How, Place Fell. Source of Redgate Gill [410165].

Redgill Head source of Red Gill which flows down to meet Whitrow Beck [143927].

Redhow alongside the minor road from Loweswater via Thackthwaite to Low Lorton [149229].

Redhow Crags see **Redhow Wood**.

Redhow Wood situated alongside the W bank of the River Cocker and between the Loweswater-Thackthwaite-Lorton road and the B5289 [153233]. In it are Redhow Crags with land to their immediate rear rising to C160m (C525ft) [152233].

Redmire off minor road, A66 to Mungrisdale [373298] ...reed mire.

Redness head of Bassenthwaite Lake [231267] ...'ness' - headland.

Redness Point small promontory head of Bassenthwaite Lake [229267].

Redscar property alongside Brook Lane, Underbarrow [458922].

Redsike Gill rises 363238 and joins Trout Beck at 363267.

Reecastle Crag prominent crag at the W foot of High Seat overlooking the Watendlath valley. Believed to have been the site of a British hill fort [273175].

Reggle Knott N Raise Beck overlooking Dunmail Raise [331121].

Renny Crags Claife Heights 216m (709ft) [365986] ...possibly diminutive of Reynold.

Renny Park Coppice N Hog House Beck, W B5286 [360016] ...see **Renny Crags** above.

Reservoir Cottage formerly connected with Kentmere Reservoir and nearby quarries but now used as a walking/climbing centre [446073].

Rest Dodd typical 'dodd' summit. On ridge between Rampsgill and Hayeswater. NNW the Knott, E Satura Crag and S the Nab. A considerable area of it is in the Martindale Deer Forest. Marshy and boggy on three flanks 696m (2284ft) [433137] ...after a steepish climb its summit could be an appropriate place on which to rest.

Rest Gill rises Crinkle Crags at 247051. Joins Yeastyrigg Gill at 238055 to form Lingcove Beck.

Restaurant in the Forest see **Grizedale Lodge Hotel**.

Resting Stone alongside the track from Rosthwaite to Watendlath. A convenient place to rest/pause [280157].

Reston Hall alongside the A591 and near Ings village. Built in 1743 and at that time christened Leghorn Hall by its builder, Robert Bateman. The story of Robert Bateman is a veritable rags to riches but one with unhappily a tragic ending. Born at Ings, Robert, with the help of villagers, made his way to London where he obtained work and ultimately became a wealthy merchant trading with Italy and particularly Leghorn where he lived for several years. He never forgot Ings and its villagers and, as previously mentioned, had Leghorn Hall built and also the present Ings Church with its Italian marble floor, and near-by almshouses. He never saw the church completed for in 1743 he was killed by the Italian captain on one of his own ships as she was sailing from Leghorn. The hall was later given its present title, Reston Hall [458986] ...'reston' - farmstead in the brushwood.

Reston Scar towering above the A591 and Reston Hall, Reston Scar shows its craggy face to motorists heading along the main road from Kendal to Windermere 255m (837ft) [460988] ...see **Reston Hall**.

Revelin Crag N face of Crag Fell overlooking Ennerdale [095145], see also **Crag Fell** ...the EPNS suggests that its origin is possibly from the word 'riveling' meaning rivulet. Ben Gill flows nearby. Another but somewhat obscure suggestion, is that it is a military term referring to a detailed work in a fortification.

Revelin Moss Thornthwaite Forest [209241] ...rivulet moss. Two streams, Grisedale Gill and Sanderson Gill, meet here.

Rheged situated at the junction of the A592 and A66. Popular visitor attraction and Europe's largest grass-covered building. Rheged includes restaurants, speciality shops, childrens' play area, artists' exhibitions, pottery demonstrations and the Helly Hansen National Mountaineering Exhibition. Free parking and entry to the building. A giant cinema screen, the size of six double-decker buses, shows three spectacular large format movies every day ...Rheged was an ancient kingdom which covered Lancashire, Cumberland and Galloway.

Rib End end of Kirkfell Crags above Beck Head [204107].

Ribby Gills several streams giving the appearance of ribs down the SE slope of Glaramara. They join Langstrath Beck [255099].

Ridding Brow slope between Heughscar Hill and Roehead [482233] ...'clearing' brow.

Ridding Gill rises Muncaster Fell at 118983 and joins the R Esk at 121975.

Ridding Wood SW shore Esthwaite Water. Car park sited between the shore and the Hawkshead-Newby Bridge road [361953] ...'rydding' - clearing.

Ridding Wood S Grizedale. A short circular walk through the wood has been made especially for those less mobile and provides forest sculptures and excellent views across the Grizedale Beck valley [338938] ...see above.

Riddings Beck rises 390222 and joins Aira Beck at 398215.

Riddings Beck rises E Ings at 314251 and joins the R Glenderamackin at 318250.

Riddings Plantation N of Gowbarrow Park [405221].

Riddings, The alongside Threlkeld to Wescoe road [313250] ...clearings.

Rigg Beck rises below Rowantree How at 155958 and joins Devoke Water at 159968.

Rigg Beck rises at the foot of Sail at 203200 and flows down a valley to join Newlands Beck at 236202.

Rigg Beck property alongside Rigg Beck [230201].

Rigg Head Yewdale Fells [301987] ...head of the ridge.

Rigg Intake Claife Heights [382985].

Rigg Intake Colthouse Heights [368972].

Rigg Screes screes below Aikin Knott and dropping down to Rigg Beck [212202].

Rigg, The see **The Rigg**.

Rigg Wood E side Coniston Water. Car parking area at foot [301922].

Rigghead approached from minor road, Guardhouse-Scales [345252].

Rigghead Quarries slate quarries opened about 1864 and, before their demise, were quite productive [237153].

Riggindale lateral dale running from Haweswater Reservoir to the High Street ridge and the Straits of Riggindale. To the N is the Kidsty Pike-Kidsty Howe ridge and to the S Riggindale Scar [460116]. At its foot can be seen the remains of Riggindale Farm.

Riggindale Beck rises slightly S of Rampsgill Head and W Kidsty Pike at 443126. Actual source is shown on the OS map as Head of Riggindale Beck. Flows down Riggindale to join Haweswater at 469118.

Riggindale Crag crags on Riggindale Scar overlooking the head of Riggindale [446114].

Riggindale Scar name given to the lengthy ridge along which virtually a straight path starts at the Rigg and climbs over or alongside Swine Crag, Heron Crag, Eagle Crag, Rough Crag, Caspel Gate, Riggindale Crag and Long Stile to the summit of High Street. Hugh's Cave (see **Haweswater**) is on its N craggy slope [443113-476116].

Riggingleys Top earlier Riddingleys Top. Near Askham, tumulus nearby [496229] ...clearing at the top.

Riggs Crags N Stone Arthur and W spur joining Great Rigg to Stone Arthur [347097] ...crags on the slope of Great Rigg.

Riggs, The see **The Riggs**.

Risebarrow E River Lowther. N Bampton Grange [521187] ...hill overgrown with brushwood.

Ritchie Crag Mardale Common, E Haweswater. The Old Corpse Road passes just to the S of it [490123].

Ritson's Force waterfall on Mosedale Beck named in memory of Will Ritson (1808-1890) of Wasdale Head [185093], see also **Wasdale Head Inn**.

River Annas its most northerly tributary rises on Waberthwaite Fell at 135934 and combines with another, Charlesground Gill, which rises on Corney Fell at 140924. As the River Annas the combination flows through Corney and Bootle. At the latter it is joined by two more substantial streams within a short distance of each other, Kinmont Beck at 108897 and the combination of Grassoms, Grassgill, Hentoe and Crookley Becks at 108881. The much enlarged river then flows past the small hamlet of Annaside and parallel with the coast before entering the sea near Selker at 074883 ...Einarr's river.

River Bank property on the bank of the River Duddon at Ulpha [196929].

River Bleng its farthest headstream, Tongue Gill, rises below Little Gouder Crag at 137108. Joined by Rossy Gill, Ill Gill, Swinsty Beck and Stare Beck it flows down to Gosforth. Turns due E and meets the River Irt [102032] which issues from Wastwater. The Irt eventually joins the Esk at Ravenglass at 081962 ...the dark river or from the Celtic 'blaen' which has several meanings including the source of a river or stream or highland/hill (Bleng Fell).

River Brathay two major headstreams, the principal one, Widdy Gill, rising near the Three Shire Stone at 278027 and the other, Wrynose Beck, rising on Wrynose Fell at 279039, meet at Widdygill Foot [288030] and become known as the River Brathay. This is joined by Bleamoss Beck before flowing down to and through Little Langdale Tarn where it is joined by Greenburn Beck. Subsequently drops over Colwith Force and shortly afterwards met by Ben Beck. Then, in and out of Elter Water where it is swelled by Great Langdale Beck. From Elter Water it flows easterly over Skelwith Force through Clappersgate to be joined by the River Rothay between Clappersgate and Waterhead at 370035. Shortly afterwards the two combined enter Windermere at 372031. The Brathay and the Rothay feature in a curious arrangement whereby the Windermere char swim up the Brathay to spawn whereas the trout from the lake head up the Rothay ...the broad river.

River Calder rises near Ennerdale Water at 103132. Subsequently joined by many tributaries including Whoap Beck, Comb Beck/Stinking Gill, Bomery Gill, Long and Ya Gills, Latterbarrow Beck, Caplecrag Beck, Sleven Beck, Friar Gill, Worm Gill, Needless Gill and Scargreen Beck. Skirts the remains of Calder Abbey and flows under Calder Bridge and alongside the Sellafield Nuclear Power Station before entering the sea at 020025 ...the rapid flowing stream.

River Caldew Rises high on the slope of Skiddaw at 266288 and flows through Mosedale, Hesket Newmarket and Dalston before joining the Eden at Botherby. The Eden then flows to Bowness on Solway where it enters the sea ...the cold water. Similar to Caldbeck which means cold stream.

River Cocker commences at the outflow of Crummock Water and flows along Lorton Vale to Cockermouth where it meets the River Derwent. En route it is joined by named substantial streams such as Liza Beck, Coldgill Beck, Hope Beck, Meregill Beck/Thackthwaite Beck, Whit Beck, Sandy Beck, Little Sandy Beck/Paddle Beck, Swinescales Beck, Bitter and Tom Rudd Becks ...crooked river.

River Derwent the Derwent rises at Sprinkling Tarn from where a stream drops down to Sty Head Tarn then into Styhead Gill. This meets Grains Gill, another headstream, at 234111 and the two combine to become a more substantial and better known River Derwent. Subsequently, on its journey along the picturesque Borrowdale, it is joined by other streams notably the substantial Hause and Combe Gills and Stonethwaite and Watendlath Becks before entering Derwent Water. Flowing out of Derwent Water it is joined by a major tributary, the River Greta. It then enters Bassenthwaite Lake at Derwent Foot. From the lake it flows through Cockermouth where it is joined by the River Cocker and eventually enters the sea at Workington ...see **Derwent Water**.

River Duddon principal headstreams rise at 271034 and 276032 on Wrynose Fell above the summit of Wrynose Pass. They join forces at 273027 to become the River Duddon which flows down its long valley to enter the sea between Haverigg Point and Walney Island. Wordsworth's favourite river and to which he wrote a sequence of 34 sonnets titled *The River Duddon*. These trace its source to its mouth ...its meaning is obscure. Either a personal name Dudd/Dudda and meaning the valley of one Dudd or Dudda or from the Celtic word 'du', dark or black, therefore the dark river.

River Eamont flows out of Ullswater at Pooley Bridge at 468243. Subsequently joined by Dacre Beck, Kirk Sike and Lady Beck before flowing under the M6 motorway at Skirsgill and under the A6 at Eamont Bridge. Joined by the River Lowther at Brougham Castle it eventually meets the River Eden at 587311. On or near its banks are several historic buildings or sites notably - Dunmallard Hill; the ancient Pooley Bridge over the river; Dalemain; the 14th century pele of Yanwath Hall; 16th century Eamont Bridge; the partly restored Norman remains of Brougham Castle; the antiquarian remains of Mayburgh Henge, and King Arthur's Round Table ...the meeting place of rivers referring to the confluence of the Eamont and the Lowther.

River Esk rises slightly S of Esk Hause (considered to be the highest pass in regular use in the Lake District) amid majestic mountain scenery. Winds its way down Eskdale being joined en route by many other streams. The principal ones are Little Narrowcove, How Beck, Lingcove Beck, Hardknott Gill, Whillan Beck, Whis Gill, Linbeck Gill, Broadoak Beck and Whitrow Beck. In its lower reaches it passes through a widening green valley, woods and pasture land before crossing a broad plain to be joined by the Rivers Irt and Mite and enters the sea at Ravenglass ...water river or possibly the river by the ash trees.

River Gilpin rises principally as Gilpin Beck, NE Gilpinpark Plantation at 439964. Joined near Mitchelland by another headstream which rises N Gilpin Lodge at 430962. The enlarged River Gilpin is subsequently joined by the outflow from Knipe Tarn, flows S to Crosthwaite where it is joined by Hollow Clough Gill. From Crosthwaite it strikes a more easterly direction through the Lyth Valley where it meets Underbarrow/Helsington Pool before joining the River Kent near Sampool at 475842 ...a case of which came first the chicken or the egg?. Did the river take its name from the ancient surname Gilpin or was it vice versa? Notable Gilpins were at Crook in the 14th century and Crosthwaite from the 16th century. Legend has it that Richard Gilpin of Kentmere Hall killed the last wild boar in England at Crook in the first half of the 14th century (see also **Wild Boar Hotel**). The possible derivation of the word Gilpin does suggest that the family took its name from the watercourse. Gilpin - a gushing stream/gulp.

River Glenderamackin rises alongside the col between Blencathra and Bannerdale Crags at 328291 and flows circuitously via Mungrisdale and the Threlkeld valley to become the R Greta slightly W of Threlkeld Bridge at 314247. The Greta joins the Derwent which flows through Bassenthwaite Lake and eventually enters the sea at Workington ...of obscure origin

River Gowan begins life at the outflow of Borrans Reservoir at 431009 and flows down through Ings and Staveley to join the River Kent at 472980 ...from surname Gawain or Gowen.

River Greta becomes the Greta at the confluence of the R Glenderamackin and St John's Beck slightly W of Threlkeld Bridge at 314247. Flows through Keswick and joins the R Derwent at 256236. This flows through Bassenthwaite Lake and eventually enters the sea at Workington ...the rocky river.

River Irt flows out of Wastwater at 145039. Joined by the River Bleng at 102032 and meanders its way to Ravenglass where it is joined by the Mite and in a very short distance joins the Esk at 082961. The rivers Ehen and Irt have been fished for freshwater pearls for over two millennia. Today, these elusive and rare moluscs still exist but are protected by statute ...no satisfactory explanation of the name.

River Kent Rises at 437101 slightly E of the High Street Roman road and flows down through Hall Cove, Kentmere Reservoir and Staveley. Subsequently joined by the Gowan, the Mint and Sprint before flowing through Kendal and later Levens Park. Shortly after this it is joined by the Gilpin and the Bela before finally entering Morecambe Bay at Arnside [454792]. Reputed to be the fastest flowing English river and some works even consider it to be the shortest. The latter is certainly not so. The River Bain flows out of Semer Water and joins the River Ure in Wensleydale, a distance of approximately 4kms (2.5 miles). More than likely there is somewhere a shorter river than that. Over its 40kms (25 mile) journey from source to estuary the Kent drops some 740m (over 2400ft) ...Aqua de Kent(e) in the 12th century. Meaning doubtful but there are indications that at one time the name could have meant a sacred river.

River Lickle two principal tributaries rise on the slope of White Pike, one at 246954, another, Yewry Sike, at 251954 and a third tributary emerges from Yaud Mire at 243952. Combine at 243945 from where the Lickle continues on down its attractive valley to be joined by the combined Broadslack Beck/Long Mire Beck, Black Moss Beck, the combined Hare Hall Beck/Red Moss Beck/Dunnerdale Beck, the substantial Appletree Worth Beck before entering the Duddon S of Duddon Bridge at 203875 ...of uncertain origin. Possibly curving, slow or bright water.

River Liza rises in the boulder strewn area below Windy Gap at 212108. Subsequently joined by Tongue Beck/Loft Beck, Sail Beck, Scarth Beck, High and Low Becks, Gillflinter Beck, Dodsgill Beck and Woundell Beck the latter incorporating Deep Gill and Silvercove Beck before discharging into Ennerdale Water ...bright or shining river.

River Lowther before the construction of the Wet Sleddale Reservoir in the 1960s the source of the Lowther was that of Sleddale Beck. However, the Lowther is now deemed to begin at the outflow of the reservoir at 553116. For 3.2kms (2 miles) of its journey the river provides part of the eastern boundary of the Lake District National Park and on its way to meet the River Eamont at Brougham it passes either through or close by Thornship, Keld, Shap Abbey, Rosgill, Hegdale, Bampton/Bampton Grange, Helton, Lowther Park and Askham. The Eamont subsequently joins the River Eden. From its source to the Eamont the Lowther is joined by named watercourses of Howe Gill, Wicker's Gill, Docker Beck,

Thornship Gill, Keld Gill, Lanshaw Sike, Swindale Beck, Haweswater Beck, Gill Beck, Whale Beck, Millkeld Sike, Keldron Spring, and Askham Beck. In his *Guide Through the District of the Lakes* Wordsworth notes that "the whole course of the Lowther, from Askham to the bridge under Brougham Hall, presents almost at every step some new feature of river, woodland, and rocky landscape." [553116-536292] ...several possibilities but one particular is the 'lather' river meaning the foaming river.

River Marron see **Leaps Beck**.

River Mint under its name the Mint does not actually flow through the Lake District National Park but its furthest headstream, Bannisdale Beck, does. This rises on Bannisdale Fell at 503057, flows down Bannisdale, under the A6 at Bannisdale Low Bridge and shortly afterwards meets Ashstead Beck at 553005. Here it becomes known as the River Mint, and subsequently joins the River Kent at 517943 ...noisy river.

River Mite rises on the slope of Illgill Head at 169046 and flows SW to eventually join the River Irt at 082962 near the latter's confluence with the River Esk at Ravenglass ...urinate or drizzle but why it is so called is obscure.

River Rothay Raise Beck rises on Dollywaggon Pike at 343128. Bifurcates at Dunmail Raise, one arm flowing N to Thirlmere and the other S to become the River Rothay at its confluence with Green Burn at 332096. The Rothay then flows down Grasmere Vale where it is joined by Tongue Gill, Greenhead Gill and Easedale Beck, before flowing alongside Grasmere village and on into Grasmere. Flows through this and Rydal Water and is subsequently joined by Rydal Beck, Scandale Beck and Stock Ghyll before meeting the River Brathay between Waterhead and Clappersgate [370035] ...the trout river.

River Sprint the Sprint actually starts at the source of its furthest headstream, Wren Gill, which rises on the ESE slope of Harter Fell at 463092. However, from the meeting of Wren Gill and the watercourses from Gatescarth and Brownhowe Bottom at 478082 the substantial stream becomes known as the River Sprint. On its journey down Longsleddale it is joined by Galeforth Gill and Stockdale Beck then by Routen Beck before joining the River Kent at Burneside at 509952 ...gushing river or bounding stream.

River Winster rises Undermillbeck Common at 415950 and flows down through the Winster Valley on a roughly parallel course to the W of the River Gilpin. For most of its journey it provided the former boundary between Lancashire and Westmorland. Eventually it joins Morecambe Bay E of Grange-over-Sands. Its southern end flows in a straight channel over the marshes. This particular section was re-constructed by noted ironmaster, John Wilkinson (1728-1808), in order to carry peat and ore to his nearby foundry. For this purpose he also built the first iron boat which today is said to lie in the mud of Helton Tarn, a swelling in the Winster. An obelisk commemorating John Wilkinson stands in Lindale-in-Cartmel alongside the road to Grange ...Ekwall suggests 'the left one' (the one to the W) as it runs on a roughly parallel course to the W of the River Gilpin. Another suggestion is that it is the white river.

Riverside Farm between Trout Beck and the A5091 [387261].

Rivings a summit in the Lord's Seat group 335m (1099ft) [198294].

Roan Wood W Greendale [144053] ...either Rowantree Wood, Roan's Wood or an abbreviation of Rowland's Wood.

Rob Rash WSW Loughrigg Tarn, alongside the A593 [339041] ...Rob's narrow piece of uncultivated land.

Robin Fold Edge rocky edge above Robin's Fold (sheepfold) [237158].

Robin Gill one headstream rises 317069 and another from the outflow of Youdell Tarn at

317068. Flows alongside Robinson Place to join Scale Gill at 310062.

Robin Gill rises slope of Illgill Head at 169045. Joined by Little Grain Gill and Great Grain Gill before entering the River Mite at 160023.

Robin Gill Tarn see **Youdell Tarn**.

Robin Hood ridge and summit between Borrowdale and Crookdale 493m (1617ft) [530059] ...the legend and folklore of Robin Hood abounds in Cumbria as well as central and other northern areas of the country. There is a Robin Hood island and wood at Helsington, a Howe Robin and Robin Hood's Graves at Crosby Ravensworth, a Robin Hood's Chair, overlooking Ennerdale Water, a Robin Hood's Farm, Bassenthwaite, and several hostelries bear the outlaw's name.

Robin Hood's Chair large block of stone at the base of Anglers' Crag, Ennerdale [100151].

Robin Lane Troutbeck-Hundreds Road [402022] ...Robin's lane.

Robin's Fold sheepfold on the slope of High Spy [239157].

Robinbank Crag ESE head of Watendlath Tarn [280157].

Robinson much earlier Robinson Fell. Highest summit on the High Snab Bank-Blea Crag-Robinson ridge. Faces its slightly smaller 'twin', Hindscarth, across Little Dale 737m (2418ft) [202169] ...named after a Richard Robinson who purchased it as part of land acquired in the time of King Henry VIII.

Robinson Crags Robinson [202173].

Robinson Place farm, Great Langdale. The farmhouse dates from the late 17th century but a barn from the early 17th century. Acquired by the NT in 1974 [312063] ...local family surname.

Robinson's Cairn a large cairn situated alongside the High Level route to Pillar and Pillar Rock and from which there is a good view of the E face of Pillar Rock. The cairn is a memorial to John Wilson Robinson, fellwalker and rock climber, who first climbed his beloved Pillar Rock in 1882 and, before he died in 1907, made more than a hundred ascents of the mountain. The cairn was built by comrades and friends in 1908. Nearby a tablet commemorating him is affixed to a rock [177124].

Robinson's Gully see **Great End**.

Robinson's Tarn Claife Heights. Small mainly marshy area slightly N of Wraymire Tarn and slightly SSE Hodson's Tarn, C190m (C623ft) [369981].

Roche Moutonee see **Deepdale**.

Rock Climbing since Samuel Taylor Coleridge completed one of the first recorded rock climbs, albeit a reverse climb down Broad Stand, Scafell Pike, in 1802 and Walter Hackett-Smith first climbed Napes Needle in 1886 rock climbing has become a substantial sport and the Lake District a mecca for climbers. Consequently numerous cliffs, crags and slabs have provided routes for both serious and novice members of the climbing fraternity. Even individual boulders such as the Pudding Stone, Coppermines Valley, and the Y-Boulder, Mosedale, have provided challenges to climbers particularly beginners and novices. The principal climbing areas, however, are Wasdale with Wasdale Head as the birthplace of British mountaineering, Borrowdale and Great Langdale. From Wasdale there are many climbs available including Scafell Crags, Scafell East Buttress, Central Buttress, Pikes Crag, Great End and Great Gable with its famous Napes Needle, Kern Knotts and Gable Crag. Borrowdale also gives access to the above climbs but alongside the valley are Shepherd's Crag, Black Crag, Troutdale Pinnacle while nearby are Gillercombe Buttress on Grey Knotts, Dove Crag and Raven Crag. The accessibility of Langdale draws many climbers particularly to Gimmer Crag, Raven Crag Buttress, Middlefell Buttress and Pavey Ark. Other areas include Ennerdale with its famous Pillar Rock, Dow Crag near Coniston, also Bowfell and, near Thirlmere, Castle Rock and Raven Crag. These are just a relatively small percentage of the considerable number of rock climbs available in the Lake District. There are many books on the subject and the Fell and Rock Climbing Club (formed 1906) has, since 1922, produced definitive guides to areas of the Lake District. These are obtainable from climbers' shops and booksellers generally.

Rodger Crag ESE summit of Muncaster Fell [118980].

Roehead off the Pooley Bridge to Howtown road [480237] ...head of a row of trees. Nearby is Roehouse.

Roehouse off the Pooley Bridge to Howtown road near Roehead [476237] ...house in or alongside a row of trees.

Roger Ground near Hawkshead [351974] ...see **Grounds**.

Roger Ridding S Thwaite Head [347901] ...personal name + clearing.

Roman Camps site of three N A66 near Troutbeck and on the Roman road which ran from Old Penrith to, it is believed, Papcastle [379273] [384273] [389277].

Roman Forts N A66 near Troutbeck [384272]; Galava, Ambleside, Brougham and Hardknott, see also **Roman Camps**.

Roman Road (High Street), Ambleside to Brougham, near Penrith, via Allen Knott and Scots Rake, or by Grandsire, Yoke, Ill Bell, Froswick, High Street, then High Raise, Loadpot Hill and Heughscar Hill

Roman Road (courses of), section visible just north of present A66 near Troutbeck. This is part of the Roman road from Old Penrith via Troutbeck fort and camps to Papcastle [389273]. High Street - Ambleside to Brougham near Penrith via Allen Knott, Scots Rake, or Grandsire, Yoke, Ill Bell, Froswick, to High Street, then High Raise, Loadpot Hill and Heughscar Hill. Kirkstone Pass - terraceway N section of Kirkstone Pass parallel to the present road and to the W of it is possibly a Roman road. Ambleside - Hardknott via Little Langdale and a section of the present route over the Whinlatter Pass is deemed to have been built on an earlier Roman road.

Rook Howe Kentmere. A beer house in 1833. In 1999, the then farmhouse, as part of the Kentmere Hall and Hartrigg Estate along with Kentmere Hall, Hartrigg Farm and Scales Farmhouse, came up for sale by private treaty [459045] ...rook hill.

Rookin House Farm between Trout Beck and the A5091. 5.5kms (3.5miles) from Ullswater and 14.5kms (9 miles) from Keswick and Penrith. Now a trekking and activity centre [382254].

Rooking Patterdale. Cluster of old cottages across Goldrill Beck and alongside the track to Hartsop. Hereabouts, Wordsworth acquired the Broad How Estate (19 acres of land and a cottage) in 1806 intending to build a house on the site or extend the original farmhouse. This, dated 1670, is now called Wordsworth's Cottage. He never built there nor did he live there and eventually sold the land in 1834. The present Broad How was built shortly after Wordsworth sold the land and property [401159] ...rough fissure or chasm.

Rooking Gill rises below Steel Edge, Place Fell, at 404163 and joins Goldrill Beck at 399158.

Roscombe Rigg on Low Birk Fell, E Ullswater. Overlooks Ullswater [410193].

Rose Bank Embleton [165294].

Rose Castle no relation to Rose Castle, Carlisle, the residence of the Bishop of Carlisle nor is it a castle. Actually, a small building E Tarn Hows which has given its name to a nearby plantation and a tarn [334999].

Rose Castle Plantation E shore Tarn Hows and surrounding Rose Castle Tarn [334002] ...takes its name from nearby Rose Castle.

Rose Castle Tarn slightly E of and above Tarn Hows. Joined to the latter by a small stream. Surrounded by Rose Castle Plantation and therefore sometimes referred to as Plantation Tarn C190m (C623ft) [333002] ...similar to Rose Castle Plantation in that it takes its name from Rose Castle, a farm building, nearby.

Rose Cottage Gosforth [082030].

Rosgill Rosgill with Hegdale comprises nearly 30 homes and lies approximately 3.2 kms (2 miles) from Shap. The confluence of Swindale Beck and the River Lowther is close by. Rosgill Hall, now a farm, was once the manor house of the de Rosghyll and later the Salkeld families. The old school, erected in 1878, closed in 1958 [537168] ...ravine of the horses.

Rosgill Hall see **Rosgill**.

Rosgill Hall Wood slightly SE Rosgill Hall [540162].

Rosgill Head ENE Rosgill. Alongside the road from Shap to Bampton Grange and Bampton. Home for centuries of the Castley family (see also **Hegdale**) [542170].

Rosgill Moor SW Rosgill [524153].

Rosley Thorns off the A5084 between Torver and Sunny Bank [289937] ...possibly 'hross' - horse and 'leah' - glade or open space in woodland.

Ross's Camp Muncaster Fell [121986] ...no connection with Romans or of any archaeological significance. It comprises a flat slab of rock positioned horizontally on several other stones and was erected by members of a shooting party as a place to partake of sustenance. The slab is inscribed 'Ross's Camp 1883'. Ross was most likely either the leader of the party or the person who had the idea to erect the 'camp'. Still a popular picnic site.

Rossett property dating from the 17th century where, at one time, packhorse ponies rested after journeying over or to the Rossett Gill and Stake Passes. Believed to have given its name to Rossett Gill rather than the other way round [293063] ...horse shelter.

Rossett Bridge Mickleden. Earlier called by locals Slops Bridge. Carries the track/path which winds its way up the slope to the S of the gill. In the late 17th and early 18th century this was a sledway. The latter was constructed to carry iron ore from the Ore Gap area down the pass [252073].

Rossett Gill rises between Hanging Knotts and Rossett Crag at 250074 and joins Mickleden Beck at 262073.

Rossett Gill Pass rises to the head of Rossett Gill and its summit overlooks Angle Tarn. Rises to C610m (C2001ft) [247076].

Rossett Pike above Rossett Gill Pass and overlooking Angle Tarn 650m (2132ft) [249076] ...possibly a corruption of Rosthwaite Pike but more than likely linked to Rossett (horse shieling/shelter) and therefore 'the peak above the horse shelter' or 'the peak above the horse pastures'.

Rossy Gill rises 140092 and joins the upper River Bleng at 136095.

Rosthwaite principal village in Borrowdale and a major walking centre. Several hotels and B&Bs, the former including the Scafell Hotel, previously a coaching inn, the Royal Oak, formerly an 18th century farmhouse which has been a walkers' hotel since 1865 and the Hazel Bank Country House Hotel, a former Victorian residence. There is a Post Office come store which was previously an inn, toilets, a well-known cafe/tea room (the Flock Inn), adjoining Yew Tree Farm. The farm was acquired by the National Trust in 1977. Nearby, on the W bank of the River Derwent is the Longthwaite YH and at its rear Johnny Wood, of special interest to naturalists and acquired with High Doat by the NT in 1964 [259148] ...clearing marked by a cairn or heap of stones.

Rosthwaite Allotment E A592. NE Ghyll Head [399932] ...similar to Rosthwaite, Borrowdale, in that it signifies a 'hreysi' a clearing. One marked by a cairn/stones or one surrounded by the same.

Rosthwaite Bridge carries the B5289 over the River Derwent [257151].

Rosthwaite Cam highest summit of Rosthwaite Fell 612m (2008ft) [256118].

Rosthwaite Farm E A592, Newby Bridge-Bowness road. A 17th century farmhouse modernised and extended. A track linking it to Rosthwaite Allotment continues alongside Rosthwaite Heights to Ghyllhead [401934].

Rosthwaite Farm Tarns not shown on the OS map but shown and described in *The Tarns of Lakeland* by John and Anne Nuttall (1996). Grid reference is given in this work as 402934. Altitude C110m (C362ft).

Rosthwaite Fell with its near neighbour, Thornythwaite Fell, it fronts the N end of the Borrowdale Fells. Upwards of 30 small tarns nestle in the hollows of its ridge, the largest and only one named being Tarn at Leaves. High point is Rosthwaite Cam at 612m (2008ft) [256118].

Rosthwaite Heights E A592 and NE Ghyllhead [398930].

Rosthwaite Tarn see **Ghyll Head Fish Pond**.

Rothay Bridge carries the A593, Ambleside-Coniston road over the River Rothay [372039].

Rothay Garden Hotel Grasmere village. Built as a private house in the mid-19th century. In the 1950s became the Rothay Bank Hotel. Expanded in the 1980s and renamed the Rothay Garden Hotel. In 1999 won the prestigious Les Routiers Hotel of the Year.

Rothay Garth Hotel Grasmere village. Erected in the 19th century as a country house. Later a school for 'gentle young ladies' and then a doctor's house before becoming a hotel in 1950.

Rothay Manor Hotel alongside Rothay Bridge, Ambleside. Formerly a large Regency house built in 1830, now an hotel [373039].

Rothay Park Ambleside. Between St Mary's Church and the R Rothay on verdant pasture land. From the W access is gained by foot across the R Rothay by Miller Bridge, a typical Lakeland packhorse bridge [372044].

Rothay Valley that along which the River Rothay flows from near Dunmail Raise through Grasmere, Grasmere Lake, Rydal Water, Ambleside to Windermere.

Rothay, River see **River Rothay**.

Rothery Sike Ennerdale. Rises 088163 and drains into Ennerdale Water at 092160.

Rottenstone Gill rises Rosthwaite Fell at 256121 and joins Combe Gill at 251124 ...appropriately named stony stream.

Rough Crag above the Green Burn and Greenburn Bottom [309107].

Rough Crag precipitous crag alongside the road around W side Thirlmere. Overlooks Hawes How Island [314154].

Rough Crag Riggindale Scar 628m (2060ft) [454112].

Rough Crag overlooks Nether Beck, Wasdale [152082].

Rough Crag Birker Moor. N Devoke Water. Trig. point at 319m (1047ft) [161978].

Rough Crag E Birker Moor Road and Sike Moss [186967].

Rough Crag Scafell Pike [219069].

Rough Crags above Greenburn [283024].

Rough Crags epitomises the Shipman Knotts area [474065].

Rough Crags N Wrynose Pass [272031].

Rough Edge steep and rough escarpment of John Bell's Banner and Caudale Moor overlooking Kirkstone Pass [408105] and [408098].

Rough Hill High Rough Hill. Off the unfenced road from Heltondale to the Bampton to Carhullan road [497192] ...rough hollow.

Rough Hill Tarn alongside the unfenced road from Heltondale to the Bampton to Carhullan road [495194].

Rough Holes rocky area E Dale Park valley [358922] ...rough hollows.

Rough Holme islet in Windermere [399979] ...rough island.

Rough How N Siney Tarn, Eskdale [162017].

Rough How alongside the track from the Birker Moor Road to Woodend [172963].

Rough How Bridge also referred to as Shoulthwaite Bridge. An old bridge carried an earlier section of the A591 over Shoulthwaite Beck while the New Rough How Bridge carrying the present A591 was built in 1965 [300206].

Rough Hows Claife Heights [372984].

Rough Hows Intake Claife Heights [371982].

Rough Intake Loughrigg Fell [358058] ...a rough piece of land taken in from waste and enclosed.

Rough Knott E of the head of Watendlath Tarn [280161].

Rough Mire S Green Mire at the head of Bassenthwaite Lake [232261].

Rough Sides afforested slope E Scandale Beck [380062].

Roughholme off the A595 2.8kms (1.75 miles) N Waberthwaite [107955].

Roughton Gill rises on N slope of Blencathra at 321280 and joins Glenderaterra Beck at 296274 ...roaring stream. At the present time the valley houses the Roughton Stone, a relic of the considerable mining thereabouts which ceased in the late 19th century. The exact purpose of the stone is not known but suggestions are that it may have been a grindstone or a sorting table. Caldbeck Parish Council have suggested that it be moved to Caldbeck churchyard to protect it from further damage. See also **Caldbeck & Uldale Commons**.

Round Hill Claife Heights [385983].

Round Hill Lowther Park [540222].

Round How below Little Carrs [266014].

Round How Great End. Overlooks Greta Gill 741m (2431ft) [219081].

Round How just below and to the S of the summit of Hartsop Dodd [411117].

Round How S Dockray. SW Bracken How 387m (1270ft) [392208].

Round How subsidiary summit of Place Fell. SSE of main summit C630 (C2067) [408166].

Round How Ormathwaite. W Mallen Dodd. NW Latrigg [273250].

Round Mount W Thirlmere overlooking Beech Grove [307184].

Round Scar E Damas Dubs [221036].

Round Table between the head of Intack Sike and Ulgill Gutter. Similar to King Arthur's Round Table (the Round Table), near Eamont Bridge; Round Table, Stainmore; Pendragon Castle, Mallerstang; and Arthuret, in that its name is derived from Arthurian legend (or is it as many believe, fact?) [493169].

Roundclose Hill alongside the junction of Hundith Hill Road and the B5282, 100m (328ft) [139284].

Roundhill Farm off Kirkstone Road [387052].

Roundley Beck rises W Black Hall, Dunnerdale, at 235012 and joins the River Duddon at 240010.

Roundthwaite Coppice slightly W of Crook Road [463968] ...the wood of the Roundthwaite family.

Routen Beck rises on Potter Fell at 509995. During its course widens into two tarns (Upper and Lower Routen Beck Tarns) and meets the River Sprint at 522985 ...similar to Routing Gill Beck in Matterdale, Rowten Beck near Glenridding and Roughton Gill at Blencathra, in that it means the roaring stream.

Routen Farm Ennerdale [105163] ...the descriptive word refers to a noisy or roaring stream. Gill Beck drops down steeply nearby.

Routing Gill on ESE slope Great Mell Fell [403252].

Routing Gill Beck rises on E slope of Great Mell Fell at 403252 and joins Dacre Beck at 412253 ...roaring + gill + beck.

Row Waberthwaite. Off the A595 [110941].

Row Bridge old narrow packhorse bridge behind the Wasdale Head Inn and near to Row Head. Crosses Mosedale Beck giving access to small fields and also provides a route for walkers up the W side of Mosedale Beck to the foot of Dorehead Screes [186088].

Row End ENE Low Rigg. Off narrow road connecting St John's in the Vale Church with minor road, B5322 to A66 [308232].

Row Farm Gosforth [178036].

Row Farm Waberthwaite [107938].

Row Head Wasdale Head. 17th century farmhouse acquired by the NT in 1962 [187089].

Rowan Tree Dub E the Park, NE High Parkamoor [314929] ...rowan tree by the pool.

Rowan Tree Hill W of and overlooking Ghyll Head Reservoir and Ghyll Head Road [395923].

Rowan Tree How SSE Cockley Beck [251006].

Rowan's Ground enclosure alongside Tongue Gill [343100] ...presumably the surname Rowan derived from the alternative name for the mountain ash.

Rowanthwaite Pond private pond lying just off the B5284 at Crook [461953].

Rowantree Beck rises N slope Great Dodd at 342210. Joined by Rowantree Gill and becomes Mosedale Beck at 350227. This eventually joins the R Glenderamackin at 350264.

Rowantree Beck rises White Moss at 200975. Subsequently becomes Smallstone Beck which combines with Highford Beck at 177987.

Rowantree Beck rises slope of Whiteless Pike at 180182. Joins Squat Beck at 174182. This combines with Rannerdale Beck which enters Crummock Water at 162191.

Rowantree Crag NNE Stone Howe. S Langhow Pike. No rowan tree remains [529128].

Rowantree Crags S High Scarf Crag 359m (1178ft) [213036].

Rowantree Fold sheepfold [344220].

Rowantree Force double waterfall in deep ravine on Rowantree Beck [145937].

Rowantree Gill rises NNW Heron Pike at 355085 and joins Greenhead Gill at 349085.

Rowantree Gill rises SE slope Clough Head at 337221 and joins Rowantree Beck at 340219.

Rowantree Gill rises With Bottom below Whitfell at 154932. Flows over Rowantree Force and later become Samgarth Beck which meets Stainton Gill and Black Beck at 121946. Becomes Mill Gill which eventually become Broadoak Beck before entering the River Esk at 099953.

Rowantree How SSE Cockley Beck [251006].

Rowantree How Miterdale Forest 177m (581ft) [136011].

Rowantree How N Wallowbarrow Crag [222973].

Rowantree How Birkby Fell C400m (C1312ft) [157959].

Rowantree Knotts Kentmere. E Saletarn Knotts, W Birk Rigg [451054].

Rowantreethwaite Mardale Banks, E Haweswater 529m (1736ft) [487122]. Has the distinction of being the longest single place name in the four maps which cover most of the LDNP.

Rowantreethwaite Beck rises Rowantreethwaite Well at 488120 and meets Hopgill Beck at 481118.

Rowantreethwaite Well E Haweswater. Source of Rowantreethwaite Beck [488120].

Rowend Bridge Gosforth. Carries the road from Gosforth to Santon Bridge over the River Bleng [078033].

Rowland Beck rises NE Blakeley Raise at 073139. Met by Oxenstone Beck at 067153 and joins the River Ehen at 068159.

Rowlandfield Plantation Lowther Park [528219] ...from the local family of Rolland/Rowland.

Rowley Wood Satterthwaite [341922].

Rowling End E steep craggy end of the Sail-Causey Pike-Newlands ridge 433m (1421ft) [229207].

Rowling End Farm below Rowling End [235205].

Rowten Beck rises between Brown Dodd and Stang at 351172 and joins Glenridding Beck at 360171 ...roaring stream.

Royal Hotel Bowness. Well over 400 years old. Earlier the White Horse but after Queen Adelaide had dinner there in 1840 it took the more grandiose title. The scene of ghostly happenings in the past and more recently. These included sightings of a young girl and a middle aged woman in period dress and ghostly hand and body imprints in beds where no guest had slept.

Royal Oak Bowness. Centuries old, originally the Ship Inn.

Royal Oak Hotel see **Rosthwaite**.

RSPB the RSPB has five nature reserves in Cumbria: Campfield Marsh, Solway Estuary; Geltside, E of Carlisle; Haweswater, E of Shap; Hodbarrow, Millom and St. Bees Head.

Rucroft Wood alongside Dacre Beck [447267] ...rye croft wood.

Ruddwent Embleton. Alongside Tom Rudd Beck [165289].

Ruddy Gill see **Grains Gill**.

Rulbuts Hill S Scout Hill. W High House, Winster 175m (574ft) [407936] ...the first element is possibly a personal name and the second 'booth/shelter'.

Rumney's Plantation off the A592 between Brackenrigg and Pooley Bridge [453238] ...family of Oswald Romeneye.

Rush Gill ravine lower Deepdale through which flows Aira Beck [366210].

Rushbearing a centuries old ceremony in which freshly-cut aromatic smelling rushes were laid over the earth floors of churches and other buildings at regular intervals. With the advent of paving, rushes were no longer needed to cover the floor and rushbearing ceased in all but a handful of churches. In the case of Grasmere, generally referred to as possessing the principal rushbearing ceremony, the floor of the church was flagged in 1841 but the ancient ceremony is still celebrated annually. Other noteable rushbearing ceremonies include those of Ambleside, Warcop and Urswick. The history of the Grasmere rushbearing ceremony is detailed in a booklet *The Rushbearing in Grasmere* (1984).

Rushmire N Matterdale End and alongside A5091 [393240].

Ruskin, John see **Brantwood**.

Ruthwaite Beck flows from Ruthwaite Cove at 346133 to join Grisedale Beck at 359138.

Ruthwaite Cove ESE High Crag and N Dollywaggon Pike and the Tongue. The 'russet cove' of Wordsworth's *Prelude*. Hard Tarn is situated on a ledge above it [347136].

Ruthwaite Lodge Grisedale. Belies its rather grand title. Originally built as a smithy and bothy for the miners from the nearby Ruthwaite Lodge and Eagle Crag Mines. These closed c1880 and the building subsequently became a shooting lodge and a place of rest for travellers and ponies on the Grisedale Pass route. Today it serves as a climbing hut. A plaque on it bears the inscription 'Restored by the Maintenance Team of Outward Bound Ullswater and dedicated 26.3.93 to the memory of Richard Read and Mike Evans Tutors from the O. B. U. killed on Mt. Cook New Zealand 31.1.88'. [355135].

Rydal the village of Rydal lies alongside, and just off, the A591 at the foot of Rydal Water and 2.4kms (1.5 miles) from Ambleside. The Rydal Estate has been owned by the le Flemings for centuries. The present owner is Major Richard le Fleming of Dorset, who was the sole beneficiary in the will of Mrs Joan Isobel Hughes Curwen (formerly le Fleming) who died in July 1991. Principal properties and attractions are Rydal Hall, Rydal Falls, Rydal Mount, Rydal Lodge, Rydal Church, Rydal Park, the Glen Rothay Hotel, Dora's Field and Nab Cottage [365062] ...the valley in which rye was grown.

Rydal Beck rises at over 640m (2100ft) at 364113 and on its meanderings down the solitary Rydale drops over several waterfalls including Buckstones Jump, High Fall and the well-known Rydal Upper and Lower Falls (alongside Rydal Hall) before joining the River Rothay alongside Rydal Bridge on the A591 at 367058.

Rydal Bridge carries the A591 over Rydal Beck [367058].

Rydal Church dedicated to St Mary it was opened by Lady le Fleming in 1824 at a cost

Rydal

of £1,500 and consecrated in August 1825. The Wordsworth family worshipped here and occupied the pew in front of the pulpit [364062].

Rydal Falls two major waterfalls on Rydal Beck near Rydal Hall, High [366068] and Lower Fall [366064], with roughly 0.5kms (0.3 mile) between them and with a middle cascade above the lower falls. The falls were a 'must' for 19th century tourists but not as much visited today although they are often painted by both amateur and professional painters and provide the subject for many photographs.

Rydal Farm off the A591 and between it and the River Rothay [369053].

Rydal Fell ridge running from Nab Scar to Fairfield. The grazing land on the slope E of Rydal Beck is also referred to locally as Rydal Fell [361091].

Rydal Hall known as Rydal House until the 17th century it has probably been the home of the le Flemings since around 1600 although a building is believed to have existed on the site prior to this date. Much enlarged during the 18th and 19th centuries. During last century used as a hotel, a boarding school and in 1963 acquired by the Diocese of Carlisle and used as a conference centre and retreat offering accommodation to groups and individuals. Adjoining the hall are the formal and rockery gardens. Rydal Beck flows alongside with its two picturesque waterfalls in close proximity to each other. The grotto, a 'viewing house' or summer house at the side of the beck and near one of the falls was erected in the 17th century by Daniel le Fleming. A ruin by 1980, it has since been restored. A sweet chestnut in the grounds has a girth of 10.46m (34ft), [366063].

Rydal Head at one time Fairfield was known as Rydal Head but today Rydal Head comprises the slope below Fairfield at the head of the Rydal Beck [363113].

Rydal Lodge Rydal. Alongside the A591. Parts date from the early 17th century and the building was the original coaching inn in Rydal. Today it is a country house hotel.

Rydal Mount originally a 16th century farmhouse but later much enlarged. Principally known as the home of William Wordsworth who rented it from Lady Diana le Fleming of Rydal Hall in 1813. He died there in 1850. Since 1970 it has been open to the general public as a memorial to Wordsworth [364065].

Rydal Old Hall remains of the hall, occupied by the le Flemings before they moved to the present Rydal Hall in about 1600, can be seen left of the A591, Ambleside-Grasmere road, approximately 500m (0.3 mile) N of Scandale Bridge [369055].

Rydal Park part of a former hunting reserve established some 7 centuries ago by Sir Roger de Lancastre [371061].

Rydal Water alongside the A591 between Ambleside and Grasmere. Used to be called Rothaymere or Routhmere, both names being derived from the River Rothay which flows through both it and Grasmere. Excluding Elterwater, called by Lake District historian Collingwood "a true lake of the lakes" but often not classified as a lake owing to its fluctuating size and unusual symmetry, Rydal Water is slightly larger than the smallest lake, Brothers Water. With a length of 1.2kms (0.75mile), a breadth of 0.4kms (0.25 mile) and a maximum depth of 17m (56ft) it lies at 55m (181ft) above sea level. Possesses two islands, Heron and Little Isle. Boating is prohibited but fishing from the bank, principally for pike, perch and eels but with some trout, is permitted. Fishing is under the jurisdiction of the WADAA with permits obtainable from tourist information centres and local tackle shops.

Between Nab Cottage and the start of Rydal village proper, a rock on the lake side of the road is said to be where Wordsworth often sat and contemplated in solitude - an impossibility in this day and age with cars and coaches speeding noisily along the A591. Rydal Water has a phenomenon infrequently seen and only in very windy weather - a water spout. Wordsworth witnessed it and wrote: "On this day, March 30th 1822, the winds have been acting on the small lake of Rydal, as if they had received command to carry its waters from their bed to the sky... Frequently an eddying wind scoops the waters out of the basin, and forces them upwards in the very shape of an Icelandic geyser, or boiling fountain, to the height of several hundred feet." Water spouts have been seen since and, as recently as Good Friday 1998, a relative travelling along the road to Grasmere on a windy day witnessed one but not apparently as tall as the one seen by Wordsworth [356062] ...Rydal Water is not in nearby Rydal (Rydale) 'valley of the rye' but is in the Rothay valley. It takes its name however from the village of Rydal.

S

Sad Gill not named on the OS map. Rises 415098 and joins Trout Beck at 424082. Two settlements (also not shown on map) N & S of Sad Gill and between the path up to Threshthwaite Mouth and Trout Beck at 423085 and 423081 respectively are scheduled as ancient monuments ...ravine with a shelter or mountain pasture nearby.

Saddle, The see **The Saddle**.

Saddle Gate col between Whiteless Edge and Whiteless Pike [181191].

Saddleback popular name for Blencathra. Takes its name from 'the saddle' between Hall's Fell Top and Foule Crag. (For more information see **Blencathra**).

Saddlebacked How Dunnerdale. Near Castle How [237007].

Saddlecrag Gill rises near Little Saddle Crag at 528084. Joined by Widepot Sike at 526094 and enters Sleddale Beck at 524099.

Sadgill furthest habitation (farm and two other properties) in Longsleddale and at the end of the tarmac road up that valley. In days long gone by the Sadgill packhorse bridge over the River Sprint (originally built in 1717) was the meeting place of drove roads up and down Longsleddale and over from Kentmere. Today, a quarry track and a path lead from Sadgill up to and over the Gatescarth Pass to Mardale Head and another track goes over to Kentmere [483057]. Sadgill features as 'High Close' in Mrs Humphrey Ward's *Robert Elsmere.* There is another Sad Gill alongside Trout Beck ...nothing sad about it. See **Sad Gill** above.

Sadgill Wood Sadgill, Longsleddale [481055].

Sadler's Knott SE Knock Murton, NE Kelton Fell [103186] ...Sadlemoor in the early 17th century. Takes its name from its shape.

Sail high fell at the end of the Rowling End-Causey Pike ridge and the Stile End-Outerside ridge. A rounded summit of heather and grass 773m (2536ft) [198203] ...swampy hill.

Sail Beck rises Baysour Slack at 196109 and meets the River Liza at 197121 ...see **Black Sail**.

Sail Beck see **Mill Beck** see also **Black Sail**.

Sail Hills Ennerdale Fell [124130] ...dark hills.

Sailing see **Boating & Sailing**.

Saint see abbreviation **St**.

St Andrews Mission Church Ecclerigg. An early 20th century wood and iron church situated midway between Windermere and Ambleside. Acquired in the summer of 1998 by the Lake District Tourism and Conservation Partnership.

St Ann's Farm Ings with Hugill [441996] ...a chapel was once attached to the farm. The church at Ings is dedicated to St Anne.

St Anne's School Windermere. Founded in 1863 and moved from St Anne's on Sea to Windermere (Browhead) in 1924. Elleray was initially rented as a junior school and subsequently purchased in 1944 from Riggs, coach and carriage proprietors and owners of the nearby Windermere Hotel. The senior school is at Browhead off the A592 and Chapel Ridding is today part of the school [408000]. From its initial opening with just 6 pupils in 1863 the school now houses around 350 students. In September 1999 it was renamed Windermere St Anne's. See also **Elleray**, **Old Elleray**.

St Bartholomew's Church see **Loweswater**.

St Catherine's mansion off the A592 and the connecting road from the A592 to the Troutbeck Bridge-Near Orrest road. Once owned by the Earl of Bradford. Nearby Chapel Riddings, a steep section of the road known as St Catherine's Brow, and St Catherine's are the only reminders of an ancient chapel dedicated to St Catherine, which stood nearby alongside the old track from Kendal via Mislet, Near Orrest, Crosses, Troutbeck Bridge and Ambleside. The chapel disappeared centuries ago [410997].

St Catherine's Church Boot, Eskdale. A leaflet describing the church and its history states "Little is known of the history of St. Catherine's Church, Eskdale." There is, however, a story that it is traditionally linked with the 13th century and that it was one of the four dale chapels belonging to St Bees Priory. It is believed to have been given parish church status in the mid-15th century. There are hints of a restoration in the 17th century but the church was definitely practically rebuilt in 1881. Until 1901 the dead from Wasdale were brought over the corpse road between Wasdale Head and Boot to be buried in the churchyard. Among the tombstones in the yard is one of Tommy Dobson, founder of the Eskdale and Ennerdale Foxhounds, and its Master for 53 years [176003].

St Catherine's Church & Tower see **Crook**.

St Herbert's Island see **Derwent Water**.

St John's Beck sometimes called The Bure. Flows from the foot of Thirlmere at 309191. Met by Beckthorns Gill and Sandbed Gill before joining the R Glenderamackin at 314247. The confluence is the start of the R Greta.

St John's Common E St John's in the Vale. W and WSW Great Dodd [330203].

St John's Fell see **High Rigg**.

St John's in the Vale scenic dale linking the A591 with the A66(T). Through it runs the

B5322. Takes its name from the Knights Hospitallers of the Order of St John who are thought to have had a church, hospice, or hermitage here in the 13th century. The present church, sited above the vale and between Low Rigg and High Rigg, is dedicated to St John and dates from the mid-19th century. In the churchyard is St John's Well. Nearby, the former school is now a Diocesan Youth Centre. Occasionally the valley is called Buredale after St John's Beck which is sometimes still referred to as the Bure [317223].

St John's Well in the churchyard of St John's Church above St John's in the Vale [306224].

St Martin's Langdale Linen Industry see **Elterwater**.

St Mary's Well Hutton John. Presumably, like several others, dedicated to St Mary Magdalene [440270].

St Michael's Church Lowther, see **Lowther Park**.

St Oswald's Grasmere. Writing 150 years ago in her *A Description of the English Lakes* Harriet Martineau refers to "the cluster of lodging-houses called St Oswald's, where a hydropathic establishment struggled on for a time, but found the Westmorland winters too long for invalids." Today, St Oswald's is leased as private property by the National Trust [332072] ...there are suggestions that at one time the property was owned by St Oswald's Church or that it was either a projected site for, or even the site of, an earlier church. A very old well (long since covered) in a field alongside is claimed to have been used by the nearby St Oswald's Church for christening purposes. Legend even has it that St Oswald himself used to conduct baptisms here.

St Oswald's Church Grasmere, see **Grasmere** also **St Oswald's** above.

St Patrick's Well alongside the A592 at Glenridding. Stone surround and slate roofed. Once thought to have healing properties and legend has it that St Patrick baptised here [388166]. NB there is also a St Patrick's Well at Bampton.

St Raven's Edge overlooking head of N section of Kirkstone Pass from the E. Highest point 593m (1946ft) [406084] ...St Raven possibly a corruption of Sattereven therefore Sattereven's Edge (see also **Sattereven**).

St Sunday Crag between Fairfield and Patterdale a long fell spreads itself roughly in a NE direction and includes Cofa Pike, Deepdale Hause, St Sunday Crag and Birks. The major height is that of St Sunday Crag. Although the latter title is generally accepted as the name of the mountain the actual summit is called the Cape. St Sunday Crag comprises a mile-long series of crags on the NNE-WSW of the Cape overlooking Grisedale. These crags are interspersed by gullies such as West Chockstone Gully, Y Gully, East Chockstone Gully and a noted arete, Pinnacle Ridge 841m (2759ft) [369134] ...why St Sunday Crag? Nothing definite. There is a St Sunday Beck in the Kent valley which, like its namesake, is possibly from St Sanctan or may even be derived from St Dominic. The latter was often referred to as St Sunday. In any case, why did this particular line of crags take its name from the saint?

Sale Fell overlooking Wythop Mill and Wythop Dale 359m (1178ft) [194297].

Sale How summit in the Skiddaw group 666m (2185ft) [276286].

Sale Pot small hanging valley through which flows Riggindale Beck shortly after leaving the head of Riggindale Beck [444122] ...possibly the shieling by the deep hole or in the valley.

Salehow Beck the watercourse formed by the meeting of Stile Gill and Pike Sike meets Kitbain Gill at 281291 and become Salehow Beck which joins the River Caldew at 296297.

Sales combe down which flows Hogget Gill. Little Hart Crag lies to its S [386108] ...possibly from 'skali' meaning shed/shieling/hut.

Saletarn Knotts Crag Quarter, Kentmere [444054] ...no tarn is shown on the current OS map but obviously at one time there was an established tarn hereabouts with a shed/shieling (scale) nearby.

Sallows summit, Kentmere Park. S Garburn Pass 516m (1693ft) [437040] ...hill of the willows. Today a very few isolated trees exist hereabouts.

Sally Hill S Ponsonby Old Hall [055046] ...possibly from 'selja' - a dairy.

Salmond's Plantation alongside the A592 between Brackenrigg and Pooley Bridge. Presumably, like nearby Rumney's Plantation, derived from a local personal name [458241].

Salt Well Manesty. Possibly the Monks of Furness Abbey extracted salt here. Certainly recorded in the mid-16th century and an analysis in 1740 notes that it had curative properties which were claimed to cure many physiological illnesses [252185].

Saltcoats across the Mite/Irt estuary from Ravenglass [077969] ...cottages/sheds where salt was dried or stored. For centuries the salt marshes of Morecambe Bay and alongside the Kent Estuary provided sites where salt was desalinated.

Saltcoats Crossing railway crossing on the line between Ravenglass and Drigg [079973].

Salutation Inn Ambleside. Old coaching inn dating back centuries.

Sam Bottom between the S ridge of Black Sails and Great How Crag and alongside Swirl Hawse Beck [279001].

Sam New Quarry N of Honister Hause. Worked from 1839. Re-activated in 1901 [224145].

Samgarth Beck continuation of Rowantree Beck which becomes Mill Beck shortly after the confluence of Stainton and Black Becks.

Samling, The see **Dove's Nest**.

Sampson's Bratful Stockdale Moor [098080] ...legend suggests that Sampson dropped a pile of stones from his brat (apron) when the string of the latter broke. However, it is more than likely that this large and lengthy cairn is an ancient tumulus (burial ground), see also **Stockdale Moor**.

Sampson's Stones large boulders between the foot of Cam Spout Crag and the River Esk [218054] ...like Sampson's Bratful legend suggests that Sampson dropped (or in this case threw) the stones here. The real answer is that the boulders were carried and dumped by a retreating glacier.

Sand Beds NW Ullock Pike. W the Edge and E of the A591 [238294].

Sand Gill rises 393145 and joins Deepdale Beck at Deepdale Bridge at 399144.

Sand Ground alongside Skinner How Lane [342993] ...see **Grounds**.

Sand Hill between Hopegill Head and Coledale Hause 756m (2480ft) [187219].

Sand Hill off the A591 [232289].

Sand Parrock N Force Forge. W Force Mills [335911] ...sand paddock.

Sandbank alongside a minor road from the A595 (Holmrook)-Santon Bridge road to Eskdale [113998].

Sandbed Gill rises S Jim's Fold (sheepfold) at 326220 and drops down to join St John's Beck at 318217.

Sandbeds Gill rises slope of Ullock Pike at 240290 but, according to the OS map, drops down as far as the A591 at 234291.

Sandbeds Moss N old coach road, St John's in the Vale-Dockray [367229].

Sanderson Gill rises below Grisedale Pike at 199232. Joins Grisedale Gill at 208242. For continuation see **Grisedale Gill**.

Sandhill Knotts W Haweswater. Alongside Measand Beck [484154].

Sandwick cluster of properties E shore Ullswater, W Hallin Fell and Howtown. The road from Pooley Bridge to Howtown continues on to Sandwick from where there is a scenic coastal path to Patterdale [423196] ...sandy creek.

Sandwick Beck Boredale Beck and Howegrain Beck join at 426194 and become Sandwick Beck which enters Ullswater at 423200.

Sandy Beck begins life after the confluence of Mosser Beck and Cat Gill. Joined by Cleaty Gill and meets the River Cocker at 137271.

Sandy Nab promontory W shore Windermere [385944] ...'nab/nabbi' - a projection.

Sandy Wyke bay W Windermere alongside Pull Wyke and, along with the latter, classed as a wildlife refuge [367023].

Sandybeck Bridge carries minor road from Brandlingill to Low Lorton over Sandy Beck [135269].

Sandyhill Staveley. Farm on the S bank of the River Kent [475977].

Santon hamlet at the meeting of minor roads, Gosforth to Santon Bridge and the A595 to Santon Bridge [099018] ...dwelling/farmstead/hamlet on sandy soil.

Santon Bridge hamlet which has grown up around a major crossing over the River Irt. The modernised Bridge Inn is the home, each November, of the World's Biggest Liar Competition which was actually started in the 19th century by Will Ritson of Wasdale Head. He earned the title by telling amazing stories so convincingly that they sounded true. On one occasion he claimed that turnips grown in Wasdale were so large that food was quarried out of them and what was left was used as shelters for the Herdwick sheep. This 'convincing lying' became a contest which continued for a considerable time before dying out. However, it was revived in 1975 and journalists and onlookers flock to the inn to listen to the raconteurs. The Santon Bridge Craft Shop was established over 40 years ago [111016] ...see **Santon**.

Santon House alongside the Santon to Gosforth road [097021].

Sara Point see **White Moss Common & Baneriggs**.

Sarah's Gate see **White Moss Common & Baneriggs**.

Sattereven fell between the summit of Kirkstone Pass and upper Woundale [407081] ...more than likely a name equivalent to Seat Sandal in that it is an inversion compound. In the case of Seat Sandal {Seat, 'saetr' (mountain pasture) of Sandulf} but in this case {Satter, 'saetr'(mountain pasture) of Even or similar but unidentified surname}.

Satterthwaite small village at the foot of the Grizedale Beck valley and at the head of the Rusland valley. It possesses a church, consecrated in 1840, and which replaced several earlier chapels; an inn, the Eagles Head; and just S of the village a school built in 1848 [339924] ...summer pasture in the clearing. This was obviously the summer pasture of one Hrolfr (modern Rolf) who gave his name to Rusland.

Satterthwaite Bridge Satterthwaite. Carries the Satterthwaite-Force Mills road over Grizedale Beck [337921].

Satterthwaite Moor E Coniston Water and above Satterthwaite [319916].

Satura Crag overlooking path between Angle Tarn and The Knott (424137) ...more than likely similar to Setterah and Satter of Sattereven in that it derives from 'saetr' - mountain pasture/shieling and therefore means the crag on the hill by the mountain pasture.

Savin Hill W slope Brim Fell [269988] ...see **Savins** below.

Savins ESE High Hartsop Dodd. Overlooks Caiston Glen and Beck [395107] ...'savin' is another name for a species of the juniper tree. Locally, however, the name is also given to other species of the same tree. Charcoal from the savin was particularly valuable in the manufacture of gunpowder.

Sawmill Cottage off the Staveley to Kentmere road. As its name implies it had an earlier association with a saw mill. This adjacent building is now a studio and gallery for Kentmere Pottery [454017].

Sawrey Ground off the road from Hawkshead Hill-Tarn Hows [335991] ...see **Grounds.** Sawrey means a wet/muddy place but is also the name of an earlier prominent local family.

Sawrey Striceley between Ashes Beck and Force Beck [340902] ...Sawrey is a personal name but also means the 'muddy place'. For Striceley see **Striceley Fell**.

Sawrey Striceley Tarn Sawrey Striceley. Artificial tarn at an altitude of C55m (C180ft) [339907] ...see **Sawrey Striceley** and **Striceley Fell**.

Sawrey's Wood rear Elterwater Hall [322045].

Sawreys see **Far Sawrey & Near Sawrey**.

Sawry Bridge carries the bridleway from Satterthwaite to Grizedale over Grizedale Beck [337924].

Scab Moss Claife Heights [378988] ...suggests a bog/swamp covered by a crust.

Scafell (Sca Fell). Second highest of the Lake District mountains and separated from the highest, Scafell Pike, by the col of Mickledore, 964m (3163ft) [207065] ...see **Scafell Pike**.

Scafell Crag impressive N to E face of Scafell comprising buttresses, pinnacles and gullies. Many early 19th century rock climbs were pioneered on the crag and today it is one of the foremost, if not the foremost, climbing ground in the Lake District with climbs of varying degrees of severity and difficulty. Prominent amongst these are Broad Stand, East Buttress, Central Buttress, Pisgah, Pinnacle, Shamrock and Tower and Deep Gill buttresses. The only experienced walkers' or scramblers' route up Scafell through the crags is that via Lord's Rake (see **Lord's Rake**) [207068].

Scafell Hotel see **Rosthwaite**.

Scafell Pike formerly 'The Pikes', 'Pikes of Scawfell' or 'Scafell Pikes' all referring to the three summits of Broad Crag, Ill Crag and Scafell Pike. The latter is the highest of the three and is also the highest mountain in England. As such it is a mecca for those walkers who wish to say that they have stood on the highest point in the country. Its extremely rocky summit is surmounted by a huge cairn on which steps lead to a flat top. In 1921 an inscribed stone was built into the N face of the cairn commemorating the gift of the peak to the NT by Lord Leconfield as a memorial to the men of Lakeland who fell in the First World War. Slightly W of the cairn is an OS trigonometrical point. As late as 1959 a neolithic stone-axe factory site was discovered near the summit. The shortest route to the top is from Wasdale via Brown Tongue but there are also popular routes from Borrowdale, Eskdale and Great Langdale. Rock climbers can perform on Pike Crags and Dow Crag (Esk Buttress) and other climbs are detailed in the Fell and Rock Climbing Club's climbing guide *Scafell, Wasdale and Eskdale*, 978m (3209ft) [216072] ...hill with a shieling/hut or possibly the bald-headed hill referring to its barren summit area.

Scafell Pike group of fells. See Reference Section: **Heights**.

Scalderskew farm on the slope of Ponsonby Fell and S of Scalderskew Wood [087078] ...Skjoldr's wood.

Scalderskew Beck two headstreams rise, one E Scalderskew at 093078 and a lengthier one alongside Sampson's Bratful, Stockdale Moor, at 098081. The combined watercourses enter the River Bleng at 089066.

Scalderskew Wood alongside Worm Gill [087088].

Scale Nether Wasdale [133047] ...the shepherd's summer hut.

Scale Beck rises 107062 and joins the River Bleng alongside Bleng Bridge at 086055.

Scale Beck rises slope of Little Dodd at 149159 and flows over Scale Force before joining Crummock Water at 157159.

Scale Bridge bridge over Scale Gill [214024].

Scale Bridge carries track to Scale over Cinderdale Beck [133045].

Scale Bridge bridge across Buttermere Dubs [168166].

Scale Crag Eskdale [154005] ...crag by the hut/small house.

Scale Force waterfall on Scale Beck, Crummock. The longest drop of any Lakeland waterfall being 38m (125ft) [150170]. Wordsworth in his Guide written nearly 200 years ago says of Scale Force that "...it is a fine chasm, with a lofty, though but slender, fall of water."

Scale Gill Cowcove Beck and Catcove Beck join forces at 210028 to become Scale Gill which joins the River Esk at 215022 ...shieling/shepherd's summer hut by the stream.

Scale Gill rises 299075 and drops down alongside Raw Head to meet Great Langdale Beck at 313058 ...gill/ravine with a shed/shieling.

Scale Green below Scale Green Intake near Satterthwaite village [329929] ...'skali' - a shieling/hut.

Scale Green Intake Grizedale Forest Park [327936].

Scale Head a summit of Claife Heights. Higher than Latterbarrow but not as high as High Blind How 253m (830ft) [376978].

Scale Head Tarn unnamed on OS map. Slightly E of Wise Een Tarn C200m (C656ft) [373975].

Scale Hill alongside the Loweswater to the B5289 road. Here was the Scale Hill Hotel of which Wordsworth nearly 200 years ago noted that "...there is a roomy Inn, with very good accommodation." Today it is holiday apartments [150216].

Scale Island Crummock Water [161174].

Scale Ivy Intakes Claife Heights. Rises to 229m (751ft) [380965] ...'scale' - shed/shieling.

Scale Knott rocky hill overlooking Scale Beck and Crummock Water. Spot height at 338m (1109ft) [150178].

Scale Knotts rocky hillocks above Scales, Kentmere [455056] ...shed/shieling by or on a rocky summit.

Scalebarrow Knott Rosgill Moor. NE Scalebarrow Tarn [520153] ...rocky hill with a shieling.

Scalebarrow Tarn obviously a small tarn at one time but now just a bog. SW Scalebarrow Knott [519151].

Scalebeck Gill rises Dodd/Skiddaw Dodd at 248272 and flows down to meet the River Derwent.

Scaleclose Coppice NT enclosure bounded on the N by combined tributaries of Scaleforce Gill and on the S by Scaleforce Gill. Hidden alongside the coppice is Scaleclose Force [247149].

Scaleclose Force waterfall on Scaleclose Gill alongside Scaleclose Coppice [248149].

Scaleclose Gill rises 237146 and joins Tongue Gill at 250150. This enters the River Derwent at 252150 ...hut near the stream.

Scalegate SW Helton and approached from it by road and track [488203] ...way to the shieling.

Scalehill Bridge carries the Loweswater to B5289 road over the R Cocker [149215].

Scalehow Beck rises Place Fell at 406173. Subsequently drops down by cascades and notable waterfall, Scalehow Force [414190], to join Ullswater at 416196 ...shieling (hut) on the hill by the stream.

Scalehow Force see **Scalehow Beck**.

Scalehow Wood E shore Ullswater. Through it flows Scalehow Beck [415194].

Scales 2kms (1.5 miles) NE Threlkeld on A66. The start of two major paths up Blencathra, one via Scales Fell and the other by Sharp Edge [344269] ...shieling - hut.

Scales alongside the road between Kentmere and Hartrigg. In 1999 the farmhouse, as part of the Kentmere Hall & Hartrigg Estate, came up for sale by private treaty [459054].

Scales slope above the head of Crummock Water [161168].

Scales High Lorton [166254.

Scales Beck flows from Scales Tarn, Blencathra, [330281] to meet the R Glenderamackin at 334283.

Scales Farm Scales. Dates from the 17th century [342269].

Scales Farm SW Helton at end of road and track from the hamlet [487201] ...shieling + farm.

Scales Fell E slope Blencathra. Bounded on the W by Scaley Gill and on the E by the R Glenderamackin and Comb Beck. Highest point is actually Doddick Fell Top at 682m (2238ft) [332279] but there is a subsidiary summit at 641m (2103ft) [335278].

Scales Tarn Blencathra 610m (2001ft). Towering above it to the W is Tarn Crags, to the N Sharp Edge and Foule Crag and to the NE Brunt Knott. Believed at one time to be bottomless but actually at its deepest is only 8m (26ft) [329281]. Set in such a deep hollow that it is said that on looking down from the crags above at midday stars can be seen reflected in the dark water.

Scales Wood an SSSI. An Atlantic oak/birch wood which supports 60 different types of mosses and liverworts [166165].

Scaley Beck flows down the S face of Blencathra from 331277 to meet the R Glenderamackin at 339260.

Scaley Moss W Blakeley Raise. Alongside Coldfell Road [060136].

Scam Matthew E Mosedale. Above bridleway between Wet Sleddale and Mosedale C520m (C1706ft) [516105] ...scam is possibly an error for a scar which is named after a local family of Matthew.

Scandale valley through which flows Scandale Beck and up which initially a track and then a footpath leads to a col and then down Caiston Glen [380079] ...short valley.

Scandale Beck two principal headstreams, one rising at Scandale Head but the furthest between Little Hart Crag and Bakestones Moss at 383100. The beck flows slightly W of Scandale Tarn, down Scandale, under High and Low Sweden Bridges before joining the R Rothay at 371045 near the confluence of the latter with Stock Ghyll.

Scandale Bottom foot of Scandale Fell before steepish ascent by Scandale Pass to col [381087]

Scandale Bottom Sheepfold [382088].

Scandale Bridge carries the A591 over Scandale Beck. Lowest of the three bridges over the beck the other two being High and Low Sweden Bridges [372051].

Scandale Fell alongside the head of Scandale [380090].

Scandale Head head of Scandale [378097].

Scandale Pass from Ambleside, initially a track and then a footpath leads alongside High Sweden Bridge, an interesting old packhorse bridge, up the dale and across part of Scandale Fell to a col between Little Hart Crag and Red Screes. It then continues down Caiston Glen either to the Brotherswater Inn or via Hartsop Hall and alongside Brothers Water to the A592 at Cow Bridge. A popular walkers' route from Ambleside to Patterdale and from the col good access to Red Screes, Little Hart Crag and Dove Crag. Highest point C520m (C1706ft) [388096] ...the pass at the head of the short valley.

Scandale Tarn sometimes known as Little Hart Crag Tarn. Slightly NW of the col at the head of Scandale Pass. On a rock overhanging the water is carved "Harry Bogle and Percy Laidlaw stocked this tarn with gudgeon fish on July 5th, 1878." Whether any still remain with the few trout it is said to contain I have no record C560m (C1837ft) [386098].

Scar Crag Birker Moor C250m (C820ft) [183979].

Scar Crags craggy face on the Rowling End-Causey Pike-Sail ridge 672m (2205ft) [208206].

Scar Foot alongside the Kendal-Underbarrow road. Used to be three cottages [482922] ...at the foot of Underbarrow Scar.

Scar Foot Farm behind Scar Foot [482922].

Scar Gill rises Hardknott at 229021 and joins the Esk at 222027.

Scar Head Torver [283947].

Scar House Lane connects Loanthwaite Lane and Colthouse [355988].

Scar Lathing S Great Moss, Eskdale 439m (1440ft) [226049].

Scar Plantation see **Knipe Scar & Knipescar Common**.

Scar Wood below Cunswick Scar [491936].

Scar Wood see **Station Scar Wood**.

Scarbrow Wood Gosforth. Alongside the Gosforth to Nether Wasdale road [099044].

Scarf Crag Harrot [160272].

Scarf Stones Derwent Water [264211] ...stones frequented by cormorants.

Scargreen in the valley of Scargreen Beck 1.6kms (1mile) from Ponsonby [066059].

Scargreen Beck rises 076061 and flows past Scargreen to join the River Calder at 054064.

Scarny Brow steep section of Coldfell Road [061143].

Scarside W Bampton Grange. Approached by lane off the Bampton Grange-Rosgill Head-Shap road [537183].

Scarside Plantation see **Knipe Scar & Knipescar Common**.

Scarth Gap gap between Seat and Haystacks through which the path from Buttermere to Ennerdale passes C450m (C1476ft) [189133] ...a tautology. Scarth (from 'skaro') also means gap.

Scarth Gap Pass pass leading over Scarth Gap from Buttermere to Ennerdale [188136].

Scartufts see **Loughrigg Fell**.

Scattering Garth alongside track off minor road from the A595 (Holmrook) to Santon Bridge [099992].

Scaw Ennerdale. Slope of Great Borne [124159] ...either wood or scar. In the latter case the steep scar below the summit of Great Borne shown on some maps and guide books as Herdus Scar.

Scaw Well above Scaw and ESE of the summit of Great Borne [127162].

Scawgill Bridge carries the B5292 over Aiken Beck [177257] ...bridge by the wooded ravine.

Sceugh E of the unfenced road between Heltondale and Rough Hill. NNW Butterwick [498198] ...wood. There is also a Skews to the NW of Bampton.

Schelly rare fish so far only confirmed to be found in England in Ullswater, Haweswater, Brothers Water and Red Tarn but with the possibility of it existing in two or three other lakes and tarns. At the time of writing there was a project to move some eggs to Blea Water and

Small Water where it is hoped they will develop and reproduce.

School Knott SE Windermere Station 232m (761ft) [426974]. School Knott Tarn lies at its foot. Wainwright writing in 1973 pointed out that the summit did not possess a cairn. Most surprising is that it still does not possess one [426974] ...the adjective 'school' could be a word corruption but more than likely it simply means the hill above the school. In the case of the latter, the school may have been either of two of the former Windermere Grammar Schools. The first occupied Laurel House (now a guest house), Bowness, from 1613-1836 and the second replaced it, also in Bowness, but in a more easterly direction from 1836-1885. Suggests the former considering that in its day and age the school would be prominent amongst the relatively few cottages which then comprised Bowness. Incidentally, the third Windermere Grammar School, alongside Princes Road, Windermere, opened in 1885, was demolished in the 1960s and replaced by another school.

School Knott Tarn on a col between School Knott and Grandsire. Trout fishing by permit from WADAA, C200m (C656ft) [428973].

School Wood near Roger Ground. Alongside the Hawkshead-Satterthwaite road [350973].

Schoolknott Plantation NE School Knott [428977].

Schwitters, Kurt artist. Born Hanover, 1887, died Ambleside 1948. An orthodox oil painter he was also a recognised poet, dramatist and musician. However, he is probably best remembered as one of the pioneers of abstract impressionist art and on settling in Ambleside after the Second World War he used an empty barn in Great Langdale as a studio and on an interior wall started a style of sculpture called a Merzbau which had three dimensional properties and utilised objects such as piping, a wheel rim and other mundane objects to create an abstract mural set in cement. This was 3.8m (12.5ft) long by 2.3m (7.5ft) high.

For many years after his death the unfinished mural remained in the barn but in October 1965, it, and the inner wall of the barn were transported by low loader to be put on public display in the Faculty of Science and Arts at Newcastle University.

Scoat Fell centre of four ridges, W to Haycock, N to Steeple, E to Pillar and S to Red Pike. Possesses two principal summits, Great Scoat Fell and Little Scoat Fell, the latter being the highest at 841m (2759ft) [160114] and the former 39m (128ft) lower at 155112. Great and Little refer to land mass ...fell with projecting ridges.

Scoat Tarn set in a glacial hollow below Red Pike (Wasdale) and Scoat Fell. Takes its name from the latter. The source of one of the two principal headstreams which combine to form Nether Beck. Believed to contain brown trout C600m (C1968ft) [159103] ...the tarn by the 'skot' - projecting piece of land/ridge (Scoat Fell).

Scogarth near Guardhouse [345262] ...shepherd's hut in the enclosure.

Scope Beck Deep Gill rises at the head of Little Dale at 205166 and with other small streams becomes Scope Beck. This enters a man-made reservoir, Scope Beck Tarn, before exiting as a more substantial Scope Beck which subsequently joins Newlands Beck at 231192 ...probably from, 'sceap' OE for sheep.

Scope Beck Tarn shown as reservoir on the OS map. Dammed at its lower end. Constructed to provide water power for the Goldscope Mine [215178].

Scope End end of the Hindscarth-High Crags ridge. Drops steeply to the Newlands valley [224183] ....see **Scope Beck** above but also, and appropriately, it is the end above the former Goldscope Mine.

Scot Crag SSE Hart Crag. Overlooks Deepdale Slack and looks across SSE to Sheffield Pike [362192].

Scot Hall Gosforth [085023].

Scot(s) Rake from the E of Thornthwaite Crag a path drops steeply down the western shoulder of Froswick to Hagg Gill. This was used by marauding Scots centuries ago and was the scene of at least one major skirmish between locals and Scots ...rough path of the Scots. There is another Scot Rake in Ravenstonedale but this takes its name from members of a local Scot(t) family.

Scothall Plantation S Scot Hall [085021].

Scott Crag craggy area alongside the path from Sail to Crag Hill [196203].

Scott Howe E A5074. Between Bryan Houses Plantation and Foxhole Wood 169m (554ft) [427929] ...surname + hill.

Scott Wood Lorton Vale. Alongside the River Cocker [153241].

Scour Rigg Kentmere Park [447037] ...shed on, or alongside, a ridge.

Scout Crag across White Gill from Swine Knott. Possesses several rock climbs of varying degrees of difficulty [298070] ...overhanging rock.

Scout Hill WSW High Mill. SE Bellman Houses [409939] ...probably similar to Scout Hills at Crook and Lupton in that it means rocky hill.

Scout Scar projecting rock on the escarpment. See **Underbarrow Scar**.

Scream Point alongside the A591 just N of Ratherheath Lane [489961] ...an interesting name but apparently of obscure origin.

Scream Point Tarn not named on the OS map. Approximately 140m (153 yards) N of Ratherheath Tarn. Narrow and shallow. Height 105m (344ft) [484960].

Screes, The see **The Screes**.

Screes Coppice across the B5289 from Mary Mount Hotel [268192].

Scrithwaite Farm Broughton Mills [220913] ...clearing by a landslip on a hillside.

Scroggs Bridge Over Staveley. Carries the road from Staveley to Kentmere over the Kent [467994] ...bridge by the brushwood.

Scroggs Farm Over Staveley. Near Scroggs Bridge [470993].

Scrow Beck lengthy stream which rises high on the E slope of Coniston Old Man at 277976 and joins Church Beck at 298977 ...for derivation of scrow see **Glossary**.

Scrubby Crag NNE of Link Hause, between Hart Crag and Fairfield [367116].

Seacross Lonnin unusual named lonnin (lane), Wythop Mill [173297].

Seal Gill rises near Broughton Moor Quarry at 258942 and joins Ash Gill Beck at 273951 ...gill by the willows.

Sealhole Grain rises at 469166 and joins Cawdale Beck at 472175. This flows down Cawdale and become Howes Beck before flowing into Haweswater Beck at 518180. Shortly afterwards this joins the River Lowther ...'seal' - willow, 'hole' - hollow, 'grain' - fork of a river or valley.

Seamew Crag in Windermere near Sandy Wyke. Most northerly of Windermere's named islets or islands [370024] ...sea gull crag. According to *Collins Dictionary* 'mew' is any sea gull but especially the common gull.

Seat subsidiary summit at the end of the Red Pike-High Stile-High Crag ridge 561m (1840ft) [186134].

Seat Farm E Ullswater off the Pooley Bridge to Howtown road [462223] ...derived either from the ON 'seati' (lofty place) and therefore the farm in a lofty place. In this case a headland overlooking Ullswater. May also be derived from ON 'saetr' meaning summer pasture.

Seat How Birker Moor. Overlooks Devoke Water from the E 311m (1020ft) [165971] ...inversion compound meaning hill of the shieling/summer pasture.

Seat How craggy area in the Lord's Seat group C490m (C1608ft) [213256] ...see **Seat How** above.

Seat Robert E Haskew Tarn, ESE Willy Winder Hill. Highest part of Ralfland Forest. Like the not too distant Branstree, nearby Yarlside and Hallsfell Top, Blencathra, it is unusual in that it possesses a sunken OS ring 515m (1690ft) [526114] ...Robert's outcrop of rocks, seat. Similar in derivation to Hugh's Seat, Lady's Seat, Lord's Seat and Simon's Seat.

Seat Sandal W Fairfield to which it is joined by Grisedale Hause and Hause Gap. "A fond lover of the clouds" in *Wordsworth's Prelude*, 736m (2415ft) [344115] ...Sandulf's shieling (summer pasture).

Seat Side overlooks Scandale Bottom from the E [385086].

Seat Tarn small tarn (shown but not named on the OS map) alongside the path from Seat to Gamlin End C530m (C1739ft) [184136].

Seatallan formerly Seat Allan. One of the lesser known and least visited mountains in the Lake District. Its cone-shaped ridge, adorned with a trig. point and a large cairn (the latter believed to be of considerable antiquity) surmounts rocky outcrops to the N and E. At the foot of its SE slope is the comparatively large Greendale Tarn. There are several routes to its grassy summit, some interesting but others tedious 692m (2270ft) [140084] ...an inversion compound similar to Seat Robert and Seat Sandal. In this case it refers to Alein's summer pasture.

Seathow Wood below Seat How and above the Braithwaite-Thornthwaite-A66 road [221259].

Seathwaite Ambleside. Alongside the road which subsequently becomes a track to Roundhill Farm [383047] ...first element is obscure. Possible interpretations include 'saetr' meaning mountain pasture or shieling; 'sef' sedges/rushes; an earlier name Sealthwaite Green could refer to 'sele' meaning willow copse. Similar to Seathwaite in the Duddon valley the whole could be the clearing by the lake. In this case the lake would be Windermere or there could be a possible reference to a widening of Stock Ghyll thereabouts.

Seathwaite largest settlement in the Duddon valley. Possesses an inn (see also **Newfield Inn**), a church, cottages and farms. The Rev Robert Walker, often referred to as 'Wonderful Walker' primarily because of his good works, was born at Seathwaite in 1702 and died there in 1802. In between these dates he ministered at the chapel for 66 years. His grave is in the churchyard. The chapel was rebuilt in the 1870s. One of Wordsworth's Duddon sonnets is dedicated to the chapel and particularly its minister and attached to the poem he wrote a *Memoir of the Rev. Robert Walker* [228960] ...either sedge clearing or clearing by the lake (Seathwaite Tarn).

Seathwaite tiny community consisting of farm, cottages and house at the end of the Seathwaite valley and the last properties in Borrowdale. The farm cottage possesses a small cafe which provides sustenance for those hardy types who pass by it on their way to or from the high fells either by Stockley Bridge, Taylor Gill Force or Sourmilk Gill. Alongside Sour Milk Gill are huge sloping rocks known as the Seathwaite Slabs [232122] which provide sport and training for rock climbing novices. Slightly N of the gill can be seen the remains of the old Borrowdale Lead Mine [230128] which for centuries produced plumbago/graphite, known locally as wad and used for many purposes but best known for the manufacture of pencils. The mine closed in the mid-19th century when cheaper imports came from abroad. See also **Pencil Manufacture**. Further down the valley near Seathwaite Bridge are the remnants of the famous Borrowdale Yews [235126] immortalised as the "Fraternal Four of Borrowdale" in Wordsworth's poem *Yew-Trees*. The bridge over the

Seathwaite, Borrowdale.

Derwent N of the farm is a war memorial provided by the Ramblers Association. Seathwaite holds the record for the wettest inhabited place in England with around 130 inches of rain per year. See also **Styhead Tarn**. Most of the farm was acquired by the NT in 1944. The rest, along with Rainguage Cottage at its rear, was given to the Trust in 1982. Just S of the farm is High House. The original 18th century building became a ruin but was later rebuilt as the K-Fellwalkers base [215121] ...either sedge clearing or clearing by a lake. Although there is no lake today it is more than likely that the flat valley between Seathwaite and Seatoller was once a substantial lake.

Seathwaite Bridge carries the road up the Duddon valley across Tarn Beck [232968].

Seathwaite Bridge carries the Seatoller to Seathwaite road over the River Derwent [240128].

Seathwaite Fell high triangular fell bounded by Styhead Gill, Grains Gill and the track from Sty Head to Rossett Gill. Three principal summits, N 601m (1972ft), S 631m (2070ft) and in the middle 632m (2073ft) [227097].

Seathwaite Slabs see **Seathwaite**, Borrowdale.

Seathwaite Stepping Stones see **Stepping Stones**.

Seathwaite Tarn a small tarn above the Duddon valley was dammed at the beginning of last century to provide a water supply for the people of Barrow. Today it is classed as the second largest tarn in the Lake District Park after Devoke Water. The source of Tarn Beck, a major tributary of the River Duddon, it is fed principally by Tarn Head Beck and Bleaberry Gill. Possesses a small rocky island and contains many brown trout. Fishing rights are owned by the Furness Fishing Association, C380m (C1247ft) [253988].

Seathwaite Tarn Mine old disused copper mine just above the head of Seathwaite Tarn and alongside Tarn Head Beck. Little historical information on it but it is best known for its reference in Richard Adams *The Plague Dogs* (1977) as the hiding place of the fugitive dogs, Rowf and Snitter, and the place where they met Tod, the fox [262993].

Seathwaite Tarns several tarns and small pools on Seathwaite Fell the largest of which now bears the name Sprinkling Crag Tarn. See slso **Sprinkling Crag Tarn**.

Seatoller hamlet at the foot of the Honister Pass and at the junction of the road to

Seathwaite. End of the bus route from Keswick through Borrowdale. Possesses a large NT car and coach park, the Yew Tree Country Restaurant (parts of which date from 1628), a converted barn which houses the LDNP Dalehead Base with its displays, study facilities, talks and during the season the starting point for guided walks. Seatoller Farm was acquired by the NT in 1959 [245138] ...either headland/promontory by the lake; summer pasture among the alder trees or Olwar's summer sheiling.

Seatoller Bridge carries the Seatoller to Seathwaite road over Hause Gill [246137].

Seatoller Fell fell area to the S of the Seatoller to Honister Hause road and W of the Seathwaite valley C460 (C1509ft) [233132].

Seaton Hall off the A595 between Corney and Bootle. Remains of a priory here, Seaton or Lekeley Priory, dating from before 1227. In the early 17th century it is recorded that Leckley is now called Seaton [107900] ...along with Seaton near Workington more than likely simply means the hamlet by the sea although both are over a mile from the sea.

Seatonhall Wood E Seaton Hall [111900].

Seavy Knott W Loft Beck [203121] ...sedgy rocky hill.

Seavy Mire Hill Claife Heights [376973] ...'sedge' mire/bog hill.

Seavy Side between Little Mosedale Beck and Mosedale Beck [497089] ...sedgy side (of ridge).

Second Moss Lane see **First, Second, Third Moss Lanes**.

Segrave, Sir Henry (1896-1930). Land and water-speed record holder. He established a water-speed record of 98.76 mph on Windermere in June 1930, before being killed on another run.

Seldom Seen terrace of former miners' cottages in the dale of Glencoyne. Certainly lives up to its name being hidden away 1.2kms (0.75 mile) up a track from the A592 [380185]. There is another Seldom Seen, a group of cottages alongside Chapel Beck, near Thornthwaite 6.4kms (4 miles) WNW of Keswick, and a former one stood below the B5345, Whitehaven-St Bees road.

Sele Bottom ESE Burnmoor. NE Buck Barrow. Logan Beck and tributaries flow through it [161919] ...either willow, mountain hut or hollow bottom.

Sella Ulpha [196925] ...either willow hill or shieling/hut on or by the hill.

Sellafield Nuclear Power Station Calder Hall Nuclear Power Station, Britain's first, opened on the site in 1956. This closed in 2003 but Sellafield, formerly known as Windscale, is still a major reprocessing plant for spent nuclear fuel [028039].

Selside flank to the SW of the Top o'Selside [306916] ...shieling/mountain pasture by the willows or possibly the shieling of a person called Seli.

Selside see **Selside Pike**.

Selside Beck Tarn Beck flows out of Arnsbarrow Tarn and becomes Selside Beck at 306911. This enters Coniston Water at 295909.

Selside Brow slope leading up from the head of Mosedale to Branstree/Artlecrag Pike. Distanced from Selside/Selside Pike but at the end of the Selside Pike-Branstree ridge [483094] ...Selside, N of Kendal, is deemed to be derived from willow copse but in this case Selside possibly means the hillside or pasture with a mountain hut on the brow.

Selside End lower slope of Selside NNE Selside Pike [494119].

Selside Pike the Pike, summit of Selside, is 2.4kms (1.5 miles) NE of Branstree and overlooks the head of Swindale. A grassy summit is surmounted by a considerable heap of stones possibly the remains of a broken rocky outcrop (the pike) 655m (2149ft) [490111] ...unlike Selside N of Kendal which is deemed to have been derived from 'sele' - willow copse, Selside Pike, above the tree level, is possibly from 'sel' mountain hut the whole meaning the sharp pointed hill with a mountain hut on its slope.

Sergeant Crag southern end of the Stainton Pike ridge [150938].

Sergeant's Crag the NNW ridge of High Raise heads over Sergeant's Crag and Eagle Crag before dropping steeply to the confluence of Greenup Gill and Langstrath Beck. Sergeant's Crag is the higher of the two rocky summits. Its sheer rock face, scarred by two gullies, overlooks Langstrath while the slope facing Greenup Gill is far more gentle. The deep gully on its W face was first climbed by the legendary O G Jones in the early 1890s 571m (1873ft) [274114] ...local family of William Sargyante mentioned in 1602.

Sergeant Man rocky summit to the E of the High Raise plateau. Normally ascended via Easedale but also approached from High Raise (High White Stones), the Blea Rigg ridge or Stickle Tarn 730m (2395ft) [286089] ...similar to Coniston Old Man, Skiddaw Man and Helvellyn Lower Man in that the word man refers to a summit cairn. Sergeant, like the not far distant Sergeant's Crag, suggests a surname/an official's title or simply owing to its fine position it was given an appropriate rank.

Sergeant Man Tarn slightly N of Sergeant Man [286091] ...see **Sergeant Man**.

Set Level Grizedale Forest Park. W Colin How, ESE Parkamoor [315922].

Settera Park S Helton [512210]. The ancient park contains a medieval moated 'camp' or 'homestead' moat which is scheduled as an Ancient Monument. Roman relics have been found here [514212] ...hill with a shieling + park.

Setterah Park Wood Setterah Park, S of Helton [512212]

Setterah Sike rises at 500200 and joins Heltondale Beck at 507206.

Settle Earth Longsleddale. Craggy, boulder strewn area below Raven Crag [476078] ...probably the lofty place where foxes go to earth. It is an area well-known to the foxhunting fraternity.

Settlements (includes ancient camps, earthworks, enclosures, field systems, forts and homesteads). Principal ones are:

070099	Tongue How (homestead)
074098	Tongue How (settlement)
097087	Stockdale Moor (field system)
098078	Stockdale Moor (field system)
132150	Ennerdale. Alongside Clews Gill (settlement)
133959	Barnscar (settlement)
185942	W Birker Moor Road (enclosure)
186951	W Birker Moor Road. Nr. Crosbythwaite Bridge (settlement)
187948	W Birker Moor Road. Nr. Crosbythwaite Bridge (enclosure)
190957	E Birker Moor Road. Nr. Crosbythwaite Bridge (field system)
240922	The Hawk (settlement)
300188	Castle Crag Hill Fort, Thirlmere.
328240	Threlkeld (settlement)
367149	Grisedale (homestead)
373034	Ambleside (Galava Roman fort)
379273, 384273 & 389277	N Troutbeck (Roman camps)
384272	N Troutbeck (Roman fort)
390199	Glencoyne Park (settlement)
398117	Near Hartsop Hall (settlement)
400142	Deepdale (settlement)

415011	Allen Knott (hill fort)
423081 & 423084	Sad Gill, Troutbeck (settlements)
423154	Heck Beck, Bannerdale (settlement)
437010	High Borrans (settlement)
440090, 452069 & 461025	Kentmere (settlements)
451244	Maiden Castle
461025	Millrigg, Kentmere (settlement)
461266	Dacre Castle (earthworks)
465234	S Gale Bay, Ullswater (moated site)
468246	Dunmallet Hill Fort
469128	Castle Crag Hill Fort, Mardale
490156	NE Measand Bridge (earthworks)
490163	Four Stones Hill (settlement)
493179	Towtop Kirk (homestead or fort)
498232 & 500234	Skirsgill Hill (settlements)
500160	W Burnbanks (homestead)
507157	SW Naddle Bridge (settlement)
514212	Setterah Park (moated camp or homestead)
525216	Cragside Wood (settlement)
529195	Knipescar Common (enclosure)
530193	Scarside Plantation (earthworks)
520029, 530029 & 532020	Bannisdale (settlements and enclosure)
542154	W-WNW Shap Abbey (earthworks)
545157	SW Shap Abbey (earthworks)
548152	Shap (remains of Shap Abbey)

Seven Wells alongside Farra Grain Gill [321924] ...no wells shown on the OS map but the name obviously refers to the numerous water outlets which serve as tributaries to Farra Grain Gill.

Sewage works

074032	(Gosforth)
152264	(Lorton)
224261	(off the A66 near the head of Bassenthwaite Lake.
235243	(Braithwaite. Off the A66)
246239	(Portinscale)
247176	(Grange-in-Borrowdale)
249139	(Seatoller)
255150	(Rosthwaite, Borrowdale)
255249	(Between the A591 and the River Derwent)
256180	(Borrowdale. W bank River Derwent)
259141	(Stonethwaite valley)
306971	(alongside Lake Road, Coniston)
326041	(Elterwater)
372041	(alongside the River Rothay, Ambleside)
385912	(E shore Windermere)
481980	(E Staveley)

Shap for origin of name see **Shap Abbey**.

Shap Abbey its remains stand in a secluded and lonely valley alongside the R Lowther

1.6kms (1 mile) W of Shap and off the Shap-Bampton road. It is open to the public. The Premonstratensians (White Canons) established themselves here about 1199 upon their removal from Preston Patrick. The Abbey was dissolved in 1540 and the buildings began to fall into ruins. Many stones were later removed to be used in the construction of other buildings in the Shap area. However, from what still remains a picture can be built up of a substantial monastic building. The high 16th century West Tower has been restored. Shap Abbey Farm adjoins [548152] ...the name Shap comes from Hep(p)(e) meaning a heap, pile of stones. A stone circle stands S of the village of Shap and the Goggleby Stone [559151] and Thunder Stone [552158] and others are all that now remain of a former long avenue of standing stones.

Shap Blue Quarry see **Shap Quarries**.

Shap Clock see **Leyland Clock**.

Shap Fells extensive area of fells between Kendal and Shap (marked on the 2.5 ins OS map at 546092) which in days gone by was traversed by predecessors of the present A6. Only on the far W fringe does any height exceed 610m (2000ft). Grey Crag (Sleddale Fell) 638m (2093ft) and Harrop Pike 637m (2090ft). In the middle of the 16th century the 'road' across the fells was quoted as being "through such wayes, as we hope we never shall againe..." and over 100 years later Thomas West described the route as "a dreary melancholy tract of twelve miles." Up to the opening of the M6 motorway the route over Shap via the A6 could be terrible in winter with dense fog, ice, and frequent blockages by snow.

In May 1994, a 3m (10ft) high piece of shap granite, suitably inscribed as a tribute to drivers and crew of commercial vehicles which used the old A6 trunk road over Shap and also to those people of Kendal and Shap village who helped the drivers during atrocious weather conditions thereabouts, was unveiled alongside the A6 at Shap summit. The predecessor of the present A6 became a stage coach route in 1763 and the route of the A6 was constructed in the 1820s. The Lancaster-Carlisle section of the railway opened in 1846 and the stretch of the M6 motorway in 1971. At its summit the A6 reaches 426m (1397ft), and the M6, 316m (1036ft). Even today the area is far from touristified, and desolate and lonely valleys like Bannerdale, Borrowdale, Crookdale, Wasdale and Wet Sleddale lead to even more desolate and remote hill and crag tops. Shap Fells comprise an area whose appeal is principally in its wildness and loneliness rather than its beauty. Certainly John Ruskin appreciated this when he wrote "Ever since I passed Shap fells, when a child, I have had an excessive love for this kind of desolation."

Ancient documents suggest that at one time there were considerable numbers of Scandinavian settlers in the area for mention is made of a Thengeheved ('council place at the head of the valley') in Swindale. This was apparently where a 'parliament' met to settle affairs of the settlers for a considerable area around it. In May 1975, an F11 crashed on the slope of Little Yarlside killing its pilot. Early this century a fighter jet crashed into a bridge just N of Shap village. In recent years there have been several sightings of a large black animal which many consider to be a panther in the Shap area. There is, however, a legend concerning a black animal, in this case a large black dog, which has been seen bounding along the Shap road. Shortly after its sightings there occurred a number of traffic accidents all of which ended in tragedy. See also **Eastern Fells** in Reference Section: **Heights**.

Shap Pink Quarry see **Shap Quarries**.

Shap Quarries Shap granite is of very high quality and exceedingly attractive and is mined at the Shap Pink Quarry [558084] and Shap Blue Quarry [564106] both of them clearly visible W of the A6 between Shap and Shap summit. Shap granite has been in demand for some considerable time and numerous buildings show examples of it. To name a few - the Albert Memorial; St Pancras Station; the Thames Embankment; Manchester Town Hall and Royal Exchange; St George's Hall, Liverpool; and the facades of many Victorian bank buildings. At the present time the Pink Quarry is mothballed and the Blue Quarry is principally used to extract ballast and aggregates.

Sharp Edge Blencathra. As its name implies an exceedingly narrow ridge which was formerly known as Razor Edge. Runs from Brunt Knott to Foule Crag providing an impressive view down into the crater-like Scales Tarn [327284]. An interesting and exhilarating route to the summit ridge of Blencathra but one that can be dangerous particularly in bad weather.

Sharp Knott ESE Lamplugh. Extensive former mining activity to the N of its summit. Forestry on its slopes to the N, W and S. Both Sharpknott Gill and Wisenholme Beck rise here 482m (1581ft) [107201].

Sharpknott Gill rises Sharp Knott at 106200 and flows down into Cogra Moss.

Sharrow Bay Ullswater. Two miles from Pooley Bridge along the Pooley Bridge to Howtown road [455219] ...'sharrow' - boundary hill + bay.

Sharrow Bay country house hotel, Sharrow Bay, Ullswater. Reputed to be the first country house hotel created in Great Britain and generally considered to be one of the top Lake District hotels. The property was erected in 1844 and greatly enlarged 10 years later. In 1948 Francis Coulson (died February 1998) opened it as an hotel and restaurant and he was later joined by Brian Sachs (died some three years after Francis Coulson). Since its inception the hotel has received considerable recognition and many national awards [456220].

Sharrow Mire E Sharrow Bay, Ullswater [460218].

Shatton Hall SE Cockermouth, off the B5292 [148281] ...possibly the hall in the point or corner of land. Both it and Shatton Lodge Farm lie in a pointed area between the B5292 and parallel road which ultimately meets the B5292.

Shatton Lodge Farm SE Cockermouth, off the B5292 [145283].

Shaw Bank served by track from A591 through Dale Bottom [301215].

Shaw Beck one of three small streams which feed Skeggles Water from the N and NW. Rises 475042 and enters Skeggles Water at 478034 ...copse through, or by which, the stream flows.

Shawbank Crag High Rigg overlooking Naddle Valley [303215].

Sheep although the native sheep of the Lake District is the thick-set, white-faced Herdwick, there are many Swaledales, a finer-bodied sheep horned in both sexes, with a dark face and grey muzzle, Rough Fell, Blackface, Dalesbred, North Country Cheviots (Northies), some other breeds and cross breeds and a few rare breeds. Herdwicks are mainly found on the high fells.

Incidentally, the origin of the hardy Herdwick is the subject of controversy. One school suggests that, from a wrecked Armada ship, "Forty little sheep swam ashore lang syne on Drigg shore... thrived... and spread all over Lakeland." The fact that there is no record of an Armada ship being wrecked on the Cumberland coast and Herdwicks were certainly farmed in the Lake District long before that era points to this as pure folklore. The most likely theory is that they were brought over by Viking settlers. One former farming family in Swindale claims to have raised Herdwicks from the late 12th to the early 19th century. The Viking theory is also given much credence by the old method of counting sheep in the Lake District and Yorkshire. The numbers up to 20 bear much similarity to Celtic/Danish words - Yan, Tyan, Tethera, Methera, Pimp, Cethera/Sethera, Lethera, Hovera, Dovera, Dick, Yan-a-dick, Tyan-a-dick, Tethera dick, Methera dick, Bumphit/Bumfit, Yan-a-bumphit, Tyan-a-bumphit, Tethera bumphit, Methera bumphit, Jigot/Giggot. Slight variations in spelling occur between different areas. Each 20 was notched up on a long stick and a 100 was signified by a pebble placed in the pocket. During this century the hardy Herdwick flocks have been declining steadily. This is due partly to cross-breeding and partly due to an annual exodus to other areas of the country. In order to establish ownership sheep are marked on their fleece with dye. These marks are called smit marks. The hundreds currently in use in Cumbria are listed in a smit book (Shepherd's Guide). This was first introduced in 1817. See also **Heaf/Heft**.

Sheep Crag above Chapel Stile [317061].

Sheep Crag SW Grey Friar [256001].

Sheep Dog Trials prominent sporting feature in Lakeland. The earliest recorded was in 1877 at Belle Isle, Windermere. The Lake District Sheep Dog Trials Association was formed in 1891.

Sheep Pens SE Fairbank Farm [456977].

Sheep Rock (Roche Moutonee), see **Deepdale**.

Sheepbone Buttress between Comb Crags and High Crag Buttress [180144].

Sheffield Pike part of the Helvellyn massif. Stands prominently between Glencoyne and Glenridding showing crags to both. Black Crag looks N over Glencoyne and Glenridding Screes and crags face Glenridding to the S ...not named after the City of Sheffield or even a person of that name but most likely a corruption of sheep fell or sheep fold 675m (2215ft) [369182].

Shelter Cairn Hindscarth [216167].

Shelter Crag Tarns see **Shelter Crags**.

Shelter Crags N Crinkle Crags and on the same ridge. Possesses two summits the N one being 775m (2543ft) and further S the major summit of the crags is 815m (2674ft) [250053]. Several small attractive tarns/pools in the vicinity. Some people suggest that as Shelter Crags lies on the same ridge as Crinkle Crags it/they should be part of Crinkle Crags.

Shepherd Bridge Coniston. Bridge across Yewdale Beck [305978].

Shepherd Crags between Mecklin Wood and Latterbarrow [121025].

Shepherd Yeat off Back Lane, Crook [436944] ...surname Shepherd + gate/opening/way.

Shepherd's Bridge carries the A593 to Hodge Close road over Yewdale Beck. One of a select band of bridges which has its name on the bridge [314999] ...conjures up a picture of the shepherd herding his flock over the bridge either from the farm or from one field to the other.

Shepherds Crag Borrowdale. High precipice between the B5289 and the foot of Watendlath Beck. A mecca for rock climbers [263185].

Sherry Gill rises just S Sleddale Pike at 536092 and joins Sleddale Beck at 537107.

Shipman Knotts rough, craggy area on ridge from Harter Fell-Kentmere Pike-Goat Scar-Stile End to Sadgill track. Usually climbed as part of the Kentmere Horseshoe 587m 1926ft [472063] ...sheepman (shepherd) rocky hilltop.

Shivery Knott Watendlath Fell [289153].

Shivery Man between Shivery Knott and Middle Crag [286156].

Shoemire Wood alongside the A595 (Waberthwaite) [103926].

Shooting How Seatallan [141087].

Shop Wood Nether Wasdale [125044].

Short Grain one of several tributaries which combine to become Worm Gill. Rises 113127.

Short Stile craggy spur at the head of Riggindale. N of, and parallel to, Long Stile. [444122].

Shoulthwaite near Thirlmere. Walkers will notice on the fellside at Shoulthwaite a strange pyramidal wooden structure. This is actually a shooting hide used in culling deer ...the clearing by the stream near the stone circle or the clearing where the mill or mill wheel stands.

Shoulthwaite Bridge see **Rough How Bridge**.

Shoulthwaite Castle see **Castle Crag Hill Fort**.

Shoulthwaite Farm off the A591 and alongside Shoulthwaite Gill [299205].

Shoulthwaite Gill lengthy watercourse which rises between High Seat and High Tove at 291173 and flows down Shoulthwaite Glen between the Benn and Iron Crag and below the Castle Crag hill fort (sometimes called Shoulthwaite Castle). In times of rain there are fine falls on this stretch of the stream. At Rough How Bridge (Shoulthwaite Bridge) [300206] it takes the name of Naddle Beck which is joined by many small streams including the named Brown and William's Becks before entering the River Greta at 303246.

Shoulthwaite Glen narrow valley down which flows Shoulthwaite Gill, see **Shoulthwaite Gill**.

Shoulthwaite Moss SW A591. *The Lake District* (Collins New Naturalist Series) points out that the moss is the only raised bog within the Lake District mountains. There is a belief that an ancient village lies below the moss and certainly there is a hill fort to its rear [305202].

Shudderstone How E Seathwaite Tarn [256987].

Shundraw alongside minor road, B5322-A66 [308235] ...Ekwall suggests look-out hill.

Side property NE slope Cold Fell [062098].

Side, The see **The Side**.

Side End side of Cold Fell overlooking the River Calder [062088].

Side Farm Patterdale. Much earlier just 'Side'. Former home of the Wordsworth's close friends, Captain and Mrs Luff, with whom they often stayed. Today the farm is a well-known riding/pony-trekking centre and camping site. Acquired by the National Trust in 1950 [398162].

Side Gates section of the fell road between the foot of Wrynose Pass and by Blea Tarn to Great Langdale [297037] ...presumably at one time the road/track was gated hereabouts.

Side House former farmhouse, Great Langdale. Below Side Pike. Given to the NT in 1929 [295060].

Side House in small valley off the minor road from Staveley to Bowston/Garnett Bridge [489985].

Side Pike NW rocky extension of Lingmoor Fell. Its N, S and E sides are precipitous and walkers heading for its summit must do so by the W ridge. The path from Lingmoor Fell to Side Pike traverses under the crags on the S side where 'the squeeze' between rocks has to be negotiated. Easy for the slim and slender but the more corpulent may experience a certain difficulty in negotiating it, 362m (1188ft) [293054] ...pointed hill(side).

Side Wood alongside the River Calder [064096].

Sike W slope Little Mell Fell [412242].

Sike Moss E Birker Moor Road [180967].

Sillathwaite slightly W of Sillathwaite Wood [060128] ...possibly Sigrior's clearing.

Sillathwaite Wood NE Lowther Park and E Sillathwaite [063125].

Silver Bay E Silver Point, Ullswater [397185].

Silver Cove ENE Caw Fell. Source of Silvercove Beck [129112].

Silver Crag/Hill Silver Hill on 1 inch Bartholomew's. E shore upper reach Ullswater. Rocky extension of Birk Fell from which it is divided by slight col. 'Silver' refers to the preponderance of silver birch trees in the area also reflected in the names of Birk Fell, Low Birk Fell, Silver Bay and Silver Point 271m (889ft) [397181].

Silver Hill W shore Derwent Water [253221].

Silver Holme island off the W shore of Windermere. The 'Cormorant Island' of Arthur Ransome's *Swallows and Amazons*. Reputed to be a horde of silver buried hereabouts and Collingwood in the *The Lake Counties* (1902) says that he was told of a "kist (chest) o'silver ligging under t'watter" [377908].

Silver How prominent low fell to the SW of Grasmere village and overlooking it, the Grasmere valley and Rydal Water. Actually the end of a long ridge which commences at High Raise then over Sergeant Man and Blea Rigg. "...the tall steep of Silver How" in Wordsworth's *To Joanna*. Several cairns adorn its hummocky summit ridge but the highest is obvious and is 395m (1296ft) at 325066 ...either the hill overlooking the place where lead/silver were mined, or the hill with silver birch trees nearby.

Silver How Birker Moor [193984].

Silver How Tarn now named on the OS map. Small tarn W of and below Silver How [321067].

Silver Knott Muncaster Fell [134995].

Silver Point rocky headland E Ullswater. Alongside low level path from Patterdale to Sandwick. Excellent viewpoint [395184].

Silverbield Crag near High Scarf Crag [217039].

Silvercove Beck rises at the head of Silver Cove at 128110. Joins with Deep Gill at 132134 to become Woundell Beck which enters the River Liza at 134140. A footbridge across the beck near its meeting with Deep Gill was provided by the Friends of the Lake District when the Nine Becks Walk was made in 1974.

Silverholme mansion W shore Windermere. Built in the 19th century. Today comprises holiday flats [375909].

Simon Kell alongside the River Calder [062105] ...Sigemund/Sigmundr's spring.

Simon Stone large boulder alongside the beck at the head of Swindale [505118].

Sinen Gill rises on Mungrisdale Common at 312288 and joins Glenderaterra Beck at 296278.

Siney Tarn Eskdale. Slightly N of Blind Tarn and, similar to the latter, it is becoming very overgrown, C220m (C722ft) [162011] ...tarn which dries up.

Sippling Crag NW Benn Man summit [301194] ...a sibling to Benn Mann.

Sites of Special Scientific Interest (SSSIs). These include: Duddon Estuary; Sandy Beck Meadow National Nature Reserve; Bowness Knott, Ennerdale; Seatoller Wood; Blelham Tarn and Bog; ClaifeTarns and Mires; Brothers Water and Low Wood; Launchy Gill; Crinkle Crags; Langdale Pikes and Stickle Tarn.

Skeel Crags below Yoke and overlooking Skeel and Bryant's Gills, Kentmere [442062] ...possibly the shieling/hut by the crags.

Skeel Gill rises Yoke at 439065 and flows down past Skeel Crags to join Bryant's Gill at 449065. This joins the River Kent nearby at 450068 ...see **Skeel Crags**.

Skeggles Water large tarn situated in hollow on ridge between Kentmere and

Longsleddale. Drained to the S by Skeggleswater Dike. Skeggles Water contains deposits of diatomite (minute vegetable organisms which form deposits with external casing of silica) used in abrasives, filters, insulation, paints, and varnishes. However, unlike Kentmere Tarn which has been commercially exploited for diatomite attempts to drain Skeggles Water and extract the diatomite have, as yet, been resisted, 305m (1001ft) [480034] ...from 'skokull' meaning a cart pole but in this case used as a nickname. Therefore, the lake/pool of Skakel/Skakull.

Skeggleswater Dike drains Skeggles Water at 480032. Becomes Hall Beck where the valley narrows alongside Staveley Head at approximately 469017.

Skelda Hill alongside the Eskmeals coast road. A very low hill with contour at 10m (33ft) [082911] ...shield hill.

Skelghyll Lane from High Skelghyll Farm to Holbeck Lane [395021] ...see **Skelghyll Wood**.

Skelghyll Wood lower SW slope Wansfell ridge. Owned by the National Trust. The wood offers a nature trail and is also on a popular walking route from Ambleside to Troutbeck. In it is Jenkyn's Crag, a viewpoint [383030] ...wood near the shed/hut by the ravine or the wood by the noisy, resounding stream referring to the nearby Hol Beck flowing down its deep chasm.

Skelgill farm and property E side of the Newlands valley. At Skelgill Mrs Tiggy Winkle, a Beatrix Potter character, washed the "woolly coats belonging to the little lambs at Skelghyl" [242208].

Skelgill Bank Cat Bells ridge [244204].

Skellerah Corney [114916] ...according to the EPNS Skellarah refers to one Celia Eme de Skelhare.

Skellerah Wood Corney. N Skellerah [114922].

Skelly fish, see **Schelly**.

Skelly Crag Ashness Fell [271185] ...'skali' - shepherds' summer hut.

Skelly Crags W slope Dunnerdale. W Castle How [233004] ...possibly the crags by the shepherds hut/shelter.

Skelly Neb promontory overlooking Ullswater near the Outward Bound School. Opposite is Geordie's Crag. Between the two is the narrowest section of the lake and many years ago fishermen used to stretch nets across to catch the Schelly (Skelly) [438209] ...*The Place Names of Cumberland* suggests its origin as being from skali meaning shed/shieling but another suggestion is that the promontory takes its name from the schelly which used to be caught in quantities thereabouts.

Skelthwaite Crag WSW Low Rigg summit overlooking Naddle valley [300226].

Skelwith bridge 4kms (2.5 miles) from Ambleside at the junction of the B5343 to Elterwater and the A593 to Coniston. A handful of houses, a hotel, the Kirkstone Galleries and a slate dressing works where green slate from the Kirkstone Quarry is cut and dressed. The Skelwith Bridge crosses the River Brathay at this point [344034] ...bridge by the ford near the noisy one. The latter obviously refers to the nearby Skelwith Force. See also **Pet's Quarry**.

Skelwith Bridge Hotel Skelwith Bridge. Alongside the A593. Built in the 17th century and known for many years as the Hare and Hounds. At its rear is the Talbot Bar. A talbot is a variety of hound formerly used for hunting [344034].

Skelwith Fold cluster of cottages at the junction of lanes from Skelwith Bridge and Clappersgate to the Drunken Duck Inn. Excellent view looking down to and over Skelwith Bridge [351028].

Skelwith Fold Caravan Park large award-winning caravan park established in a former country estate of 130 acres once owned by the Marshall family. The mansion which stood on part of the site was erected in 1890 and was demolished in the 1950s just a few years after the daughter of its builder left the estate. Much conservation work has been undertaken by its new owners [353027].

Skelwith Fold Farm off Bog Lane which runs between Brathay and Skelwith Fold [352032].

Skelwith Force on the R Brathay just above Skelwith Bridge. One of the smallest drops of Lakeland waterfalls being only some 4.5m (15ft) but with the broadness of the river hereabouts and particularly when in spate it is a very impressive cataract [341035].

Skelwith Pool a widening of the R Brathay below Skelwith Bridge has the appearance of a small tarn [350034].

Skew Gill ravine and stream Great End. The stream rises in Skew Gill gully at 223090 and joins Spouthead Gill at 219092.

Skews NW Bampton [504188] ...wood. A small woodland and a Woodfoot nearby. There is also a Sceugh W Butterwick.

Skiddaw usually pronounced 'Skidda'. N of Keswick and E of Bassenthwaite. Fourth highest mountain in the Lake District after Scafell Pike, Scafell and Helvellyn or if Ill Crag on the Scafell Pike massif is classed as a separate height then it takes fifth place. Its ridge comprises several summits the highest being High Man or Skiddaw Man with a trig. point at 931m (3054ft) [260291]. A few yards to its N is North Top at 922m (3025ft) [261292] and to its S Middle Top 928m (3045ft) [261288] and South Top 925m (3035ft) [261285] while to its SSE Little Man/Low Man rises to 865m (2838ft) [267278]. The Lake District has possessed several hermits living in various localities over the centuries one of which, known as the Skiddaw Hermit or the Dodd Man, lived in a 'nest' amongst the rocks of Scalebeck Gill on Dodd/Skiddaw Dodd. His real name was George Smith (C1825-1876), a native of Banffshire who, after numerous wanderings made his home on the slope of Skiddaw for many years during which time he earned a living by painting portraits and dabbling in phrenology. Later he lived in a small tent on the shores of Windermere before returning to his native Banffshire where he died.

Alongside the normal tourist route from the end of Gale Road and shortly after the track turns to ascend above and parallel to Whit Beck there is a monument to three shepherds while slightly higher are the scant remains of a refreshment hut which used to provide sustenance for those hardy earlier travellers on their journey to the summit. Today, reaching the summit via the tourist route is considered relatively easy along a well-defined path but Harriet Martineau writing in her *Guide to the Lakes* (1855) implored everyone considering the climb to take a guide. The young Ruskin wrote of a typical Victorian ascent by the same route as "a busy, bustling affair of guides, ponies, spare riding skirts for the ladies, cloaks, mantles, tied-on-hats, sips of brandy and huge quantities of food" ...there are several possible derivations. The second element is obviously hill but the first could refer to archer, projecting rock, craggy hill or even from 'skeio' meaning racecouse.

Skiddaw Forest extensive hollow and fell slopes to the E of Skiddaw and drained principally by the River Caldew. To its W rises the Skiddaw massif, to the E Blencathra and to the N Great Calva and Knott. Once part of Lord Leconfield's estates and comprised some 3,000 acres. The estate was broken up in 1957. In ancient times and similar to many other forests it was a sporting reserve. Today, it is virtually tree-less apart from the odd rowan, birch or juniper and the conifer windbreak by Skiddaw House [275291].

Skiddaw House Skiddaw Forest, Back o'Skidda'. For many years Skiddaw House was two properties, one for a shepherd and the other for a gamekeeper. The gamekeeper subsequently left and the last resident shepherd and the last known person to live there was Pearson Dalton who made it his home for 45 years before he retired in 1969 at the age of 72. After his retirement he went to live not far away at Fellside. He died in May 1974, and is buried in Caldbeck churchyard. Skiddaw House then remained derelict for nearly 25 years before it became at youth hostel which is open from late March to the end of October. Skiddaw House and Black Sail are the two remotest youth hostels in the Lake District [287291].

Skiddaw Little Man see **Skiddaw**.

Skiddaw range of fells, see Reference Section: **Heights**.

Skiing when conditions are right there is good skiing in the vicinity of Raise on the Helvellyn ridge, where the old-established Lake District Ski Club has a hut and tow (snow can fall here as early as November and Savages Gully has been known to provide skiing as late as June); on the slopes of the Dodds and at Dunmail Raise. The High Street ridge and Barton Fell are possibilities and, in deep snow, the S slope of Catstycam. A small area of the fellside just N of the Kirkstone Pass Inn is suitable for this recreation, particular for beginners to the sport. There are many other areas where skiing is possible but care must be taken at all times as crags and precipices may be encountered at the end of seemingly innocuous grassy slopes.

Skiing (Grass) see **Grass Skiing**.

Skill Beck rises E slope Dodd /Skiddaw Dodd at 249274. Joined by Gable Gill at 246277 and flows into Bassenthwaite Lake at 225288.

Skilling Crag foot of Ill Crag. Above Little Narrowcove and upper reach of the R Esk [227068] ...possibly, like Skill Beck (Bassenthwaite Lake), derives its name from the ON 'skiallr' meaning noisy, resounding. In this case the noise is from the two watercourses nearby.

Skinner How Lane connects the Knipe Fold-High Cross road with the B5285 [345901].

Skirsgill Hill near Askham. Two settlements here [498232]. Scheduled as Ancient Monuments ...probably the haunted ravine by the hill. There is another Skirsgill just outside Penrith.

Skitwath Beck one of the two principal headstreams of Dacre Beck. Rises in Greystoke Moor Plantation at 416296. Joined by Hatter's Syke, Swinescales Beck and Wham Sike before joining Dacre Beck at Hutton at 435265 ...filthy ford on the stream.

Skreel Side steep slope overlooking Measand Beck [467159].

Skull Gill rises slope of Pike o'Blisco at 277044 and joins Oxendale Beck at 275054 ...with nearby Grave Gill suggests a connection with death.

Slack Wood Dale Park [357943] ...wood in, or by, the hollow.

Slades Beck rises Skiddaw Little Man at 259276. For continuation see **Tongues Beck**.

Slape Crag Barf [216266] ...slippery crag.

Slape Scar W shore Windermere [389979] ...slape is a North Country expression meaning smooth or slippery. It occurs elsewhere in Cumbria as Slape Crag, Slape With, Slapestone Edge and Slapestones.

Slapestone Edge overlooks Easedale Tarn [303088] ...slippery stone edge.

Slapestones alongside minor road from the A595-Santon Bridge road to Eskdale Green [120001] ...see **Slape Scar**.

Slat Gill rises on the N slope of Lonscale Fell 285278 and joins Salehow Beck at 285285.

Slate Crag Bowfell. The central crag will interest rock climbers [240065].

Slate Hill N Wet Sleddale Reservoir dam 291m (955ft) [553125] ...slate cutting and dressing were frequently practised in the 17th and 18th centuries.

Slate Knott Hardknott [235019].

Slater(s) Bridge Little Langdale. Picturesque slate and stone footbridge over the R Brathay near Little Langdale Tarn. Generally considered to have been built to provide quarrymen access to the many quarries S of the Brathay [312030] ...appropriately named Slater(s) Bridge after the slaters who used it but the EPNS suggests that the title is derived from the family of John Sleyther mentioned in the late 14th century.

Sleathwaite alongside the minor road from the A595-Santon Bridge road to Eskdale Green [123001] ...sloe clearing. The sloe is the blue black fruit of the blackthorn.

Sleddale Beck rises SSW Brown Howe at 517081. Joined by Brownhow Gutter, Saddlecrag Gill, Tonguerigg Gill and Sherry Gill, before entering Wet Sleddale Reservoir at 543112. Previous to the construction of the reservoir the source of Sleddale Beck was the start of the River Lowther but today the Lowther is deemed to start at the reservoir's outflow ...sled and dale both mean valley - so valley, valley stream.

Sleddale Fell large fell area to the E of the higher reach of Longsleddale. Rocky outcrops lead to the highest point, Grey Crag, at 638m (2093ft) [497072].

Sleddale Forest to the W of Longsleddale. At one time much afforested and like the other eastern Lakeland forests Fawcett, Grisedale, Ralfland and Thornthwaite principally owned by the Barony of Kendal and used as a hunting reserve. Today, only comparatively few areas of woodland, alongside Longsleddale and Kentmere, remain to remind us of a once substantial wooded area. Highest point is spot-heighted at 429m (1408ft) [488016].

Sleddale Grange Wet Sleddale. Once, as the name implies, an outlying farm belonging to Shap Abbey. Now used as barns [544117].

Sleddale Hall Wet Sleddale. Former old hall, at one time possibly the home of the centuries-old Sleddale family [540114].

Sleddale Pike Shap Fells. N Wasdale Pike. Between the upper reaches of Tonguerigg Gill and Sherry Gill. Small tarn to S, C500 (C1640ft) [536094].

Sleathwaite alongside minor road from the A595-Santon Bridge road to Eskdale Green [123001] ...sloe clearing'. Sloe is the blue black fruit of the blackthorn.

Slee, Lanty like Moses Rigg of Moses Trod fame, a reputed whisky/graphite smuggler, Lanty Slee was a notorious whisky smuggler whose domain was the Little Langdale/Wetherlam fell area and although he did much local trade a large quantity of his illicit whisky went over Wrynose and Hardknott Passes to the coast. Born in 1802 he died at his home, Greenbank Farm, Little Langdale, in 1878. Several of his stills and storage places have been unearthed notably ones at Low Fell; Hall Garth; Atkinson Coppice; Far Arnside and Betsy Crag but there are possibly quite a few stills and hideouts so well hidden that they have yet to be found.

Sleet Cove cove below Deepdale Hause, head of Deepdale [363124].

Sleet Fell northernmost shoulder of Place Fell rising steeply above Sandwick and up to Low and High Dodds. Cairn at 378m (1240ft) [422188].

Sleet Hause col between Rowling End and Causey Pike [225207] ...see **Sleet How** below. In this case the hause is relatively level as opposed to the ascent of Rowling End and Causey Pike.

Sleet How on the ridge from Braithwaite via Kinn to the summit of Grisedale Pike [207228] ...ON 'sletta/slettr' meaning smooth/level (hill). Sleet How is not exactly level but in comparison with the final ascent to Grisedale Pike and the initial ascent to Sleet How it certainly is.

Sleven Beck rises alongside Lowther Park, Uldale, at 058116 and joins the River Calder at 065109.

Slew Tarn ENE Skelwith Fold. Possibly originally a smaller tarn enlarged as a fish pond for the former owners of the estate, the Marshall family C70m (C230ft) [356030].

Slight Side shouler of Scafell 748m (2454ft) [210052] ...level pasture with a mountain shieling/hut.

Sling Beck several streams rise on the slope leading up to Great Worm Crag and combine at 207961 to become Sling Beck which enters the River Duddon at 213955.

Slops Beck rises near Height House at 233907 and joins Galloper Pool at 231889. The latter subsequently enters the Duddon Estuary below Foxfield.

Smaithwaite (Smeathwaite), between A591 and minor road alongside W shore Thirlmere [312197] ...small clearing.

Smaithwaite Banks alongside minor road around W shore of Thirlmere. Foot of slope leading up to Benn Man [307193].

Smaithwaite Fell between A591 and minor road alongside W shore Thirlmere 205m (673ft) [313197].

Small Water cradled in corrie NW Harter Fell and E Mardale Ill Bell. At one time believed to be unfathomable but its maximum depth is actually 16m (52ft). Free fishing for brown trout and perch. On the track alongside it are three small stone shelters (just room enough for pigmies) presumably built many years ago for small travellers. Situated at an altitude of 452m (1483ft) [455100].

Small Water Beck flows out of Small Water at 457101 and after its confluence with Blea Water Beck at 463106 becomes Mardale Beck which enters Haweswater at 468109.

Small Water Crag overlooks Small Water from the S [454098].

Smallstone Beck rises as Rowantree Beck on White Moss at 200975. Becomes Smallstone Beck in the region of 187983. Joins the combined Little and Highford Becks at 177987. Arminghow Gill meets at 176992 and the watercourse becomes Birker Beck which flows over Stanley Force whence it becomes Stanleygill Beck. This meets the R Esk at 173002.

Smallthwaite Band ridge running down from Red Screes to Middle Dodd [395092].

Smallthwaite Knott Kentmere. Nan Bield Pass passes below it [452081] ...small clearing on the rocky hill.

Smeathwaite see **Smaithwaite**.

Smithy Beck rises between Hausegreen Crag and Water Crag at 152060 and joins Wastwater at 154057. An ancient bloomery once stood alongside the beck.

Smithy Beck Ennerdale. Rises N Latterbarrow ridge at 136148. Joined by Starling Gill and Clews Gill before entering Ennerdale Water at 122146 ...at one time a bloomery or smithy was situated at the mouth of the beck.

Smithy Beck Forest Trail Ennerdale. Two routes. The full route is approximately 5.4kms (3.4 miles) and the shorter 3.3kms (2 miles).

Smithy Brow on N section of the Kirkstone Pass above Barker Brow [404094] ...smithy and barker suggest a smithy/forge and a tanners. However, these are more than likely surnames rather than actual occupations.

Smithy Fell in the Fellbarrow Group. Rises to C390m (C1279ft) [133237].

Smithy Green alongside the A66 where the latter runs alongside Bassenthwaite Lake [211294].

Smithy Hill between Neds Low Wood and Birks Brow [410921].

Smithy Mire alongside Whis Gill [166994].

Smithymire Island at the confluence of Greenup Gill and Langstrath Beck. Site of an ancient bloomery. Langstrath was once exceptionally wooded but most of the wood was cut down centuries ago to provide fuel for the bloomery [274130].

Smooth Beck shown but not named on the OS map. Farthest headstream rises at 370984 and flows through Hodson's and Robinson's Tarns to join Esthwaite Water at 359974.

Smooth Beck Bridge carries the B5285 over Smooth Beck [360975].

Smooth Knott near Satterthwaite [325922] ...somewhat of a contradiction in terms as it means the smooth rocky hillock.

Snarker Moss between Snarker Pike and Red Screes [390080].

Snarker Pike on ridge from Ambleside to Red Screes 644m (2113ft) [390075] ...the pointed hill frequented by snakes. Obviously named at a time when snakes, particularly adders, were more frequent in the Lake District as exemplified by Hagworm Close/Gill/Hole/Wood, Hermons Hill, Snarker Moss, Ulm Gill, Walm Home, Walmgate, Worm Gill/How, Wormpots and Wormrigg Wood.

Sneckyeat off the Brandlingill to Randle Cross road [121272] ...sneck is a dialect word for latch and yeat is gate/way. Jennings of Cockermouth brew a beer called Snecklifter.

Snipes How W A591 and slightly N of Bracken Riggs [296212] ...hill frequented by snipe.

Snipeshow Tarn small tarn in hollow between Bracken Riggs and Snipes How [296211].

Snow Cove Gill rises alongside Snarker Moss at 392080 and flows under the Struggle to meet Stock Ghyll at 397073 ...the cove/gill in which snow lingers.

Snowder to the E of the A595 [078014].

Snowdrift Slack NNE Grey Friar (262008) ...the hollow into which the snow drifts.

Society of Friends (Quakers), see **Fox, George** (1624-91).

Sorrowstones alongside the Santon to Gosforth road [096022] ...sorrow is usually deemed to refer to the sorrel plant. However, according to tradition, a criminal on his way to the gallows at Hanging How or Gallows Hill was given a last drink of ale at the house to drown his obvious sorrows.

Sosgill foot of High Rigg. W St John's Beck [315210] ...muddy shieling(s).

Sosgill area on the NW boundary of the NP [103240] ...see above.

Sosgill Bridge elegant slender packhorse bridge which crosses St John's Beck at 316211.

Sosgill Farm Sosgill. Adjoining the NW boundary of the NP [102241].

Souland Gate farm alongside the minor road from the A592 to Dacre [466257] ...way to the sour lands.

Soulby hamlet alongside minor road on Soulby Fell. Near Pooley Bridge [463252]. There is a village of the same name 4kms (2.5 miles) NW of Kirkby Stephen ...maybe Sula's farmstead or farmstead constructed of posts.

Soulby Fell W Pooley Bridge. WSW hamlet of Soulby. Near its summit are the remains of an ancient fort called Maiden Castle. Highest point C290m (C951ft) [451245].

Soulby Fell Farm Soulby Fell [456251].

Sour Howes highest point of Applethwaite Common. The fell top comprises grassy and tuffety mounds. Far from fertile ground as the 'sour' implies 483m (1585ft) [428032].

Sour Milk Gill Force see **Sourmilk Gill** below.

Sourfoot Fell in the Fellbarrow group. Rises to C410m (C1345ft) [135233].

Sourmilk Gill actually a section of Easedale Beck between Easedale Tarn outflow and the confluence with Far Easedale Beck. Takes its name from Sourmilk Gill Force [318088] which cascades down it. The Wordsworths referred to the fall as Churnmilk Force. The gill is joined by Little Brinhowe Gill and Far Easedale Beck whence it continues as Easedale Beck to meet the R Rothay at 336080 ...similar to several other Sour Milk waterfalls, including the well-known ones at Buttermere and Seathwaite, in that the name is derived from the white milky foam appearance (epitomising milk being churned) when the stream is in spate.

Sourmilk Gill rises at the head of Gillercomb at 219112 and after flowing through Gillercomb drops over spectacular waterfalls before reaching the River Derwent at 234122.

Sourmilk Gill Buttermere. Rises Bleaberry Tarn and drops steeply for approximately 396m (1300ft) over impressive cascades in times of spate. The gill joins Buttermere Dubbs near its outflow from Buttermere at 173163. Of the fall Father West wrote: "Among the variety of waterfalls that distinguish this awful boundary of rock, one catches the eye at a distance that exceeds the boasted Lowdore, in height of rock and unity of fall..."

Souterstead off the A593 [274936] ...sheep farm.

South Crag Stonethwaite Fell between Ribby Gills and Black Wall [257102].

South East Gully see **Great End**.

South Top see **Skiddaw**.

Souther Fell between R Glenderamackin and the old road from Scales to Mungrisdale. N Top 522m (1713ft) [354291), S Top 495m (1624ft) [351281]. On two occasions in the 1730s and one in the 1740s people witnessed an army of soldiers, horsemen and coaches appearing at one end of the fell and disappearing over the other end. A similar scene was witnessed on Helvellyn on the eve of the Battle of Marston Moor (July 1644) ...'shoemaker's hill', 'sheep hill' or 'under hill'.

Southerfell alongside old road Scales-Mungrisdale [360279].

Southerndale valley between Skiddaw and Ullock Pike down which flows Southerndale Beck [248292].

Southerndale Beck rises at the head of Southerndale. Joins with Barkbeck Gill at 342311. Subsequently becomes Chapel Beck which flows alongside Chapel and joins Bassenthwaite Lake at 212309.

Southwaite Beck rises 447248 and joins Dacre Beck at 452261 ...clay clearing by the stream beck.

Southwaite Bridge S of Cockermouth. Carries minor road over the River Cocker [131283].

Southwaite Farm off minor road from Dacre to Sparket [448258].

Southwaite Farm S of Cockermouth. W bank of the River Cocker [130281].

Southwaite Green S of Cockermouth. W of the River Cocker [127282].

Southwaite Mill S of Cockermouth. W bank of the River Cocker [130283].

Sowermyrr Gosforth [085040] ...the muddy/swampy ground.

Sowler's Tower above Far Sawrey [382957].

Sparholme Wood Calder Bridge. Alongside the Calder Bridge to Ennerdale Bridge road [044063].

Sparket area E of Thackthwaite alongside the Dacre-Thackthwaite road [431256] ...the place where brushwood is found.

Sparket Farm N Thackthwaite-Dacre road [431257]

Sparket Mill Sparket. Alongside Dacre Beck [437264].

Sparrow How Wood E Garnett Wood and W Far Sawrey-High Cunsey road [377946].

Speaking Crag W shore of Haweswater. End of small afforested promontory across bay from the Rigg [473122] ...echoing crag. There is another named 'echoing' crag, Gouther Crag, alongside Swindale.

Spedding Crag above Walthwaite and alongside path from there to Silver How or Grasmere [326058] ...most likely a surname + crag.

Spicka Coppice W of the foot of Blelham Tarn. E B5286 [359002] ...possibly the coppice at the foot of the pike.

Spigot House Crook. Today a private residence but centuries ago it was one of three local factory workshops turning out wooden baskets, etc [437949] ...spigot - a stopper for the vent hole of a cask, or a tap usually made of wood and fitted to a cask. Hence the proverb 'spare at the spigot and spill at the bung' meaning to be parsimonious on trifles and wasteful on great matters.

Spoon Hall Coniston [298966].

Spothow Gill its farthest tributary rises below Dow Crag at 207992 and the gill joins the R Esk at 203007.

Spout Crag Grisedale. End of ridge from Dollywaggon Pike over the Tongue. Above confluence of Ruthwaite Beck and Grisedale Beck [354134] ...a spout refers to a small stream/spring outlet. The crag in this case immediately overlooks the source of a small stream which joins Ruthwaite Beck.

Spout Force also known as Force Spout. Waterfall in a gorge on Aiken Beck [181260].

Spout Head crags near Sty Head and the source of Spouthead Gill [223092] ...headland above the spout, water outlet. The latter presumably the source of Spouthead Gill.

Spout House Crosthwaite. A late 16th century farmhouse [445918] ...see **Spout Crag**.

Spout House Farm Eskdale [157003] ...see **Spout Crag**.

Spoutcrag Quarry large disused quarry E slope Lingmoor Fell [307051] ...see **Spout Crag**.

Spouthead Gill rises below Spout Head Crags at 221093, joined by Skew Gill and other streams before joining Lingmell Beck at 212092.

Spring Bank W minor road A66-Matterdale End [410256].

Spring Bank Braithwaite. Alongside the Braithwaite-Thornthwaite-A66 road [230243].

Spring Hag wooded area alongside the Staveley to Bowston/Burneside road. Major portion given to the Cumbria Wildlife Trust in 1969 with a further extension added in 1995 [484982].

Spring House off minor road from Corney to the A595 (Cross House) [113903].

Spring Keld Gosforth. E River Bleng. A well is shown adjoining [085047].

Spring Plantation adjoining Miterdale Forest [133013].

Spring Wood adjoining Rulbuts Hill [404935] ...plantation wood.

Spring Wood behind Wad's Howe, Longsleddale [494031].

Spring Wood Colthouse. Believed to be that referred to by Wordsworth in his *Prelude* (Book VIII) "There was a Copse/ An Upright bank of wood and woody rock/ That opposite our dwelling stood..." [362981].

Springs Coppice Eskdale [133982].

Springs Wood Castlerigg [277226].

Sprinkling Crag Tarn alternative name Great Slack Tarn. Shown but not named on the OS map. Its present title, which has been adopted by other writers, was given to it by the late W H Cooper. Situated above Sprinkling Crags and just below the S summit of Seathwaite Fell, C620m (C2034ft) [228095].

Sprinkling Crags N Sprinkling Tarn [230095].

Sprinkling Tarn sizeable tarn at the foot of Seathwaite Fell. Nearly seven centuries ago it was called 'Prentibiountern', a lengthy name which legend suggests meant that the tarn was associated with one Bjorn, an outlaw, who was branded (prenti) for his crimes. However, scholars disagree with this explanation and consider that more probably it was derived from 'Sprentaborntern' equated with sprint in the former Westmorland and meaning the tarn by the gushing or sparkling stream. It became Sparkling Tarn in 1774 and was later corrupted or altered to Sprinkling Tarn. Considered to be the actual source of the R Derwent. A stream from it drops down to Styhead Tarn then into Styhead Gill which meets Grains Gill, another headstream, and the two combine to become an enlarged R Derwent. Fishing is for brown trout 597m (1959ft) [228091].

Sprint, River see **River Sprint**.

Spy Crag Over Staveley 219m (718ft) [475988] ...crag used as a look-out point.

Spying How overlooking Glencoyne Park, Ullswater [383197].

Square Covert ENE Holmrook. Rectangular on the OS map [090998].

Squat Beck rises head of Rannerdale at 177179. Subsequently joined by Rowantree Beck before meeting Rannerdale Beck which enters Crummock Water at 162191.

Squat Knotts crags E Hindscarth-High Crags-Scope End ridge [222170].

Squeeze, The see **Side Pike**.

Squirrels today there are believed to be 10,000 red squirrels in Cumbria and half as many greys.

Stable Harvey W Coniston Water. Situated alongside a lane, once the main road from Blawith to Torver. Today a farm but once a hamlet nicknamed 'the City'. For many years there was a school here [284917] ...Hervi's stable. A stable for packhorses and the monks of Furness Abbey on their way to and from Hawkshead. As far back as 1332 there is mention of Richard, son of Adam de Stabilhervy.

Stable Harvey Moss Torver Low Common. W Stable Harvey [278918].

Stable Hills on promontory E shore Derwent Water [267219].

Stack House Wet Sleddale. Nearby is Stackhouse Brow. A footpath sign at the Longsleddale end of the Gatescarth Pass points the way to Stack House [547124].

Stackers Brow alongside the Eskdale to Ulpha fell road [158992].

Stackhouse Brow overlooks Stack House and Wet Sleddale [543123].

Stags Head Hotel Bowness. Old established hostelry.

Stagshaw Gardens .8kms (0.5 mile) S Ambleside off the A591. An 8 acre woodland garden created by the late Cubby Acland, regional agent for the National Trust, and now owned by the National Trust. Many trees, shrubs and plants and particularly a fine collection of azaleas and rhododendrons [381029].

Stainton alongside Stainton Beck [127947] ...stony farmstead/hamlet.

Stainton Beck rises Stainton Fell at 152946 and joins with Black and Samgarth Becks at 121946 to become Mill Gill and subsequently Broadoak Beck which joins the R Esk at 099953.

Stainton Fell craggy ridge to the ENE Waberthwaite and W and SW of Hesk Fell. The highest point is Stainton Pike with two principal summits, the higher at 498m (1634ft) [153943] and the lower at 491m (1611ft) [153941].

Stainton Ground ruined farm off the fell road from Broughton Mills to Seathwaite [220923] ...see **Stainton Ground Quarries** and **Stephenson Ground**.

Stainton Ground Quarries large disused quarries approached by track from the Broughton Mills to Seathwaite fell road [220935/222934] ...appropriately named for a quarry area as Stainton means stony farmstead. The latter, Stainton Ground, lower down the valley is, like nearby Carter Ground, Jackson Ground and Stephenson Ground, derived from the name of an original settler.

Stainton Ling W Stainton Fell [139944] ...ling is heather/gorse.

Stainton Pike see **Stainton Fell**.

Stair hamlet situated on both sides of Newlands Beck and generally considered to be the start of the Newlands Pass. A flour mill operated here until the 1880s and one of the properties has a datestone 1647 and initials TF above its doorway. The TF is reputed to have been Sir Thomas Fairfax, parliamentarian and one of Cromwell's generals who lived here for a while [236212] ...possibly from OE 'staeger' meaning to climb and referring to the steepness of the road hereabouts.

Stair Knott Ennerdale Fell. Overlooks the head of Ennerdale Water [125136].

Staithwaite Borrow W Starnthwaite, Crosthwaite. Similar to Starnthwaite in that the first name refers to a local family called Stern(e) [430923].

Stake area of fell N of the summit of the Stake Pass [265092].

Stake Beck rises Martcrag Moor at 273079 and parallels part of Stake Pass before joining Langstrath Beck at 264099.

Stake Gill rises in Langdale Combe near the summit of the Stake Pass at 263087 and joins Little Gill and Rossett Gill at 262073 to become Mickleden Beck.

Stake Pass from Mickleden, Great Langdale, to Stonethwaite, Borrowdale. A popular walkers' route between the two valleys but in days gone by an even more busy route with pedlars, packhorse trains and the transportation of iron ore from Ore Gap to the bloomery near the foot of the Langstrath valley. The Cumbria Way follows the Stake Pass route from Mickleden to Rosthwaite. The pass rises to C480m (C1576ft) [265087] ...the pass was originally marked by stakes.

Stake Pass Tarn shown but not named on the OS map. Large tarn near the summit of the Stake Pass C450m (C1476ft) [265088].

Stakes Bridge carries the road to Priorling, Low and High Prior Scales and Thornholme over the River Calder [056068].

Stalkinghouse Plantation N Ullswater and between Collierhagg Beck and Kirkstyle Gill [420214].

Stallion Head Seathwaite Fells. Not far distant is Horse How [251972].

Stanah farm E of the southern end of the B5322. Start of Sticks Pass which crosses Helvellyn range and continues to Ullswater [320190] ...stone.

Stanah Gill rise Stanahgill Head between Watson's Dodd and Stybarrow Dodd at 339191 and drops steeply over waterfalls to Stanah where it enters a water race at 321190 and is diverted to Thirlmere to enter the latter at 313169.

Stanahgill Head between Watson's Dodd and Stybarrow Dodd [339191].

Stand Crag W of the Corridor Route [218087].

Stand Crags rocky headed crags alongside Stangs. Overlook Sales and Hogget Gill [382109] ...crags alongside the stang. Stang refers to a post usually placed to denote a boundary.

Standing Crag ENE Ullscarf [296134].

Standing Stone large boulder W Whitfell and alongside the ancient track from Waberthwaite to Ulpha [161936].

Standing Stone between Red Pike and High Stile [165148].

Standing Stones off Coldfell Road [061130].

Standy Gill rises 150082 and joins Nether Beck at 153084.

Stanegarth dwelling N bank Cawdale Beck and opposite the latter's confluence with Willdale Beck [497177] ...stone enclosure.

Stang E of ridge situated between Sticks Gill and Glenridding Beck 655m (2149ft) [355176] ...stang means a post usually placed to denote a boundary.

Stang Dub in the River Derwent between the confluence of Tongue Gill and the Crook (Stonethwaite Beck) [252152].

Stang End as its name implies it is the end of Stang. Overlooks Swart Beck and Glenridding Beck [361176].

Stang End farm, Little Langdale. Bequeathed to the National Trust by Beatrix Potter [319028] ...boundary marked by a stang - a post.

Stang How alongside Honister Pass W [220140].

Stang Moss Bethecar Moor [310907] ...see **Stang** above.

Stangends S River Irt. Adjacent Great Coppice [118036] ...stang - usually a pole or stake denoting a boundary.

Stanger area to the SE Cockermouth between the B5292 and the River Cocker and comprisisng principally High Stanger Farm [139279], Low Stanger Farm [136277], Stanger Farm [137277], Stanger How 79m (259ft) [143272] and a Stanger Spa (holy well) at 141272. The spa, now disused, was an old saline spring contained in a well. It was reputed to be a cure for rheumatism and skin diseases and bottles of water from it were sent all over the world. Years ago the well was enclosed in a stone building but this is now in a dilapidated condition. Today the water is free but at one time it cost 6d (2p) a bottle ...a stake or pole used as a landmark or denote a boundary or a shieling with a pole.

Stanger Farm see **Stanger**.

Stanger How see **Stanger**.

Stanger Spa (holy well), see **Stanger**.

Stangs sometimes the Stangs. End of a spur which projects into Dovedale and bifurcates the head of that dale [382112] ...stangs - posts usually referring to boundary posts.

Stanley Force waterfall, Eskdale. Also called Dalegarth Force or Stanley Gill Force. After flowing down from Birker Moor, Birker Beck drops over a 18m (60ft) fall in to a deep wooded ravine, Stanley Gill [174995] ...named after the Stanley family who owned the nearby Dalegarth Hall (in the 13th century called Auestwait) for centuries.

Stanley Ghyll House Boot. Opposite Beckfoot Halt on the Ravenglass to Eskdale railway line. Built over 100 years ago and used as a base for guided walking tours for many years.

Stanley Gill Force see **Stanley Force**.

Stanleygill Beck see **Birker Beck**.

Star Crag E ridge between Yoke and Ill Bell [440071] ...sedge crag.

Stare Beck rises Starebeck Knotts at 122075 and joins the River Bleng at 116083 ...the reedy/sedgy stream.

Starebeck Knotts Nether Wasdale Common. Source of Stare Beck [124074].

Starling Dodd on the ridge between Great Borne and Red Pike 633m (2077ft) [142158] ...not a roost for starlings but an inversion compound meaning the rounded hill by Alein's path.

Starling Gill rises below Thiefstead at 529138 and joins Swindale Beck at 526144 ...possibly Alein's path by the ravine.

Starling Gill rises slope of Starling Dodd (from which it takes its name) at 137156 and joins Smithy Beck at 134149.

Starnthwaite Crosthwaite. Between the River Gilpin and the Back Lane to the B5284 at Crook [436921] ...see **Staithwaite Borrow**.

Starnthwaite Ghyll Starnthwaite, Crosthwaite. Originally one of the old mills which received their water power from the River Gilpin. A centuries old fulling mill later became a paper mill, bobbin mill and in the 1880s converted to a corn and saw mill. In 1892 became a 'home colonisation society' where unemployed men were taught a useful trade and worked on the estate. Later became a home for epileptic boys and in 1935 Starnthwaite became an approved school. Ceased as such in 1973 and became a residential intermediate treatment centre. This work continued until the 1980s in which year the property was converted into flats [435922].

Starnthwaite Ghyll School see **Starnthwaite Ghyll**.

Station Coppice W A591 3.6kms (2.25 miles) N Wythburn Church. Car park with nearby viewpoint [317170] ...not a railway or bus station but like West's 'stations' a specific place with a fine viewpoint.

Station Scar Wood W Windermere (Lake) [388957], see also **West's Stations**.

Staveley large village situated at the foot of the Kentmere valley alongside the R Kent. Up to its being by-passed in 1988 Staveley was bisected by the main road from Kendal to Windermere. The village is about 700 years old and for centuries the fast-flowing waters of the Kent were used principally to power fulling mills hereabouts. At one time there were as many as 60 mills in operation on the Kent or its tributaries. Much later Staveley's unique position, alongside the river and in a well-wooded area, made it an excellent place for bobbin making and the opening of the not far distant Kendal-Lancaster-Preston canal at the beginning of the 19th century, the opening of the Lancaster-Carlisle section of the railway in 1846 and the inception of the Oxenholme-Kendal-Windermere line the following year helped even more to increase trade between the Lancashire mills and Staveley. In the mid-19th century Staveley had six bobbin mills operating on the Rivers Gowan and Kent. However, consequent on the decline of the textile industry in the 20th century, Staveley's bobbin making industry declined. Later, other wood working crafts took over particularly the making of handles for hammers, brooms, etc. Since then diversification of industry has taken place particularly on a central industrial estate.

Buildings of note include the 14th century tower of St Margaret's Church (the nave was demolished in 1865) a former bobbin mill (c1820s) a former corn mill (c1790) a former cotton mill (1785-9), St James' Church (consecrated in 1865), Working Men's Institute building (established 1874), the Abbey (now an old people's home) built as an hotel in 1844 and Staveley Park Farm (a listed building). At the rear of the former Staveley Wood Turning Mill a fish pass was constructed on the Kent in 1985. This has resulted in three times as many salmon being caught hereabouts as previously were caught. Another fish pass is sited approximately 500m (546 yards) higher on the weir above Barley Bridge. Writing in October 1802, on returning from a journey to Hawes, Yorkshire, Dorothy Wordsworth wrote: "I am always glad to see Staveley; it is a place I dearly love to think of..." For further reading consult *A Lakeland Valley Through Time: A History of Staveley, Kentmere and Ings* published by the Staveley and District History Society (1995) [471982] ...the wood or glade where staves are obtained. See also **Nether Staveley**, **Over Staveley**. There is another Staveley - Staveley-in-Cartmel - near Newby Bridge.

Staveley By-pass opened 1988.

Staveley Crossing level crossing over the Kendal-Windermere railway line. Originally gates were opened and closed by the crossing keeper who lived alongside [477974].

Staveley Head Fell Over Staveley [473017].

Staveley Park Staveley. Farm and listed building. Takes its name from a park which existed hereabouts from the 14th century to hunt deer and provide grazing for cattle in summer [474982].

Staveley Station on the Oxenholme to Windermere line. Has been an unmanned halt since 1971 [479981].

Steel Brow W Floutern Tarn [121170] ...stile by the brow of the hill.

Steel Edge initially a relatively easy but later becoming steep slope leading from Dry Cove Bottom up to the Wetherlam S ridge. At its summit and to the right of the path leading to the top of Wetherlam lies Wetherlam Tarn [294006] ...steep ('stigel') edge.

Steel Edge steep slope leading up to Round Howe, Place Fell [406165].

Steel End (Stile or Style End). Wythburn. Farm at the foot of Steel Fell and alongside the road around the W side of Thirlmere. Since nearby West Head Farm was closed by the water authority many years ago Steel End has been renamed West Head [322128].

Steel End northern extremity of Steel Knotts [443193] ...steep, or from the local family of Steel.

Steel Fell large fell to the WSW Dunmail Raise. Triangular in shape, bounded on the E by the A591 and on the other two sides by the Wyth Burn and Green Burn respectively. The actual summit is called Dead Pike 553m (1814ft) [320112] ...the steep path up the fell.

Steel Knotts narrow ridge running roughly S from Howtown between Fusedale and Howe Grain. Its summit is Pikeawassa 432m (1417ft) [440181] ...from 'stile' meaning steep, or from the local family of Steel.

Steel Pike overlooking the head of Longsleddale from the W [474080] ...from family named Steel(e).

Steel Rigg ridge S Wrengill Quarry, N Steel Pike [475083] ...from family named Steel(e).

Steel Rigg Kentmere. W Reservoir Cottage [443073] ...surname Steel(e) ridge.

Steelfield Hall Gosforth [066038].

Steeple a rocky mountain N of Scoat Fell and W of Pillar. Actually, the summit is on a spur of Little Scoat Fell which drops down steeply over Long Crag and between High and Low Becks to Ennerdale 819m (2687ft) [157117] ...not exactly a steeple but a rocky tower.

Steeple, The see **Eskdale Needle**.

Steers Pool continuation of Lord's Gill [252912] ...personal name or pool/stream in which steers were washed.

Stegcroft Bridge carries the Felldyke to Lamplugh road over Rakegill Beck [084204].

Stencher Beck rises Wansfell ridge 388038 and flows down through Skelghyll Wood to join Windermere at 378027 ...doesn't sound very sweet smelling but derivation is actually the stony or rocky stream.

Stenkin Wythburn. Originally shepherd's cottage owned by nearby West Head Farm [320131] ...stony road.

Stenners Crag overlooks Stythwaite Steps, Far Easedale [316093] ...possibly surname Stenner derived from the OE 'staener' meaning rocky place or from the ON 'stein' meaning stone.

Step, The see **The Step**.

Step Gill rises between May Crag and Squat Knotts at 220171 and joins Newlands Beck at 228174.

Step Hills above the Stepping Stones across the upper River Bleng [122082].

Stephead Close Seathwaite [234959].

Stephead Gill rises slope White Pike at 242955. Joins Wash Dub Beck at 233962 and this meets Tarn Beck at 230963.

Stephen How house on the A593 Skelwith Bridge-Coniston road [338029].

Stephen How on Park Fell E of the A593 Skelwith Bridge-Coniston road [339025].

Stephenson Ground situated alongside a minor road from Broughton Mills. One of several 'grounds' in the immediate area. Others are Carter Ground, Jackson Ground and Stainton Ground [235931] ...writing in 1774 Father West, one of the earliest writers of Lake District guides, noted that "inclosures were called the grounds of the person that first enclosed them and some retain the same name at present." This enclosure took place at the beginning of the 16th century.

Stephenson Haw WNW Stephenson Ground [226934].

Stepping Stones guest house, former Victorian home, with four self-contained letting apartments opposite the stepping stones across the River Rothay. Until 1969 it had been owned by the Wordsworth family for over 100 years [365055].

Stepping Stones stones across the R Rothay [366055].

Stepping Stones across the R Esk to and from St. Catherine's Church, Boot [176002].

Stepping Stones below Step Hills and across the upper River Bleng [122085].

Stepping Stones across the R Duddon at Seathwaite. Thought to be those mentioned by Wordsworth in one of his Duddon sonnets [224963].

Stepping Stones across the R Duddon below Fickle Crag. See **Fickle Steps**.

Stepping Stones across the R Duddon near its confluence with Tommy Gill [209942].

Stepping Stones across Bull Haw Moss Beck [205948].

Stepping Stones across the R Duddon near New Close [202937].

Stepping Stones across Torver Beck near Delicars and Sunny Bank. Now replaced by a footbridge [287927].

Stepping Stones Pow Beck [243232].

Steps End Rydal [363061].

Steps Hall just across the R Lowther at the end of the track from the A6 at Shap which passes Brackenber Lodge. Paths continue to Wet Sleddale and Thornship [560136] ...originally reached by stepping stones across the R Lowther.

Stewardson Nab E shore Windermere between Beech Hill Hotel and Ghyll Head. Stewardson Ground nearby [390925] ...surname + projection.

Stickle Breast breast of the fell below Pike o'Stickle [271071].

Stickle Brow Rosthwaite Fell [261117].

Stickle Ghyll/Gill commences at the dam at the S end of StickleTarn at 288075. Often referred to and shown on some maps as Mill Gill. The latter, however, rises E of Stickle Gill high up on the slope of Blea Rigg and flows alongside Millbeck to join Stickle Gill at 295066. The combined watercourse meets Great Langdale Beck at 298064. Mill Gill and Millbeck are named from an early mill believed to have stood near the foot of the gill.

Stickle Pike pyramidical-shaped peak of the Dunnerdale Fells 375m (1230ft) [212927].

Stickle Tarn originally dammed at its S end where a closed sluice allowed water to rise to a high level before it was opened to enable a head of water to rush down the valley to eventually turn wheels and activate machinery at the Elterwater Gun Powder Works (this closed in 1930), 469m (1539ft) [287076]. In 1999 it was declared an SSSI because of its archaeological importance as a site quarried in the Neolithic period for the production of stone axes ...tarn below the stickle ie. Harrison Stickle.

Stickle Tarn below Stickle Pike, Dunnerdale Fells. The source of Hare Hall Beck, C300 (C984ft) [214928].

Stickletongue Beck rises E Great Stickle at 214916 and joins the River Lickle at 217904.

Sticks Gill (E) flows E from 344182 near the summit of Sticks Pass. Enters former Sticks Tarn reservoir (now principally a marshy area) at 356181. Emerges as Swart Beck which joins Glenridding Beck at 366174.

Sticks Gill (W) rises below summit of Sticks Pass at 340182 and joins Brund Gill at 328180. From confluence becomes Fisherplace Gill.

Sticks Pass next to Esk Hause it is claimed to be the highest popular pass in the Lake District. Starts from Stanah (B5322) [318190] and traverses the 8kms (5 miles) to Ullswater which it reaches at either the foot of Glencoyne [388187] or Glenridding [387170]. At its highest point 738m (2421ft) it crosses the Helvellyn range. For many years ore was carried by pack horse from the Greenside Mine and over the pass to a smelter at Keswick. Takes its name from a line of stakes which used to mark the highest part of the route.

Sticks Tarn below Sticks Pass and above the former Greenside Lead Mine. When the mine was working a small tarn in the hollow was enlarged to supply water to it and was known by locals as the Top Dam. At one time its surface area was not far below that of Angle Tarn, Langdale, but since the closure of the mine the tarn has diminished and to all intents and purposes is just a marshy area 575m (1886ft) [357181].

Stile End end/beginning of the pass [467048] which carries the former drove road and today a bridleway between Kentmere and Sadgill, Longsleddale. Pass rises to C350m (C1148ft) [476050] ...end of the steep path/track.

Stile End across Barrow Door from Barrow 447m (1466ft) [221219].

Stile Gill rises WSW of the summit of Sale How at 270284 and combines with Pike Sike at 277281. The combined watercourse joins with Kitbain Gill at 281281 to become Salehow Beck.

Stinking Gill an unfortunate name. Rises between Heckbarley and Grike at 080140. Joined by Comb Beck before meeting the River Calder at 075129.

Stirrup Crag Yewbarrow. Initial steep rocky ascent from Dore Head to the summit of Yewbarrow passes over Stirrup Crag [176094] ...W A Poucher states that "its most apt name is only fully appreciated when it is observed from Looking Stead." According to the EPNS the name refers to the hill on which ewes were pastured.

Stock Beck alongside the confluence of Appletree Worth Beck and the River Lickle [236918].

Stock Bridge crosses the River Irt at 087007 ...bridge by the tree stumps.

Stock Ghyll rises nonchalantly at the foot of the red screes (which give Red Screes its name) at 397083. It then flows under the Struggle at Pet's Bridge and shortly afterwards is joined by Snow Cove Gill. Subsequently swelled by many streams flowing down the valley sides it assumes a sizeable proportion and drops down swiftly through Ambleside to join the R Rothay at 371045. One of Ambleside's tourist attractions is Stockghyll Force [383046] set in the wooded Stockghyll Park behind the Salutation Inn. This waterfall drops some 27m (90ft) in two steps. A footbridge above the falls provides a grand view of the cascading waters. At the end of the 19th century there was a refreshment shelter nearby and there was an admission charge to enter the park and see the falls. Today's visitors can see both free. Another tourist attraction is the tiny building, Bridge House, spanning the ghyll to the W of the A591. This, probably erected in the 17th century as a summer house, has had several uses, a cobbler's workshop, an antiques shop and earlier the home of a man, his wife and six children. Today it is owned by the National Trust and houses an information centre.

Over the centuries the force of the water in the lower reaches of Stock Ghyll provided Ambleside with much industry and at the turn of the 18th century there was quite an industrial estate hereabouts with six mills plying various trades, fulling, cotton or flax (later bobbins), corn, bark and woollen. In fact, the rattling noise made by the waterwheels caused this area to become known as Rattle Gill. Of the six mill premises three are today occupied wholly or partly by a glass blower; shopping premises and holiday flats. A building known as the Glass House is a restaurant where can be seen an old water wheel and two drive shafts ...tree-stump stream.

Stockbridge alongside the road from the A595 (Waberthwaite) to the Eskmeals coast road [093935].

Stockdale valley and former farm off Longsleddale. There is an outdoor pursuits centre, a private residence and a holiday cottage here and, until several years ago, a machine-knitting workshop and salesroom. This closed in November 1998. At Stockdale the Mardale Tunnel carrying water from Haweswater Reservoir under the fells ends and a pipe-line continues under Longsleddale to the water treatment plant at Selside. Evidence of tunnelling in the form of debris and soil can be seen slightly W of Stockdale Beck. This small valley has given its name to the Stockdale Shales of the Silurian Period. In the dale stands an 18th century lime kiln [492054] emphasising the proximity at this point of the Carboniferous Limestone to the shales [491053] ...tree-stump valley.

Stockdale Beck not named on the OS map. Rises Sleddale Fell at 492071. Met by Brow Gill at 492056 and joins the R Sprint at 490050.

Stockdale Bridge carries the road up Longsleddale over Stockdale Beck [490050].

Stockdale Head the head is nearly 4kms (2.5 miles) from the summit of Stockdale Moor and is really the head of Blengdale. Hereabouts, Tongue Gill, the farthest headstream of the R Bleng, is joined by several small streams [136099] ...similar to many other place names beginning with stock, the word refers to tree trunks and brings to mind an era when areas so called were considerably tree clad.

Stockdale Moor moorland end of the SW ridge of Caw Fell. Acquired by the NT in 1958. Those persons with an experienced eye may spot much evidence of early man in the shape

STONETHWAITE

of ancient cairns, field systems and the long cairn of Sampson's Bratful C290m (C951ft) [103083].

Stockghyll Force see **Stock Ghyll**.

Stockhow Bridge carries the road around the W side of Thirlmere over the Wyth Burn [321129].

Stockley Bridge carries the track from Seathwaite Farm over Grains Gill to join paths alongside the Grains and Ruddy Gills and also one alongside Styhead Gill. An old packhorse bridge on the route between Borrowdale and Wasdale it was widened in the late 19th century and rebuilt after severe flooding in 1966 [235109] ...at one time the valley around the bridge was heavily wooded and this aspect is reflected in the origin of the name - tree stumps in a woodland clearing.

Stocks Bridge footbridge over the R Esk [131978].

Stoddah E minor road A66-Matterdale End. Alongside road to Hutton [415268] ...stud/herd of horses.

Stoddah Bank hill E minor road A66-Matterdale End. W Stoddahgate [415264].

Stoddah Bank property E minor road A66-Matterdale End. Adjacent road to Hutton [415268].

Stoddah Farm E minor road A66-Matterdale End. Alongside minor road to Hutton [418263].

Stoddahgate E minor road A66-Matterdale End. Adjacent the road to Hutton [418265].

Stone Arthur sometimes referred to as Arthur's Chair. Group of rocks at end of spur leading down from Great Rigg. The subject of William Wordsworth's poem *There is an Eminence of these our hills* 504m (1654ft) [348092] ...Arthur who? W G Collingwood notes that "if that be an ancient name, it is the only hint that our southern dales could have been the scenes of idylls of the King." Reference to King Arthur. However it is possibly derived from the celtic 'ar torr' and therefore meaning stone(s) on the hill.

Stone Chair Hill between Griddle How and Stone Chair Intake. E A593 [329013] ...presumably, like the Perch below Hartsop Above How, a compatible, albeit stony hill on which to perch or sit.

Stone Chair Intake between the A593 and the old road from Hawkshead to High Cross [328011].

Stone Circles Cumbria possessed approximately 65 stone circles of the late Neolithic and early bronze age period around one quarter of all those which exist or are known to have existed in England. Nearly 50 are still in either complete or incomplete state within the county boundary, 16 of them within the confines of the Lake District National Park. The one on Swarth Fell is easily the highest stone circle in Cumbria at 560m (1837ft) above sea level and today consists of approximately 65 fallen stones. It is not quite the largest in Cumbria. This honour goes to Long Meg and Her Daughters with originally 69 stones of which over a third are still standing. Works to consult include *The Stone Circles of Cumbria* by John Waterhouse (1985), *The Stone Circles of the British Isles* by Aubrey Burl (1976) and *The Reason for the Stone Circles in Cumbria* by Ray Seton. Also stone circles are mentioned individually in the *Transactions of the Cumberland and Westmorland Archaeological and Antiquarian Society*.

Stone Cove on slope E Rydal Fell. SSE Great Rigg [357102].

Stone Cove on slope E Rydal Fell. SSE Greatrigg Man [357102].

Stone Guard How [251999] ...hill with a stone enclosure.

Stone Hause W Thirlmere. SW Brown Rigg [304145].

Stone Howe remains of tumulus slightly SW of Shap Abbey at 545149.

Stone Howe rocky summit WNW Great Ladstones, NE Glede Howe [527125].

Stone Ivens Plantation below Black Brows and alongside the Hawkshead-Newby Bridge road [367930].

Stone Pike Swainson Knott [078078] ...stony pointed hill.

Stone Walls some of Lakeland's stone walls are believed to be upwards of 1,000 years old, others were completed in the 12th and 16th centuries, but the majority date from about 1750-1850 during the Enclosure Acts. One of the oldest and well documented is that frequently passed by fell walkers climbing the Fairfield ridge from Rydal. The tumbled down remains of what was originally a substantial wall follow alongside the present path between Nab Scar summit and Heron Pike. This was erected in 1277 by Roger de Lancaster to delineate a deer park between the two spurs of high land on each side of Rydal Beck. At the time of the Enclosure Acts the cost of constructing 7 yards (6.3m) was 8 shillings (40p). This was to include transport and collecting the stones. Today, to build a similar type and length of wall would cost several hundred pounds. Writer Hugh Walpole appropriately described Lakeland walls "as running like live things about the fells." It is estimated that there are 15,000kms (9,320 miles) of dry stone walls in Cumbria.

Stonebarrow Gill flows down alongside Boredale Hause from 409152 to join Goldrill Beck at 400156.

Stonegarth Wood Ulpha [191925].

Stonehills Tarn also known as Barrow Plantation Tarn. Privately owned tarn lying slightly S of the rough track from Lindeth Lane running E past Barrow Plantation. Possesses an island and has a dam at its southern end, C110m (C361ft). Stonehills (house) nearby [418944].

Stoneraise W minor road Scales-Guardhouse [348267].

Stonestar property below the Duddon Bridge to Ulpha road [201912] ...steep stony/rocky hill.

Stonesty Gill rises SE Stonesty Pike 251037 and joins Moasdale (Mosedale) Beck at 242030.

Stonesty Pike S Crinkle Crags [249069] ...steep stony peak.

Stonesty Pike Tarns several tarns between Crinkle Crags and Stonesty Pike [250042].

Stonethwaite attractive hamlet of cottages and farms and an inn, the latter, the Langstrath Country Inn. A popular walking centre. The Cumbria Way passes on the other side of the beck [263137] ...land cleared of stones.

Stonethwaite Beck Greenup Gill and Langstrath Beck combine at 274130 to become Stonethwaite Beck. This flows down the Stonethwaite valley through Rosthwaite and along a section known as the Crook before joining the R Derwent at 253154.

Stonethwaite Bridge bridge across Stonethwaite Beck from Stonethwaite [263138].

Stonethwaite Fell between Glaramara and Langstrath [260106].

Stonethwaite Valley the upper reach of Borrowdale bifurcates at Rosthwaite one arm continuing to Seatoller and Seathwaite and the other up the Stonethwaite valley past Stonethwaite to Langstrath and Greenup Edge [262140].

Stoneycroft Stair [233213].

Stony Beck rises Wansfell at 404052 and joins Trout Beck at 420043.

Stony Beck rises E Irton Park at 105017 and flows through Irton Park and alongside Irton Hall to join the R Irt.

Stony Brow Grizedale Forest Park [349957].

Stony Cove Pike see **Caudale Moor**.

Stony Rigg below Holly Crag and above Deepdale Beck [383126].

Stony Rigg E of path between Boredale Hause and Angletarn Pikes C490m (C1608ft) [411151].

Stony Tarn Eskdale. Secluded tarn surrounded by rocky fells including Peelplace Noddle, Whin Crag and Dawsonground Crag C300m (C984ft) [199205].

Ston(e)ycroft Stair [233213].

Stonycroft Gill rises below Outerside at 211212 and flows by Stoneycroft and Stair to join Newlands Beck at 236212. Alongside the gill near the bridge which carries the Braithwaite to Buttermere road over it is the former Stonycroft Mine. This dates from c1680 to 1854 [231212].

Stonycroft Mine see **Stonycroft Gill**.

Stool E Nether Beck [153092] ...possible resemblance to a stool or seat.

Stool End last farm in Great Langdale. Farmhouse dates from the 17th century. At various times called Stealend and Style End. Along with Wall End Farm and the Old Dungeon Ghyll Hotel presented to the NT by Prof. G M Trevellyn in 1929 [276057] ...the EPNS suggests a derivation from the OE 'stol' meaning stool/seat an allusion to the resemblance at the foot of the Band while the NT's *Great Langdale: A History of Land Use* (Vol 1) also refers to its position at the foot of the Band, in this case, derived from 'stile' suggested as meaning ditch. Certainly old names of nearby areas, Dykelands, Great Moss and Little Moss Dykes agree with this interpretation. Stool may also be derived from stile/steale from the OE 'stigel', a steep path, a high ridge and therefore the habitation at the end/foot of the steep ridge, the latter being the Band.

Stords slope Swainson Knott [077081].

Stord's Hill Birkby Fell. S Devoke Water 384m (1260ft) [155962].

Storms alongside minor road off the A66 [292244].

Stormwater Bridge under minor road from Portinscale to B5289 [255239].

Storrs large area to the S of Bowness. Includes the extensive Storrs Park, Storrs Hall and many fine properties [397937-501954] ...young wood/plantation.

Storrs Hall Hotel situated on a promontory E shore Windermere 3.2kms (2 miles) S of Bowness and off the A592. The hall was built for Sir John Legard of Ganton Hall, Yorkshire, in 1790. From 1806-37 it was owned by John Bolton, a shipping merchant. Much enlarged 1811. Its last private occupant was the Rev Thomas Stansfield, first stroke of the first Oxford boat which won against Cambridge in the first Oxford-Cambridge boat race held at Henley in 1829. He died late 19th century and the hall subsequently became a hotel. Called the Grand Hotel at the turn of the last century but later reverted to Storrs Hall (Hotel). In the hands of the North British Trust Hotel chain from 1940-97 when it was acquired by two businessmen who completely renovated the building. Recently acquired by the English Lakes Hotel group which also includes the Low Wood Hotel, between Windermere and Ambleside; the Waterhead Hotel, Waterhead and the Wild Boar, Crook. In October, 1997, scenes for the ITV comedy *Neville's Island* were shot at the hotel [393941].

Storrs Temple (Temple Of Heroes). Octagonal tower at the end of a stone jetty E shore Windermere. Erected in 1804, a year previous to Nelson's victory and death at Trafalgar, by Sir John Legard of nearby Storrs Hall in honour of Admirals Duncan, Howe, Vincent and Nelson and commemorated the British naval victories of the Napoleonic Wars. Owned today by the National Trust [390941].

Storthes area through which Holehouse Gill and attendant tributary Storthes Gill flows

[167940] ...similar to Stord in that it means an area of brushwood/wood thereby signifying that centuries ago the area was well wooded.

Storthes Gill rises W slope Hesk Fell at 169948 and joins Holehouse Gill at 169938.

Stott Park Bobbin Mill see **Thurs Gill Mill**.

Straighthead Gill rises slope of Illgill Head at 176057 and joins Wastwater at 179068.

Straining Well water purifying station between the A591 and Thirlmere. 1.6kms (1 mile) N Wythburn Church. A castellated structure [321150]. See also **Thirlmere**.

Straits of Riggindale a strait is a narrow part, place or passage. In this case it is the narrowest part of the High Street ridge between the crags at the head of Riggindale and the steep fellside down to Hayeswater and Hayeswater Gill [440122].

Strands see **Nether Wasdale**.

Strands Beck farthest headstream rises Blawith Fells at 275910. Joined by Climb Stile Beck and meets Steers Pool/Lord's Gill at 243897.

Strands Bridge carries the B5289 over the River Derwent [231137].

Strandshag Bay Derwent Water [266221] ...shore of the bay frequented by shag/cormorants.

Strawberry Gill dry gill descending E from the summit of Base Brown [228114].

Strawberry Wood lower slope Wansfell ridge, E Waterhead [382035].

Striceley Fell Thwaite Head [345908] ...possibly the stirk/heifer pasture on the fell.

Striceley Intake WSW Thwaite Head. SE Force Forge [339903] ...intake land pastured by the stirks/heifers.

Strickland Ees promontory W shore Esthwaite Water. A large drumlin [359964] ...Strickland - land on which stirks or young cattle were pastured. For the definition of Ees see **Ees**.

Strickland Ketel large area to the W of the River Kent. Nearly 150 years ago it was described as containing part of the village of Burneside, Bonning-Yeat, Green-bank, Bouston Bridge, Gowan Head, Plumgarths, Aikrigg End and Sparrowmire. At one time formed a manor with Strickland Roger but possibly divided in the late 12th century [486960] ...Strickland refers to a pasture ground for stirks and other young cattle. Ketel was the grandson of Ivo de Tailbois who was granted much land in Kendal and district by William the Conqueror. Subsequently Ketel succeeded to this part of his grandfather's estate.

Strickland Roger large area on the E side of the River Kent extending as far as the Sprint and N to Potter Fell [506984] ...this portion of a larger manor was probably granted to Roger by Ketel. See also **Strickland Ketel**.

Striddle Crag large crag S Fleetwith Gully on Fleetwith Pike [204139].

Striding Edge narrow arete running up to Helvellyn. S of Red Tarn which lies well below. An interesting route to the summit in fine weather but in snow, ice, or high wind, it is best avoided unless the person is an experienced hill walker or climber. On the summit edge of Helvellyn is the Gough Memorial (erected 1890) which records the death of Charles Gough in 1805 and the faithful dog which kept vigil by his body for 3 months. Also on the edge, overlooking Nethermost Cove, stands the iron Dixon memorial to a huntsman who fell from the spot in 1858. In February 1945, a Mosquito fighter/bomber crashed on Striding Edge. Its crew of 2 were killed [347150].

Strudda Bank W River Calder [059082] ...at one time a marshy area overgrown with brushwood.

Struggle, The see **Kirkstone Pass**.

Strutta Wood adjoining Low Strutta and between the Watendlath road and the B5289.

From its edge there is another 'surprise view' over Borrowdale and Derwent Water [269197] ...possibly similar to Strudda (strod) and meaning the marshy land overgrown with brushwood.

Stub Hill W side of Derwent Water above Copperheap Bay C100m (C328ft) [252217] ...tree-stump hill.

Stubb Place alongside the minor road from Bootle to Eskmeals [082907].

Stubby Hest between Swindale Beck and Starling Gill [524143].

Stubshead Hill Gosforth. E A595. SE Gallows Hill [077021] ...tree-stump pasture.

Stubthwaite Crag large crag ESE Low Water [281980].

Stunfell Howe lower slope of Sallows, S of Garburn Pass [441043].

Sty Beck lower reach of Stanah Gill below falls [319189].

Sty Head Sty Head simply means the head of the (steep) path being that which crosses the col, Styhead Pass, en route from Borrowdale to Wasdale. Centuries ago the pass was called Edderlanghals which both the EPNS and Robert Gambles agree could refer to the long path over the pass by the rapidly flowing stream. Extremely popular with walkers and climbers who have the choice of several routes from it to Borrowdale, Eskdale, Great Langdale, the Scafell massif, Great Gable, etc. The summit of the pass at 228094 is situated at an altitude of 488m (1601ft) [218094]. Sty Head and its pass are generally busy paricularly during the summers months with fell walkers heading in all directions but if either of two schemes proposed in the late 19th and early 20th centuries had come to fruition the area would have been noisy, polluted, and gone would be the peace and quite it enjoys today. The first scheme was for a carriageway from Seathwaite to Wasdale Head and the second a carriageway from Seathwaite to Sty Head where it would be met by a tramway ultimately to run from Seascale to Keswick via Wasdale Head and Sty Head.

Stybarrow Crag impressive high cliff bedecked with trees that overhangs the A592 N Glenridding. It is actually the very end of a lengthy ridge which runs from Stybarrow Dodd over Green Side, Sheffield Pike and Glenridding Dodd. Before part of the crag was blasted away to make way for the present-day metalled road a rough track passed over the top and it was here, centuries ago, that a Patterdale Mounsey obtained the hereditary King of Patterdale title after organising a band of local dalesmen in a successful defence against border raiders [387178] ...sty (from 'stig' or 'stigel') - steep path.

Stybarrow Dodd second highest and most southerly of the Helvellyn Dodds. Grassy. Immediately N of Sticks Pass which traverses its lower slopes for a considerable distance 843m (2766ft) [343189].

Stybeck Fall on lower reaches of Stanah Gill [319189].

Stybeck Farm off A591 between Dale Head and junction with B5232 [320188].

Styhead Gill a stream considered by many to be the source of the R Derwent drops down from Sprinkling Tarn to Styhead Tarn from where Styhead Gill emerges to descend over Taylor Gill Force to join Grains Gill at 234111. The substantial watercourse then becomes better known as the R Derwent.

Styhead Tarn set in a glaciated hollow just below Sty Head and at the foot of Great End, Great Gable and Seathwaite Fell. A welcome sight for walkers heading for nearby Sty Head. A major feeder flows steeply from Sprinkling Tarn while from its outlet Styhead Gill, a major headstream of the R Derwent, begins its descent to join Grains Gill near Stockly Bridge. Styhead Tarn has the rather dubious honour of being the wettest place in Britain. In 1954, 4391mm (172.9ins) of rain fell thereabouts, C440m C1443ft) [222099].

Stythwaite Steps originally Far Easedale Gill was crossed here by stepping stones but a wooden bridge now serves this purpose [318094] ...steps by the steep path by the clearing.

Sulphury Gill an unusual name. Possibly derived from the sulphur content of the ore-bearing minerals in the rocks thereabouts. Rises as Well Gill between Rampsgill Head and the Knott at 438127 and cascades down its lower reach to join Hayeswater Gill at 425129.

Summer Grove Plantation alongside the B5284 and across the road from the Windermere Golf Course [427961].

Summers Cove Beck rises N Walna Scar Road at 278968. Joined by Hussey Well Beck at 282961 and the combined watercourse joins Torver Beck at 282958.

Sunny Bank area and properties at the foot of Torver Beck and alongside the A5084. A bobbin mill operated here from the early 19th century until the 1930s [289925].

Sunny Bank Cottage Sunny Bank [290923].

Sunny Brow off the Knipe Fold-Drunken Duck Inn road. Below Limestone Hill [343004].

Sunny Pike Seathwaite Fells. E Tongue House and above Sunny Pike Gill [241974].

Sunny Pike Gill rises Seathwaite Fells near Lingy Stone at 247977 and joins Tarn Beck at 236973.

Sunnybrow Crook. Property off the B5284 [443952].

Sunnythwaite Grizedale Forest Park [344956].

Surprise View viewpoint alongside the road to Watendlath. Here, where the road curves there is a breathtaking panoramic view over Borrowdale, up Derwent Water and over to Bassenthwaite and Skiddaw [268189].

Survey Posts see **Pillars**.

Swainsey Crag W of unfenced road over Rosgill Moor from Bampton/Bampton Grange to Swindale. SSE Scalebarrow Tarn [521149]

Swainsley Hall NE Force Mills. Long since lay in ruins but even these have now disappeared in the forest [343914]

Swainson Knott E Scalderskew Wood C340m (C1115ft) [080084] ...possibly the shepherd's hill or a surname + hill.

Swaledale Sheep see **Sheep**.

Swallow Hole Out Scar, Knipescar. Hole which swallows the water emerging from a nearby spring [549188].

Swallow Scar Beck not named on the OS map. Rises Steel Edge at 294007 and joins Henfoot Beck at 296010.

Swallow Scarth E Helvellyn ridge. N Nethermost Pike [344145].

Swallowhurst Corney. Alongside minor road off the A595 [103910] ...wooded hill frequented by swallows.

Swallowhurst Hall Corney. Alongside the A595 [102915].

Swan (Mv) built by Vickers of Barrow in 1938. Subsequently dismantled and transferred to Lakeside in sections where she was reassembled. Replaced an earlier *Swan* (launched 1869, broken up 1938).

Swan Dub deep pool on Langthwaite Beck [264103] ...pool frequented by swans.

Swan Hotel Grasmere. Alongside the A591. Originally built as a coaching inn over three centuries ago but added to over the succeeding years. "Who does not know the famous Swan? Object uncouth, and yet our boast, For it was painted by the Host" (Wordsworth's *The Waggoner*). The host who painted the original inn sign and referred to by Wordsworth was Anthony Wilson, landlord of the Swan Inn for over 30 years until his death in 1831. An anecdote concerning the hostelry is:- that Walter Scott while staying with the Wordsworths at Dove Cottage would step down from his bedroom window and repair to the Swan where he enjoyed a fuller breakfast than was provided in the Wordsworth household. A similar story suggests that while staying with the Wordsworths he would surreptitiously visit the Swan for a strong drink. However, this secret meeting with alcoholic beverage came to light one morning while Scott and Wordsworth were walking past the hostelry. Unfortunately for Scott they met the landlord who obviously embarrassed the former by stating that he was somewhat early for his drink that day [340082].

Swan Hotel Powter How, Thornthwaite. A former coaching inn built in 1678 on the old Keswick-Cockermouth road. Situated at the foot of Barf on which slope stands the prominent whitewashed rock known as Bishop Rock or the Bishop of Barf [222265]. See also **Bishop of Barf**.

Swanesty How alongside the track from Stonethwaite to Watendlath [263158] ...steep hill of the swine.

Swanesty How Grange-in-Borrowdale [247175].

Sware Gill rises Graystones at 175265 and joins Whit Beck at 174256.

Swart Beck Swart Beck emerges from the former reservoir which served the Greenside Mine at 357181, disappears underground and surfaces well before joining Glenridding Beck at 366174 ...the dark or black stream.

Swarth Beck rises 458190 between Loadpot Hill and Swarth Fell. Alongside its head at 457191 is a stone circle. Flows down a deep ravine, over the cataracts in Swarthbeck Gill and alongside Swarthbeck to join Ullswater at 449211 ...the black or dark stream.

Swarth Beck rises S Lank Rigg at 091109 and joins Worm Gill at 096101.

Swarth Fell rises to the E of Howtown and lies to the N of Loadpot Hill. The whole fell is sometimes referred to as Bonscale Pike or Toughmoss Pike. However, Bonscale Pike is simply a subsidiary peak on a line of crags overlooking Ullswater. From Howtown and Ullswater the top of the crags appears to be the summit but this is set well back and like others on the lengthy High Street ridge it is grassy. Traversed by the Roman Road it is the last height of note on the ridge prior to dropping down to Pooley Bridge, Askham or Helton. On its W slope it possesses what was one of the largest stone circles in Cumbria [457191] which today consists of approximately 65 fallen stones and is scheduled as an Ancient Monument C560m (C1837ft) [461197]. In 1942 the pilot of a Spitfire was killed when his plane crashed on the fell ...as one 19th century writer stated "its dark and sombre hue merits the name which has been bestowed on it" - black or dark hill.

Swarth Fell between Lowther Park and the River Calder 335m (1099ft) [065120] ...dark/black hill.

Swarthbeck E Ullswater alongside Swarth Beck [453209].

Swarthbeck Gill see **Swarth Beck**.

Swarthfield E shore Ullswater below Swarth Fell [447205].

Swear Gill rises 525130 and joins Swindale Beck at 520134 ...neck of land, col or hollow on a ridge by a stream.

Sweden Crag near High Sweden Bridge and to the W of the path leading over Low Pike [375069] ...the crag above the moorland cleared by burning.

Sweeten Crag S Kitty Crag on the S ridge of Wetherlam 435m (1427ft) [295988].

Sweetenthwaite Hill Hawkshead Moor, Grizedale Forest Park [340968].

Swift (Mv) built at Glasgow in 1900. Originally coal-fired but converted to diesel in 1956. Docked at Lakeside for many years.

Swinburn's Park between Hagg Wood/Gate Crags and Kirksty Brow/Kirkstyle Gill [420220].

Swindale lonely rugged valley running E of and parallel to Mardale. Although there is a road and track to the last habitation, Swindale Head, the dale is really a walkers' area. Walkers' routes and paths approach the dale from Bampton, Bampton Grange, Mardale, Rosgill, Shap, Wet Sleddale and the Gatescarth Pass via Mosedale. At one time Swindale had a church and adjoining school at Truss Gap. Both have gone, the church (erected in 1749) was demolished in 1938 and the school (founded in 1703) was abandoned many years earlier and demolished in the 1960s. Manchester Corporation Waterworks intended to build a reservoir in the dale and, in fact, by a Private Act of Parliament dated 1919 the Corporation was empowered to buy the watersheds of Mardale, Swindale and Wet Sleddale. Mardale and Wet Sleddale have been turned into reservoirs but as yet Swindale has been saved this fate and today water is solely extracted from the beck below Truss Gap where there is a water treatment works, small dam, a weir and an unseen tunnel through which water is carried from Haweswater under Hugh Laithes Pike, across the Naddle valley then via the Harper Hills reservoir. John Hodgson (1780-1845), the historian of Northumberland, was born in Swindale and a former local family, the Baxters, claim to have raised Herdwick sheep here from the end of the 12th century until the early 19th. Ancient documents concerning Swindale certainly suggest that many centuries ago the dale was not as lonely as it is today. Reference is made to Thengeheved, the modern interpretation of which is 'the council place at the head of the valley'. Swindale was obviously an important place, a place where a 'parliament' met to settle the affairs of Scandinavian settlers in and around the area. Incidentally, a similar moot, the Thingmount at Fell Foot Farm, Little Langdale, was designated a Scheduled Ancient Monument in 1977. Today there are only two working farms in the dale [513129] ...the valley where swine grazed.

Swindale Beck Mosedale Beck rises 486089. Drops down over the Forces (Swindale Falls) into Swindale where it is met by Hobgrumble Gill and becomes Swindale Beck. On its way to join the R Lowther at 535164 Swindale Beck is joined by Dry Groove Gill, Black Crag Gill, Gouthercrag Gill/Haskew Beck, Swear Gill, Mere Sike, Starling Gill and Tailbert Gill.

Swindale Common E head of Swindale and lower Mosedale [512114].

Swindale Falls see **Forces**.

Swindale Foot area and farm at the foot of Swindale. The farm is one of the two remaining working farms in Swindale [522138].

Swindale Foot Crag overlooks Swindale Foot. S Bewbarrow Crag C380m (C1247ft) [520139].

Swindale Head former farm near the head of Swindale. For many years the home of the Sewell family. The old corpse road from Mardale drops into Swindale here. The track up the valley ends here but a path continues up to and into Mosedale and on to the Gatescarth Pass [505125].

Swindale Lane Swindale [519135].

Swine Crag alongside Riggindale Scar [468113].

Swine Gill rises 505109 and joins Mosedale Beck at 508109.

Swine Knott/Crag across White Gill from Scout Crag [297069] ...the hill frequented by swine.

Swinescales alongside minor road A66-Matterdale End [415271].

Swinescales Beck rises at 406273 and joins Skitwath Beck at 419275.

Swinescar Hause from the hause to the W of Swinescar Pike a stream, also named Swinescar Hause, rises at 313072 and flows down to Blindmoss Tarn. Subsequently Blindmoss Gill flows out of the tarn area to join Easedale Beck at 325083.

Swinescar Pike above Swinescar Hause [314072].

Swineside Knott overlooks Spying How, Glencoyne Park and Ullswater 553m (1814ft) [379197].

Swinklebank Crag overlooks Longsleddale [498046]. Spot height on ridge at rear 553m (1814ft) [501049] ...swine bank crag.

Swinklebank Wood Longsleddale. Above High Swinklebank Farm and below Swinklebank Crag [495046] ...see **Swinklebank Crag** above.

Swinside off Coldfell Road [061149] ...summer pasture where pigs were grazed.

Swinside on the ridge rising from High Swinside Farm to Hopegill Head 509m (1670ft) [177239] ...see above.

Swinside rounded fell in afforested area to the S of Ullock. Spot heighted at 244m (800ft) with a lesser summit at 213m (699ft) [243244].

Swinside Newlands valley. Foot of the fell of that name and at a road junction from the Newlands Pass. Farm and inn. The latter a country pub popular with tourists and locals [243218].

Swinside End off Coldfell Road [058147].

Swinside End Farm Scales, High Lorton [168254].

Swinside Gill rises slightly N of Newlands Hause at 192178 and joins Sail Beck at 187178.

Swinside Houses alongside the Whinlatter Pass [188246].

Swinside Lodge Swinside [247215].

Swinside Plantation betwen Swinside and the Whinlatter Pass (B5292) [183241].

Swinsty Beck rises Nether Wasdale Common at 132076 and joins the R Bleng at 119084 ...stream by the pigs' steep path.

Swinsty Gill rises WNW Stonesty Pike Tarns at 249043 and joins Lingcove Beck at 236044 ...stream by the pigs' steep path.

Swinsty How Dunnerdale Forest [231986] ...pig sty hill.

Swirl Band shoulder leading up from Levers Hause to Swirl How [272001].

Swirl Hawse col between Swirl How/Prison Band and the path up to the summit of Wetherlam C620m (C2034ft) [278008].

Swirl Hawse Beck rises Swirl Hawse at 278007 and joins Levers Water at 280995.

Swirl How second highest peak of the Coniston range 802m (2631ft) [273006]. In March 1944, an Avro Anson crashed on the slope of Swirl How killing its crew of 3. Close by a Spitfire was discovered with its dead pilot ...the hill around which the wind swirls and no doubt it can be a very draughty place. It could also be the hill by the neck/col. The latter being Swirl Hawse.

Swirle Crag between the upper reaches of Captain Whelter Beck and Hopgill Beck [486108] ...possibly the crag around which the wind whirls/swirls.

Swirls, The see **Swirls Forest Trail** below.

Swirls Forest Trail made by the NWWA. Commences at Swirls car park and picnic area to the E of the A591 and 3.6kms (2.25 miles) N Wythburn Church. The Swirls (Swirrel Wood) is a wooded eminence nearby [317168] ...in this case the forest inhabited by squirrels. Swirl is an old local name for a squirrel.

Swirral Edge rocky ridge leading down from Helvellyn to col and then continuing more sedately to Catstye Cam. Well-trodden paths from Patterdale and Glenridding join E Red Tarn, climb N of the tarn and over Swirral Edge to the summit of Helvellyn [343154] ...most unlikely in this case to refer to the squirrel. Possibly the edge across which the wind swirls or from the OE 'swira' meaning neck or col.

Swirrel Wood see **Swirls Forest Trail**.

Swithin Crag W Dobgill Bridge, Thirlmere [312140].

Sword House Eskdale. House and kennels (Eskdale & Ennerdale foxhounds) alongside the Eskdale to Ulpha fell road [148991] ...earlier Sword Hows (sword hill) but origin of sword is unknown.

Syke Side National Trust farm off Loanthwaite Lane [360994].

Sykes off the road between the A591 which passes St. John's Church and joins the road up St. John's in the Vale [300244] ...from OE 'sic', a small stream. Two flow alongside.

Sykeside behind Brotherswater Inn. Noted camping site with amenities [403119].

Symonds Knott subsidiary summit of Scafell [208067].

T

Taggleshaw Tarns Potter Fell. Low Taggleshaw Tarn is much overgrown. Lies about 183m (200 yards) SSE of Gurnal Dubs C290m (C951ft) [505989]. Middle Taggleshaw Tarn lies E of Gurnal Dubs C300m (C984ft) [507993]. High Taggleshaw Tarn NNE of Gurnal Dubs contains a small island C310m (C1017ft) [505994] ...Taggleshaw is probably 'disordered copse' which is appropriate to the higgledy piggledy nature of the terrain thereabouts.

Tail Crag W Tarn Head Beck valley [263999].

Tail Crag ESE Caw. W River Lickle [237942].

Tail End Grasmere, see **Dale End**.

Tail o'Ling N Measand Beck [474160].

Tailbert properties, including a farm, WSW Shap from which they are approached by road and track through Keld. Tailbert Gill flows through narrow wooded valley alongside on its way to join Swindale Beck [534145] ...of obscure origin but could possibly be from 'taefl-board'- a flat table board as used for dice or chess. In which case could mean a rectangular flat-topped hill or similar.

Tailbert Bank slope leading up from Swindale Beck to Tailbert Head [528144].

Tailbert Beck rises Ralfland Forest at 533130 and flows down alongside Tailbert to join Swindale Beck at 533155.

Tailbert Gill rises Ralfland Forest at 533130 and flows alongside Tailbert to join Swindale Beck at 533155.

Tailbert Head W Tailbert 328m (1076ft) [530143].

Tansey Gill rises Tarn at Leaves, Rosthwaite Fell, at 258122 and enters Langstrath Beck at 267115 ...gill in which the tansy (herb) grows.

Tanyard Beck rises from a spring in Great Spring, foot of Underbarrow Scar at 482914 and joins Underbarrow Pool at 469905 ...suggests the stream alongside the tannery but may have another meaning.

Tarbarrel Moss SW Ullister Hill 493m (1617ft) [206253].

Tarn what is the difference between a lake and a tarn? A subject of much controversy. Generally speaking a lake occupies a valley while a tarn is situated much higher. However, a tarn is not necessarily smaller ie Devoke Water, the largest Lakeland tarn, is roughly the same size as Rydal Water but as wide and longer than Brothers Water. On the other hand, Devoke Water at 235m (770ft) is lower than the highest lake, Haweswater 240m (788ft). In fact, many tarns are far lower than either Haweswater or Thirlmere 179m (588ft). The best scientific distinction is that suggested many years ago by T T Macan of the Freshwater Biological Association. His research showed that the most common emergent plant in tarns tended to be the bottle sedge whereas in lakes it is often the common reed. Having said that, some tarns and lakes contain both. There is obviously no definite rule as to which water is which. Factors already quoted play a part in distinguishing one from the other along with regional and historical records and, in the case of tarns, the degree of permanency. Tarns were, however, named centuries ago. Angle Tarn, Patterdale, was 'Angilter(n)ey' over 700 years ago and the word tarn comes from the ON 'tjorn' meaning tear. The number of tarns in the Lake District is emphasised by a record set up by two Grasmere men, Colin Dodgson and Timothy Tyson, who, between 1951 and 1966 plunged into 730 lakes, ponds, but mainly tarns. Only permanent waters were used and those in which they could manage a couple of strokes. See also under individual tarns and list in the Reference Section.

Tarn at Leaves Rosthwaite Fell. Below Bessyboot C500m (C1640ft) [258122] ...unknown origin. Possibly the tarn by the laithes/tarn by the barns. This could also fit in with a suggestion for Bessyboot nearby - Bessy's sheepfold or booth/shelter or both.

Tarn Beck flows out of Seathwaite Tarn at 251988 and through rocky pools and over delightful waterfalls to join the River Duddon near Seathwaite at 225961. The 'Tributary Stream' of Wordsworth's Duddon sonnets.

Tarn Beck rises Arnsbarrow Tarn at 310917. Subsequently becomes Selside Beck at 306911 which joins Coniston Water at 295909.

Tarn Brow alongside Seathwaite Tarn [251991].

Tarn Close Crook. Off the Crook to Staveley road. Believed to have been built around 1820 for the Fell family. Has its own tarn adjoining [462959].

Tarn Close Crag crag just S of Blea Tarn, Langdale, from which it takes its name 219m (718ft) [293041].

Tarn Crag E Longsleddale and NE Buckbarrow Crag. Takes its name from Greycrag Tarn which lies on col nearby. On its summit stands one of Manchester Corporation Waterworks former survey posts (see also **Pillars**) 664m (2179ft) [488078].

Tarn Crag near the head of Grisedale. N Grisedale Tarn from which it takes its name. Adjoining Falcon Crag [352126].

Tarn Crag overlooks Easedale Tarn from which the crag has obtained its name. On the Sergeant Man-Tarn Crag-Greathead Crag-Stenners Crag ridge 550m (1804ft) [303093].

Tarn Crag SE StickleTarn from which it takes its name [290073].

Tarn Crag Birker Moor. Above Low Birker Tarn 291m (955ft) [193996].

Tarn Crags Blencathra ridge above Scales Tarn 829m (2720ft) [324280].

Tarn Crags W Thirlmere. Overlooking Harrop Tarn [308134].

Tarn Foot farm and caravan and camping site alongside Loughrigg Tarn [346041].

Tarn Head Beck two major tributaries rise between Grey Friar and Swirl How at 266005 and 269004 respectively. The beck subsequently flows alongside the former Seathwaite Tarn copper mine and its spoil heaps before entering Seathwaite Tarn at 258992.

Tarn Hill NW Hollow Stones. No tarn shown on the OS 1:25000 map but possible connection with not too far distant Tarnside and Tarnside Farm [449921].

Tarn Hill Dunnerdale Fells. NW Great Stickle. SSW Stickle Pike. Takes its name from the 8 tarns shown on the OS map. These are not named but are usually given the collective title of Tarn Hill Tarns. The summit of Tarn Hill is at 313m (1027ft) and the small tarns nestling between its many crags lie at an altitude of 260 to 300ms (853 to 984ft) [210921].

Tarn Hill Tarns see **Tarn Hill**.

Tarn Hows extremely popular beauty spot situated 3.2kms (2 miles) NE of Coniston off the Coniston-Skelwith Bridge road (A593). Originally three small tarns which were dammed at their SW end in the 19th century by James Marshall of Monk Coniston Hall (who also dammed nearby Yew Tree and High Arnside Tarns) and became the present 0.8kms (0.5 mile) long and indented tarn of today. Popularly known as Tarn Hows, other names have been Highlow Tarns, Monk Coniston Tarns, Three Tarns and the Tarns. It is still called the latter on OS maps. The name Tarn Hows seems to be somewhat inappropriate meaning tarn 'hills' or the 'hills above the tarn' but actually it is believed to have taken its name from Tarn Hows Farm to its SW, the latter name being a misnomer for the much earlier name Tarn House (Tarnhouse). The tarn was presented to the National Trust in 1930 as a memorial to Sir James and Lady Anne Scott, a fact commemorated on a stone set on top of a crag E of the tarn. Sited at an altitude of 188m (617ft) it has a maximum depth of 9m (29.5ft). Fishing is private but consists of pike, perch, roach and rudd. The LDNP Board opened its first car park at Tarn Hows in 1954 [331000] ...see **Tarn Hows Cottage**.

Tarn Hows Cottage off the lane which leaves the B5285 opposite Monk Coniston Hall and passes Tarn Hows to meet the B5285 again at Hawkshead Hill [320994] ...it has been suggested that Tarn Hows took its name from the earlier Tarn Hows Farm, the latter name being a misnomer for Tarn House (Tarnhouse).

Tarn Hows Hotel Victorian hotel, built in the 1880s, and situated off the High Cross-Knipe Fold road. Tarn Hows is less than 0.8kms (1 mile) away. The hotel is also a registered riding and pony trekking centre [339993].

Tarn Hows Intake SW Tarn Hows [324994].

Tarn Hows Wood National Trust woodland between Low Yewdale and Tarn Hows Cottage [317992].

Tarn Intake named after the nearby Grizedale Tarn(s) [346946].

Tarn Moor alongside Moor Divock. Deep under the moor a 2.74kms (3,000 yards) long tunnel, completed in 1969, carries water from Ullswater to Heltondale en route to Manchester [487216] ...pond on the moor. There are several ponds or small tarns in the area.

Tarn Moss S A66. 1km (0.75 mile) ENE of former Troutbeck Station [399274].

Tarn Riggs alongside Strands Beck and Hodge Wife Gill [269907].

Tarn Wood alongside Fell Lane, Muncaster Fell [105973].

Tarnside alongside the A5074-High Birks-Bowland Bridge road. An old established tarn nearby (del Terne in 1374) but not named on the OS map [433908].

Tarnside Farm off the A5074 [435910] ...see **Tarnside**.

Taw House farm, Eskdale. Rebuilt at the beginning of the 19th century. Purchased by the NT in 1942 [211016]. Coleridge said that the name meant 'the toes of Scafell' and it is indeed situated at the foot of the long S ridge running down from Scafell. The most probable explanation is that it refers to Tower's place after a local 18th to early 19th century family of that name who occupied the property. A footbridge carrying a path across the Esk to Taw House was rebuilt in 1969 in memory of Dick Marsh (Eskdale Outward Bound School).

Taylor Fold sheepfold [375191].

Taylor Gill lower section of Styhead Gill down which Taylor Gill Force drops ...see **Taylor Gill Force**.

Taylor Gill Force spectacular waterfall in Taylor Gill over which Styhead Gill drops some 43m (140ft) from a hanging valley [230110] ...the Taylor in question was probably William Taylor of Crosthwaite whose family was registered in 1718. Other names nearby probably asociated with early families are Aaron Crag/Slack, Airey Bridge, Mitchell Cove/Gill, Patterson's Fold and Wilkinson's Dub.

Teal (Mv) Windermere steamer operated seasonally by the Bowness Bay Boat Co. Built by Vickers at Barrow. Subsequently dismantled and transferred to Lakeside where she was reassembled and launched in July 1936. Replaced an earlier *Teal* (1879-1927). Converted to diesel in 1956.

Television Channels see **Media**.

Television Mast Claife Heights [383981].

Tent Cottage see **Townson Ground**.

Tent Lodge Georgian house E side of Coniston Water. In the garden of the nearby Townson Ground Elizabeth Smith (1776-1806), scholar, translator and linguist, slept in a tent because, as a tuberculosis sufferer, she might benefit from the fresh air. Tent Lodge was built after her death and its name commemorates her habitation. Later the Lodge became a holiday home and Alfred Tennyson spent part of his honeymoon here in 1850. He returned in 1857 [318974].

Tent Lodge Plantation above Tent Lodge E side of Coniston Water [322972].

Tent Lodge Tarn in Grizedale Forest Park above Tent Lodge and Tent Lodge Plantation. Lodge Head Tarn in *Exploring Lakeland Tarns* by Don Blair but Tent Lodge Tarn in *The Tarns of Lakeland* by John and Anne Nuttall C240m (C787ft) [327972].

Tenter Hill a fulling mill is recorded at Hawkshead Hill in the 16th century and at the nearby Tenter Hill the wet cloth was hung on a tenter (a frame by which cloth retained its shape while drying). The word tenter as a place name appears frequently throughout Cumbria as in Tenter Close, Tenter End, Tenter Garth, Tenter How(e), Tenterbrook Wood and Tenterfield [338989].

Tenter Howe Longsleddale [512007] ...tenter - a person who stretches cloth on a tenter (a frame by which cloth retains its shape while drying). Kendal and district were dominant in the textile industry and particularly famous for Kendal Green cloth.

Tenter Howe Tarn on flat shoulder of Tenter Howe, Longsleddale. Not named but shown on OS map. Little open water and what is left is becoming overgrown with sedge C250m (C820ft) [507007].

Tern (Mv) launched in 1891. Built by Forrests of Wyvenhoe, Essex, and is the oldest passenger steamer operating on Windermere. Originally coal-fired but converted to diesel in 1956. Requisitioned during the Second World War as a lake patrol boat and also served as a base for testing mine laying techniques. Then operated under the name *HMS Undine.*

Terrace Farm Lorton. Off the B5292 [159264].

Tewet Tarn N Low Rigg [305236]. Stream issuing from it joins Naddle Beck at 301241 ...tewet - peewit, another name for the lapwing or green plover.

Tewfit Mire SW Steps Hall. Between Lingy Hill and Reamer Bank [556133] ...possibly mire frequented by plovers (peewits).

Tewit How N Haycock. W Steeple 610m (2001ft) [146119] ...hill frequented by peewits/plovers.

Tewit Moss Birker Moor. ENE Devoke Water [168974] ...moss frequented by peewits/plovers.

Tewsett Pike Low Fell, Shap Fells [562109] ...possibly the hill frequented by peewits (plovers).

Thack Bottom Scandale. Below Thack Bottom Edge and Scandale Head [378092] ...rushes or reeds in the bottom of the valley.

Thack Bottom Edge edge of ridge overlooking Thack Bottom, Scandale [375094].

Thackmell Crags W Thirlmere. S of and overlooking Launchy Gill [308155].

Thackthwaite hamlet 1km (0.75 mile) E minor road A66-Matterdale End [423255] ...clearing from which thatching material is obtained.

Thackthwaite community comprising houses and farms alongside the minor road which connects Low Lorton with Loweswater [148237].

Thackthwaite Beck shown on the 2.5 ins OS map as a section of Dacre Beck NW Thackthwaite and flowing roughly between 412253 and 422262. See also **Dacre Beck**.

Thackthwaite Beck rises 148233. Joined by Meregill at 152243 and the combined watercourse meets the R Cocker at 151252.

Thackthwaite Gill headwaters rise from springs on Little Mell Fell [421244] [422246] [420248]. Joins Thackthwaite Beck (Dacre Beck) at 421259.

Thackthwaite Wood Thackthwaite, Lorton Vale. Adjoining Wilderness Wood [147233].

The Almshouses Ulpha, see **Ulpha Almshouses**.

The Band Great End. Grassy ridge leading up the N face of that mountain to the head of Skew Gill. A walkers' route to the summit of Great End ascends by the Band and slope above Skew Gill to a rocky ascent to the summit cairn [226089].

The Band ridge of Bowfell which divides Mickleden from Oxendale. Provides a popular walkers' route to and from the Three Tarns, Crinkle Crags and Bowfell from Great Langdale. The route up the Band was exceptionally stony and heavily used and after three years work the path was eventually realigned and landscaped and completed at the end of 2000 [266059] ...the word 'band' refers to a long ridge from a high fell (Bowfell) or an elevated tract of land between two valleys, in this case Mickleden and Oxendale.

The Bell below Beck Fells. Rises to 335m (1099ft) [288979].

The Benn SW Shoulthwaite Moss [302198].

The Bield Little Langdale. Large property formerly a farmhouse called Low Bield [302036] ...shelter/hut/dwelling.

The Bishop see **Bishop of Barf**.

The Bog off minor road, Troutbeck-Wallthwaite [372266].

The Bog exceedingly swampy area, possibly once a tarn, through which the Wyth Burn flows [299113].

The Broom property, Underbarrow, alongside Broom Lane [458925].

The Brow SE Cockley Beck [250010].

The Brow Low Lorton [145255].

The Bungalow Ramps Gill. Alongside Mell Beck and above Rampsgill Beck. With its red roof and its secluded situation among trees it looks like a tea planter's residence. Originally a shooting lodge and near it, in 1912, the Kaiser shot a stag [439162].

The Cabin indentation in coastline E shore Coniston Water [302934].

The Cape ...sharp headland of a lofty ridge. See **St Sunday Crag**.

The Castle hill on Whitestone Moor. No visible signs of a former castle or indeed any other remains [471205].

The Causeway Farm alongside the road between the Ings-Troutbeck road and Troutbeck bridge. Dating from circa mid 17th century and similar to several farms in the Windermere and adjoining area once owned by a member of the Philipson family [416000] ...the name Causeway (raised way) along with Broadgate (broad way) and Crosses has led authorities to believe that the present road could have been more or less on the line of an old Roman road from Watercrook, Kendal, to Galava, Ambleside.

The Churn see **Watendlath Beck**.

The Clerk see **Clerk, The**.

The Close between Troutal and Little Blake Rigg [239990].

The Cockpit see **Moor Divock**.

The Combe Borrowdale Fells. Rises to Combe Door and Combe Head. Down it flows Combe Gill on its journey to join the R Derwent [251124].

The Common E of Alice Howe (A591) to Ings-Troutbeck road [425996].

The Common SE Grizedale Tarn [348942].

The Common Farm see **Common Farm**.

The Coombs small valley between Hallin Fell and N extremity of Steel Knotts. Road over the Hause from Howtown to Martindale passes to its W [438192].

The Cove marshy area traversed by the path from the Walna Scar Road to Goat's Hawse [267968].

The Cove Seathwaite Fells. Long House Gill flows through it [253968].

The Crook Duddon valley [209950] ...nearby is a substantial bend in the R Duddon.

The Crook winding section of Stonethwaite Beck which joins the R Derwent at 253154. See also **Stonethwaite Beck**.

The Cross Grizedale Forest Park [354942].

The Dodd on High Street ridge E of the Roman road [466194].

The Drunken Duck Inn see **Drunken Duck Inn**.

The Dubs S Little Fell [320024] ...'dub(b)s' - pools. Marshy area and pool hereabouts.

The Edge slightly WNW of Ullock Pike. A section of the Allerdale Ramble passes along the top of it [242292].

The Ferry House see **Ferry House**.

The Forces spectacular waterfalls over which Measand Beck falls from hanging valley [485156].

The Forest see **Fawcett Forest**.

The Forge in the first half of the 17th century a bloomsmithy (an open hearth where iron ore was smelted using charcoal and a water-powered trip hammer) was established alongside Cunsey Beck 0.8kms (0.5 mile) from the shore of Windermere. Shown on the present OS map as the Forge [377936]. Iron ore was principally transported from Low Furness up Windermere to its W shore (Collingwood says that Hammer Hole was the landing place) and then over land via Little Ore Gate and Great Ore Gate. All that remains today are parts of a leat and slag heaps.

The Gap Nether Wasdale [120048] ...over 450 years ago it was 'del gap'.

The Glebe see **Bowness-on-Windermere** and **The Rectory**.

The Glen Nether Staveley. Off the Crook (B5284)-Borwick Fold road [453968].

The Grange Hotel alongside the Loweswater to Mockerkin road [116227].

The Green Lamplugh [089209].

The Green Station Eskdale Green. On the Ravenglass & Eskdale Railway [145998].

The Grove Ravenglass [088966].

The Hause on lower slope of spur leading down from Low Kop to Cawdale Beck. Between Cawdale and Willdale [485174].

The Hause pass between Hallin Fell and Steel Knotts up and over which the road zig zags between Howtown and Martindale [436192].

The Hause pass on minor road which runs between Little Mell Fell and Priest's Crag fell [424235].

The Hawk craggy outcrop in afforested area between the R Lickle and Appletree Worth Beck. Ancient settlement here [240923].

The Haws E Birker Fell road and Crosby Gill [198948].

The Headlands Keswick. The Headlands, the Heads, Heads Road overlook Hope and Crow Parks and Derwent Water [264233].

The Heald bungalow alongside the road running by the E side of Coniston Water. Home of famous author Arthur Ransome from 1940-45 [308946] ...similar to the Heald, Claife Heights and Heald Wood, Troutbeck, in that 'heald' means a slope.

The Heald Claife Heights [385979] ...the slope (see also **Crier of Claife**).

The Height between Red Scar and Great Worm Crag [191968].

The Heights Farm, Ings with Hugill [452997].

The High Farm off the A 5074 [438901].

The Hill off the Low Lorton-Thackthwaite-Loweswater road [146241].

The Hope alongside the minor road from the B5292 to Hopebeck [167240].

The How cottages alongside Loughrigg Tarn [345046] ...the hill.

The How Borrowdale. Hill above Rosthwaite [258147].

The Howe Crook. Alongside the B5284 [439951].

The Howe off the A592 S of Church Bridge, Troutbeck [413024].

The Howes craggy hilly area alongside Howes Beck, Bampton [508180] ...the hills.

The Hows enclosed hilly area near Troutal, Duddon valley [237991].

The Hummers adjoining Hummer Lane. WSW Torver [266936] ...writing over a century ago the Rev. T E Ellwood suggested that the name meant 'a grassy slope by the side of a river'.

The Hundreds see **Troutbeck Hundreds**.

The Ings NT area E shore Derwent Water [268221] ...the meadows/water meadows.

The Intake E Stainton [132945].

The Kennels Grizedale [333951].

The Knight a figurative name for a stony subsidiary summit and small ridge on Place Fell between the latter's summit and Birk Fell [404176].

The Knoll Ambleside. Off the Rydal road. Built by Harriet Martineau (1802-76) in 1846 and she lived there until her death. She was a journalist, novelist and hostess to many literary and prominent figures. In 1855 she wrote the well-known *Complete Guide to the English Lakes*. In 1960 the house was divided into two private apartments.

The Knott head of Swindale 297m (974ft) [505120].

The Knott seen from the A592, Hartsop, or Hayeswater, the W face of the Knott is most impressive with rocky outcrops bisected by a scree gully rising to a cone-like summit. However, from the E it is merely a slight protuberance at the end of a short spur from the main High Street ridge. Provides exceptional views of Hayeswater 317m (1040ft) below, 739m (2425ft) [437127].

The Knott W Wallowbarrow Coppice [211962].

The Knott SW Pool Scar [257910].

The Knott W Ball Hall 284m (932ft) [224920].

The Knott in afforested area E River Lickle [244932].

The Knott Birkby Fell 331m (1086ft) [144951].

The Knotts N Ullswater and NNW of the hamlet of Knotts 274m (899ft) [435217].

The Knowe subsidiary peak of Harter Fell. Usually climbed as part of the W ridge of the Kentmere Horseshoe, C760m (C2493ft) [459088] ...knoll or hilltop.

The Labyrinth W side of Coniston Water. A circular copse on private farmland but originally dug out in a series of ditches or paths resembling a maze by earlier owners of Monk Coniston Hall. Consequently called the Labyrinth and by some locals the Wigwam [312979].

The Lea between Red Bank Road, Grasmere, and Grasmere (lake) [334064] ...the clearing.

The Lodge Howe Grain, Martindale [432188].

The Lodge originally the lodge/gate house to Wasdale Hall [144043].

The Lodge Borrowdale. S Hollows Farm [247168].

The Low Duddon valley [206944].

The Mill Ennerdale. Ancient mill alongside the River Ehen. Now a residence [082153].

The Moors Torver [282952].

The Nab projection NE summit of Birkhouse Moor [370165].

The Nab S shore of Elter Water [335040] ...projection. Where the R Brathay enters Elter Water its delta forms a promontory.

The Nab years ago the Nab was a barricaded area with much barbed wire and many 'Keep Out' notices on its slopes. Today, however, the notices and barbed wire have to all intents and purposes disappeared and several modern-day fell walking guides incorporate the Nab in their itineraries. From this it would seem that walkers are now welcome, however those hardy souls who wish to 'notch up' this fell should request permission in advance from the Dalemain Estate Office. This may or may not be granted. The reason for all this is that the Nab is an integral part of the Martindale Deer Forest which is delineated by a 'forest wall' bounding Ramps Gill, Bannerdale, Bannerdale Head, the Nab and the N slope of Rest Dodd. It is managed by the Dalemain Estates as a sporting reserve and is the only deer forest of its kind in England. The 'wall' obviously does not contain the deer which roam far and wide but within its confines they have sanctuary 576m (1890ft) [434152].

The Nick a stream which flows from Nick Head at 364183 down a nick to join Deepdale Slack and Wintergroove Gill at 366187. The three then become Glencoyne Beck.

The Nook Kentmere [455044].

The Nook alongside the minor road from the A595 (Corney) to the Bootle to Eskmeals road [091907].

The Nursery W Scrithwaite Farm [218912].

The Oaks property off the Ludderburn-Hartbarrow road [405909].

The Old Rectory Lamplugh [089210].

The Park craggy area E side of Coniston Water. Rises to 302m (991ft) [311935].

The Park Dacre. Alongside Dacre Lodge Farm [458260].

The Park in Grizedale Forest Park. Lawson Park to its W [322952].

The Park between Swinside and Stub Hill [248217].

The Pen on slope leading down from Loadpot Hill towards Heltondale [481185].

The Pen between Wallowbarrow Crag and Wallowbarrow Heald [216970].

The Perch between Gill Crag and Dovedale slabs [388119] ...suggests a place on which one can perch comfortably.

The Peewits on the ridge between High Tove and High Seat [289171] ...place frequented by peewits/plovers.

The Pike subsidiary summit of Birker Fell ridge C450m (C1476ft) [200986].

The Pike steep craggy hill overlooking Ulpha 370m (1214ft) [186934].

The Prison area to the W of Swirl Hawse Beck valley [276997] ...see **Prison Band**.

The Rake shallow gully between Glenridding Screes and S slope of Glenridding Dodd [379174].

The Rake section of the River Cocker at Southwaite [131281].

The Rectory/Rectory Farm Bowness-on-Windermere. Rectory Farm adjoining the Rectory is now owned by the National Trust [399963]. The glebe alongside once belonged to the rector and the dictionary definition of such land is 'that granted to a clergyman as part of his benefice'. The word glebe is from the Latin 'gleba/glaeba' meaning a clod, land, soil. See also **Bowness-on-Windermere**.

The Rigg afforested peninsular at the foot of Riggindale Scar [475116]

The Rigg E Walna Scar Road and S Boo Tarn [284967].

The Riggs W Helton. Tumulus nearby [498219] ...ridges.

The Saddle depression between Red Pike summit and Dodd [162156].

The Samling see **Dove Nest**.

The Scar between Sail and Crag Hill [196202].

The Screes the high ridge to the S of Wastwater falls initially by cliffs and gullies and then in steep scree slopes down to the lake. The whole drop is an impressive 549m (1800ft) [154045] ...ON 'skreio/skrio(a)' - landslide/landslip.

The Seat outcrop below Seat How [168970] ...shieling/summerpasture.

The Squeeze see **Side Pike**.

The Stake ESE Skiddaw House [296288].

The Stangs see **Stangs**.

The Steeple see **Eskdale Needle**.

The Step behind Greenhow End and on an experienced scramblers route (in fine weather) from Deepdale to Fairfield [369120].

The Struggle see **Kirkstone Pass**.

The Swirls Swirrel Wood, see **Swirls Forest Trail**.

The Tarns see **Tarn Hows**.

The Tongue alongside Caudale. E Caudale Beck [409112].

The Tongue ridge leading ENE from Dollywaggon Pike [349132].

The Tongue substantial tongue of land between Trout Beck and Hagg Gill 364m (1194ft) [422064].

The Vicarage Little Town [236198].

The Wyke property off Red Bank Road, Grasmere. Wyke Plantation above [333065] ...similar to 'wick' in that it means a creek or inlet. The small valley of Wyke Gill and its attendant stream drops down alongside the Wyke to join Grasmere (lake) and form a creek.

Theatre by the Lake Keswick. Between 1952 and 1975 the Century Theatre, consisting of mobile caravans and nicknamed 'The Blue Box', toured the country. In 1975 it established itself in Keswick on the E side of Derwent Water near the foot of the lake and after sterling service to theatregoers the Blue Box was dismantled at the end of 1996 and made its final move to Snibson Discovery Park, Leicestershire, as the centrepiece of an exhibition of touring and travelling theatre. Building of a new theatre began on the former site in 1998 and Keswick's present Theatre by the Lake opened in August 1999, with *Charley's Aunt* alternating with *The Lakers*.

Theatre in the Forest see **Grizedale Forest Park**.

Thick Side between Blea Crag and Langstrath Beck [266105].

Thick Wood Duddon valley. Alongside the River Duddon [201914].

Thickholme alongside Bridge Lane which connects Town End, Troutbeck, with Troutbeck Bridge [405014]. Cottages hereabouts were originally part of the Holehird estate but were given to the county council in 1945. They were sold by public auction in 1971.

Thickholme Bridge bridge across Trout Beck [407016].

Thiefstead Ralfland Forest, E Swindale Foot [530139] ...with nearby Outlaw Crag it certainly suggests that at one time the area was wild and dangerous for travellers.

Thin Side NNW slope of High Hartsop Dodd. Between Bull Crag and Dovedale Beck [392112].

Third Gill rises Wandope at 184195 and joins Sail Beck at 190187.

Third Moss Lane see **First, Second, Third Moss Lanes**.

Thirlmere the original narrow and smaller lake, practically divided into two by the promontory of Armboth and the land below Dalehead Hall, was variously called Leathes Water, Wythburn Water, Bradmere (Brackmere), Thurlesmere or Thirlmere. The valley was flooded at the end of the 19th century to provide a reservoir for Manchester Corporation and a 163kms (102 mile) aqueduct linked it with that city. This scheme cost £1.5 million and at one time there were 570 men working on the reservoir and up to 3,000 employed on the aqueduct. Water commenced to flow in October 1894. This travels along the aqueduct at a speed of about 2 miles per hour with a fall of 20 inches per mile or 1 in 3168. The reservoir has a holding capacity of 9,000 million gallons. Just below the road on the E side of the lake is the straining well into which water is drawn to start its journey to Manchester. The water drops into a cylindrical well 19.8m (65ft) deep and 10.6m (35ft) wide. From the tower it flows to the water treatment works at Dunmail Raise. Many trees were planted on the W side mainly larch accompanied by spruce and Douglas fir.

Thirlmere Water by Norman Hoyle and Ken Sankey, published in 1994, tells the story of Thirlmere and its construction. All that is now left of the village of Wythburn (often referred to as 'the City') are the 17th century church which was rebuilt in the 18th century and restored and extended in 1872, and West Head Farm (previously called Steel End Farm) at the head of the reservoir. The village of Armboth completely disappeared under the water and exists in name only. Of the 12 farms in Wythburn and Armboth listed in the 1851 census only one remains. Flooding of the valley raised the water level by 15m (50ft). Just over 6kms (3.75 miles) in length Thirlmere stands 179.1m (587.7ft) above sea level, the second highest of the lakes. Maximum depth is 46m (151ft), between Hause Point and Hawes How Island. The old road along Thirlmere is now under the reservoir and the present section of the A591 was built to replace it by M/C Waterworks in the 1880s. In more recent times motorists driving along the section by the reservoir will notice above their heads three rope ladders stretched from trees either side of and over the road. These are squirrel ladders positioned by United Utilities to help these animals cross the busy road to woods on either side. Also in the 1880s a new road, approximately 8.4kms (5.25 miles), less busy and more scenic, was built around the W side of Thirlmere.

Launching for canoes, dinghies and sailboards is available at Armboth on application to the water authority. Thirlmere contains two islands - Deergarth How Island and Hawes How Island both of which were rocky promontories prior to flooding. The lake and its environs are not without their ghosts. A huge black dog is said to swim across the lake and roam the area and nearby Harrop Tarn is reputed to be haunted by a headless spectre [322131-310190]. Contains perch, pike and trout. There is mention in Dorothy Wordsworth's *Lakeland Journals* of William catching a 4.75lbs pike in Wythburn Water in June 1800, and John catching two small pike in the same lake in August 1800. Wythburn Water later became part of Thirlmere Reservoir ...the former name is presumed to mean the lake with a hollow, possibly referring to the narrow waist of the original lake which was spanned by Wath Bridge, an old pack horse bridge, consisting of several stone piers supporting wooden structures. The stone columns now lie well below the surface of the reservoir. W G Collingwood, historian and archaeologist, suggests Thorolf's mere for the present title.

Thirlmere Leat/Water Race consequent on the construction of Thirlmere Reservoir in the 19th century the engineers realised that the waters of several substantial becks which flowed down from the Helvellyn ridge never reached Thirlmere and flowed into St John's Beck. They therefore constructed a water race or leat along the foot of the slope. This trapped and diverted Ladknott Gill, Mill Gill, Stanah Gill, Fisherplace Gill and Helvellyn Gill and carried them by gravitation to Thirlmere by a tunnel under the A591 to enter the reservoir at a point [313169] WSW Station Coppice car park. To the S of Legburthwaite those waters which escape the race join How Beck below Great How and enter St John's Beck near Smaithwaite/Smeathwaite Bridge.

Thirlmere Youth Hostel small hostel in what was the village school, Legburthwaite [318190].

Thirlspot an old name for it was 'Trespath'. E of the A591. Principally comprises a hotel (King's Head) and Thirlspot Farm. A popular cairned pony-track route over White Side and Lower Man to Helvellyn starts here [317177] ...giant's pool or pot.

Thirlspot Farm Thirlspot [317177].

Thistle Grasmere Hotel alongside Grasmere (lake) and the A591. Established in 1855. Previous to 1999 was called the Prince of Wales Hotel. Earlier still it was the Lake Hotel. A stone boathouse nearby is dated 1843 but replaced an earlier structure erected in the early 1800s.

Thompson's Holme island in Windermere near Belle Isle and second largest to the latter [391971] ...from the T(h)ompson family of Undermillock.

Thorn Cottage near Bannisdale High Bridge. Off the A6 and alongside the old road from Kendal-Shap [542013].

Thorn Crag Great Langdale. E Loft Crag, S Harrison Stickle [281072].

Thorn How Birker Moor [191973].

Thorn Knott SW slope of Seatallan [125067].

Thornbank Gosforth. Off the A595 [074025].

Thorney Bank Wet Sleddale [556122].

Thorney How Grasmere. Former farmhouse opened as a youth hostel in 1932 [332084] ...thorn hill.

Thorneythwaite farm, Seatoller, Borrowdale [246134].

Thornflatt off the A595 [088977] ...thorny flat/level piece of ground.

Thornholme alongside the River Calder [068089] ...the thorn tree(s) on an 'island' or spit of land. In this case, the latter lies between the River Calder and Worm Gill.

Thornhow farmstead, Grisedale, overlooked by Thornhow Crag [383156].

Thornhow Crag overlooks Thornhow and Grisedale [382154].

Thornhow End a major path from Patterdale over Birks and St Sunday Crag to Fairfield rises steeply from the valley to excellent viewpoint at Thornhow End overlooking Glenamara Park and Ullswater. It is actually the commencement of Birks Ridge [386153].

Thorns Lane Underbarrow. Named after Thorn(e)s Villa (now Greenriggs) [474920].

Thorns Villa see **Greenriggs**.

Thornsgill Beck rises at 377219. Joined by Groove Beck, Blake Sike and White Sike, and is generally accepted as becoming Trout Beck at the confluence with the latter at 377235.

Thornship just over the boundary of the Lake District National Park. SSW Shap and approximately 2.1kms (1.3 miles) by road via Keld from that village [557141] ...'Forni's' (surname) + Shap (the latter from 'Hep(p)(e)' meaning pile or heap of stones).

Thornship Gill Peathill Gill rises from Gambling Well at 532115. Subsequently joined by Mirk Gill and the combination becomes Thornship Gill at 543128 before entering the R Lowther at 556141.

Thornthwaite small scattered community on the section of the old road W of Bassenthwaite Lake and between Braithwaite and the A66. Includes settlement of Powter How at the foot of Barf. Chapel Beck flows through the village and passes the parish church of St. Mary's, the latter built in 1764. In days gone by the stream powered machinery for a lead mine and a bobbin/sawmill. Thornthwaite, similar to several other places, possesses a Seldom Seen which, in this case, originally housed miners.

Thornthwaite Galleries, a 300 year old building, contains examples of fine art, a tea shop and at times demonstrations by exhibiting artists. Ladstock Country House Hotel, set in its seven acres, dates back over 200 years and the Swan Hotel at Powter How is a former coaching inn built in 1678 [223254].

Thornthwaite Crag on the High Street range and across Threshthwaite Mouth from Stony Cove Pike. Good views from various points on its summit which is capped by a slender 4m (14ft) stone column marked on the map as a beacon. The best known Roman road in the Lake District, that along High Street, skirts the crag to the E, 784m (2572ft) [432100] ...crag by the thorn clearing.

Thornthwaite Force waterfall on Haweswater Beck below Naddle Bridge. Described by West in 1793 as 'a fine cataract' ...[511160].

Thornthwaite Galleries see **Thornthwaite**.

Thornthwaite Hall S Bampton, ENE Burnbanks and Naddle Gate [513163]. As the name Thornthwaite - clearing in the thorn trees - implies the manor of that name was once a large forest vestiges of which can still be seen in and around the area (not to be confused with

the Thornthwaite Forest W of the A66 between Keswick and Bassenthwaite). The present Elizabethan Hall, converted in the 19th century into a farmhouse was probably built by the Curwen family of Workington and later passed into the hands of the Howard family. One of the latter, Lord William Howard, 'Belted Will' in Sir Walter Scott's *The Lay of the Last Minstrel*, is believed to have died here. The hall is suggested by some to be the setting for Anthony Trollope's novel *Can You Forgive Her?* and was called 'Vavasor Hall' in the book.

Thorny Knott overlooks Swindale Head and Swindale [503129].

Thorny Slack WSW Force Forge [331903] ...thorny hollow.

Thornyfields property in the Gilpin valley between Gilpin Mill and Crook Foot [431939].

Thornythwaite adjacent A5091. Between Matterdale End and Dockray [394223].

Thornythwaite Fell along with neighbour Rosthwaite Fell provides the N extremity of the Borrowdale Fells. Its summit is a rocky protuberance alongside the path to Glaramara which starts from the B5289, 574m (1883ft) [245118].

Thrang Crag Beda Fell. Below Ewe Crag. Overlooks Howe Grain [434174] ...crag alongside the narrow defile.

Thrang Crag Chapel Stile, Great Langdale [319057] ...the crag overlooking the narrow steep-side valley.

Thrang Crag large sheep farm below Thrang Crag, Howe Grain, Martindale [434175].

Thrang Crag Quarry Chapel Stile [320056].

Thrang Crag Wood W shore Coniston Water [289915] ...wood by the crag by the narrow defile (that of Black Beck).

Thrang Crags Hen Comb [137181].

Thrang Farm Chapel Stile, Great Langdale [319053].

Thrang Force see **Throng/Thrang Force**.

Thrang Gill rises W Thirlmere and joins the reservoir at 305175.

Three Dubs Crags Claife Heights, above Three Dubs Tarn [378976].

Three Dubs Tarn Claife Heights. As its name suggests at one time possibly three 'dubs' - ponds. Later a small reservoir dating from about 1908, 206m (676ft) [378974].

Three Pit Stone boulder alongside the upper reaches of Mere Beck [266914] ...pit is one definition of poll/pol which also means either pond/pool or stream. Therefore more than likely refers to the stone by the pits or channels of the three streams which have their sources nearby.

Three Shires Stone at a point alongside the road E Wrynose Pass the three counties of Cumberland, Lancashire and Westmorland met and from at least 1671 until the late 19th to early 20th century three small stones stood at this spot to mark the meeting of the boundaries. These were inscribed with C, L and W respectively. In 1816 William Field of Cartmel had a limestone monument carved with, on its S side, the word Lancashire and on the reverse the initials and date WF 1816. However, this post was not erected on its site until after his death in 1860. In July 1997, the pillar was found damaged. Intricate repairs to the stone were carried out and in the summer of 1998 the monolith and three facsimile stones were placed in position behind a raised turf embankment to protect them from damage by vehicles [278028].

Three Shires Inn Little Langdale. 19th century inn built on the packhorse route over the Wrynose and Hardknott Passes to the coast. Originally the Tourists Rest but as it stood no great distance from the then meeting of the three shires, Lancashire, Cumberland and Westmorland, it was renamed the Three Shires Inn in the mid-20th century [317034].

Three Tarns lie on the col between Bowfell and Shelter/Crinkle Crags and at the point where the path from Eskdale to Bowfell meets those from the Band and Hell Gill. Sometimes referred to as the Tarns of Buscoe as they are situated at the head of Buscoe and Buscoe Sike rises nearby. Normally three shallow tarns but in dry weather there may be only two and at the other extreme there could be four or five. In his *Walking in the Lake District* (1933) H H Symonds writes: "The man who counted the three tarns was a pessimist: but in calling them tarns he was an optimist." 720m (2363ft) [248060].

Three Tarns see **Tarn Hows**.

Threefooted Brandreth on the ridge N of High Seat [287183] ...Brandreth from 'brandreio' refers to a grate/tripod/trivet and suggests that there was once a beacon here lit on a three-legged receptacle. Also, three ancient boundaries met here. See also **Brandreth**.

Threepow Raise Moor Divock [482219]. Two round barrows on it are scheduled as ancient monuments ...disputed boundary marked by a tumulus (cairn).

Threlkeld village 0.4km (0.25 mile) off A66 and 6kms (4 miles) E of Keswick. Also the name given to a valley. The village is situated at the foot of Blencathra and is a centre for climbing that mountain. Possesses two old inns, the Horse and Farrier and the Salutation, and its church dates from the second half of the 18th century. Two major industries of the past were the Gategill Lead Mines, which at one time employed 100 men, and the Threlkeld Granite Quarry. The former closed in 1928 (plant sold and dismantled during the 1939-45 war) and the latter closed in 1982 (see also **Threlkeld Quarry**). The kennels of the Blencathra foxhounds are now at Gategill. Threlkeld was at one time one of the four intermediate stations on the Keswick-Penrith line which closed in March 1972 [324255] ...Thrall's Spring. Nearby there is still an old well, Hailhead Well.

Threlkeld Bridge crosses R Glenderamackin and St John's Beck [315247].

Threlkeld Common E, ESE, SE Threlkeld [346244].

Threlkeld Hall former fortified manor house and home of the Threlkeld family. Mentioned in Wordsworth's *Benjamin the Waggoner*. Now a farm [330257].

Threlkeld Knotts NW Clough Head. E St John's in the Vale 514m (1686ft) [330230].

Threlkeld Leys off the Brandlingill to Randle Cross road [117272] ...spring on or by the pasture/meadow land.

Threlkeld Quarry large quarry worked from the 1860s until 1982. Now a mining museum and shop and the home of four mining locomotives titled Nellie, Nick the Greek, Pinkie and Silver Band [327243].

Threshthwaite Cove there is a steep descent NNW from Threshthwaite Mouth into the cove which is the source of Pasture Beck [424108]. A legend suggests that a party of raiding Scots who reached the cove were forced to flee after Hugh Hird, the giant of Troutbeck, shot arrows of rails at them from his bow of the bough of a large yew tree. In June 1937 a Hawker Hird failed to clear the summit of the cove and crashed killing its 2 crew ...cove by the clearing where threshing took place.

Threshthwaite Crag SW Threshthwaite Mouth. E Stony Cove Pike. Overlooks path from Troutbeck to Threshthwaite Mouth [424099].

Threshthwaite Mouth col between Caudale Moor (Stony Cove Pike) and Thornthwaite Crag and between Park Fell Head and Threshthwaite Cove c600m (C1968ft) [427103].

Throng Close above Throng/Thrang Force [239982].

Throng/Thrang Force waterfall on Tarn Beck [240985] ...waterfall in the narrow valley or defile.

Throstle Garth between the R Esk and Lingcove Beck and below Throstlehow Crag [227040] ...enclosure frequented by thrushes or surname + enclosure.

Throstle Shaw alongside the A591 near Derwent Foot [238271] ...thrush wood.

Throstlehow Crag between the R Esk and Lingcove Beck 404m (1325ft) [227044].

Throstlegarth Bridge see **Lingcove Bridge**.

Thrushbank alongside the Loweswater to Mockerkin road. High Thrushbank nearby [132215].

Thrushwood alongside the A591 N Great Crosthwaite. The Allerdale Ramble passes through [261248].

Thunacar Knott an undistinguished protrusion on the High Raise plateau between the Langdale Pikes and High White Stones. Its eastern escarpment, Pavey Ark, is better known. Possesses two summits with a small tarn in between. The N cairned summit is 717m (2351ft) while slightly S the land rises to 723m (2372ft) [279080] ...Robert Gambles in his *Lake District Place-Names* suggests that a probable explanation could be the craggy hill of the thin man.

Thunacar Knott Tarn situated between the two summits of Thunacar Knott [279081].

Thurs Gill its farthest headstream rises in Grizedale Forest at 333976 and flows past a former bobbin mill and under the B5285 to meet Black Beck at 346991 ...possibly after Thor meaning thunder. By the former bobbin mill the water thunders through a deep ravine.

Thurs Gill Mill near Hawkshead Hill. Thurs Gill supplied the water power for this former bobbin mill [341988] one of many throughout the High Furness woods in the 19th century. These mills supplied bobbins for the Lancashire cotton mills and, like the Thurs Gill Mill, many barrels, hoops and swills. One bobbin mill, that at Stott Park, 0.8kms (0.5 mile) N of Finsthwaite on the Newby Bridge-Hawkshead road, built in 1835, closed in 1971, but has been preserved as a working unit and a reminder of a once common Lakeland industry. Owned by English Heritage it is open daily from mid-March to the end of October.

Thurston property E side of Coniston Water. Earlier known as Coniston Bank. Today the 'Thurston Experience' run by South Tyneside Metropolitan Borough Council [314965]

...Coniston Water was once known as Thurstonmere or Thurston Water.

Thurston Water see **Coniston Water**.

Thwaite Band Ashness Fell. Above Thwaite House and Thwaitehouse Beck [274181].

Thwaite Cottage Coniston. 17th century cottage off the B5285 and near the lake shore. A bed & breakfast establishment [310977].

Thwaite Head community at the foot of Dale Park and head of the Rusland valley [348906] ...clearing at the head.

Thwaite Head Bridge Thwaite Head. Carries the Thwaite Head-Rusland road over Ashes Beck [347905].

Thwaite Head Fell above Thwaite Head [353912].

Thwaite House Coniston. Off the B5285 and near the lake shore. Built 1821 [309977].

Thwaite House alongside the Watendlath road [270180].

Thwaitehill off the road from Pooley Bridge to Howtown [458218] ...clearing on the hill.

Thwaitehill Bay Ullswater. Ullswater Yacht Club has its headquarters here [456225].

Thwaitehill Knotts Thornthwaite Forest [218253].

Thwaitehill Neb Ullswater. Across the narrows from Castlehows Point [455224].

Thwaitehouse Beck near Thwaite House and Thwaite Bank. Rises W slope High Seat at 282180 and joins Watendlath Beck at 270178.

Thwaites W bank River Calder [063107] ...parcels of land/clearings.

Thwatterden Hall see **Crook**.

Tilberthwaite hamlet principally comprising High [308014] and Low Tilberthwaite [305011] reached by road which leaves the A593 2.4kms (1.5 miles) NE of Coniston. A much quarried area in the past and today the start of many walkers' routes. Tilberthwaite Gill [301007] down which flows Yewdale Beck, is an impressive ravine with an attractive waterfall. High Tilberthwaite Farm was purchased by the National Trust from Beatrix Potter in 1930 and early in the 20th century it was the headquarters of the Langdale Linen Industry (for more information on the latter see **Elterwater**) ...clearing by Tilli's fort.

Tilberthwaite Fells fell area to the N, W and NW of High and Low Tilberthwaite [286019]. A section of the fells called Tilberthwaite High Fells lies slightly N of the summit of Wetherlam [286014].

Tilberthwaite Gill see Tilberthwaite.

Tilberthwaite High Fells see **Tilberthwaite Fells**.

Till's Hole Longsleddale [485051] ...Matilda's hollow.

Timley Knott E of the road to Bursting Stone Quarry. N Walna Scar Road [283971].

Tim's Tarn Eskdale. Shown but not named on the OS map. In a plantation alongside the R Esk and alongside a path to Low Birker, Low Birker Tarn and Tarn Crag [183001] ...named after Tim Ward one of its two makers.

Tindle Crag Brackenthwaite. NT property [151219].

Tinkler Crags Irton Park [115007].

To Stone or To'ther Shap Fells. W Long Fell and ENE Wasdale Pike. Boulder perched on granite rock [548090] ...should surely be 'To Stone on T'other' referring to a totting stone resting on another stone. Totting means liable to topple over or looking very unsteady. There are many precariously placed boulders in the Lake District. Of particular note are the Totting Stone, Launchy Gill, Thirlmere, and the famous Borrowdale Bowder Stone.

Toad How Great Gable. Near Sty Head and alongside the track from Wasdale to the former [216095].

Toadhowe Well a spring E Kentmere Reservoir and alongside the Nan Bield Pass track

[451084] ...the well nearby or on the toad hill.

Toathmain alongside junction of Rosgill to Bampton via Bomby road and unfenced road to Swindale [530168] ...obscure but possibly from a surname such as Todman, Toleman or Totheman.

Tod Crag NNW Hart Crag and overlooks Deepdale [356202].

Tod Crag Moss below Tod Crag. Part of Deepdale [357204].

Tod Gill NNE Gowbarrow Fell. Head of Todgill Sike [410225].

Tod Hole Nether Wasdale Common [133077] ...fox hole/hollow.

Todcrags overlook Sleddale Beck [524103] ...fox crags

Todd Crag see **Loughrigg Fell**.

Todd Crag Todd Fell. Overlooking Longsleddale [510018].

Todd Fell E Longsleddale of which valley it provides a good viewpoint 401m (1316ft) [512020] ...either from a local family Tod(d) or meaning the fell frequented by foxes.

Todd Fell between Lord's Seat and Broom Fell [200269].

Todd Rigg ridge E of minor road A66-Matterdale End. N Stoddahgate 277m (909ft) [417268].

Toddell alongside the minor road from Aikbank Mill to Randle Cross [122264] ...fox holes.

Toddell Bridge carries minor road over Sandy Beck [122265].

Toddle Bank S Cleator Moor to Ennerdale Bridge road [054151] ...bank frequented by foxes.

Toddle Cottage alongside the road from Bampton to Helton [511187] ...cottage by the fox holes.

Toddle Gutter stream which rises NNW Bampton village near Toddle Cottage at 512187. Subsequently becomes Pow Beck in the region of 513193. This joins Gill Beck at 513197 and enters the Lowther at 515200 ...the watery channel by the fox holes.

Todgill N Gowbarrow Fell on minor road connecting Thornythwaite with A66-Matterdale End road to the A592 [410228].

Todgill Sike rises at 410222 and joins small tarn from which Blackdike Beck emerges at 407230.

Toll Bar Cottage dated 1764. Behind Scar Foot on the Underbarrow Road. One of four former toll bars on the Kendal to Kirkby Ireleth turnpike road [482922].

Tom Butt Ennerdale Bridge [071161].

Tom Fox Crag NE Slight Side [211053] ...personal name or an allusion to an episode concerning a fox.

Tom Gill wooded glen, also romantically called Glen Mary, a name attributed to have been given by Alfred Tennyson who loved the area and stayed at Tent Lodge, Coniston, for part of his honeymoon in 1850 and returned 7 years later. Tom Gill, the stream which drops down it from the foot of Tarn Hows, has impressive cataracts and waterfalls and joins Yew Tree Beck at 320999 ...Tom who?

Tom Heights western background to Tarn Hows and E of the A593, 269m (883ft) [328005].

Tom Heights Intake Plantation foot of Tom Heights [330003].

Tom Rudd Beck lengthy stream with many tributaries rising on Wythop Moss and Embleton High Common. Flows initially N then W before joining the R Cocker at Cockermouth. A fast flowing stream which once had several mills operating along its banks.

Tom Winder's Loom pool alongside the R Lowther between Helton and Whale [517214]

...either one of two Thomas Winders recorded late 18th and early 19th centuries respectively or, according to a note to the 1859 OS map, from an insane man who committed suicide here ...loom/lumm - a pool.

Tommy Gill rises from well at 221940 and joins the River Duddon at 209941.

Tom's Howe farm, Longsleddale [486050] ...personal name + hill.

Tongue ENE Little Mell Fell [434243].

Tongue tongue of land between the River Esk and Calfcove Gill [230077].

Tongue tongue of land between Tongue Beck and the River Liza. Centuries ago called Brinttenng. There is a Brin Crag facing across Tongue Beck [206116].

Tongue Beck rises below Gillercomb Head at 215111 and joins the River Liza at 200119.

Tongue Brow Coniston Fells. Above Coppermines Valley [287988].

Tongue Gill rises on Fairfield Brow at 354114. Subsequently joined by Little Tongue Gill and flows down over Tonguegill Force to join the R Rothay at 334091.

Tongue Gill rises NW Bigert Mire at 175929 and joins Holehouse Gill at 183926.

Tongue Gill rises Rigg Head at 235154 and after being joined by Lavery Gill meets the R Derwent at 252150.

Tongue Gill see **River Bleng**.

Tongue Head between Allencrags Gill and Angletarn Gill and alongside the Angle Tarn to Sty Head bridleway [240065].

Tongue House Kentmere. Alongside a subsidiary track E River Kent from Overend via Whether Fold to Smallthwaite Knott and below Tongue Scar. There is an ancient settlement alongside [452068].

Tongue House alongside Tarn Beck. The farm was purchased by the NT in 1983 [236975].

Tongue House Close adjoining Throng Close and above the path from Tongue House to Seathwaite Tarn [242981].

Tongue House High Close S Tongue House Close [242977].

Tongue How E River Calder and N lower section of Worm Gill. Much evidence of early habitation with ancient cairns, a homestead and a settlement [071099].

Tongue Intake Plantation National Trust land W of the A593, Skelwith Bridge-Coniston road [329023] ...intake - plantation on a tongue of land. For derivation of intake, see **Arnside Intake**.

Tongue Moor tongue of moorland, Burn Moor [172039].

Tongue Pot pool in the R Esk near confluence with Lingcove Beck [227035].

Tongue Rigg ridge between Sleddale Beck and Tonguerigg Gill [528099].

Tongue Scar Kentmere. Above Tongue House and a settlement [453071].

Tonguegill Force picturesque waterfall on Tongue Gill [339096].

Tonguerigg Gill rises NNW Wasdale Pike at 535088 and joins Sleddale Beck at 536106.

Tongues Beck rises between Skiddaw Little Man and Broad End at 262279. Joined by Slades Beck at 259275 and subsequently this is met by Black Beck at 261271 before becoming Mill Beck. The latter joins Wath Beck and the watercourse enters the R Derwent at 243260.

Tongues Gills several gills which rise on Buckbarrow Moss, S slope Seatallan, and combine to join Greendale Gill at 143064.

Tonguesdale Moss Birker Moor [169990].

Toot Hill on the NP boundary N of the Mockerkin to Loweswater road [102234] ...the hill from which one can toot or look-out.

Tooth How Plantation S Harrot [163272].

Top Dam see **Sticks Tarn**.

Top of Broad Slack between Swirl How and Great Carrs (270006) ...see **Broad Slack**.

Top o' Selside E Coniston Water. Highest point of Bethecar Moor 335m (1099ft) [309919].

Torver village approximately 4.8 kms (3 miles) SW of Coniston on the A593 and at the junction with the A5084. Comprises houses, cottages, some scattered throughout the area, a post office, a converted railway station (the railway came to Torver in 1859 and ceased in 1958), two hostelries (Church House Inn and the Wilson Arms Country Inn), and a church (founded as a chapel in the 12th century. The present church, built in 1884 and dedicated to St Luke, replaced one which had a relatively short life in the 19th century). Before 1538 the dead of Torver had to be carried over mountainous country and in all sorts of weather to Ulverston. A school, closed in 1927, is now the parish room.

Torver High Common with its ancient cairns, dyke and enclosure, emphasises the fact that there was much life hereabouts in prehistoric times. Peat bogs on the Common and Torver Back Common are designated as SSSI and lend credence to at least one of the meanings of the word Torver [284942] ...either Torfi's shieling; hut/shed with a turf roof or hut/shed where peat is cut and stacked.

Torver Back Common similar to many other commons in the Lake District, including Torver High and Low Commons. They are hilly and in places wet areas, a reminder of the time, centuries ago, when local people held in common the right to graze cattle, catch fish or collect wood and peat in any land not under cultivation. Today, the three Torver Commons are owned by the Lake District National Park and designated access land but stock levels and ideas for conservation are projected and often carried out by the Torver Commoners Association. Torver Back Common has a frontage to Coniston Water and the Cumbria Way passing along its eastern edge. It possesses, along with Torver High Common, several peat bogs with limestone flushes which are designated as SSSI. Two tarns are accessible to the general public, Kelly Hall and the long and thin Long Moss Tarn [294937].

Torver Beck centuries ago referred to as the River Torver. Rises below Goat's Hawse at 267980 and flows in and out of Goat's Water before dropping steeply over several spectacular waterfalls for some 518m (1700ft) to join Coniston Water at 292923.

Torver Bottom Torver High Common. Marshy area through which flow many streams [267956].

Torver Common Wood Torver Back Common [298947].

Torver High Common stretches from the A593 to Goat's Hawse is a hilly and at times very boggy area rising to a mountain ridge in the N. Apart from its peat bogs designated as SSSI there are signs of occupation by early man in the shape of ancient cairns and an enclosure [265952].

Torver Intake E Tarn Hows (the Tarns) [336004] ...similar to Torver S of Coniston the name has several interpretations. The second element is generally accepted as 'erg' (shieling/shelter) and the whole possibly refers to the shelter with the turfed roof in which peat is stored and which was owned by a person called Torfi.

Torver Low Common S and E of the A593. The OS map shows 11 tarns nestling among its hillocks. The largest and the only one named on the map, Torver Tarn, shown as a reservoir (disused) is a natural tarn. Of the other tarns the principal two are Torver Low Common Tarn and Birk Haw Tarn [276925].

Torver Low Common Tarn W Torver Tarn, Torver Low Common C150m (C492ft) [276926].

Torver Tarn also called Thrang/Throng Moss Reservoir or Torver Reservoir. Largest and only one of the 11 tarns on Torver Back Common shown on the OS map that is named albeit shown as reservoir (disused). A natural tarn that was enlarged to supply water to the mill at Sunny Bank. The latter ceased operating in the 1930s. A small stream from its outflow joins Mere Beck which subsequently joins Torver Beck, 114m (374ft) [281926].

Tosh Tarn S of the Gosforth to Wastwater high road, C90m (C295ft) [128053]. Tosh Tarn Farm which stood nearby was once an important and influential farm. It is now no longer in existence ...Toshtorne in the late 16th century.

Tottle Bank NW Stable Harvey [282920] ...look-out hill.

Touchstone Interiors originally began as Kirkstone Galleries in 1964 to sell the Kirkstone green slate, but after a complete refurbishment in January 2004, re-opened under its present title. Slate products are still on sale but the present name reflects a new identity in the sale of contemporary furniture and furnishings.

Tourist Attractions numerous individual leaflets available, including yearly *Best of Lakeland* which designates over 60 places to visit. See also **Cumbria's Top 20 Tourism Attractions**.

Tower Bank Arms Near Sawrey, see **Near Sawrey**.

Tower Brow between the A593 and the A5084 and above Moor Farm [281935].

Tower Hotel Portinscale [253236].

Tower Wood Outdoor Pursuits Centre alongside the A592, Newby Bridge-Bowness road [387910].

Town Bank slope of Lank Rigg above Worm Gill [077102].

Town Cass Keswick. Adjoining Crow Park [261229].

Town End Far Sawrey. Alongside Far Sawrey-High Cunsey road [378951].

Town End farm, Colthouse. Small brewery in barn here [359981].

Town End Grasmere. Hamlet to the S of the village as opposed to Town Head to the N. Principally a cluster of mainly old buildings alongside the side road up and over White Moss (much earlier part of the Ambleside-Keswick road). Most notable buildings are Dove Cottage and the adjoining Wordsworth Museum, Sykeside Farm (Sykeside), home of Agnes Fisher, sister-in-law of Molly Fisher, daily help to the Wordsworths; Ashburner's Cottage, home of Thomas and Peggy Ashburner; Rose Cottage, lodgings for nearly 11 years of Hartley Coleridge; Sykeside Cottage, home of John Dawson, Dorothy Wordsworth described a funeral there in September 1800; How Foot, Victorian house, once the holiday home of the Rev William Spooner of 'Spoonerism' fame, today a well-known hotel [344071].

Town End NT property, Troutbeck [407023], see **Troutbeck**.

Town End southern end of Troutbeck as opposed to Town Head at the northern end [407021].

Town End slightly NNE of Ponsonby [054058].

Town End alongside the A593 SW Torver [261924].

Town End Bridge carries the A593 over Lord's Gill [263926].

Town Head N Grasmere village and just off the A591. In yesteryears a toll gate was positioned hereabouts on the old turnpike road from Ambleside to Keswick [333099].

Town Head Troutbeck. Yeoman's house dated 1693 and other properties at the head of Troutbeck village as opposed to Town End at the beginning of the village. Here the minor road through the village meets the A592 [415038].

Town Head Farm Penruddock [423275].

Town Yeat alongside the Underbarrow-Crosthwaite road. Two adjoining cottages one of which reverted to its original name of Town Yeat Cottage in 1999. A barn here once housed the Lyth Gallery [453911] ...in the past it was the way/gate to the town. In this case the town was that of Church Town, Crosthwaite, village by or near the church.

Townfield Bridge crosses R Glenderamackin at 320248. Name commemorates the former town field which occupied 14 acres between the village and the R Glenderamackin.

Townson Ground E side of Coniston Water. 16th century property now a guest house, long known as Tent Cottage [318974], see also **Tent Lodge**.

Towtop/Towtop Kirk Towtop Kirk [493179] is an ancient stone enclosure and scheduled ancient monument, possibly an early homestead or a fort, at the end of a ridge which descends over the Hause and Hause End and on its lower section is called Towtop [492178] ...the term 'kirk' here refers either to a ring of stones or stones once thought to have been the remains of a former church. However Towtop is not easily explained. Top is obviously the top of a hill but 'Tow' could either be t'how(e) meaning the hill or possibly meaning witchcraft. There is, incidentally, another Tow Top on Newton Fell near Lindale.

Tranearth Beck Ash Gill Beck and Bull Haw Moss Beck join at 276951 and become Tranearth Beck which joins Torver Beck at 283957 ...stream alongside the ground frequented by cranes.

Tranthwaite Hall farm, Underbarrow [470930] ...clearing used by cranes or maybe Trani's clearing.

Trantrams E Knipescar and on E boundary of the National Park [547198] ...pond frequented by cranes. There is a pond nearby.

Trantrams Wood near Trantrams [547200].

Trap Knotts N slope of Maiden Moor. Site of the highest workings of the former Yewthwaite Mine [243189].

Travellers Rest inn, Glenridding. Believed to be well over 300 years old. In the past its principal clientelle was miners and other workers from the Greenside Mine [383170].

Travellers Rest Inn old coaching inn alongside the A591 N Grasmere village. Originally three cottages dating from the late 16th century. The middle one subsequently became an inn and as the other two cottages became available they were incorporated into the hostelry. Further extension took place in 1854 [336089].

Tray Dub near Swan Dub on Langstrath Beck. Hereabouts a footbridge crosses over a waterfall in a ravine [264101].

Tre(i)stermo(u)nt see **Cross Dormont**.

Trees, Tallest & Widest alongside the road near the Armboth car park there is a signpost to the giant tree of Thirlmere. This, a silver fir, planted in 1821, rises to 46m (151ft). I am indebted to Dr J B Holdsworth of the Tree Register of the British Isles organisation for the information on the tallest and greatest girth trees in Cumbria. As far as is known the tallest is situated near Aira Force, Ullswater. Also a silver fir it rises to 50m (164ft). However, this bears no comparison to the tallest tree in Great Britain, a Douglas fir at the Hermitage, Dunkeld, Tayside, which rises to a height of 64.6m (212ft) and, according to experts, is still growing. The tallest tree currently standing is a coast Douglas fir in Oregon which towers over this with a height of 100.3m (329ft). Again, as far as is known, the tree with the largest girth in Cumbria is a sweet chestnut in the grounds of Rydal Hall. This has a circumference of approximately 10.45m (34ft). In the wood behind Merewood at 392014 there is another sweet chestnut with a girth of 10.96m (36ft). This is not registered as a tree in the strict sense of the word as it cannot be measured at the accepted height being comprised of an old coppiced stool with nine separate trunks. Here again, the largest girths for Britain and the world are 13.33m (43.75ft) and 35.8m (117.6ft) respectively although baobab trees of Africa have had girth measurements of up to 54.5m (180ft) attributed to them.

Trough Head E Birks. Depression between that mountain and Arnison Crag. Source of Hag Beck. The wall which encloses Glenamara Park comes to a point just below the Head and is climbed by an exceedingly high metal stile. From this a path descends through the park 430m (1411ft) [389142] ...the valley head, the valley being that of Hag Beck which flows through Glenamara Park.

Trough House Bridge Eskdale, see **Beckfoot Bridge**.

Troughton Beck rises Martcrag Moor at 269080 and joins Mickleden Beck at 266069 ...trough/valley/settlement/stream. Therefore the stream which flows down to the settlement in the valley.

Troughton Gill Two tributaries rise at 263006 and 266007 and the beck joins the R Duddon at 267020.

Troughton Hall alongside the A593 [256919] ...personal name + hall.

Trout Beck rises Threshthwaite Mouth 427101 and flows down through Troutbeck Park, Troutbeck valley, Troutbeck and Troutbeck Bridge to join Windermere near Calgarth Hall at 395996 ...the trout stream. Once abounded with trout and salmon.

Trout Beck upper course is Thornsgill Beck and it is from this that it is sometimes called Gills Beck. Generally deemed to become Trout Beck at the confluence with White Sike at 377235. It flows N to near the former Troutbeck Station and then W to join the R Glenderamackin at 358268.

Trout Farm see **Hawkshead Trout Farm**.

Troutal small hamlet alongside the R Duddon and the road up the Duddon valley [235988] ...presumably takes its name either from a trout pool in the nearby Duddon or from Seathwaite Tarn, a substantial trout pool. Eckwall mentions that the first element may be a personal name.

Troutal Fell fell area above Seathwaite Tarn [249995] ...see **Troutal**.

Troutal Tongue Duddon valley. Between Tarn Beck and the Duddon [236982].

Troutbeck not to be confused with the Troutbeck in the former Cumberland alongside the A66. Village recorded in the 13th century as Trutebek. Today consists principally of 17th and 18th century farms and houses stretching for nearly 2.4kms (1.5 miles) alongside a minor road from Troutbeck Bridge to Town Head on the A592 and on the W slope of the Troutbeck Valley. Properties originally drew their water from various wells, several of which still exist, ie St James's, St John's, St Margaret's and Shady Well. The church, consecrated in 1562 as Jesus Chapel, later became Jesus Church. Rebuilt in 1736 with further major restoration work and alterations in 1861 it has an interesting E window in that it was the combined work of Edward Burne-Jones, William Morris and Ford Maddox Brown. Town End at the S end of the village was built in 1626 by George Browne, a 'statesman'. Owned by the Browne family until the 1940s when it was acquired by the National Trust. It is now open to the public. Two hostelries at the N end of the village are the Mortal Man and the Queen's Head Hotel. The township originally consisted of three divisions called 'the Hundreds' (see **Troutbeck Hundreds**) [410034] ...from the nearby Trout Beck which centuries ago is said to have abounded with trout and salmon.

Troutbeck comprising several properties S of former Troutbeck Station and alongside A5091. This is the Troutbeck mentioned in the famous hunting song *D'ye Ken John Peel* and not the other Troutbeck near Windermere [386262].

Troutbeck Bridge hamlet alongside the A591, Windermere to Ambleside road, and

1.6kms (1 mile) N of Windermere Station. For centuries various highways have passed over Troutbeck Bridge, the principal bridge over the Trout Beck. These have included the present A591, the earlier Kendal-Windermere road N of Orrest Head, and possibly even a medieval road and Roman road. An old fulling mill was situated on the bank of the Trout Beck just behind the former W A Fell works alongside the A591. This was converted into a corn mill in the late 14th century, a paper mill in the 17th century and a bobbin mill during the boom era of bobbin making in the early 19th century. Today it houses a firm of monumental masons. The firm of W A Fell closed in November 1994, after 135 years. The building was demolished in 1996 and a Post Office sorting office was built on its site. This began making deliveries to the people of Windermere and Ambleside areas in September 1997. Troutbeck Bridge boasts two major schools, the Lakes School, opened in October 1965, and St Anne's School. The Sun Hotel, today an extended former coaching inn, was a favourite of Hartley Coleridge. Troutbeck Bridge swimming pool was opened by public subscription in 1974 and redesigned and upgraded in 1999. At Troutbeck Bridge there was a branch of St Martin's Langdale Linen Industry. This continued until after the First World War [403003], see also **Holehird**.

Troutbeck Church see **Troutbeck**.

Troutbeck Giant see **Hird House**.

Troutbeck Hundreds in former years the common pastures at Troutbeck were divided into three Hundreds, the Upper, Middle and Lower. These were reached by drove roads such as the present Nanny Lane and the Hundreds Road. Hundreds were not only confined to Troutbeck. They were present throughout England and each hundred originally comprised 100 hides, the latter being the amount of land deemed to be able to support a peasant family. In the 12th and 13th centuries this usually meant 50 hectares (120 acres) of arable land. However, over the succeeding centuries inflation must have risen considerably for Bulmer in his *History, Topography, and Directory of Westmorland* (1885) notes that Troutbeck township: "comprises three divisions called hundreds, each of which has 600 cattlegates of two acres each on the extensive common, and there were a bull, constable, and bridge to each hundred." Hence originated the saying that 'Troutbeck has 300 bulls, 300 constables, and 300 bridges' to which a cynic from a neighbouring valley added 'and many hundred feuls (fools)'.

Troutbeck Park farm, Troutbeck Park. Purchased by Beatrix Potter in 1924 and used in several of her illustrations. One of 15 farms bequeathed to the National Trust on her death. Not open to the general public [420057].

Troutbeck Park the Troutbeck valley and surrounding areas were once extensively forested and in early feudal times the whole area was a huge park. Large parks like Troutbeck Park were areas in which deer were confined for hunting purposes. Later this park was divided amongst its inhabitants with a smaller park of 2,000 acres called the New Park retained for hunting. Today the area is that principally farmed by Troutbeck Park farm once owned by the author and illustrator Beatrix Potter and left by her to the National Trust. Two cairns S of Bluegill Fold between Trout Beck and Blue Gill [425077] are scheduled as ancient monuments as is a stone circle roughly 1.6kms (1 mile) N of Troutbeck Park Farm [423069].

Troutbeck Park Quarry see **Park Quarry**.

Troutbeck Station S A66. Formerly on Penrith-Keswick line (now defunct) [390271].

Troutdale subsidiary valley off Borrowdale. Contains Troutdale Cottages. Down the dale flows Combe Gill. Acquired by the NT in 1965 [262176] ...takes its name from a long since disused trout hatchery which was established in the 19th century.

Troutdale Cottages Troutdale [260177].

Truss Gap Swindale. Equidistant between Swindale Foot and Swindale Head. There is a farm here, also a footbridge and ford across Swindale Beck, a small dam and water treatment works. Former grammar school and church were sited here [514132].

Trussgap Brow steep hillside E Truss Gap and Swindale Beck, Swindale [523134].

Tullithwaite Hall farm, Underbarrow [473909] ...personal name + clearing + hall.

Tullythwaite House Underbarrow. Formerly famous restaurant and a favourite eating place of notable Lake District chefs, John Tovey of Miller Howe and Brian Sack and Francis Coulson of Sharrow Bay Country Hotel. Today it is a noted bed and breakfast establishment which, in 1997, won the best bed and breakfast award in Cumbria Tourist Board's Awards for Excellence [472915] ...see Tullithwaite Hall.

Turdypack Gill an unusual named ravine down which Kid Beck flows [115053].

Turner Hall Close between Stephead Gill and Low Bridge Beck [238958].

Turner Hall Farm Tarn Beck valley. NE Seathwaite. Campsite adjoining [233964].

Turnerhow Brackenthwaite. Alongside the short connecting road between the B5289 and that to Scale Hill and Loweswater [155223] ...Tannerhow in 1821.

Twopenny Crag head of Riggindale and below the Straits of Riggindale. Obviously not worth a fortune [442124]. There is a field in the Ormside area called Tippeny and meaning a piece of land worth twopence, and a Five Shillings Piece in the Bampton district probably referring to a rent or service.

Tyson Wood Sunny Bank [287923] ...Tyson is a common Cumberland/Westmorland surname.

U

Ulcat Row N Gowbarrow Fell on minor road connecting Thornythwaite with A66-Matterdale End road to A592 [405226] ...owl cottage corner.

Ulgill Gutter rises between head of Intack Sike and Willdale Beck at 490167 and flows down into marshy area at 491171 ...either wolf or owl channel.

Ulgra Beck rises Hesk Fell at 176950 and joins Woodend Pool/Crosby Gill at 184956.

Ulgraves a summit of Potter Fell. Not spot-heighted on the OS map but on the 1:63360 (1 ins) map given as 332m (1090ft) [511996] ...wolf pits.

Ullister Hill in the Lord's Seat group of fells. Two spot heights at 520m (1706ft) [209259] and 525m (1722ft) [209260] ...appertaining to wolves.

Ullock hamlet near Portinscale [244230] ...place where wolves play.

Ullock Moss between Portinscale and Ullock [249230].

Ullock Pike cone-shaped peak on humpy ridge running WNW from Carlside Col over Longside Edge 692m (2270ft) [244288] ...the pike on which the wolves play.

Ullscarf mountain between Greenup Gill and Thirlmere and near the S end of a lengthy ridge running From Castlerigg (Kendal) to the Wyth Burn. Steep and craggy slopes on three sides but its summit is grassy 726m (2382ft) [292122] ...wolf's pass.

Ullscarf Gill rises Ullscarf at 294126 and enters Harrop Tarn at 311135.

Ullscarf Ridge (Ullscarf-Bleaberry Fell), see Reference Section: **Heights**.

Ullstone large perched boulder to the E of the path up to the summit of the Nan Bield Pass [455081] ...at least one source suggests the boulder on which the owl perches but more than likely it is the boulder frequented by wolves.

Ullstone Gill rises Band Knott, Kentmere, at 456082 and flows alongside Ull Stone to join the R Kent at 454066.

Ullswater Ulf's or Ulfr's lake. Pooley Bridge is situated at its foot and Patterdale at its head. Second longest of the lakes being nearly 11.8kms (7.3 miles) in length. Maximum depth is 62.5kms (205ft) nearly 0.8kms (0.5 mile) NE Silver Point. At 145m (476ft) above sea level it is the fourth highest of the lakes. Fishing for trout, perch, pike, char and schelly with some salmon which enter from the River Eamont. Two steamers, *Lady of the Lake* (launched 1877) and *Raven* (launched 1889) operate a daily scheduled service from Glenridding Pier to Howtown and Pooley Bridge and back in the season. On Ullswater on 23 July 1955, the late Donald Campbell established a world water speed record of 202.32mph and a plaque marking the place where he launched his *Bluebird* on that day was unveiled in October 1977, by his daughter, Gina. Donald Campbell died on Coniston in January 1967, while attempting another record. His body was recovered 34 years later. Two aircraft crashed into the lake, one in December 1940, and the other in June 1945, resulting in the deaths of 1 crew member. Ullswater contains 4 islands - Cherry Holm, Lingy Holm, Norfolk Island (House Holm) and Wall Holm. In March 1969, the final break through was made to the Tarn Moor tunnel between Ullswater and Heltondale. This, thousands of feet below the moor and 2.74kms (3,000 yards) long, carries millions of gallons of water daily to Manchester via the Selside Water Treatment Plant [388164-468243]. Wordsworth suggested the lake "as being, perhaps, upon the whole, the happiest combination of beauty and grandeur, which any of the Lakes affords," while poet Richard Cumberland exclaimed:

Thee, savage Thirlmere, now I hail:
Delicious Grasmere's calm retreat,
And Stately Windermere I greet
And Keswick's sweet fantastic vale;
But let her Naiads yield to thee,
And lowly bend the subject knee -
Imperial lake of Patterdale!

Principal bays - Blowick, Gale, Glencoyne, Gowbarrow, Howtown Wyke, Mossdale, Oldchurch, Purse, Sandwick, Sharrow, Silver, Thwaitehill.

Principal promontories - Aira Point, Castlehows Point, Devil's Chimney, Geordie's Crag, Glenridding Beck delta, Kailpot Crag, Old Church, Purse Point, Sandwick Beck delta, Silver Point, Skelly Neb, Stybarrow Crag, Thwaitehill Neb.

Ullswater Canoeing & Kayaking Centre the Spit, Glenridding [390171].

Ullswater Fox Hounds formed in 1873 on amalgamation of a pack at Matterdale with one at Patterdale. The pack covers Helvellyn, Fairfield, Martindale, High Street, and sometimes part of the Pennines. Kennels are at Grassthwaite Howe, Patterdale. Most famous huntsman was Joe Bowman 'Auld Hunty', born at Matterdale in 1850 and died at Glenridding in 1940. Another, who held the post from 1971-96, was Dennis Barrow with close to 2,000 kills to his credit.

Ullswater Hotel see **Inn on the Lake**.

Ullswater Outward Bound Centre see **Hallsteads**.

Ullthwaite Bridge carries track from Browfoot Lane, Kentmere, to Staveley-Kentmere road over the River Kent. Old bridge with, at one time, Ullthwaite Mill, one of many in the Staveley area, sited nearby [456012] ...the bridge by the clearing frequented by wolves.

Ulpha hamlet in the Duddon valley with a church, post office and shop. Formerly known as Ulpha Kirk. Its 17th century church, dedicated to St John, was restored in the late 19th

century and 1934 and is the subject of one of Wordsworth's Duddon sonnets which begins: "The Kirk of Ulpha, to the pilgrim's eye, is welcome as a star." Ulpha Old Hall, a ruined pele tower, is situated alongside Holehouse Gill. The old Ulpha corn mill, in woodland with a riverside setting, was converted and renovated into a private residence in the 1950s. Ulpha once boasted a hostelry, the Traveller's Rest, now a private residence, at the start of the Ulpha to Eskdale fell road. Wordsworth and Coleridge stayed there in 1802 [197934] ...wolf's hill or Ulfr's hill.

Ulpha Alms Houses Ulpha [198935].

Ulpha Bridge carries the Duddon Bridge to Cockley Beck road over the River Duddon [197930].

Ulpha Church House Ulpha [197933].

Ulpha Fell apparently the fell equivalent of a moveable feast. Several maps show Ulpha Fell to the NW of Ulpha with Hesk Fell as its highest point while others, including the current OS map, name it alongside Green Crag. The 1864/5 OS map prints the name alongside Wallowbarrow Heald and the noted climber and author Bill Birkett in his *Complete Lakeland Fells* notes that it connects the Birker Fell ridge with the road over Birker Moor.

Ulpha Park SSW Ulpha. N Penn [187911].

Ulpha School Ulpha [198930].

Ulthwaite Rigg between Little Mosedale Beck and upper reaches of Sleddale Beck C500m (C1640ft) [515093] ...wolf clearing ridge.

Under Crag below Hollin House Haw, Tarn Beck valley. The birthplace of 'Wonderful Walker', the Rev. Robert Walker, curate of Seathwaite for 66 years [233967].

Under Crag Torver [279942].

Under Howe E A66-Mungrisdale road [372284].

Underbank Eskdale [178999].

Underbarrow & Bradleyfield township and parish to the W of Kendal covering an area of roughly three miles square. A quiet and unspoilt area. Underbarrow, as its name implies, is 'under the hill' (Underbarrow Scar atopped by Helsington Barrows, Bradley Field and Cunswick Fell). Today it is principally a scattered agricultural community with a nucleus of a village in a triangle of land bounded by the Kendal-Crosthwaite road, the Crook to Underbarrow road and the minor road to the E of the latter. However in 1829 there were diverse industries in Underbarrow as shown by the following list of occupations in the parish - 2 corn mills; 3 maltsters; 2 tanneries; 2 wheelwrights; a blacksmith; a joiner; a stone mason; a bleaching mill; a shoemaker; a bobbin mill; a bone crushing mill and a charcoal burnery. Here are All Saints Church (1869) which was rebuilt on the site of one erected in 1708; an unusual corrugated iron village hall (erected in 1904); a former school building and a hostelry, the Punch Bowl, last of three inns at Underbarrow which used to serve travellers on the former packhorse/turnpike road from Kendal to Ulverston. Not to be confused with the Punch Bowl at nearby Crosthwaite. Oldest habitation in the parish is Cunswick Hall [476926]. Bradleyfield to the E of Underbarrow Scar is today principally represented in name by Bradley Field, Bradleyfield House, and Bradleyfield. It was owned in ancient times by the Bradley family (who came from Bradley in Lancashire). One of this family married into the Leybourne family of Cunswick Hall ...Bradley actually means broad clearing in a stretch of open country and refers appropriately to the present-day Bradleyfield atop Underbarrow Scar. See also **Underbarrow Scar**.

Underbarrow Beck one headstream rises ENE Bonfire Hall but the farthest and major one rises near Long Wood at 478942 and meets Chapel Beck at 465917 to become Underbarrow Pool. The latter joins the R Gilpin.

Underbarrow Mill see **Low Mill House**.

Underbarrow Moss W Underbarrow Pool [464903].

Underbarrow Pool Underbarrow Beck and Chapel Beck join forces at 465917 to become Underbarrow Pool. This joins the R Gilpin which in turn joins the R Kent.

Underbarrow Road section of the Kendal to Underbarrow road over and down from Underbarrow Scar. Formerly part of the packhorse route to Newby Bridge and Ulverston which became a turnpike road in 1763 and was extended to Kirkby Ireleth. The old toll bar cottage (dated 1764) still stands alongside the present road [492925].

Underbarrow Scar old maps show Underbarrow Scar as the whole escarpment from near Brigsteer to the end of Cunswick Scar and *The Place Names of Westmorland* notes it as "forming the long ridge between Underbarrow Beck and the Kent." Not named at all on the current 1:25000 (2.5 ins) map but the OS 1:63360 (1 inch) and Bartholomew's delineates it as most of the 3kms (2 miles) ridge from near Brigsteer to Underbarrow Road. Today this section of the ridge is commonly called Scout Scar although the latter is actually a cliff on the southern section. Scout Scar is surmounted by a canopied stone shelter with a stone seat surround. This was erected in 1912 as a memorial to King George V and was restored in 1969. In 2002 a specially built stainless steel dome was positioned over the shelter. Known locally as either 'the umbrella' or 'the mushroom' it was originally provided with a view indicator. However, vandals saw to its demise but in 2002 a stainless steel panorama map was fixed beneath the rim of the dome. The ridge provides an excellent viewpoint, particularly westerly, northerly, and down into, and over, the Lyth and Underbarrow valleys to many of the high Lakeland peaks and southerly to the Morecambe Bay area.

In 1937 the Friends of the Lake District successfully fought a Central Electricity Board scheme to take pylons over the scar. Alfred Wainwright in his *Outlying Fells of Lakeland* poses the question: "Where does all the rain go that falls on Scout Scar?" and for that matter we can include Cunswick Scar. "No streams, no major springs," he says. The answer, however, lies to a great degree in the fact that there are many springs and wells in the vicinity whereby rain which falls on the scars can ultimately emerge. Within a distance of 3.2kms (2 miles) W of Underbarrow Scar there are over 30 springs (one of which is the source of Tanyard Beck and another feeds Cunswick Tarn), 15 wells and a spout, shown on the OS map. Needless to say, there are obviously many more that are not shown. A trig. point is sited at 229m (751ft) but the highest point is at the N end of what is termed Scout Scar at 235m (771ft) [487922].

Underhelm below Helm Crag on the Easedale Road to Low Mill Bridge road [333086].

Underhill House Longsleddale [489045].

Underhill Wood Longsleddale [489042].

Undermillbeck Common in ancient times the manor of Undermillbeck was once of considerable extent and included much land above the Mill Beck. Incorporated in it were the hamlets of Langden, Loughrigg, Grismere, Hamelside, Troutbeck, Applethwaite, Crosthwaite, Stirkland Ketel and Hoton. Today, the name Undermillbeck with appendage Common appears on the OS map as a rough area to the S of the B5284 and Windermere Golf Course. To its N Capple Barrow rises to C190m (C623ft) and overlooks the golf course and the B5284 [420955] ...the land under the Mill Beck. See also **Mill Beck**.

Undermillbeck Common Tarns many of varying sizes and all on private ground. The largest lies to the NE of Barrow Plantation and is used for sporting purposes [424951].

Underscar Applethwaite. Now houses 25 time-ownership homes. Also there is a 19th century coach house and walled gardens [270256].

Underwood SE Little Mell Fell. Alongside minor road from A66-Matterdale End road to A592 [428233].

Underwood Mosser [109248].

Unnamed Summit ENE Artlecrag Pike and W Howes, 673m (2208ft) [488103].

Upper Routen Beck Tarn on Routen Beck, Potter Fell C260m (C853ft) [511992].

Uskdale Gap gap through which the path from Yew Tree Farm and through Harry Guards Wood ascends between high ground before a left turn to the summit of Holme Fell [319008].

Uzzicar see **Farm Uzzicar**.

V

Vale of Grasmere part of the Rothay Valley and being that section which sweeps down from Dunmail Raise to, and including, Grasmere (lake). Thomas Gray in his journal of 1769 described the view from Dunmail Raise down the valley as, 'one of the sweetest landscapes that art ever attempted to imitate.'

Valley View alongside the Kendal to Underbarrow Road [473992].

Valve Houses foot of Thirlmere overflow [310191].

Vaugh Steel WNW Bampton, NW Hullockhowe [499186] ...Vaugh is of obscure origin but Steel is from 'stile' meaning steep.

Vicarage Beckfoot, Eskdale [170004].

Vicarage Dacre Alongside minor road from the A592 to Dacre [463260].

Vicarage near Dale Bottom alongside the A591 [296217].

Vicars property S of the River Brathay and across the river from Fell Foot (farm) [298030].

Vicar Swa Waterfall on the River Esk near its confluence with Lingcove Beck [227036].

Vickers How on slope of Illgill Head above Wastwater [163051].

Victoria Bay Derwent Water [253206].

Village Quarry Lowther [535218].

Virgin Mary Well in the grounds of the former Holmrook Hall [081003].

Waberthwaite village alongside the A595 between Bootle and Muncaster. Its ancient church, dedicated to St. John, is situated at Hall Waberthwaite some 2.8kms (1.75 miles) by major and minor road from Waberthwaite itself. At one time a huge granite quarry at Broad Oak employed about 50 men, locals and others, but to all intents and purposes this closed in 1946. However, one industry still thrives. In 1828 Hannah Woodall opened the village shop which over the years expanded into producing prize ham, bacon and sausages and today Woodalls possesses a Royal Warrant for its traditional and famous Cumberland sausage [105934] ...although acknowledging that its precise origin cannot be established the EPNS and other works suggest that the most likely meaning is the clearing by the hunting or fishing booth/hut. Another suggestion is that it takes its name from the old ford across the Esk and is therefore the ford (wath) by the clearing while there is even a suggestion of it being Wyburgh's clearing.

Waberthwaite Fell large fell area E Waberthwaite. Corney Fell to its S [138935].

Waberthwaite Marsh WSW Hall Waberthwaite and adjoining Newbiggin Marsh [098946].

Wad's Howe Longsleddale. W bank River Sprint across Wad's Howe Bridge [495032] ...personal name + hill.

Wad's Howe Bridge Longsleddale. Packhorse bridge over the River Sprint. At the bridge the old drove road along the W side of Longsleddale crossed to the E and in the middle of the 18th century the bridge was referred to as being, 'in the high road from Ambleside to Appleby' [497033].

Wadcrag Wythop Mill. Alongside the road to Routenbeck and the A66 [182298].

Wain Lane bridleway between the A591 and Holbeck Lane [401014] ...an old wagon route, a 'wain' being a former wagon or cart.

Wainwright, Alfred (1907-1991). Noted author and illustrator. The best known of his many works are the 7-volume *Pictorial Guide to the Lakeland Fells* (1955-66) and the companion volume *The Outlying Fells of Lakeland* (1973). Of these eight works five cover the particular area in this work - *The Central Fells*, *The Northern Fells*, *The Eastern Fells*, *The Far Eastern Fells* and *The Outlying Fells of Lakeland.* Hunter Davies wrote a biography *Hunter Davies's Wainwright: The Biography* (published by M Joseph) in 1995. There have been suggestions that a memorial be erected on Haystacks, his favourite fell, or on Orrest Head, the fell he first visited. However, there is a permanent memorial to him in Buttermere Church. A plaque below a window which looks out towards Haystacks is inscribed, 'Pause and Remember Alfred Wainwright. Fellwalker, Guide Book Author and Illustrator, Who Loved This Valley. Lift Your Eyes To Haystacks, His Favourite Place. 1907-1991.' His many works are also a fitting tribute to him. His ashes were scattered at Innominate Tarn, Haystacks. An inaugural meeting of a Wainwright Society took place on 9 November 2002.

NB - In his 7 guides to the Lake District Fells Wainwright lists 214 summits. At the time of writing the record time for completing all the summits is 6 days, 23 hours and 11 minutes from the first summit to the last. This was established in 1985 by Jos Naylor of Wasdale.

Wainwright's Coast to Coast Walk from St Bees via Ennerdale, Rosthwaite, Grasmere, Patterdale, Shap, Orton, Kirkby Stephen, Keld, Reeth, Richmond, Danby Wiske, Ingleby Cross, Clay Bank Top, Blakey, Glaisdale and Grosmont, to Robin Hood's Bay. Highest point on the walk is Kidsty Pike at 780m (2559ft) and the lowest, excluding, the extremities, is Danby Wiske at 33.5m (110ft) above sea level. Distance from the shore at St Bees to the Bay Hotel, Robin Hood's Bay, 192 miles.

Wainwright's Inn Chapel Stile. Its licence was transferred from the White Lion, Chapel Stile, in the 1930s to a former farmstead called Grassings. The extended building became the Langdales Hotel and more recently Wainwright's Inn, named after the notable author and illustrator Alfred Wainwright [322052].

Waite Howes alongside Gouthercrag Gill [519129] ...wet hills.

Walk Mill a former fulling mill at Broughton Mills [224905] ...see also **Fulling Mills**.

Walker Ground Hawkshead. One of the original 'grounds' (see **Grounds**) of Furness Abbey and dating from around the 15th century. Extended and updated in the 18th and considerable refurbishment since [349980].

Walking see **Fell Walking**.

Wall End 17th century farmhouse at the head of Great Langdale. At one time the Holiday Fellowship had a hostel in several wooden chalets at Wall End. These were demolished in the mid-1960s and have been replaced by a NT camping site at the head of the valley. Along with Stool End and the Old Dungeon Ghyll Hotel, Wall End was presented to the NT by Prof. G M Trevellyn in 1929 [283055] ...near the end of an ancient enclosure.

Wall End at end of the track from the A592 up Deepdale. A path continues up the dale from here. In 1991 a detached cottage and small garden at Wall End were bequeathed to the National Trust [393137].

Wall Holm one of Ullswater's four islands [391175] ...centuries ago it was walled round.

Walla Crag much earlier Wallow Crag. Impressive crag with bare rock summit. Situated to the E of Derwent Water and above Great Wood. An excellent viewpoint looking over Derwent Water and to its N and S. The fell is actually the rocky NW face of Bleaberry Fell. A steep gully down the face of the crag just S of its summit is called Lady's Rake and is reputed to be the route by which Lady Derwentwater fled from Lord's Island in 1715 on hearing of the impending execution of her husband for his part in the Jacobite Rising of that year. There is, however, considerable doubt as to the authenticity of this story. In the 19th century a hoard of pennies dated betwen 1272 and 1327 were discovered just below the gully and this find could point to a much earlier ascent 379m (1243ft) [277213] ...hill of the British. The Castlerigg Stone Circle is situated not far distant. Could also mean dark grey or grey crag.

Wallhead Crag Harter Fell [218999].

Wallow Crag Naddle Forest. Overlooks the foot of Haweswater. Once the haunt of eagles. There is also a Walla (Wallow) Crag overlooking Derwent Water and a Wallowbarrow in the Duddon Valley [496151] ...dark grey or grey crag.

Wallowbarrow Coppice W High Wallowbarrow Farm [216962].

Wallowbarrow Crag impressive high crag between Rake Beck and the R Duddon. Its summit provides magnificent views down the Duddon valley and of Harter Fell and many other mountains and its cliff face provides sport for rock climbers. Given to the NT in 1929. Rises to 292m (958ft) [222968] ...hill of the British but could also mean grey hill.

Wallowbarrow Heald NW Wallowbarrow Crag and E Iron Crag [216972] ...see also **Wallowbarrow Crag**. 'Heald' - a slope.

Walloway adjoining minor road A66-Matterdale End [412255].

Walls see **Stone Walls**.

Walls Castle see **Ravenglass**.

Walls Plantation Ravenglass [088960].

Wallthwaite minor road from Troutbeck to Scales (A66) [354262] ...in the 16th century there is record of a mill in the parish and possibly the name refers to a clearing where the process of fulling (cloth/yarn made more compact during manufacture through shrinking and pressing) was in operation.

Walm Howe between Dennyhill and Walmgate alongside Bampton to Haweswater road [517173].

Walmgate farm alongside Bampton to Haweswater road [516171] ...either the way to the spring or the snake way.

Walmgate Foot in the angle formed by meeting of road from Bampton to Haweswater and that from Bampton Grange to Walmgate Foot [517175].

Walmgate Head NE Burnbanks village alongside the Bampton to Haweswater road. The former Measand Grammar School building was re-erected here as a private residence [512165].

Walna Scar on the continuation of the Dow Crag-Buck Pike-Brown Pike ridge to White Maiden and White Pike. Rises to 621m (2037ft) [258963] ...either hawks' crag or hill of the British. Suggesting the latter there are certainly ancient cairns and early settlements on the fells and moors nearby.

Walna Scar Quarries disused quarries on the W slope of Walna Scar [248958/9].

Walna Scar Road ancient track then packhorse road and later used as an access road to quarries. Runs from Coniston to Seathwaite over the Walna Scar ridge and down Walna Scar Side. Its summit is 606m (1988ft). Nearby is the summit of Walna Scar [259965].

Walna Scar Side slope W side Walna Scar. Traversed by the Walna Scar Road [270969].

Walpole, Hugh see **Watendlath & Manesty**.

Walthwaite farm and property alongside the old road from Chapel Stile to Grasmere [324056] ...walled clearing.

Walthwaite Bottom Elterwater. Between the B5343 and the old road from Chapel Stile to Grasmere [331051].

Wander Scar E of the ridge and path between Froswick and Thornthwaite Crag [435091]. Certainly not a place to 'wander' off the track.

Wandope mountain with grassy summit but with extremely craggy E face and steep and craggy scree slope to its W, 772m (2533ft) [188197] ...takes its name from the valley where ossiers (willows) grow.

Wandope Moss Wandope [186199].

Wansfell extensive area of fell between Stock Ghyll and Trout Beck valleys with a distinctive and well-defined ridge. Paths from Ambleside and Troutbeck meet at Wansfell Pike 484m (1588ft) [394042], a rocky outcrop thought by many to be the summit. However, this lies NE of the pike at 487m (1598ft) [404053]. Wordsworth wrote a sonnet to the fell ...of obscure origin but most likely a surname such as Wanny (Wansbeck, Northumbria) or as also suggested similar to Wansdyke (Bath) and referring to the god, Woden. Therefore possibly Woden's Fell.

Wansfell Holme 0.8kms (0.5 mile) S of Waterhead off the A591. At the foot of the Wansfell ridge [380027].

Wansfell Pike see **Wansfell**.

Wanthwaite St John's in the Vale. Alongside minor road, B5322-A66(T) [314232].

Wanthwaite St John's in the Vale. E B5322 [319229] ...the clearing in which angelica grows.

Wanthwaite Bank W slope Threlkeld Knotts [324231].

Wanthwaite Bridge carries minor road B5322-A66(T) over St John's Beck. Nearby, off the B5322, is the start of the old coach road to Dockray [314231].

Wanthwaite Crags E B5322. WSW Clough Head. Spectacular crags overlooking Fisher's Wife's Rake and Bramcrag Quarry [324221].

Wardless E Sour Howes and S Sallows [435032] ...origin unknown.

Wardwarrow off the minor road, A595 to Santon [089014].

Warnscale overlooking Warnscale Bottom from the W [190142].

Warnscale Beck rises between Grey Knotts and Brandreth at 215123. Joined by principal tributary which rises on the slope of Grey Knotts and then flows through Warnscale Bottom to join Buttermere at 188150.

Warnscale Bottom below Hay Stacks. Valley through which Warnscale Beck flows [195142].

Wartches Area between Helton Fell and Swarth Fell [468202] ...possibly Watt's share of land

Wartches Beck rises Wartches at 470201 and joins Brown Beck at 473199.

Wasdale large valley which encloses Wastwater. A centre for climbers and walkers. The latter can find climbs of varying severity on many crags and cliffs including Scafell buttresses, Pikes Crag, and the aretes, cliffs and pinnacle (Napes Needle) of Great Gable and Gable Crag. For winter ice and snow climbing the gullies of Great End provide much sport. Wasdale has its own brewery, the Great Gable Brewery at the Wasdale Head Inn, and also

Wasdale Springs natural spring water is bottled at Windsor Farm. See also **Wastwater**.

Wasdale not to be confused with its much larger western namesake. Valley which commences at Shap Wells crosses the A6 and continues westward into the Shap Fells where it is bounded by Gargill, Little Yarlside, Great Yarlside, Wasdale Pike and Long Fell. No habitation W of the A6 as Wasdale Head farm is now derelict [544073] ...valley with a lake. No lake now but at one time may have possessed one which has been drained. However, the name could also refer to a large stream, in this case, Wasdale Beck, fed in its upper reaches by many tributaries.

Wasdale Beck farthest headstream rises E Great Yarlside at 528077. Joins Blea Beck (earlier Longfell Gill) at 579096. The enlarged stream becomes Birk Beck which ultimately flows into the R Lune.

Wasdale Fell lower slope of Kirk Fell overlooking Lingmell Beck and Wasdale Head [194095].

Wasdale Hall foot of Wastwater. Dates from 1829 with a S wing added 10 years later. Acquired by the National Trust in 1959 and is now a youth hostel [145045]. The hall and surrounding area is said to be haunted by a mother and child. The latter, an early occupant of the house, was accidentally drowned in the lake.

Wasdale Head Wasdale. Derelict farm now in dangerous condition as emphasised by warning notice [550082].

Wasdale Head the alluvial plain at the head of Wastwater where a scattered settlement comprises a hotel, farms and a tiny church (St Olaf's, claimed to be the smallest in England but actually believed to be the third smallest). In the summer the population is boosted considerably by occupants at campsites and farmhouse accommodation. The hotel, a noted centre for walkers and climbers, is also famous for its 19th century landlord, Will Ritson (see **Wasdale Head Inn**). The Wasdale valley area is often quoted as possessing the highest mountain in England (Scafell Pike), the deepest lake (Wastwater), the smallest church (see above) and at least two winners of the World's Greatest Liar competition - Will Ritson and Joss Naylor [186088] ...head of the valley with a lake.

Wasdale Head Hall Farm head of Wastwater. Acquired by the NT in 1959 [180068].

Wasdale Head Inn Wasdale Head. Began its life as a farmhouse, Row Foot, the birthplace of Will Ritson (1808-1890). He extended the farmhouse in the mid-19th century and turned it into the Huntsman's Inn. Ritson retired in 1879 and the inn was rebuilt by one of the local Tyson family in the 1880s with part of the original building as an annex. Renamed the Wastwater Hotel it later acquired its present title. In its early days the inn became famous as a base for prominent climbers and many a famous classic route was pioneered by those staying at Wasdale Head. Will Ritson's fame not only grew from his connections with top class climbers and other notable personalities but he was also a farmer, huntsman, mountain guide, wrestler, raconteur and above all the 'world's greatest liar' a title he acquired through the many outrageous stories which he always insisted were true. The inn has a Ritson's Bar and also in his memory, a waterfall on Mosedale Beck is named Ritson's Force. The inn possesses its own micro brewery. The World's Greatest Liar competition is now held annually at Santon Bridge [186088].

Wasdale Mouth pass from Wasdale to Crookdale which crosses between Whatshaw Common and Little Yarlside. Rises to 419m (1375ft) at 535065.

Wasdale Pike Shap Fells. N Yarlside and upper reach of Wasdale Beck. Twin-cairned summit 565m (1854ft) [536084].

Wash Dub Beck rises below White Pike at 246957. Joined by Stephead Gill before entering Tarn Beck at 230963 ...pool in which sheep were washed.

Washfall Beck rises slightly W Black Crag, Black Fell, at 339016 and flows down and under the A593 alongside Colwith Brow to join Ben Beck at 331029 ...the stream in which sheep were washed. There is a sheepfold near its lower reach.

Washfold sheepfold alongside Woundale Beck [410071] ...sheep would be washed in the nearby stream.

Washfold Point slight promontory Devoke Water. Ruined boathouse here [162970].

Waste Wood Calderbridge [048060].

Waste Wood Birkby [124968].

Wast Water see **Wastwater**.

Wastwater OS Wast Water. Large lake in Wasdale. Seventh longest of the lakes being 4.8 kms (3 miles) in length but by far the deepest 76m (249ft). An impressive sheet of water with the famous Screes rising sheer from its surface to a height of approximately 549m (1800ft). In January 1945, a Grumman Avenger flew into the Screes. Its crew of three were killed. In March 1973, a Cherokee crashed on the steep face of Illgill Head and four persons were killed. Two small rocky islands are a favourite haunt of black-headed gulls. Illgill Head and Whin Rigg rise above the Screes while to the lake's N are Middle Fell and Yewbarrow and past the head of the lake Kirk Fell, Great Gable and Lingmell tower above the valley. The view of the latter three has been adopted as the emblem of the Lake District National Park. Wastwater was acquired by the NT in 1979 as part of its 30,400 acres share of the Leconfield Commons named after their former owner Lord Leconfield.

Similar to Coniston Water, Wastwater has its 'Lady in the Lake' scenario. After a furious row in October 1976, a man killed his wife. He wrapped the body in bedsheets and polythene and drove to Wasdale. On the edge of Wastwater he inflated a rubber dinghy, rowed out and tipped the body into the lake. Nearly 8 years later, in February 1984, while police divers were searching for a missing French student they discovered the body on a ledge below the surface. From various clues the husband was arrested and in March 1985, he was acquitted of murder but found guilty of manslaughter and sentenced to 4 years in prison. Police admitted that if the corpse had been thrown into the lake a few score yards from where it was found it would have sunk into the deepest part of the lake and would not have been found.

A granite epitaph on a small knoll slightly E of the lake and the road up to Wasdale Head reads:

William Curwen Porter
Master Eskdale and Ennerdale Fox Hounds
Fell Here Salvers Hunt 1 Nov 1952 and died 29 Nov 1952

The NT allow rowing boats and canoes on Wastwater with a maximum of 15 at any one time. Contains trout, perch and char, 61m (200ft) [164062] ...Wasdale Water. As Wasdale means the valley with a lake the 'water' is superfluous.

Watbarrow Point W shore Windermere near Wray Castle. Promontory at the foot of a wooded slope [378010] ...probably watch hill or look-out hill.

Watch Crag Thornthwaite Forest, Bassenthwaite. Alongside the A591 [234278] ...look-out crag.

Watching Crag Sourfoot Fell. Overlooks Lorton Vale and the River Cocker [139232] ...the crag from which to watch or look-out.

Watching Gill below Watching Crag [140231].

Watendlath secluded hamlet in the fells at the end of a road which leaves the B5289 at Ashness Gate. A delightful spot with its three farms and cottages, a tarn, a packhorse bridge and the infant Watendlath Beck cascading over a rock step. The hamlet and tarn are owned by the NT and the three farms, Stepps End (formerly Watendlath Farm), Fold Head and Caffle How were purchased in 1960. Today Watendlath is a farming community and a mecca for tourists and afficiendos of Hugh Walpole's (1884-1941) novels (particularly *Judith Paris* (1931) whose fictional home it was) but in days gone by with its farms, a woollen mill and a staging post for pack horses, it was also a thriving place. Its old picturesque bridge over the beck was provided with parapets in the last century. Watendlath was actually the last hamlet in the Lake District to receive a mains electricity supply. This was in 1978 the same year as the telephone arrived [276163] ...of uncertain origin. Possibly the barn by the water's end (Watendlath Tarn) or Gwendolen's lake.

Watendlath Beck rises Watendlath Tarn and shortly afterwards flows through a narrow fissure and into a bowl in the rocks known as the Churn or Devil's Punchbowl. Continues down the Watendlath valley where it is joined by Emblesteads Gill and Thwaitehouse Beck before dropping down a rocky gorge and over the High Lodore Falls and the more famous Lodore Falls to meet Derwent Water at 266193.

Watendlath Farm see **Stepps End Farm**.

Watendlath Fell large fell area S Watendlath [283148].

Watendlath Tarn Watendlath. Fed from the S by Bleatarn Gill. Its outflow is Watendlath Beck. No private craft are permitted and fishing for trout is by permit 263m (863ft) [275162].

Water Barnetts Tarn see **Barngates Tarn**.

Water Crag slightly WNW of the top of Swirral Edge. Overlooks Brown Cove [341153].

Water Crag foot of Middle Fell. Alongside the road along Wastwater [156060] ...the crag overlooking/above Wastwater.

Water Crag above Devoke Water 305m (1001ft) [154975].

Water Park W shore Coniston Water. S Coniston Hall. Site of two old bloomeries (see also **Bloomeries**) [303957].

Water Park a Georgian mansion set in 65 acres on the E side of lower Coniston Water. The house has played host to royalty, been owned by the Duke of Albermarle and been in the possession of the Harrison family for three centuries from 1578. It then passed to the Brydson family of which the last Brydson in line died in the 1970s. Subsequently passed by inheritance to Arthur Hatton and his family before being acquired in the late 1990s by philanthropist and multi-millionaire Eric Wright. Today it is an outdoor centre for underprivileged children from the north west and is operated under the terms of the Eric Wright Trust [293903].

Water Side alongside Esthwaite Water [356976].

Water Side Woods alongside Esthwaite Water [364968]

Water Works Duddon valley [209947]; Ormathwaite [275255].

Water Yeat Bridge also known as Stephenson Ground Bridge. Carries minor road over the River Lickle [239930] ...Water Yeat (water gate) is a hamlet alongside the A5084 N Blawith.

Waterbarrow W shore Windermere near Sandy Nab [383946].

Waterend the N end of Loweswater but by its position should surely be Waterhead [116225], see also **Loweswater**.

Waterfalls the four OS maps show many falls, waterfalls or named drops. In times of considerable precipitation cascades appear. Those named in the area are individually listed. Most falls are worth viewing particularly when in spate, but it must be emphasised that some will be on private land and others only available to the seasoned walker or even the scrambler. *A Naturalist's Guide to Lakeland Waterfalls Throughout the Year - Book 1*

Southern Lakeland by Mary Welsh (1985) describes over 40 falls, and *Walks to Lakeland Waterfalls* obtainable from tourist information offices for a small price, lists 13 of Lakeland's waterfalls with directions and descriptions. The highest fall in the Lake District is Scale Force, Crummock, with a total drop of 52m (172ft) [151171].

Waterfoot Caravan Park large caravan site alongside Waterfoot Hotel Farm [462246].

Waterfoot Hotel Farm Soulby [460246]. There is a large caravan site alongside.

Watergate Farm foot of Loweswater. Purchased by the NT in 1985 [127211].

Waterhead 1.6kms (1 mile) S of Ambleside at the head of Windermere. Principally hotels (the Wateredge Hotel was originally two 17th century fishermen's cottages which have been combined), guest houses and a pier from which in the season boats operate services to Bowness, Lakeside, and return, a 21-mile round trip. There is also a public launching jetty for boats under 5hp. Galava Roman Fort is nearby. Since the Windermere Steam Yacht Co opened its boat terminus at Waterhead in 1845 the then two separate villages of Waterhead and Ambleside have expanded to meet each other. At Waterhead the A5075 leaves the A591 to meet the A593 (Ambleside-Coniston road). Ambleside Youth Hostel is sited at Waterhead between the A591 and the lake. In 1970 the first car park charges by the LDNP authority were introduced at Waterhead - ls (5p) a day [376034].

Waterhead Coniston. Country guest house alongside the B5285 and near the lake. Replaced an older inn situated at the head of the lake. This was destroyed by fire in 1860 and the New Waterhead Hotel was built nearer to Coniston village [310975].

Waterhead Pier W shore Coniston Water [311972].

Waterhouse N A66 [363275].

Watermill Inn Ings, see **Ings with Hugill**.

Watermillock scattered village between Glenridding and Pooley Bridge alongside and off the A592. Stretches for l.6kms (l mile) up the fellside and the parish extends for 3 sq miles. Just over 100 years ago there were 46 farms covering the area. These have depleted over the years and today a third of the farms and buildings that remain are holiday homes and camping and caravan sites. The boating, sailing and windsurfing fraternity are particularly well catered for hereabouts with a marina and boat park near Rampsbeck and a sailing section at the Outward Bound School Centre at Hallsteads. The Church of All Saints is sited up the fell under Priest's Crag. Opened in 1882 it replaced a 'new' church which had replaced an ancient one at Old Church alongside Ullswater [446225] ...the bare hill on which wethers grazed.

Watermillock Common between Dowthwaitehead and Glencoyne Park, Ullswater 540m (1772ft) [379202].

Watermillock House Watermillock. Off the A592 [446224]

Waternook NW Howtown alongside Howtown Bay [440199].

Waterside House E shore Ullswater alongside the Pooley Bridge to Howtown road. A working farm which welcomes visitors and provides other attractions [463230].

Waterson Ground Farm alongside the B5286 between Outgate and Hawkshead Hall. Camping and caravan side adjacent [351994] ...Waterson is an old local surname. A John Waterson, mole catcher, was renowned for his long feet. A clog made for him measured 0.5m (20 inches) in length, over 0.2m (8 inches) in width at the bottom, 0.4m (16 inches) across the front and 0.56m (22 inches) round the back. For meaning of 'ground' see **Grounds**.

Waterson Intake High Wray [371993] ...see **Waterson Ground Farm**.

Waterson Moss Outgate. Near Waterson Ground Farm [352998].

Wath Beck tributaries rise at 255248 and 253250. Subsequently joined by Applethwaite

Gill and Mill Beck before joining the River Derwent by High Stock Bridge at 243260.

Watness Coy Devoke Water [158967].

Watson's Dodd on the Helvellyn range between Great Dodd and Stybarrow Dodd 789m (2589ft) [336196] ...who was the Watson who gave his name to this unspectacular grassy mountain?

Watson's Park Great Wood, Borrowdale [276220].

Waver Beck short stream which rises at 147097 and joins Nether Beck at 151096 ...possibly, similar to its larger namesake, the River Waver, it means the wandering stream.

Web Stone see **Launchy Gill**.

Welcome Nook off the minor road from the A595 S to Corney. Corney's most famous son, Edward Troughton, was born and brought up here (see **Corney**) [119931].

Well Farm alongside the Bootle to Eskmeals road. A well is shown nearby at Marshside [085905].

Well Foot Longsleddale [492038]. Well shown alongside.

Well Gill see **Sulphury Gill**.

Well in Crag spring alongside the Walna Scar Road [278964].

Wellfoot Wood Longsleddale [491037].

Wellington area adjoining Gosforth. Has grown up around Wellington Bridge which carries the Gosforth to Nether Wasdale road over the River Bleng [077039]. The site of an old Walk Mill (for the origin of the name see **Fulling Mills**) and area around it is now occupied by a large garden centre.

Wellington Bridge Wellington, Gosforth. Carries the road from Gosforth to Nether Wasdale over the River Bleng [080040].

Wescoe hamlet 2kms (1.25 miles) W Threlkeld [304250] ...the west wood.

Wescoe Farm Wescoe [303251].

Wescoe Wood near Wescoe. Alongside N bank R Greta [307247].

West Chockstone Gully St Sunday Crag [366134].

West Greenriggs Plantation southern end of Lowther Park. Nearby is Greenriggs Head Plantation and Back Greenriggs [537202].

West Head Wythburn. Alongside the road around the W side of Thirlmere. Last of the farms which once comprised the village off Wythburn and hamlet of Armboth. The original West Head Farm [318133] was closed by the water authority many years ago and today is just a pile of stones. The nearby Steel End Farm now bears the name West Head Farm [322128].

West Nab overlooking Borrowdale and West Nab Gill [528048].

West Nab Gill rises Fawcett Forest at 529045 and joins Borrow Beck at 535049.

West Park see **East/West Park**.

West, Father Thomas antiquarian and doyen of Lake District guides. Born in Scotland in 1720 but later moved to the Furness area and became chaplain of Tytup Hall, Dalton, in the early 1760s. Wrote the *Antiquities of Furness* (1774) and *A Guide to the Lakes* (1778). Died in 1779.

West's Stations in his popular *Guide to the Lakes* (1778) Thomas West outlined various select 'stations' (view points) from which the traveller could see the best views of and over particular lakes Derwent Water (8 stations), Windermere (5 stations), Coniston (4 stations) and Bassenthwaite (5 stations). Of Windermere's 5 stations the first was on the W shore of the lake on Claife Heights in Station Scar Wood [387956] near the ferry. Originally the viewing area was just a rock but in the 1770s the appropriately named Belle View, an elaborate tower was built. It fell into disuse in the 19th century. A short walk up a steep path from the rear of the car park near the ferry brings one to the remains of this station, a dilapidated tower and a Gothic archway. Today, the height of the trees thereabouts precludes a view of the lake and the old stations nearest equivalent is probably the summit of High Blind How cleared to provide a viewpoint. West's other Windermere Stations are 2 on Belle Isle S and W sides respectively, Rawlinson's Nab and E shore of Windermere 1.6kms (1 mile) E of Ferry Point near the present day golf course.

Westing near Mungrisdale [375296].

Westmorland the district of those living west of the moors, the moors in this case being the North Yorkshire Pennines. Joined with Cumberland and part of Lancashire in 1974 to become the present-day Cumbria. Previously the boundary between Cumberland and Westmorland had traversed Dunmail Raise then up to Dollywaggon Pike. It then followed the ridge placing Helvellyn just in Westmorland and Helvellyn Lower Man in Cumberland and on to Stybarrow Dodd where it turned E to Glencoyne and into Ullswater. Leaving Ullswater it crossed Pooley Bridge and then followed the E bank of the R Eamont. In 1726 Daniel Defoe referred to 'Westmoreland' as: 'a country eminent only for being the wildest, most barren and frightful of any that I have passed over in England, or even in Wales itself.'

Westmorland Cairn southern end of the summit plateau of Great Gable and above Westmorland Crags. Built in 1876 by the brothers Westmorland. From it there is a most impressive view looking down to and over Lingmell Beck and Wasdale [211102].

Westray Embleton [152230] ...possibly named after a Roger de Westwra mentioned in 1292.

Wet Gill rises Dunnerdale Forest at 222987 and joins the R Duddon at 229978.

Wet Knotts on the craggy E face of Fleetwith Pike [217140].

Wet Side Edge ridge N of Great and Little Carrs [273020].

Wet Sleddale lonely valley running approximately 4kms (2.5 miles) SW from the A6 into the Shap Fells. The source of the R Lowther. Once it was owned by Shap Abbey. The appellation 'wet' to Sleddale (the latter tautologically means 'valley dale') suggesting a high

percentage of rain thereabouts appeared centuries before the present reservoir was filled in 1966. Two farms, Beckside and Howe, were drowned in the making of the reservoir. The latter was built to increase the stock and yield of the Haweswater system and supplies water to Haweswater reservoir and thence to Watchgate Water Treatment Works. Incidentally, it was 47 years earlier that under a Private Members Act of Parliament Manchester was empowered to buy the watersheds of Mardale, Swindale and Wet Sleddale. The reservoir has a length of 1km (0.6 mile) and lies at an altitude of 275m (902ft) [550115]. A tarmac road goes as far as the dam and a bridleway, once an old drove road, continues over the fells to Mosedale, and a path crosses Ralfland Forest to Truss Gap, Swindale. Before the construction of the reservoir the source of the R Lowther was high up on the Shap Fells but today, from its source to the head of the reservoir the stream is called Sleddale Beck and the Lowther is deemed to commence at the dam outflow. Of particular interest at the head of the dale and positioned alongside Sleddale Beck between Tonguerigg Gill and Sherry Gill are two adjoining ancient stone-walled deer enclosures scheduled as an ancient monument [556116] ...the wet valley dale.

Wet Sleddale Reservoir see **Wet Sleddale**.

Wether Hill crossed by the High Street Roman road. Between Keasgill Head and Loadpot Hill C670m (C2198ft) [456167] ...a wether is a castrated ram.

Wether How on the Great Carrs to Little Carrs ridge [267011] ...hill of the wether (castrated ram).

Wether How N of the head of Seathwaite Tarn [259999].

Wetherlam impressive mountain S Greenburn and Wrynose Pass, N Coniston Fells, W Tilberthwaite and E Swirl How and Great Carrs. It has been much quarried and mined particularly on its E slope 762m (2500ft) [288011] ...wether means castrated ram.

Wetherlam Edge steep rocky escarpment to the summit of Wetherlam from Birk Fell Hawse [291014].

Wetherlam Tarn S ridge of Wetherlam [292003].

Wetside Glenridding. Group of cottages alongside a path to Lanty's Tarn, Keldas and Grisedale [383167].

Wha House Bridge across the R Esk near Wha House Farm [204009].

Wha House Farm Eskdale. Along with Taw House it was purchased by the NT in 1942 to stop possible afforestation of the area [200008] ...'Whawes/Whaes' in the 16th century.

Whale hamlet within the parish of Lowther and just off the Askham-Bampton Grange road. Principally a farming community [522215] ...rounded hill. This hill is the prominent one between Whale and Lowther village.

Whale Beck rises at 533216 and joins the R Lowther at 518214.

Whale Farm Whale [522217].

Whalebone Arch originally a popular landmark to the left of the road which preceeded the A591 by-pass near Plumgarths. Today the arch is situated to the right of the A591 on Tolson Hall land not far from the Elba Monument. It is now only half its original height and half hidden in bushes. Who was responsible for its erection? No one is absolutely sure. Suggestions are that it was once a gift to the Cropper family from a Norwegian wood-pulp supplier or that it was erected by a member of the Bateman family, former owners of the hall. The whale bones were probably taken from a finback whale otherwise known as razorback or common rorqual (balaenoptera physalus).

Whalemoor SE Whale [531206].

Whalemoor Head S Whalemoor [532203].

Wham Sike rises ENE slope Great Mell Fell at 401255 and joins Skitwath Beck at 419275 ...stream in the marshy hollow.

Whams Moss N High Brow. S Groove Beck [365218] ...moss in the marshy hollow.

Wharton Tarn also known as High Cross Tarn and much earlier Jenny Greenteeth Tarn (so called by local children because the tarn was said to be haunted by an ugly old woman). Approximately 183m (200 yards) NW of High Cross on the Hawkshead-Coniston road. Lies at a height of C180m (C590ft) [331988].

Whasdike farm S Windermere-Kendal railway line [434979].

Whatshaw Common W A6 between Crookdale and Wasdale. Two spot-heights 485m (1591ft) and 484m (1588ft) [542061].

Whatshaw Pike on slope of Whatshaw Common overlooking Crookdale [543057].

Wheel Fell slope Swainson Knott [075079] ...from either OE or ON and referring to an early stone circle.

Wheelmire Hill Wet Sleddale [558115].

Whelp Side slope WSW/SW Helvellyn [334146].

Whelpside Gill flows down Whelp Side from Brownrigg Well [338150] near the summit of Helvellyn. Before flooding of the valley the gill joined Wyth Burn. Today it is culverted under the road and enters Thirlmere at 323137.

Whelpside Gill Spring see **Brownrigg Well**.

Whelpsty How WSW High Craghall 244m (800ft) [178915] ...steep hill frequented by whelps (young offsprings of a fox).

Whelter Beck rises Whelter Crags, W Haweswater, at 460139 and flows through Whelter Bottom to join Haweswater at 471132. Pre-flooding of Mardale the beck flowed under the old road to the W of Haweswater near the tiny community of Whelter. This, and the road, are now under the waters of the reservoir. Between the outflow of the beck and Castle Crag there is a tumuli ...the beck in the hollow or combe.

Whelter Bottom combe above Whelter Knotts and below Whelter Crags, W Haweswater. Through it flows Whelter Beck. In the combe are remains of original Norse shielings and at its foot under grassy hummocks are the graves of a Scottish raiding party ambushed thereabouts centuries ago [466137].

Whelter Crags a spur from High Raise ends at the imposing Whelter Crags which, in part, rise nearly 305m (1000ft) above Whelter Bottom and nearly 457m (1500ft) above Haweswater Reservoir [460138] ...the crags above the hollow or combe.

Whelter Knotts rise from the W shore of Haweswater. At the rear is the combe of Whelter Bottom [471136].

Whether Fold sheepfold alongside the R Kent below Kentmere Reservoir [448076] ...whether - a male sheep especially a castrated ram.

Whillan Beck rises Burnmoor Tarn at 187046. Joined by Hardrigg Gill, Ramshaw Beck and Brockshaw Beck before meeting the R Esk at Beckfoot at 169003.

Whin Ben low subsidiary summit of Whiteside. S Whiteside End and SW Gasgale Crags 413m (1355ft) [166213].

Whin Crag Eskdale. Overlooks Stony Tarn [200023] ...gorse crag.

Whin Fell in the Fellbarrow group. Its summit is Hatteringill Head at 385m (1263ft) [134248].

Whin Garth W Guards Head [092053] ...gorse/whin enclosure.

Whin Rigg ridge and summit which rises above the Screes to the S of Wastwater. The ridge posseses two summits, Illgill Head, the highest, to the NE and Whin Rigg to the SW.

Looking down from the ridge there are exceptional views down deep ravines and over scree to Wastwater 457m (1500ft) below, 535m (1755ft) [152034] ...gorse/whin ridge.

Whin Rigg Birker Moor [172989].

Whin Rigg Tarns shown but not named on the OS map. A short distance from the summit of Whin Rigg and alongside the path from the latter to Illgill Head. There are several peat moss tarns hereabouts but only three of any reasonable size. The largest is known as Whin Rigg Tarn C480m (C1575ft) [156039].

Whincop Birker Moor. NE Low Ground [178990] ...whin covered hill.

Whincop Bridge carries track to Whincop over combined watercourse of Smallstone, Highford and Little Becks [177988].

Whinfell property off the B5286 between Near and Far Sawrey [373955] ...the whin/gorse covered hill.

Whinfell Hall Low Lorton [150254].

Whinfield Ground alongside the Duddon Bridge to Ulpha road W of the Duddon [180913].

Whinlatter N of the Whinlatter Pass with its highest point Whinlatter Top at 525m (1722ft) [197249] ...gorse covered hill/slope/fell or possibly animal's lair in the whin/gorse bushes.

Whinlatter Crag Whinlatter [197246].

Whinlatter Gill rises Thornthwaite Forest near the visitor centre at 205244. Joins Hobcarton Gill at 185247 and becomes an enlarged Blaze Beck. For continuation see **Blaze Beck** and **Whit Beck**.

Whinlatter Pass leaving Braithwaite the B5292 heads over the Whinlatter Pass to High Lorton and in its upper reaches passes through the extensive Thornthwaite Forest. An earlier turnpike road over the pass was described by William Hutchinson in 1794 as 'the Steep and Alpine pass of Whinlatter'. A section of the old Roman road from old Penrith to Papcastle also utilised the pass. In 1919 the Forestry Commission began their first Lake District planting at Hospital Plantation near the head of the pass. The tree-clad area, the Thornthwaite Forest, today covers over 10 square miles. The Whinlatter Visitor Centre alongside the pass was opened in 1977 and from it, and nearby parking areas, there are miles of walks of varying lengths in and through much of the forest. The pass rises to C300m (C984ft) at 198245.

Whinlatter Top Whinlatter 525m (1722ft) [197249].

Whinlatter Visitor Centre 3.2 kms (2 miles) W of Keswick just off the B5292. Opened in 1977 it offers parking, displays, film and audio-visual programmes, a shop, local information, books, guides, maps, food, beverages, forest trails and picnic areas. At the time of writing live pictures from a camera overlooking the ospreys' nest alongside Bassenthwwaite Lake were being relayed to the centre [208245].

Whinnah E Sosgill Farm [107240] ...whin/gorse hill.

Whinnerah Gosforth. Above and to the W of the R Bleng [082053] ...possibly derived from whin/gorse. Whin Garth lies to its E just across the river.

Whinny Brow between the A66 and Latrigg [274244] ...the gorse hillside.

Whinny Crag NW Arthur's Pike and overlooking Ullswater [459209] ...gorse crag.

Whinny Howe E Longmire Road and above Latrigg Tarn [417019] ...whin (gorse) hill.

Whinny Ridding Loweswater [141219] ...land cleared of whin/gorse.

Whinnyhill Coppice off minor road from the A595 (Holmrook) to Santon Bridge [097997] ...coppice on or by the whin/gorse covered hill.

Whins small hill between the A593 and Hummer Lane [269933] ...whin/gorse covered hill.

Whins Ennerdale [099167].

Whinscales Eskdale Fell 425m (1394ft) [197033] ...the whin/gorse by the shepherd's summer hut.

Whinscars N Carter Ground [229926] ...gap/pass through the whin/gorse or windy gap. A bridleway from the fell road between Broughton Mills and Seathwaite passes through a gap between rocky outcrops on its way to Long Mire via Jackson Ground.

Whirl Howe Longsleddale. A tumulus on the E bank of the R Sprint below Sadgill [486053] ...circular hill.

Whis Gill rises below High Bank at 169996. Joins Red Gill at 158992 and the combined watercourse subsequently joins the R Esk.

Whistling Green Ulpha. Off the Duddon Bridge to Ulpha road [196927].

Whit Beck rises to the W of Lonscale Fell at 280272 and joins Glenderaterra Beck at 295252 ...either willows by the stream or the white stream.

Whit Beck a stream with many lengthy tributaries including Aiken Beck/Drycloff Gill and Blaze Beck/Whinlatter Gill/Hobcarton Gill/Littlethwaite Gill. Aiken Beck meets a substantial Blaze Beck alongside Scawgill Bridge and the combined watercourse becomes Whit Beck. Sware Gill enters shortly afterwards and the beck continues past High Lorton where it is joined by Eller Beck before entering the R Cocker at 153248 ...more than likely the white stream with reference to the white foam of the 'roaring' stream.

Whit Crags Corney Fell [135910].

Whitbeck Bridge carries the B5289 over Whit Beck [156249].

Whitbysteads SW Askham [506228] ...site of Wyle's or Witeby's house.

White Bog marshy area between Howe Grain and Atkinson's Grain [462172].

White Bridge Dalemain Estate private bridge across the River Eamont [479267].

White Cap slightly E Rowantree Crag [530129].

White Cove between Sheepbone Buttress and Comb Crags [178142].

White Crag behind Raven Crag, W A591 [413047].

White Crag Great Langdale. W Raven Crag [281065].

White Crag NNW Sleddale Hall. Overlooks Wet Sleddale [539117].

White Crag Ralfland Forest [545135].

White Crag S slope of Helm Crag above Easedale [326089].

White Crag Birker Moor. Between Rowantree Beck and Highford Beck [195975].

White Crag WSW Dock Tarn [269141].

White Crag N arete of Mellbreak [143199].

White Craggs see **Clappersgate**.

White Crags between Stanah Gill and Fisherplace Gill overlooking Dale Head [325185].

White Crags W Thirlmere adjoining Rough Crag [312153].

White Crags overlooking Langstrath from the W [265119].

White Cross Bay E shore of Windermere. During the war years a large factory occupied the land adjoining the bay and bungalows housed many families. Here, Sunderland Flying Boats were built, tested on the lake, and serviced. Today, various types of boats have replaced the flying boats on the lake and the area left when the buildings were demolished provides hard standing for luxury holiday homes and touring caravans. The whole is now known as the White Cross Bay Leisure Park and Marina. Much earlier the bay was known as Craam's Bay but consequent on the drowning of two young men nearby in 1853 a small white cross was erected as a memorial and the bay and foreshore consequently became known by its present title. Years ago the cross fell into deep water in the bay but was retrieved in 1969 and re-set on its plinth. In late 1999 the White Cross Bay Leisure Park was bought by John Morphet, managing director of South Lakeland Caravans Ltd., for £10,000,000 from the TJH group [393004].

White Esk fellside N of the upper reach of the River Calder [082132] ...white ash tree.

White Gill rises Low Wythow, Yewdale Fells, at 305992 and joins Yewdale Beck at 308986.

White Gill rises on the southern slope of Blea Rigg at 297075 and for a considerable distance downwards enjoys a subterranean existence under boulders and scree. Joins Great Langdale Beck at 304062 ...the white, dry, open gill.

White Hole below Rowantree Knotts, Kentmere [449053] ...dry hollow.

White Horse Bent SE Bannerdale Crags. Steep slope leading to R Glenderamackin [343282] ...bent either refers to the curved hillside or to a type of grass called bent but whose was the white horse?

White How SSW Wormshell How. WNW Iron Crag 444m (1457ft) [205975].

White How above Pike How, Pike How Close and the River Duddon [241993].

White How Due E of Great Paddy Crag. S Plough Fell [163908].

White Howe alongside Pinch Crags and overlooking Scandale from the E [382079] ...the dry, white hill.

White Howe Fawcett Forest. E Bannisdale Head. Trig. point at 530m (1739ft) [524042].

White Knott Barton Fell, E Ullswater. SW on the escarpment of Swarth Fell is White Knotts [469215] ...white, dry, open + rocky hill.

White Knotts E Howtown on steep escarpment of Swarth Fell. NE on the escarpment of Barton Fell is White Knott [450196].

White Lion Hotel Patterdale. Early 19th century. In its brochure the hotel claims that Wordsworth was in its bar as news arrived that Nelson had died at Trafalgar. However, he and Dorothy were staying nearby at Side Farm with their friends the Luffs and it was actually there, at breakfast time that they heard of the victory at Trafalgar and of the death of Lord Nelson [397159]. For more information see Wordsworth's *A Guide Through the District of The Lakes* and *Portrait of the Wordsworth Country* by Robert Sands.

White Maiden of the three principal summits on Walna Scar ridge White Maiden is the middle one at 608m (1995ft) [254957].

White Moss Sleddale Forest. Spot-heighted at 392m (1286ft) [480020].

White Moss WSW Brat's Moss [169022].

White Moss adjoining White How [202974].

White Moss Common & Baneriggs between Grasmere and Rydal. White Moss (called by Thomas West over 200 years ago 'Grasmere Hill') is a low fell its summit being only 142m (466ft) [346067]. However, nearby there is an excellent viewpoint particularly over Rydal. Baneriggs (earlier Bainriggs) is the wooded area between White Moss Common and Rydal Water and is bisected by the A591 [345062]. The name Baneriggs in this case means 'the short ridge' referring to that from White Moss Common to the present A591 and Grasmere (lake).

Two roads and a track lead to Grasmere from Rydal. The highest, and most picturesque, is the old coffin track or trail by which, in early times, coffins were carried from Rydal to Grasmere. This was named by Dr Arnold 'Old Corruption'. It is a favourite of many walkers. The middle road, over White Moss, the old turnpike road before the low level road was built in 1825/6, and was nicknamed 'Bit by Bit Reform' and the low level route, the present

A591, was 'Radical Reform'.

Both White Moss Common and Baneriggs were favourites of the Wordsworths and this is reflected by names in William's poems: Glow-Worm Rock; John's Grove; Mary Point and Sara Point and the Wishing Gate (Sarah's Gate). For more information on these and directions to them consult *Wordsworth and the Lake District* by David McCracken or enquire at the Wordsworth Museum, Grasmere.

White Moss House Hotel alongside the A591 near Rydal Water. Built in 1730 and acquired by William Wordsworth for his son Willie. Subsequently owned by the Wordsworths until the 1930s [351066].

White Moss Quarry foot of White Moss Common. Today a car park [348065].

White Moss Tarn described by W Heaton Cooper in his *The Tarns of Lakeland* as a 'small reedy pool'. It lies alongside the old coffin trail from Grasmere to Rydal over White Moss Common and below Nab Scar. Situated at an altitude of 114m (374ft) [347068]. There is another White Moss Tarn outside the National Park alongside the rough track between Bouth and Low Hay Bridge W of the foot of Windermere.

White Napes rocky area SW slope Great Gable [208101].

White Oak rocky outcrop to the SSE of Gavel Pike [119181].

White Pike NE Clough Head between it and Old Coach Road [339230].

White Pike lowest of the three summits on the Walna Scar ridge 598m (1962ft) [249956].

White Pike Birkby Fell 442m (1450ft) [151956].

White Pike on the ridge running NW from Pillar 782m (2566ft) [169124].

White Pike on the slope of Red Pike (Buttermere) S of its summit [160149].

White Raise large cairn on Moor Divock [489224].

White Raise tumuli, Ralfland Forest [535134].

White Side W slope Helvellyn range leading up to Whiteside Bank [337166]. The actual summit on the Helvellyn ridge is not named but is usually referred to as White Side. Summit cairn 863m (2831ft) [338167].

White Sike rises alongside the Old Coach Road from Wanthwaite to Dockray at 367226 and joins Thornsgill Beck at 377235.

White Stile on path between Field Head and Low Dale Park/Thwaite Head [360913].

White Stones a summit on the Band, 568m (1863ft] [261061].

White Stones summit above Green Side. E Stybarrow Dodd. W Glencoyne Head 795m (2608ft) [353187].

White Stones property alongside the A591 [242266].

White Stones crags S Carl Side [253272].

White Wall wall of rock E of the Birker Moor Road and Sike Moss [185967].

Whiteacre Crag between the road E Haweswater and the reservoir shore. Below Mardale Banks [479123].

Whitebanks foot of Toddle Bank. Off the Cleator Moor to Ennerdale Bridge road [051151].

Whitegill Crag alongside White Gill and a favourite of rock climbers [297072].

Whitehowe Wood alongside the R Kent, Kentmere valley [460005].

Whiteless Breast lower slope of Whiteless Pike which levels out at 439m (1440ft) [182183] before final steep ascent to the summit of Whiteless Pike.

Whiteless Edge narrow ridge between Wandope and Whiteless Pike [183195].

Whiteless Pike a lower summit of Wandope approached from the latter by the narrow Whiteless Edge and the col of Saddle Gate 660m (2165ft) [180190] ...unknown origin.

Whiteoak Beck rises Whiteoak Moss at 122176. Met by Highnook Beck at 130206 and the combined watercourse meets Park Beck at 135210.

Whiteoak Moss boggy area enclosed by Floutern Kop, White Oak and Hen Comb. Source of Whiteoak Beck which flows N to Park Beck and Grain Gill which flows W to join with other streams to become Croasdale Beck [126177].

Whiteside extensive area of land between Longsleddale and Bannisdale [522013]. Summit is Whiteside Pike, a distinctive rocky cairned dome summit spot-heighted at 397m (1302ft) [521016]. A lower height is 369m (1211ft) at 524016 ...the dry, open hillside.

Whiteside third highest peak on the Grisedale Pike-Hopegill Head-Gasgale Crags-Whiteside ridge 707m (2319ft) [170219] ...white mountain shieling (summer pasture).

Whiteside Bank see **White Side**.

Whiteside End Kentmere Park [450030] ...end of the white, dry, open hillside.

Whiteside End end of Whiteside overlooking Lorton Vale and the foot of Crummock Water [164219].

Whiteside Pike see **Whiteside**.

Whiteside Plantation alongside Longmire Road, E slope Troutbeck valley [417024].

Whiteside Wood small plantation ESE slope Whiteside Pike and above road to Bannisdale [530011].

Whitesike Moss N Sandbeds Moss [368235].

Whitestone Moor Helton Fell [474207] ...the white stone moss referring to the limestone exposed hereabouts.

Whitestones Waberthwaite [112932].

Whitesyke Nether Wasdale [122044].

Whitfell highest point in an isolated range running N from the Corney to Duddon Bridge fell road to the ancient track between Waberthwaite and Ulpha. A large cairn crowns its summit at 573m (1880ft) with nearby a trig. point just 1m (3.3ft) lower [158930] ...white hill.

Whitrow Beck rises Waberthwaite Fell at 148934. Met by Red Gill at 138939 and flows by Row Farm to join the R Esk alongside Waberthwaite Marsh at 096947.

Whittern Gill rises 127232 and joins Dub Beck at 114228. The latter enters Loweswater.

Whity Head W Swirl Band [270001].

Whoap unusual named fell to the NE of Lank Rigg and rising above Whoap Beck, a tributary of the R Calder, and Red Gill, a tributary of Worm Gill. Rises to a grassy domed summit at 511m (1676ft) [099129].

Whoap Beck rises between Lank Rigg and Whoap at 095124 and joins the R Calder at 084130.

Whorl Gill gill alongside Sillathwaite Wood [065129] ...the EPNS suggests that the title may be derived from 'hwyfel' which means circle as it lies below the circular Blakeley. On the other hand it could be derived from 'quarrel' meaning quarry.

Whorney Side above Whorneyside Force on Buscoe Sike and below Crinkle Crags [259052].

Whorneyside Force spectacular waterfall below Hell Gill, Buscoe Sike, and sometimes referred to as Hell Gill Force [261054].

Widdy Gill rises near the Three Shire Stone at 278027. Meets Wrynose Beck at Widdygill Foot at 288030 and from the confluence the water takes the name R Brathay ...possibly the wide stream.

Widdygill Foot see **Widdy Gill**.

Wide Close Torver [276945].

Widepot alongside Widepot Sike [525095] ...the white, dry, open deep hole or hollow.

Widepot Sike rises WNW Great Saddle Crag at 522088. Joins Saddlecrag Gill at 526094 and this joins Sleddale Beck at 524099.

Widewath Heltondale [501210]. Nearby two bridges over Heltondale Beck are scheduled as ancient monuments [503208] [501208] ...the ford (across Heltondale Beck) by the willows.

Widow Hause NE of the summit of Graystones. Rises to 404m (1325ft) at 183270.

Wilcock Wood Winster Valley [411933].

Wild Boar Hotel Crook. Built as a farmhouse about 1660 it later became an inn. Its name is derived from the legend that Richard Gilpin slaughtered the last wild boar in England on or near the site of the hotel. However, this deed is also attributed to Sir Richard Musgrave on Wild Boar Fell and more than likely to other persons and places throughout the country [435954].

Wilderness Wood adjoning Thackthwaite Wood [146231].

Wilfin Beck source Three Dubs Tarn at 377973. Fed by stream from Moss Eccles Tarn. Joins Windermere at 384941.

Wilkes How subsidiary summit of the Fellbarrow Group. WSW Fellbarrow 263m (863ft) [120240]. Disused quarry lies just N of its summit on the 260m (853ft) contour.

Wilkinson's Dub River Derwent, Borrowdale [254163].

Wilkinson's Wood alongside the Nether Wasdale to Gosforth road [109047].

Wilkinsyke Farm Buttermere [176169].

Willdale E Bampton. Separated from Cawdale by the Hause and Hause End [487172] ...wild valley.

Willdale Beck rises head of Willdale at 482165. Joined by Intack Sike before meeting Cawdale Beck at 497177. The latter becomes Howes Beck which joins Haweswater Beck. This subsequently meets the R Lowther.

William's Beck rises High Rigg at 306219 and flows down to meet Naddle Beck at 297221.

Williamson Memorial/Monument see **High Knott**.

Willie Wife Moor WSW/SW slope Dollywaggon Pike [337126] ...whoever she was, Willie's wife has been commemorated in the name of a large area of fellside.

Willy Fold sheepfold alongside Peathill Gill [536119] ...Willy Winder's sheepfold?

Willy Gill rises the Forest at 529042 and joins Borrow Beck alongside Borrowdale Head at 544041.

Willy Scrow W Coniston [291975] ...personal name. See **Glossary** for the derivation of 'scrow'.

Willy Winder Hill N Haskew Tarn, WNW Seat Robert [522116] ...possibly Willy Winder of Wet Sleddale.

Willybrag Gill rises Whinlatter at 194252 and joins Aiken Beck at 194258.

Willygrass Gill rises Dock Tarn and joins Stonethwaite Beck at 268134 ...Willy's land by the stream. On the other side of Stonethwaite Beck is Alisongrass, Alison's land.

Wilson's Bield sheepfold between Dale Head and High Spy [232155].

Wilson Knott W Belle Grange [380990].

Wilson Place farm, Little Langdale [318034] ...Wilson's dwelling, presumed to be Isaac Wilson of the late 17th and early 18th centuries and reputed to have connections with the Kendal mint cake family of that name.

Wilson, Prof. John see **Elleray**.

Wilton Hill W A66-Mungrisdale road [367285].

Wind Gap pass between Pillar and Little Scoat Fell C760m (C2493ft) [168118] ...an obvious name similar to Windy Gap between Great Gable and Green Gable.

Wind Hall Gosforth [073043].

Windebrowe formerly Old Windebrowe and once owned by Raisley Calvert. Between the River Greta and the A66. Today owned by the Calvert Trust Keswick. The old Windebrowe Tithebarn alongside was restored by the Calvert Trust in 1980 [277240]. See also **Calvert, Raisley** and **Calvert Trust**.

Winder Green alongside High Winder [493238] ...the shieling offering shelter from the wind + grassy spot.

Winder Hall Farm E Pooley Bridge. SW Celleron. Off the minor road from the B5320 to Askham. At one time called Low Winder. Main block dated 1612 [492245].

Winder Hill SW Bampton, WNW Littlewater 315m (1033ft) [502172] ...wind-swept shelter or pasture + hill.

Winder Wood W Winder Hall Farm [485245].

Windermere the village of Windermere (yes! a village - in April 1996, the council decided unanimously to keep village status for Windermere and Bowness) lies 2.4kms (1.5 miles) from the large expanse of water from which it takes its name. Bowness is actually on the lake shore. With the coming of the railway from Oxenholme in 1847 it was originally intended to continue it to Ambleside but opposition to this was so intense that the company finished it at the little hamlet of Birthwaite. However, to attract tourists to the scenic lake the station was also named Windermere and from that date the hamlet and later the village became Windermere. Over the succeeding years expansion of both Bowness and Windermere has resulted in a continuous stretch of buildings joining the two places together.

Across the road from the station approach Rigg's, coach proprietors, built the Windermere Hotel in 1847 at a cost of £1,327. It opened as Riggs Windermere Hotel. Windermere Station was a substantial girdered structure until the mid-1980s when a new smaller station was built. The old station was sold to Booth's supermarket which opened after considerable conversion in April 1985. The former railway sidings nearby are now occupied by Lakeland Ltd., formerly Lakeland Plastics. Windermere and its surrounding area boasts many country house hotels, hotels and guest houses most of which are listed in the current *Cumbria: The Lake District* published by the Cumbria Tourist Board. Principal attractions include the Windermere Steamboat Museum; World of Beatrix Potter Attraction, Bowness; Brockhole, the National Park Visitor Centre; the gardens of the Lakeland Horticultural Society at Holehird, or a leisurely walk up to Orrest Head 238m (781ft) from the summit of which there are marvellous views [414993]. Suggested reading - *Portrait of Windermere* by Christopher D Taylor (1983) and *Windermere in the 19th century* by Oliver M Westall (1991).

Windermere lake Most popular of the Cumbrian lakes and the largest expanse of inland water in England. It is 16.9kms (10.5 miles) in length and at its widest 2kms (1.25 miles) between Pull Wyke and Low Wood. Deepest point in the top basin lies centrally off White Cross Bay and is 64m (210ft). This depth is only exceeded by Wastwater 76m (249ft) and Blea Water 68m (223ft). In the S basin below Cockshot Point the greatest depth is 42m (138ft). It was near the deepest section in the N basin that Sir Henry Seagrave lost his life in June 1930, while attempting to break his own world water speed record of 98.76 mph. Actually, he was very badly injured when his boat flipped over during a run and he died later that day at Belle Grange. The greatest tragedy, however, occurred in October 1635, when 47 passengers, horses and ferryman drowned when the ferry capsized in rough weather, (see also **Windermere Ferry** below). For the statistically minded the lake contains approximately 70,000 million gallons. Twenty two islands or islets (see under individual names) are named on the OS map, from Seamew Crag in the N to Blake Holme in the S and ranging in size from the extremely small Maiden Holme to relatively sizeable islands such as Thompson's Holme or the largest Belle Isle. *The Place Names of Westmorland* identifies 8 others Bull Head, Costrells Rocks, David Wyke, Haws Holme, Matson Shoal, Ringing Crag, Skirtful Crags and Snake Holme.

Principally Windermere is fed by the rivers Brathay and Rothay, Pull Beck, Stencher Beck, Hol Beck, Blelham Beck, Trout Beck, Cunsey Beck and the lake itself feeds into the R Leven at Newby Bridge where a weir maintains the water level. At Calgarth a pumping station, built in 1972, extracts water and transfers it to the Watchgate Treatment Plant where it is distributed to parts of South Cumbria, Lancashire and Manchester.

During the season, April-November, regular boat services are operated by the Bowness Bay Boating Co. (who bought the Windermere Iron & Steamboat Co. in 1993) with *MV Swan*, *MV Teal*, *MV Tern* and launches *Miss Cumbria*, *Miss Lakeland* and *Miss Westmorland* between Lakeside (where connections can be made with the Lakeside-Haverthwaite railway) and Bowness and Waterhead. A 34kms (21 mile) trip around the lake can also be made. Boats can also be privately chartered. At Lakeside there is the notable Aquarium of the Lakes which, according to its brochure, has over 30 displays under one roof including the UK's largest collection of freshwater fish. Windermere is fished for brown trout, pike, perch, eels and char.

Last century Windermere has been the scene of much seaplane activity. At Hill of Oaks a seaplane school was operated by the Northern Aircraft Co (wound up in November 1916). Slightly earlier it had been requisitioned by the Royal Navy Air Service. In the early 1900s the 'step' float for seaplanes and float planes was developed at Hill of Oaks by Captain Wakefield. A factory at Cockshot Point for the Northern Aircraft Co later became the HQ of the Royal Navy Air Service. The latter completed a move to Hill of Oaks in 1916. For a period after the First World War Cockshot Point was used as a base by the Avro Transport Co who also operated pleasure and passenger flights. During the Second World War at a large factory at White Cross Bay, 35 Short Sunderland Flying Boats were built, tested on the lake and serviced by a workforce of 1500 personnel. There are stories that at least one flying boat was scuttled in the lake in 1944. On February 3 1943, a Falcon 2 glider made its first successful take off from Windermere. The glider is now exhibited in the Windermere Steamboat Museum. Thirty two years earlier the first successful hydro-aeroplane had also flown from Windermere.

In 1998 Windermere had three bathing water sites designated by the EC - Fell Foot, Millerground and YMCA Lakeside. Unfortunately, in 2001 two of the sites, Fell Foot and Lakeside, failed to meet stringent water quality standards.

In January 2001 a helicopter pilot escaped when his plane crashed into the lake 0.8 kms (0.5 mile) from Storrs Point. He managed to exit from the flooded cabin and swam to the shore. The aircraft was subsequently recovered by salvage experts.

Windermere Ferry for well over 500 years there has been a ferry across Windermere on the present route. Originally oar driven the last of this kind, *Mary Ann*, plied until 1869 when she was replaced by the first steam and chain operated ferry. The *Mary Ann* and her huge oars can now be seen in the grounds of the Windermere Steamboat Museum. A second steam ferry was commissioned in 1914. This was replaced by *Drake* (named after the county surveyor for Lancashire, Mr C D Drake) in 1954. Six years later this was converted to diesel.

Taken out of service in 1990 and replaced in that year by the present larger *Mallard*. In 1635 47 passengers (including a wedding party), horses and ferryman drowned when the ferry sank in rough weather. *The Windermere Ferry: History, Boats, Ferrymen and Passengers* by Dick White was published in 2002.

Windermere Golf Club Cleabarrow, Windermere. Alongside the B5284. Founded in 1891. A hilly, heathland course of 18 holes, one of only two 18-hole courses in the Lake District National Park. The other is Keswick Golf Club [420962].

Windermere Hotel see **Windermere**.

Windermere Iron Steamboat Co established in 1848. Operates *Swan*, *Teal* and *Tern* on Windermere. Company bought by the Bowness Bay Boat Co in 1993.

Windermere Marina Village E shore Windermere 1.6kms (1 mile) S Bowness. Time ownership luxury cottages built around a substantial marina [399958].

Windermere St Anne's School Windermere, see **St. Anne's School**.

Windermere Steamboat Museum Rayrigg Road, Windermere. Opened in the 1970s and houses a unique collection of steam, motor and sailing boats. These include *Dolly*, built in 1850, the oldest mechanically powered boat in the world; *Esperance*, built for industrialist H W Schneider, and which he used daily to travel from his home at Bowness to Lakeside. This served as a model for Captain Flint's house boat in Arthur Ransome's *Swallows and Amazons*; and a 1780 sailing yacht. Open daily from Easter to October inclusive.

Windermere Youth Hostel High Cross, Bridge Lane, Troutbeck [405103].

Windgap Cove Ennerdale side of Wind Gap. Source of High Beck [164121].

Winds strong gusty winds and gales often affect the high fells when the valleys below are relatively calm and the mountain rescue services are sometimes called out to help people blown over and consequently injured or bruised. On occasion I have been compelled to cling to rocks or boulders or even lie flat on the ground until an extremely strong gust has passed and then edge forward to repeat the process. Similarly, a colleague returning from Great Gable via Windy Gap (not called that for nothing), Green Gable and Brandreth was blown over so many times he lost count and was quite exhausted after his experience. People are frequently blown over and receive minor or substantial injuries. As an example, in April 1994, a fell walker was blown over by a gust of wind at Sty Head and suffered a fracture. The following October another fell walker received mild hypothermia as a result of being overcome by effects of severe prolonged gusting wind on Scafell. In October 1995, three people each suffered a fracture after being blown over in extremely windy conditions at Castle Nook, Newlands. Mountain rescue parties were called to the Knott, Ullswater, when a fell walker was blown off balance and as a result sustained a fractured ankle. In the same month another walker was blown over by a gust of wind on the Band and received head, leg and arm injuries and suffered shock. Of course, added to all this in winter is the significant and unpleasant wind chill factor. Although generally speaking valleys are calm in relation to mountain tops some valleys are known for sudden winds. Those in the NE of Lakeland for example such as Mardale can, at times, feel the effects of the Helm Wind blowing down from the Cross Fell area. Ridges at the head of valleys are particularly prone to be frequently blasted by the wind funnelling up the valley and increasing in intensity as it does so. The ridges at the head of Kentmere provide a notable example of this. Rydal Water has its own phenomenon in very windy weather, a water spout (see **Rydal Water**).

Winds Gate point where the fenced Birker Moor Road passes between walls and becomes an unfenced road [185958].

Windsor Farm off the Gosforth to Wastwater high road. Home of the Wasdale Springs natural spring water [121057].

Windsurfing see **Boating & Sailing**.

Windy Gap col between Green Gable and Great Gable. A very windy place at times. In neolithic times was probably a route taken to transport stone-axes from nearby 'factories' to West Cumberland and beyond C750m (C2461ft) [215105].

Windyhowe Hill N Hubbersty Head. Ridge rises to 103m (338ft) [426918].

Winscale Hows E slope Seatallen [146086] ...shieling/hut on the windy hill.

Winster attractive village alongside the A5074, Bowness-Levens road and nestling in the valley of the R Winster from which it takes its name. Many little whitewashed cottages one of which, in the centre of the village, is now a private residence, earlier known as Compston House but more commonly known today as the old post office. This dates from 1600. The local hostelry, the Brown Horse, dating from the early 1800s, is a popular eating and drinking establishment. The present church, dedicated to Holy Trinity and consecrated in 1875, replaced a much earlier building on an adjacent site. Near to the church the Winster School building possesses a datestone 1849. Two notables associated with the village and valley were Jonas Baber, former clockmaker (see **Bryan House Farm**) and William Pearson (1780-1856), naturalist and poet and close friend of William Wordsworth. Not far distant, noted childrens' author Arthur Ransome lived at Low Ludderburn from 1925-35. Electricity only reached Winster in 1949. During the 1960s Manchester Corporation Waterworks submitted plans to build a huge reservoir in the valley but these plans were not approved [419935] ...see **River Winster**.

Winster House Georgian property W slope Winster valley [410928].

Winster Vicarage built 1904 and used as a vicarage until 1978 when it passed into private ownership. Now called Crag House from its proximity to Cat Crag nearby [419938].

Winster, River see **River Winster**.

Winter Crag farm, Martindale. Alongside Howe Grain Beck and near Martindale old church [433183].

Winter Crag on N ridge of Beda Fell. Serrated crags overlooking Winter Crag Farm and Howe Grain Beck [431184].

Wintergroove Gill rises E Scot Crag and ESE/SE Hart Side at 365193. Joins Deepdale Slack and the Nick at 366187 to become Glencoyne Beck.

Winterseeds Grasmere. Property off the A591 [338089] ...winter area of sown grass.

Wise Een Tarn largest of the tarns on Claife Heights with a dam and boat-house at its N end. Once used for research by the Freshwater Biological Institute but now privately owned. Fishing prohibited C200m (C656ft). Footpaths from Near and Far Sawrey pass Moss Eccles Tarn and then between Wise Een and Scale Head Tarns to join the old pack-horse track from Hawkshead via Colthouse to Belle Grange [370976] ...tarn among the willow trees.

Wisenholme Beck rises Sharp Knott at 109201. Subsequently becomes Wood Beck which joins the R Marron at 065211.

Wishing Gate see **White Moss Common & Baneriggs**.

Wistow Crags on slope of Pillar overlooking Mosedale [174117].

Withe Bottom below and to the W of Whitfell [152932].

Withered Howe Kentmere [465061] ...possibly the hill frequented by the weasel/stoat.

Withesike Bay Derwent Water [253203] ...the bay into which flows the stream bounded by willows.

Wolf Crags overlooking old coach road from St John's in the Vale-Dockray [355222]. A Bristol Beaufighter crashed here in 1943 killing its two aircrew.

Wolf Howe slightly W A6 and E Lamb Pasture 331m (1086ft) [543024] ...wolf hill.

Wolfcrag Fold sheepfold [349222].

Wolfcrag Moss between Wolf Crags and old coach road (St John's in the Vale-Dockray) [358226].

Wolfhowe Gill rises the Forest, Fawcett Forest, at 541034 and flows alongside then through Wolfhowe Plantation and under the A6 to meet Ashstead Beck at 551019.

Wolfhowe Plantation on slope of Wolf Howe [545027].

Wolt Bridge Scales-Hutton Moor End-A66 road. Crosses Trout Beck at 358268.

Wonder Hill Birker Moor. N High Ground. SSW Low Ground 196m (643ft) [174986] ...possibly 'Under Hill'.

Wood Bank W Thirlmere. S Fisher Crag [307161].

Wood Close above Town End and Dove Cottage, Grasmere [345070].

Wood Close Point southern projection of High Wray Bay, Windermere [378003].

Wood End alongside track off minor road from A595 (Holmrook) to Santon Bridge [102992].

Wood End W shore Bassenthwaite Lake off the minor road from Braithwaite to the A66 [221271].

Wood Farm slightly W River Winster and adjoining Fox Crag Plantation [410914].

Wood Farm Troutbeck. Alongside Mirk Lane and adjoining Newclose Wood. Originally Lowwood Farm but name changed to avoid confusion with the Lowwood Hotel. 17th century but much altered and enlarged and the house has been a private residence for over 70 years. Over the centuries many generations of Troutbeck Birketts made it their home. Of the 48 tenements recorded for the manor of Troutbeck in 1675 no less than 20 were occupied by Birketts [394016].

Wood Farm alongside the minor road from Aikbank Mill to Brandlingill [120262].

Wood Heads Grizedale Forest Park [330951].

Wood Hill above the confluence of Mossy Beck and Heltondale Beck [494205].

Wood House SE Pickthall Ground [212902].

Wood House Buttermere. Overlooks Crummock Water and is 0.8 kms (0.5 mile) from Buttermere village. 17th century property acquired by the NT in 1993. Leased from the Trust and is now a guest house [169174].

Wood Howe Haweswater's only island. Prior to flooding it was a projection from the Rigg [477119].

Wood Knotts Slope Hesk Fell [177955].

Wood Moss Tarn Grizedale Forest Park. Largest of the Grizedale tarns. Also known as Hob Gill Tarn. Hob Gill flows in and out of it C160m (C525ft) [328918].

Wood Nook SE Naddle Bridge and W Woodnook Gill [513156].

Wood Side upper edge of afforestation below Gale Crag and above Hartsop Hall [395122].

Woodbank Gill rises 283160 and meets Bleatarn Gill at 276159 just before the latter joins Watendlath Tarn.

Woodcock Stone off A591. On low south slope of High Rigg [310204].

Woodend farm and cottage near Devoke Water. Once a sizeable Quaker settlement with a Quaker House and school. In the 19th century 17 families lived here. Between the farm and the tarn are Quaker graves [167964].

Woodend W shore Bassenthwaite Lake alongside the minor road from Braithwaite to the A66. Woodend Brow lies to its NW and Wood End to its SE [219273].

Woodend Bridge carries the road over Birker Moor across the upper reach of Crosby Gill [179963].

Woodend Brow above Hursthole Point, Bassenthwaite Lake [215276].

Woodend Height Birkby Fell. SW Woodend C480m (C1575ft) [157954].

Woodend Pool rises SW Woodend at 166962 but does not flow into Devoke Water. Instead flows N then E before being joined by small streams including Little and Great Gills, Freeze Beck and Ulgra Beck to become Crosby Gill which enters the R Duddon at 201937.

Woodfell Gill steep slope of Branstree, E of Mardale Head. A stream is shown on the map flowing down most of the gill but apparently disappearing before it reaches Haweswater [475106].

Woodfoot NW Bampton [509189].

Woodfoot Ennerdale [080165].

Woodgate Waberthwaite [111943].

Woodhouse Islands Crummock Water [166176].

Woodhow farm alongside the Nether Wasdale to Wastwater road. The curved red sandstone porch bears the date 1757 [140042].

Woodhow Tarn Nether Wasdale. In depression WNW Woodhow. Said to contain pike and perch C60m (C199ft) [136043].

Woodhowe Moss between the head of Naddle valley and Hare Shaw. As its name suggests it is a marshy area [498136].

Woodland Grove E A593 [248909].

Woodlands alongside the B5292 NW Braithwaite [225241].

Woodnook Gill rises 516154 and joins Haweswater Beck at 513160.

Woodside E of the Pooley Bridge to Howtown road and alongside Aik (oak) Beck [473230].

Woodside off minor road from the A595 S to Corney [119943].

Woodside Road connects the A5074-Bowland Bridge road with Cowmire Hall [426901].

Woody Crag E Seathwaite Tarn [256984].

Woof Crag above the Old Corpse Road between Mardale and Swindale. WSW Hare Shaw C490 (C1608) [493129] ...named after local family of James Woofe.

Woof Gill rises S Great Hollow at 256113 and joins Langstrath Beck at 264108.

Woof Stones alongside Woof Gill [263111] ...stones frequented by wolves or from local family name, Woof.

Woolpack Inn Eskdale. Like its predecessor, the Pyet's Nest at Penny Hill, the centuries-old Woolpack was built to serve the packhorse routes through Eskdale. Its name, like other Woolpacks throughout the country, signifies the large trade in the transport of wool [190010]. A wool pack consisted of 240lbs.

Wordsworth Hotel Grasmere. Formerly the Rothay Hotel. The latter was last used as such in 1970. The building subsequently became very dilapidated and years later the Wordsworth Hotel rose from its 'ashes'. No direct connection with Wordsworth but his memory lingers on through the names of the Prelude Restaurant and the Dove and Olive Branch lounge bar [337075].

Wordsworth, William (1770-1850). Described as the greatest poet of the English Romantic movement he was Poet Laureate 1843-50 and was a true lover of the Lake District. He lived at Grasmere from 1799-1813 and at Rydal from 1813-50. During these years William, more often than not accompanied by his sister Dorothy, made many journeys into and over the local mountains, along valleys and over passes. For a comprehensive account of places visited by him and also those reflected in his poetry consult *Wordsworth and the Lake District: A Guide to the Poems and Their Places* by David MacCracken; *Portrait of the Wordsworth County* by Ronald Sands; *Guide Through the District of the Lakes in the North of England* by William Wordsworth, and the *Grasmere Journals* by Dorothy Wordsworth. Wordsworth geneology: William (1770-1850); Dorothy [sister] (1771-1855); Mary [wife] born 1770, married William 1802, died 1859; John [William's brother] (1772-1805); Christopher [William's brother] (1774-1846); children of William and Mary - John (1803-75), Dora (1804-47), Thomas (1806-12), Catherine (1808-12) and William (1810-83).

Wordsworth's Cottage see **Rooking**.

Work How E Stock Ghyll and on slope of Wansfell [396052] ...'Walkhowe' in 1707.

World's Biggest Liar Competition see **Santon Bridge**.

Worm Gill rises E Whoap at 103129. Joined by Short Grain, Red Gill, Hole Gill, Bleaberry Gill, Long Grain, Swarth Beck, Cawfell Beck and Caw Gill before joining the R Calder at 106090 ...snake ravine.

Worm How alongside Tarn Beck [236980] ...snake hill.

Wormhole Hill Bethecar Moor [313904] ...snake (hagworm) hollow on the hill.

Wormshell How Birker Fell. ESE Green Crag [207979] ...possibly snake hill from 'wyrm', a snake.

Woundale valley down which Woundale Beck flows before it joins Trout Beck [411076] ...probably valley with the twisting stream.

Woundale Beck rises at the head of Woundale at 409085 and joins Trout Beck at 417063.

Woundale Raise alongside the A592, W Woundale Beck [407068] ...in 1777 it was described as 'another (heap of stones) supposed to have been a British sepulchre'. Raise, (hreysi), a cairn or heap of stones.

Woundell Beck Ennerdale. Silvercove Beck and Deep Gill join forces at 132134 and become Woundell Beck which flows into the R Liza at 134140 ...stream in the snake valley.

Wray consists of two hamlets, High and Low Wray [373000 and 372012 respectively] on the W side of Windermere. Low Wray Farm, rebuilt in the 19th century, has been owned by the National Trust since 1948 and the Trust has a camping site here. The Wray area also includes Wray Castle and Wray Church. An early incumbent of the latter was Canon Rawnsley, founder and first secretary of the National Trust. High Wray lies to the S of Low Wray. High Wray Farm was bequeathed to the National Trust by Mr W Heelis (husband of Beatrix Potter) after his death in 1945. Although swimming is not generally recommended in Windermere, High Wray Bay is often used as a swimming area ...secluded nook/remote corner of land.

Wray Castle Low Wray, W shore Windermere. Castellated mansion built in the 1840s for a Liverpool surgeon, Dr James Dawson. For many years a residence and Beatrix Potter spent holidays here. Given to the National Trust in 1929 by Sir Noton Barclay to commemorate his term as Lord Mayor of Manchester (the nearby Dower House formerly known as Wray Cottage was acquired by the Trust in 1948). The castle has served as a youth hostel, headquarters of the Freshwater Biological Association (now at Ferry House, Far Sawrey), a Merchant Navy radio officer cadets' school 'RMS Wray Castle' and today a specialist electronics and telecommunications training centre. There are many interesting trees in its grounds one of which, a mulberry, was planted by William Wordsworth in 1845. The grounds are open to the general public but not the castle [375010].

Wray Crag N of track from Stile End, Kentmere, to Sadgill, Longsleddale, and alongside the path from this track to Shipman Knotts [473053] ...'roebuck' crag.

Wray Crag W shore Windermere [377014].

Wray Crags W slope Brim Fell ridge [268988] ...possibly the crags frequented by deer.

Wray Gill rises Silver How at 325067 and flows down over several spectacular cataracts to join Grasmere at 334071 ...either from 'ra' meaning roebuck and therefore the gully frequented by deer or from 'vra' referring to a nook or corner of land.

Wraymires Tarn 183m (200 yards) N Wise Een Tarn, C190m (C623ft) [369979] ...the tarn in a remote boggy area.

Wreay adjoining Bennethead [445238] ...secluded nook or corner.

Wren Crag on High Rigg overlooking St John's in the Vale 311m (1020ft) [316201]. Known locally as 'Wern Crag'.

Wren Gill off the head of Longsleddale. Originally called Wrangdayll or Wrangdale becoming Wren Gill sometime during the late 18th or early 19th century. Down it flows Wren Gill, the farthest headstream of the R Sprint, and at its foot is the long-disused Wrengill Quarry [468088] ...originally the twisting valley and later the twisting ravine.

Wren Gill the farthest headstream of the R Sprint. Rises on the ESE slope of Harter Fell at 463092 and takes the name Sprint when it joins watercourses from Gatescarth and Brownhowe Bottom at 478082.

Wrengill Quarry alongside Wren Gill off the head of Longsleddale. Possibly the earliest, or at least one of the earliest slate quarries in the Lake District. Disused since Italian prisoners of war working it were sent home [474086].

Wrestling see **Cumberland & Westmorland Wrestling**.

Wrighthow W edge Foxbield Wood. S Wrighthow Crags [108035].

Wrighthow Crags W edge of Foxbield Wood. N Wrighthow [108036].

Wrynose Beck three major tributaries rise on Wrynose Fell at 277038, 279039 and

282039 and combine at 283035 to become Wrynose Beck. This meets Widdy Gill at 288030 and together they become the R Brathay ...for origin of name see **Wrynose Pass**.

Wrynose Bottom near the foot of Wrynose Pass. Here a present-day footpath joins and follows the old Roman road for a distance before the latter probably forded the Duddon just before Cockley Beck [260022].

Wrynose Breast breast of fell N Wrynose Pass [267026].

Wrynose Bridge bridge which carries the road over Wrynose Pass across Wrynose Beck [285033].

Wrynose Fell large fell area to the N of the Wrynose Pass. From it streams flow N and S to join Great Langdale Beck and the R Brathay respectively [278041].

Wrynose Pass connects Little Langdale with the Duddon valley, a distance of 6kms (4 miles). At Cockley Beck on the W side the pass meets the Hardknott Pass road. The present road down the valley parallels the old Roman road from Galava, Ambleside, to Ravenglass via Hardknott Fort. Wrynose Pass rises to 393m (1289ft) at 277027 near the Three Shire Stone. Years ago pack horse trains would ascend and descend the pass to and from Greenodd or Ravenglass and it was also a major drove road. In the 19th century when smuggling was rife hereabouts illicit whisky was taken across the pass and it is recorded that there was "many a brush with the Excise men. Straw or sacks would be tied to the wagon wheels to reduce the noise, but if the Excise men pursued them they (the smugglers) had boulders ready to roll down the steep hillside." Both Wrynose and Hardknott Passes were part of a military training area during the Second World War and both road surfaces were seriously damaged. Much restoration work was undertaken before the pass road was reopened in 1947 ...pass of the stallion(s) or the pass over the twisted headland.

Wyke, The see **The Wyke**.

Wyke Gill see **The Wyke**.

Wyke Plantation Grasmere. Above the Wyke [331063].

Wyth Burn rises below Greenup Edge at 388201. Joined by Flour Gill, Birks Gill, Mere Beck, Cat Gills, Blackcrag Gill and Ill Gill, before entering Thirlmere at 322131. Practically all Lakeland streams are either becks or gills but Wyth Burn and nearby Green Burn appear to have what is unusual for Lakeland streams, a Scottish derivation. However, this is not so, as the burn is believed to be derived from the OE 'burna'. Similarly, there are four apparent Scottish glens alongside or near Ullswater - Glenamara, Glencoyne, Glenridding and Caiston Glen. Here the derivation, according to the English Place Name Society, is from the Welsh 'glyn'.

Wythburn prior to flooding of the Thirlmere valley the village of Wythburn, just N of Dunmail Raise, comprised two inns (the Nag's Head [earlier the Horse Head] and the Cherry Tree), a large hall, a church, and several farms. The Cherry Tree Inn was described by Wordsworth in his lengthy poem *The Waggoner*. The Nag's Head closed in 1928. All that now remains as a result, directly or indirectly, of the flooding of the valley is the church (a 17th century church was rebuilt in the 18th century and restored and extended in 1872), a farm now called West Head but earlier Steel End Farm (the original West Head Farm was closed by the water authority many years ago and now lies in ruins), and the Wyth Burn. The shortest walking route, but a steep one, to the summit of Helvellyn starts from the car park at Wythburn alongside the A591. This badly eroded footpath was repaired in 2003. Today there is much afforestation around the area but there was probably even more two centuries ago when it was said by Wythburnians that a squirrel might have gone from Wythburn Chapel to Keswick without alighting on the ground [322130] ...willow valley.

Wythburn Fells fells and crags W and SW Wythburn [315129].

Wythburn Head Tarns five pools on the Wyth Burn at the foot of an area known as the Bog. From here the Wyth Burn flows steeply over a series of waterfalls on its way to join Thirlmere [305115].

Wythe Gill Whiteside. Stream emerging from it at 165224 drops down to be joined by Coldgill Beck and this joins Hope Beck just before the latter enters the R Cocker at 154237 ...willows by the stream.

Wythe Gill rises from a spring on the slope of Kirk Fell at 169265 and ultimately joins the R Cocker at Low Lorton.

Wythe Sike SW Wythop Hall [200282].

Wythop Beck Wythop Beck and Beck Wythop rise within yards of each other S Wythop Hall. The latter flows E into Bassenthwaite Lake near Beck Wythop cottages. Wythop Beck's two farthest headstreams rise at 196276 and 201276 respectively on the N slope of Lord's Seat and the stream flows NW through Wythop Mill and then E as Dubwath Beck to join Bassenthwaite Lake near its foot at Dubwath.

Wythop Dale/Valley the valley opens up at Wythop Mill and continues to its head near Wythop Hall. A peaceful valley along which flows Wythop Beck. It is described by Alfred Wainwright as "...a charming and secluded natural sanctuary in an idyllic setting, a place of cal" ...willow valley, wooded valley or, as it appeared in the 16th century as 'wed', 'wid' - wide, would suggest wide valley. See also **Wythop Mill**.

Wythop Hall see **Wythop Dale/Valley**.

Wythop Mill hamlet in the Wythop valley in close proximity to the village of Embleton. The mill from which the hamlet takes its name was once used to provide timber for the Wythop Estate. Today, restored and renovated, it displays woodworking machinery and hand tools and along with an adjoining coffee shop is popular with tourists. At the head of the valley is the 17th century Wythop Hall built on the site of an earlier property. To the Hall's S are the substantial remains of a silica works which had a short life in the 1930s. Mid-valley, near Kelswick, are the remains of an ancient chapel one wall of which is inscribed 'Site of Wythop Old Church'. The present church, built in 1864-5 and dedicated to St Margaret, is situated on the N side of Sale Fell alongside the road to Routenbeck and the A66. Wythop Beck flows through the hamlet [178298].

Wythop Moss large boggy/marshy area in the Lord's Seat Group [183278] ...either the boggy area above the willow valley or that above the wide valley C320m (C1050ft) [179271].

Wythop Woods W bank of Bassenthwaite Lake [210291].

Y

Y Boulder huge boulder, split by a Y-shaped crack, in Mosedale. Provided much sport for early climbers and today basic and short climbs for beginners in rock climbing [177104].

Y Gully St Sunday Crag [366135].

Ya Gill rises Kinniside Common at 084118 and joins Long Gill at 077123. This meets the River Calder at 073124 ...obscure origin.

Yachting see **Boating & Sailing**.

Yarlside slope leading up from Wasdale Beck towards Wasdale Pike. W Hazel Bank [538078] ...Earl's seat similar to Hugh Seat, Simon Seat, Lord('s) Seat which are named after members of the de Morville family, early Barons of Westmorland.

Yarlside Crag Great Yarlside, overlooking Crookdale [525073].

Yaud Mire below Dawson Pike [241952].

Yeastyrigg Crags overlooking Yeastyrigg Gill [237064] ...crags to the E of the ridge running S from Esk Pike and between the R Esk and Yeastyrigg Gill/Lingcove Beck.

Yeastyrigg Gill rises just below Ore Gap at 240071 and joins Lingcove Beck at 238056.

Yew Band band of crags W side Holme Fell [311007].

Yew Bank Hardknott [233032].

Yew Bank Blawith Fells. E The Knott. Rises to 207m (679ft). Ancient cairn E summit [262910].

Yew Barrow Dunnerdale Fells [206920].

Yew Beck rises ENE Arnsbarrow Hill at 315913 and joins with Bell Beck at 331892. The combined watercourse meets Grizedale Beck at Rusland at 327889.

Yew Crag High Rigg overlooking A591 and Naddle Valley [307208].

Yew Crag overlooks Blindtarn Moss [314078].

Yew Crag W of the A592 and middle reaches of Ullswater. Summit of the crag approached by stone steps up its face. An excellent viewpoint overlooking Dobbin Wood and Ullswater, with a memorial seat to rest one's weary bones after a short but exhilarating climb [415206].

Yew Crag S slope Yewbarrow [174075] ...crag frequented by ewes.

Yew Crag NE Rosthwaite. E track to Watendlath [264152].

Yew Crags foot of Hardknott overlooking Eskdale [222022].

Yew Crags WSW Elterwater village [324047].

Yew Pike Yewdale Fells [300986].

Yew Pike Dunnerdale Fells. SE Ulpha [204926].

Yew Tree N of the Gosforth to Wastwater high road. E Kid Beck [118055].

Yew Tree Beck see **Yewdale Beck**.

Yew Tree Farm alongside narrow road connecting St John's in the Vale church with minor road, B5322-A66. ENE Low Rigg summit [309230].

Yew Tree Farm Crook. To its N is an ancient look-out point called the Monument [451956].

Yew Tree Farm Yewdale, see **Yew Tree Tarn**.

Yew Tree Farm Rosthwaite, see **Rosthwaite**.

Yew Tree Tarn alongside the A593, Coniston to Skelwith Bridge road, and NNE of the well-known and much painted and photographed Yew Tree Farm from which it takes its name. An 1891 OS map shows the site of the old yew tree behind the farm. This was blown down during a violent storm in December 1894. Yew Tree Farm was purchased by the

National Trust in 1930. The tarn, also the property of the National Trust, was created in the 19th century by James Marshall of Monk Coniston Hall who dammed a stream and marshy area. Today, fishing for brown and rainbow trout, is controlled by the Coniston and Torver Angling Association, 107m (351ft) [322004]. The first of the National Trust's holiday cottages was sited alongside the tarn, a timber chalet on the W bank.

Yewbarrow a mountain which suggests a huge whale or the upturned hull of a boat rises to the W of Wasdale Head and its ridge drops down to Wastwater. This long rough ridge is practically enclosed by crags but there is relatively easy scrambling from its N and S 628m (2060ft) [173085] ...the hill on which ewes are pastured.

Yewbarrow Hall up to the 19th century called Ubarrow Hall. The oldest building in Longsleddale, a medieval pele tower, is incorporated in the 17th century hall [504026] ...yew hill hall.

Yewbarrow Wood on slope behind Yewbarrow Hall, Longsleddale [506027].

Yewcrag Quarries N Honister Hause. Worked from 1848 [223142].

Yewdale attractive valley NNE of Coniston along which flows Yewdale Beck and for over 3.2kms (2 miles) runs the A593, Coniston to Skelwith Bridge road. Yewdale was a particular favourite of Wordsworth, Ruskin, Tennyson and Arthur Ransome. Wordsworth in his epistle to Sir G H Beaument writes of Yewdale:

Descend and reach in Yewdale's depths, a plain
With haycocks studded, striped with yellowing grain -
An area level as a Lake and spread
Under a rock too steep for man to tread...

Ruskin wrote his *Yewdale and its Streamlets* (1888) and Arthur Ransome spent a holiday there and consequently Low Yewdale farmhouse became Dixon's Farm in *Winter Holiday* [314994] ...one of many place names derived from its association with the yew tree. This particular one 8m (27ft) in circumference is said to have been blown down by a violent storm in the late 19th century.

Yewdale Beck streams which flow down and through the inappropriately named Dry Cove and Dry Cove Bottom between Blake Rigg and Wetherlam Edge and others which rise alongside the path N of Hole Rake and on Yewdale Fells eventually combine to form Yewdale Beck. The principal tributaries, however, are Henfoot Beck which rises below Hen Tor on the slope of Wetherlam at 292008 and its major tributary Swallow Scar Beck. Another headstream is Crook Beck, the combination of two streams one of which rises near Hole Rake at 292993 and the other at 297992. Yewdale Beck flows through the deep and attractive Tilberthwaite Gill and on down Yewdale. Subsequently joined by Yew Tree Beck (a combination of Guards Beck and Tom Gill) and White Gill before entering Coniston Water near Water Head Pier at 310971.

Yewdale Crag impressive buttress overlooking Yewdale and the A593 [308993].

Yewdale Crag Moss Yewdale Fells. N Yewdale Crag [306996].

Yewdale Fell Side steep side of Yewdale Fells overlooking Yewdale [310996].

Yewdale Fells W Yewdale. The fells end with fine crags and buttresses overlooking Yewdale. The most impressive being Yewdale Crag [305995].

Yewdale Moss Yewdale Fells [301998].

Yewdel Knott N Ellers [248181].

Yewgrove Gill rises N of Rest Dodd at 431141 and joins Bannerdale Beck at 425148.

Yewry Sike rises at 251954 and joins the R Lickle at 243945.

Yews ENE Grandsire, NW Borwick Fold [437975].

Yews the *Guinness Book of Records* points out that the oldest British tree is the yew and that the oldest is approximately 3,500 years old. Conversely the erudite *Encyclopaedia Britannica* notes that estimates of longevity of such trees have been based on the fusion of close growing trunks none of which is more than 250 years old. However, the Lake District claims many very old yews including the Lorton Yew under which George Fox preached in 1653; the Borrowdale Yews; the Martindale yew and one in Armathwaite Hall grounds. The Lorton Yew is claimed to be 1,200 years old and the other three over 2,000 years of age. That in the grounds of the Old Church Hotel, Ullswater, is possibly 1,500 years old and there are several old-established ones in the churchyard of St Olaf's, Wasdale Head. *The Cumbria Yew Book* by Ken Mills (1999) provides many details on yews generally and lists 27 of Cumbria's ancient yews.

Yews off the A5074 [401949].

Yews Mire between Winder Hill and Howes Beck [504175]. Second element suggests that it was once a mire or bog but today the name appears on the 2.5" map over scrubland.

Yewthwaite Comb between Cat Bells and Maiden Moor. Source of Yewthwaite Gill [242190].

Yewthwaite Gill rises Yewthwaite Comb at 241190 and joins Newlands Beck at 234199.

Yewthwaite mine sited on the slope of Cat Bells [240194] with a high level on Trap Knotts [243189]. Earliest record is the mid-19th century and the mine was abandoned in 1893.

Yewtree Cottage alongside narrow road connecting St John's in the Vale Church with minor road, B5322-A66. ENE Low Rigg summit [309229].

YMCA Centre Lakeside. Celebrated its Golden Jubilee in 2002.

Yoadcastle highest summit of Birkby Fell 494m (1621ft) [157952] ...possibly the hill where nags were pastured.

Yoke ridge and peak between the Garburn Pass and Ill Bell. Highest summit is at 706m (2316ft) [438067] but there is a lower cairned summit at C660 (C1265ft) [436062]. Normally climbed as part of the Kentmere Horseshoe ...origin unknown but could take its name from the possible resemblance of a yoke between its two summits.

Yorkshire Rake Crags Ill Crag [226072].

Youdell Tarn on the ridge between Great Langdale and Easedale. Shown but not named on the OS map. It was at one time a large tarn formed by peat digging but encroaching plant life has diminished its size. Takes its name from an early owner of Robinson Place, John Youdell. Other names given to it include Lang How, Robin Gill, Yew Crag, Brigstone and Silver How. However, the latter two are tarns in their own right, 369m (1211ft) [318068].

Youth Hostels there are 28 YHs in the Lake District and those within this work are:

Ambleside, Waterhead	Black Sail, Ennerdale
Borrowdale (Longthwaite)	Buttermere
Coniston (Coppermines House & Holly How)	Derwent Water (Barrow House)
Elterwater	Ennerdale (Gillerthwaite)
Grasmere (Butterlip How & Thorney How)	Eskdale (Boot)
Hawkshead	Helvellyn (Glenridding)
Honister Hause	Keswick
Langdale (High Close)	Patterdale (Goldrill House)
Skiddaw House	Thirlmere (Legburthwaite)
Wastwater (Wasdale Hall)	Windermere (High Cross)

For grid references and further information consult individual entry.

LAKELAND GLOSSARY

Ay a stream, eg Brathay, Rothay.

Band an elevated tract of land forming a division between two areas of less elevation, eg the Band between Oxendale and Mickleden.

Barrow a small hill. Sometimes a tumulus, eg Whitbarrow, Gowbarrow, Stybarrow or from ON 'erg' eg Berrier, Bethecar, Rannerdale, Winder.

Beck a brook or stream, eg Aira Beck, Scaleforce Beck.

Bent coarse fell grass, eg Bents, Benty Howe.

Bield a shelter for animals or humans, eg Aaron's Bield, Fox Bield, Nan Bield, Pate Bield and numerous unnamed bields.

Birk birch tree, eg Birk Fell, Birkrigg, Birks.

Blea dark, dark blue, eg Blea Tarn, Blea Water.

Borran a heap of stones or burial ground, eg High and Low Borrans.

Both a herdsman's hut or cottage, eg Armboth.

Brant steep, eg Branstree, Brant How, Brant Street, Brantwood.

Brock badger, eg Brockhole, numerous Brock Crag(s).

Bull like 'lad' 'bull'is sometimes given to individual boulders or crags. In the case of boulders those exceptionally large eg Bull Crag, Gray Bull.

By a village, a hamlet, or an isolated farmstead, eg Aldby, Appleby, Bybeck.

Caer fort or castle, eg Carhullan, Carlisle.

Caester ancient fortification, eg Huncaster, Muncaster.

Cairn a pile of stones either marking a way up to the summit of a fell or on the summit itself.

Cam/Camb crest of a hill, eg Catstye Cam (Catstycam).

Cape sharp headland of a lofty ridge, eg the Cape (St Sunday Crag).

Capel/Capell/Caple/Capple horse, nag or stallion, eg Capel Crags, Capell Crag, Caple Crag, Capplebarrow.

Caw/Calva calf, eg Caw Fell, Great Calva.

Caw/Cau cold, eg Caudale, Cawdale.

Clapper large flat stones used to make a rough bridge, eg Clappersgate.

Cock woodcock/blackcock, eg Cockup, Cocklakes Hill, Cockley Beck, Great Cockup,

Comb(e) a hollow enclosed on three sides by a hill or hills, eg Black Combe, Mousthwaite Combe.

Cop top, crest, summit of a hill, eg Kinniside Cop.

Crag a rocky cliff, eg Brock Crag, Stybarrow Crag.

Cuddy a donkey or ass, eg Cuddy Beck.

Demesne Land see **Main(s)**.

Den similar to dale or dean and means a valley, eg Mickleden.

Dodd bare rounded summit, eg Great Dodd, Rest Dodd, Stybarrow Dodd, Watson's Dodd.

Dore opening or gap in a ridge between walls of rock, eg Great Dore, Mickledore.

Dow wood pigeon/dove or in some cases dark or deer, eg Dow Crag, Dowthwaite.

Drumlin see **Gazetteer**.

Dub a pool in a river, eg Dubhow Beck, Meethom Dub, Plum Dub.

Dun a hill fort or stronghold, eg Dunmallard Hill.

Dungeon deep fissure or cavern, eg Dungeon Ghyll.

Edge a narrow ridge or arete, eg Sharp Edge, Striding Edge, Swirral Edge.

Elter whooper swan, eg Elter Water, Elterwater.

Emel caterpillar, eg Embleton.

Erne eagle, eg Erne Nest Crag (head of Deepdale), possibly Arnison Crag (Ernes) Crag.

Esk water, eg Esk (river). Possibly also means 'ash'.

Fell from the ON 'fj(i)all' meaning hill or mountain, eg Bowscale Fell, Place Fell, Souther Fell.

Force a substantial waterfall, eg Aira Force, High Force, Rowantree Force, Scalehow Force.

Foulmart/Foumart polecat, eg Foul Mart, Foulmart Hill, Foumart Gill.

Garth enclosed small piece of land, eg Garth Heads, Gatesgarth, Scogarth.

Gate a way or gap between fells or crags when it follows a word, eg Caspel Gate, Walmgate. Goat or goats when preceding a word, eg Gatebeck, Gatescarth.

Gavel looking like a gable end, eg Great Gable (old name Great Gavi(e)l, Gavel Pike.

Gawk/Gouke/Gauk/Gowk/Cawk cuckoo, eg Cawk Cove, Gowk Hill.

Gill/Ghyll usually a short narrow ravine or gully. In most cases, the name is given to the stream which flows down it, eg Dungeon Gill and countless other gills.

Gimmer female sheep that has not yet borne a lamb, eg Gimmer Crag.

Grain the fork of a stream or the bisected head stream of a river, eg Howe Grain, Sealhole Grain.

Grise wild boar or pig but also refers to a place where pigs were pastured, eg Grisedale, Mungrisdale.

Ground see **Gazetteer**.

Gutter stream/rivulet in a channel, eg Red Gutter, Toddle Gutter, Ulgill Gutter.

Hag/Hagg/Hogg clearing in a wood, eg Collier Hagg, Hagg Wood. Hag/Hagg occasionally refers to a snake. See below.

Hag/Hagworm a snake, eg Hagworm Gill.

Hause head of a pass, a col, or a connecting ridge, eg Deepdale Hause, Esk Hause, the Hause.

Haver/Hafri oats, eg Haverbrack, Haverigg Holme.

Haw(s) usually hill/hills but in some cases enclosure, eg Bull Haw Moss, Hollin House Haw.

Hell from the Norse and means - rushing. Signifies very swift flowing water, eg Hell Gill.

Heron in low regions it refers to the heron but when the name is given to crags or other high places it refers to the golden eagle or the sea eagle, eg Heron Crag, Heron Pike (eagle), Heron Island, Rydal Water (heron).

Hesk/Hest horse, eg Hesk Fell.

Holm/Holme an island in a lake, a water meadow or resembling an island, eg Cherry Holm (Ullswater), Grass Holme (Windermere), Haverigg Holme.

Homestead ancient habitation.

Hop/Hope/Op small valley, eg Hartsop, Wandhope.

How a low hill, eg Gummers How, Round How, Silver How.

Ing/Ings meadows, outlying pastures, eg Ings (near Windermere and near Threlkeld). Ing may also be used as a connecting participle as in Distington, Frizington, Killington.

Intack/Intake a piece of land taken in from waste and enclosed, eg Great Intake, Intack Sike.

Keld/Kel spring, eg Keld, Threlkeld.

Knott a rocky outcrop on a hill, eg Bell Knott, Knott Halloo, Swineside Knott.

Lad frequently applied to individual boulders and crags. Derived from 'hlaed' meaning pile, eg Lambert Lad, Ladstones, Lad Crags.

Lath/Laithe a barn, eg Hugh Laithes Pike, Laithwaite.

Ling heather, eg Lingmell, Lingmoor Fell, Lingy Holm.

Lonnin/Lonning lane or by-road, eg Green Lonning.

Main(s) demesne land. Land surrounding a house or manor retained by the owner for his own use, or a farm (home farm) attached to a mansion house, eg Mains Farm, Mainsgate.

Man a summit cairn. Sometimes a height just below the summit of the range, eg Benn Mann, Helvellyn Lower Man, Little Man (Skiddaw), Skiddaw Man.

Mart pine marten, eg numerous Mart Bield, Mart Crags.

Meal sandhills, dunes, eg Eskmeals, Meolbank.

Mere a lake, eg Buttermere, Thirlmere, Windermere.

Nab/Neb a promontory, an extremity, a projection of a hill, eg Nab Scar, Skelly Neb, The Nab, Thwaitehill Neb.

Naddle point or sharp end of a ridge or hill. Also there is a slight possibility that it refers to snake being derived from the ON 'naor' meaning adder, eg Naddle Beck, Naddle Forest.

Ness/Nese nose. A projection on a lake, eg Bowness.

Nether lower, eg Nether How, Nether Stainton, Nether Wasdale.

Park see **Gazetteer**.

Pen a hill, head, a summit, eg the Pen, Penruddock.

Pie/Piot magpie, eg Piot Crag.

Pike a hill or mountain with a prominent peak, eg Dollywaggon Pike, Pike of Blisco, Scafell Pike.

Pinfold a pund/pound, enclosure enclosed by stones, eg Pinfold, Pinstones Point.

Pound 'pund', an enclosure.

Raise a heap of stones or a tumulus. A high place usually on a ridge, eg High Raise, Raise.

Rake a straight steep passage or fissure through rocks or rough ground, eg Hole Rake, Jack's Rake (Pavey Ark), the Rake (Sheffield Pike).

Ridding clearing, eg Glenridding, Riddings.

Rigg usually a ridge but can also refer to a field name as a cultivated strip of land, eg Birk Rigg Park, Birk Riggs, High Rigg, Matterdale Rigg, Riggindale.

Roche Moutonee bedrock or protuberance that has been shaped by glacier overriding. The side facing the oncoming ice is smooth and formed by glacial abrasion while the side away from the moving ice is steep and rough and is considered to be the result of the plucking action of the glacier.

Ros/Ross horse, eg Rosgill and more than likely Rossett Gill and Rossett Pike.

Saetr see **Shieling**.

Sca/Scar a cliff or rock face, eg Knipescar, Scafell.

Scale a rough hut or shelter, eg Scaleforce Beck, Scales, Scales Fell,

Scarth a notch in a ridge, eg Gatescarth, Scarth Gap.

Scree rough debris between cliffs. Loose stones which have fallen from cliffs, eg Blue Screes, Helvellyn Screes, Red Screes.

Scrow dialect word meaning disorder, untidyness. In the case of land an untidy or higgledy piggledy area, eg Dixon Scrow, Foul Scrow, Willy Scrow.

Shieling hut or shelter (sometimes temporary) used by those tending cattle or sheep on high or remote ground, or a summer pasture for grazing. From ON 'saetr' and usually expressed as seat, side or sett, eg Ambleside, Rossett, Satterthwaite, Seat Sandal. See also **Side** below.

Side side of a hill, eg Side Farm [farm on the side of a hill (Place Fell)], Side House & Pike.

Sike/Syke a small stream usually flowing through marshy ground or one which drains marshy ground, eg Black Sike, Layburn Sike, Skeggleswater Sike.

Skelly/Schelly a rare fish, eg Skelly Neb.

Slack a slight depression/hollow between two elevations, eg Deepdale Slack, Witherslack

Slape smooth or slippery, eg Slape Stone, Slapestone Edge.

Snarker snake, eg Snarker Moss, Snarker Pike.

Spout a waterfall, eg Cam Spout.

Spring as an adjectival word usually refers to a plantation/copse of young trees, eg Spring Plantation, Springs Hill, Springs wood.

Stand/Stang formerly a pole or stake usually positioned to signify a boundary, eg Stand Crags, Stang End, Stangs.

Steel/Stile steep, eg Steel Fell, High Stile. In certain cases may refer to a family name.

Stickle a sharp peak, eg Harrison Stickle, Pike of Stickle.

Stile see **Steel/Stile**.

Sty a steep path or ladder-like path.

Tarn in **Gazetteer**, eg Angle Tarn, Grisedale Tarn, Red Tarn.

Tewit plover/lapwing, eg Tewfit Mire, Tewit Tarn.

Thwaite a clearing. A piece of cleared ground, eg Bassenthwaite, Dowthwaite, Esthwaite, Legburthwaite, Stonethwaite.

Tod/Todd fox, eg numerous Tod Crags, Tod Rigg.

Ton/Tun enclosure , farmstead, village, town, eg Bampton, Broughton, Dalton, Workington.

Ul/Ull wolf, eg Ullock Pike, Ullscarf, Ulpha.

Ul/Ull occasionally an owl, eg Ulcat Row, Ulgill Gutter.

Walla grey or darkish coloured or place of the British, eg Walla Crag, Wallabarrow, Wallow Crag.

Wath/With a ford or wood, eg Crookwath, Langwathby, Skitwath Beck, Wath or Witherslack.

Wether a castrated ram, eg High Wether Howe, Wether Hill, Wetherlam.

Whelp wolf, eg Whelp Side, Whelpside Gill.

Wic/Wick building/dairy farm, eg Butterwick, Cunswick, Keswick.

Wick/Wyke creek or bay, eg Bleawick, Sandwick, the Wyke.

Worm snake. From the OE 'wyrm' or 'wurm', eg Great/Little Worm Crag, Wormshel.

Wyth willow, eg Wythburn, Wythop.

Wray landmark. Also the reverse, a secluded piece or corner of land, eg High Wray, Low Wray, The Wray, Wray Quarter. Less frequently derived from 'roe-buck' ie Wray Crag and possibly Wray Gill.

Yew an refer to either the yew tree (OE 'iw'), eg Fallen Yew, Yewbarrow Hall & Wood (Longsleddale), Yewdale or to the ewe (OE 'eowu') when it becomes a corruption of ewe, eg Yew Crag (Watermillock), Yewbarrow (Wasdale).

Place Names

Representative names signifying flora and fauna or which could possibly suggest the same. Several names may have alternative meanings and consequently appear under different headings

When, after an initial name a / appears the word after it follows the original adjective i.e. Ash Crags/Hill/Knott refers to Ash Crags, Ash Hill, Ash Knott or Cockley Beck Bridge/Fell/Gill refer to Cockley Beck Bridge, Cockley Beck Fell and Cockley Beck Gill.

Adder see **Snake**.

Alder Elder Beck/Coppice/Cottage; Eller Beck/Dubs/How; Elleray; Elleray Bank/Farm; Ellerbeck; Ellerbeck Bridge/Farm; Ellergarth; Ellerhow; Ellerhow Moss; Ellers; Ellers Beck/Bridge; Ellerwood; Little Ellers; Old Elleray; Seatoller.

Angelica Wanthwaite.

Apple Tree Applethwaite; Applethwaite Common/Gill; Appletree Worth; Appletree Worth Beck; Black Apple Tree; Crab Tree Dale Wood; Crabtree Beck/Brow/Cottages; Crabtreebeck.

Ash Tree Ash; Ash Banks/Crag(s)/Gill/Hill/Knott/Spring/Tarn; Ash Gill Beck; Ashes; Ashes Beck/Coppice/Lane; Ashcrag Holme; Ashley Green; Ashleymoor Plantation; Ashness Bridge/Farm/Fell/Gill/How/Wood; Askham; Askill; Askill Knott; Belt Ash Coppice; Esk; Esk Hause; Eskin; Esthwaite; Hesket Farm/Wood; Pots of Ashness, White Esk.

Aspen Tree Esp Ford; Esps Farm.

Badger Badger Rock; Brock Barrow/Bield/Crag(s)/How; Brock Stone; Brockhole; Brockle Beck; Brocklebank Ground; Brockstones; Brockhole Hag; Brockshaw Beck; High Brock Crag(s); Low Brock Crag(s); Low Pate Crag; Pate Bield.

Barberry Barbary Rigg.

Barley Barley Bridge; Barton; Bigert Mire; Bigertmire Pasture.

Bass perch family, see **Perch**.

Bee Bee Holme; Honeybee Wood.

Beech Beech Grove; Beech Hill.

Bent Grass see **Grass**.

Bilberry see **Bleaberry/Bilberry**.

Birch Tree Birch Crag(s); Birch How; Bird Dyke; Birk Bank/Crag/Dub/Fell/Field/Force/Hagg/Haw/How/Knott/Moss/Rigg(s)/Side; Birker Beck/Fell/Force/Moor; Birkerthwaite; Birket(t); Birkett Bank/Cottage; Birkett Wood Farm; Birkhead; Birkhouse Moor; Birkin Knott; Birkmoss Plantation; Birkrigg; Birkrigg Brow; Birkriggs Wood; Birks; Birks Bridge/Brow/Coppice/Gill/Head/Plantation/Road/Wood; Birkthwaite Beck; High Birk; High Birk How(e); Birthwaite Road; Burthwaite Bridge; Burtness Comb/Wood; High Birkin Knott; High Birks; Low Birks; Old Burtness; Silver Bay/Crag/Point.

Bird Bird How.

Bird Cherry Hegdale.

Blackcock/Woodcock Cock Cove/Hag/Point; Cockhag Plantation; Cocklakes Hill; Cocklaw Fell; Cockle Hill; Cocklethwaite; Cockley Beck/How/Moss; Cockley Beck Bridge/Fell/Gill/Great Intake/How; Cockly Crag/Pike; Cockrigg Crags; Cockshot Point; Cockshott Wood; Woodcock Stone.

Blackthorn see **Sloe**.

Bleaberry/Bilberry Bleaberry Crag/Fell/Gill/Haws/Hill/How/Knott/Tarn; High Bleaberry Knott; Low Bleaberry Knott.

Boar see **Pig/Boar**.

Bog Myrtle see **Gale**.

Box Tree Boxtree.

Bracken Ain House; Ainhouse Plantation; Bracken Gill/Hause/How(e)/Platt/Riggs/Wreay; Brackenbarrow Farm; Brackenburn; Brackenclose; Brackenrigg; Brackenthwaite Fell/Hows; Brackenwife Knotts; Briar Rigg/Shot; Briery; Briery Close; Brier's Intake Coppice.

Broom Bannel Head; Bramley; Bramley Seat; Broom Bank/Fell/Hill/Lane/Riggs; Broomhill Plantation; Glenridding; The Broom.

Bull see **Cattle**.

Burdock Cleabarrow.

Burtree see **Elder/Burtree**.

Buzzard Buzzard Crag/Knott; High Buzzard Knott; Low Buzzard Knott.

Cabbage Kail Pot.

Calf see **Cattle**.

Cat see **Wildcat**.

Caterpillar Embleton.

Cattle Bowness; Bull Close/Coppice; Bull Close Coppice; Bull Crag; Bull Haw Moss; Bull Haw Moss Beck; Bulman Strands; Butharlyp How (Butterlip How); Calf Close/Cove/Crag/Hole/Wood; Calfclose Bay/Wood; Calfcove Gill; Calfgate Gill; Calfhow Pike; Calfhowe Crag; Calflay Wood; Calgarth Hall/Park; Caw; Caw Fell/Gill/Moss/Tarn; Cawfell Beck; Cawk Cove; Cow Bridge/Brow/Close Gill; Cowcove Beck; Cowperthwaite Intake; Cowrake Head; Cowsty Knotts; Fusethwaite Yeat; High Bull Crags; Kye Wood; Low Bull Crags; Striceley Fell/Intake; Strickland Ees/Ketel/Roger.

Cherry Cherry Holm.

Chestnut Chestnut Hill.

Chicken Chicken Rock.

Cock Cockpit; Cockpit Hill.

Cormorant/Shag Calfclose Bay; Scarf Stones; Strandshag Bay.

Corn Cornclose Land; Cornhow.

Cow see **Cattle**.

Crab Apple see **Apple**.

Crane Frank Tranearth; Matthew Tranearth; Tranearth Beck; Trantrams; Tranthwaite Hall.

Crow Crackhill Nook; Cracoe Close; Crow Holme/Park; Crowhow End; Crowmire.

Crowberry Crowberry Haws/Hill.

Cuckoo Cawk Cove; Cuckoo Brow Wood; Gowbarrow Fell/Hall/Park; Gauk Hill, Gowk Hill.

Curlew Carlew Crag; Curlew Crag.

Damson Damson Dene Hotel; Damson Valley (Lyth Valley).

Deer Buck Barrow; Buck Castle/Crag(s)/Moss/Pike/Stone/Well; Buckbarrow; Buckbarrow Crag/Moss/Well; Buck Stone; Buckholme; Buckstone Hows; Buckstones; Buckstones Jump; Calf Screes; Deer Bield Crag; Deer Bields/Howe; Deer Enclosure; Deerclose Cottage; Doe Green; Doe House Gill; Dow Crag; Fawn Crag; Great Hartbarrow;

Hart Crag/Head Farm/Hill/Side; Hartcrag; Hart Howe; Harter Fell; Hartley Beck; Hartrigg; Hartsop; High Buck How; High Hartsop Dodd; Hind Crag/Gill/Side; Hindscarth; Hindscarth Crags/Edge; Little Hartbarrow; Little Hart Crag; Little Harter Fell; Low Buck How; Rayrigg Bank/Hall/Wood/Wyke; Rayside; Wray Crag(s)/Gill.

Dill Delicars.

Dock Dock Tarn; Docker Nook; Dockernook Crag/Gill/Wood; Dockray; Dockray Nook.

Dog/Hound Dog Crag; Dog Hill; Dog How; Houndshope Cove.

Donkey/Ass Cuddy Beck/Crag.

Dove/Pigeon Dove Cottage; Dove Crag(s)/Nest/Nest Wood; Dovecote Wood; Dovedale; Dovenest Crag; Dow Bank/Crag; Dowthwaite; Dowthwaite Head.

Duck Drunken Duck Inn.

Eagles Ancrow Brow; Arnison Crag; Eagle Crag (numerous); Erne Crag; Erne Nest Crag; Heron Crag(numerous)/Heron Pike/Stones.

Eel Eel Beck/Coop/House; Eel House Bridge/Intake; Pod Net; Podnet Tarn.

Elder Burtree Bank/Scar.

Elm Tree Elmhow.

Ewe Ewe Close/Crag.

Falcon Falcon Crag.

Fern Ferney Green; Ferngill Crags; Fernwood.

Field Mouse Mousthwaite.

Fir Tree Fir Island.

Fish Bass How/Rock; Fish Ladder; Fisherty How; Guerness Gill/Wood; Loup; Louper Weir; Naddle; Rothay; Skelly Neb; Trout Beck; Troutal; Troutal Fell/Tongue;Troutbeck; Troutdale.

Flax Limefitt.

Flowers Flour Gill.

Fowl see **Chicken, Cock, Duck, Geese**.

Fox Fox Bield/Crag(s)/Fold/Ghyll/Haw/How/How Farm; Fox Crag Plantation; Foxbield Moss/Wood; Foxes Tarn; Foxhole Bank/Wood; Foxwell; Horn Crag; Low Todrigg; Settle Earth; Tod Crag/Fell/Gill/Hole/Rigg; Todcrags; Todd Fell; Toddell; Toddell Bridge; Toddle Cottage/Gutter; Tom Fox Crag; Whelp Side; Whelpside Gill; Whelpside Gill Spring; Whelpsty How.

Gale (Sweet Gale, Bog Myrtle) Gale Bay; Galemire Bay; Galesyke; Myrtle Bay.

Garlic Ramp Holme; Ramps Gill; Rampsgill Head; Rampshaw Beck; Rampsholme Island.

Geese Goose Crag/Howe; Goosewell Farm; Goosey Foot Tarn; Gosforth; Gosforth Crag/Moss; Gosforth Hall Plantation.

Glow Worm Glow Worm Rock.

Goats Buckbarrow; Buckbarrow Moss; Gaitkins; Gaitscale; Gaitscale Close/Gill; Gasgale Crags/Gill; Gaterigghow Bridge; Gatescarth; Gatescarth Beck/Pass; Gatesgarth; Gatterigghow; Goat Crag(s)/Gill(s); Goatfoot Crags; Goat House Scar; Goat's Crag/Hawse/Water; High Goat Gill; High Kid Crag; Keskadale; Kid Beck; Kidbeck Bridge/Farm/How/Moor/Moss; Kidshowe Beck/Bridge; Kidson How; Kidsty Howes/Pike; Little Gatesgarth; Low Gait Crags; Low Goat Gill; Low Kid Crag; Lower Gatescarth; Nanny Brow/Lane.

Gorse Great Whinscale; Whin Ben/Fell/Garth/Rigg/Tarns; Whincop; High & Low Whineray Ground; Whinfell; Whinfell Hall; Whinfield Ground; Whinlatter; Whinlatter

Pass/Top; Whinnah; Whinnerah; Whinny; Whinny Brow/Ridding; Whinnyhill Coppice; Whins; Whinscales; Whinscales Crag/Howe.

Grass Bent Haw; Benty Howe; Fogmire; Fogmire Beck; Grasmere; Grass Holme; Grassgarth; Grassthwaite How; Green Quarter; Hare Bennett; Winterseeds. Also numerous other places with suffix 'Green'.

Grouse see **Blackcock/Woodcock**.

Gull Seamew Crag.

Hagworm see **Snake**.

Hare Askew Rigg Farm; Hard Rigg; Hardrigg Gill; Hare Bennett/Crag(s)/Gill/Hall/Raise/Shaw; Harrop Tarn.

Hart see **Deer**.

Hawk Hawk Bridge/Crag/Rigg; Hawkbarrow Cottage/Farm; Hawkearth Bank; Hawkrigg Farm; The Hawk; Walna Scar;Walna Scar Road; Walna Scar Side.

Hawthorn Back Hawthorn Riggs, Fore Hawthorn Riggs, see also **Thorn**.

Hay Haber Hill/Tarn; Haycock; Haycote Farm; High Hay Wood.

Hazel Blackhazel Beck; Blennerhazel; Coledale; Hazel Bank/Hall/Head/Lodge/Seat Wood/Shaw; Hazelhow End; Hazelseat.

Heather/Ling Bradlingill; High Ling Crag; Ling Comb/Crag/Fell/Holme/How; Lingcomb Edge; Lingcove Beck/Bridge; Lingholm; Lingholm Islands; Lingmell; Lingmell Beck/Col/Crag/End/Gill/Scars; Lingmoor Fell/Tarn; Lingy Acre/Bank/Crag/End/Holm/Stone; Lining Crag; Low Ling Crag; Stainton Ling; Tail o'Ling.

Heckberry Hegdale.

Hemp Hemp Rake; Hempgarth Wood/Plantation.

Hen/Water Hen see **Moorhen**.

Heron Corney; Heron Island.

Hog Hog Gill/Hole; Hoggill Brow.

Holly Bannerdale; Bannerside; Bennethead; Boredale; Broad Hollins; High Hollin Bank; High Hollins; Hollens Farm; Hollin; Hollin Bank/Crag/How(e)/Root; Hollin Band Plantation; Hollin Head Cottage; Hollin House Haw/Tongue; Hollinghead Bank/Crag; Hollins; Hollins Bridge; Hollinthwaite; Holly Crag; Low Hollins; Mosedale Holly Tree.

Horse Burnt Horse; Capell Crag/Gill; Caple Crag; Caplecrag Beck; Capple Barrow/Beck/Crags/Howe/Rigg; Capplebarrow; Capplebarrow Crag; Capplefall; Capplerigg; Capplerigg Lane; Caspel Gate; Colthouse; Colthouse Heights/Plantation; Great Horse Crag; Horse Crag/How/Parks/Pasture Wood; Hesk Fell; Horse Close; Horseclose Wood; Horseholme Wood; Horsehow Crags; Horseman Bridge; Horsemire Head; Kepple Crag; Little Horse Crag; Roscombe Rigg; Rosgill; Rosley Thorns; Rossett; Rossett Bridge/Crag/Gill/Pike; Rossett Gill Pass; Stallion Head; Wrynose Beck/Bottom/Breast/Bridge/Fell/Pass; Stoddah; Yoadcastle.

Hound Houndshope Cove; Hundhowe; Talbot Bar (Skelwith).

Ivy Iving Howe; Ivy Crag/Knott; Scale Ivy Intakes.

Jackdaw Jackdaw Crag.

Juniper Savin Hill; Savins.

Kail Kail Pot.

Kite Glede How; Kitt How; Kitty Crag.

Lad Lad Crags, Ladstones, Lambert Lad.

Larch Tree Larch.

Laurel Laurel Bank.

Lily Lily Pond. Possibly others with the adjectival Lily although these could refer to a personal name or 'little'.

Lime Tree Linbeck; Linbeck Gill; Lindeth Farm/Fell Hotel/Howe Hotel/Lane/Tarn; Lindreth Brow; Lincomb Tarns; Linthwaite House Hotel; Low Lindeth; Merklins.

Ling see **Heather**.

Madder Matterdale.

Magpie Piot Crag; Pyet's Nest; Pye Howe.

Marsh Marigold Goldrill Beck.

Moorhen Hen Crag/Holme/Tor; Henfoot Beck; Henhow.

Mountain Ash see **Rowan Tree**.

Mouse Mousthwaite.

Nettle Nettle Cove/Crag/Slack; Nettlehowe Crag.

Nut Tree Nuttera Beck.

Oak Tree Aik Beck; Aika Hill/Sike; Aikbank Farm/Mill; Aiken; Aiken Beck/Knott/ Plantation; Aikin; Aikin Knott; Broad Oak; Broadoak Beck; Derwent Water; Great Oaks Wood; Lyzzick; Oak Bank/Hill/Howe; Oak Howe Needle; Oak Isle; Oakbank; Oakhowe Crag; Oakland; Oaks; Oakenthorpen Wood; River Derwent; The Oaks; White Oak; Whitoak Beck/Moss.

Oats Haverigg Holme.

Osier (Willow) Wandope; Wandope Moss; Wythburn.

Otter Otter Bank; Otter Island; Otterbield Bay/Island.

Owl Green Owlett; Owlet Wood; Ulcat Row.

Oxen High Oxen Fell; Low Oxen Fell; Ox Pike; Oxen Fell; Oxen House Bay;Oxendale; Oxendale Beck.

Perch Bass How/Rock.

Peewit see Plover/Peewit.

Pig/Boar Far Swine Crag; Goat Scar (although in the case of the one alongside Longsleddale this is believed to originate from ON 'goltr' - wild boar); Grasmoor; Grisedale; Grisedale Gill/Pike; Grizedale; Grizedale Beck/Moor/Tarn; Grizedale Forest Park; High Swinklebank Farm; High Swinside Farm; Hog Gill/Hole; Hogg Park; Hoggill Brow; Low Swinklebank; Low Swinside; Mungrisedale; Near Swine Crag; New Close Piggery; Swanesty How; Swindale; Swine Crag/Gill/Knott; Swinescales; Swinescar Hause/Pike; Swineside Knott; Swinklebank Crag/Wood; Swinside; Swinside House/Lodge/ Plantation; Swinsty Beck/Gill/How.

Pigeon see **Dove/Pigeon**.

Pike Dollywaggon Pike.

Pine Martin Mart Bield/Crag(s); Martcrag Moor; Martcrag Moor Tarn; Martindale.

Pine Tree Pinethwaite.

Plover/Peewit Tewet Tarn; Tewfit Mire; Tewit Moss; Tewsett Pike; The Peewits.

Plum Trees Low Plumgarths; Plum Dub; Plumgarth(s).

Polecat Foul Mart; Foumart Gill.

Potato Potato Peg Plantation.

Poultry Low Hen Croft.

Rabbit Cunsey Beck; Pillow Mounds; Rabbit Cat How; Rabbit How/Warren.

Ram see **Sheep**.

Ramsons Ramp Holme; Ramps Gill; Rampsgill Head.

Rat Rattan Haw.

Raven High Rannerdale; High Raven Crag; Low Raven Crag; Rainsbarrow Wood; Rainsborrow Cove/Crag; Ramps Gill; Rampshaw Beck; Rannerdale; Rannerdale Beck/Bridge/Farm/Knotts; Raven Crag/Howe/Nest; Raven Crag Tarn/Tarns; Raven Crags; Raven Nest How; Raven Tor; Ravenscar Plantation.

Red Kite see **Kite**.

Reeds see **Rushes/Reeds**.

Rook Rook Howe; Rookin House Farm.

Rose Rose Bank; Rose Castle; Rose Castle Plantation/Tarn; Rose Cottage.

Rowan Tree Roan Wood; Rowan's Ground; Rowan Tree Dub/Hill/How; Rowanthwaite Pond; Rowantree Beck/Crag(s)/Gill/Hill/How/Knotts; Rowantreethwaite.

Rushes/Reeds Glencoyne; Reamer Bank; Redmire; Seathwaite; Seathwaite Fell/Tarn(s); Seavy Knott/Mire Hill/Seavy Side; Star Crag; Stare Beck; Starebeck Knotts;Thack Bottom; Thack Bottom Edge.

Rye Rucroft Wood; Rydal; Rydal Beck/Fell/Water.

Savin see **Juniper**.

Sedge see **Rushes/Reeds**.

Shag see **Cormorant**.

Sheep Alisongrass Hoghouse; Briar Shot; Caw; Ewe Close/Crag(s)/How; Gimmer Crag; High Wether Crag/How; Hog Bank; Hog House Beck; Hogs Earth; Lamb Bridge/Howe/Pasture; Lambfoot Dub; Lambford Bridge; Lambground; Lambhowe Hill/Plantation; Lambing Knott; Low Wether Crag; Ramps Gill; Rams Slack; Rampsgill Head; Rams Beck; Ramshaw Beck; Ramsteads; Scope Beck/End; Sheep Crag/Pens; Sheepbone Buttress; Shepherd('s) Bridge; Shepherd Crag; Shepherd Yeat; Shepherds Crag; Shipman Knotts; Souterstead; Watermillock; Wether Hill/How; Wetherlam; Wetherlam Edge/Tarn; Whether Fold; Yew Bank/Barrow/Beck/Crag(s)/Pike; Yewbarrow; Yewdel Knott; Yewthwaite Comb/Gill.

Skelly/Schelly (Fish) Skelly Neb.

Sloe Sleathwaite.

Snake Great Worm Crag; Hermons Hill; Little Worm Crag; Naddle; Snake Holme; Snarker Moss/Pike; Walmgate; Worm Gill/How; Wormhole Hill; Wormshell How, Woundell Beck.

Snipe Snipes How; Snipeshow Tarn.

Sorrel Dockray.

Sparrow Sparrow How Wood.

Sparrow Hawk Hawk Crag/Rigg; Hawkearth Bank; Hawkrigg Farm.

Squirrel Swirrel Wood.

Stoat Withered Howe.

Strawberry Strawberry Gill/Wood.

Swallow Swallow Scar Beck; Swallowhurst; Swallowhurst Hall.

Swan Elter Holme; Elter Water; Eltermere; Elterwater; Elterwater Common/Hall/Quarry; Far Swan Beck; Middle Swan Beck; Near Swan Beck; Swan Dub.

Sweet Gale see **Gale**.

Tansy Tansy Gill.

Thistle High Thistleton; Low Thistleton.

Thorn Back Hawthorn Riggs; Beauthorn; Beckthorns Gill; Fore Hawthorn Riggs; Haws Holme/Wood; Higher Thorny Bank; Rosley Thorns; Thorn Cottage/Crag/How/Knott; Thornbank; Thorney Bank/Knott; Thorneythwaite; Thornflatt; Thornholme; Thorny How;

Thornhow; Thornhow Crag/End; Thorns Lane/Villa; Thornsgill Beck; Thornship; Thornthwaite Crag; Thorn(y)thwaite; Thorny Slack; Thornyfields.

Thrush High Thrushbank; Throstle Garth/Shaw; Throstlehow Crag; Thrushbank; Thrushwood.

Toad Paddock Wray; Toad How; Toadhowe Well, Toadpool.

Trees Cotra; Cotra Breast; Stockdale; Stockdale Beck/Bridge. See also individual tree names.

Trout Rothay; Rothaymere/Routhmere (former names of Rydal Water); Trout Beck; Troutal; Troutal Fell/Tongue; Troutbeck; Troutbeck Park/Tongue; Troutdale.

Water Hen see **Moorhen**.

Weasel Withered Howe.

Whin see **Gorse**.

Wild Cat Cat Bank/Bells/Bields/Cove/Crag/Gill(s)/How; Cat's Crag; Catcove Beck; Catgill Bridge; Cathow Bridge; Catstycam; High Cat Crag; Low Cat Crag; Rabbit Cat How.

Wild Fowl Fewling Stones.

Wild Garlic see **Garlic**.

Willow Sallows; Seal Gill; Sealhole Grain; Sele Bottom; Sella; Selside; Top o'Selside; Wandope; Wandope Moss; Whit Beck; Widewath; Wise Een Tarn; Withersike Bay; Wythburn; Wythe Gill; Wythop.

Wolf Hullockhow; Ulgill Gutter; Ulgraves; Ull Stone; Ullister Hill; Ullock; Ullock Moss/Pike; Ullscarf; Ullstone Gill; Ulpha; Ulthwaite Bridge/Rigg; Whelpside Gill; Wofa Holes; Wolf Crags; Wolf Howe; Wolfcrag Moss; Wolfhowe Gill/Plantation; Woof Gill/Stones.

Wood Pigeon see **Dove/Pigeon**.

Woodcock see **Blackcock/Woodcock**.

Yew Borrowdale Yews; Fallen Yew; Green Yew; High Yewdale; Low Yewdale; Low Yews; Yew Band/Bank/Barrow/Beck/Crag(s)Mire/Pike/Tree; Yew Tree Beck/Farm/Tarn; Yewbarrow Hall/Wood; Yewdale; Yewdale Beck/ Crag; Yewdale Crag Moss; Yewdale Fell Side; Yewdale Fells; Yewdale Moss; Yewdel Knott; Yewgrove Gill;Yewry Sike;Yews; Yewthwaite Comb/Gill.

See also *Out of the Forest: The Natural World and the Place Names of Cumbria* by Robert Gambles (1989).

In the case of Bull Crag(s), Gray Bull, High and Low Bull Crags the name usually represents the size of the crag and not necessarily to it or its area having been frequented by bulls. Similarily Great Horse and Little Horse Crags may refer to the size of the crags and not a preponderance of horses thereabouts.

HEIGHTS

To calculate a six-figure grid reference number:-

1:25000 (2.5 inches = 1 mile) maps are divided into squares of 4 cms (1.56 ins) with each square representing 1km in length. To calculate the grid reference number read the number of the vertical line to the west of the place required and add to it the estimated tenths eastward eg Satterthwaite is 33 + 9 therefore 339. Likewise, read the number of the line at the foot or southern end of the square and again calculate the tenths. In this case Satterthwaite reads 92 + 4. The full grid reference number is therefore 339924.

Heights in feet were last published as a series on the 1:63360 (one inch to one mile) maps of the area:- 82 Keswick, 83 Penrith, 88 Barrow, and 89 Lancaster and Kendal. Subsequently these figures were converted to metric and the result rounded up or down to the nearest metre. Hence Scafell Pike at 3210 feet becomes 978.41987 metres rounded down to 978m while Helvellyn at 3118ft becomes 950.37793 rounded down to 950m.

In this work and in the general text I have first and foremost listed heights in metres as given on the current Outdoor Leisure 1:25000 (2.5 inches to one mile) maps but for those like myself who still understand feet and have an affinity with these as a measurement of altitude I have included heights in feet calculated by multiplying each metre by 3.2808992 feet and then rounding up or down to the nearest foot.

Where no specific height has been given on the current map and yet by the hill or mountain's position or character it has been felt necessary to include a figure this is given to the nearest contour line and preceded by the capital letter C.

Those interested in heights in feet will notice discrepancies in many generally accepted heights. These are due to:

1 Revisions by map makers over the years.

2 Conversion from current maps whose heights have been rounded up or down to three figures and do not include decimals. Two examples of the latter are Helvellyn, 3118ft and Scafell Pike, 3210ft. In the case of Helvellyn, as previously stated, this figure converted to metres = 950.37793 rounded down to 950m. However, the 950m converted back to feet becomes 3116.85424 rounded up to 3117ft. Similarly, England's highest mountain Scafell Pike, 3210 feet, becomes 978.41987 rounded down to 978m. Here again, conversion from 978 back to feet gives a figure of 3209 when rounded up. The two examples are reflected in many heights throughout the text but where they occur the resulting discrepancy is so minor considering the footage involved that, in the interest of consistency, I have given the metric conversion to feet as calculated even though this leaves mountains like Helvellyn and Scafell Pike a foot each short of their genererally accepted heights.

In the case of ranges, most mountains fit into a precise geographical pattern as outliers or spurs of major peaks but there are exceptions to this rule. Red Screes is not part of the Fairfield range neither does Bowscale Fell belong to Blencathra or indeed, Great and Little Mell Fell to Helvellyn. Also, the Grasmoor range has been alloted a much expanded area. However, arbitrarily they can be considered to be part of that particular range and in the interest of practicality that is how those groupings and others have been decided.

* Writing on page 89 of his *Exploring Lakeland Tarns* (1993) Don Blair notes that "According to the OS it is not possible to give an accurate height for either of them [these tarns]."

HEIGHTS (ALPHABETICAL)

Heights over 152m (500ft) except in high ridge groupings when heights are either given at over 700m (2297ft) in the case of the Scafell Pike range or for lesser heights 500m (1640ft) or 350m (1148ft)

	m	ft	grid ref
A5091	342	1122	389246
A591	238	781	327117
A592	455	1493	401082
A6	426	1398	554064
A66	288	945	395275
Adam Seat	666	2185	471091
Alcock Tarn	365	1198	349079
Allen Crags	785	2575	236085
Angle Tarn (Hartsop)	480	1575	417144
Angle Tarn (Bowfell)	570	1870	244076
Angletarn Pikes: N summit	567	1860	413148
Angletarn Pikes: S summit	565	1854	414147
Ard Crags	581	1906	207198
Arlecdon Reservoir see Cogra Moss			
Armboth Fell	479	1571	297160
Arnison Crag	433	1421	394150
Arnsbarrow Hill	322	1056	312911
Arnsbarrow Tarn	295	968	310917
Arnside Heights	297	974	337013
Arthur's Pike	532	1745	461207
Artlecrag Pike (Branstree)	713	2339	478100
Askill Knott	284	9932	123227
Atkinson Pike (Foule Crag)	845	2772	324283
Banks	303	994	269940
Banna Fell	456	1496	116174
Banner Rigg	C270	C886	427995
Bannerdale Crags	683	2241	335290
Bannisdale Fell (Long Crag)	493	1617	516052
Barf	468	1535	215268
Barrow	455	1493	227218
Base Brown	646	2119	225115
Beacon Fell	255	837	278907
Beacon Tarn	163	535	274901
Beckhead Tarn	C620	C2034	205107
Beda Head	509	1670	428170
Bell, The see The Bell			
Bell Crags	558	1831	298143
Benn Man	446	1463	302193
Bennethead Banks	295	968	444243

Bessyboot	C540	C1772	258125
Bethecar Moor	335	1099	309919
Birk Fell (Place Fell)	C510	C1673	401182
Birk Fell (Wetherlam)	526	1726	296019
Birk Haw Tarn	C160	C525	270924
Birkby Fell	494	1621	157952
Birkby Fell group of fells, principal heights over 350m (1148ft)			
Yoadcastle	494	1621	157952
Woodend Height	C480	C1575	157954
White Pike	442	1450	151956
Rowantree How	C400	C1312	157959
Stord's Hill	384	1260	155962
Birker Fell	489	1604	200983
Birker Fell, group of fells, principal heights over 350m (1148ft)			
Green Crag	489	1604	200983
Crook Crag	469	1539	200989
The Pike	C450	C1476	200986
White How	444	1457	205975
Great Worm Crag	427	1401	194969
Great Whinscale	425	1394	198990
Little Worm Crag	C400	C1312	193971
Broad Crag	372	1220	195978
Birker Moor Road	C260	C853	176972
Birkett Fell	C720	C2362	365198
Birkhouse Moor	718	2356	364160
Birks	622	2041	380144
Black Brows	268	879	363926
Black Crag (Red Pike Ridge)	801	2628	166101
Black Crag (near Skelwith Bridge), see Black Fell			
Black Crag (Whinlatter)	527	1729	199241
Black Crags	588	1929	256081
Black Fell	323	1060	340016
Black Sails	C740	C2428	283007
Blackbeck Tarn	C490	C1608	202128
Blake Fell	573	1880	110197
Blawith Fells	255	837	278907
Blea Crag	630	2067	237171
Blea Rigg	541	1775	301078
Blea Tarn (Langdale)	C190	C623	293044
Blea Tarn (Eskdale)	C220	C722	166010
Blea Tarn (Watendlath)	C480	C1575	291141
Blea Water	483	1585	449108
Bleaberry Fell	590	1936	286196
Bleak Hill	438	1437	533121
Blease Fell (Knowe Crags)	804	2638	312270
Bleatarn Hill	C280	C919	168013
Blencathra (Saddleback)	868	2848	323277

Blencathra group of fells, principal heights over 500m (1640ft)			
Blencathra (Hallsfell Top)	868	2848	323277
Gategill Fell Top	851	2792	318273
Foule Crag (Atkinson Pike)	845	2772	324283
Tarn Crags	829	2720	324280
Blease Fell (Knowe Crags)	804	2638	312270
Bowscale Fell	702	2303	333305
Bannerdale Crags	683	2241	335290
Doddick Fell Top	682	2238	332279
Scales Fell	641	2103	335278
Mungrisedale Common	633	2077	312292
Scales Tarn	610	2001	329281
Souther Fell	522	1713	354291
Bleng Fell	253	830	079060
Blind Tarn (Eskdale)	C220	C722	161010
Blind Tarn (Coniston)	C560	C1837	262967
Boat How	337	1106	177034
Bolton's Tarn	C190	C623	448935
Boo Tarn	280	919	282968
Bonscale Pike	524	1719	453201
Border End	522	1713	228019
Boredale Hause	384	1260	408157
Borrans Reservoir	C200	C656	429010
Bowfell	902	2959	245064
Bowfell and adjoining ridges, principal heights over 500m (1640ft)			
Bowfell	902	2959	245064
Crinkle Crags	859	2818	249049
Little Stand	727	2385	251032
Three Tarns	720	2363	248060
Pike of Blisco	705	2313	271042
Cold Pike	701	2300	263036
Great Knott	696	2283	260043
Cold Pike: W summit	683	2241	259036
Cold Pike: WNW summit	C650	C2132	256037
White Stones, The Band	568	1863	261061
Bowness Knott	333	1093	112155
Bracken How	C370	C1214	393211
Brackenthwaite Hows	208	682	154214
Brandreth	715	2346	215119
Brandreth Three Tarns	C660	C2165	215115
Branstree	711	2333	478100
Branstree (Artlecrag Pike)	713	2339	478100
Brant Fell	191	627	410962
Brantrake Crags	259	850	149982
Brigstone Tarn	C370	C1214	319068
Brim Fell	796	2611	271986
Broad Crag (Scafell)	930	3051	219076

Broad Crag (Birker Fell)	372	1220	195978
Broad End (Skiddaw)	831	2726	261298
Broadcrag Tarn*	820-830	2690-2723	213069
Broadmoor Hill	286	938	143246
Brock Crag (Eskdale)	342	1122	215029
Brock Crags (Hartsop)	561	1841	417137
Broom Fell	511	1676	194272
Brothers Water	158	520	403127
Brown Cove Tarn	625	2051	343160
Brown Crag	610	2001	328177
Brown Hill	262	860	553140
Brown Hills	C590	C1936	372193
Brown How (Lingmoor)	469	1539	303046
Brown How (Ennerdale)	C320	C1050	116158
Brown How (Whinlatter)	517	1696	191251
Brown Howe (E Kentmere)	C700	C2297	463083
Brown Howe (Shap Fells)	C560	C1837	519085
Brown Pike	682	2237	261966
Brown Rigg	463	1519	305146
Brownhow Hill	305	1001	408266
Brownrigg Well (Helvellyn)	853	2799	338150
Brownthwaite Crag	444	1457	443173
Brund Fell	415	1362	264162
Brunt Knott	427	1401	484006
Buck Barrow	549	1801	152910
Buck Crags	579	1900	506072
Buck Pike (Rossett Pike Ridge)	606	1988	253078
Buck Pike (Dow Crag Ridge)	744	2441	262973
Buckbarrow	420	1378	136061
Burnbank Fell	475	1558	110209
Burnmoor Tarn	C250	C820	184044
Burthwaite Heights	318	1043	189283
Butter Crag	C400	C1312	350083
Calf Crag	530	1739	302104
Calfhow Pike	C660	C2165	331211
Capple Barrow	C190	C623	422958
Capple How	445	1460	432029
Capplebarrow	512	1680	509035
Carl Side	746	2447	255281
Carling Knott	544	1785	121206
Carlside Tarn	C720	C2362	256282
Carron Crag	314	1030	325943
Castle Crag, Borrowdale	290	951	249159
Castle Crag, Kentmere	490	1608	446052
Castle Head	162	531	270227
Castle Rock (Castle Rock of Triermain)	339	1112	322197
Castlerigg Fell	460	1509	291206

Castlerigg Stone Circle	210	689	292236
Cat Bells	451	1480	244199
Cat Crag	369	1211	209031
Catstye Cam	890	2920	348158
Caudale Head/Moor Tarn	745	2444	415101
Caudale Moor (Stony Cove Pike)	763	2503	418100
Causey Pike	637	2090	219209
Caw	529	1735	230944
Caw Fell	C690	C2264	132110
Caw Moss Tarn	C390	C1280	252949

Central Fells - these have been expanded to include the larger area lying between Great Langdale/Mickleden to the S, Stake Pass and Langstrath Beck to the W, the A592 to the E and the Wyth Burn and Greenup Gill to the N. Principal heights over 500m (1640ft)

High Raise	762	2500	281095
Harrison Stickle	736	2415	282074
Sergeant Man	730	2395	286089
Thunacar Knott	723	2372	279080
Pike o'Stickle	709	2326	274074
Pavey Ark	700	2297	285079
Loft Crag	C670	C2198	277072
Rossett Pike	650	2132	249076
Sergeant's Man	571	1873	274114
Steel Fell (Dead Pike)	553	1814	320112
Tarn Crag	550	1804	303093
Martcrag Moor	547	1795	268083
Blea Rigg	541	1775	301078
Calf Crag	530	1739	302104
Eagle Crag	521	1709	276121

Claife Heights	270	886	382973
Cleabarrow Tarn	C170	C558	424962
Clough Head	726	2382	334225
Cocklakes Hill	C270	C886	408273
Cocklaw Fell	365	1198	481039
Cockley Moor	455	1493	381225
Codale Head	C710	C2329	289092
Codale Tarn	466	1529	297088
Cofa Pike	C820	C2690	359121
Cogra Moss (Arlecdon Reservoir)	C230	C755	095195
Cold Pike	701	2300	263036
Coldbarrow Fell	675	2215	289129
Coledale Hause	C600	C1968	189212
Colthouse Heights	218	715	368973
Common Fell	C540	C1772	383204

Coniston Old Man, see Old Man of Coniston

Coniston range (including Wetherlam), principal heights over 500m (1640ft)

Old Man of Coniston	803	2634	272978
Swirl How	802	2631	273005

Brim Fell	796	2611	271986
Great Carrs	780	2558	270009
Dow Crag	778	2552	262978
Grey Friar	770	2526	260004
Wetherlam	762	2499	288011
Buck Pike	744	2441	262972
Black Sails	C740	C2428	283007
Little Carrs	C730	C2395	270012
Fairfield	695	2280	261966
Hell Gill Pike	692	2270	270014
Brown Pike	682	2237	261966
Wet Side Edge	579	1900	274021
Corney Fell Road	400	1312	150896
Crag Fell	523	1716	097144
Crag Hill	839	2753	193204
Crinkle Crags	859	2818	249049
Crook Crag	469	1539	200989
Crook Reservoir	C200	C656	445957
Cunswick Fell/Scar	207	679	492943
Dale Head	753	2471	223153
Dale Head group of fells, principal heights over 500m (1640ft)			
Dale Head	753	2471	223153
Robinson	737	2418	202169
Hindscarth	727	2385	216165
High Spy	653	2142	234162
Blea Crag	630	2067	237171
Littledale Edge	576	1890	208161
Maiden Moor	576	1890	237182
High Scawdel Tarn	550	C1804	231147
High Snockrigg	526	1726	187169
Low Scawdel	521	1709	242162
Dale Head Tarn	C500	C1640	230152
Dale Park	268	879	363926
Darling Fell	391	1283	128225
Dawson Ground Crags	397	1302	204027
Dead Pike (Steel Fell)	553	1814	320112
Demming Crag	525	1722	222002
Devoke Water	C240	C787	158969
Dikey Hill	242	794	113239
Dock Tarn	C410	C1345	274144
Dockey Tarn	C380	C1247	353073
Dod Hill	451	1480	411053
Dodd (Buttermere)	641	2103	164158
Dodd (Skiddaw)	502	1647	244274
Dodd (Whiteside)	454	1489	169231
Dodd Crag	460	1509	291206
Doddick Fell Top	682	2238	332279

Dollywaggon Pike	858	2815	346131
Dore Head	C490	C1608	175095
Dove Crag	792	2598	375104
Dow Crag (Coniston)	778	2552	263978
Dow Crag (Ulpha)	404	1325	204994
Dubbs Reservoir	228	748	421017
Dunmail Raise	238	781	327117
Eagle Crag (Langstrath/Greenup)	521	1709	276121
Easedale Tarn	290	951	308087
Eastern Fells (between Shap and Longsleddale), principal heights over 500m(1640ft)			
Artlecrag Pike	713	2339	478100
Branstree	711	2333	478100
Tarn Crag	664	2179	488078
Selside Pike	655	2149	490111
Sleddale Fell (Grey Crag)	638	2093	497072
Harrop Pike	637	2090	501078
Great Yarlside	C590	C1936	524077
Howes: W summit	C580	C1903	499104
Buck Crags	579	1900	506072
Little Saddle Crag	C570	C1870	527083
Wasdale Pike	565	1854	536084
Great Saddle Crag	C560	C1837	326087
Howes: E summit	544	1785	503105
Red Crag	539	1768	508067
High Wether Howe	531	1742	515109
White How	530	1739	524042
Rowantreethwaite	529	1736	487122
Lord's Seat	524	1719	519066
Scam Matthew	C520	C1706	516015
Little Yarlside	516	1693	532072
Seat Robert	515	1690	526114
Capplebarrow	512	1833	509036
Hare Shaw	503	1650	498131
Sleddale Pike	C500	C1640	536094
Ulthwaite Rigg	C500	C1640	515093
Eel Crag	C800	C2625	190207
Eel Tarn	C210	C689	189019
Embleton High Common	294	964	169281
Erne Crag	621	2037	360087
Esk Hause	759	2490	233080
Esk Pike	885	2903	237075
Eskdale Fell	522	1713	192038
Eycott Hill	345	1132	387295
Fairfield(Coniston)	695	2280	266007
Fairfield (Fairfield Range)	873	2864	359118
Fairfield Range, principal heights over 500m (1640ft)			
Fairfield	873	2864	359118

St Sunday Crag	841	2759	369134
Hart Crag	822	2697	368113
Cofa Pike	C820	C2690	359121
Dove Crag	792	2598	375104
Gavel Pike	784	2572	373134
Red Screes	776	2546	396088
Great Rigg Man	766	2513	356104
Seat Sandal	736	2415	344115
High Bakestones	C710	C2329	379099
High Pike	656	2152	374088
Middle Dodd	654	2146	397095
Snarker Pike	644	2113	390075
Nan Bield Pass	640	2100	453096
Little Hart Crag	637	2090	387100
Birks	622	2041	380144
Rydal Fell	621	2037	357087
Heron Pike	612	2008	356083
Hartsop Above How	570	1870	385121
Scandale Tarn	C560	C1837	386098
Scandale Pass Col	C520	C1706	388096
High Hartsop Dodd	519	1703	394107
Gale Crag	512	1680	392124
Low Pike	508	1667	374078
Stone Arthur	504	1654	348092
Fawcett Forest	528	1732	528036
Fellbarrow (Mosser Fell)	416	1365	132242
Fellbarrow group of fells, principal heights over 350m (1148ft)			
Low Fell	423	1388	137226
Fellbarrow	416	1365	132242
Sourfoot Fell	C410	C1345	135233
Darling Fell	391	1283	128225
Smithy Fell	C390	C1279	133237
Hatteringill Head (Whin Fell)	385	1263	134248
Loftbarrow	C350	C1148	131231
Fleetwith Pike	648	2126	205142
Floutern Cop	451	1480	122174
Floutern Pass	C410	C1345	121172
Floutern Tarn	C380	C1247	125170
Flusco Hill	177	581	472259
Foule Crag (Atkinson Pike)	845	2772	324283
Four Stones Hill	415	1362	492162
Fox Haw	385	1263	223936
Fox Tarn (Foxes Tarn)*	820-830	2690-2723	209064
Froswick	720	2362	435085
Gale Crag	512	1680	392124
Gale Fell	518	1699	134164
Garburn Pass	447	1467	436044

Garner Bank	244	800	158986
Gasgale Crags	719	2359	175221
Gate Crag	283	928	184997
Gategill Fell Top	851	2792	318273
Gatescarth Pass	594	1949	474092
Gavel Fell	526	1726	117184
Gavel Pike	784	2572	373134
Gaze Stone How	395	1296	255014
Ghyll Pool	220	722	497984
Gibson Knott	420	1379	321099
Glade How	C430	C1411	134064
Glaramara	783	2569	246105
Glaramara group of fells, principal heights over 500m (1640ft)			
Allen Crags	785	2575	236085
Glaramara	783	2569	246105
Glaramara: lower summit	775	2543	246102
Rosthwaite Cam	612	2008	256118
Thornythwaite Fell	574	1883	245118
Racom Band	541	1775	261123
Glede How	476	1562	521120
Glencoyne Wood	451	1480	379180
Glenridding Dodd	442	1450	381176
Goat House Scar	407	1335	450046
Goat Scar	626	2054	473069
Goat's Hawse	649	2129	266983
Goat's Water	503	1650	266976
Godworth	365	1197	101183
Gowbarrow Fell	481	1578	408218
Gowk Hill	C470	C1542	445167
Grandsire	251	823	432973
Grange Fell	415	1362	264162
Grasmoor	852	2795	175203
Grasmoor group of fells, principal heights over 500m (1640ft)			
Grasmoor	852	2795	175203
Crag Hill	839	2753	193204
Eel Crag	C800	C2625	190207
Grisedale Pike	791	2595	199226
Sail	773	2536	198203
Wandhope	772	2533	188197
Hopegill Head	770	2526	186222
Sand Hill	756	2480	187219
Gasgale Crags	719	2359	175221
Whiteside	707	2319	170219
Ladyside Pike	703	2306	185227
Scar Crags	672	2205	208206
Whiteless Pike	660	2165	180190
Causey Pike	637	2090	219209

Hobcarton End	634	2080	195235
Coledale Hause	C600	C1968	189212
Ard Crags	581	1906	207198
Outerside	568	1863	211215
Knott Rigg	556	1824	197189
Gray Crag: north summit	699	2293	428117
Gray Crag: south summit	710	2329	430110
Graystones	456	1496	178264
Great Bank	329	1079	144019
Great Barrow	232	761	187017
Great Birkhouse Hill	C380	C1247	493163
Great Borne	616	2021	124164
Great Carrs	785	2575	270009
Great Crag	C320	C1050	187978
Great Dodd	857	2812	342206
Great End	910	2986	227085
Great Gable	899	2949	211103
Great Gable group of fells, principal heights over500m (1640ft			
Great Gable	899	2949	211103
Kirk Fell	802	2631	195105
Green Gable	801	2628	215017
Brandreth	715	2346	215119
Grey Knotts	697	2287	217126
Fleetwith Pike	648	2126	205142
Base Brown	606	2119	225115
Hay Stacks	597	1959	193132
Great Round How	554	1818	207128
Great How (Eskdale Fell)	522	1713	197040
Great How (Thirlmere)	335	1099	314188
Great How (Little Langdale)	211	692	322026
Great Howe	494	1621	489064
Great Knott	696	2283	260043
Great Knott (Skiddaw)	445	1460	248299
Great Ladstones	C440	C1444	532124
Great Meldrum	437	1434	415223
Great Mell Fell	537	1762	397254
Great Paddy Crag	532	1745	150909
Great Rigg (Greatrigg Man)	766	2513	356104
Great Round How	554	1818	207128
Great Saddle Crag	C560	C1837	526087
Great Scoat Fell	802	2631	155112
Great Stickle	305	1001	212916
Great Whinscale	425	1394	198990
Great Worm Crag	427	1401	194969
Great Yarlside [contour]	C590	C1936	524077
Great Yarlside [spot height]	585	1919	524077
Green Crag (Birker Fell)	489	1604	200983

Green Crag (Hay Stacks Ridge)	528	1732	202131
Green Gable	801	2628	215017
Green Hill	161	528	405920
Green How (Torver)	185	607	272924
Green How (Birker Moor)	200	656	172992
Green How (Birker Moor)	C270	C886	184988
Green Side, see White Stones			
Greendale Tarn	C410	C1345	147074
Greenup Edge	C610	C2001	286106
Grey Crag (Grasmere)	350	1150	348076
Grey Crag (Sleddale Fell)	638	2093	497072
Grey Crag (Buttermere)	807	2648	170148
Grey Friar	770	2526	260004
Grey Knotts	697	2287	217126
Greycrag Tarn	595	1952	492076
Grike	488	1601	085141
Grisedale Pike	791	2595	199226
Grisedale Pass	588	1929	349117
Grisedale Tarn	539	1768	350120
Grizedale Forest Park	314	1030	325943
Grizedale Tarn	C210	C689	346944
Guinea Hill	243	797	336967
Gurnal Dubbs	C290	C951	502992
Hagg Pond	190	623	367982
Hagg Wood	342	1122	428220
Hallin Fell	388	1273	433198
Hallsfell Top (Blencathra)	868	2848	323277
Hard Knott	549	1801	232024
Hard Tarn (Ruthwaite)	716	2349	346138
Hardknott Pass	393	1289	231015
Hare Crag	538	1765	277299
Hare Shaw	503	1650	498131
Harper Hills	419	1375	508143
Harrison Stickle	736	2415	282074
Harrop Pike	637	2090	501078
Harrop Tarn	290	951	311136
Harrot	292	958	160275
Hart Crag	822	2697	368113
Hart Side	756	2480	359197
Harter Fell (Mardale)	778	2553	460093
Harter Fell (Eskdale)	653	2142	219997
Hartsop Above How	570	1870	385121
Hartsop Dodd (Low Hartsop Dodd)	618	2028	411118
Haskew Tarn	C470	C1542	521113
Hatteringill Head (Whin Fell)	385	1263	134248
Haweswater Reservoir	240	787	480140
Hay Stacks	597	1959	193132

Haycock	797	2615	145107
Hayeswater	422	1385	432122
Hazel Bank	427	1401	545077
Hell Gill Pike	692	2270	270014
Helm Crag: highest point	405	1329	326093
Helm Crag: OS point	398	1306	327093
Helvellyn	950	3117	342151
Helvellyn range of fells, principal heights over 500m (1640ft)			
Helvellyn	950	3117	342151
Lower Man	925	3035	337155
Nethermost Pike	891	2923	344142
Catstye Cam	890	2920	348158
High Crag	884	2900	343137
Raise	883	2897	343174
White Side	863	2831	338167
Dollywaggon Pike	858	2815	346131
Great Dodd	857	2812	342206
Stybarrow Dodd	843	2766	343189
White Stones (Green Side)	795	2608	353187
Watson's Dodd	789	2589	336196
Little Dodd	C780	C2559	337204
Hart Side	756	2480	359197
Sticks Pass	738	2421	342182
Clough Head	726	2382	334225
Birkett Fell	C720	C2362	365198
Randerside	C720	C2362	349211
Red Tarn	718	2356	349152
Birkhouse Moor	718	2356	364160
Hard Tarn	716	2349	346138
Sheffield Pike	675	2215	369182
Calfhow Pike	C660	C2165	331211
Stang	655	2149	355176
Brown Cove Tarn	625	2051	343160
Brown Crag	610	2001	328177
Brown Hills	C590	C1936	372193
High Brow	575	1887	368214
Swineside Knott	553	1814	379197
Keppel Cove	C550	C1804	345165
Watermillock Common	540	1772	379202
Common Fell	C540	C1772	383204
Great Mell Fell	537	1762	397254
Threlkeld Knotts	514	1686	330230
Little Mell Fell	505	1657	423240
Hen Comb	509	1670	132181
Herdus	562	1844	118163
Heron Pike	612	2008	356083
Hesk Fell	477	1565	176947

Heughscar Hill	C370	C1214	488231
High Arnside Tarn	168	551	331011
High Bakestones	C710	C2329	379099
High Blind How	270	886	382973
High Brow	575	1887	368214
High Crag	158	518	355009
High Crag (Buttermere)	744	2441	180140
High Crag (Helvellyn)	884	2900	343137
High Craghall	225	738	180917
High Crags (Hindscarth Ridge)	529	1736	217175
High Crags (Newlands)	412	1352	237190
High Doat	283	928	247144
High Dodd	501	1644	416182
High End	488	1601	281024
High Fell	532	1745	162091
High Hartsop Dodd	519	1703	394107
High House Bank	495	1624	543048
High Hows	313	1027	096202
High Knott	C270	C886	454001
High Light Haw	263	863	303905
High Man	282	925	328965
High Man Tarn	C260	C853	329965
High Nook	488	1601	120189
High Nook Tarn	C220	C722	124199
High Pen	475	1558	110189
High Pike	656	2152	374088
High Pike Haw	354	1161	264949
High Pikehow	574	1883	144100
High Raise (High Street)	802	2631	448134
High Raise (Central Fells)	762	2500	281095
High Rigg: central top	343	1125	308215
High Rigg: E top	307	1007	311211
High Rigg: N top	357	1171	309220
High Rigg: S top	311	1020	316201
High Saddle	675	2215	289129
High Scarf Crag	487	1598	215044
High Scawdel Tarn	C550	C1804	231147
High Seat	608	1995	287180
High Snockrigg	526	1726	187169
High Spy	653	2142	234162
High Stile	807	2648	170148
High Stile ridge, principal heights over 500m (1640ft)			
High Stile	807	2648	170148
Red Pike	755	2477	161154
High Crag	744	2441	180140
Dodd	641	2103	164158
Starling Dodd	633	2077	142158

Great Borne	616	2021	124164
Little Dodd	590	1936	149155
Herdus	562	1844	118163
Seat	561	1840	186134
Gale Fell	518	1699	134164
High Street	828	2717	441110
High Street range of fells, principal heights over 500m (1640ft)			
High Street (Racecourse Hill)	828	2717	441110
High Raise	802	2631	448134
Rampsgill Head	792	2598	443128
Thornthwaite Crag	784	2572	432100
Kidsty Pike	780	2559	447126
Harter Fell	778	2553	460093
Caudale Moor (Stony Cove Pike)	763	2503	418100
Mardale Ill Bell	C760	C2493	448101
Ill Bell	757	2484	436077
Low Raise	754	2474	456137
The Knott	739	2425	437127
Kentmere Pike	730	2395	465078
Froswick	720	2362	435085
Red Crag	711	2333	450152
Gray Crag: S summit	710	2329	430110
Raven Howe	C710	C2329	450146
Yoke	706	2316	438067
Gray Crag: N summit	699	2293	428117
Rest Dodd	696	2284	432137
Loadpot Hill	672	2205	457181
Wether Hill	C670	C2198	456167
Little Harter Fell	C670	C2198	470093
Adam Seat	666	2185	471091
Lingmell End	C660	C2165	446092
Place Fell	657	2156	406170
Round How	C630	C2067	408166
Rough Crag	628	2060	454112
Hartsop Dodd (Low Hartsop Dodd)	618	2028	411118
St Ravens Edge	593	1946	406084
Shipman Knotts	587	1926	472063
The Nab: N summit	576	1890	434152
Low Kop	572	1877	474165
Angletarn Pikes: N summit	567	1860	413148
Angletarn Pikes: S summit	565	1854	414147
Brock Crags	561	1841	417137
Swarth Fell	C560	C1837	461197
Arthur's Pike	532	1745	461207
Bonscale Pike	524	1719	453201
Sallows	516	1693	437040
The Nab: S summit	515	1690	435145

Buck Crag	514	1686	439052
Birk Fell	C510	C1673	403183
Beda Head	509	1670	428170
High Dodd	501	1644	416182
High Taggleshaw Tarn	C310	C1017	505994
High Tove	515	1690	289165
High Wether Howe	531	1742	515109
High White Stones	762	2500	281095
Highs Moss Tarn	C220	C722	375980
Hindscarth	727	2385	216165
Hobcarton End	634	2080	195235
Hodson's Tarn	C200	C656	369982
Holehouse Tarn	C470	C1542	154940
Hollow Moor	426	1398	469040
Hollow Stones	188	617	450919
Holme Fell	317	1040	315006
Holme Ground Tarns	230	755	215011
Honister Hause	C360	C1181	225136
Hooker Crag	231	758	112983
Hopegill Head	770	2526	186222
Horsehow Crags	433	1421	225009
How Top	277	909	377285
Howe Hill	177	581	413003
Howes: E summit	544	1785	503105
Howes: W summit	C580	C1903	499104
Hugh Laithes Pike	426	1397	502152
Hugill Pike	273	896	459931
Ill Bell	757	2484	436077
Ill Crag (Scafell Pike)	935	3068	223073
Ill Crag (Newlands Hause)	546	1791	200192
Illgill Head	609	1998	169049
Innominate Tarn	525	1722	197129
Ireland Wood	244	800	511179
Iron Crag	408	1339	211972
Irton Fell	395	1296	144026
Irton Pike	C220	C722	121016
Jenkin Hill	C730	C2395	274275
Juniper Tarn	C200	C656	340964
Keldas	311	1020	385163
Kelton Fell	311	1020	095182
Kemp Tarn	C220	C722	464989
Kentmere Pike	730	2395	465078
Kentmere Reservoir	290	951	445080
Keppel Cove	C550	C1804	345165
Keppel Crag	328	1076	199999
Kerris Hill	230	755	460963
Kidsty Pike	780	2559	447126

Kiln Bank Cross	259	850	215933
King's How	392	1286	258167
Kinmont Buckbarrow	535	1755	147910
Kinniside	375	1230	078116
Kinniside Common	541	1775	085119
Kinnisdie Kop	180	590	041146
Kirk Fell (Wasdale)	802	2631	195105
Kirk Fell (Lord's Seat group)	438	1437	173266
Kirkstone Pass Inn	C450	C1476	401080
Kirkstone Pass summit	455	1493	401082
Knipescar Common	342	1122	536191
Knock Murton	447	1467	095191
Knott Rigg	556	1824	197189
Knotts	234	768	309021
Knowe Crags (Blease Fell)	804	2638	312270
Lad Hows	426	1398	172193
Ladies Table	296	971	209288
Ladyside Pike	703	2306	185227
Lag Bank	393	1289	247943
Lamb Pasture	367	1204	534021
Lang How	414	1358	318071
Langdale Pikes: Pike of Stickle	709	2326	274074
Langdale Pikes: Harrison Stickle	736	2415	282074
Langfield Banks	173	568	468261
Lank Rigg	541	1775	092120
Lanthwaite Hill, see Brackenthwaite Hows			
Lanty Crag	273	896	500202
Lanty's Tarn	276	906	384163
Latrigg	368	1207	279247
Latrigg Tarn	245	804	417018
Latter Barrow (Birkby)	166	545	129966
Latterbarrow (Kinniside Common)	354	1161	074115
Latterbarrow (W Irton Fell)	C200	C656	127027
Latterbarrow (Ennerdale)	273	896	130147
Latterbarrow (Claife Heights)	244	804	367991
Latterbarrow (Wasdale)	C200	C656	127027
Launchy Tarn (High Scawdel)	C550	C1804	233150
Levers Hause	C680	C2231	271994
Levers Water	414	1358	279993
Lily Fell	182	597	464977
Lily Pong	C200	C656	368983
Lily Tarn	200	656	364040
Lincombe Tarns	684	2244	241094
Ling Fell	373	1224	180286
Lingmell	800	2625	209082
Lingmell (Ennerdale)	435	1427	142130
Lingmell End	C660	C2165	446092

Lingmoor Fell	469	1539	303046
Lingmoor Tarn	C390	C1280	301051
Lingy Hill	C250	C820	558135
Little Arming How	244	800	182992
Little Birkhouse Hill	C400	C1312	494165
Little Carrs	692	2270	270015
Little Crag	C280	C919	184977
Little Dodd (Helvellyn range)	C780	C2559	337204
Little Dodd (Ennerdale)	590	1936	149155
Little Hart Crag	637	2090	387100
Little Harter Fell	C670	C2198	470093
Little Ladstones	C390	C1280	535126
Little Meldrum: N summit	424	1391	425233
Little Meldrum: S summit	404	1325	422228
Little Mell Fell	505	1657	423240
Little Round How	494	1621	207132
Little Saddle Crag	C570	C1870	527083
Little Scoat Fell	841	2759	160114
Little Stand	727	2385	251032
Little Worm Crag	C400	C1312	193971
Little Yarlside	516	1693	532072
Littledale Edge	576	1890	207161
Littlewater Tarn	259	850	509170
Loadpot Hill	672	2205	457181
Lofshaw Hill	312	1024	387278
Loft Crag	C670	C2198	277072
Loftbarrow	C350	C1148	131231
Long Crag (Bannisdale Fell)	493	1617	516052
Long Crag (W Duddon Valley)	C410	C1345	204989
Long Fell (Shap): N summit	424	1391	558091
Long Fell (Shap): S summit	452	1483	557085
Long Fell (Embleton)	319	1047	167275
Long Moss Tarn	C130	C426	291936
Long Side (Longside Edge)	734	2408	249284
Long Top (Crinkle Crags)	859	2818	249049
Lonscale Fell	715	2346	286271
Looking How	164	538	403906
Looking Stead	627	2057	186118
Lord's Lot	209	686	446929
Lord's Seat	524	1719	519066
Lord's Seat (NW Fells)	552	1811	204266
Lord's Seat group of fells, principal heights over 350m (1148ft)			
Lord's Seat	552	1811	204266
Ullister Hill	525	1722	209260
Whinlatter Top	525	1722	197249
Brown How	517	1696	191251
Broom Fell	511	1676	194272

Tarbarrel Moss	493	1617	206253
Seat How	C490	C1608	213256
Barf	468	1535	215268
Graystones	456	1496	178264
Kirk Fell	438	1437	173266
Widow Hause	404	1325	183270
Ling Fell	373	1224	180286
Sale Fell	359	1178	194297
Lorton Fells	525	1722	197249
Lothwaite	345	1132	203297
Loughrigg Fell	335	1099	347051
Low (Tilberthwaite) Fell	397	1302	302021
Loweswater Fell (Fellbarrow group)	412	1352	136223

Loweswater Fell/Blake Fell range of fells [an extensive area bounded on the W by the Croasdale-Fangs Brow road, on the N by Loweswater, E by Crummock Water and S by the Floutern Pass track]. Principal heights over 350m (1148ft)

Blake Fell	573	1880	110197
Carling Knott	544	1785	121206
Gavel Fell	526	1726	117184
Mellbreak	512	1680	149186
Hen Comb	509	1670	132181
Sharp Knott	482	1581	107201
Burnbank Fell	475	1558	110209
High Pen	475	1558	110189
Banna Fell	456	1496	116174
Floutern Cop	451	1480	122174
Knock Murton	447	1467	095191
Owsen Fell	409	1342	101210
Godworth	365	1197	101183
Low Fell (Shap Fells	349	1145	560107
Low Fell (Fellbarrow group)	423	1388	137226
Low Hartsop Dodd, see Hartsop Dodd			
Low How	497	1631	374215
Low Kop	572	1877	474165
Low Pike	508	1667	374078
Low Raise	754	2474	456137
Low Rigg	277	909	303277
Low Saddle	656	2152	288133
Low Scawdel	521	1709	242162
Low Taggleshaw Tarn	C290	C951	505989
Low Tarn	C520	C1706	162093
Low Water	544	1785	275983
Lower Routen Beck Tarn	C250	C820	514991
Maiden Moor	576	1890	237182
Mardale Ill Bell	C760	C2493	448101
Martcrag Moor	547	1795	268083
Martcrag Moor Tarn	C540	C1772	267081

Mellbreak: N top	509	1670	143195
Mellbreak: S top	512	1680	149186
Mickle Moss	232	761	444014
Mickledore	C840	C2756	210069
Middle Crag	C480	C1575	288158
Middle Dodd	654	2146	397095
Middle Fell	582	1909	151072
Middle How	483	1585	296110
Middle Taggleshaw Tarn	C300	C984	507993
Mill Moor	176	577	479255
Millrigg Knott	300	984	461013
Moor Howe	229	751	397911
Moss Eccles Tarn	C170	C558	372968
Mosser Fell	416	1365	132242
Muddy Brow	279	915	547015
Muncaster Fell	231	758	112983
Muncaster Tarn	C160	C525	106978
Mungrisedale Common	633	2077	312292
Murton Fell	447	1467	095191
Mustard Hill	263	863	320935
Nab Crags	508	1667	314125
Nab Scar	C450	C1476	356072
Nan Bield Pass	640	2100	453096
Nethermost Pike	891	2923	344142
New Road (Dockray)	C430	C1411	384222
Newlands Hause	333	1092	192177
Oak Howe Crag	417	1368	305055
Old Coach Road (Dockray-Wanthwaite)	C440	C1443	384223
Old Man of Coniston	803	2634	272978
Ore Gap	C770	C2526	240072
Orrest Head	238	781	414994
Outerside	568	1863	211215
Owlet Wood	212	695	440969
Owsen Fell	409	1342	101210
Oxen Fell	228	748	326017
Park Fell	284	932	339024
Pavey Ark	700	2297	285079
Pen (Scafell Pike)	768	2520	220069
Penn (Whiteside)	C550	C1804	168224
Pike	C360	C1181	286218
Pike de Bield	810	2657	236068
Pike of Blisco	705	2313	271042
Pike of Stickle	709	2326	274074
Pikeawassa	432	1417	440181
Pikes	469	1539	238947
Pikes Crag	877	2877	210072
Pillar	892	2926	171121

Pillar group of fells, principal heights over 500m (1640ft)			
Pillar	892	2926	171121
Scoat Fell	841	2759	160114
Red Pike	826	2710	165106
Red Pike: lower summit	821	2628	166101
Steeple	819	2687	157117
Black Crag	801	2628	166101
Haycock	797	2615	145107
Looking Stead	692	2270	140084
Caw Fell	C690	C2264	132110
Seatallan	627	2057	186118
Place Fell	657	2156	406170
Plough Fell	448	1470	162912
Ponsonby Fell	C310	C1017	082071
Potter Fell	395	1296	490998
Potter Tarn	C250	C820	494989
Powley's Hill	465	1526	505135
Priest's Crag	424	1391	424233
Racom Bands	541	1775	261123
Raise (Helvellyn)	883	2897	343174
Rake Crags	506	1660	313113
Rampsgill Head	792	2598	443128
Randerside	C720	C2362	349211
Rannderdale Knotts	355	1165	167182
Raven Crag (Thirlmere)	461	1512	304188
Raven Crag (Birkby)	199	653	133969
Raven Howe	C710	C2329	450146
Red Crag (Eastern Fells)	539	1768	508067
Red Crag (High Street)	711	2333	450152
Red Pike (Buttermere)	755	2477	161154
Red Pike (Wastwater)	826	2710	165106
Red Pike: lower summit	801	2628	166101
Red Screes	776	2546	396088
Red Screes Tarn	774	2539	396087
Red Tarn (Helvellyn)	718	2356	349152
Red Tarn (Langdale)	C530	C1739	268037
Redbrow Bank	162	531	161995
Redcrag Tarn	700	2298	451150
Redhow Crags	C160	C525	152233
Renny Crags	216	709	365986
Rest Dodd	696	2284	433137
Reston Scar	255	837	460988
Rivings	335	1099	198294
Robin Hood	493	1617	530059
Robinson	737	2418	202169
Robinson's Tarn	C190	C623	369981
Rose Castle Tarn	C190	C623	333002

Rossett Gill Pass	C610	C2001	247076
Rossett Pike	650	2132	249076
Rosthwaite Cam	612	2008	256118
Rosthwaite Fell	612	2008	256118
Rough Crag (Riggindale)	628	2060	454112
Rough Crag (Birker Moor)	319	1047	161978
Round How (Dockray)	387	1270	392208
Round How (Place Fell)	C630	C2067	408166
Round How (Great End)	741	2431	219081
Rowantree Crags	359	1178	213036
Rowantree How (Birkby Fell)	C400	C1312	157959
Rowantree How (Miterdale)	177	581	136011
Rowantreethwaite	529	1736	487122
Rowling End	433	1421	229207
Rulbuts Hill	175	574	407936
Sail	773	2536	198203
Sale Fell	359	1178	194297
Sale How	666	2185	276286
Sallows	516	1693	437040
Sand Hill	756	2480	187219
Scafell	964	3163	207065
Scafell Pike	978	3209	216072
Scafell Pike group of fells, principal heights over 700m (2297ft)			
Scafell Pike	978	3209	216072
Scafell	964	3163	207065
Ill Crag	935	3068	223073
Broad Crag	930	3051	219076
Great End	910	2986	227085
Esk Pike	885	2903	237075
Lingmell	800	2625	209082
Esk Hause	759	2490	233080
Slight Side	748	2454	210052
Round How	741	2431	219081
Scale Head	253	830	376978
Scale Head Tarn	C200	C656	373975
Scale Ivy Intakes	229	751	380965
Scale Knott	338	1109	150178
Scales Fell	641	2103	335278
Scales Tarn	610	2001	329281
Scam Matthew	C520	C1706	516105
Scandale Pass Col	C520	C1706	388096
Scandale Tarn	C560	C1837	386098
Scar Crag	C250	C820	183979
Scar Crags	672	2205	208206
Scar Lathing	439	1440	226049
Scarth Gap	C450	C1476	189133

School Knott	232	761	426974
School Knott Tarn	C200	C656	428973
Scoat Fell	841	2759	160114
Scoat Tarn	C600	C1968	159103
Scott Howe	169	554	427929
Scout Scar	235	771	487922
Seat	561	1840	186134
Seat How (Lord's Seat group)	C490	C1608	213256
Seat How (Birker Moor)	311	1020	165971
Seat Robert	515	1690	526114
Seat Tarn	C530	C1739	184136
Seat Sandal	736	2415	344115
Seatallan	692	2270	140084
Seathwaite Fell	632	2073	227097
Seathwaite Tarn	C380	C1247	253988
Seatoller Fell	C460	C1509	233132
Selside Pike	655	2149	490111
Sergeant Man	730	2395	286089
Sergeant's Crag	571	1873	274114
Shap Fells, see Eastern Fells (Shap to Longsleddale)			
Sharp Knott	482	1581	107201
Sheffield Pike	675	2215	369182
Shelter Crags	815	2674	250053
Shipman Knotts	587	1926	472063
Side Pike	362	1188	293054
Silver Crag/Hill	271	889	397181
Silver How	395	1296	325066
Siney Tarn	C220	C722	162011
Skeggles Water	305	1001	480034
Skiddaw: High Man	931	3054	260291
Skiddaw: middle top	928	3045	261288
Skiddaw: south top	925	3035	261285
Skiddaw: north top	922	3025	261292
Skiddaw Little Man/Low Man	865	2838	267278
Skiddaw range of fells, principal heights over 500m (1640ft)			
Skiddaw: High Man	931	3054	260291
Skiddaw: middle top	928	3045	261288
Skiddaw: south top	925	3035	261285
Skiddaw: north top	922	3025	261292
Skiddaw Little Man/Low Man	865	2838	267278
Broad End	831	2726	261298
Carl Side	746	2447	255281
Long Side	734	2408	249284
Jenkin Hill	C730	C2395	274275
Carlside Tarn	C720	C2362	256282
Lonscale Fell	715	2346	286271
Ullock Pike	692	2270	244288

Sale How	666	2185	276286
Hare Crag	538	1765	277299
Dodd (Skiddaw Dodd)	502	1647	244274
Slate Hill	291	955	553125
Sleddale Fell (Grey Crag)	638	2093	497072
Sleddale Fells, see Eastern Fells			
Sleddale Forest	429	1408	488016
Sleddale Pike	C500	C1640	536094
Sleet Fell	378	1240	422188
Slight Side	748	2454	210052
Smaithwaite Fell	205	673	313197
Small Water	452	1483	455100
Smithy Fell	C390	C1279	133237
Snarker Pike	644	2113	390075
Soulby Fell	C290	C951	451245
Sour Howes	483	1585	428032
Sourfoot Fell	C410	C1345	135233
Souther Fell: N top	522	1713	354291
Souther Fell: S top	495	1624	351281
Sprinkling Crag Tarn	C620	C2034	228095
Sprinkling Tarn	597	1959	228091
Spy Crag	219	718	475988
St Raven's Edge	593	1946	406084
St Sunday Crag	841	2759	369134
Stainton Pike	498	1634	153943
Stake Pass	C480	C1575	265087
Stake Pass Tarn	C450	C1476	265088
Stang	655	2149	355176
Starling Dodd	633	2077	142158
Steel Fell (Dead Pike)	553	1814	320112
Steel Knotts	432	1417	440181
Steeple	819	2687	157117
Stickle Pike	375	1230	212927
Stickle Tarn (Dunnerdale Fells)	C300	C984	214928
Stickle Tarn (Great Langdale)	469	1540	287076
Sticks Pass	738	2421	342182
Sticks Tarn	575	1886	357181
Stile End (Barrow Door)	447	1466	221219
Stile End Pass (Kentmere to Longsleddale)	C350	C1148	476050
Stockdale Moor	C290	C951	103083
Stone Arthur	504	1654	348092
Stony Cove Pike	763	2503	418100
Stony Rigg	C490	C1608	411151
Stony Tarn	C300	C984	199205
Stord's Hill	384	1260	155962
Stybarrow Dodd	843	2766	343189
Styhead Pass	488	1601	218094

Styhead Tarn	C440	C1443	222099
Swainson Knott	C340	C1115	080084
Swarth Fell	C560	C1837	461197
Sweeten Crag	435	1427	295988
Swindale Foot Crag	C380	C1247	520139
Swineside Knott	553	1814	379197
Swinklebank Crag Ridge	553	1814	501049
Swinside (above High Swinside Farm)	509	1670	177239
Swinside (S Ullock)	244	800	233244
Swirl Hawse	C620	C2034	278008
Swirl How	802	2631	273006
Taggleshaw Tarn: High	C310	C1017	505994
Taggleshaw Tarn: Low	C290	C951	505989
Taggleshaw Tarn: Middle	C300	C984	507993
Tailbert Head	328	1076	530143
Tarbarrel Moss	493	1617	206253
Tarn at Leaves	C500	C1640	258122
Tarn Close Crag	219	718	293041
Tarn Crag (E Longsleddale)	664	2179	488078
Tarn Crag (Birker Moor)	291	955	193996
Tarn Crag (Easedale)	550	1804	303093
TarnCrags	829	2720	324280
Tarn Hill	313	1027	210921
Tarn Hows	188	617	331000
Tent Lodge Tarn	C240	C787	327972
Tenter Howe Tarn	C250	C820	507007
Tewit How	610	2001	146119
The Bell	335	1099	288979
The Knott (High Street)	739	2425	437127
The Knott (Broughton Mills)	284	932	224920
The Knott (Birkby Fell)	331	1086	144951
The Knott (Swindale)	297	974	505120
The Knotts	274	899	435217
The Knowe	C760	C2493	459088
The Nab	576	1890	434152
The Park (E Coniston Water)	302	991	311935
The Pike (Birker Fell)	C450	C1476	200986
The Pike (Duddon Valley)	370	1214	186934
The Tongue (Troutbeck)	364	1194	422064
Thirlmere Reservoir	179	587	322131
Thornthwaite Crag	784	2572	432100
Thornythwaite Fell	574	1883	245118
Three Dubs Tarn	206	676	378974
Three Tarns	720	2363	248060
Threlkeld Knotts	514	1686	330230
Throstlehow Crag	404	1325	227044
Thunacar Knott	723	2372	279080

Todd Fell	401	1316	512020
Todd Rigg	277	909	417268
Tom Heights	269	883	328005
Top o'Selside	335	1099	309919
Trough Head	430	1411	389142
Ulgraves	332	1090	511996
Ullister Hill	525	1722	209260
Ullock Pike	692	2270	244288
Ullscarf	726	2382	292122
Ullscarf ridge - Ullscarf to Bleaberry Fell, principal heights over 500m (1640ft)			
Ullscarf	726	2382	292122
High Saddle	675	2215	289129
Low Saddle	656	2152	288133
High Seat	608	1995	287180
Bleaberry Fell	590	1936	286196
High Tove	515	1690	289165
Rake Crags	506	1660	313113
Ulthwaite Rigg	C500	C1640	515093
Underbarrow Scar	235	771	487922
Undermillbeck Common	C190	C623	420955
Upper Routen Beck Tarn	C260	C853	511992
Walla Crag	379	1243	277213
Wallowbarrow Crag	292	958	222968
Walna Scar	621	2037	259965
Walna Scar Road	606	1988	259965
Wandhope	772	2533	188197
Wansfell	487	1598	404053
Wansfell Pike	484	1588	394042
Wasdale Mouth	419	1375	535065
Wasdale Pike	565	1854	536084
Watendlath Tarn	263	863	275162
Watermillock Common	540	1772	379202
Watson's Dodd	789	2589	336196
Wet Sleddale Reservoir	275	902	550115
Wether Hill	C670	C2198	456167
Wetherlam	762	2500	288011
Wharton Tarn	C180	C590	331988
Whatshaw Common	485	1591	542061
Whelpsty How	244	800	178915
Whin Ben	413	1355	166213
Whin Fell	385	1263	134248
Whin Rigg	535	1755	152034
Whin Rigg Tarn	C480	C1575	156039
Whinlatter Pass	C300	C984	198245
Whinlatter Top	525	1722	197249
Whinscales	425	1394	197033
White How	444	1457	205975

White Howe	530	1739	524042
White Maiden	608	1995	254957
White Moss (Sleddale Forest)	392	1286	480020
White Pike (Coniston)	598	1962	249956
White Pike (Pillar Ridge)	782	2566	169124
White Pike (Birkby Fell)	442	1450	151956
White Side (Helvellyn)	863	2831	338167
White Stones (Green Side)	795	2608	353187
White Stones (The Band)	568	1863	261061
Whiteless Breast	439	1440	182183
Whiteless Pike	660	2165	180190
Whiteside	707	2319	170219
Whiteside Pike	397	1302	521016
Whitfell	573	1880	158930
Whoap	511	1676	099129
Widow Hause	404	1325	183270
Wilkes How	263	863	120240
Wind Gap	C760	C2493	168118
Winder Hill	315	1033	502172
Windy Gap	C750	C2461	215105
Wise Een Tarn	C200	C656	370976
Wolf Howe	331	1086	543024
Wonder Hill	196	643	174986
Wood Moss Tarn	C160	C525	328918
Woodend Height	C480	C1575	157954
Woof Crag	C490	C1608	493129
Wraymires Tarn	C190	C623	369979
Wren Crag (High Rigg)	311	1020	316201
Wrynose Pass	393	1289	277027
Wythop Moss	C320	C1050	179271
Yew Bank (Blawith Fells)	207	679	262910
Yewbarrow	628	2060	173085
Yoadcastle	494	1621	157952
Yoke: high summit	706	2316	438067
Yoke: low summit	C660	C2165	436062
Youdell Tarn	369	1211	318068

CONVERSIONS

1 metre	=	3.2808992 ft
2 metres	=	6.5617984
3	=	9.8426976
4	=	13.1235968
5	=	16.4044960
6	=	19.6853952
7	=	22.9662944
8	=	26.2471936
9	=	29.5280928
10	=	32.808992
20	=	65.617984
30	=	98.426976
40	=	131.235968
50	=	164.044960
60	=	196.853952
70	=	229.662944
80	=	262.471936
90	=	295.280928
100	=	328.08992
200	=	656.17984
300	=	984.26976
400	=	1312.35968
500	=	1640.44960
600	=	1968.53952
700	=	2296.62944
800	=	2624.71936
900	=	2952.80928
1000	=	3280.8992

1 foot = 0.3048037 metres
1 mile = 1.609344 kilometres

Abbreviations

AD	Anno Domini
C	A capital C preceding a height refers to the nearest contour line
c	A lower case c after a number means century
c	A lower case c preceeding a number means 'circa'
CAMRA	Campaign for Real Ale
CHA	Countrywide Holidays Association
CTC	Cyclists Touring Club
E	East
ENE	East North East
EPNS	English Place Name Society
ESE	East South East
ha(s).	Hectare(s)
km(s).	Kilometre(s)
LDNP	Lake District National Park
M/C	Manchester Corporation
ME	Middle English
N	North
NNE	North North East
NNW	North North West
NP	National Park
NRL	National Rod Licence
NT	National Trust
NW	North West
NWWA	North West Water Authority
OE	Old English
ON	Old Norse
OS	Ordnance Survey
RSPB	Royal Society for the Protection of Birds
S	South
SL	Sea Level
SSSI	Site of Special Scientific Interest
SSW	South South West
SW	South West
Trig. Point	Ordnance Survey triangulation point
W	West
WADAA	Windermere, Ambleside and District Angling Association
WNW	West North West
YHA	Youth Hostels Association

Principal Dales/Valleys

Aira Beck
Bannerdale (2)
Bannisdale
Barkbethdale
Blengdale
Boredale
Borrowdale
Buttermere
Caiston Glen
Calder
Caudale
Cawdale
Coledale
Croasdale
Crookdale
Deepdale (2)
Dovedale
Duddon
Dunnerdale
Easedale
Embleton
Eskdale
Far Easedale
Fusedale
Gillercombe
Glencoyne
Glenderamackin
Glenderaterra
Glenridding
Great Langdale
Greenburn
Greendale
Grisedale
Grizedale
Hartsop
Heltondale
Howe Grain
Kentdale
Keskadale
Langstrath
Little Dale
Little Langdale
Little Mosedale
Long Mire
Longsleddale
Lorton Vale
Lyth Valley
Mardale
Martindale
Matterdale
Mickleden
Miterdale
Mosedale (3)
Naddle (2)
Newlands
Oxendale
Patterdale
Ramps Gill
Rannerdale
Rothay Valley
St John's in the Vale
Scandale
Seathwaite
Shoulthwaite Glen
Southerndale
Stockdale
Stonethwaite
Swindale
Thirlmere
Threlkeld
Troutbeck (2)
Troutdale
Vale of Grasmere
Warnscale Bottom
Wasdale (2)
Wet Sleddale
Willdale
Winster Valley
Woundale
Wythop
Yewdale

For further information consult individual entry in the gazetteer.

Heights of Principal Cols/Passes

	metres	feet	grid ref
Beck Head	C620	C2034	206107
Birker Moor Road	C260	C853	176972
Black Sail	C550	C1804	192114
Boredale Hause	384	1260	408157
Broughton Mills to Seathwaite	259	850	215932
Coledale Hause	C600	C1968	189212
Corney Fell Road	400	1312	150896
Dore Head	C490	C1608	175095
Dunmail Raise	238	781	327117
Esk Hause	759	2490	233080
Floutern	C410	C1345	121172
Garburn	447	1467	436044
Gatescarth	594	1949	474092
Goat's Hawse	649	2129	266983
Grisedale Hause	588	1929	349117
Hardknott	393	1289	231015
Honister Hause	C360	C1181	225136
Kirkstone	455	1493	401082
Levers Hawse	C680	C2231	271994
Mickledore	C840	C2756	210069
Nan Bield	640	2100	453096
Newlands Hause	333	1092	192177
Ore Gap	C770	C2526	240072
Rossett Gill	C610	C2001	247076
Scandale	C520	C1706	388096
Scarth Gap	C450	C1476	189133
Stake	C480	C1575	265087
Sticks	738	2421	342182
Stile End (Kentmere to Sadgill)	C350	C1148	476050
Styhead	488	1601	218094
Swirl Hawse	C620	C2034	278008
Threshthwaite Mouth	C600	C1968	427103
Wasdale Mouth	419	1375	535065
Whinlatter	C300	C984	198245
Wind Gap	C760	C2493	168118
Windy Gap	C750	C2461	215105
Wrynose	393	1289	277027

For further information consult entry in gazetteer.

Lakes

Bassenthwaite Lake
Brothers Water
Buttermere
Coniston Water
Crummock Water
Derwent Water
Elter Water
Ennerdale Water
Esthwaite Water
Grasmere
Haweswater
Loweswater
Rydal Water
Thirlmere
Ullswater
Wast Water
Wet Sleddale
Windermere

For more information consult individual entry in gazetteer.

Islands (named)

Coniston Water
Fir Island
Peel Island

Crummock Water
Holme Islands
Iron Stone
Scale Island
Woodhouse Islands

Derwent Water
Derwent
'Floating'
Lingholm
Lord's
Otter
Otterbield
Rampsholme
St Herbert's
Scarf Stones

Haweswater
Wood Howe

Rydal Water
Heron Island
Little Isle

Thirlmere
Deergarth How Island
Hawes How Island

Ullswater
Cherry Holm
Lingy Holm
Norfolk Island (House Holm)
Wallholme

Windermere
Belle Isle
Blake Holme
Brathay Rocks
Chicken Rock
Crow Holme
Curlew Crag
Grass Holme
Green Tuft Island
Hartley Wife
Hen Holme
Lady Holme
Liles of the Valley
Ling Holm
Maiden Holme
Ramp Holme
Rough Holme
Seamew Crag
Silver Holme
Thompson's Holme

MINES, PRINCIPAL (DISUSED)

The only operational haematite (specialist ore mine) in Europe is the Florence Mine, Egremont. The first sod of the No 1 shaft was cut in January 1914, by Florence, wife of the then company's chairman. At the same time she christened the mine 'Florence'. Underground tours are available and there is a Heritage Centre and museum.

Bannerdale Crags [336295] [340291]

Barrow [234217]

Boot Nab Gill, [175012]

Caudale E Caudale Beck, [409107]

Force Crag Coledale, [193214/200216]

Dovedale Hartsop or Hartsop Hall Mine. Closed 1942, [395119]

Dubhow Gill disused copper mine workings just S of the gill, [409144]

Eagle Crag Eagle Crag Mine. Closed 1877, [358142]

Egremont Florence Mine, see introduction above.

Gategill [324262]

Glenderamackin Valley upper reach Glenderamackin, [333286]

Glenridding Greenside Mine, closed 1962, [364177]

Grasmere Providence Mine, Little Tongue Gill (not shown on OS 2.5 ins Outdoor Leisure map, [339105]

Grasmere Fairfield Mine, Tongue Gill. (not shown on OS 2.5 ins Outdoor Leisure map), [340098]

Grasmere upper Greenhead Gill. Mine closed about 1573 (not shown on OS 2.5 ins Outdoor Leisure map), [350087]

Hartsop Hall Mine see **Hartsop Mine**

Hartsop Mine (Harstop Hall Mine) Dovedale. Closed 1942 [395119].

Helvellyn Helvellyn or Wythburn Mine. Alongside Mines Gill which drops down W slope of Helvellyn to Thirlmere, [325148]

Hesk Fell (Copper), [178942]

Kentmere [459008]

Kentmere E Millrigg Knott, [463014]

Kentmere WSW Wrengill Quarry, [471084]

Logan Beck [173916]

Longsleddale [329149]

Low Harsop Mine see **Myers Head Mine**

Mousthwaite Comb [344275]

Myers Head Mine (Low Hartsop Mine) situated at the confluence of Pasture Beck and Hayeswater Gill. 1868 to c1878 [416126].

Newlands Valley Castlenook, [227170]

Newlands Valley Goldscope, [226185] [230184]

Newlands Valley Little Mine, [233191]

Scope End Pan Holes, [226186]

The Pike (Copper), [189936]

Stonycroft Stonycroft Gill, [231212]

Tilberthwaite S Tilberthwaite Gill, [304005]

Wythburn copper mine, Birkside Gill, [330126]

Yewthwaite slope Cat Bells, [240194] [243189]

Detailed information on these and other mines, levels, trials in the area is principally given in *Mines of the Lake District Fells* by John Adams, 1988. Much information can be found in *Mines & Mining in the English Lake District* by John Postlethwaite, 1877 with later editions; *Mining in the Lake Counties* by W T Shaw, first published 1970; *Beneath the Lakeland Fells: Cumbria Mining Heritage* by the Cumbria Amenity Trust Mining Society, 1992; *Lakeland's Mining Heritage: The Last 500 Years* by the Cumbria Amenity Trust Mining History Society, 2000 and *Cumbrian Mining* by Ian Taylor (2001).

Quarries Disused

055061 slope in fell, N Ponsonby
065055 SSW Scargreen
077042 Wellington
094040 off the Gosforth to Nether Wasdale road
102978 Muncaster Fell
107906 S of the A595 to Corney Hall road
112944 Broad Oak, Waberthwaite
116028 alongside Santon Bridge to Nether Wasdale road
120240 Wilkes How
124242 slope of Fellbarrow
126222 slope Darling Fell
129245 slope of Fellbarrow
131236 Smithy Fell. Alongside a tributary of Mosser Beck
141211 Loweswater
152008 Eskdale
154212 Brackenthwaite Hows (Lanthwaite Hill)
154222 Brackenthwaite
159004 Eskdale
162283 Embleton. Slope of Long Fell
164004 Beckfoot, Eskdale
172287 slope of Ling Fell
177258 alongside the B5292 near Scawgill Bridge
185128 Dub's Quarry, Ennerdale
196284 Darling How
200245 Whinlatter. Alongside the B5292.
202295/6 Slope Lothwaite
203947 Duddon valley
204132 S Warnscale Beck. Between Green Crag and Little Round How
204293 Lothwaite Side
205282 SE Wythop Hall
210135 Dubs Quarry, Fleetwith
210194 Keskadale
210293 Wythop Wood
212139 slope Fleetwith Pike. Above Hopper Quarry
212228 alongside the ridge between Kinn and Sleet How
213137 Hopper Quarry, Fleetwith
213140 Ash Gill Quarry, Honister
215280 King's Wood
215927 below Stickle Tarn outflow
216139 Bull Gill, Honister
217276 Woodend Brow above Woodend
219943 Brock Barrow
220935 Stainton Ground Quarries
222934 Stainton Ground Quarries
223142 Yewcrag Quarries, N Honister Hause
223145 Quey Foot Quarry, N Honister Hause
223185 W slope Scope End
224145 Sam New Quarry, N Honister Hause
228202 foot of Rowling End. Alongside Rigg Beck
228948 Caw Quarry
229912 alongside the River Lickle
235275 rear of Kiln How
237153 Rigghead
240267/8 alongside the A591 on the slope of Dodd (Skiddaw Dodd)
242938 in afforested area E River Lickle
244236 Portinscale
248958/9 Walna Scar Quarries
249166 Dalt Wood, N Castle Crag, Borrowdale
250961/2 Walna Scar Side
251160 High Hows, Castle Crag, Borrowdale
252951 N Broughton Moor Quarry
253167 Quayfoot, Borrowdale
254945 Broughton Moor Quarry
255930 Alongside Hummer Lane
256938 S Broughton Moor Quarry
261939 Lord's Low Allotment
262965 E slope Brown Pike
269955 Ash Gill Quarry between Red Gill and Ash Gill Beck
271971 E slope Coniston Old Man
271974 E slope Coniston Old Man
272958 Flask Brow, Torver
277979 Flask Brow, Torver

278959 alongside Torver Beck
279961 between Summers Cove Beck and Torver Beck
279973 Bursting Stone Quarry, Coniston
279981 E slope Coniston Old Man
280962 between Summers Cove Beck and Torver Beck
282983 between Summers Cove Beck and Torver Beck
283952 WNW Little Arrow
284984 WNW Little Arrow
288909 alongside the A5084
289969 Banishead
292276 slope Lonscale Fell
293275 slope Lonscale Fell
294956 alongside A593, Torver to Coniston road
294985 E Levers Water Beck, N Miners Bridge
295987 E Levers Water Beck, N Miners Bridge
296995 below Long Hill, Yewdale Fells
297974 Coniston
297996 below Long Hill, Yewdale Fells
298145 E head of Blea Tarn (Watendlath)
299973 Coniston
300035 alongside Little Langdale to head of Great Langdale road
304017 Low Fell, near Betsy Crag
305008 Tilberthwaite
305010 Low Tilberthwaite
305019 Betsy Crag, Low Fell (2)
305020 Betsy Crag, Low Fell
305021 Betsy Crag, Low Fell
306007 Tilberthwaite
306022 Betsy Crag, Low Fell
306042 Lingmoor Fell
307160 N Launchy Gill, Thirlmere
307023 Betsy Crag, Low Fell
307024 Betsy Crag, Low Fell
307051 Spoutcrag Quarry, Lingmoor Fell
307160 N Launchy Gill
307236 Low Rigg
308001 S Goat's Crag
308047 Colt Howe Quarry, Lingmoor Fell
308198 foot of Smaithwaite Banks
308205 S Yew Crag, High Rigg
309014 near High Tilberthwaite
309027 Atkinson Coppice, Little Langdale
309040 Lingmoor Fell
309043 Lingmoor Quarry, Lingmoor Fell
310020 E Knotts. NNE High Tilberthwaite
310040 Lingmoor Fell (2)
310942 Heald Brow, E side of Coniston Water
311019 E Knotts. NNE High Tilberthwaite
311022 E Knotts. NNE High Tilberthwaite
311028 Little Langdale (2)
311041 Lingmoor Fell
312015 between High Tilberthwaite and Hodge Close
312024 Moss Rigg Quarry, Moss Rigg Wood
312042 Lingmoor Fell
312985 Guards Wood
313016 between High Tilberthwaite and Hodge Close
313017 between High Tilberthwaite and Hodge Close
314027 Little Langdale
314028 Little Langdale
316044 Banks Quarry, Lingmoor Fell
316194 Legburthwaite
317013 Holme Fell
317017 Hodge Close
317261 Gategill Fell
318018 Hodge Close
318037 off the old road from Little Langdale to Elterwater
318041 Howe Banks Quarry, Lingmoor Fell
320019 Hodge Close
320220 Bramcrag Quarry, St John's in the Vale
320056 Thrang Crag Quarry, Chapel Stile
321230/1 Hilltop Quarries, St John's in the Vale
321233 Hilltop Quarries, St John's in the Vale
322933 between Farra Grain Heights and Mustard Hill

323043 SW Elterwater
323044 SW Elterwater
323045 SW Elterwater
323237 W slope Threlkeld Knotts
324049 Elterwater Quarry (still being worked)
324087 Easedale, below Jackdaw Crag
324917 Satterthwaite Moor
325079 James's Quarry, WNW Grasmere
325946 below Carron Crag
327243 Threlkeld Quarry, Thelkeld
330991 alongside Hawkshead Hill-Tarn Hows road
332995 SW Rose Castle
333997 SW Rose Castle
334941 Grizedale
334996 S Rose Castle
334997 SSW Rose Castle
335990 alongside Hawkshead Hill-Tarn Hows road
337936 alongside Grizedale-Satterthwaite road
342999 Knipe Fold
345063 White Moss Common
347007 adjoining the Drunken Duck Inn-Knipe Fold road
347010 W Drunken Duck Inn-Knipe Fold road
347910 alongside Thwaite Head-Dale Park road
348065 White Moss Quarry
348913 junction of Force Mills-Dale Park road and that from Thwaite Head-Dale Park
350001 between Field Head House and Ramsteads
352026 SSE Skelwith Fold
353003 alongside Drunken Duck Inn-Outgate road
355058 Loughrigg Quarries, Loughrigg Fell
356010 slope High Crag. Other quarries in vicinity
358015 Brathay Quarries
359182 above Greenside Mine
359186 above Greenside Mine
362009 off the B5286 near Randy Pike
362909 alongside Graythwaite-Thwaite Head road
364016 adjoining B5286. Near Pull Woods
366168 above Moor Side, Birkhouse Moor
367916 alongside unfenced track Field Head-Home Farm
372959 Near Sawrey
372989 Claife Heights
373918 angle between Hawkshead-Newby Bridge road and Cunsey-Graythwaite road
379961 N Far Sawrey
381039 below Redbank Wood, Grasmere
385250 E Bank of Trout Beck
386227 Matterdale. Between New Road and the A5091
386982 Heald Quarry (Crier of Claife)
387021 behind the Lowwood Hotel
388084 WSW slope Red Screes over looking Scandale Bottom
392073 Kirkstone Quarry (Pet's Quarry) (still being worked)
392224 W Thornythwaite A5091
393073 Pet's Quarry (Kirkstone Quarry) - working quarry - below Snarker Pike E
393231 Matterdale End
396008 off the A591, near Quarry Garth Country House Hotel
397170 between Side Farm and Blowick, Ullswater
400028 off Hundreds Road, Troutbeck
400162 behind Side Farm, Ullswater
404948 ENE junction A5074/B5360
407082 between Sattereven and St Raven's Edge
408177 Place Fell (Slate Workings)
409108 Caudale Quarry, W Caudale Beck
413183 E Low Moss Gill. Foot of High Dodd
414052 below Dodd Hill, W A592
416059 between the A592 and Hird Wood.
417050 E A592, near Ings Bridge, Troutbeck valley
422231 SSW of The Hause
423063 slope of the Tongue, Troutbeck Park
424034 Applethwaite Quarry, Garburn Road
424237 SSE slope Little Mell Fell

Quarries Disused

427063	Park Quarry, Troutbeck Park
428965	alongside road from the B5284 (opposite Windermere Golf Course) - Borwick Fold
429239	E slope Little Mell Fell
430070	E Hagg Gill
431215	NW Gowbarrow Hall
433056	E Hagg Gill. Above Lowther Brow
435038	slope Sallows (3 quarries)
440070	between Rainsborrow Crag and Star Crag
441069	behind Rainsborrow Crag, Kentmere
442070	behind Rainsborrow Crag, Kentmere
445071	Kentmere, S Reservoir Cottage
445073	Kentmere, S Reservoir Cottage
446073	Kentmere, adjoining Reservoir Cottage
448917	E Spout House
449074	Kentmere, E River Kent, below reservoir dam
450038	Kentmere, adjoining Hall Wood
451072	above Tongue Scar, Kentmere.
453105	between Blea Water and Small Water, N Piot Crag
456079	above Ullstone Gill
457080	below Kentmere Pike, E Ullstone Gill
458077	above Ullstone Gill
459107	alongside Blea Water Beck
467082	WSW Wrengill Quarry, Longsleddale
474086	Wrengill Quarry, Longsleddale
475020	Sleddale Forest
477042	Cocklaw Fell
477048	Cocklaw Fell (N slope)
479082	Longsleddale
478163	N Measand Beck
480090	below Selside Brow
482090	E Gatescarth Pass
482231	W Heughscar Hill
483235	W Heughscar Hill
486186	Pen End
489057	E Sadgill, Longsleddale
491095	Mosedale
492246	Winder Hill Farm
493055	Stockdale, Longsleddale
494097	Mosedale Quarry, Mosedale
494217	W Helton
494945	Plumgarths
496196	W Butterwick, E Cockle Hill
496250	S Celleron
497098	Mosedale
498917	Bradleyfield
500220	W Helton
501242	between Askham and Celleron
503213	SW Helton
504180	above the Howes, Bampton
507220	W Helton
509244	NNW Askham
512040	SW Bannisdale Head
520044	E Bannisdale Head
525199	Knipescar
526195	Knipescar
528184	Bampton Grange
528187	Bampton Grange
532193	Knipescar Common
532204	between Whalemoor and Whalemoor Head
536238	Village Quarry, Lowther
539182	Scarside
542221	Hackthorpe High Plantation, Lowther Park
544119	Wet Sleddale
545167	E Rosgill
547023	adjoining A6, N Kidshowe Bridge
547191	Outscar
558084	Shap Pink Quarry, Shap Fells, see Shap Quarries in Gazetteer
564106	Shap Blue Quarry, Shap Fells, see Shap Quarries in Gazetteer

The number of quarries still operating in the whole of the Lake District can be counted on two hands but the above list of disused quarries in this area shows the extent of quarrying in past years.

TARNS

Principal tarns in the area (where just a single tarn is mentioned the word 'tarn' is omitted)

Acre
Alcock
Allen Crags Tarns
Angle (2)
Arnsbarrow
Ash Crags
Barngates
Beacon
Beckhead
Birk Haw
Blackbeck
Blea (3)
Blea Water
Bleaberry
Blelham
Blind (2)
Blindtarn Moss
Bolton's
Boo
Borrans Reservoir
Borwick Fold
Brandreth Tree Tarns
Brigstone
Broadcrag
Brown Cove
Burnmoor
Carlside
Caspel Gate
Caudale Head
Caudale Head/Moor
Caw Moss
Codale
Codale Head Tarns
Cogra Moss
Combe Door Tarns
Combe Head Tarns
Crook Reservoir
Cunswick
Dale Head
Devoke Water
Dock
Dockey
Dry
Dubbs Reservoir
Easedale
Eel
Eskdale Green
Flag Pots
Flass
Floutern
Four Stones
Foxes (Fox)
Galls
Ghyll Head Fish Pond
Ghyll Head Reservoir
Ghyll Pool
Goat's Water
Goosey Foot
Great Castle How Tarns
Great How Tarns
Great Moss
Greendale
Green Hows
Greenburn Reservoir
Grey Crag
Grisedale
Grizedale
Gurnal Dubs
Haber
Hagg Pond
Hard
Hardknott Tarns
Harrop
Haskew
Hayeswater
High Arnside
High House
High Man
High Nook
High Scawdel
Highs Moss
Hodson's
Holehird
Holehouse
Holme Ground
Holmes Head
Innominate
Jenny Dam
Juniper
Kelly Hall
Kemp
Kentmere
Kentmere Reservoir
Kepple Cove
Kirkfell
Knipe
Lambfoot Dub
Lanty
Lanty's
Latrigg
Launchy (2)
Levers Water
Lily
Lily Pond
Lincomb Tarns
Lindeth
Lingmoor
Little Langdale
Littlewater
Long Moss
Loughrigg
Low
Low Birker
Low Eskholme
Low Ludderburn
Low Water
Low Routen Beck
Martcrag Moor
Middle Fairbank
Middlerigg
Moor
Mortimere
Moss Eccles

Tarns

Moss Side
Muncaster
Out Dubs
Parkgate
Peat Pot
Pike Tarns
Podnet
Pots of Ashness
Potter
Priest Pot
Rainsbarrow
Ratherheath
Raven Crag
Raven's Crag
Ravencrag Tarns
Red (2)
Red Screes
Redcrag
Robinson's
Rose Castle
Rosthwaite Farm Tarns
Rough Hill
Rowanthwaite Pond
Sawrey Striceley
Scale Head
Scalebarrow
Scales
Scandale
School Knott
Scoat
Scope Beck
Scream Point
Seat
Seathwaite
Seathwaite Tarns
Sergeant Man
Shelter Crag Tarns
Silver How
Siney
Skeggles Water
Slew
Small Water
Snipeshow
Sprinkling
Sprinkling Crag
Stake Pass
Stickle (2)
Sticks
Stonehills
Stonesty Pike Tarns
Stony
Styhead
Taggleshaw Tarn: High
Taggleshaw Tarn: Low
Taggleshaw Tarn: Middle
Tarn at Leaves
Tarn Hill Tarns
Tarn Hows
Tent Lodge
Tenter Howe
Three Dubs
Three Tarns
Thunacar Knott
Tim's
Torver
Torver Low Common
Tosh
Undermillbeck Common
Upper Routen Beck
Watendlath
Wetherlam
Wharton
Whin Rigg Tarns
White Moss
Wise Een
Wood Moss
Woodhow
Wythburn Head

For more information and positions of other tarns consult the five principal works on Lakeland tarns - *The Tarns of Lakeland* by W Heaton Cooper (first published 1960), *Exploring Lakeland Tarns - A Complete Guide* by John Blair (1993), *A Guide to the Lakeland Tarns* by H E Winter (1991), the more technical *Concentrations of Major Ions in Lakes and Tarns of the Lake District (1953-1978)* by T R Carrick & D W Sutcliffe, published by the Freshwater Biological Association (1982), *Tarns of Lakeland* Vol 1 - West (1995), Vol 2 - East (1996) by John and Anne Nuttall and *Tarns of the Central Lake District* by the Freshwater Biological Association and the Brathay Exploration Group (2003). The latter lists 49 tarns and Rydal Water and covers their history and vegetation.

PROMINENT WATERFALLS

Aira Force Aira Beck
Barrow
Birker Force Birker Beck
Buckstones Jump Rydal Beck
Cam Spout Eskdale
Colwith Force River Brathay
Dalegarth Force Eskdale
Dungeon Ghyll Force Great Langdale
Esk Falls Eskdale
Force Falls Force Mills
Force Jump River Kent, Kentmere
Forces Falls (Swindale Falls) Mosedale Beck
Fordingdale Force Measand Beck,
Galleny Force
Gill Force Eskdale
Hell Gill Force see Whorneyside Force
High Force Aira Beck
High Force Pudding Beck
High Lodore
Holme Force
Levers Water Beck
Lodore
Low Force Aira Beck
Low Force Pudding Beck
Moss Force
Ritson's Force Wasdale Head
Rowantree Force
Rydal Falls Rydal Beck
Scale Force Crummock
Scaleclose Force
Scalehow Force Scalehow Beck
Skelwith Force River Brathay, Skelwith
Sourmilk Gill Buttermere
Sourmilk Gill Force Easedale Beck
Spout Force (Force Spout)
Stanley Force Eskdale
Stanley Gill Force see Stanley Force
Stockghyll Force Stock Ghyll, Ambleside
Stybeck Fall Stanah Gill
Taylor Gill Force Borrowdale
The Forces Deepdale Beck
The Forces Measand Beck
Thornthwaite Force Haweswater Beck
Throng/Thrang Force
Tonguegill Force Tongue Gill
Vicar Swa Eskdale
Whorneyside Force Oxendale

For possible additional information consult individual entry in gazetteer.

Springs and Wells

053056 (S) Ponsonby
055046 (S) alongside Sally Hill
056067 (S) near Stakes Bridge which crosses the River Calder
057100 (S) Friar Well, source of Friar Gill
059087 (S) on Cold Fell N Strudda Bank
062105 (S) alongside the River Calder
063094 (S) Cold Fell, adjoining Side Wood
073041 (W) Holy Well, Gosforth
075043 (S) Gosforth, E Wind Hall, SW Bank House Farm
076071 (S) Farmery
079074 (S) between Swainson Knott and Ponsonby Fell
080073 (S) between Swainson Knott and Ponsonby Fell
081003 (W) Virgin Mary Well.
081165 (S) Woodfoot, Ennerdale
085047 (W) alongside Spring Keld, Gosforth
085047 (S) Gosforth, E River Bleng
086204 (S) between Dockray Nook and Fitz Bridge
090151 (S) W shore Ennerdale Water.
090204 (S) alongside the track from Dockray Nook N to Lamplugh
091038 (S) ESE Rainors
091161 (S) alongside Rothery Sike
093036 (S) W Murthwaite Moor Wood
093983 (S) NE A595, WSW Gaskell
094177 (S) slope Kelton Fell. Small stream issuing forth joins Croasdale Beck
095212 (S) slope Owsen Fell
096214 (S) slope Owsen Fell
097051 (S) between Guards and Losca
097215 (S) slope Owsen Fell
097951 (S) E Beacon Plantation, Muncaster
097962 (S) Muncaster
098171 (S) SE Croasdale
098180 (S) source of small tributary of Croasdale Beck
099205 (S) short stream issuing from it joins Wisenholme Beck
099214 (S) slope Owsen Fell
101165 (S) alongside the minor road from Croasdale to Bowness (Ennerdale)
101905 (W) Marshside
101919 (S) E A595, NW Middle Bank
103919 (S) E A595, N Middle Bank
104924 (S) alongside Borrowdale Wood
106206 (S) short stream issuing from it joins Wisenholme Beck
106927 (S) Far Bank, Waberthwaite
107030 (S) near Hollins
107998 (S) near Crag Farm
108039 (W) Gatterigghow
108202 (S) short stream issuing from it joins Wisenholme Beck
108908 (S) N A595 to Corney Hall road
108936 (W) alongside the A595
108952 (S) E Hall Waberthwaite, W A595
109033 (W) alongside track from Santon Bridge-Nether Wasdale road to Wrighthow
109271 (S) alongside Palace How
109939 (W) Waberthwaite, between Row Farm and the A595.
110236 (S) alongside path between Bramley and Graythwaite
110970 (S) Muncaster, alongside the A595
111917 (W) Corney, across minor road from Moorside
112935 (S) Waberthwaite, between the A595 and minor road S to Corney
112942 (S) alongside minor road from the A595 to Woodgate
112948 (S) W A595 near Broad Oak
112955 (S) between Glenwood and the A595
112998 (S) between Crag Farm and Sandbank
113905 (S) SE Corney Hall, Spring House nearby
114243 (S) Mosser, SW Mossergate Farm
114915 (S) S Skellerah

114925 (S) W How End
114936 (S) Waberthwaite, between the A595 and the minor road S to Corney
114941 (S) Waberthwaite, between the A595 and the minor road S to Corney
115034 (S) SW Stangends
116022 (S) alongside Mecklin Beck and near Gill House
116272 (S) alongside Threlkeld Leys
116918 (S) Corney
117918 (2S) Corney
118051 (S) N of Gosforth to Wastwater high road
118226 (S) SW Askill
118922 (S) slightly W Charlesground
118952 (S) High Dyke Wood
119945 (S) alongside Mill Gill
119949 (S) S High Dyke Wood
120029 (S) alongside the Santon Bridge to Nether Wasdale road, stream from it joins Mecklin Beck
120223 (S) head of Loweswater
120917 (S) near Lambground, Corney
120945 (S) alongside Mill Gill
121037 (W) Cold Well, Great Coppice
121916 (W) Lambground, Corney
122223 (S) near Loweswater Hall, Loweswater
122248 (S) Mosser, near Fellside Farm
127162 (W) Scaw Well, ESE summit of Great Borne
132033 (S) SE Flass Tarn
133067 (W) Cold Well WSW of the summit of Seatallan
137217 (S) Loweswater
138251 (S) alongside the track to Hatteringill, stream emerges from it to joins the Cocker
139253 (S) near the track to Hatteringill, stream emerging from it joins the Cocker
141228 (S) lower slope Raven Crag, Low Fell
141272 (S & W) Stanger Spa Holy Well
142235 (S) E slope Sourfoot Fell
143205 (S) Loweswater, stream from it joins Park Beck
143223 (S) S Pottergill
144023 (W & S) Caddy Well, above Great Bank, Miterdale, Merebeck originates here.
145283 (W) Shatton Lodge Farm
147200 (S) between Green Wood and Crummock Water
148217 (S) alongside the R Cocker near Scale Hill
152240 (S) Lorton Vale
159261 (W) High Lorton, alongside the B5292
160261 (S) Hole Mire, High Lorton
162260 (2W) Hole Mire, High Lorton, alongside the B5292
163194 (S) between Fall Crag and Cinderdale Beck
164071 (W) alongside Bowderdale, Wasdale
164195 (S) between Fall Crag and Cinderdale Beck
165196 (S) between Fall Crag and Cinderdale Beck
165292 (W) alongside Beck House Farm, Embleton
167237/169236/169237 (4S) foot of Dodd, Whiteside
168245 (3S) SW High Swinside Farm
168280 (S) Embleton High Common
168286 (S) Embleton
169240 (S) foot of Swinside
169243 (S) alongside the minor road from the B5292 to Hopebeck
169246 (2S) High Swinside Farm
169290 (S) W Green Lonning between Wythop and Embleton
170239/170240 (2S) foot of Swinside
170241 (3S) foot of Swinside
170258 (S) alongside the B5292
170291 (S) W Green Lonning between Wythop and Embleton
171251/172252/173252 (3S) slope Swinside, N minor road from the B5292 to Hopebeck
171272 (S) near head of major tributary of Tom Rudd Beck
171290 (S) W Green Lonning between Wythop and Embleton
173288 (S) slope Ling Fell

173294 (S) Low Abbey, Wythop Mill
175004 (S) SSE Dalegarth, Eskdale
175272 (2S) Wythop Moss
178282 (S) Bladder Keld, slope Ling Fell
178298 (S) Wythop Mill
182272 (S) Wythop Moss
182282 (S) slope Ling Fell
184932 (S) Pike Side
190276 (S) slope Broom Fell
192280 (S) E fringe Wythop Moss
194282 (2S) E Burthwaite Heights
194284 (S) E Burthwaite Heights
195947 (S) Brighouse, off the Birker Fell road
198281 (S) SW Wythop Hall, W Wythe Sike
199281 (S) SW Wythop Hall, W Wythe Sike
200278 (2S) WSW Wythop Hall
201008 (S) Wha House Farm, Eskdale
203904 (2S) E Low Whineray Ground, S Raven's Crag
203905 (S) E Low Whineray Ground, S Raven's Crag
204276 (S) S Wythop Hall
204292 (S) Lothwaite Side
204901 (S) near Hutton
205293 (S) Lothwaite Side
211229 (W & S) Lanty Well between Kinn and Sleet How
213942 (S) near High Kiln Bank Farm
219917 (S) Keskadale
219917 (W) Keskadale
220935 (S) E Park Head Road, source of Dunnerdale Beck
220946 (S) source of Black Sike, Duddon
221917 (S) near Dry Hall, Dunnerdale Beck valley
221940 (W) source of farthest headstream of Tommy Gill
223901 (S) Broughton Mills
224902 (S) Broughton Mills
226903 (S) Broughton Mills
227919 (S) alongside the Broughton Mills to Stephenson Ground road
228919 (S) alongside the Broughton Mills to Stephenson Ground road
228905 (S) Broughton Mills
228911 (S) alongside the River Lickle
229187 (W) Low Snabb
229911 (S) alongside the River Lickle
233274 (S) Derwent Foot
233296 (S) between the A591 and minor road to Scarness and Chapel
235276 (S) Little Crosthwaite
235276 (W) Little Crosthwaite
235277 (S) Little Crosthwaite
235914 (S) between Stock Beck and Lind End Bridge
236902 (S) near Low Hen Croft
236905 (W) just off the A593, W Baskell
237205 (W) Ghyll Bank, Newlands valley
238904 (W) off the A593, SE Baskell
240292 (S) below the Edge, Bassenthwaite
240293 (S) below the Edge, Bassenthwaite
240295 (S) above Raven Crag, Bassenthwaite
241208 (W) Skelgill
244209 (S) between Skelgill and Gutherscale
246196 (S) Cat Bells
246203 (S) Skelgill Bank
247192 (S) E slope Cat Bells
247202 (S) foot of Skelgill Bank
248193 (S) foot of Skelgill Bank
248195 (S) foot of Skelgill Bank
248202 (S) foot of Skelgill Bank
248206 (S) foot of Skelgill Bank
250905 (S) adjoining Crag Wood
252185 (W) Salt Well, Manesty
253250 (S) between the A591 and the River Derwent
257265 (S) stream emerging joins Mill Beck
261919 (W) near Haverigg Holme
270206 (S) E shore Derwent Water
275226 (2S) between Springs Wood and Castlehead Wood
276940 (S) near Brocklebank Ground, Torver
277939 (W) Brocklebank Ground off the A593
278964 (S) Well In Crag, alongside the Walna Scar Road
279224 (S) Castlerigg
280229 (S) stream emerging from it becomes Cuddy Beck
281224 (W) Castlerigg
282224 (W) Castlerigg
282945 (S) Torver
283259 (S) short stream emerging joins Whit Beck

284259 (S) short stream emerging joins Whit Beck
283950 (S) the Moors, Torver
284245 (S) wooded area N River Greta
284949 (S) W Torver Beck
285947 (S) Crook, Torver
288940 (S) off the A5084
289948 (S) alongside the A593, Torver-Coniston road
291201 (S) N end of Goat Crag
291952 (S) High Ground, alongside the A593
292242 (W) S A66 and Storms
293202 (S) N end of Goat Crag
293256 (S) stream emerging joins Whit Beck
299972 (S) Coniston
300203 (S) slightly S Shoulthwaite Farm
300241 (S) alongside loop road which crosses Naddle Bridge
300255 (S) foot of Blease Fell
300256 (2S) foot of Blease Fell
300257 (S) foot of Blease Fell
301215 (W) Shaw Bank, foot of High Rigg
301971 (S) Coniston, between Bowmanstead and Cat Bank
303981 (W) Far End, Coniston
306211 (S) High Rigg
306218 (S) High Rigg
306220 (S) High Rigg
306224 (W) alongside St John's Church, St John's in the Vale
306983 (S) Back Guards Plantation, Coniston
307217 (S) High Rigg
307218 (S) High Rigg
307219 (S) High Rigg
308212 (S) High Rigg
308218 (S) High Rigg
309207 (S) below Yew Crag, High Rigg
309257 (S) foot of Blease Fell
310195 (W) foot of Smaithwaite Banks
310210 (S) High Rigg
310217 (S) High Rigg
310255 (S) foot of Blease Fell
311202 (S) slope of High Rigg, N A591
311986 (S) Yewdale
312203 (S) High Rigg
312221 (S) Rake How, High Rigg
313217 (S) W St John's Beck
313989 (S) Yewdale
314211 (S) W St John's Beck
314213 (S) W St John's Beck
314216 (S) W St John's Beck
314220 (S) W St John's Beck
314985 (S) near Boon Crag Farm, Coniston
315208 (S) W St John's Beck
316207 (S) W St John's Beck
318218 (S) W B5322 St John's in the Vale
318219 (S) W B5322 St John's in the Vale
318971 (W) E side Coniston Water
319216 (S) E B5322 St John's in the Vale
319230 (S) E B5322 St John's in the Vale
319974 (S) E side Coniston Water
320185 (S) Fisher Place
320191 (S) Legburthwaite
320192 (S) Legburthwaite
320213 (S) near Bram Crag, St John's in the Vale
320237 (S) E B5322 St John's in the Vale
322149 (W) E shore Thirlmere
322977 (W) E side Coniston Water, across road from Atkinson Ground
324056 (W) Walthwaite
325082 (W) Easedale
325242 (W) Threlkeld Quarry
326086 (W) Easedale
330085 (W) grounds of Lancrigg, Grasmere
330259 (W) Hailhead Well, Threlkeld
331068 (W) Grasmere, W Red Bank Road
331903 (S) alongside Force Forge-Ickenthwaite road
332070 (W) Grasmere, W Red Bank Road
332100 (S) Town End, W A591
332100 (S) alongside Raise Beck near Town Head
334019 (S) Low Arnside
335078 (W) Easedale
335990 (W) alongside Hawkshead Hill-Tarn Hows road
335997 (W) S Rose Castle
338031 (S) alongside Cumbria Way near Skelwith Bridge
338074 (W) Grasmere, alongside the R Rothay.

338150 (W) Brownrigg Well, Helvellyn
339235 (W) alongside Old Coach Road
339909 (W) Force Mills
339989 (S) Tenter Hill, near Hawkshead Hill
340922 (S) Rowley Wood, Satterthwaite
340946 (S) Grizedale
341043 (S) W Loughrigg Tarn
341997 (W) Knipe Fold
342012 (S) Pullscar Plantation
342266 (S) between Scales and Guardhouse Bridge
342920 (S) below Pennington Height SE Satterthwaite
342929 (S) Breasty Haw
343015 (S) Pullscar Plantation, Pull Beck feeder
343018 (S) E Great Cobble, Pull Beck feeder
343032 (W) Skelwith Bridge, alongside the A593
343920 (S) below Pennington Height SE Satterthwaite
344027 (W) alongside minor road Bull Close-Brow Coppice
344275 (S) Mousthwaite Comb
345012 (S) Pullscar Plantation
345925 (S) E Satterthwaite, WNW Brock Crag
345929 (S) Breasty Haw
346013 (S) Pullscar plantation
346036 (S) Skelwith Bridge, between Mill Brow and the A593
346918 (S) alongside bridleway Low Dale Park-Satterthwaite
347000 (S) near Field Head House
347909 (S) Thwaite Head
348008 (S) Barngates Tarn feeder
348020 (S) E Drunken Duck Inn - Skelwith Fold road, Pull Beck feeder
348926 (S) Lawrence Scar Wood, W Dale Park Beck
349016 (S) E Drunken Duck Inn Skelwith Fold road, Pull Beck feeder
349926 (2S) Lawrence Scar Wood, W Dale Park Beck
350923 (S) across Dale Park Beck from Middle Dale Park
351027 (W) Skelwith Fold
351915 (S) SE Low Dale Park
351916 (S) SE Low Dale Park
351978 (2S) W Hannakin
352913 (S) SSE Low Dale Park
353006 (S) between the Outgate-Drunken Duck Inn road and Cold Well Intake
353010 (S) E Drunken Duck Inn, across road Outgate-Drunken Duck Inn
353017 (S) Great Brathay
353991 (W) alongside Loanthwaite Lane
354015 (S) Great Brathay
354965 (W) W Fold Gate
355018 (S) Great Brathay, Pull Beck feeder
355910 (S) Horse Pasture Wood
355914 (S) Low Dale Park Plantation
355966 (W) between Esthwaite Lodge and Fold Gate
355966 (W) Outgate
355992 (S) Loanthwaite
356019 (S) SW Pull Wyke, Pull Beck feeder
356976 (W) adjacent Water Side, W Esthwaite Water
356991 (S) alongside Loanthwaite Lane
356997 (W) Outgate
357011 (S) Cowperthwaite Intake
357914 (S) Low Dale Park Plantation
358258 (S) E Mosedale Beck and Mosedale Viaduct
358919 (S) Low Dale Park Plantation
358938 (S) NE High Dale Park, E Dale Park Beck
358939 (S) NE High Dale Park, E Dale Park Beck
359008 (S) E B5286, N Dan Becks
359010 (S) NE slope High Crag
360922 (S) between Bleaberry Fell and Rough Holes
360923 (S) Middle Dale Park Plantation
360930 (S) between High Dale Park and Black Brows
360985 (S) between Colthouse Plantation

and Colthouse-High Wray road
361920 (S) below Bleaberry Fell
361926 (S) Middle Dale Park Plantation, W Black Brows
361929 (S) between High Dale Park and Black Brows
361938 (S) High Dale Park Plantation
363246 (W) E Mosedale Beck, ESE Lobbs
363915 (S) Ausin Fell Coppice
363916 (S) Ausin Fell Coppice
363996 (W) alongside Colthouse-High Wray road
364005 (S) alongside Blelham Tarn which it feeds
364914 (2S) Ausin Fell Wood
364920 (S) below Bleaberry Fell
364998 (W) High Tock How
365019 (S) Pull Woods
365918 (S) W Field Head
365920 (S) below Bleaberrry Fell
365925 (S) below Black Brows. W Hazelseat
365928 (S) Black Brows, Dale Park
365989 (S) Latterbarrow
366919 (S) W Field Head
366928 (S) below Brack Brows, Dale Park
366939 (S) near Eel House
367918 (S) W Field Head
367931 (S) W Little Ore Gate, slightly W Hawkshead-Newby Bridge road
367939 (S) near Eel House
367984 (S) slightly N Colthouse-Belle Grange track
369029 (S) W shore Windermere, near Brathay Hall
369937 (2S) S Eel House, slightly W Hawkshead-Newby Bridge road
371932 (S) Little Ore Gate
375921 (S) Moss End Wood
375921 (S) Moss End Wood
375933 (S) W Low Cunsey Farm
378056 (W) alongside track, Grasmere-Scandale
379999 (2W) Balla Wray
380027 (W) Wansfell Holme
380218 (W) E Little Pike, W Cuddy Crag
380954 (W) Far Sawrey
381278 (S) W Lofshaw Hill. N A66
381946 (2S) alongside Far Sawrey-High Cunsey road near Crabtree Cottages
382928 (S) alongside Cunsey-Graythwaite road near Hammer Hole
383957 (S) Far Sawrey
384278 (S) W Lofshaw Hill, N A66
385052 (S) adjoining Kirkstone Road, W Roundhill Farm
387028 (S) alongside track Skelghyll Wood-High Skelghyll
387975 (W) W shore Windermere
388016 (W) below Holbeck Lane. E A592
388166 (W) St Patrick's Well, Glenridding
389012 (W) N Brockhole, alongside A591
389964 (S) W shore Windermere opposite landing stage W shore Belle Isle
390029 (S) High Skelghyll
390222 (S) W Thornythwaite, A5091
390922 (S) E A592. N Beech Hill Hotel
392215 (W) Dockray
393222 (W) Thornythwaite
393922 (S) between Beech Hill Hotel and Rowantree Hill
394026 (W) adjoining Low Skelghyll
395293 (S) SW Eycott Farm
396020 (W) between Skelghyll Lane and Holbeck Lane
396231 (S) Matterdale End
397008 (S) off the A591, near Quarry Garth Country House Hotel
397021 (S) between Robin Lane and Skelghyll Lane
397271 (S) Troutbeck, S A66
397942 (W) between Storrs Hall Hotel and Bellman Ground and the A592 and B5360
398961 (S) E shore Windermere, SE Cockshot Point
400219 (S) E Riddings Beck
400902 (S) between Looking How and Moor How Park
401912 (S) Ludderburn, between Moor How and Ludderburn Hill
401914 (S) between Cote Hill and Ludderburn Hill
401948 (2S) near junction A5074/B5360

402904 (S) between Looking How and Moor How Park
402945 (W) angle between the A5074 and B5360
402942 (2W) alongside track between Bellman Ground and Barker Knott Farm
403020 (S) between Robin Lane and Holbeck Lane
403082 (S) slightly E summit of Kirkstone Pass, slope St Raven's Edge.
404017 (W) alongside Wain Lane
404023 (S) Troutbeck, alongside Robin Lane
405003 (S) Troutbeck Bridge
405906 (S) slope of Looking How
405909 (W) alongside the Oaks, Cartmel Fell
405913 (W) foot of Fox Crag
405932 (S) S Rulbuts Hill
405935 (S) edge of Spring Wood adjoining Rulbuts Hill
405967 (S) alongside Brantfell Road, Bowness
406979 (S) Rayrigg Wood
407012 (S) alongside Bridge Lane near Broad Oaks
407037 (S) Troutbeck, E Nanny Lane
407246 (S) foot of Great Mell Fell
407902 (W) adjoining Bryan Beck
407921 (S) foot of Green Hill
407964 (S) Post Knott, Bowness
408016 (W) Thickholme Bridge
408033 (S) Troutbeck village
408906 (W) between Great and Little Hartbarrow
408907 (W) adjoining Little Hartbarrow
408910 (S) N Little Hartbarrow
408952 (S) W Lindeth Farm
409031 (W) Troutbeck village
409033 (W) Troutbeck village
409937 (S) W High House, Winster
410000 (W) top of St Catherine's Brow, near Troutbeck Bridge
410034 (2W) Troutbeck village
410928 (W) Winster House
410946 (3S) alongside footpath between the A5074 and Lindeth Lane
411015 (W) adjoining Moorhowe Road
411037 (W) Troutbeck village
411926 (S) E boundary Neds Wood
411952 (W) Lindeth Farm
412926 (S) W River Winster
413242 (S) W slope of Little Mell Fell
413244 (S) W slope of Little Mell Fell
414031 (S) Troutbeck, adjoining A592 opposite Limefitt Park
414991 (W) S slope Orrest Head
415012 (S) alongside Moorhowe Road. Near Allen Knott
415032 (W) Troutbeck, alongside Trout Beck
415927 (W) S track from Winster House to Winster-Birks Bridge road
416229 (S) between Old Park and Great Meldrum
416238 (S) Lowthwaite
416968 (S) Home Farm, Bowness
417929 (S) across road from Bryan House Farm
418900 (S) near Haycote Farm
418933 (W) Green Yew, Winster
418970 (W) W Lickbarrow Road
419934 (S) Winster
420025 (S) adjoining Dubbs Road
420248 (S) head of Thackthwaite Gill
420925 (S) between Hawkearth Bank and the A5074
420955 (2S) Undermillbeck Common
420964 (W) Low House Farm, Cleabarrow
421244 (S) Low House Farm, Cleabarrow
421903 (W) S of Low Fell Plantation
421954 (S) Undermillbeck Common
422246 (S) Undermillbeck Common
422916 (W) S Lamb Howe
422918 (S) alongside track from the A5074 to Lamb Howe
422951 (W) Undermillbeck Common
422996 (W) across the road from the Common Farm
423226 (S) Little Meldrum
423906 (S) S Low Fell Plantation
423965 (S) Cleabarrow
423973 (S) School Knott
423976 (S) School Knott

424018 (S) E Dubbs Reservoir and Dubbs Road
424236 (S) Little Mell Fell
424904 (S) S Low Fell Plantation
425905 (S) ESE Low Fell Plantation
425916 (W) Hubbersty Head
426226 (S) Little Meldrum
426234 (S) The Hause
426236 (S) N The Hause
427229 (S) near Priest's Crag
427230 (S) near Priest's Crag
427978 (S) Schoolknott Plantation
428225 (S) between Little Meldrum and Hagg Wood
428226 (S) slope Little Meldrum
428237 (S) Little Mell Fell
428901 (W) near Low Birks
428972 (S) alongside School Knott Tarn
428977 (S) Schoolknott Plantation
428978 (2S) Schoolknott Plantation
429228 (S) near Watermillock Church
430229 (W) near Watermillock Church
430230 (S) foot of Priest's Crag
430231 (S) foot of Priest's Crag
430935 (S) near Crook Foot
430975 (S) Schoolknott Plantation
431906 (S) SW Tarnside
431924 (S) S Foxhole Bank
432217 (S) between Birk Crag and the Knotts
432237 (S) Cove
432946 (S) near Bateman Fold
432970 (S) S slope Grandsire
433903 (S) S Tarnside
433908 (W) Tarnside
433913 (W) N A5074-Crosthwaite road
433925 (S) S Foxhole Bank
433926 (S) Foxhole Bank
433969 (S) W Outrun Nook
433976 (S) E Schoolknott Plantation
434191 (W) Hause Farm, near Howtown
434912 (S) N Tarnside Farm
434916 (W) Crosthwaite
434930 (S) Bulman Strands
434944 (S) near Shepherd Yeat
434971 (S) SE slope Grandsire
434979 (W) Whasdike
435194 (S) Hallin Fell
435914 (S) Crosthwaite
435930 (S) Bulman Strands
436069 (S) W slope Yoke. Emergent stream joins Hagg Gill
436918 (W) Hardriggs
436946 (S) slightly W bridleway between Back Lane and Spigot House
436965 (S) near Crag House
437917 (W) Crosthwaite
438907 (S) E Mireside, alongside Mill Lane
438911 (S) ENE Tarnside Farm
438982 (S) NE Whasdike
439220 (S) Leeming Farm, Watermillock
439260 (S) SSE Sparket Mill, E minor road
439906 (S) alongside the A5074 SE Mireside
440244 (S) W Bennethead Banks
440270 (W) St Mary's Well, Hutton John
440271 (W) Hutton John
440904 (W) off the A5074 alongside tracks to The High Farm
440912 (S) Crosthwaite
440921 (S) E Starnthwaite
440922 (S) E Starnthwaite
440938 (W) Birk Moss
441026 (S) ESE Capple Howe, ENE Red Crags
441912 (3S) Crosthwaite
442904 (S) alongside the A5074
442911 (S) Crosthwaite
442996 (S) near St Anne's Farm, Ings
443220 (W) Horrock Wood Farm, Watermillock
443937 (S) W Cock Hag
444905 (W) alongside bridleway, A5074-Esp Ford
444907 (S) Esp Ford
444914 (S) Crosthwaite, slightly E of track to Spout House
445000 (S) just below and to the S of Williamson's Monument
445232 (S) alongside Longthwaite Beck
445913 (S) Cartmell Fold, Crosthwaite
445921 (S) feeder Hollow Clough Gill
445958 (S) slightly N Crook Reservoir.

446072 (S) alongside track Hartrigg-Kentmere Reservoir, near Reservoir Cottage
446072 (S) W River Kent, near Kentmere Reservoir
446233 (S) alongside A592 to Bennethead
447065 (S) foot of Rainsborrow Crag, Kentmere
447910 (S) off Mill Lane, Crosthwaite
447913 (2S) near Cartmell Fold, Crosthwaite
447938 (S) Cock Hag
448906 (S) Little Moss Side
448962 (W) WSW Fell Plain
449240 (S) alongside Ramps Beck
449906 (W) Little Moss Side
449969 (S) S Middle Fairbank Tarn
449999 (S) near the Heights, Hugill
450906 (W) Moss Side
450965 (S) near Fell Plain
451084 (S) Toadhowe Well, E Kentmere Reservoir
451911 (W) W Town Yeat. N Underbarrow-Crosthwaite road
451914 (W) Fell Edge
451915 (S) Fell Edge
451938 (S) near High Leys, Crook
452044 (S) Kentmere, S Garburn Pass track
452244 (S) Soulby Fell
453015 (W) near Croft Head, Kentmere
453260 (W) alongside Dacre Beck near High Bridge
453962 (2S) slightly W of B5284 (Crook) -Borwick Fold road
453968 (W) alongside the Glen, SSE Middle Fairbank Tarn
454962 (2S) slightly W of B5284 (Crook) -Borwick Fold road
454089 (S) W slope the Knowe, emergent stream joins Lingmell Gill
454961 (S) slightly W of B5284 (Crook)-Borwick Fold road
454991 (W) Raw Ghyll, Ings with Hugill
455920 (S) W Broom Lane, Underbarrow
455929 (S) between Cockhag Plantation and Mountjoy Wood
455943 (S) near Crook Hall
455961 (S) slightly W of B5284 (Crook)-Borwick Fold road
455972 (S) E Middle Fairbank Tarn
456210 (S) between Auterstone and Swarthbeck
456914 (S) near Blakebank, Underbarrow
456916 (S) alongside Broom Lane, Underbarrow
456951 (W) slope Cockpit Hill, Crook
456970 (S) ESE Middle Fairbank Tarn
457086 (S) Black John Hole
458901 (S) W Cock Moss
459045 (W) Kentmere, near Rook Howe
460028 (S) Kentmere, between Long Houses and Nuttera Beck
460081 (S) W slope Brown Howe
460934 (S) W Crook-Underbarrow road, N Mountjoy Wood
460998 (S) slope Hugill Fell, W Fellfoot
461980 (S) E Brownspring Coppice
462036 (W) Kentmere, alongside Cornclose Lane
462938 (W) Beckside
463928 (S) between Chapel House and All Saints Church, Underbarrow
463979 (S) E Brownspring Coppice
464921 (S) near Kirkby House, Underbarrow
464925 (W) S All Saints Church and along side the Crook-Underbarrow road
464926 (S) near All Saints Church, Underbarrow
464981 (S) Staveley, alongside the A591.
464992 (S) Hygill Fell below Black Crag
465086 (S) emergent stream feeds upper tributary of Wren Gill
465924 (W) Underbarrow, alongside track to Nook Farm
465940 (2S) W Bell Hill
466923 (S) Underbarrow
467066 (W) NNW Low Fold, Over Staveley
467233 (S) Hodgson Hill
467937 (Spout) Lindreth Brow
467996 (S) near Scroggs Bridge, Over Staveley
468922 (W) behind Punch Bowl,

Underbarrow
468975 (2S) alongside Staveley to Crook road
468987 (S) Staveley
469001 (W) ESE Elf Howe, Over Staveley
469923 (S) Underbarrow
469935 (W) Lindreth Brow
471949 (S) W Capple Rigg
472991 (S) near Scroggs Farm
473909 (S) Tullithwaite Hall
473922 (W) alongside Valley View, Underbarrow
473945 (S) alongside Capplerigg Lane
474231 (S) between Aik Beck and Elder Beck
474921 (S) alongside Thorns Lane, Underbarrow
474983 (S) N Staveley Park
474998 (S) along. Hall Lane to Staveley road
475010 (S) alongside High House, Over Staveley
475909 (W) SW Garthrow
475911 (W) WSW Garthrow
475918 (W) alongside Greenriggs (Thorns Villa)
475935 (W) Bonfire Hall, Underbarrow
475992 (S) near Scroggs Farm
476005 (W) near Ghyll Bank, Over Staveley
476910 (W) SSW Garthrow
476910 (S) SSW Garthrow
476914 (W) Garthrow
476916 (S) W Garth Row Lane
476944 (S) Long Wood
476945 (S) adjoining Long Wood
476992 (S) near Scroggs Farm
478076 (W & S) Buckbarrow Well, Longsleddale
478916 (S) E Garth Row Lane
478920 (S) alongside Garth Row Lane
478962 (S) Ratherheath Plantation
479205 (W) Jeanie Brewster's Well
479931 (W) Cold Harbour, Underbarrow
479982 (S) E Staveley Park
479988 (S) slope Spy Crag. Near Piked Howe
480916 (S) E Garth Row Lane
480954 (W) off Ratherheath Lane
481923 (W) behind Scar Foot, Underbarrow Road
482914 (S) Great Spring, source of Yanyard Beck
482922 (W) adjoining Foxwell, Underbarrow Road
483942 (S) W track Cunswick Hall to B5284
483993 (S) near Littlewood Farm
484902 (S) foot of Underbarrow Scar
485916 (2S) below Hodgson's Leap, Scout Scar
485947 (S) W track Cunswick Hall to B5284
485962 (S) alongside Ashes Lane
487201 (S) Scales Farm
488120 (W) Rowantreethwaite Well, E Haweswater
489929 (S) below and to W of Cunswick Scar
489956 (S) S Ratherheath Lane
490267 (S) NE Barton
490930 (S) alongside Gamblesmire Lane
490982 (S) between Hundhowe and Side House
490983 (S) between Hundhowe and Side House
491039 (W) Well Foot, Longsleddale
491937 (S) Scar Wood, feeds Cunswick Tarn
494234 (S) S High Winder
494928 (S) alongside Bank Head.
495924 (W) alongside Bradleyfield House
496209 (S) near Howebill House
496926 (S) alongside Bank Head.
499191 (S) Rough Hill
500169 (W) NW Aika Hill
500919 (W) Bradley Field
502211 (W) Dub Hill, Heltondale
506219 (W) Helton
507170 (W) Littlewater Well
508987 (S) Potter Fell
509219 (W) Helton
510196 (S) Butterwick
511221 (W) Mark's Well, Helton
512008 (S) Longsleddale, between Tenter

Howe and the R Sprint.
512182 (W) St Patrick's Well (Mab Well), Bampton
512998 (S) NNE Ulgraves, above Longsleddale
513998 (S) NNE Ulgraves, above Longsleddale
514213 (W) Setterah Park, alongside moat
514216 (S) Millkeld Sike, near Helton
514999 (S) Millkeld Sike, near Helton
515227 (S) near Helton
515999 (S) NE Ulgraves, above Longsleddale
516225 (S) Keldron Spring, Helton.
517218 (S) near Helton, alongside R Lowther
517240 (S) Lady Well, Askham
518197 (S) Knipe
519212 (S) SSW Whale
520177 (W) Bomby
520982 (S) alongside road to Garnett Bridge, below Hollin Crag
520993 (S) Garnett Bridge Wood
521993 (S) Garnett Bridge Wood
522987 (S) alongside road to Garnett Bridge, near East View
523990 (S) alongside road to Garnett Bridge, near East View
524234 (W) Peg Huck Well, Lowther Castle Garden
524992 (S) Garnett Bridge
530020 (S) near Dryhowe Bridge, Bannisdale
531167 (W) near Toathmain, W River Lowther
532114 (W) Gambling Well
534171 (W) Hegdale
536155 (W) Kilhow Well, Rayside
536184 (W) Low Scarside
537183 (S) Scarside
538182 (S) Scarside
539011 (W) near Bannisdale High Bridge
543015 (S) near Thorn Cottage
543169 (W) Rosgill Head
548187 (S) Out Scar, Knipescar
553144 (S) see main text under Keld
557141 (W) Thornship
561140 (S) Thornship

WATERCOURSES

Becks, burns, gills, grains, gutters, nicks, rivers, sikes and slacks.

Becks

Addacombe
Aik
Aiken
Aira
Angletarn
Appletree Worth
Arndale
Ash Gill
Ashes
Askham
Bannerdale (2)
Bannisdale
Barrow (2)
Beck Leven
Beck Wythop
Bell (2)
Belle Grange
Ben
Birker
Birkett
Birkthwaite
Black (21)
Black Moss
Blackdike
Blackhazel
Blake
Blaze
Blea
Blea Moss
Blea Water
Bleacove
Blelham
Boredale
Borrow
Bowscale
Braidy
Bright
Brimful
Broadoak
Broadslack
Brockle
Brockshaw
Brown (2)
Browndale
Bryan
Buckbarrow
Bull Haw Moss
Caiston
Caplecrag
Capple
Captain Whelter
Caral
Carlhowe
Castlehow
Catcove
Caudale
Cawdale
Cawell
Cawfell
Chapel (2)
Cinderdale (2)
Cinderhill
Climb Stile
Coal
Coegill
Coldgill
Coledale
Collierhagg
Comb (3)
Cooper
Countess
Cove
Cowcove
Crabtree
Croasdale
Crook
Crookdale
Cuddy
Cunsey
Dacre
Dale Park
Dead
Deepdale
Dodd
Doddickgill
Dovedale (Hartsop)
Dub
Dubbs
Dubhow
Dunnerdale
Dunney
Easedale
Eden
Eel
Elder
Eller
Ellers
Esthwaite Hall
Far Ruddy
Far Swan
Fogmire
Force
Freeze (2)
Frith
Fusedale
Gable
Gatescarth
Gatescarthdale
Gatescarthgill
Gatherstone
Gill (4)
Glencoyne
Glenderaterra
Glenridding
Gobling
Goldrill
Gray
Great Langdale
Greaves
Greenburn
Grisedale
Grizedale
Groove (3)
Groovegill
Hag
Hagg
Hale

Watercourses

Hall (2)
Hallgarth
Hare Hall
Hartley
Haskew
Hassnesshow
Haweswater
Heck
Heltondale
Henfoot
High Hole
Highford
Highnook
Hoathwaite
Hog House
Hol
Hole
Hollow
Hollow Moss
Holme
Hope
Hopgill
How (3)
Howegrain
Howes
Hussey Well
Inkern
Keskadale
Kid
Kidshowe
Kilnhow
Kinmont
Kirkstone
Ladcrag
Lair
Langstrath
Latterbarrow
Leaps
Levers Water
Light
Lingcove
Lingmell
Little
Little Grain
Little Mosedale
Little Mossy
Little Sandy
Liza
Logan
Long
Long Mire
Longgrain
Longthwaite
Low Bridge
Low Water
Lowthwaite
Marchbank
Mardale
Masmill
Matterdale
Measand
Mecklin
Mell
Mellfell
Mere (4)
Meregill (2)
Mickleden
Middle Swan
Mill (4)
Mires
Moasdale
Mosedale (4)
Moss
Mossdale
Mosser
Mossy
Mouldry Bank
Naddle (2)
Naddles
Near Ruddy
Near Swan
Nesgillhow
Nether
Nethermostcove
Newlands
Nunnery
Nuttera
Old Park
Oliver
Over
Oxendale
Paddle
Park (2)
Pasture
Pencilmill
Penrose
Pierce How
Pow (2)
Pudding
Pull
Raise (2)
Rake (2)
Rakegill
Ramps
Rampsgill
Rampshaw
Rams
Ramshaw
Randale
Rannerdale
Red (2)
Red Dell
Red Gill
Red Moss
Red Tarn
Riddings (2)
Rigg (2)
Riggindale
Robin
Roundley
Routen
Routing Gill
Rowantree (3)
Rowantreethwaite
Rowten
Ruthwaite
Rydal
Sail (2)
Salehow
Samgarth
Sandwick
Sandy
Scale (2)
Scalderskew
Scalehow
Scales
Scaley
Scandale

Scargreen
Scope
Scrow
Selside
Shaw
Skill
Skitwath
Slades
Sleddale
Sling
Slops
Small Water
Smithy
Smooth
Southerndale
Southwaite
St John's (The Bure)
Squat
Stainton
Stake
Stare
Stencher
Stickletongue
Stockdale
Stony (2)
Straighthead
Strands
Sty
Summers Cove
Swallow Scar
Swart
Swarth
Swindale
Swinescales
Swinsty
Swirl Hawse
Tanyard
Tarn (2)
Tarn Head
Thackthwaite (2)
Thornsgill
Thwaitehouse
Tom Rudd
Tongue (2)
Tongues
Torver
Tranearth
Troughton
Trout
Ulgra
Underbarrow
Warnscale
Wartches
Wasdale
Wash Dub
Washfall
Watendlath
Wath
Waver
Whale
Whelter
Whillan
Whit
Whiteoak
Whitrow
Wilfin
Willdale
William's
Wisenholme
Woundale
Wrynose
Wythop
Yew Tree
Yewdale

Burns

Green
Wyth

Di(y)kes

Bird
Layburn
Skeggleswater

Gills

Allen
Allencrags
Angletarn
Applethwaite
Arminghow
Arnison
Ash
Ashness
Barkbeth
Barnes
Barrow
Beckstones
Beckthorns
Bessy
Big Stranger
Birks
Birkside
Black (2)
Black Crag
Black Gills
Blackcrag
Bleatarn
Bleaberry (3)
Blease
Blindtarn
Blue
Bowdergate
Bracken
Broad
Broadslack
Brow
Browney
Brund
Bryant's
Burr
Bursting Gills
Calfcove
Calfgate
Capell
Cat (3)
Cat Gills
Caw
Charlesground
Cleaty
Clews
Cockley Beck
Coldcove
Comb (4)
Cow Close
Cragsteads
Crinkle
Crosby
Dale Head

Deep
Dob
Dockernook
Dodd
Doddick
Dodknott
Doe House
Dowthwaite
Driedley
Dry Grove
Dry (3)
Drycloff
Drygrove
Dryhowe
Dubhow
Dudmancombe
Dungeon Ghyll
Emblesteads
Far
Far Broadgill
Far Easedale
Far Tongue
Farra Grain
Fisher
Fisherplace
Flour
Footmoorgate
Fother
Foumart
Friar
Frith
Gable
Gaitscale
Gale
Galeforth
Gasgale, see Liza Beck
Gate
Goat
Goat Gills
Gouthercrag
Grain
Grains (2)
Grassguards
Grave
Great
Great Grain
Greathall
Greendale
Greenhead
Greenhow
Greenup
Greta
Grisedale
Groove (3)
Grove
Grunting
Guerness
Hagg
Hall
Hardknott (2)
Hardrigg
Hare (2)
Hause (2)
Hayeswater
Hell (2)
Helvellyn
High Bridge
High Goat
High Keld
Hind
Hob
Hobgrumble
Hog
Hogget
Holehouse
Hollinhow
Hollow
Hollow Clough
How
Howe
Ill (6)
Isaac
Keld
Kill
Kirkstyle
Kitbain
Ladknott
Launchy (Deergarth)
Lavery
Lewthwaite
Linbeck
Lingmell
Little
Little Brinhowe
Little Grain
Little Stanger
Little Tongue
Long House
Longfell
Lord's
Low Goat
Low Keld
Low Moss
Lurge
Mealhowe
Megs
Mere (2)
Merebeck
Middlesteads
Miles
Mill
Mines
Mirk
Mitchell
Moor
Moss
Mosshause
Near
Near Broadgill
Near Tongue
Needless
Newhouse
Parkhouse
Parrocks
Peathill
Piers
Poorhag
Priest
Prison
Raise
Ramps
Red (3)
Redacre
Redgate
Redsike
Rest
Ribby Gills
Ridding

Robin
Rooking
Rossett
Rossy
Rottenstone
Roughton
Rowantree
Ruddy
Sad
Saddlecrag
Sand
Sandbed
Sandbeds
Sanderson
Scale (2)
Scalebeck
Scaleclose
Scar
Seal
Sharpknott
Sherry
Shoulthwaite
Sinen
Skeel
Skew
Skull
Slat
Snow Cove
Sourmilk (3)
Spothow
Spouthead
Stake
Stanah
Standy
Starling (2)
Step
Stephead
Stickle
Sticks (2)
Stile
Stock
Stonebarrow
Stonesty
Stonycroft
Storthes
Strawberry
Styhead
Sulphury
Sunny Pike
Swear
Swine
Swinside
Swinsty
Tailbert
Tansy
Thackthwaite
Third
Thornship
Thrang
Thurs
Tilberthwaite
Tom
Tommy
Tongue (3)
Tongue Gills
Tonguerigg
Troughton
Ullscarf
Ullstone
Well
West Nab
Wet
Whelpside
Whinlatter
Whis
White (2)
Whittern
Widdy
Willy
Willybrag
Willygrass
Wintergroove
Wolfhowe
Woodbank
Woodfell
Woodnook
Woof
Worm
Wray
Wren
Wythe (2)
Ya
Yeastyrigg
Yewgrove
Yewthwaite

Grains

Atkinson's
Far
Farra
Howe
Sealhole

Gutters

Brownhowe
Fleet
Lee Haw
Long
Quarry
Red
Toddle
Ulgill

Miscellaneous

Buttermere Dubs
Damas Dubs
Huntpot Dub
Little Narrowcove

Nicks

The Nick
Hause
Swinescar

Pools

Baysbrown
Galloper
Low Birker
Steers
Underbarrow
Woodend

Rivers

Bleng
Brathay
Calder
Caldew

WATERCOURSES

Cocker
Derwent
Duddon
Eamont
Esk
Gilpin
Glenderamackin
Gowan
Greta
Irt
Kent
Lickle
Liza
Lowther
Marron
Mint
Mite
Rothay
Sprint
Winster

Sikes

Aika
Annas
Birrel
Black (2)
Blackshaw
Blaika
Blake (2)
Buscoe
Christan
Clemety
Greenriggs
Greenup
Intack
Keasgill
Lanshawe
Laythwaite
Mere
Millkeld
Mother
Nook
Pike
Polsgill
Pounder
Red
Rothery
Setterah
Todgill
Wham
White
Widepot
Yewry

Slacks

Deepdale

Waters

Light

For further information including grid references consult the individual watercourse in the gazeteer section.

Mountain Accidents and Rescues

Note that comparatively few accidents happen on high rocky summits while rock climbing or scrambling. In fact, most occur on well-defined paths, tracks, or steep (wet) grassy slopes. So take care at all times whether just out for a low level walk or on a substantial fell walk and heed the basic advice on safety on the fells as given by the Lake District Search and Rescue Association:-

Clothing - This should be colourful, warm, windproof and waterproof. Wear boots with nails or moulded rubber soles, not shoes, plimsolls, or gum-boots. Take a woollen cap and spare jersey; it is always colder on the tops.

Food - In addition to the usual sandwiches, take chocolate, dates, mint cake or similar sweet things which restore energy quickly. If you don't need them yourself, someone else may.

Equipment - This must include map, compass, and at least one reliable watch in the party. A whistle, torch and spare batteries and bulbs (six blasts or flashes repeated at minute intervals signal an emergency), and, in winter conditions, an ice-axe and survival bag are essential. Climbers are all urged to wear helmets.

Company - Don't go alone, and make sure party leaders are experienced. Take special care of the youngest and weakest in dangerous places.

Emergencies - Don't press on if conditions are against you - turn back even if it upsets your plan. Learn first aid, and keep injured or exhausted people warm until help reaches you. Get a message to the police for help as soon as possible. Report changes of route or time-table to them if someone is expecting you. The police will do the rest.

The Lake District Search and Mountain Rescue Association consists principally of 15 teams including the **Search and Rescue Dog Association** (SARDA). All members are volunteers and rely for all financial assistance on bequests, annual donations by authorities, groups, societies or individuals, deeds of covenant, collecting boxes, etc. Individual groups publish accidents and rescues during the year but the overall body, the Lake District Search & Mountain Rescue Association publishes a yearly report covering all its members' turnouts. A leaflet issued by the Lake District National Park *Enjoy the Fells in Safety* is also freely available.

SELECTED PEOPLE ASSOCIATED WITH THE LAKE DISTRICT

Arnold, Mathew (1822-1888) son of Thomas Arnold.

Arnold, Thomas (1795-1842) headmaster of Rugby School. See also **Fox How**; **White Moss Common** & **Baneriggs**.

Beaumont, Sir G (1753-1827) patron of the arts, landscape painter and illustrator. See also **Applethwaite**.

Bonington, Sir Chris see **A-Z**.

Bragg, Melvyn see **A-Z**.

Calvert Raisley (1773-1795) Wordsworth's benefactor and friend. See also **Calvert Trust** and **Windebrowe**.

Christian, Fletcher (c1764-c1794) Mutiny on the *Bounty* leader. Born Cockermouth.

Clarkson, Thomas (1760-1846) lifelong campaigner against slavery. See also **Eusemere**.

Coleridge, Hartley (1796-1849) eldest son of S T Coleridge. See also **Clappersgate**.

Coleridge, Samuel Taylor (1772-1834) Man of letters, poet and dramatist. See also **Broad Stand**, **Eusemere**; **Films & film making**; **Greta Hall**, **Ulpha**.

Collingwood, W G (1854-1932) painter, historian, archaeologists, author. See also **A-Z**.

Constable, John (1776-1837) landscape painter. Toured the Lake District sketching in 1806.

Dalton, John (born and lived in Eaglesfield) scientist. Discoverer of the Atomic Theory.

Davey, Sir Humphrey (1778-1829) scientist. Inventor of the miner's safety lamp.

Davies, Hunter (1936-) notable author, see **A-Z**.

De Quincey, Thomas (1785-1859) journalist. See also **Dove Cottage**; **Fox Ghyll**; **Kirkstone Pass Inn**; **Nab Cottage**.

Keats, John (1795-1821) poet. Toured through the Lake District to Scotland in 1818.

Lamb, Charles (1775-1834) essayist.

Martineau, Harriet (1802-1876) writer. See also **Lake District Guide Books**; **Red Lion Hotel, Grasmere**; **St. Oswald's, Grassmere**; **The Knoll**.

Nicholson, Norman (1914-1987) author and poet. See **A-Z**.

Potter, Beatrix (1866-1943) illustrator, writer and sheep farmer. See **A-Z**. Also many references in the general text.

Quillinan, Edward (1791-1851) poet.

Ransome, Arthur (1884-1967) author. See **A-Z**.

Rawnsley, Canon H (1851-1920) one of the founders of the National Trust and its first secretary. See also **Allan Bank**; **Crosthwaite Church**; **Elterwater' Friar's Crag**; **Grisedale Tarn**; **Wray**.

Ruskin, John (1819-1900) poet, art critic, artist, philosopher. See also **A-Z**.

Scott, Sir W (1771-1832) poet and novelist. See also **Castle Rock**; **Patterdale Hotel**; **Swan Hotel**, **Grasmere**.

Southey, Robert (1774-1843) poet. See also **Blencathra**; **Crosthwaite Church**; **Grange-in-Borrowdale**; **Greta Hall**; **Lodore Falls**, **Mirehouse**.

Wordsworth, William (1770-1850) poet (poet laureate 1843-50). See also **A-Z**.

See also - **Art in the Lake District**; **Lake District Guide Books** and **Literary Lakeland** in the general text.

Roads (A & B class)

A591 from Sizergh roundabout via Kendal and Staveley by-passes, Windermere-Ambleside-Grasmere and Keswick to the A595 at Bothel.

A592 Newby Bridge to A66(T) Penrith via Windermere-Kirkstone Pass-Patterdale-Glenridding and Watermillock.

A593 Ambleside-Skelwith Bridge-Coniston-Torver to Broughton-in-Furness.

A595 Dalton-in-Furness-Askham-in-Furness-Kirkby-in-Furness-Broughton-in-Furness-Silecroft-Bootle-Ravenglass-Cleator Moor-Cockermouth-Bothel-Thursby-Carlisle.

A5074 A591 Windermere) to A590 (Gilpin's Bridge) via Winster and Lyth valleys.

A5075 Waterhead (A591) to the Ambleside-Coniston road (A593).

A5084 Torver-Blawith-A5092 Lowick Green.

A5086 Egremont-Cleator Moor-Cockermouth. Short section borders the LDNP between 103266 and 109279.

A5091 A66-Troutbeck-Matterdale End-A592.

A6 for approximately a third of its 26 miles between Kendal and Penrith the A6 skirts the National Park boundary. It crosses Shap summit at 426m (1398ft).

A66 Scotch Corner (A1)-Brough-Penrith-Keswick-Cockermouth-Workington.

B5284 from the A5074 S Bowness via Crook to the Plumgarths roundabout.

B5285 A5074-Windermere ferry-Far Sawrey-Near Sawrey-Hawkshead to Coniston.

B5286 Clappersgate (A593) to Hawkshead (B5285).

B5287 Town End (Grasmere) through Grasmere to the A591 (Swan Inn).

B5288 A66-Motherby-Greystoke-Penrith.

B5289 A66 (Portinscale)-Keswick-Borrowdale-Buttermere-Low Lorton-B5292..

B5292 A66-Braithwaite-Whinlatter Pass-Lorton-Cockermouth .

B5320 Pooley Bridge (A592)-Eamont Bridge (A6).

B5322 through St Johns in the Vale-A66-A591.

B5343 Skelwith Bridge (A593) to the head of Great Langdale.

B5360 A592 to the A5074.

HIGHEST, LARGEST, LONGEST, SMALLEST, SHORTEST, DEEPEST

Highest Mountain	Scafell Pike 978m (3209ft) .
Highest Spring/Well	Brownrigg Well 853m (2799ft) Helvellyn..
Highest Tarn	Broadcrag Tarn - the OS brackets Broadcrag Tarn and Foxes/Fox Tarn in the same height range but Broadcrag is generally considered to be slightly higher within that range.
Deepest Tarn	Blea Tarn, Mardale 68m (223ft).
Highest Lake above SL	Haweswater 240m (788ft).
Deepest Lake	Wastwater 76m (249ft).
Longest Lake	Windermere 17kms (10.5 miles).
Lowest Lake above SL	Windermere 39.3m (129ft).
Highest named pass	Mickeldore C840m (C2756ft).
Highest named pass most frequented	Considered to be Esk Hause 759m (2490ft).
Highest Road Pass	A592 over Kirkstone Pass 455m (1493ft).
Steepest Road Pass	Hardknott with sections 33.3% (1 in 3).
Largest Tarn	Devoke Water followed by Seathwaite Tarn and Burnmoor.
Smallest Lake	Generally accepted as Brothers Water. However, the smallest 'lake' is often quoted as Elterwater but this is also frequently referred to as a tarn.
Waterfall with longest drop	Scale Force near Buttermere with a drop of 38m (125ft).
Shortest names	Y (Boulder and Gully) and Ya (Gill).
Longest single name	Rowantreethwaite

Bibliography

Ordnance Survey Leisure Maps: The English Lakes (1:25,000) NE, NW, SE, SW
Ordnance Survey Leisure Guide to the Lake District, lst edition, 1984
OS Sheet 35/31 1:25000, Provisional Edition, 1950
OS Sheet 35/41 1:25000, Provisional Edition, 1950
Bartholomew Lake District 1 inch map 1971
Cumbria English Lake District Touring Map issued by the Cumbria Tourist Board.
Tourist Map of the Lake District published by Gall & Inglis (no date)
The Travellers Guide to the Lake District 1st edition, 1965
The Lake District by W T Palmer. Revised edition 1936
A Description of the English Lakes, Harriet Martineau, 1858, reprinted 1974.
Wordsworth and the Lake District, David McCracken, 1984
The Lake District, Roy Millward and Adrian Robinson, 1970
Mining in the Lake Counties W T Shaw, 3rd edition, 1975
Mines and Mining in the Lake District, John Postlethwaite, 1877.
Coniston Copper, Eric G Holland, 1987
Prose of Lakeland, compiled by B L Thompson, 1954
The Hidden Places of Cumbria, 1990
The Lake District: A Century of Conservation, Geoffrey Berry and Geoffrey Beard, 1980
The Lake Counties, W G Collingwood, edited and revised by William Robinson, 1988
Brief Guide to the Lake District, 1974, Eric Delderfield
Inside the Real Lakeland, A H Griffin, 1965
Discovery Guide to The Lake District, Caroline Hillary, Pamela Grant & Malcolm Parker, 1991?
A Walk around the Lakes, Hunter Davies, 1979
The Lakeland Peaks, W A Poucher, 9th edition, 1983
Companion Guide to the Lake District, Frank Welsh, 1989
The Lake District, originally compiled by M J B Baddeley, 24th ed., edited by R J W Hammond, 1971
The Lake District, edited by R J W Hammond, 2nd edition, 1975
The English Lakes, F G Brabant, revised by B L Thompson, 4th edition, 1952
Guide to the Lake District, Geographia Ltd. (no date)
The Ancient Ways of Lakeland, Richard Sale and Arthur Lees, 1986
The Penguin Guide to the Lake District, W T Palmer, 1947
The Tarns of Lakeland, W Heaton Cooper, 3rd edition, 1983
The Lakes, W Heaton Cooper, 3rd edition, 1987
Roads and Trackways of the Lake District, Brian Paul Hindle, 1984
Lakeland Valleys, Robert Gambles, 1978
Lake District Place-Names, Robert Gambles, 1985
Out of the Forest: The Natural World and the Place-names of Cumbria, Robert Gambles, 1989
On High Lakeland Fells, Bob Allen, 1987
Lakeland Villages, Jim Watson, 1988
The Lake District National Park, ed. by the Countryside Commission, 1975
The Lake District National Park, John Wyatt, 1987

A Pictorial Guide to the Lakeland Fells, A Wainwright, 7 vols., 1955-1966
The Outlying Fells of Lakeland, A Wainwright, 1973
Cumbria: The Lake District, published by the Cumbria Tourist Board, 1997
Westmorland Gazette - various articles
Cumbria magazine - various editions
The Lake District, (Collins New Naturalist Series), W H Pearsall & Winifred Pennington, 1989
The Laker's ABC, David Scott, 1955
Portrait of the Wordsworth Country, Robert Sands, 1984
The Lake Mountains, (1) - Skiddaw and Blencathra to Black Combe, Terry Marsh, 1987
The Good Guide to the Lakes, Hunter Davies, 1984
Walking Through the Lake District, Michael Dunn, revised paperback ed., 1987
Highways and Byways in the Lake District, A G Bradley, 1980
The Cumbria Village Book compiled by the Cumbria Federation of Women's Institutes, 1991
Lake District Map Companion, compiled by Elizabeth Ledward, 1978
The Best Pubs in Lakeland, Mike Dunn, 1989
Historic and New Inns of Interest in Westmorland and Cumberland, Weardale Press Ltd., 1968.
Inns of Character and Hotels in the Lake District, produced by D G Jackson, (no date)
Lake District Walks for Motorists Northern Area: Keswick, Borrowdale and Ullswater, John Parker, 1978
Walk the Lakes: 40 Easy Walks, selected and described by John Parker, 1983
Depth Charts of the Cumbria Lakes, A E Ramsbottom (Freshwater Biological Association Scientific Publications No.33), 1976
Concentration of Major Ions in Lakes and Tarns of the English Lake District (1953-1978), T R Carrick and D W Sutcliffe (Freshwater Biological Association Occasional Publications No.18), 1982
A Guide Through the District of the Lakes in the North of England, William Wordsworth, 1835
Letters of William Wordsworth: a new selection, edited by Alan G Hill, 1984
Dorothy Wordsworth's Illustrated Lakeland Journals, 1987
Letters of Dorothy Wordsworth, a selection edited by Alan G Hill, 1981
The Place-Names of Cumbria, Parts I, II, III, (English Place-Name Society), Vols XX, XXI (1950), XXII (1952)
The Place-Names of Westmorland, Parts I and II (English Place-Name Society), Vols XLII and XLIII (1967)
The Place-Names of Lancashire, Eilert Ekwall, (1922)
The National Trust Guide, compiled by Robin Fedden and Rosemary Joekes, 1973
Selected Poems of William Wordsworth, (The Worlds Classics Series), 1913
Thirlmere Across the Bridges to Chapel 1849-1852: From the diary of Rev Basil R Lawson, Curate of Wythburn, 1989
Guide to Ullswater, Harry Appleyard, 1970
A Pictorial and Descriptive Guide to the English Lake District, (Ward Lock & Co Ltd. publishers), c1924
Lake District Search & Mountain Rescue Association - Mountain Accidents - various years.
Cumbria, John Parker, 1977
Mardale: The Drowned Village, David and Jean Hay, 1976
History, Topography, and Directory of Westmorland, ed. by T F Bulmer, 1885

BIBLIOGRAPHY

The Stone Circles of Cumbria, John Waterhouse, 1985
The Curious Traveller Through Lakeland, Jessica Lofthouse, 2nd edition, 1973
Collins Guide to English Parish Churches, John Betjeman, 1958
A Love of the Lakes, Geoffrey Berry and Brian Redhead, 1988
The Lakeland Landscape, Geoffrey Clark and W Harding Thompson, 1938
Pageant of Lakeland, A H Griffin, 1967
Tramping in Lakeland, W T Palmer, 1934
The Folklore of the Lake District, Marjorie Rowling, 1976
The Discovery of the Lake District, the Victoria and Albert Museum, 1984
Cumbria Real Ale Guide, published by CAMRA (Campaign for Real Ale)
Exploring Lakeland Tarns: A Complete Guide, Don Blair, 1993
The English Lakes, W T Palmer, 1943
A Literary Guide to the Lake District, Grevel Lindop, 1993
Inns, Hotels & Restaurants in the Lake District & Cumbria, produced by D G Jackson Advertising Services (no date)
Secrets & Legends of Old Westmorland, Dawn Robertson and Peter Koronka, 1992
A History, Topography and Directory of Westmorland; and the Hundreds of Lonsdale and Amounderness in Lancashire, Mannex & Co, 1851, reprinted 1978
On Lower Lakeland Fells, Bob Allen, 1990
A Lakeland Notebook, A H Griffin, 1975
A Tour to the Lakes in Cumberland: John Ruskin's Diary for 1830, edited by James S Dearden, 1990.
The Lake Counties, Arthur Mee, 1994 ed.
The Westmorland Lakes in Old Photographs, collected by John Marsh, 1992
Towns and Villages of the Lake District and Cumbria, Alan Bryant, 1994
Beatrix Potter: Artist, Storyteller and Countrywoman, Judy Taylor, 1986
Windermere Grammar School: A History, 1936
The National Trust: A Century in the Lake District, compiled by Susan Denyer and Janet Martin, 1995
Tales of a Lakeland Valley - Langdale, Sheila Richardson, 1997
The Greens of Grasmere: a narrative, Dorothy Wordsworth edited by Hilary Clark, 1987
The Ancient Ironworks of Coniston Lake, W G Collingwood, 1902
The Book of Coniston, W G Collingwood, 1900
Windermere in the 19th century, ed. by C M Westall, 1991
Air crashes in the Lake District 1936-76, M J Hurst, 1997
Cumberland and Westmorland Wrestling, George Ion, 1955
An Aeronautical History of the Cumbria, Dumfries and Galloway Region: Part I, 1825-1914; Part II, 1915-1930, Peter Conron, 1984
Beneath the Lakeland Fells: Cumbria Mining Heritage, Cumbria Amenity Trust Mining Society, 1992
Industrial Archaeology of the Lake Counties, J D Marshall and Michael Davies-Shiel, 1977
Countrygoers North, Jessica Lofthouse, 1965
Wainwright in the Valleys of Lakeland, 1992
Old Lakeland: Some Cumbria Social History, J D Marshall, 1971
The Lake Counties of 100 Years Ago, John Marsh and John Garbett, 1994

Ings With Hugill: A Westmorland Village, 1993
A Lakeland Valley Through Time: A History of Staveley, Kentmere and Ings, Staveley and District History Society, 1955
Staveley Village History Trail, Staveley and District History Society, 1991
Transactions of the Cumberland and Westmorland Antiquarian and Archaeological Society
The National Trust Properties in the Lake District, Bruce L Thompson, 1930
The Gosforth District: Its Antiquities and Places of Interest, C A Parker, 1904
Torver, John Dawson, 1985
Lake District Grid Squares Explored, Peter B Danby, 1994
Lakeland Geology, E H Shackleton, 1966
The Cumbria Yew Book, Ken Mills, 1999
Keswick: The Story of a Lake District Town, George Bott, 1994
Lakeland's Mining Heritage: the Last 500 Years, Cumbria Amenity Trust Mining History Society, 2000.
A History of Cockermouth, J Bernard Bradbury, 1981
Keswick Mountain Rescue Team 'Call Out: The First 50 Years', George Bott
The Story of Coniston, Alastair Cameron and Elizabeth Brown, 2002
At Lakeland's Heart, John Carnie, 2002
Lakeland Birds: a Visitor's Handbook, W R Mitchell and R W Robson, 1974
Lakeland Mammals: A Visitors Handbook, W R Mitchell and Peter Delap, 1974
Wordsworth's Birds, Stanley Finch, 1986
Complete Lakeland Fells, Bill Birkett, 1994
Cumbrian Coastal Railways, David Joy, 1968.